Family Living™

Our Best Cookbook
COLLECTION
Book 2

Black Forest Cheesecake, p. 14

910 RECIPES

for Brunches, Suppers, Snacks, Side Dishes, Breads & Muffins, Party Foods, Chocolate, Cookies, Desserts, and Food Gifts.

ISBN13: 978-1-60900-340-1

910 recipes for snacks, meals & gifts!

Get ready to treat yourself! Here are tantalizing tastes for the **chocolate** lover, fresh-baked **breads** from savory to sweet, delicious **brunch foods** to start leisurely days, and hearty choices for everyday **family meals**. There also are **side dishes** to add unforgettable flavor to casual suppers or fancy feasts, plus shortcuts for making fabulous, **easy desserts**. For munching between meals, there are **cookies** and other grab-and-go **snacks** of all kinds. When it's time to party, guests will love the wide range of **appetizers**, sweets, and beverages. And for **gifts** that show how much you care, what could be more personal than your loved ones' favorite foods? You'll reach for this great treasury of recipes time after time!

Leisure Arts, Inc.
Little Rock, Arkansas

Cherry Sugarplums, page 55

Surprise Muffins (left), page 78, and Praline Biscuits, page 96

Simply Delicious Chocolate
Page 11

Tantalizing Treats for the Chocolate Lover

- Pies & Cakes
- Candy
- Cookies
- Pudding
- Cheesecake

Simply Delicious Breads & Muffins
Page 57

Flavorful and Fresh from the Oven

- Quick Breads
- Muffins
- Biscuits
- French Toast
- Sweet Rolls

Chocolate-Mint Torte, page 20

Cinnamon-Carrot Bread, page 68

*aked Spiced Fruit (left) and
anana-Raisin Bran Muffins, page 107*

*Corn Salad with Roasted Garlic
Dressing, page 167*

imply Delicious
runches
age 103

*elicious Foods
Start the Day!*

Entreés
Side Dishes
Fruits
Sweets
Breads

Simply Delicious
Suppers
Page 149

*Casual Choices
for Family Meals*

• Main Dishes
• Grills
• Casseroles
• Soups
• Breads

*e and Barley Pilaf and
opered Ham, page 106*

Four-Cheese Quiches, page 167

Green Bean Sauté, page 212

Ice Cream Sundae Cake, page 278

Simply Delicious Side Dishes
Page 195

Add Unforgettable Flavor to Your Meals

- Garden Veggies
- Casseroles
- Salads
- Soups
- Rice
-

Simply Delicious Easy Desserts
Page 241

Shortcuts to Making Fabulous Desserts!

- Pies & Tarts
- Cakes
- Cobblers
- Fun for Kids
- Creamy Confections
-

Tortilla Soup, page 199

Banana Cream Tart, page 245

oconut Fruitcake Bars, page 291

Soft Breadsticks and Madeira Cheese Spread, page 375

imply Delicious ookies
age 287

Big Variety—Because veryone Loves Cookies!

Crisp or Chewy
Moist or Flaky
Bar Cookies
Slice-and-Bake Cookies
Iced Cookies

Simply Delicious Snacks
Page 333

Grab-and-Go Goodies for Every Appetite!

• Snack Mixes
• Muffins
• Cheese Spreads
• Fruits
• Sweet Stuff

zelnut Cookies, page 290

Caramel Crackers (from left), Cinnamon-Apple Popcorn, and Caramel Corn Puffs, page 370

Blue Cheese and Port Wine Spread (left) and Deviled Crab Eggs, page 386

Hot Seafood Dip (left), page 459, and Spinach Puffs, page 468

Simply Delicious Party Snacks
Page 379

Foods and Beverages for Casual Entertaining!

- Tasty Canapés
- Snack Mixes
- Mini Sandwiches
- Sweets of All Kinds
- Selections for Kids
- Index, page 572

Simply Delicious Party Foods
Page 425

Appetizers and Drinks for Your Guests

- Creamy Dips
- Cheese Balls
- Spicy Meatballs
- Flavored Teas
- Rich Coffees
- Index, page 573

Tropical Granola Snack Mix (left) and Cinnamon Candy Corn, page 416

Sunrise Mimosas (left), page 429, and Chilled Asparagus Mousse, page 464

hicken-Onion Soup, page 511

Gingerbread Mix, page 523

imply Delicious Gifts for Friends
'age 471

asty Treats to Honor ll Your Loved Ones

Candy
Cookies
Cakes
Soups
Breads & Jams

Simply Delicious Food Gifts
Page 517

Creative Gift Mixes That Deliver Good Tastes

• Cookies
• Breads
• Soups
• Seasonings
• Teas & Coffees

oney-Almond Cookies, page 480

Cheese Spreads, page 546

Simply Delicious
CHOCOLATE

Nothing highlights a delicious meal better than a sweet surprise at the end. Whether your tastes run to velvety chocolate pies and rich, moist pound cakes or luscious, fruity treats and refreshingly tart sauces, the recipes in this extravagant collection are sure to satisfy. The hardest part will be deciding which to try first!

Black Forest Cheesecake, page 14

DEATH BY CHOCOLATE CAKE

CAKE

1 package (18¼ ounces) devil's food cake mix without pudding in the mix
1 package (3.9 ounces) chocolate fudge instant pudding mix
3 eggs
1¼ cups water
½ cup vegetable oil
1½ cups semisweet chocolate chips

FILLING

1 can (20 ounces) evaporated milk, divided
1½ cups sugar
5 tablespoons all-purpose flour
4 egg yolks
2 tablespoons butter or margarine, melted
1 teaspoon vanilla extract
½ teaspoon almond extract
2 ounces semisweet baking chocolate

FROSTING

½ cup butter or margarine
6 tablespoons sour cream
¼ cup cocoa
3½ cups confectioners sugar
1 teaspoon vanilla extract
1 cup chopped pecans
1 package (12 ounces) semisweet chocolate chips for chocolate curls

Preheat oven to 350 degrees. For cake, combine cake mix, pudding mix, eggs, water, and oil in a large bowl.

Using low speed of an electric mixer, bea until moistened. Increase speed of mixer to medium and beat 2 minutes. Stir in chocolate chips. Pour batter into 2 greased and floured 9-inch round cake pans. Bake 30 to 35 minutes or until cake begins to pull away from sides of pan and springs back when lightly pressed. Cool in pans 10 minutes; invert onto a wire rack to cool completely. Slice each layer in half horizontally. Separate layers with waxed paper and wrap in plastic wrap. Freeze layers until firm.

For filling, combine ¼ cup evaporated milk, sugar, flour, egg yolks, butter, and extracts in a small bowl; set aside. Combine chocolate and remaining evaporated milk in a medium saucepan. Stirring constantly, cook over medium heat until chocolate melts. Pour sugar mixture into chocolate mixture. Stirring constantly, bring to a boil; boil 3 to 4 minutes or until thickened. Remove from heat. Cover and refrigerate until well chilled.

Place 1 layer of cake on serving plate Spread one-third of filling evenly over cake layer. Repeat with remaining filling and second and third cake layers. Place remaining cake layer on top. Cover and refrigerate until ready to frost.

For frosting, combine butter, sour cream, and cocoa in a large saucepan. Stirring occasionally, bring to a boil over medium heat. Remove from heat. Add confectioners sugar and vanilla; beat un smooth. Spread warm frosting on top and sides of cake. Press pecans onto side of cake. Allow frosting to cool completel

For chocolate curls, melt chocolate chips in a small saucepan over low heat, stirring constantly. Pour onto a baking

The ultimate treat for a chocoholic, Death by Chocolate Cake features layers of moist cake and creamy filling topped with yummy fudge frosting and lots of chocolate curls.

heet, spreading chocolate to form an x 11-inch rectangle. Refrigerate until set ut not firm.

To make curls, pull a chocolate curler r vegetable peeler across surface of hocolate (curls will break if chocolate is too firm). Remelt and cool chocolate as necessary to form desired number of curls. Arrange curls on top of cake. Store cake in an airtight container in refrigerator.

Yield: about 20 servings

Shown on page 11: *A wonderful variation of a favorite dessert, Black Forest Cheesecake is a luscious chocolate cheesecake with a sweet cherry topping. Each slice has a garnish of whipped cream, a cherry, and a delicate chocolate lattice.*

BLACK FOREST CHEESECAKE

Cheesecake must be made 1 day in advance.

CHOCOLATE DECORATIONS
1/2   cup semisweet chocolate chips

CRUST
1   package (12 ounces) vanilla wafer cookies, finely crushed
3/4   cup butter or margarine, melted

FILLING
1   package (12 ounces) semisweet chocolate chips, divided
20   ounces cream cheese, softened
3/4   cup sugar
3   eggs
1   egg yolk
2   tablespoons whipping cream
1   tablespoon vanilla extract
2   teaspoons all-purpose flour

TOPPING
2   cans (16 ounces each) tart red pitted cherries, undrained
1/4   cup cornstarch
1   cup sugar

DECORATIVE TOPPING
2   tablespoons water
1 1/2   teaspoons unflavored gelatin
2   tablespoons sugar
1/2   cup whipping cream
   Maraschino cherries with stems

For chocolate decorations, melt chocolate chips in a small saucepan over low heat, stirring constantly. Spoon chocolate into a pastry bag fitted with a small round tip. For each decoration, pipe chocolate onto waxed paper, forming a 2 1/2-inch-high triangle. Randomly pipe chocolate inside triangle, making sure piped lines overlap. Repeat to make 16 decorations. Allow chocolate to harden. Store in a cool, dry place until ready to decorate cake.

For crust, combine cookie crumbs and butter. Press into bottom and halfway up sides of a greased 9-inch springform pan. Cover and refrigerate.

For filling, melt 1 cup chocolate chips in a small saucepan over low heat, stirring constantly; remove from heat. Adding 1 package at a time, beat cream cheese 25 minutes in a large bowl. Preheat oven to 500 degrees. Add sugar and melted chocolate to cream cheese; beat 5 minutes longer. Add eggs and egg yolk, 1 at a time, beating 2 minutes after each addition. Beat in flour, vanilla, and whipping cream. Stir in remaining 1 cup chocolate chips. Pour filling into crust. Bake 10 minutes. Reduce heat to 200 degrees. Bake 1 hour. Turn oven off and leave cake in oven 1 hour without opening door. Cool completely on a wire rack. Remove sides of pan.

For topping, drain cherries, reserving 1/4 cup juice. In a small bowl, combine cornstarch and reserved cherry juice. In a medium saucepan, combine cherries and sugar. Stirring occasionally, cook over medium heat until sugar dissolves and mixture comes to a boil. Stirring constantly, add cornstarch mixture and cook until thickened. Remove from heat; cool to room temperature. Spoon cherry mixture over cheesecake. Store in an airtight container 8 hours or overnight in refrigerator.

For decorative topping, place a large bowl and beaters from an electric mixer in freezer until well chilled. In a small saucepan, combine water and gelatin; let stand 1 minute. Stir in sugar; cook over low heat, stirring until gelatin and sugar dissolve. Remove from heat. In chilled bowl, beat cream until soft peaks form. Add sugar mixture and beat until stiff peaks form. Spoon whipped cream mixture into a pastry bag fitted with a large star tip and pipe on cake. Carefully peel waxed paper from chocolate decorations. Place chocolate decorations and cherries on cake. Store in an airtight container in refrigerator.
Yield: about 16 servings

CAPPUCCINO BROWNIES

1 teaspoon instant espresso powder
2 tablespoons warm water
1 package (10.25 ounces) brownie mix
1 egg
3 tablespoons vegetable oil
1/2 teaspoon ground cinnamon

Preheat oven to 350 degrees. In a medium bowl, combine espresso powder and warm water. Add remaining ingredients; stir until well blended. Spread batter into a greased 8-inch square baking pan. Bake 18 to 22 minutes. Cool in pan on a wire rack. Cut into 1 1/2 x 2-inch bars.
Yield: about 1 1/2 dozen brownies

CHOCOLATE-HAZELNUT SANDWICH COOKIES

1 package (9 1/2 ounces) brown-edge wafer cookies
1 jar (6.5 ounces) chocolate-hazelnut spread
1/3 cup semisweet chocolate chips

Place half of cookies bottom side up on waxed paper. Place 1 teaspoon hazelnut spread in center of each cookie. Top with remaining cookies; gently press together. Transfer cookies to a wire rack with waxed paper underneath.

In a small microwave-safe bowl, microwave chocolate chips on high power (100%) 1 minute or until chocolate softens; stir until smooth. Spoon into a resealable plastic bag. Snip off 1 corner of bag. Drizzle chocolate over cookies.
Yield: about 2 dozen sandwich cookies

DOUBLE CHOCOLATE CAKE

CAKE

1½ cups butter or margarine, softened
2¼ cups sugar
4 eggs, separated
1 tablespoon vanilla extract
3½ cups all-purpose flour
1½ teaspoons baking powder
1 teaspoon baking soda
½ teaspoon salt
2 cups buttermilk
1 cup chopped pecans, toasted
3 ounces white baking chocolate, melted
6 ounces semisweet baking chocolate, melted

FROSTING

½ cup butter or margarine, softened
11 ounces cream cheese, softened
4 ounces white baking chocolate, melted and cooled
5½ cups confectioners sugar

GLAZE

3 tablespoons whipping cream
3 ounces semisweet baking chocolate, finely chopped
2 tablespoons butter or margarine

Preheat oven to 350 degrees. For cake, grease three 9-inch round cake pans. Line bottom of pans with waxed paper; grease waxed paper. Lightly flour pans. In a large bowl, cream butter and sugar until fluffy. Add egg yolks and vanilla; beat until smooth. In a medium bowl, combine flour, baking powder, baking soda, and salt. Alternately beat dry ingredients and buttermilk into creamed mixture, beating until well blended. Stir in pecans. In a medium bowl, beat egg whites until stiff peaks form; fold into batter. Transfer 3 cups batter to a medium bowl; stir in melted white chocolate. Stir melted semisweet chocolate into remaining batter. Spread semisweet batter into 2 prepared pans. Spread white chocolate batter into remaining prepared pan. Bake 30 to 35 minutes or until a toothpick inserted in center of cake comes out clean. Cool in pans 10 minutes. Remove from pans and cool completely on a wire rack. Carefully remove waxed paper.

For frosting, cream butter and cream cheese in a large bowl until fluffy. Add melted white chocolate and beat until well blended. Gradually add confectioners sugar, beating until smooth. Place one dark cake layer on a serving plate; spread top of layer with about ½ cup frosting. Repeat with light cake layer. Top with remaining dark cake layer. Spread remaining frosting over top and sides of cake.

For glaze, place whipping cream in a small microwave-safe bowl. Microwave on high power (100%) just until it begins to boil. Add chocolate and butter; stir until glaze is smooth, thick, and glossy. Pour glaze in center of cake, spreading until glaze runs down sides of cake. Let glaze harden. Store in an airtight container in refrigerator.

Yield: about 16 servings

...ouble Chocolate Cake is a melt-in-your-mouth delight with white chocolate frosting
...nd dark chocolate glaze.

FUDGE BROWNIE CAKE

CAKE
- 1 1/2 cups butter or margarine
- 6 ounces unsweetened baking chocolate, chopped
- 6 eggs
- 1 1/2 teaspoons vanilla extract
- 3 cups sugar
- 1 3/4 cups all-purpose flour
- 2 cups chopped pecans

ICING
- 3 3/4 cups confectioners sugar, divided
- 1/2 cup butter or margarine
- 6 tablespoons milk
- 3 tablespoons cocoa
- 1 teaspoon vanilla extract
- 1 cup finely chopped pecans
- 2 cups whipping cream
- Chocolate curls to garnish

Preheat oven to 325 degrees. For cake, grease three 8-inch round cake pans. Line bottoms of pans with waxed paper; grease waxed paper. Place butter and chocolate in the top of a double boiler over simmering water. Stirring frequently, heat just until mixture melts. Remove from heat. In a large bowl, beat eggs and vanilla until blended. Stirring constantly, gradually add melted chocolate mixture to egg mixture. In a medium bowl, combine sugar and flour. Gradually stir dry ingredients into chocolate mixture just until blended. Stir in pecans. Spread batter into prepared pans. Bake 25 to 30 minutes or until cake is firm to touch. Cool in pans on a wire rack.

For icing, place 3 1/2 cups confectioners sugar in a large bowl. In a heavy small saucepan, combine butter, milk, and cocoa. Stirring constantly, cook over medium heat until butter melts. Remove from heat; stir in vanilla. Pour chocolate mixture over confectioners sugar; stir until smooth. Stir in pecans. Let icing cool about 15 minutes or until firm enough to spread. Spread icing between layers and on top of cake.

In a medium bowl, beat whipping cream until soft peaks form. Gradually adding remaining 1/4 cup confectioners sugar, beat until stiff peaks form. Ice sides and top edge of cake with whipped cream. Store in an airtight container in refrigerator. To serve, garnish with chocolate curls.

Yield: about 16 servings

RASPBERRY COFFEE

- 1 cup half and half
- 2/3 cup sugar
- 1 quart hot, strongly brewed raspberry-flavored coffee

For hot coffee, place half and half and sugar in a small saucepan over medium-low heat. Stirring frequently, heat about 10 minutes or until hot. Combine coffee and half and half mixture in a 1 1/2-quart heatproof container; serve hot.

For iced coffee, combine coffee and sugar in a 1 1/2-quart heatproof container. Stir until sugar dissolves; cover and chill. To serve, stir half and half into coffee mixture; serve over ice.

Yield: about 5 cups coffee

Scrumptiously rich, three-layer Fudge Brownie Cake is enhanced with chocolate frosting and whipped cream. Whether served hot or cold, Raspberry Coffee is a sweet indulgence.

Shown on page 4: A chocolate fancier's delight, elegant Chocolate-Mint Torte layers buttermilk chocolate cake with a crème de menthe filling. Curls of mint-chocolate candy embellish this exquisite offering.

CHOCOLATE-MINT TORTE

CAKE
- $1/2$ cup butter or margarine, softened
- $1^3/4$ cups sugar
- 2 eggs
- 1 teaspoon vanilla extract
- 2 cups all-purpose flour
- 1 teaspoon baking powder
- 1 teaspoon baking soda
- $1/4$ teaspoon salt
- $3/4$ cup buttermilk
- $1/2$ cup coffee-flavored liqueur
- 4 ounces unsweetened baking chocolate, melted

FILLING
- 4 egg whites
- $1/2$ cup sugar
- 1 tablespoon water
- $1/4$ teaspoon cream of tartar
- $1/8$ teaspoon salt
- 8 ounces semisweet baking chocolate, melted
- 1 cup whipping cream
- 2 tablespoons crème de menthe
- 15 individually wrapped chocolate wafer mints to garnish

Preheat oven to 350 degrees. For cake, cream butter and sugar in a large bowl until fluffy. Add eggs and vanilla; stir until smooth. Sift flour, baking powder, baking soda, and salt into a medium bowl. Alternately add buttermilk, liqueur, and dry ingredients to creamed mixture; beat until well blended. Stir in melted chocolate. Line bottoms of 3 ungreased 9-inch round cake pans with waxed paper. Divide batter evenly in pans. Bake 20 to 25 minutes or until a toothpick inserted in center of cake comes out clean. Cool in pans 10 minutes; remove from pans and cool completely on a wire rack.

For filling, chill a small bowl and beaters from an electric mixer in freezer. In top of a double boiler over simmering water, combine egg whites, sugar, water, cream of tartar, and salt. Whisking constantly, cook until mixture reaches 160 degrees on a thermometer (about 8 minutes). Transfer to a large bowl and beat until stiff peaks form. Gently fold melted chocolate into cooked mixture. In chilled bowl, beat whipping cream and créme de menthe until stiff peaks form. Gently fold into chocolate mixture. Refrigerate until ready to use.

To assemble cake, place 1 cake layer on a cake plate; spread one-third of filling on cake layer. Repeat with remaining layers and filling. To garnish, use a vegetable peeler to shave chocolate curl from mints; place on top of cake. Cover and store in refrigerator.

Yield: about 12 servings

RASPBERRY-CHOCOLATE CAKE

CAKE
- 1 cup cocoa
- 2 cups boiling water
- 1 cup butter or margarine, softened
- 2¹/₂ cups sugar
- 4 eggs
- 1¹/₂ teaspoons vanilla extract
- 2³/₄ cups sifted all-purpose flour
- 2 teaspoons baking soda
- ¹/₂ teaspoon baking powder
- ¹/₂ teaspoon salt

FILLING
- 3¹/₂ cups confectioners sugar
- 6 tablespoons butter or margarine, softened
- 6 tablespoons raspberry-flavored liqueur

ICING
- 1 package (6 ounces) semisweet chocolate chips
- 1 cup butter or margarine
- ¹/₂ cup half and half
- 2¹/₂ cups confectioners sugar
- Gumdrop raspberry candies and silk leaves to garnish

For cake, grease and lightly flour three 9-inch round cake pans. In a medium bowl, combine cocoa and boiling water; whisk until smooth. Cool cocoa mixture completely.

Preheat oven to 350 degrees. In a large bowl, cream butter and sugar until fluffy. Add eggs and vanilla; beat until smooth. In a medium bowl, combine flour, baking soda, baking powder, and salt. Alternately beat dry ingredients and cocoa mixture into creamed mixture just until blended (do not overbeat). Pour batter into prepared pans. Bake 25 to 30 minutes or until a toothpick inserted in center of cake comes out clean. Cool in pans 10 minutes. Remove from pans and cool completely on a wire rack.

For filling, beat confectioners sugar, butter, and liqueur in a medium bowl until smooth and fluffy. Spread filling evenly between layers. Chill 2 hours.

For icing, combine chocolate chips, butter, and half and half in a medium saucepan over medium heat. Stirring constantly, cook about 6 to 8 minutes or until mixture is smooth. Remove from heat and whisk in confectioners sugar. Transfer icing to a medium bowl placed over a bowl of ice; beat about 8 minutes or until icing holds its shape. Spread icing on top and sides of cake, using back of a spoon to swirl icing. Store in an airtight container in refrigerator until ready to serve. To serve, garnish with candies and leaves.

Yield: about 16 servings

FRENCH QUARTER CAKE

CAKE
- 1½ cups all-purpose flour
- 1¼ cups sugar
- 3 tablespoons cocoa
- 2 teaspoons baking soda
- ½ teaspoon salt
- 4 eggs
- ½ cup buttermilk
- ½ cup coffee-flavored liqueur
- ⅓ cup vegetable oil
- 1 teaspoon vanilla extract
- 2 packages (3 ounces each) cream cheese, softened
- 6 ounces semisweet baking chocolate, melted

FILLING
- ½ cup whipping cream
- 2 teaspoons instant espresso powder
- 2 ounces semisweet baking chocolate, finely chopped

ICING
- 3 cups confectioners sugar
- ⅔ cup butter or margarine, softened
- 3 tablespoons cocoa
- 2 to 3 tablespoons milk
- 1 teaspoon vanilla extract

DECORATING ICING
- 2 cups confectioners sugar
- 2 tablespoons plus 1 teaspoon cocoa, divided
- 3 to 4 tablespoons coffee-flavored liqueur
- 1 teaspoon vanilla extract

Preheat oven to 350 degrees. For cake, grease three 8-inch round cake pans. Line bottoms with waxed paper; grease waxed paper. In a large bowl, combine flour, sugar, cocoa, baking soda, and salt. In a medium bowl, whisk eggs, buttermilk, liqueur, oil and vanilla. Add egg mixture to dry ingredients; stir until well blended. In a medium bowl, beat cream cheese and chocolate until well blended. Beat cream cheese mixture into batter. Pour batter into prepared pans. Bake 18 to 23 minutes or until a toothpick inserted in center of cake comes out clean. Cool in pans 10 minutes; remove from pans and cool completely on a wire rack.

For filling, combine whipping cream and espresso powder in a small saucepan. Bring to a boil over medium-high heat; pour mixture into a small bowl. Add chocolate; stir until smooth. Chill 10 minutes or until chocolate is cool but not set. Beat chocolate mixture until thickened (about 5 minutes). Spread filling between cake layers. Cover cake and chill 15 minutes or until filling is set.

For icing, combine confectioners sugar, butter, cocoa, milk, and vanilla in a large bowl; beat until smooth. Spread icing on top and sides of cake.

For decorating icing, combine confectioners sugar, 2 tablespoons cocoa, liqueur, and vanilla in a medium bowl; stir until smooth. Spoon icing into a pastry bag fitted with a small round tip. Using a toothpick, mark a 4-inch-diameter circle at center top of cake. Beginning at edge of circle, pipe connecting swirls onto top and sides of cake. Fill in circle with decorating icing. Pipe a small bead border around circle and top edge of cake. Allow icing to harden.

)ecorated with icing curlicues and an elegant monogram, French Quarter Cake is a dark, weet ending to any meal. Three layers of decadent cake are separated by an espresso-lavored chocolate filling, capturing the unique flavor of Bourbon Street.

Transfer remaining decorating cing to a small bowl. Add remaining teaspoon cocoa to icing to darken; stir until smooth. Return icing to pastry bag. Pipe desired initial in center of cake. Store in an airtight container in refrigerator. Serve at room temperature. **Yield:** about 16 servings

CHOCOLATE-CINNAMON ROLLS

DOUGH
- 1 package quick-acting dry yeast
- 1 cup warm water
- 2$3/4$ cups all-purpose flour
- $1/2$ cup cocoa
- $1/2$ cup sugar
- 1 teaspoon salt
- $1/4$ cup egg substitute
- 1$1/2$ tablespoons vegetable oil
  Vegetable cooking spray

FILLING
- 3 tablespoons sugar, divided
- 4 teaspoons ground cinnamon, divided
- 3 tablespoons reduced-calorie margarine, divided
- 1$1/3$ cups reduced-fat chocolate chips, divided
  Vegetable cooking spray

GLAZE
- $1/2$ cup confectioners sugar
- 2 teaspoons water

For dough, dissolve yeast in 1 cup warm water in a small bowl. In a large bowl, combine flour, cocoa, sugar, and salt. Add egg substitute, oil, and yeast mixture to dry ingredients; stir until a soft dough forms. Turn onto a lightly floured surface and knead about 3 minutes or until dough becomes smooth and elastic. Place in a large bowl sprayed with cooking spray, turning once to coat top of dough. Cover and let rise in a warm place (80 to 85 degrees) 1 hour or until almost doubled in size.

For filling, combine 1$1/2$ tablespoons sugar and 2 teaspoons cinnamon in a small bowl; set aside. Turn dough onto a lightly floured surface and punch down. Divide dough in half. Roll out half of dough to a 10 x 16-inch rectangle. Spread 1$1/2$ tablespoons margarine over dough; sprinkle sugar mixture and $2/3$ cup chocolate chips over dough. Beginning at 1 long edge, roll up tightly. Cut into 1-inch-wide slices and place, cut side down, in a lightly sprayed 8-inch square baking dish. Repeat with remaining ingredients. Lightly spray tops of dough with cooking spray, cover, and let rise in a warm place 1 hour or until almost doubled in size.

Preheat oven to 375 degrees. Bake 18 to 23 minutes.

For glaze, combine confectioners sugar and water in a small bowl; stir until smooth. Drizzle over warm rolls; serve warm.

Yield: 32 cinnamon rolls

HONEY-CINNAMON COFFEE

- 1$1/2$ tablespoons ground coffee
- $1/2$ teaspoon ground cinnamon
- 3 cups water
- 6 tablespoons honey
- $1/4$ cup warm half and half

Combine coffee and cinnamon in a coffee filter. Pour water into a drip coffee maker and brew coffee. Stir honey and half and half into brewed coffee; serve immediately.

Yield: about 3 cups coffee

CHOCOLATE-NUT COFFEE CAKE

1/2 cup firmly packed brown sugar
1/2 cup semisweet chocolate mini chips
1/2 cup finely chopped walnuts
1 tablespoon ground cinnamon
3/4 cup butter or margarine, softened
1 1/2 cups granulated sugar
3 eggs
1 tablespoon instant coffee granules dissolved in 1 tablespoon hot water
2 teaspoons vanilla extract
3 cups all-purpose flour
1 1/2 teaspoons baking powder
1 1/2 teaspoons baking soda
1/4 teaspoon salt
1 1/2 cups sour cream

Preheat oven to 350 degrees. In a medium bowl, combine brown sugar, chocolate chips, walnuts, and cinnamon; set aside. In a large bowl, cream butter and sugar until fluffy. Add eggs, 1 at a time, beating well after each addition. Add coffee and vanilla; beat until well blended. In a medium bowl, combine flour, baking powder, baking soda, and salt. Alternately stir dry ingredients and sour cream into creamed mixture, stirring just until well blended. Spoon one-third of batter into bottom of a greased and floured 10-inch tube pan with a removable bottom. Spoon one-third of chocolate chip mixture over batter. Repeat layers, ending with chocolate chip mixture. Bake 1 hour or until a toothpick inserted in center of cake comes out clean. Cool cake in pan on a wire rack 10 minutes. Run a knife around edge of pan; remove sides of pan. Allow cake to cool completely. Run knife around bottom of cake and remove bottom of pan. Store in an airtight container.
Yield: about 16 servings

S'MORE CHOCOLATE BARS

1 package (21.1 ounces) brownie mix
1/2 cup vegetable oil
1/2 cup water
1 egg
7 graham crackers (2 1/2 x 5-inch rectangles), coarsely crumbled
1 1/2 cups semisweet chocolate chips
3 cups miniature marshmallows

Preheat oven to 350 degrees. In a large bowl, combine brownie mix, oil, water, and egg; stir until well blended. Pour into a greased 9 x 13-inch baking pan. Sprinkle cracker crumbs over batter. Bake 20 minutes. Sprinkle chocolate chips over brownies; top with marshmallows. Bake 8 to 10 minutes longer or until marshmallows begin to brown. Cool in pan on a wire rack. Use an oiled knife to cut into 1 x 2-inch bars. Store in an airtight container.
Yield: about 4 dozen bars

CHOCOLATE SHORTBREAD

1 cup butter, softened
2/3 cup confectioners sugar
1 teaspoon vanilla extract
1 1/2 cups all-purpose flour
1/4 cup cocoa
1/4 teaspoon salt
Confectioners sugar

In a large bowl, cream butter, confectioners sugar, and vanilla until fluffy. In a small bowl, combine flour, cocoa, and salt. Add flour mixture to creamed mixture; stir until well blended. Wrap dough in plastic wrap and chill 30 minutes.

Preheat oven to 300 degrees. Press dough into a 10 1/2 x 15 1/2-inch jellyroll pan. Bake 30 minutes. Remove from oven and use a 2-inch-wide heart-shaped cookie cutter to cut out warm shortbread. Transfer cookies to a wire rack with waxed paper underneath to cool. Sift confectioners sugar over cooled cookies. Store in an airtight container.
Yield: about 2 dozen cookies

CHOCOLATE-TOFFEE BARS

1 package (18 ounces) refrigerated sugar cookie dough
1 cup almond brickle chips
1 cup semisweet chocolate chips
1/2 cup finely chopped pecans

Preheat oven to 350 degrees. Cut cookie dough into large pieces; press into bottom of a greased 9 x 13-inch baking pan. Sprinkle remaining ingredients evenly over dough. Bake 20 to 25 minutes or until edges are lightly browned. Cool in pan on a wire rack. Cut into 1 x 2-inch bars. Store in an airtight container.
Yield: about 4 dozen bars

CHEWY CHOCOLATE BARS

CRUST
4 cups old-fashioned oats
3/4 cup dark corn syrup
1 cup firmly packed brown sugar
2/3 cup butter or margarine, melted
1/2 cup crunchy peanut butter
2 teaspoons vanilla extract

TOPPING
1 package (12 ounces) semisweet chocolate chips
2/3 cup crunchy peanut butter
1 cup coarsely chopped peanuts

Preheat oven to 350 degrees. For crust, combine oats, corn syrup, brown sugar, melted butter, peanut butter, and vanilla in a medium bowl. Press mixture into a lightly greased 9 x 13-inch baking pan. Bake 12 to 15 minutes; cool in pan.

For topping, melt chocolate chips and peanut butter in top of a double boiler over hot, not simmering, water. Stir in peanuts. Spread topping over crust. Cut into bars. Cover and chill until chocolate is firm. Store in refrigerator.
Yield: about 4 dozen bars

Easy-to-make Chocolate Shortbread (top) is a light and flaky confection. Guests will love the home-baked appeal of rich Chewy Chocolate Bars.

27

TURTLE BROWNIES

BROWNIES
1 cup butter or margarine
4 ounces unsweetened baking
  chocolate
4 eggs
2 cups sugar
1 teaspoon vanilla-butter-nut
  flavoring
1¹/₂ cups all-purpose flour
¹/₂ teaspoon salt

TOPPING
1 package (14 ounces) caramels
2 tablespoons milk
1¹/₂ cups finely chopped toasted
  walnuts
1 package (6 ounces) semisweet
  chocolate chips
2 teaspoons vegetable
  shortening

Preheat oven to 350 degrees. For brownies, melt butter and chocolate in top of a double boiler over simmering water; remove from heat and allow to cool. In a large bowl, lightly beat eggs. Add sugar and vanilla-butter-nut flavoring to eggs; beat until smooth. Combine chocolate mixture with sugar mixture. In a small bowl, combine flour and salt. Add dry ingredients to chocolate mixture; stir until smooth. Spread batter into a greased and floured 9 x 13-inch baking pan. Bake 25 to 30 minutes or until set in center. Place pan on a wire rack to cool.

For topping, place caramels and milk in top of a double boiler over medium heat. Stir until caramels melt. Stir in walnuts. Spoon caramel mixture over warm brownies, spreading evenly. Allow brownies to cool. In a small microwave-safe bowl, microwave chocolate chips on high power (100%) 2 minutes, stirring after each minute. Add shortening; stir until well blended. Spread over caramel topping. Allow chocolate to harden. Cut into 1¹/₂-inch squares. Store in an airtight container.

Yield: about 3 dozen brownies

CHOCOLATE GRAHAM CRUNCH

12 chocolate graham crackers
  (2¹/₂ x 4³/₄ inches each)
2 cups finely chopped peanuts
1 cup butter
1 cup firmly packed brown sugar
³/₄ cup semisweet chocolate mini
  chips

Preheat oven to 400 degrees. Arrange graham crackers in a single layer with sides touching in bottom of a greased 10 x 15-inch jellyroll pan. Sprinkle peanuts evenly over crackers. In a heavy small saucepan, combine butter and brown sugar. Stirring constantly, cook over medium heat until sugar dissolves and mixture begins to boil. Continue to boil syrup 3 minutes longer without stirring; pour over crackers. Sprinkle chocolate chips over syrup. Bake 8 to 10 minutes or until top is bubbly. Cool completely in pan. Break into pieces. Store in an airtight container.

Yield: about 2¹/₄ pounds candy

CHOCOLATE-PEANUT BUTTER GRANOLA SQUARES

1 package (7 ounces) bran muffin mix
1/2 cup old-fashioned oats
1/4 cup firmly packed brown sugar
1/2 cup butter or margarine, softened
1/4 cup crunchy peanut butter
1/2 cup semisweet chocolate chips

Preheat oven to 325 degrees. In a medium bowl, combine muffin mix, oats, and brown sugar. With a pastry blender or 2 knives, cut in butter and peanut butter until mixture is well blended and crumbly. Stir in chocolate chips. Press into 7 x 11-inch greased baking pan. Bake 28 to 32 minutes or until golden brown and firm. Cool in pan on a wire rack. Cut into 1 1/2-inch squares. Store in an airtight container.
Yield: about 2 dozen squares

PEANUT BUTTER HOT COCOA

9 cups milk, divided
1/2 cup smooth peanut butter
1/2 cups chocolate mix for milk
Whipped cream to garnish

In a Dutch oven, combine 1 cup milk and peanut butter. Stirring frequently, cook over low heat until smooth. Increase heat to medium. Slowly stir in remaining cups milk and chocolate mix. Stirring occasionally, cook just until mixture simmers. Garnish each serving with whipped cream; serve immediately.
Yield: about 9 1/2 cups cocoa

CHOCOLATE-RASPBERRY SQUARES

1 cup butter or margarine, softened
1 1/2 cups sugar, divided
2 egg yolks
2 1/2 cups all-purpose flour
1 jar (12 ounces) raspberry jelly
1 cup semisweet chocolate mini chips
4 egg whites
1/4 teaspoon salt
2 cups coarsely ground hazelnuts

Preheat oven to 350 degrees. In a medium bowl, cream butter and 1/2 cup sugar until fluffy. Add egg yolks to butter mixture; beat until smooth. Stir in flour until well blended. Press dough into bottom of a greased 10 x 15-inch jellyroll pan. Bake 15 to 20 minutes or until lightly browned. Spread jelly over hot crust; sprinkle chocolate chips over jelly. Beat egg whites until foamy. Gradually add remaining 1 cup sugar and salt; beat until stiff peaks form. Fold in hazelnuts. Gently spread egg white mixture over chocolate layer. Bake 20 to 25 minutes or until lightly browned on top. Cool completely in pan. Cut into 2-inch squares. Store in an airtight container.
Yield: about 3 dozen squares

In a large bowl, cream butter and sugar until fluffy. Add egg, milk, and extracts; beat until smooth. In a small bowl, combine flour, baking powder, and salt. Add dry ingredients to creamed mixture; stir until a soft dough forms. Shape dough into a ball. Wrap in plastic wrap and chill 1 hour.

Preheat oven to 375 degrees. On a lightly floured surface, use a floured rolling pin to roll out dough to $1/8$-inch thickness. Use a $2^1/4$-inch-diameter fluted-edge cookie cutter to cut out cookies. Transfer to a greased baking sheet. Bake 7 to 9 minutes or until bottoms are lightly browned. Remove from oven and immediately place 1 mint on top of each hot cookie; allow to soften. Spread softened mint evenly over each cookie. Decorate each cookie with a cherry half. Transfer to a wire rack to cool completely. Store in an airtight container.
Yield: about 4 dozen cookies

Soft and chewy, Chocolate Mint-Topped Cookies pair almond-flavored cookies with a chocolate-mint candy icing.

CHOCOLATE MINT-TOPPED COOKIES

- $3/4$ cup butter or margarine, softened
- $3/4$ cup sugar
- 1 egg
- 4 teaspoons milk
- 1 teaspoon vanilla extract
- $1/2$ teaspoon almond extract
- 2 cups all-purpose flour
- $1^1/2$ teaspoons baking powder
- $1/4$ teaspoon salt
- 1 package (12 ounces) individually wrapped layered chocolate mints
  Green candied cherry halves to decorate

POPCORN CAKE S'MORES

- $1/2$ cup marshmallow creme
- 6 tablespoons smooth peanut butter
- 6 caramel corn cakes (about 4-inch diameter)
- $1/3$ cup semisweet chocolate mini chips

In a small bowl, stir marshmallow creme and peanut butter with a wooden spoon until well blended. Spread on top of caramel corn cakes. Sprinkle chocolate chips over cakes, lightly pressing chips into topping.
Yield: 6 servings

CHOCOLATE-CARAMEL CHEWIES

3/4 cup butter or margarine, softened
1/2 cup firmly packed brown sugar
2 eggs
1 teaspoon vanilla extract
1 1/2 cups all-purpose flour
1/4 teaspoon baking soda
1/4 teaspoon salt
1 1/2 cups chopped pecans
1 cup milk chocolate chips
22 caramel candies, quartered

Preheat oven to 350 degrees. In a medium bowl, cream butter and brown sugar until fluffy. Add eggs and vanilla; stir until smooth. In a small bowl, combine flour, baking soda, and salt. Add dry ingredients to creamed mixture; stir until a soft dough forms. Stir in pecans, chocolate chips, and caramel pieces. Drop tablespoonfuls of dough 2 inches apart onto a greased baking sheet. Bake 8 to 10 minutes or until edges are lightly browned. Allow cookies to cool slightly on pan; transfer to a wire rack to cool completely. Store in an airtight container. **Yield:** about 4 dozen cookies

Chocolate-Caramel Chewies (right) are a nutty delight. Striped with vanilla candy coating, Chocolate Squares have a hint of almond flavor (recipe on page 32).

CHOCOLATE SQUARES
(Shown on page 31)

1/2 cup butter or margarine, softened
1 cup sugar
1/3 cup (about 4 ounces) almond paste
2 eggs
1 teaspoon vanilla extract
1 teaspoon chocolate extract
1 3/4 cups all-purpose flour
3/4 cup cocoa
1 teaspoon baking powder
1/4 teaspoon salt
4 ounces vanilla candy coating

In a medium bowl, cream butter and sugar until fluffy. Add almond paste, eggs, and extracts. Beat 2 minutes at high speed of an electric mixer. In a small bowl, combine flour, cocoa, baking powder, and salt. Add dry ingredients to creamed mixture; stir until a soft dough forms. Shape dough into 2 balls. Wrap in plastic wrap and chill 1 hour.

Preheat oven to 350 degrees. On a lightly floured surface, use a floured rolling pin to roll out each half of dough to 1/4-inch thickness. Using a sharp knife, cut dough into 2-inch squares. Transfer to a greased baking sheet. Bake 10 to 12 minutes or until firm. Transfer to a wire rack to cool completely.

In a small saucepan, melt candy coating over low heat, stirring constantly. Spoon candy coating into a pastry bag fitted with a medium round tip. Pipe stripes on cookies. Allow coating to harden. Store in an airtight container.

Yield: about 4 dozen cookies

CHOCOLATE-PEANUT BUTTER PUFFS

1 package (6 ounces) semisweet chocolate chips
1 cup peanut butter chips
1/2 cup coarsely chopped peanuts
30 marshmallows

In a medium microwave-safe bowl, combine chocolate and peanut butter chips. Microwave on medium-high power (80%) 2 minutes or until mixture softens; stir until smooth. Stir in peanuts. Drop about 4 marshmallows at a time into chocolate mixture; stir to completely cover marshmallows. Place coated marshmallows on a baking sheet covered with waxed paper. Chill until chocolate hardens.

Yield: 2 1/2 dozen pieces candy

CARAMEL MOCHA

1 can (14 ounces) sweetened condensed milk
1 container (12 ounces) caramel ice cream topping
1/2 cup chocolate-flavored syrup
2 1/2 quarts hot, strongly brewed coffee (we used espresso roast coffee)

In a small Dutch oven, combine sweetened condensed milk, caramel topping, and chocolate syrup. Stirring constantly, cook over medium-low heat about 8 minutes or until mixture is well blended and hot. Add coffee; stir until blended. Serve hot.

Yield: about 12 cups coffee

CHOCOLATE BREAD PUDDING MUFFINS

1 can (12 ounces) refrigerated
   buttermilk biscuits, baked
   according to package directions
2 cups milk
3 eggs
3 tablespoons butter or margarine,
   melted
2 teaspoons vanilla extract
3/4 cup sugar
1/4 cup cocoa
1 cup (6 ounces) semisweet
   chocolate chips

Preheat oven to 350 degrees. Tear biscuits into small pieces. In a large bowl, stir biscuits and milk; set aside. In medium bowl, beat eggs, butter, and vanilla until well blended. Add sugar and cocoa; beat until well blended. Stir in chocolate chips. Add chocolate mixture to biscuit mixture; stir until well blended. Let stand 5 minutes. Spoon batter into paper-lined muffin pans, filling each tin three-quarters full. Bake 40 minutes or until a toothpick inserted in center comes out clean. Serve warm.
Yield: about 18 muffins

DOUBLE DELIGHT SANDWICH COOKIES

1 jar (7 ounces) marshmallow
   crème
1/3 cup smooth peanut butter
1 package (12 ounces) round
   butter-flavored crackers
16 ounces chocolate candy
   coating, chopped
1 package (6 ounces) semisweet
   chocolate chips

In a small bowl, beat marshmallow crème and peanut butter until well blended. Spoon about 1 teaspoon filling onto half of crackers. Place remaining crackers on top of filling; lightly press crackers together. In a heavy medium saucepan, melt candy coating and chocolate chips over low heat. Remove from heat. Place each cracker sandwich on a fork and dip into chocolate, covering completely. Place on waxed paper and allow chocolate to harden. Store in an airtight container in a cool place.
Yield: about 4 dozen sandwich cookies

PEAR AND CHOCOLATE TRIFLE

- 24 ladyfingers
- 1/2 cup seedless raspberry jam
- 1 can (29 ounces) pear halves, drained
- 2 packages (4 ounces each) milk chocolate instant pudding mix
- 2 cups half and half
- 1/4 cup sugar
- 1 cup whipping cream
- 4 ounces semisweet baking chocolate, shaved

Split ladyfingers in half lengthwise and spread cut sides with jam. Line sides of a trifle or serving bowl with ladyfingers, placing every other one with jam-side facing side of bowl. Line bottom of bowl with ladyfingers, jam side up. Place pears on ladyfingers in bottom of bowl. Beat pudding mix with half and half until thickened. Pour into bowl. Gradually adding sugar, beat whipping cream until stiff peaks form. Spoon whipped cream mixture over top. Sprinkle with shaved chocolate. Cover loosely and refrigerate until ready to serve.
Yield: about 8 servings

Easy-to-assemble Pear and Chocolate Trifle introduces a delightful flavor combination.

CANDY BAR CHEESECAKE

CRUST
- 1 1/2 cups chocolate graham cracker crumbs
- 6 tablespoons butter, melted
- 2 tablespoons sugar

FILLING
- 4 packages (8 ounces each) cream cheese, softened
- 1 cup firmly packed brown sugar
- 3 eggs
- 1 teaspoon vanilla extract
- 2 chocolate-covered caramel, peanut, and nougat candy bars (2.07 ounces each), chopped
- 2 tablespoons caramel ice-cream topping

Preheat oven to 350 degrees. Wrap aluminum foil under and around outside of a 9-inch springform pan. For crust, combine cracker crumbs, melted butter, and sugar in a medium bowl; stir until well blended. Press into bottom and

...ndy Bar Cheesecake is rich and satisfying with its chocolate graham cracker crust and ...eces of caramel-peanut-chocolate bars.

...lfway up sides of prepared pan. Bake 5 ...inutes; cool completely.

Preheat oven to 350 degrees. For ...ing, beat cream cheese in a large bowl ...til fluffy. Gradually beat in brown ...gar. Add eggs, one at a time, beating ...ell after each addition. Stir in vanilla. ...ur batter over crust. Bake one hour or

until filling is set. Sprinkle with chopped candy bars. Bake 7 minutes or until candy softens. Cool on a wire rack. Remove sides of pan. Drizzle with caramel topping. Store in an airtight container in refrigerator.

Yield: 10 to 12 servings

CHOCOLATE PETITE CHEESECAKES

CRUST
- 1³/4 cups chocolate graham cracker crumbs (about twelve 2¹/2 x 5-inch crackers)
- ¹/4 cup butter or margarine, softened
- 2 tablespoons sugar

FILLING
- 2 packages (8 ounces each) cream cheese, softened
- ³/4 cup sugar
- 4 eggs
- 1 package (12 ounces) semisweet chocolate chips, melted
- 1 cup whipping cream
- 1 teaspoon vanilla extract
- 1 can (21 ounces) cherry pie filling

Line a muffin pan with aluminum foil muffin cups. For crust, combine graham cracker crumbs, butter, and sugar in a medium bowl. Press a tablespoonful of mixture into bottom of each muffin cup.

Preheat oven to 350 degrees. For filling, beat cream cheese in a large bowl until fluffy. Gradually beat in sugar. Add eggs, one at a time, beating well after each addition. Beat in melted chocolate chips. Add whipping cream and vanilla; beat until smooth. Spoon about ¹/4 cup filling over crust in each muffin cup. Bake 18 to 22 minutes or until centers are set. Cool in muffin pan. Remove cheesecakes from pan; chill overnight. To serve, spoon 1 tablespoon pie filling in center of each cheesecake.

Yield: about 2 dozen cheesecakes

HOT FUDGE SUNDAE CAKE

Hot Fudge Sundae Cake is ready in minutes — with the fudge topping baked right in. Garnish individual servings with whipped cream, chopped nuts, and cherries.

- 1 cup all-purpose flour
- ³/4 cup granulated sugar
- ¹/2 cup cocoa, divided
- 2 teaspoons baking powder
- ¹/4 teaspoon salt
- ¹/2 cup milk
- 2 tablespoons vegetable oil
- 1 teaspoon vanilla extract
- 1 cup firmly packed brown sugar
- 1³/4 cups hot brewed coffee
- Whipped cream, chopped pecans, and maraschino cherries to serve

Preheat oven to 350 degrees. In a medium bowl, combine flour, sugar, ¹/4 cup cocoa, baking powder, and salt. In a large bowl, combine milk, oil, and vanilla; stir in flour mixture. Spread batter into an ungreased 9-inch square baking pan; sprinkle with brown sugar and remaining ¹/4 cup cocoa. Slowly pour hot coffee over mixture (do not stir). Bake 35 to 40 minutes or until cake begins to crack on top and pull away from sides. Cool in pan on a wire rack 15 minutes. To serve, spoon cake into serving dishes, top with whipped cream, pecans, and cherries.

Yield: about 10 servings

BROWNIE TRIFLE

Layers of bite-size mocha brownie pieces are alternated with chocolate-covered toffee bits, instant chocolate pudding, and almond-kissed whipped topping. Chocolate curls crown this rich dessert.

1 package (21.2 ounces) brownie
   mix
1/2 cup vegetable oil
2 eggs
1/4 cup water
1/4 cup coffee-flavored liqueur or
   4 tablespoons strongly
   brewed coffee and 1
   teaspoon sugar
3 packages (3.9 ounces each)
   chocolate instant pudding
   mix
6 cups milk
1/2 teaspoon almond extract
1 container (12 ounces) frozen
   non-dairy whipped topping,
   thawed
1 package (9 ounces) snack-size
   chocolate-covered toffee
   candy bars, crushed and
   divided

   Chocolate curls to garnish

Preheat oven to 350 degrees. Prepare brownie mix with oil, eggs, and water in a large bowl according to package directions. Spread batter into a greased x 13-inch baking pan and bake 24 to 26 minutes. Use a wooden skewer to poke holes about 1 inch apart in top of warm brownies; drizzle with liqueur. Cool completely.

Prepare pudding mixes with milk in a large bowl according to package directions; set aside. In a medium bowl, fold almond extract into whipped topping; set aside. In a 4-quart serving bowl, break half of brownies into bite-size pieces. Sprinkle half of crushed candy bars over brownies. Spread half of pudding over candy pieces. Spread half of whipped topping mixture over pudding layer. Repeat layers, ending with whipped topping mixture. Cover and chill. Garnish with chocolate curls.
Yield: about 20 servings

FUDGE ICE CREAM TOPPING

1 package (12 ounces)
   semisweet chocolate chips
1 cup butter or margarine
4 cups (1 pound) confectioners
   sugar
2 2/3 cups evaporated milk
2 1/2 teaspoons vanilla extract
1/8 teaspoon salt

Combine chocolate chips and butter in a large saucepan over low heat. Stir constantly until melted. Gradually add sugar and evaporated milk, blending well. Increase heat. Stirring constantly, bring to a boil and cook 8 minutes. Remove from heat. Stir in vanilla and salt. Store in an airtight container in refrigerator. Serve warm.
Yield: about 5 1/2 cups sauce

CHOCOLATE CUSTARD

CUSTARD
- 3 eggs, beaten
- 1 package (6 ounces) semisweet chocolate chips
- 1¹/₂ cups milk
- ¹/₂ cup sugar
- ¹/₄ teaspoon ground cinnamon

CHOCOLATE CURLS
- 1 package (6 ounces) semisweet chocolate chips

DECORATIVE TOPPING
- 2 tablespoons water
- 1¹/₂ teaspoons unflavored gelatin
- 2 tablespoons sugar
- ¹/₂ cup whipping cream

Preheat oven to 325 degrees. For custard, place eggs in a small bowl. In a medium saucepan, melt chocolate chips over low heat. Stir in milk, sugar, and cinnamon. Increase heat to medium. Stirring constantly, bring to a simmer and cook until sugar dissolves. Add about ¹/₂ cup chocolate mixture to eggs; stir until well blended. Gradually add egg mixture to chocolate mixture in saucepan, stirring until well blended. Remove from heat. Place a greased 9-inch pie plate in a shallow roasting pan. Pour chocolate mixture into pie plate. Fill roasting pan with very hot water to come halfway up side of pie plate. Bake 55 to 60 minutes or until a knife inserted near center of custard comes out clean. Cool completely on a wire rack. Cover and refrigerate until well chilled.

For chocolate curls, melt chocolate chips in a small saucepan over low heat, stirring constantly. Pour onto an ungreased baking sheet, spreading chocolate to form a 3 x 6-inch rectangle. Refrigerate until set but not firm. To make curls, pull a chocolate curler or vegetable peeler across surface of chocolate (curls will break if chocolate is too firm). Remelting and cooling chocolate as necessary, form desired number of curls. Refrigerate curls until ready to decorate.

For decorative topping, place a medium bowl and beaters from an electric mixer in freezer until well chilled. In a small saucepan, sprinkle gelatin over water; let stand 1 minute. Stir in sugar. Stirring constantly, cook over low heat about 5 minutes or until gelatin and sugar dissolve. Remove from heat. In chilled bowl, beat whipping cream until soft peaks form. Add sugar mixture and beat until stiff peaks form. Spoon topping into a pastry bag fitted with a large star tip; pipe decorations on custard. Garnish with chocolate curls. Store in an airtight container in refrigerator.

Yield: about 10 servings

MAKING CHOCOLATE CURLS
Making chocolate curls for garnishes is not difficult, but it does take a little practice. The chocolate should be the correct firmness to form the curls, neither too soft nor too hard. Different types of baking chocolates may be used, but the most common ones are semisweet and unsweetened. They are packaged in boxes containing 1-ounce squares.
Continued on page 40

weetened whipped cream and chocolate curls top incredibly rich Chocolate Custard.

Continued from page 38
There are several methods for making chocolate curls. To make small, short curls, hold a baking chocolate square in your hand for a few minutes to slightly soften chocolate. Rub chocolate over shredding side (large holes) of a grater to form curls. For medium-size curls, use a vegetable peeler or chocolate curler (available in kitchen specialty shops) to shave the wide side (for wide curls) or thin side (for thin curls) of a chocolate square.

To make long, thin, loosely formed curls, melt 6 chocolate squares and pour into a foil-lined 3¹/₄ x 5¹/₄-inch loaf pan. Chill until chocolate is set (about 2 hours). Remove from pan and remove foil. Rub chocolate over shredding side (large holes) of a grater to form curls.

To make large curls, melt 5 chocolate squares and pour onto an ungreased baking sheet to form a 3 x 5-inch rectangle. Chill about 10 minutes. Scrape across surface of chocolate with a long metal spatula, knife, teaspoon, or chocolate curler to form curls. The spatula and knife will form long, thin curls and the teaspoon and curler will form shorter curls. Return pan to refrigerator if chocolate becomes too soft. Use a toothpick to pick up curls. Refrigerate curls until ready to decorate.

CHOCOLATE PÂTÉ

16 ounces semisweet baking chocolate, chopped
1¹/₄ cups butter, cut into pieces
8 eggs, separated
¹/₂ cup orange-flavored liqueur
1 cup sugar
2¹/₂ tablespoons water
¹/₂ teaspoon cream of tartar
¹/₄ teaspoon salt

Stirring occasionally, melt chocolate and butter in top of a double boiler over hot water; pour into a medium bowl. In another medium bowl, beat egg yolks and liqueur until mixture lightens in color. Transfer egg mixture to top of a double boiler over simmering water. Stirring constantly, cook until mixture reaches 160 degrees on a thermometer (6 to 8 minutes). Fold yolk mixture into chocolate mixture; chill 45 minutes.

Combine egg whites, sugar, water, cream of tartar, and salt in top of a double boiler. Whisking constantly, cook over simmering water until mixture reaches 160 degrees on a thermometer (about 25 minutes). Transfer mixture to a large bowl and beat until stiff peaks form. Fold into chocolate mixture. Pour into a 5 x 9-inch loaf pan lined with plastic wrap; cover and freeze until firm.

To serve, remove frozen pâté from pan. Use a knife dipped in hot water to cut into thin slices. Serve immediately.
Yield: 10 to 12 servings

CHOCOLATE CREAM PIE

CRUST

- 1¹/₂ cups all-purpose flour
- ¹/₂ teaspoon salt
- ¹/₂ cup shortening
- 3 to 4 tablespoons cold water

FILLING

- 1 cup sugar
- ¹/₄ cup cocoa
- ¹/₄ cup cornstarch
- 1³/₄ cups milk
- 3 tablespoons butter or margarine
- 3 egg yolks, beaten
- 2 tablespoons orange-flavored liqueur
- 1 teaspoon vanilla extract

MERINGUE

- 4 egg whites
- ¹/₂ teaspoon cream of tartar
- 1 teaspoon orange-flavored liqueur
- ¹/₂ cup sifted confectioners sugar

For crust, combine flour and salt in a medium bowl. Using a pastry blender or 2 knives, cut in shortening until mixture resembles coarse meal. Sprinkle with water; mix until a soft dough forms. On a lightly floured surface, use a floured rolling pin to roll out dough to ¹/₈-inch thickness. Transfer to a 9-inch pie plate and use a sharp knife to trim edge of dough. Prick bottom of crust with a fork. Chill 30 minutes.

Preheat oven to 450 degrees. Bake crust 10 to 12 minutes or until lightly browned. Cool completely on a wire rack. For filling, combine sugar, cocoa, and cornstarch in a heavy medium saucepan. Stir in milk and butter. Stirring constantly, cook over medium heat until mixture thickens and begins to boil. Continuing to stir, boil 1 minute. Remove from heat. Add about ¹/₂ cup chocolate mixture to egg yolks; stir until well blended. Gradually add egg mixture to chocolate mixture in saucepan, stirring until well blended. Return to medium heat and bring to a boil; boil 1 minute or until mixture coats the back of a spoon. Stir in liqueur and vanilla. Remove filling from heat; pour into crust.

Preheat oven to 350 degrees. For meringue, beat egg whites and cream of tartar in a medium bowl until foamy. Add liqueur. Gradually add confectioners sugar, beating until stiff peaks form. Spread meringue over filling. Bake 10 to 15 minutes or until golden brown. Serve warm or chilled. Store in an airtight container in refrigerator.

Yield: about 10 servings

HOT CHOCOLATE MIX

Make each cup of hot chocolate to order!

6¼ cups nonfat milk powder
1 jar (16 ounces) non-dairy powdered creamer
1 package (16 ounces) confectioners sugar
1 container (15 ounces) chocolate mix for milk
½ cup cocoa

In a very large bowl, combine all ingredients. Store in an airtight container.

To serve, pour 6 ounces hot water or hot coffee over 2½ heaping tablespoons chocolate mix; stir until well blended. If desired, add one or more of the following variations to each cup of hot chocolate.
Yield: about 14 cups mix

VARIATIONS:
Flavored syrups
Marshmallows
Ground cinnamon
Flavored coffee creamers

CREAMY MOCHA LIQUEUR

1 can (14 ounces) sweetened condensed milk
1 cup whipping cream
1 cup coffee-flavored liqueur
½ cup chocolate-flavored liqueur

Pour sweetened condensed milk, whipping cream, and liqueurs in a blender. Process until blended. Pour into gift bottle. Store in refrigerator. Serve chilled.
Yield: about 3⅔ cups liqueur

CHOCOLATE-RUM COFFEE

2 quarts brewed coffee
3 cans (12 ounces each) evaporated milk
1 can (16 ounces) chocolate syrup
½ cup firmly packed brown sugar
1 cup rum

Cinnamon sticks to garnish

In a Dutch oven, combine coffee, milk, chocolate syrup, and brown sugar. Stirring occasionally, cook over medium-high heat until sugar dissolves and mixture begins to boil; remove from heat Stir in rum. Pour into mugs and garnish with cinnamon sticks.
Yield: about twenty 6-ounce servings

CINNAMON MOCHA

6 ounces semisweet baking chocolate, chopped
½ cup half and half
¼ cup sugar
½ teaspoon ground cinnamon
1½ quarts hot brewed coffee

Combine chocolate, half and half, sugar, and cinnamon in top of a double boiler over hot water; stir until chocolate melts. Transfer chocolate mixture to a large heat-resistant container. Pour brewed coffee over chocolate mixture; whisk until frothy. Pour into cups and serve hot.
Yield: about ten 6-ounce servings

CHOCOLATE CRÈME BRÛLÉE

- 1 quart whipping cream
- 1 cup firmly packed brown sugar, divided
- 2 tablespoons granulated sugar
- 8 ounces premium-quality milk chocolate, chopped
- 7 egg yolks
- 1 teaspoon vanilla extract

Sweetened Whipped Cream to serve (recipe on this page)

Preheat oven to 350 degrees. In a heavy saucepan over medium-high heat, bring cream, ¹/₂ cup brown sugar, and granulated sugar to a boil. Add chocolate and remove from heat; stir until chocolate is melted. Allow to cool slightly.

In a medium mixing bowl, whisk egg yolks and vanilla until blended. Whisk ¹/₄ cup chocolate mixture into eggs. Pour in remaining chocolate mixture and whisk until blended. Pour mixture through a strainer into a 13 x 9 x 2-inch glass baking dish. Place dish in a larger baking pan. Add hot water to larger pan to come halfway up sides of baking dish. Bake 1 to 1¹/₂ hours or until knife inserted in center comes out clean. Cool to room temperature. Cover with plastic wrap and refrigerate 6 to 8 hours.

Set oven on broil. Pat top of dessert with paper towel to remove excess moisture. Cover top evenly with remaining ¹/₂ cup brown sugar. Place dessert under broiler just until sugar begins to melt, about 5 minutes. (Watch dessert carefully; sugar will melt very

Once you've tasted this custard-like Chocolate Crème Brûlée, you'll want to serve it at all your special dinners — and just for the family, too!

quickly.) Serve warm or chilled with Sweetened Whipped Cream.
Yield: 12 to 15 servings

SWEETENED WHIPPED CREAM

- 1 cup whipping cream
- ¹/₂ cup granulated sugar
- 1¹/₂ teaspoons vanilla extract

Place all ingredients in a large mixing bowl. Beat at high speed until soft peaks form.

ULTIMATE CHOCOLATE PUDDING

3 ounces semisweet baking
   chocolate, coarsely chopped
3 ounces unsweetened baking
   chocolate, coarsely chopped
1/4 cup butter or margarine
3 cups milk
1 1/4 cups sugar, divided
2 eggs
4 egg yolks
1/2 cup cocoa
2 teaspoons cornstarch
2 cups whipping cream, divided
1 teaspoon vanilla extract
1 tablespoon finely chopped
   bittersweet baking chocolate
   and fresh mint leaves to
   garnish

In a double boiler over simmering water, melt chocolates and butter, stirring until well blended. Remove from heat and allow to cool. In a heavy large saucepan over medium heat, whisk milk, 1 cup sugar, eggs, and egg yolks. Attach a candy thermometer to pan, making sure thermometer does not touch bottom of pan. Stirring constantly, cook until mixture reaches 180 degrees or begins to thicken. Strain custard through a fine- mesh strainer into a large bowl. In a heavy small saucepan, sift cocoa and cornstarch into 1 cup whipping cream. Stirring constantly, bring mixture to a boil; cook until slightly thickened. Add chocolate mixture, cornstarch mixture, and vanilla to custard; stir until blended. Pour into individual serving dishes; cover and chill.

To serve, chill a small bowl and beaters from an electric mixer in freezer. In chilled bowl, beat remaining 1 cup whipping cream and remaining 1/4 cup sugar until stiff peaks form. Spoon mixture into a pastry bag fitted with a large star tip. Pipe whipped cream mixture onto pudding. Garnish with chopped bittersweet chocolate and mint leaves.

Yield: 8 to 10 servings

TOFFEE SAUCE

1 1/2 cups sugar
1 cup evaporated milk
1/4 cup butter or margarine
1/4 cup light corn syrup
   Dash of salt
1 package (6 ounces) chocolate-
   covered toffee bits

Cake or ice cream to serve

In a heavy medium saucepan, combine sugar, evaporated milk, butter, corn syrup, and salt. Stirring constantly, cook over medium heat until butter melts. Increase heat to medium-high and bring to a boil; boil 1 minute. Remove from heat and cool 15 minutes. Stir in toffee bits. Serve warm over cake or ice cream. Store in an airtight container in refrigerator.

Yield: about 3 cups sauce

CHOCOLATE CHIP BARS

1 package (7 ounces) bran
   muffin mix
1/2 cup butter or margarine,
   melted
1/4 cup firmly packed brown sugar
2 eggs
1 cup semisweet chocolate mini
   chips
1 cup chopped pecans

Preheat oven to 325 degrees.
Combine muffin mix, melted butter,
brown sugar, and eggs in a medium bowl;
stir until well blended. Stir in chocolate
chips and pecans. Spread mixture into a
greased 7 x 11-inch baking pan. Bake
25 to 30 minutes or until lightly browned.
Cool in pan on a wire rack. Cut into
1 x 2-inch bars.
Yield: about 2 1/2 dozen bars

CHOCOLATE PEPPERMINT CUPS

1 package (9 ounces) round
   peppermint candies
1 quart vanilla ice cream,
   softened
1/2 cup plus 1 heaping tablespoon
   semisweet chocolate chips
4 ounces chocolate candy
   coating
10 aluminum foil muffin cups

Place candies in a resealable plastic
bag and coarsely crush; reserve 1/4 cup for
garnish. Finely crush remaining candies
and combine with ice cream in a medium
bowl. Cover and place in freezer.

Combine chocolate chips and candy
coating in the top of a double boiler over
simmering water until chocolate mixture
melts. Invert foil cups onto a baking
sheet. Spoon chocolate mixture into a
pastry bag fitted with a small round tip
(#4). Randomly pipe chocolate onto foil
cups. Place pan in freezer until chocolate
hardens.
To serve, carefully remove foil cups
from chocolate. Spoon ice cream into
chocolate cups; garnish with reserved
crushed candies.
Yield: 10 servings.

CONFETTI SNACK MIX

1 package (22 ounces) jelly
   beans
1 package (14 ounces) star-
   shaped milk chocolate
   candies
1 package (10 ounces) small
   peanut butter sandwich
   cookies
4 cups small pretzel twists
4 cups bite-size frosted wheat
   cereal

In a very large bowl, combine all
ingredients. Store in an airtight container.
Yield: about 16 cups snack mix

An attractive arrangement of pecan halves accents our Chocolate-Pecan Tart, which is loaded with chocolate chips and pecans baked in a sweet filling.

CHOCOLATE-PECAN TART

CRUST

- 1¹/₄ cups all-purpose flour
- 2 tablespoons sugar
- ¹/₄ teaspoon ground cinnamon
- ¹/₄ cup butter or margarine, softened
- ¹/₄ cup shortening
- 1 egg yolk
- ¹/₂ teaspoon vanilla extract

FILLING

- ¹/₂ cup semisweet chocolate mini chips
- 1¹/₄ cups pecan halves
- 3 tablespoons granulated sugar
- 3 tablespoons firmly packed brown sugar
- ¹/₈ teaspoon salt
- 3 tablespoons butter or margarine, melted
- ¹/₂ cup dark corn syrup
- 3 eggs
- 1 teaspoon vanilla extract

For crust, combine flour, sugar, and cinnamon in a medium bowl. Using a pastry blender or 2 knives, cut in butter and shortening until mixture resembles coarse meal. Add egg yolk and vanilla; mix just until blended. Firmly press pastry into bottom and up sides of a 9-inch-diameter tart pan with a removable bottom. Chill 30 minutes.

Preheat oven to 400 degrees. Prick bottom of tart shell with a fork. Bake 5 minutes. Allow to cool 15 minutes.

For filling, reduce oven temperature to 350 degrees. Sprinkle chocolate chips over cooled crust. Arrange pecan halves on chocolate chips. In a medium bowl, combine sugars and salt. Stir in melted butter and corn syrup. Add eggs and vanilla; whisk until well blended. Slowly pour mixture over pecans in crust. Bake 40 to 45 minutes or until filling is almost set. Place tart on a wire rack to cool. Remove sides of pan to serve.
Yield: about 10 servings

CHOCOLATE TOFFEE MUD PIE

1 quart coffee ice cream, softened
4 bars (1.4 ounces each) chocolate-covered toffee, broken into bite-size pieces (about 1 cup)
1 purchased chocolate sandwich cookie pie crust (6 ounces)
1 container (12 ounces) fudge ice cream topping
2 tablespoons coffee-flavored liqueur

Toasted almond slices to garnish

In a medium bowl, combine ice cream and toffee pieces. Spoon into crust. Cover and freeze about 3 hours or until firm.

To serve, place fudge topping in a small microwave-safe bowl and microwave on high power (100%) 1 minute or until topping melts. Stir in liqueur. Spoon mixture over each serving and garnish with almond slices.
Yield: about 8 servings

Chocolate Toffee Mud Pie gets its mouth-watering taste from a winning combination of coffee ice cream, candy bars, fudge sauce, and coffee liqueur in a chocolate crust.

WHITE CHOCOLATE-ORANGE DREAM COOKIES

- 1 cup butter or margarine, softened
- 2/3 cup firmly packed light brown sugar
- 1/2 cup granulated sugar
- 1 large egg
- 1 tablespoon grated orange zest
- 2 teaspoons orange extract
- 2 1/4 cups all-purpose flour
- 3/4 teaspoon baking soda
- 1/2 teaspoon salt
- 1 package (12 ounces) white chocolate chips

Preheat oven to 350 degrees. In a mixing bowl, beat first 3 ingredients at medium speed of an electric mixer until creamy. Add egg, orange zest, and orange extract, beating until blended.

Combine flour, baking soda, and salt; gradually add to sugar mixture, beating just until blended after each addition. Stir in chips. Drop dough by rounded tablespoonfuls onto ungreased baking sheets. Bake 10 to 12 minutes or until edges are lightly browned. Cool on baking sheets 2 minutes; transfer to wire racks to cool completely.

Yield: about 3 1/2 dozen cookies

MOCHA CRUNCH COOKIES

- 1/2 cup butter or margarine, softened
- 1/4 cup vegetable shortening
- 1/2 cup plus 2 tablespoons granulated sugar, divided
- 1/2 cup firmly packed brown sugar
- 1 egg yolk
- 1 1/2 teaspoons vanilla extract
- 1 3/4 cups all-purpose flour
- 1 tablespoon instant coffee granules
- 1/4 teaspoon baking powder
- 1/4 teaspoon baking soda
- 1/4 teaspoon salt
- 1/2 cup semisweet chocolate mini chips

Preheat oven to 375 degrees. In a large bowl, cream butter, shortening, 1/2 cup granulated sugar, and brown sugar until fluffy. Add egg yolk and vanilla; beat until smooth. In a small bowl, combine flour, instant coffee, baking powder, baking soda, and salt. Add dry ingredients to creamed mixture; stir until a soft dough forms. Stir in chocolate chips. Shape dough into 1-inch balls; place 2 inches apart on an ungreased baking sheet. Flatten cookies with bottom of a glass dipped in remaining 2 tablespoons granulated sugar. Bake 10 to 12 minutes or until edges are lightly browned. Allow cookies to cool on pan 2 minutes; transfer cookies to a wire rack to cool completely. Store in an airtight container.

Yield: about 4 dozen cookies

CHOCOLATE FRUITCAKE

CAKE

- 1/2 cup butter
- 1/2 cup granulated sugar
- 1/2 cup firmly packed brown sugar
- 2 eggs
- 1 teaspoon vanilla extract
- 1/2 cup buttermilk
- 4 ounces semisweet baking chocolate, melted
- 2 1/2 cups all-purpose flour
- 1 teaspoon baking powder
- 1 teaspoon baking soda
- 1 teaspoon salt
- 3/4 cup cherry preserves
- 1/4 cup brandy
- 1 cup chopped red candied cherries
- 1 cup chopped dates
- 1 cup coarsely chopped pecans

GLAZE

- 1/4 cup water
- 1 1/2 tablespoons cornstarch
- 1/2 cup sugar
- 3 tablespoons cocoa
- 2 1/2 tablespoons butter
- 2 tablespoons brandy
- 1/2 teaspoon vanilla extract
  Candied cherry and pecan halves to decorate

Preheat oven to 350 degrees. For cake, cream butter and sugars in a large bowl. Add eggs and vanilla; beat until smooth. Stir in buttermilk and melted chocolate. In a medium bowl, combine flour, baking powder, baking soda, and salt. Add dry ingredients to creamed mixture; stir until well blended. Add preserves and brandy; stir until well blended. Stir in cherries, dates, and pecans. Spoon batter into a well-greased 10-inch fluted tube pan. Bake 50 to 60 minutes or until a toothpick inserted in center of cake comes out clean. Cool in pan 10 minutes. Invert cake onto a serving plate.

For glaze, combine water and cornstarch in a small saucepan; stir until cornstarch dissolves. Stir in sugar and cocoa. Stirring frequently, cook over medium heat until mixture begins to boil; add butter, brandy, and vanilla. Remove from heat and stir until butter melts; allow glaze to cool 5 minutes. Pour glaze over warm cake. Decorate with cherry and pecan halves. Cool completely. Store in an airtight container.

Yield: about 16 servings

TOFFEE COOKIES

1 cup butter or margarine, softened
3/4 cup granulated sugar
3/4 cup firmly packed brown sugar
2 eggs
1 tablespoon vanilla extract
2 1/4 cups all-purpose flour
1 teaspoon baking soda
1 teaspoon salt
2 cups coarsely chopped chocolate-covered English toffee bars

Preheat oven to 350 degrees. In a large bowl, cream butter and sugars until fluffy. Add eggs and vanilla; beat until smooth. In a medium bowl, stir together flour, baking soda, and salt. Add dry ingredients to creamed mixture; stir until a soft dough forms. Stir in toffee pieces. Drop by heaping teaspoonfuls 2 inches apart onto a greased baking sheet. Bake 8 to 10 minutes or until edges are lightly browned. Transfer to a wire rack to cool completely. Store in an airtight container.
Yield: about 6 1/2 dozen cookies

CHERRY-TOPPED CHOCOLATE COOKIES

1 jar (10 ounces) maraschino cherry halves
1 package (18.25 ounces) devil's food cake mix
1/2 cup sour cream
1 egg
2 tablespoons confectioners sugar

Preheat oven to 375 degrees. Drain cherries; place on a paper towel and pat dry. In a large bowl, beat cake mix, sour cream, and egg with an electric mixer until light in color (batter will be stiff). Use greased hands to shape dough into 1-inch balls and place 2 inches apart on a greased baking sheet. Press 1 cherry half into center of each cookie. Bake 8 to 10 minutes or until edges are set. Cool cookies on pan 2 minutes; transfer to a wire rack to cool completely. Sift confectioners sugar over cookies.
Yield: about 5 dozen cookies

GERMAN CHOCOLATE FUDGE

4 packages (4 ounces each) German baking chocolate, chopped
1 can (14 ounces) sweetened condensed milk
1 cup chopped pecans, toasted
1 cup flaked coconut
2 teaspoons vanilla extract

Line an 8-inch square baking pan with aluminum foil, extending foil over 2 sides of pan; grease foil. Combine chocolate and sweetened condensed milk in a large microwave-safe bowl. Microwave until chocolate softens; stir mixture until chocolate melts. Stir in pecans, coconut, and vanilla. Spread mixture into prepared pan. Cover and chill 2 hours or until firm.
Use ends of foil to lift fudge from pan. Cut into 1-inch squares. Store in an airtight container in a cool place.
Yield: about 4 dozen pieces fudge

BRANDIED FRUIT BALLS

1   pound dried fruit (we used a
      mixture of cherries, peaches,
      dates, prunes, cranberries,
      and apricots)
1   cup chopped walnuts
1/4 cup brandy
1/2 cup sifted confectioners sugar
3/4 cup semisweet chocolate chips
7   ounces chocolate candy
      coating, chopped

Process dried fruit, walnuts, and brandy in a food processor until finely chopped. Chill in an airtight container 1 hour.

Shape brandied fruit into 1-inch balls; roll lightly in confectioners sugar and place on a baking sheet. In a heavy medium saucepan over low heat, melt chocolate chips and candy coating. Remove chocolate from heat. Placing each fruit ball on a fork and holding over saucepan, spoon chocolate over balls. Transfer to a baking sheet covered with waxed paper. Chill until chocolate hardens. Store in an airtight container in refrigerator.
Yield: about 4 dozen fruit balls

CHOCOLATE-BUTTERSCOTCH CANDY

1   package (11 ounces)
      butterscotch chips
1   package (12 ounces)
      semisweet chocolate chips
1/2 cup raisins
1/2 cup chopped pecans

Line a 7 x 11-inch pan with waxed paper. In separate small saucepans, melt butterscotch and chocolate chips over low heat, stirring constantly. Remove from heat. Stir raisins into butterscotch chips; spread into prepared pan. Stir pecans into chocolate chips; spread over butterscotch mixture. Allow candy to harden. Cut into 1-inch squares. Store in an airtight container in a cool, dry place.
Yield: about 5 dozen pieces candy

MICROWAVE ROCKY ROAD FUDGE

4 1/2 cups sifted confections sugar
1/2 cup butter or margarine
1/3 cup cocoa
1/4 cup milk
1/4 teaspoon salt
1/2 cup chopped pecans
1/2 cup miniature marshmallows
1   teaspoon vanilla extract

Line an 8-inch square baking pan with aluminum foil, extending foil over 2 sides of pan; grease foil. In a large microwave-safe bowl, combine confectioners sugar, butter, cocoa, milk, and salt. Microwave on high power (100%) 2 to 2 1/2 minutes or until butter is melted. Add pecans, marshmallows, and vanilla; stir until well blended. Pour into prepared pan. Chill about 1 hour or until firm. Use ends of foil to lift candy from pan. Cut into 1-inch squares and store in an airtight container.
Yield: about 1 1/2 pounds fudge

No-bake Chocolate-Nut Truffles are easy to prepare with rich chocolate-flavored liqueur, vanilla wafer crumbs, and toasted pecans. Rolled in confectioners sugar, the treats are melt-in-your-mouth good!

CHOCOLATE-NUT TRUFFLES

    2 cups vanilla wafer crumbs
    2 cups sifted confectioners sugar
    1 cup finely chopped
         pecans, toasted
    2 tablespoons cocoa
  4¹/₂ tablespoons whipping cream
  4¹/₂ tablespoons chocolate-
         flavored liqueur
       Sifted confectioners sugar

In a large bowl, combine vanilla wafer crumbs, 2 cups confectioners sugar, pecans, and cocoa. Add whipping cream and liqueur; stir until well blended. Shape into 1-inch balls; roll in confectioners sugar. Store in an airtight container in a cool place.

Yield: about 5 dozen candies

HONEY-NUT FUDGE

  ¹/₄ cup butter or margarine
    3 ounces unsweetened baking
         chocolate
  ¹/₂ cup honey
    1 tablespoon water
    1 teaspoon vanilla extract
    1 package (16 ounces)
         confectioners sugar
    1 cup chopped pecans

Line an 8-inch square baking pan with aluminum foil, extending foil over 2 sides of pan; grease foil. In a heavy large saucepan, melt butter and chocolate over medium-low heat. Add honey, water, and vanilla to chocolate mixture; stir until well blended. Remove from heat. Add confectioners sugar; stir until smooth. Stir in pecans. Spread mixture into prepared pan. Chill until firm. Use ends of foil to lift fudge from pan. Cut into 1-inch squares. Store in an airtight container in a cool place.

Yield: about 4 dozen pieces fudge

Connoisseurs of fudge will love Honey-Nut Fudge, a sweet treat that gets its unique flavor from pecans and honey.

PEANUT BUTTER BARS

1 package (16 ounces)
    confectioners sugar
1¹/₂ cups graham cracker crumbs
1 cup smooth peanut butter
1 cup butter or margarine
8 chocolate-covered caramel,
    peanut, and nougat candy
    bars, chopped (2.07
    ounces each)
1 tablespoon milk

Combine confectioners sugar and
graham cracker crumbs in a large bowl. In
a medium microwave-safe bowl, combine
peanut butter and butter. Microwave on
medium-high power (80%) 2 minutes or
until mixture melts, stirring after each
minute. Pour peanut butter mixture over
graham cracker mixture; stir until well
blended. Press mixture into bottom of an
ungreased 9 x 13-inch baking dish. Place
candy bar pieces and milk in a medium
microwave-safe bowl. Microwave on
medium power (50%) 3 minutes or until
candy melts, stirring after each minute.
Spread melted candy mixture over
peanut butter mixture. Cool 20 minutes
or until candy mixture hardens. Cut into
-inch squares.

Yield: about 8 dozen bars

*Peanut Butter Bars are quick to make
in the microwave and feature a peanut
butter-graham cracker crust topped with a
melted candy bar mixture.*

CREAMY CHOCOLATE CARAMELS

2 cups sugar
1¹/₂ cups whipping cream, divided
1 cup light corn syrup
¹/₄ cup butter
4 ounces unsweetened baking chocolate, chopped
1 teaspoon vanilla extract

Line a 9-inch square baking pan with aluminum foil, extending foil over 2 sides of pan; grease foil. Butter sides of a heavy Dutch oven. Combine sugar, ³/₄ cup whipping cream, corn syrup, and butter in Dutch oven. Stirring constantly, cook over medium-low heat until sugar dissolves. Add chocolate; stir until melted. Using a pastry brush dipped in hot water, wash down any sugar crystals on sides of pan. Attach a candy thermometer to pan, making sure thermometer does not touch bottom of pan. Increase heat to medium; continue to stir and bring mixture to a boil. Gradually stir in remaining ³/₄ cup whipping cream. Stirring frequently without touching sides of pan, cook until mixture reaches firm-ball stage (approximately 242 to 248 degrees). Test about ¹/₂ teaspoon mixture in ice water. Mixture will roll into a firm ball in ice water but will flatten if pressed when removed from water. Remove from heat and stir in vanilla. Pour mixture into prepared pan. Cool several hours at room temperature.

Use ends of foil to lift candy from pan. Use a lightly oiled heavy knife to cut candy into 1-inch squares. Wrap in waxed paper and store in a cool place.
Yield: about 6¹/₂ dozen caramels

BOURBON PECAN BALLS

2 cups chopped pecans
³/₄ cup bourbon
¹/₂ cup butter or margarine, softened
1 teaspoon vanilla extract
9 to 11 cups confectioners sugar
8 ounces unsweetened baking chocolate, chopped
8 ounces chocolate candy coating, chopped

Combine pecans and bourbon in an airtight container. Allow to stand at room temperature 48 hours, stirring occasionally.

In a large bowl, combine butter and vanilla. Stir in nuts. Gradually add confectioners sugar until mixture is stiff. Shape mixture into ³/₄-inch balls. Place on a baking sheet lined with waxed paper; cover tightly with plastic wrap. Chill 1 hour.

Melt chocolate and candy coating in top of a double boiler over hot, not simmering, water. Dip balls into chocolate. Place on a baking sheet lined with waxed paper. Chill until chocolate hardens. Store in an airtight container in refrigerator.
Yield: about 10 dozen balls

CHOCOLATE PEPPERMINT PATTIES

7 cups confectioners sugar
7 tablespoons cocoa
1 can (14 ounces) sweetened
   condensed milk
1/2 cup butter, softened
1 teaspoon peppermint extract
24 ounces chocolate candy
   coating, chopped
1 package (12 ounces)
   semisweet chocolate chips

In a large bowl, combine confectioners sugar and cocoa. Add sweetened condensed milk, butter, and peppermint extract; beat until well blended. Shape mixture into 1-inch balls and flatten each ball to make a 1 1/2-inch-diameter patty. Place patties on baking sheets lined with waxed paper. Freeze patties 30 minutes or until thoroughly chilled.

In top of a double boiler, melt candy coating and chocolate chips over hot, not simmering, water. Remove double boiler from heat. Remove 1 dozen patties at a time from freezer. Placing each patty on a fork and holding over saucepan, spoon chocolate mixture over patties. Return to baking sheets lined with waxed paper.

Let chocolate harden. Store in an airtight container in refrigerator.

Yield: about 7 1/2 dozen patties

Shown on page 4: Cherry Sugarplums feature candied cherries wrapped in creamy cherry-flavored fondant and drenched in luscious dark chocolate.

CHERRY SUGARPLUMS

1/3 cup butter, softened
1/3 cup light corn syrup
1 teaspoon cherry flavoring
   Liquid red food coloring
4 cups sifted confectioners sugar
1 container (4 ounces) red
   candied cherries, halved
6 ounces chocolate candy coating
4 ounces bittersweet baking
   chocolate

In a medium bowl, cream butter and corn syrup until fluffy. Stir in cherry flavoring; tint pink. Beating with an electric mixer, gradually add confectioners sugar to butter mixture until too stiff to beat. Stir in remaining sugar. Pour mixture onto a dampened smooth surface. Knead until very smooth and creamy. Using teaspoonfuls of candy mixture, shape balls around cherry halves. Place balls on waxed paper. Lightly cover with waxed paper and allow to dry overnight at room temperature.

In a heavy medium saucepan over low heat, melt candy coating and bittersweet chocolate. Remove chocolate from heat. Placing each ball on a fork and holding over saucepan, spoon chocolate over balls. Place balls on a baking sheet covered with waxed paper. Place in refrigerator to allow chocolate to harden. Store in an airtight container in a cool place.

Yield: about 5 1/2 dozen candies

Fruit, nuts, pretzels, and cake are fun to dip in easy-to-make Chocolate Fondue and liqueur-flavored White Chocolate Fondue.

CHOCOLATE FONDUE

 ½ cup light corn syrup
 ½ cup whipping cream
 1 package (6 ounces) bittersweet
   baking chocolate, chopped

In a heavy medium saucepan, combine corn syrup and whipping cream. Bring mixture to a boil over medium heat. Remove from heat and add chocolate; stir until chocolate melts. Serve warm or store in an airtight container in refrigerator.

To reheat, place sauce in a medium microwave-safe bowl and microwave on medium-high power (80%) 2 minutes or until chocolate softens; stir until smooth. Serve warm.

Yield: about 1½ cups sauce

WHITE CHOCOLATE FONDUE

 3 cups whipping cream
 ½ cups sugar
 ¼ cup white crème de cacao
 1½ teaspoons vanilla extract
 12 ounces white chocolate,
   chopped

In a heavy large saucepan, combine whipping cream and sugar over medium heat. Stirring frequently, bring mixture to a boil. Reduce heat to medium low and simmer about 25 minutes or until liquid has been reduced to 2 cups. Remove from heat. Stir in crème de cacao and vanilla. Add white chocolate; stir until melted. Serve warm or store in a microwave-safe container in refrigerator.

To reheat, microwave sauce on medium power (50%) 8 minutes or until smooth, stirring after each minute. Serve warm.

Yield: about 3 cups sauce

Simply Delicious
BREADS & MUFFINS

Pineapple Upside-Down
Cinnamon Rolls, page 72

Entice your family with the wonderful aroma of fresh-baked breads! There are selections here for every taste, from savory to sweet. Choose from quick breads, muffins, biscuits, French toast, sweet rolls, and more.

CORN BREAD LOAF

6 tablespoons butter or margarine
1 cup chopped green onions
3/4 cup chopped celery
4 cups corn bread crumbs
4 cups finely crumbled white bread
10 slices bacon, cooked and
    crumbled
1 1/2 teaspoons ground sage
3/4 teaspoon salt
1/2 teaspoon ground black pepper
6 eggs, beaten
1 cup chicken broth

Preheat oven to 350 degrees. In a large skillet, melt butter over medium-high heat. Stir in onions and celery; sauté 8 minutes or until soft. In a large bowl, combine bread crumbs. Stir in onion mixture and next 4 ingredients. Stir in eggs and chicken broth. Spoon evenly into a greased and floured 4 x 12-inch loaf pan. Bake 30 to 40 minutes or until top is brown. Unmold onto serving plate and slice. Serve immediately.
Yield: about 10 servings

HERB BREAD

Fresh sage leaves to decorate
2 packages dry yeast
1/3 cup warm water
5 cups bread flour
1 cup whole-wheat flour
2 tablespoons dried rosemary
    leaves, crushed
1 tablespoon dried thyme leaves,
    crushed
2 1/2 teaspoons salt
1 1/2 cups warm milk
1/2 cup honey
1/4 cup vegetable oil
    Vegetable cooking spray
1 egg, beaten

Press fresh sage leaves between paper towels 8 hours or overnight.

In a small bowl, dissolve yeast in 1/3 cup warm water. In a large bowl, combine bread flour, whole-wheat flour, rosemary, thyme, and salt. Add yeast mixture, milk, honey, and oil to dry ingredients. Stir until a soft dough forms. Turn onto a lightly floured surface and knead 5 minutes or until dough becomes smooth and elastic. Place in a large bowl sprayed with cooking spray, turning once to coat top of dough. Cover and let rise in a warm place (80 to 85 degrees) 1 hour or until doubled in size.

Turn dough onto a lightly floured surface and punch down. Divide dough into thirds. Shape each piece of dough into a loaf and place in a greased 5 x 9-inch loaf pan. Spray tops of loaves with cooking spray, cover, and let rise in a warm place 1 hour or until doubled in size.

Preheat oven to 350 degrees. Brush tops of loaves with egg. Arrange pressed sage on tops of loaves; brush sage with egg. Bake 25 to 30 minutes or until bread sounds hollow when tapped. Serve warm or transfer to a wire rack to cool completely. Store in an airtight container. Serve with Herb Butter.
Yield: 3 loaves bread

loaf that's meant to be savored, Herb Bread is flavored with rosemary and thyme, and
as a fresh sage garnish. It's extra delicious when served with creamy Herb Butter.

HERB BUTTER

1 tablespoon plus 2 teaspoons
   dried rosemary leaves,
   crushed
1 tablespoon dried thyme leaves,
   crushed
$1/2$ teaspoons ground cardamom
$1/2$ cups butter, softened
$1/2$ cup whipping cream

Process rosemary, thyme, and cardamom in a food processor until finely ground. In a medium bowl, use an electric mixer to cream butter until fluffy. With electric mixer running, gradually add whipping cream; beat until fluffy. Stir in herb mixture. Spoon into jars or small ramekins. Cover and chill. Serve with Herb Bread.

Yield: about $2^1/2$ cups herb butter

CHALLAH

For a non-dairy bread, use water and oil.

- 2 cups milk **or** water
- 1/2 cup butter or margarine **or**
     1/3 cup vegetable oil
- 1/3 cup sugar
- 2 packages dry yeast
- 3 eggs
- 8 cups all-purpose flour
- 2 teaspoons salt
     Vegetable cooking spray
- 1 egg
- 2 teaspoons poppy seed

In a medium saucepan, combine milk, butter, and sugar; heat to 110 degrees. Remove from heat. Stir in yeast and cool 10 minutes.

Pour milk mixture into a large bowl. Add 3 eggs; beat until well blended. Add flour and salt; stir until a soft dough forms. Turn onto a lightly floured surface and knead until dough becomes smooth and elastic. Place in a large bowl sprayed with cooking spray, turning once to coat top of dough. Cover and let rise in a warm place (80 to 85 degrees) 1 hour or until doubled in size.

Turn dough onto a lightly floured surface and punch down. Divide dough in half. Use a floured rolling pin to roll each half into a 9 x 13-inch rectangle. Cut each rectangle lengthwise into 3 equal strips. For each loaf, braid 3 strips of dough together; transfer to a separate baking sheet sprayed with cooking spray. Spray tops of loaves with cooking spray. Let rise in a warm place 1 hour or until doubled in size.

Preheat oven to 350 degrees. In a small bowl, beat 1 egg. Brush loaves with egg. Sprinkle poppy seed evenly over both loaves. Bake 25 to 30 minutes or until golden brown and bread sounds hollow when tapped. Serve warm.
Yield: 2 loaves bread

SWISS CHEESE BREAD

- 4 cups all-purpose flour
- 2 tablespoons sugar
- 1 tablespoon baking powder
- 1 1/2 teaspoons salt
- 1/2 cup chilled butter or margarine, cut into pieces
- 4 cups (16 ounces) shredded Swiss cheese
- 1 tablespoon dried dill weed
- 2 cups milk
- 2 eggs

Preheat oven to 400 degrees. In a large bowl, combine flour, sugar, baking powder, and salt. Using a pastry blender or 2 knives, cut in butter until mixture resembles coarse meal. Stir in cheese and dill weed. In a medium bowl, whisk together milk and eggs. Add milk mixture to flour mixture; stir just until moistened. Pour batter evenly into 7 greased 3 x 5 1/2-inch loaf pans. Bake 20 to 25 minutes or until a toothpick inserted in center of bread comes out clean. Cool 10 minutes in pans. Remove from pans and serve warm or cool completely on a wire rack.
Yield: 7 mini loaves bread

WHOLE GRAIN BREAD

MIX

1 1/2 cups all-purpose flour
1/2 cup whole-wheat flour
1/4 cup old-fashioned oats
2 tablespoons yellow cornmeal
2 tablespoons wheat germ
2 tablespoons unprocessed bran
2 tablespoons firmly packed
    brown sugar
1 teaspoon salt
1 package quick-rise dry yeast

Combine flours, oats, cornmeal, wheat germ, bran, brown sugar, salt, and yeast in a large bowl; stir until well blended. Store in an airtight container in a cool place. Prepare with bread instructions below.

Yield: about 2 1/2 cups bread mix, makes loaf bread

To bake bread: Place bread mix in a large bowl. In a small saucepan, heat cup milk and 2 tablespoons vegetable oil until very warm (120 to 130 degrees). Add milk mixture to bread mix; stir until soft dough forms. Turn onto a lightly floured surface and knead 5 minutes or until dough becomes smooth and elastic. Cover and allow dough to rest 0 minutes. Shape dough into a loaf and place in a greased 4 1/2 x 8 1/2-inch loaf pan. Spray top of dough with cooking spray, cover, and let rise in a warm place 80 to 85 degrees) 50 minutes or until doubled in size.

Preheat oven to 375 degrees. Brush top of loaf with a beaten egg. Bake 25 to 30 minutes or until bread is golden brown and sounds hollow when tapped. Serve warm or transfer to a wire rack to cool completely. Store in an airtight container.

PARMESAN BREAD STICKS

1 package of dry yeast
1 teaspoon sugar
1 1/4 cups warm water
2 1/2 to 2 3/4 cups all-purpose flour,
    divided
1/2 teaspoon salt
1 tablespoon olive oil
    Vegetable cooking spray
2 tablespoons freshly grated
    Parmesan cheese

In a small bowl, dissolve yeast and sugar in warm water. In a large bowl, combine 1 cup flour and salt. Add yeast mixture and oil to dry ingredients; beat with an electric mixer about 3 minutes. Add 1 1/2 cups flour; stir until well blended. Turn dough onto a lightly floured surface. Knead about 5 minutes or until dough becomes smooth and elastic, using remaining flour as necessary. Place in a large bowl sprayed with cooking spray, turning once to coat top of dough. Cover and let rise in a warm place (80 to 85 degrees) 1 hour or until doubled in size.

Turn dough onto a lightly floured surface and punch down. Roll dough into a 12 x 16-inch rectangle. Cut dough into 1 x 12-inch strips. Twist and press ends onto an ungreased baking sheet. Lightly brush strips with water. Sprinkle with Parmesan cheese. Lightly cover strips and let rise in a warm place 45 minutes or until almost doubled in size.

Preheat oven to 400 degrees. Bake 12 to 17 minutes or until bottoms are lightly browned. Serve warm.
Yield: 16 bread sticks

Here's a delicious mid-morning snack or coffee break treat! Pineapple-Pumpkin Bread is prepared with pound cake mix, canned pumpkin, and crushed pineapple and loaded with chopped pecans.

PINEAPPLE-PUMPKIN BREAD

- 1 package (16 ounces) pound cake mix
- 2 teaspoons pumpkin pie spice
- 1 teaspoon baking soda
- 1 cup canned pumpkin
- 1 can (8 ounces) crushed pineapple
- 2 eggs
- 1 cup chopped pecans

Preheat oven to 325 degrees. Grease bottoms of two 4¹/₂ x 8¹/₂-inch loaf pans and line bottoms with waxed paper. Grease and flour waxed paper and sides of pans. In a large bowl, combine cake mix, pumpkin pie spice, and baking soda. Add pumpkin, undrained pineapple, and eggs; beat until well blended. Stir in pecans. Spoon batter into prepared pans. Bake 45 to 55 minutes or until a toothpick inserted in center of bread comes out clean. Cool in pans 20 minutes. Remove from pans and serve warm or cool completely on a wire rack.
Yield: 2 loaves bread

Sprinkled with caraway seed, Easy Pumpernickel Bread is a hearty addition to meal.

EASY PUMPERNICKEL BREAD

- 1   package (16 ounces) hot roll mix
- ³/₄   cup warm (105 to 115 degrees) strongly brewed coffee
- 2   eggs
- ¹/₄   cup molasses
- ³/₄   cup rye flour
- 3   teaspoons caraway seed, divided
- 2   teaspoons cocoa
    Vegetable cooking spray
- 1   egg white, lightly beaten

In a small bowl, sprinkle yeast from roll mix over coffee; allow yeast to soften. Stir in eggs and molasses. In a medium bowl, combine roll mix, rye flour, 2 teaspoons caraway seed, and cocoa. Add yeast mixture; stir until a soft dough forms. Place in a large bowl sprayed with cooking spray, turning once to coat top of dough. Cover and let rise in a warm place (80 to 85 degrees) about 1 hour or until doubled in size.

Turn dough onto a lightly floured surface and knead 3 minutes or until dough becomes smooth and elastic. Shape dough into 2 round loaves and place on a greased baking sheet. Spray tops of dough with cooking spray, cover, and let rise in a warm place 1 hour or until doubled in size.

Preheat oven to 350 degrees. Brush dough with egg white and sprinkle with remaining 1 teaspoon caraway seed. Bake 25 to 30 minutes or until bread is golden brown and sounds hollow when tapped. Transfer to a wire rack to cool completely. Store in an airtight container.

Yield: 2 loaves bread

SUPER MEXICAN CORN BREAD

1 cup all-purpose flour
3/4 cup yellow cornmeal
1 1/2 teaspoons baking powder
1 teaspoon sugar
1 teaspoon salt
1/2 teaspoon baking soda
1 cup buttermilk
1 can (8 1/2 ounces) cream-style
   corn
1/4 cup vegetable oil
2 eggs, beaten
2 tablespoons seeded and chopped
   jalapeño peppers
1 cup (4 ounces) shredded sharp
   Cheddar cheese
6 slices bacon, cooked and
   crumbled

Preheat oven to 375 degrees. In a medium bowl, combine flour, cornmeal, baking powder, sugar, salt, and baking soda. Stir in buttermilk, corn, oil, eggs, peppers, cheese, and bacon. Pour into 4 1/2-inch-wide greased star-shaped baking pans or greased muffin cups. Bake 25 to 30 minutes or until a toothpick inserted in center of corn bread comes out clean. Serve warm. Store in an airtight container.
Yield: about 8 corn bread stars or 15 muffins

PUMPKIN NUT BREAD

3 cups all-purpose flour
1 tablespoon ground cinnamon
1 teaspoon baking soda
1 teaspoon ground cloves
1 teaspoon ground nutmeg
1/2 teaspoon salt
3 cups sugar
1 cup vegetable oil
1 can (16 ounces) pumpkin
2 eggs
1 cup chopped pecans

Preheat oven to 350 degrees. In a medium bowl, combine flour, cinnamon, baking soda, cloves, nutmeg, and salt. In a large bowl, mix together sugar, oil, and pumpkin. Beat in eggs one at a time. Add dry ingredients to pumpkin mixture; stir until smooth. Stir in pecans. Pour batter into two 5 x 9-inch greased and floured loaf pans. Bake 50 to 60 minutes or until toothpick inserted in center comes out clean. Cool in pans 10 minutes. Remove from pans and cool on a wire rack. Store in an airtight container.
Yield: 2 loaves bread

SNOWMAN BREAD

2 cups water
1 cup old-fashioned rolled oats
6 cups all-purpose flour
1/2 cup nonfat dry milk powder
2 1/2 teaspoons salt
2 packages dry yeast
1/3 cup warm water
1/2 cup honey
1/4 cup vegetable oil
   Vegetable cooking spray
1 egg, beaten
   Raisins
   Candied cherry
   Pretzels

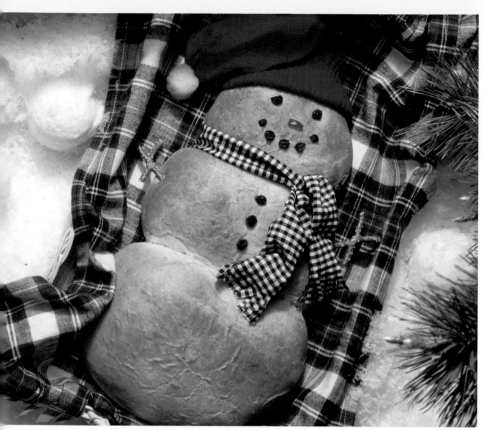

Enriched with oats and honey and "dressed" in a scarf and cap, a loaf of Snowman Bread is a fun treat to serve on a cold winter day.

In a medium saucepan, bring 2 cups water to a boil. Remove from heat; stir in oats. Cool to room temperature.

Sift next 3 ingredients into a large bowl. In a small bowl, dissolve yeast in ⅓ cup warm water. Add oat mixture, yeast mixture, honey, and oil to dry ingredients. Stir until a soft dough forms. Turn onto a lightly floured surface and knead until dough becomes smooth and elastic. Place in a large bowl sprayed with cooking spray, turning once to coat top of dough. Cover and let rise in a warm place (80 to 85 degrees) 1 hour or until doubled in size.

Turn dough onto a lightly floured surface and punch down. Divide dough in half. Referring to photo, shape each half of dough into 3 balls, graduated in size. Arrange each set of balls on a greased baking sheet to resemble a snowman. Brush dough with egg. For each snowman, use raisins for eyes, mouth, and buttons and a small piece of candied cherry for nose. Break pretzels into twig shapes. Insert 1 broken pretzel into each side of snowmen for arms. Spray dough with cooking spray, cover, and let rise in a warm place 1 hour or until doubled in size.

Preheat oven to 350 degrees. Bake 25 to 30 minutes or until bread sounds hollow when tapped. Transfer to a wire rack to cool. Store in an airtight container. **Yield:** 2 loaves bread

HONEY-BUTTERMILK BREAD

    3 cups all-purpose flour
1 1/2 teaspoons salt
    1 package active dry yeast
  3/4 cup buttermilk
  1/2 cup warm water
    3 tablespoons honey
    1 tablespoon butter or margarine,
       melted
    1 teaspoon almond-flavored extract

In a large bowl, stir together first
3 ingredients. In a medium bowl, whisk
together remaining ingredients. Add
buttermilk mixture to dry ingredients;
knead until a soft dough forms. Turn
dough onto a lightly floured surface;
knead about 5 minutes or until dough
becomes soft and pliable. Place in a
greased bowl; grease top of dough.
Cover and let rise in a warm place
(80 to 85 degrees) 1 hour or until
doubled in size.

Turn dough onto a lightly floured
surface and punch down. Divide dough
in half; shape each half into an 18-inch
long log shape. Pinch together ends of
1 log shape to form a ring; transfer to a
greased baking sheet. Interlocking 1 ring
with the other, repeat with remaining log
shape. Grease top of dough. Cover and
let rise in a warm place 1 hour or until
doubled in size.

Preheat oven to 350 degrees. Bake
30 to 35 minutes or until golden brown.
Transfer to a wire rack to cool completely.
Store in an airtight container.
Yield: 1 loaf bread

ORANGE-PECAN BREAD

    3 cups all-purpose flour
  3/4 cup finely chopped pecans
    1 package dry yeast
1 1/2 teaspoons sugar
1 1/2 teaspoons salt
    1 teaspoon dried grated orange
       peel
    1 cup plus 1 tablespoon milk
  1/4 cup butter or margarine
    1 teaspoon orange extract
       Vegetable cooking spray

In a large bowl, combine flour, pecans,
yeast, sugar, salt, and orange peel. In
a small saucepan, combine milk and
butter. Stirring occasionally, cook over
medium-low heat until milk mixture
reaches 130 degrees. Remove from heat;
stir in orange extract. Add milk mixture
to dry ingredients; stir until a soft dough
forms. Turn dough onto a lightly floured
surface and knead about 5 minutes
or until dough becomes smooth and
elastic. Place in a large bowl sprayed with
cooking spray, turning once to coat top of
dough. Cover and let rise in a warm place
(80 to 85 degrees) 1 hour or until doubled
in size.

Turn dough onto a lightly floured
surface and punch down. Place in a
greased 5 x 9-inch loaf pan. Spray top
of dough with cooking spray, cover, and
let rise in a warm place 1 hour or until
doubled in size.

Preheat oven to 375 degrees. Bake
30 to 35 minutes or until golden brown.
Cool completely on a wire rack. Store in
an airtight container.
Yield: 1 loaf bread

CINNAMON-BANANA BREAD

BREAD
- 1 cup firmly packed brown sugar
- 1 cup butter or margarine, divided
- 2 ripe bananas, cut into small pieces
- 1/2 cup chopped pecans
- 1/2 cup granulated sugar
- 2 eggs
- 1 3/4 cups all-purpose flour
- 2 tablespoons ground cinnamon
- 1 teaspoon baking powder
- 1/2 teaspoon baking soda

FROSTING
- 1 1/4 cups confectioners sugar
- 1 package (3 ounces) cream cheese, softened

Preheat oven to 350 degrees. For bread, combine brown sugar and 1/2 cup butter in a medium saucepan over medium heat, stirring until butter is melted. Add bananas and pecans, stirring until well coated. Cool to room temperature.

In a large bowl, cream remaining butter and granulated sugar until fluffy. Beat in eggs. In a small bowl, sift together remaining ingredients. Stir dry ingredients into creamed mixture. Stir in banana mixture. Divide batter evenly between 2 greased 3 1/2 x 6 3/4-inch loaf pans. Bake 45 to 50 minutes or until a toothpick inserted in center of bread comes out clean. Cool in pans 10 minutes. Transfer to a wire rack to cool completely.

For frosting, combine confectioners sugar and cream cheese in a medium bowl. Using medium speed of an electric mixer, beat until smooth. Drizzle frosting over bread. Store in an airtight container.
Yield: 2 loaves of bread

CARROT-ORANGE BREAD

- 4 eggs
- 2 cups granulated sugar
- 1 1/4 cups vegetable oil
- 3 cups all-purpose flour
- 2 teaspoons baking powder
- 1 1/2 teaspoons baking soda
- 1/2 teaspoon salt
- 1 teaspoon ground nutmeg
- 2 teaspoons ground cinnamon
- 2 cups loosely packed shredded carrots
- 1 can (11 ounces) mandarin oranges, drained and chopped
- 2 teaspoons grated orange peel

Preheat oven to 350 degrees. In a large mixing bowl, beat eggs and sugar. Slowly add oil and continue beating until smooth. Sift together flour, baking powder, baking soda, salt, nutmeg, and cinnamon. Add flour mixture to egg mixture, beating until smooth. Stir in carrots, oranges, and orange peel. Pour batter into two well-greased 5 x 9 x 3-inch loaf pans. Bake 45 to 50 minutes or until a wooden toothpick inserted in the center comes out clean. Remove from pans and cool on wire rack.
Yield: 2 loaves of bread

Shown on page 4: *A mini loaf of moist, nutty Cinnamon-Carrot Bread has irresistible appeal. The yummy streusel topping is a snap to make using graham cracker crumbs.*

CINNAMON-CARROT BREAD

BREAD
- 3/4 cup coarsely crushed cinnamon graham crackers (about five 2 1/2 x 5-inch crackers)
- 3/4 cup chopped pecans
- 1 cup sugar
- 3/4 cup vegetable oil
- 2 eggs
- 1/2 teaspoon orange extract
- 1 cup shredded carrots
- 1 1/3 cups all-purpose flour
- 1 teaspoon ground cinnamon
- 1/2 teaspoon salt
- 1/2 teaspoon baking powder

ICING
- 3/4 cup confectioners sugar
- 1 tablespoon water
- 1/2 teaspoon orange extract

Preheat oven to 350 degrees. For bread, grease four 2 1/2 x 5-inch loaf pans. Line pans with waxed paper; grease waxed paper. In a medium bowl, combine cracker crumbs and pecans; set aside. In a large bowl, combine sugar, oil, eggs, and orange extract; beat until blended. Stir in carrots. In a small bowl, combine flour, cinnamon, salt, and baking powder. Add flour mixture to oil mixture; stir just until moistened. Spoon half of batter into prepared pans. Sprinkle about 3 tablespoons crumb mixture over batter in each pan; swirl mixture with a knife. Spoon remaining batter over crumb mixture. Sprinkle remaining crumb mixture on top. Bake 38 to 43 minutes or until a toothpick inserted in center of bread comes out clean and top is golden brown. Cool in pans 10 minutes. Remove from pans and cool completely on a wire rack.

For icing, combine confectioners sugar, water, and orange extract in a small bowl stir until smooth. Drizzle icing over bread Allow icing to harden. Store in an airtight container.

Yield: 4 loaves bread

SOFT PRETZELS

- 1 1/2 cups warm water
- 1 package dry yeast
- 1 tablespoon granulated sugar
- 4 1/2 cups all-purpose flour
- 1 1/2 teaspoons salt
- 1 egg, lightly beaten
- Coarsely ground kosher or sea salt

Combine water, yeast, and sugar in a mixing bowl. Allow to stand until yeast is dissolved and begins to foam (about 5 minutes). Stir in flour and 1 1/2 teaspoon salt. Turn out onto lightly floured surface and knead 8 to 10 minutes or until dough is smooth and elastic. Separate dough into 16 equal pieces. Roll each piece into a 20-inch-long rope and form into a pretzel shape. Place on a lightly greased baking sheet. Cover and let rise 20 minutes.

Preheat oven to 425 degrees. Brush pretzels with egg and sprinkle with coarsely ground salt. Bake 15 minutes or until golden brown. Remove pretzels from baking sheet and cool on wire rack

Yield: 16 pretzels

...rved warm, Golden Monkey Bread is simple to make with frozen dinner rolls. Cinnamon, ...own sugar, and butterscotch chips melt in the oven to form a rich glaze over this pull-...art bread.

OLDEN MONKEY BREAD

1 cup firmly packed brown sugar
1 teaspoon ground cinnamon
1 package (25 ounces) frozen
     white dinner yeast rolls, thawed
/2 cup butter or margarine, melted
/2 cup butterscotch chips, divided
/2 cup chopped pecans, divided

n a small bowl, combine brown sugar
d cinnamon. Tear each roll into 3
eces. Dip each piece into melted butter
d coat with brown sugar mixture.
ace half of dough pieces in a greased
-inch fluted tube pan. Sprinkle

¹/₄ cup butterscotch chips and ¹/₄ cup pecans over dough. Place remaining dough pieces in pan. Sprinkle remaining butterscotch chips and pecans over dough. Cover and let rise in a warm place (80 to 85 degrees) about 2¹/₂ hours or until doubled in size.

Preheat oven to 375 degrees. Bake 25 to 30 minutes or until golden brown. Cover with aluminum foil if bread begins to brown too quickly. Cool in pan 10 minutes. Invert bread onto a serving plate. Serve warm.
Yield: 10 to 12 servings

69

CREAM PUFF RING

PASTRY
- 1 cup water
- 1/2 cup butter or margarine
- 1 cup all-purpose flour
- 1/8 teaspoon salt
- 4 eggs

PASTRY CREAM
- 3 egg yolks
- 1/2 cup sugar
- 2 tablespoons all-purpose flour
- 3/4 cup milk
- 1/4 cup orange-flavored liqueur
- 1 cup whipping cream, whipped

GLAZE
- 2 ounces unsweetened baking chocolate
- 1 tablespoon butter or margarine
- 2 cups sifted confectioners sugar
- 1/4 cup boiling water
- 2 tablespoons orange-flavored liqueur

Preheat oven to 400 degrees. For pastry, combine water and butter in a medium saucepan over medium heat. Cook until butter melts. Stir in flour and salt until well blended. Stirring constantly, cook over medium heat until mixture forms a ball. Remove from heat; cool 10 minutes. Add eggs, 1 at a time, beating well after each addition. Line a 9-inch round cake pan with aluminum foil. Drop eight 1/4 cupfuls of dough in pan 1/2 inch apart, forming a circle. Bake 30 minutes. Reduce oven to 375 degrees; bake pastries 20 minutes longer. Cut slits in ring to allow steam to escape. Continue baking 20 minutes longer. Remove from pan; cool on foil.

For pastry cream, beat egg yolks and sugar until mixture is light in color. Stir in flour and milk. Transfer mixture to a heavy large saucepan. Stirring constantly bring to a boil over medium heat. Cook until very thick (about 4 minutes). Remove from heat and stir in liqueur; cool completely, stirring occasionally. Fold in whipped cream.

For glaze, melt chocolate and butter in top of a double boiler. Remove from heat and beat in confectioners sugar, water, and liqueur; set aside. Carefully slice tops from pastries. Pull soft dough from insides. Fill with pastry cream. Replace tops and spoon glaze over ring.
Yield: 8 servings

SANTA BREAD
(Shown on page 92)

BREAD
- 4 1/2 cups all-purpose flour, divided
- 1/2 cup granulated sugar
- 2 packages dry yeast
- 2 teaspoons grated orange peel
- 2 teaspoons ground cinnamon
- 1 teaspoon salt
- 1 cup milk
- 1/2 cup butter or margarine
- 1/4 cup plus 1 tablespoon water, divided
- 2 eggs
- 1 egg white
  Red paste food coloring

ICING
- 2 1/2 cups confectioners sugar
- 3 to 4 tablespoons hot water
- 1/2 teaspoon vanilla extract
  Raisins and candied cherry halves

For bread, combine 1¼ cups flour,
ugar, yeast, orange peel, cinnamon, and
alt in a large mixing bowl; set aside.
  In a small saucepan, heat milk, butter,
nd ¼ cup water just until butter melts.
dd milk mixture to dry ingredients,
eating until smooth. Beat in 2 eggs and
¼ cups additional flour. By hand, stir in
nough of remaining flour to make a stiff
ough. Turn dough onto a floured surface
nd knead until smooth and elastic,
bout 8 to 10 minutes. Place dough in a
reased bowl, turning once to grease top.
over and let rise 1 hour or until doubled
 size.
  Preheat oven to 350 degrees. Punch
own dough; divide in half and refer to
hoto to form two Santa heads. Place on
reased baking sheet. In a small bowl,
ombine egg white, remaining
 tablespoon water, and food coloring.
se pastry brush and food coloring
ixture to paint hats. Bake 40 to 45
inutes or until bread sounds hollow
hen tapped. Remove from pan and cool
 wire rack.
  For icing, combine confectioners sugar,
ater, and vanilla in a medium bowl. Ice
eards. For eyes and noses, use dots of
ing to attach raisins and cherries.
  eld: 2 loaves of bread

CHRISTMAS BREAD

  ¼ cup butter or margarine,
       softened
  ½ cup granulated sugar
  2 eggs
  ⅓ cup applesauce
  1 teaspoon vanilla extract
  2 cups all-purpose baking mix
1½ cups chopped candied fruit (we
       used pineapple and green
       and red cherries
  ½ cup chopped pecans
  ⅔ cup sifted confectioners sugar
  1 tablespoon milk

  Preheat oven to 350 degrees. In a
large bowl, cream butter and granulated
sugar until fluffy. Add eggs, applesauce,
and vanilla; beat until well blended. Add
baking mix; stir just until moistened. Stir
in candied fruit and pecans. Spoon batter
into 4 greased and floured 3 x 5½-inch
loaf pans. Bake 25 to 30 minutes or until
a toothpick inserted in center of bread
comes out clean. Cool in pans 5 minutes.
Remove from pans and place on a wire
rack with waxed paper underneath.
  For glaze, combine confectioners
sugar and milk in a small bowl; stir until
smooth. Drizzle glaze over warm bread.
Allow glaze to harden. Store in an airtight
container.
Yield: 4 mini loaves bread

PINEAPPLE UPSIDE-DOWN CINNAMON ROLLS

1 can (15¼ ounces) crushed
   pineapple, drained
1 cup firmly packed brown sugar
3 tablespoons butter
1 can (11.5 ounces) refrigerated
   cinnamon rolls
   Maraschino cherry halves to
   garnish

Preheat oven to 375 degrees. In a 10½-inch heavy ovenproof skillet, combine drained pineapple, brown sugar, and butter. Place in oven 10 minutes or until butter melts. Remove pan from oven; stir pineapple mixture to blend. Place rolls on top of pineapple mixture. Bake in lower half of oven 16 to 18 minutes or until rolls are lightly browned. Immediately invert onto a serving plate. Garnish with cherry halves. Serve warm.
Yield: 8 cinnamon rolls

Shown on page 57: Garnished with maraschino cherry halves, Pineapple Upside-Down Cinnamon Rolls have the familiar flavor of the classic cake, but they're so much easier to make! Just bake refrigerated cinnamon rolls in a brown sugar-pineapple mixture and enjoy.

PECAN-RAISIN WREATH

½ cup butter or margarine,
   softened and divided
½ cup firmly packed brown sugar
1 tablespoon corn syrup
18 pecan halves
⅓ cup chopped pecans
⅓ cup raisins
3 tablespoons granulated sugar
¼ teaspoon ground cinnamon
10 frozen uncooked white dinner
   rolls, thawed

Preheat oven to 350 degrees. In a small saucepan, combine ¼ cup butter, brown sugar, and corn syrup over medium heat. Cook, stirring constantly, until sugar dissolves. Pour sugar mixture into a greased 8-inch ring mold. Place pecan halves upside down on sugar mixture.

Melt remaining butter in a small saucepan. In a small bowl, stir together pecans, raisins, granulated sugar, and cinnamon. Dip each roll into melted butter and place in nut mixture. Spoon nut mixture over, covering each roll completely. Arrange rolls, with sides touching, in pan. Sprinkle remaining nut mixture over tops of rolls. Bake 35 to 40 minutes or until golden brown. Cool in pan 15 minutes. Turn onto a wire rack to cool completely. Store in an airtight container.

Bread may be served warm or at room temperature. To reheat, preheat oven to 350 degrees. Bake uncovered on an ungreased baking sheet 3 to 5 minutes until heated through.
Yield: about 10 servings

his delectable Pecan-Raisin Wreath is ideal to take to a holiday hostess! Easy to make with ozen yeast rolls, the bread is enhanced by pecans, raisins, and cinnamon. A simple basket akes a convenient carrier. Shiny bells attached to the basket liner will jingle all the way to ur friend's house!

TASTY PECAN MUFFINS

1 cup all-purpose flour
3/4 cup whole-wheat flour
3 tablespoons sugar
2 teaspoons baking powder
1 teaspoon salt
1 cup milk
2 eggs
1/2 cup butter or margarine, melted
2/3 cup chopped pecans, toasted
   and coarsely ground

Preheat oven to 350 degrees. In a medium bowl, combine flours, sugar, baking powder, and salt. Make a well in center of dry ingredients. In a small bowl, combine milk, eggs, and melted butter; beat until well blended. Add to dry ingredients; stir until well blended. Stir in pecans. Fill greased muffin cups about two-thirds full. Bake 25 to 28 minutes or until a toothpick inserted in center of muffin comes out clean and edges of muffins are lightly browned. Cool in pan 5 minutes. Serve warm or cool completely.
Yield: about 1 dozen muffins

PEANUT BUTTER AND JELLY MUFFINS

1 package (18.25 ounces) white
   cake mix
1 teaspoon baking soda
1 cup crunchy peanut butter
3/4 cup water
2 eggs
1/3 cup strawberry jam

Preheat oven to 350 degrees. In a large bowl, combine cake mix and baking soda. Add peanut butter, water, and eggs; beat just until blended. Fill paper-lined muffin cups about two-thirds full. Place a teaspoonful jam in center of batter in each muffin cup. Bake 18 to 23 minutes o until a toothpick inserted in muffin come out clean. Serve warm.
Yield: about 1 1/2 dozen muffins

CINNAMON PUFFINS

1 1/2 cups all-purpose flour
1 1/2 teaspoons baking powder
1 teaspoon ground nutmeg,
     divided
1/2 teaspoon salt
1 cup sugar, divided
1/3 cup shortening
1 egg
1/2 teaspoon vanilla extract
1/2 cup milk
1/2 cup butter or margarine
1 teaspoon ground cinnamon

Preheat oven to 350 degrees. In a medium bowl, combine flour, baking powder, 1/2 teaspoon nutmeg, and salt. In another medium bowl, beat 1/2 cup sugar, shortening, egg, and vanilla until well blended. Add flour mixture to creamed mixture; beat in milk until smooth. Fill each cup of a lightly greased 12-cup muffin pan two-thirds full with batter. Bake 20 minutes or until light golden brown. Melt butter in a small saucepan. In a small bowl, combine remaining 1/2 cup sugar, cinnamon, and remaining 1/2 teaspoon nutmeg. While puffins are warm, dip in butter, then in sugar mixture, coating thoroughly. Store in an airtight container.
Yield: 1 dozen puffins

STREUSEL MUFFINS
(Shown on page 76)

STREUSEL
5 tablespoons firmly packed
     brown sugar
2 tablespoons all-purpose flour
1 1/4 teaspoons ground cinnamon
2 tablespoons butter or margarine
1/3 cup chopped pecans

MUFFINS
1 package (18.25 ounces) yellow
     cake mix
3/4 cup applesauce
3 eggs
1/2 cup vegetable oil
1/2 cup cream cheese ready-to-
     spread frosting

Preheat oven to 350 degrees. For streusel, combine brown sugar, flour, and cinnamon in a small bowl. Using a pastry blender or 2 knives, cut in butter until mixture is crumbly. Stir in pecans.

For muffins, combine cake mix, applesauce, eggs, and oil in a large bowl; beat just until blended. Spoon about 1 1/2 tablespoons batter into each paper-lined muffin cup. Sprinkle 1 teaspoon streusel over batter. Repeat with remaining batter and streusel. Bake 18 to 23 minutes or until a toothpick inserted in center of muffin comes out clean. Cool in pan 5 minutes. Transfer muffins to a wire rack with waxed paper underneath.

In a small microwave-safe bowl, microwave frosting on high power (100%) 15 to 25 seconds or until frosting melts. Drizzle frosting over warm muffins. Serve warm.
Yield: about 1 1/2 dozen muffins

Streusel Muffins (recipe on page 75) are prepared with a cake mix, cinnamon, pecans, and apples. Glazed with a simple icing, Dandy Doughnuts are cut from canned biscuits.

DANDY DOUGHNUTS

2 cups sifted confectioners sugar
3 tablespoons water
1/2 teaspoon vanilla extract
Vegetable oil
1 can (10 biscuits) refrigerated
biscuits

In a small bowl, combine confectioners sugar, water, and vanilla; stir until smooth.

In a heavy medium saucepan, heat 1 to 1 1/4 inches of oil over medium-high heat. Using the middle of a doughnut cutter or a small cookie cutter, cut out centers of biscuits. Fry doughnut and holes in oil until lightly browned on both sides; drain on paper towels.

Dip hot doughnuts and holes into glaze and place on a wire rack with waxed paper underneath. Serve warm.
Yield: 10 doughnuts and 10 doughnut holes

Chocolate fudge cake mix helps make Raspberry-Chocolate Danish Squares (recipe on page 84) irresistible! Bursting with pecans, miniature Nut Muffins are quick to make using pantry staples.

NUT MUFFINS

1¹/₂ cups firmly packed brown sugar
1¹/₂ cups chopped pecans
¹/₂ cup all-purpose flour
¹/₈ teaspoon salt
3 eggs, beaten
¹/₂ teaspoon vanilla extract
Vegetable cooking spray

In a medium bowl, combine brown sugar, pecans, flour, and salt. Stir in eggs and vanilla just until blended (batter will be lumpy). Heavily spray miniature muffin cups with cooking spray. Fill cups about two-thirds full. Place muffin pans in a cold oven. Turn temperature to 300 degrees and bake 25 minutes. Cool 1 minute; run a knife gently around edge of each muffin cup to loosen muffins. Allow to sit in pan another 5 minutes; transfer muffins to a wire rack to cool completely.

Yield: about 3 dozen mini muffins

Shown on page 4: *A creamy chocolate-peanut butter filling is hidden in the center of taste-tempting oat bran Surprise Muffins.*

SURPRISE MUFFINS

1/2 cup smooth peanut butter
1/2 cup semisweet chocolate chips
1 1/2 cups all-purpose flour
1 cup oat bran
1/2 cup firmly packed brown sugar
2 1/2 teaspoons baking powder
1/4 teaspoon salt
1 cup milk
1/3 cup vegetable oil
2 eggs
1 teaspoon maple extract

Preheat oven to 425 degrees. In a small bowl, combine peanut butter and chocolate chips; set aside.

In a medium bowl, combine flour, bran, brown sugar, baking powder, and salt. In a small bowl, whisk milk, oil, eggs, and maple extract. Make a well in center of dry ingredients and add milk mixture; stir just until moistened. Spoon about 2 tablespoons batter into each cup of a greased muffin pan. Spoon about 2 teaspoons peanut butter mixture over batter in each cup. Spoon remaining batter over peanut butter mixture, filling each cup three-fourths full. Bake 15 to 18 minutes or until muffins pull away from sides of pan. Remove from pan and cool completely on a wire rack. Store in an airtight container. Muffins may be served at room temperature or reheated.

To reheat, cover and bake in a preheated 350-degree oven 5 to 8 minutes or until heated through.
Yield: about 1 dozen muffins

ORANGE-PUMPKIN MUFFINS

1 3/4 cups all-purpose flour
1 1/2 teaspoons pumpkin pie spice
1 teaspoon baking soda
1/2 teaspoon baking powder
1/2 teaspoon salt
1 cup granulated sugar
1/2 cup firmly packed brown sugar
2 eggs
1/3 cup vegetable oil
1 cup canned pumpkin
1/3 cup orange juice
1 teaspoon grated orange zest
1/2 cup chopped walnuts

Preheat oven to 350 degrees. In a small bowl, combine flour, pumpkin pie spice, baking soda, baking powder, and salt. In a large bowl, combine sugars, eggs, and oil. Add pumpkin, orange juice, and orange zest to sugar mixture; beat until well blended. Stir in dry ingredients just until blended. Fill paper-lined muffin cups about two-thirds full. Sprinkle about 1 teaspoon walnuts over batter in each cup. Bake 20 to 23 minutes or until a toothpick inserted in center of muffin comes out clean. Transfer muffins to a wire rack to cool. Store in an airtight container.
Yield: about 1 1/2 dozen muffins

CRANBERRY MUFFINS

MUFFINS
- 3 cups all-purpose flour
- 3/4 cup granulated sugar
- 1 tablespoon baking powder
- 1/2 cup milk
- 1/2 cup butter or margarine, melted
- 2 eggs
- 1 tablespoon vanilla extract
- 1 1/2 cups chopped fresh cranberries
- 3/4 cup chopped pecans
- 1 tablespoon grated orange peel

TOPPING
- 1/4 cup granulated sugar
- 1 1/2 teaspoons grated orange peel
- 1 teaspoon ground cinnamon
- 1/4 cup chopped pecans

Preheat oven to 375 degrees. For muffins, combine flour, sugar, and baking powder in a large mixing bowl. Make a well in center of mixture and add milk, butter, eggs, and vanilla. Stir just until all ingredients are moistened (batter will be lumpy). Stir in cranberries, pecans, and orange peel. Fill greased or paper-lined muffin cups two-thirds full with batter.

For topping, combine sugar, orange peel, and cinnamon in a small bowl. Stir in pecans. Sprinkle topping over muffins. Bake 25 to 30 minutes or until muffin springs back when gently pressed.
Yield: about 2 dozen muffins

LEMON-PECAN MUFFINS

- 1/2 cup butter or margarine, softened
- 1/2 cup plus 2 tablespoons sugar
- 2 eggs
- 1 teaspoon vanilla extract
- 1 teaspoon lemon extract
- 1 teaspoon freshly grated lemon zest
- 1/2 cup all-purpose flour
- 1/2 teaspoon baking powder
- 1/8 teaspoon salt
- 2 cups finely chopped pecans

Preheat oven to 325 degrees. Line a muffin pan with paper muffin cups. In a medium bowl, cream butter and sugar until fluffy. Add eggs, extracts, and lemon zest; beat until well blended. In a small bowl, combine flour, baking powder, and salt. Add dry ingredients to creamed mixture; stir until just moistened. Stir in pecans. Fill muffin cups about two-thirds full. Bake 25 to 30 minutes or until a toothpick inserted in center of muffin comes out clean. Serve warm or cool completely on a wire rack. Store in an airtight container.
Yield: about 1 dozen muffins

Cinnamon-Orange Sticky Buns are drenched in a buttery brown sugar topping enhanced with orange marmalade and chopped pecans.

CINNAMON-ORANGE STICKY BUNS

2 cans (11.5 ounces each) refrigerated cinnamon rolls with icing
1/2 cup orange marmalade
3 tablespoons chopped pecans
1 cup firmly packed brown sugar
1/3 cup butter or margarine, melted

Preheat oven to 350 degrees. In a small bowl, combine icing from cinnamon roll cans, marmalade, and pecans; spread into bottom of a greased 10-inch fluted tube pan. Place brown sugar in another small bowl. Dip each roll into melted butter and coat with brown sugar. Stand rolls on ends in pan. Sprinkle with remaining brown sugar. Bake 35 to 40 minutes or until golden brown. Cool in pan 5 minutes. Invert onto a serving plate. Serve warm.
Yield: 16 sticky buns

The rich flavors of ginger and molasses in the batter will make Gingerbread Pancakes a family favorite.

GINGERBREAD PANCAKES

1¹/₂ cups all-purpose flour
  ¹/₄ cup sugar
   1 teaspoon ground ginger
   1 teaspoon baking powder
   1 teaspoon baking soda
  ¹/₂ teaspoon salt
   1 cup buttermilk
   3 eggs, beaten
  ¹/₃ cup butter or margarine, melted
  ¹/₄ cup molasses
     Butter or margarine
     Butter and syrup to serve

In a large bowl, combine flour, sugar, ginger, baking powder, baking soda, and salt. In a medium bowl, whisk buttermilk, eggs, ¹/₃ cup melted butter, and molasses. Add to dry ingredients and stir just until blended.

Melt 2 tablespoons butter in a large skillet over medium heat. For each pancake, pour about ¹/₄ cup batter into skillet and cook until pancake is full of bubbles on top and underside is lightly browned. Turn with a spatula and cook until other side is lightly browned. Transfer to a warm plate, cover with aluminum foil, and place in a 200-degree oven until ready to serve. Add butter to skillet as necessary between batches. Serve hot with butter and syrup.

Yield: about 1¹/₂ dozen pancakes

SWEDISH PANCAKES

2 cups milk
2 eggs
1¹/2 tablespoons sugar
¹/4 teaspoon salt
1¹/2 cups all-purpose flour
4 tablespoons butter
Garnish: Sweetened Whipped
  Cream (recipe on page 43) fresh
  strawberries and blueberries,
  and powdered sugar

Whisk first four ingredients together.
Add flour, ¹/2 cup at a time, to milk
mixture, whisking until smooth. Melt
butter in a small skillet or crepe pan; cool.
Whisk butter into milk mixture. For each
pancake, pour about ¹/2 cup batter into
the hot pan, tilting pan until batter covers
the bottom of pan. Turn pancake over
when lightly browned. Place on waxed
paper to cool. (Pancakes can be frozen
between layers of waxed paper.)

To serve, roll up pancakes and garnish
with whipped cream, fresh fruit, and
powdered sugar, if desired.

Yield: about 21 six-inch pancakes

DANISH PASTRIES

CAKE
1¹/2 cups butter, softened and
  divided
3 cups all-purpose flour, divided
¹/8 teaspoon salt
¹/4 cup cold water
1 cup milk
¹/4 cup granulated sugar
1 teaspoon almond extract
3 eggs

GLAZE
1¹/2 cups confectioners sugar
2 tablespoons butter, softened
1 tablespoon milk
2 teaspoons vanilla extract

TOPPING
1 cup sliced almonds, toasted
2 tablespoons confectioners
  sugar

For cake, use a pastry blender or two
knives to cut 1 cup butter into 2 cups
flour in a medium mixing bowl until
mixture resembles coarse meal. Stir in
salt and water to make a dough. Divide
dough into eight equal portions. Pat out
each portion of dough into a 3 x 4-inch
oval on an ungreased baking sheet.
Refrigerate until ready to use.

Preheat oven to 350 degrees. In a large
heavy saucepan, combine remaining
¹/2 cup butter and milk over medium
heat. Bring to a boil. Add remaining 1 cup
flour, sugar, and almond extract. Quickly
stir until mixture forms a ball; remove
from heat. By hand, beat in eggs, one at
a time, until well blended. Spread a thick,
even layer of dough over chilled ovals.
Bake 40 to 45 minutes or until puffy and
golden.

For glaze, combine confectioners sugar and butter in a small bowl; stir until well blended. Stir in milk and vanilla until mixture is smooth.

For topping, mix almonds with confectioners sugar in a small bowl.

Spread glaze evenly over warm pastries. Sprinkle each pastry with topping. Serve warm or at room temperature.

Yield: 8 pastries

EGGNOG FRENCH TOAST

SYRUP
- $1/2$ cup sugar
- 1 tablespoon cornstarch
- 1 cup boiling water
- $1/2$ cup chopped walnuts
- 1 tablespoon butter
- Dash of salt
- $1/4$ cup maple syrup
- 1 tablespoon bourbon

FRENCH TOAST
- Vegetable oil
- 2 cups eggnog
- 2 eggs
- 1 teaspoon vanilla extract
- $1/2$ teaspoon orange extract
- $1/4$ teaspoon ground nutmeg
- 1 loaf (16 ounces) French bread, cut into $3/4$-inch slices

For syrup, combine sugar and cornstarch in a heavy medium saucepan. Stirring constantly over medium heat, gradually add boiling water. Add walnuts, butter, and salt; cook about 7 minutes or until mixture thickens. Remove from heat. Stir in maple syrup and bourbon.

For French toast, heat a small amount of oil in a medium skillet over medium heat. Combine eggnog, eggs, extracts, and nutmeg in a medium bowl. Dip each bread slice into eggnog mixture. Cook bread slices until each side is lightly browned. Add additional oil to skillet as necessary. Serve warm with warm syrup.

Yield: about 7 servings

FLAVORED BUTTERS

HONEY-ORANGE BUTTER
- $1/2$ cup butter, softened
- $1/4$ cup honey
- 2 tablespoons orange marmalade

CINNAMON-MAPLE BUTTER
- $1/2$ cup butter, softened
- 2 tablespoons maple syrup
- $1/2$ teaspoon ground cinnamon

STRAWBERRY BUTTER
- $1/2$ cup butter, softened
- $1/3$ cup strawberry preserves
- $1/2$ teaspoon lemon juice
- $1/2$ teaspoon confectioners sugar

For each flavor of butter, whip butter with electric mixer in a small bowl until smooth and fluffy; gradually add remaining ingredients. Store in an airtight container in refrigerator.

Yield: three flavored butters; about $3/4$ to 1 cup each.

Johnny Cakes (also called Journey Cakes) were early American favorites.

RASPBERRY-CHOCOLATE DANISH SQUARES

(Shown on page 77)

1 package (8 ounces) cream cheese, softened
1/2 cup seedless raspberry jam, divided
1 package (18.25 ounces) chocolate fudge cake mix with pudding in the mix, divided
3 eggs
1 1/2 cups sour cream
1 tablespoon butter or margarine
1/2 cup slivered almonds
2/3 cup sifted confectioners sugar
2 to 3 teaspoons water
1/4 teaspoon vanilla extract

Preheat oven to 350 degrees. Combine cream cheese and 2 tablespoons raspberry jam in a small bowl. Reserve 1/2 cup of dry cake mix; set aside. In a medium bowl, lightly beat eggs. Stir in sour cream and remaining cake mix (mixture will be slightly lumpy). Spread mixture in a greased 10 1/2 x 15 1/2 x 1-inch jellyroll pan. On 18 evenly-spaced places across top of batter, spoon about 2 teaspoons each of cream cheese mixture onto batter. In a small bowl and using a pastry blender or 2 knives, cut butter into reserved cake mix until it resembles coarse meal. Stir in almonds. Sprinkle mixture over batter. Bake 20 to 25 minutes or until a toothpick inserted in cake comes out clean. Place about 1 teaspoon raspberry jam into each indentation in cake. In a small bowl, combine confectioners sugar, water, and vanilla; stir until smooth. Drizzle icing over cake. Cut into 18 squares; serve warm.
Yield: 18 servings

JOHNNY CAKES

4 cups cornmeal
3 cups boiling water
2 eggs, lightly beaten
1/4 cup firmly packed brown sugar
2 tablespoons butter, softened
1 teaspoon salt
Butter and maple syrup or molasses to serve

Preheat oven to 400 degrees. In a medium mixing bowl, combine cornmeal and water, stirring well by hand (mixture will be very thick). Stir in remaining ingredients. Using about 1/2 cup mixture for each cake, spread mixture into circles about 4 inches in diameter on greased baking sheets. Bake 20 to 25 minutes or until centers are set. Serve warm with butter and maple syrup or molasses.
Yield: 10 to 12 Johnny Cakes

An eye-opening variation of a traditional favorite, Maple-Cinnamon French Toast offers a yummy way to greet the day.

MAPLE-CINNAMON FRENCH TOAST

Assemble French toast the day before baking to let flavors blend.

- 12 cups 1-inch cubes of French bread (about one 16-ounce loaf)
- $1/2$ cup golden raisins
- 1 package (8 ounces) cream cheese, softened
- 2 cups whipping cream
- $1/2$ cup maple syrup
- 12 eggs
- 1 teaspoon vanilla extract
- $1/2$ teaspoon ground cinnamon
- $1/8$ teaspoon salt

Divide bread cubes evenly into 2 greased $8^3/8$ x $12^3/8$ x $1^1/8$-inch aluminum foil baking pans with plastic lids. Sprinkle raisins evenly over bread. In a large bowl, beat cream cheese until fluffy. Gradually beat in whipping cream and maple syrup; beat until well combined. Beat in eggs, vanilla, cinnamon, and salt. Pour mixture over bread, pressing bread into mixture, if necessary. Cover and chill 8 hours or overnight.

To bake: Allow pan to stand at room temperature 30 minutes. Cover pan with aluminum foil. Bake in a 375-degree oven 25 minutes. Remove foil and bake 18 to 22 minutes longer or until center is set and top is golden brown. Serve warm with maple syrup.

Yield: about 6 servings in each pan

FRUIT-NUT MUFFINS

1 cup milk
1 package (6 ounces) diced dried
   mixed fruits
2 eggs
1/4 cup vegetable oil
3 cups all-purpose baking mix
3/4 cup chopped walnuts
1/2 cup quick-cooking oats
1/2 cup granulated sugar
1/2 cup firmly packed brown sugar
1 teaspoon ground cinnamon

Preheat oven to 400 degrees. In a small microwave-safe bowl, combine milk and dried fruits. Microwave on high power (100%) 1 minute; set aside. In a large bowl, beat eggs and oil; add fruit mixture and remaining ingredients. Stir just until moistened. Line muffin pan with aluminum foil muffin cups; fill cups half full. Bake 15 to 20 minutes or until golden brown. Serve warm or cool completely on a wire rack. Store in an airtight container.
Yield: about 2 dozen muffins

CRANBERRY-BLUEBERRY BREAD

3 cups all-purpose flour
1 teaspoon baking soda
1 teaspoon baking powder
1 teaspoon salt
1 cup granulated sugar
1/2 cup butter or margarine, softened
2 eggs
1 cup buttermilk
1 cup whole-berry cranberry sauce
1 cup fresh or frozen blueberries,
   thawed if frozen

Preheat oven to 375 degrees. Combine flour, baking soda, baking powder, and salt; set aside. In large mixing bowl, cream sugar and butter. Beat in eggs and buttermilk. Stir in flour mixture, blending well. Stir in cranberry sauce and blueberries. Pour batter into a greased 5 x 9 x 3-inch loaf pan. Bake 1 hour and 10 minutes or until a toothpick inserted in the center comes out clean. Remove from pan and cool on wire rack.
Yield: 1 loaf of bread

SUGARPLUM TARTS

CRUST
- 3/4 cup butter or margarine, softened
- 1/2 cup sugar
- 2 egg yolks
- 1 3/4 cups all-purpose flour
- 1/8 teaspoon salt
- 3/4 teaspoon vanilla extract

FILLING
- 1 jar (10 ounces) red plum jam
- 1 cup sugar
- 1/4 cup all-purpose flour
- 1/8 teaspoon salt
- 1 cup whipping cream
- 1/2 cup half and half
- 2 teaspoons vanilla extract

Preheat oven to 350 degrees. For crust, cream butter and sugar in a large bowl until fluffy. Add egg yolks 1 at a time, beating well after each addition. Add remaining ingredients; stir until a soft dough forms. Press about 1 1/2 teaspoons dough into bottoms and up sides of greased miniature muffin tins.

For filling, spoon about 1/2 teaspoon jam into bottom of each crust; set aside. Sift next 3 ingredients into a large bowl. Add remaining ingredients. Using highest speed of an electric mixer, beat cream mixture until thick and fluffy, about 4 to 5 minutes. Spoon about 1 tablespoon cream mixture into each crust. Bake 30 to 35 minutes or until filling is set in center and crust is brown. Cool in pan 10 minutes. Transfer to a wire rack to cool completely.

Yield: about 5 dozen tarts

CHOCOLATE-ALMOND BISCOTTI

- 1/2 cup butter or margarine, softened
- 1/2 cup firmly packed brown sugar
- 1/2 cup granulated sugar
- 3 eggs
- 1 teaspoon almond extract
- 2 1/2 cups all-purpose flour
- 1 teaspoon baking powder
- 1/2 teaspoon baking soda
- 1/8 teaspoon salt
- 1 cup semisweet chocolate mini chips
- 1 cup coarsely ground almonds, toasted

Preheat oven to 375 degrees. In a large bowl, cream butter and sugars until fluffy. Add eggs and almond extract; beat until smooth. In a medium bowl, combine flour, baking powder, baking soda, and salt. Add dry ingredients to creamed mixture; stir until a soft dough forms. Stir in chocolate chips and almonds. Divide dough in half. On a greased and floured baking sheet, shape each piece of dough into a 2 1/2 x 10-inch loaf, flouring hands as necessary. Allow 3 inches between loaves on baking sheet. Bake 20 to 24 minutes or until loaves are firm and lightly browned; cool 10 minutes on baking sheet.

Cut loaves diagonally into 1/2-inch slices. Lay slices flat on an ungreased baking sheet. Bake 5 to 7 minutes; turn slices over and bake 5 to 7 minutes longer or until golden brown. Transfer cookies to a wire rack to cool. Store in a cookie tin.

Yield: about 3 dozen cookies

OATMEAL-WALNUT SCONES

1 cup all-purpose flour
2/3 cup whole-wheat flour
1/3 cup sugar
1 1/2 teaspoons baking powder
3/4 teaspoon baking soda
1/4 teaspoon salt
3/4 cup chilled butter or margarine,
    cut into pieces
1 1/4 cups quick-cooking oats
3/4 cup finely chopped walnuts,
    toasted
3/4 cup buttermilk
1/2 teaspoon vanilla extract
1 egg, lightly beaten

Preheat oven to 350 degrees. Combine flours, sugar, baking powder, baking soda, and salt in a large bowl. Using a pastry blender or 2 knives, cut in butter until mixture resembles fine meal. Stir in oats and walnuts. Add buttermilk and vanilla; stir just until mixture is blended. On a lightly floured surface, pat dough to 1/2-inch thickness. Use a 3-inch-diameter round cookie cutter dipped in flour to cut out scones. Place 1 inch apart on a lightly greased baking sheet. Brush tops of scones with beaten egg. Bake 18 to 22 minutes or until scones are lightly browned. Serve warm.
Yield: about 15 scones

FRUITCAKE SCONES WITH DEVON CREAM

DEVON CREAM
1 cup whipping cream, divided
1/4 cup butter
1 tablespoon honey
1/2 teaspoon vanilla extract

SCONES
1/4 cup butter or margarine, softened
1/2 cup granulated sugar
2 eggs
1 1/2 cups all-purpose flour
1 1/2 teaspoons baking powder
1/2 teaspoon baking soda
1/8 teaspoon salt
1/2 cup ricotta cheese
1 cup dried mixed fruit bits
1/2 cup coarsely chopped pecans
1/4 cup water
1 teaspoon vanilla extract
1 teaspoon grated orange peel
2 tablespoons brandy

For Devon cream, combine 1/4 cup cream and butter in a small saucepan. Place pan over low heat, stirring constantly, until butter is melted. Remove pan from heat and stir in honey and vanilla; cool to room temperature.
In a mixing bowl, beat remaining 3/4 cup cream until soft peaks form. Gradually beat in butter mixture. Beat 5 minutes at high speed of electric mixer (mixture will appear to be thin). Refrigerate 3 hours.
Skim thickened cream from top of mixture and place in serving bowl. Discard remaining liquid in bottom of bowl. (Devon cream may separate slightly at room temperature, but stirring will correct this. Devon cream will keep in refrigerator 24 hours.)
Preheat oven to 350 degrees. For scones, cream butter and sugar in a large mixing bowl. Beat in eggs, one at a time, beating well after each addition. In a separate bowl, combine flour, baking powder, baking soda, and salt. Stir dry ingredients into butter mixture alternately with ricotta cheese. Stir in fruit, pecans, water, vanilla, and orange peel. Drop about 1/3 cup of dough for each scone onto a lightly greased baking sheet. Bake 12 to 15 minutes or until

Bursting with citrus flavor, Orange-Oatmeal Rolls begin with a hot roll mix. This recipe makes two pans.

tops are golden brown and a toothpick inserted into a scone comes out clean. Sprinkle warm scones with brandy. Serve scones warm or at room temperature with Devon cream.

Yield: about 8 scones

ORANGE-OATMEAL ROLLS

1 package (16 ounces) hot roll mix
1 cup sweetened crunchy oat cereal
1 cup very warm orange juice
   (120 to 130 degrees)
2 tablespoons honey
2 tablespoons butter or margarine, melted
1 egg
1 tablespoon grated orange zest
1/2 cup coarsely ground pecans
   Vegetable cooking spray
1 cup sifted confectioners sugar
5 teaspoons orange juice

In a large bowl, combine hot roll mix and yeast from roll mix with cereal. Stir in 1 cup very warm orange juice, honey, melted butter, egg, and orange zest; stir until well blended. Stir in pecans. Turn onto a lightly floured surface and knead 3 minutes or until dough becomes smooth and elastic. Cover dough; allow to rest 10 minutes. Shape dough into eighteen 2-inch balls. Place in 2 greased 8 x 5-inch aluminum foil baking pans. Spray tops of dough with cooking spray, cover, and let rise in a warm place (80 to 85 degrees) 1 hour or until almost doubled in size.

Preheat oven to 375 degrees. Bake 15 to 20 minutes or until golden brown. Cool in pans. Combine confectioners sugar and 5 teaspoons orange juice in a small bowl; stir until smooth. Drizzle icing over rolls. Allow icing to harden. Store in an airtight container.

Yield: 2 pans rolls, 9 rolls each

GOLDEN WHOLE-WHEAT ROLLS

3/4 cup milk
3/4 cup water
1/3 cup butter or margarine
1/3 cup honey
2 packages dry yeast
2 3/4 cups whole-wheat flour, divided
2 3/4 cups all-purpose flour, divided
1/2 cup yellow cornmeal
1 1/2 teaspoons salt
3 eggs, beaten
Vegetable cooking spray
1 egg, beaten

Combine milk, water, and butter in a small saucepan. Stir over medium heat until butter melts; stir in honey. Remove from heat and allow liquid mixture to cool to 110 degrees. Add yeast; stir until dissolved. In a large bowl, combine 2 1/2 cups whole-wheat flour, 2 1/2 cups all-purpose flour, cornmeal, and salt. Add yeast mixture and 3 beaten eggs to flour mixture; stir until a soft dough forms. Turn dough onto a lightly floured surface. Knead 6 to 10 minutes or until dough becomes smooth and elastic, using additional flour as necessary. Place in a large bowl sprayed with cooking spray, turning once to coat top of dough. Cover and let rise in a warm place (80 to 85 degrees) 1 hour or until doubled in size.

Turn dough onto a lightly floured surface and punch down. Shape dough into 24 balls and divide between two greased 9-inch round cake pans. Spray tops of rolls with cooking spray, cover, and let rise in a warm place 1 hour or until doubled in size.

Preheat oven to 400 degrees. Brush rolls with remaining beaten egg. Bake 12 to 15 minutes or until golden brown. Serve warm or transfer to a wire rack to cool completely.
Yield: 2 dozen rolls

REFRIGERATOR YEAST ROLLS

2 packages dry yeast
2 cups warm water
6 1/2 cups all-purpose flour, divided
1/2 cup sugar
2 teaspoons salt
1 egg
1/4 cup vegetable shortening
Vegetable cooking spray
Melted butter

In a small bowl, dissolve yeast in warm water. In a large bowl combine 2 cups flour, sugar, and salt. Add yeast mixture to flour mixture; beat 2 minutes or until well blended. Beat in egg and shortening. Adding 1 cup at a time, beat in 2 cups flour. Stir in remaining 2 1/2 cups flour by hand. Turn onto a lightly floured surface and knead about 5 minutes or until dough becomes smooth and elastic. Place in a large bowl sprayed with cooking spray, turning once to coat top of dough. Cover and let rise until doubled in a warm place (80 to 85 degrees) about 2 hours or dough can rise in refrigerator overnight. (Dough may be stored in refrigerator up to 1 week.)

Turn dough onto a lightly floured surface and punch down. For cloverleaf rolls, shape dough into 1 1/4-inch balls. Place 3 balls of dough in each cup of a greased muffin pan. Spray tops of dough with cooking spray, cover, and let rise in a warm place 1 to 1½ hours or until doubled in size.

Preheat oven to 350 degrees. Bake 18 to 22 minutes or until golden brown. Brush with melted butter and serve warm.

Yield: about 2 dozen rolls

PEPPERED CHEESE BISCUITS
(Shown on page 92)

⅔ cup grated Parmesan cheese
1½ teaspoons ground black pepper
2 cups all-purpose flour
1 tablespoon baking powder
1 teaspoon baking soda
½ teaspoon salt
⅛ teaspoon ground red pepper
1 teaspoon dried minced onion
¼ cup chilled butter or margarine, cut into pieces
⅔ cup sour cream
⅓ cup half and half
½ pound thinly sliced deli ham
2 tablespoons butter or margarine, melted

Process cheese and black pepper 5 to 10 seconds in a food processor until well blended. Sift flour, baking powder, baking soda, salt, and red pepper into a large bowl. Stir cheese mixture and onion into dry ingredients. Using a pastry blender or 2 knives, cut chilled butter into dry ingredients until mixture resembles coarse meal. Stir in sour cream and half and half; knead until a soft dough forms. On a lightly floured surface, use a floured rolling pin to roll out dough to a ¼-inch-thick rectangle. Place ham on dough. Beginning at 1 long edge, roll up dough jellyroll style. Pinch seam to seal. Wrap in plastic wrap and chill 1 hour.

Preheat oven to 450 degrees. Use a sharp knife to cut roll into ½-inch-thick slices. Transfer to a greased baking sheet. Brush with melted butter. Bake 10 to 12 minutes or until golden brown. Serve warm.

Yield: about 2 dozen biscuits

Thinly sliced ham is a tasty surprise rolled inside hearty Peppered Cheese Biscuits (recipe on page 91).

Sweet Santa Bread (recipe on page 70) is sure to delight both children and adults! Because every loaf rises differently while baking, each Santa will have his own distinct personality.

weet Potato Biscuits stuffed with ham taste great served hot from the oven.

SWEET POTATO BISCUITS

*ill these fragrant biscuits with smoked ham
r turkey for a delicious treat.*

1 sweet potato (10 -12
   ounces), baked and peeled
1/2 cups sifted all-purpose flour
2 1/2 teaspoons baking powder
1/2 teaspoon salt
1/2 teaspoon ground cinnamon
1/2 teaspoon freshly grated
   nutmeg
1/4 teaspoon ground ginger
1/3 cup firmly packed dark brown
   sugar
1/2 cup unsalted butter, cut into
   pieces and softened
3 tablespoons whipping cream,
   divided
1 egg

Purée potato in a food processor or
ash until smooth. Reserve 3/4 cup of
otato and cool.

Position rack in upper third of oven. Preheat oven to 450 degrees. Sift flour, baking powder, salt, cinnamon, nutmeg, and ginger into a medium bowl. Stir in brown sugar. Using a pastry blender or 2 knives, cut butter into dry ingredients until mixture resembles coarse meal. Add reserved sweet potato and 2 tablespoons whipping cream; stir just until moistened. Turn onto a lightly floured surface and knead gently just until dough holds together. Use a floured rolling pin to roll out dough to 1/2-inch thickness. Use a 2-inch-diameter biscuit cutter to cut out biscuits. Place biscuits on an ungreased baking sheet, spacing 1/2-inch apart. In a small bowl, combine egg and 1 tablespoon whipping cream. Brush tops with egg mixture. Bake 12 to 15 minutes or until golden brown. Cool 5 minutes before serving.
Yield: about 18 biscuits

CRANBERRY-NUT COFFEE CAKES

TOPPING
2¹/₂ cups finely chopped fresh
      cranberries
2¹/₂ cups finely chopped pecans
  ³/₄ cup sugar
1¹/₄ teaspoons ground cinnamon
  ³/₄ teaspoon ground allspice

CAKES
  1 cup butter or margarine, softened
¹/₂ cup vegetable shortening
2¹/₂ cups sugar
  4 eggs
  1 tablespoon orange extract
  1 tablespoon grated orange zest
3¹/₄ cups all-purpose flour
  1 teaspoon baking powder
³/₄ teaspoon baking soda
  1 cup buttermilk

For topping, combine cranberries, pecans, sugar, cinnamon, and allspice in a medium bowl.

Preheat oven to 350 degrees. For cakes, grease a 6-mold fluted tube pan. In a large bowl, cream butter, shortening, and sugar until fluffy. Add eggs; beat until well blended. Stir in orange extract and orange zest. In a medium bowl, combine flour, baking powder, and baking soda. Add dry ingredients alternately with buttermilk to creamed mixture; beat until smooth. Sprinkle 1 tablespoon topping into each mold. Spoon 2 tablespoons batter over topping in each mold. Repeat with 1 tablespoon topping and 2 tablespoons batter in each mold. Bake 22 to 27 minutes or until a toothpick inserted in center of cake comes out clean. Cool in pan 5 minutes. Invert onto a wire rack and cool completely. Repeat with remaining topping and batter. Store in an airtight container.
Yield: about twenty-two 6-inch cakes

PECAN BISCUITS

2¹/₂ cups biscuit baking mix
¹/₂ cup chopped pecans
  1 cup whipping cream
  2 tablespoons butter or
      margarine, melted

Preheat oven to 450 degrees. In a large bowl, combine baking mix and pecans. Add cream and stir just until a soft dough forms. On a lightly floured surface, use a floured rolling pin to roll out dough to ¹/₂-inch thickness. Use a floured 2-inch biscuit cutter to cut out dough. Transfer biscuits to a greased baking sheet and brush tops with melted butter. Bake 7 to 10 minutes or until light brown.
Yield: about 2 dozen biscuits

CANDIED GINGER BISCUITS

2 cups all-purpose flour
1 tablespoon baking powder
1 teaspoon salt
1/3 cup vegetable shortening
1/2 cup finely minced crystallized
    ginger
2 tablespoons firmly packed brown
    sugar
1 teaspoon ground ginger
1/2 teaspoon ground cinnamon
1 cup milk
2 tablespoons butter, melted

Preheat oven to 450 degrees. In a large bowl, combine flour, baking powder, and salt. Cut in shortening with a pastry blender or two knives until mixture resembles coarse meal. Stir in crystallized ginger, brown sugar, ground ginger, and cinnamon. Add milk and stir just until blended. Turn dough onto a lightly floured surface and gently knead just until dough holds together. Pat out dough to about 1/2-inch thickness. Use a 1/2-inch biscuit cutter to cut out biscuits; place on an ungreased baking sheet. Bake 15 to 20 minutes or until golden brown. Remove from oven and brush with melted butter.
Yield: about 20 biscuits

FREEZER BISCUITS

4 cups all-purpose flour
2 tablespoons baking powder
1 1/2 teaspoons salt
1 teaspoon sugar
1/2 teaspoon baking soda
1 container (16 ounces) sour cream
1/2 cup chilled butter, cut into pieces
3 teaspoons water

In a large bowl, combine flour, baking powder, salt, sugar, and baking soda. Using a pastry blender or 2 knives, cut sour cream and butter into dry ingredients until mixture begins to cling together. Add water, 1 teaspoonful at a time, to moisten dough; shape into a ball. On a lightly floured surface, use a floured rolling pin to roll out dough to 1-inch thickness. Use a 2-inch biscuit cutter to cut out biscuits. Transfer to an ungreased baking sheet. Cover and freeze 1 hour. Transfer frozen biscuits to a resealable plastic freezer bag.

To bake: Place frozen biscuits on an ungreased baking sheet. Bake in a 425-degree oven 15 to 17 minutes or until tops are lightly browned. Serve warm.
Yield: about 2 dozen biscuits

Shown on page 4: *Delectable pinwheel Praline Biscuits feature a luscious swirl of chopped pecans and brown sugar.*

PRALINE BISCUITS

1 cup chopped pecans
1/4 cup firmly packed brown sugar
3 tablespoons butter or
    margarine, melted
1 teaspoon maple extract
2 cups all-purpose flour
2 teaspoons granulated sugar
1 teaspoon baking powder
1/2 teaspoon baking soda
1/4 teaspoon salt
1/2 cup vegetable shortening
3/4 cup milk

In a small bowl, combine pecans, brown sugar, butter, and maple extract; set aside.

In a medium bowl, combine flour, granulated sugar, baking powder, baking soda, and salt. Using a pastry blender or 2 knives, cut shortening into dry ingredients until mixture resembles coarse meal. Add milk, stirring just until moistened. Turn dough onto a lightly floured surface and knead about 2 minutes. Use a floured rolling pin to roll dough into an 8 x 12-inch rectangle; spread pecan mixture over dough. Beginning at 1 long edge, roll up dough jellyroll style. Using a serrated knife, cut into twelve 1-inch-thick slices. Place slices with sides touching in a greased 7 x 11-inch baking dish. Cover and refrigerate until ready to bake.

Preheat oven to 400 degrees. Uncover biscuits and bake 22 to 25 minutes or until lightly browned. Serve warm.
Yield: 1 dozen biscuits

LEMON-DILL BISCUITS

2 cups all-purpose flour
1 tablespoon baking powder
1/4 teaspoon salt
1/4 teaspoon ground black pepper
1/3 cup chilled butter or margarine, cu
    into pieces
3/4 cup milk
1 tablespoon chopped fresh
    dill weed
1 teaspoon grated lemon zest

Preheat oven to 425 degrees. In a medium bowl, combine flour, baking powder, salt, and pepper. Using a pastry blender or 2 knives, cut butter into dry ingredients until mixture resembles coarse meal. In a small bowl, combine milk, dill weed, and lemon zest. Add to dry ingredients; stir just until moistened. On a lightly floured surface, use a floured rolling pin to roll out dough to 1/2-inch thickness. Use a 2-inch-diameter biscuit cutter to cut out biscuits. Transfer to an ungreased baking sheet. Bake 11 to 13 minutes or until golden brown. Serve warm.
Yield: about 1 1/2 dozen biscuits

SPICY PASTRAMI ROLLS

2 packages (8 ounces each)
    refrigerated crescent rolls
1/2 pound deli pastrami, sliced paper-
    thin
1/2 cup soft cream cheese with chives
    and onions
1/3 cup Dijon-style mustard

Preheat oven to 375 degrees. Separate crescent rolls into triangles. Cut triangles in half lengthwise to make 2 smaller triangles. Cut pastrami into 1 x 2-inch strips. Spread 1 teaspoon cream cheese and $1/2$ teaspoon mustard on each triangle. Leaving about $1/4$ inch of the pointed end uncovered, stack 3 pieces of pastrami at wide end of the triangle. Beginning at the wide end, roll up triangle and place on an ungreased baking sheet with point side down. Bake 12 to 15 minutes or until golden brown. Serve warm.

Yield: 32 rolls

CROSS STITCH SANDWICH ROLLS

1 package (11 ounces) refrigerated
   soft breadsticks
1 egg yolk
1 tablespoon cold water

Preheat oven to 350 degrees. Unroll dough and separate into 8 strips. Cut each strip into 4 pieces. On lightly greased baking sheets, make "cross stitches" by placing one dough strip diagonally on a baking sheet and overlapping with a second dough strip. Continue forming 16 "cross stitches." Combine egg yolk with 1 tablespoon cold water. Using a pastry brush, brush tops of rolls with yolk mixture. Follow directions on breadstick package for cooking. Remove rolls from pans and allow to cool. With a serrated knife, split each roll in half for sandwiches.

Yield: 16 cross stitch sandwich rolls

BRIOCHE ROLLS

2 packages dry yeast
$1/4$ cup warm water
$1/2$ cup butter or margarine,
   softened
$1/3$ cup granulated sugar
$1/2$ teaspoon salt
$1/2$ cup evaporated milk
$3^1/2$ cups all-purpose flour, divided
4 eggs
1 tablespoon granulated sugar

Dissolve yeast in warm water. In a medium mixing bowl, cream butter, $1/3$ cup sugar, and salt until fluffy. Stir in milk and 1 cup flour. In another medium bowl, beat 3 eggs and 1 egg yolk (reserve egg white). Add yeast and eggs to creamed mixture, beating until well blended. Stir in remaining $2^1/2$ cups flour. Turn out dough onto a lightly floured surface and knead 3 to 5 minutes or until dough holds together. Place in lightly greased bowl, turning to coat entire surface. Cover and let rise in a warm place 1 hour or until doubled in size.

Punch down dough. Divide dough into fourths. Reserving one fourth, pull remaining dough into 24 equal pieces. Roll pieces into balls and place in greased muffin pans or fluted tart pans. Pull reserved dough into 24 pieces and roll pieces into small balls. Make indentation with thumb in top of each larger roll and press smaller ball into each indentation. Cover and let rise 45 minutes or until doubled in size.

Preheat oven to 375 degrees. Lightly beat reserved egg white with 1 tablespoon sugar; brush on tops of rolls. Bake 20 to 25 minutes or until golden brown.

Yield: 2 dozen rolls

Our Coffee Break Cake (recipe on page 101) is ready in a jiffy! Ordinary spice cake mix is combined with carrots, walnuts, and coconut to create Spicy Carrot Cupcakes.

SPICY CARROT CUPCAKES

1 package (18.25 ounces) spice cake mix
1 1/3 cups water
3 eggs
1/3 cup vegetable oil
1 3/4 cups finely shredded carrots (about 4 carrots)
3/4 cup finely chopped toasted walnuts, divided
1 cup flaked coconut, toasted and divided
2 packages (3 ounces each) cream cheese, softened
1/3 cup butter or margarine, softened
3 tablespoons sifted confectioners sugar
1 1/2 tablespoons maple syrup

Preheat oven to 350 degrees. In a large bowl, combine cake mix, water, eggs, and oil. Beat at low speed of an electric mixer 30 seconds. Beat at medium speed 2 minutes. Stir in carrots, 1/2 cup walnuts, and 1/2 cup coconut. Fill paper-lined muffin cups about three-fourths full. Bake 15 to 20 minutes or until a toothpick inserted in center of cupcake comes out clean. Transfer cupcakes to a wire rack to cool.

In a small bowl, beat cream cheese and butter until fluffy. Add confectioners sugar and maple syrup; continue to beat until smooth. Ice cupcakes. Sprinkle remaining 1/4 cup walnuts and 1/2 cup coconut over icing. Store in an airtight container in refrigerator.

Yield: about 2 1/2 dozen cupcakes

hock-full of almonds and zippy crystallized ginger, crunchy Gingerbread Toasts are light, avorful sweets.

GINGERBREAD TOASTS

.¹/₂ cups all-purpose flour
¹/₄ cup finely minced crystallized
      ginger
3 teaspoons baking powder
³/₄ teaspoon salt
¹/₂ teaspoon ground ginger
¹/₄ teaspoon ground cinnamon
¹/₂ cup butter or margarine,
      softened
³/₄ cup granulated sugar
2 eggs
1 teaspoon vanilla extract
²/₃ cup blanched whole almonds,
      toasted and coarsely chopped
2 teaspoons milk
      Granulated sugar

Preheat oven to 375 degrees. Combine our, crystallized ginger, baking powder, lt, ground ginger, and cinnamon in medium bowl. In a large bowl, beat butter and sugar until fluffy. Beat in eggs and vanilla. Stir in flour mixture and almonds. Divide dough in half and shape each half into a 12 x 2-inch strip on a foil-lined baking sheet. Smooth surface of each strip. Brush each with milk; sprinkle with sugar. Bake 18 to 20 minutes or until light golden brown and firm to the touch. Remove from oven and reduce temperature to 300 degrees. Place strips on a wire rack and cool 15 minutes.

Place strips on a cutting board and use a serrated knife to cut each strip crosswise on the diagonal into ¹/₂-inch-thick slices. Place slices on a baking sheet and bake 10 minutes. Turn slices over and bake 10 minutes more. Turn off heat and allow toasts to cool in oven, leaving door slightly ajar.
Yield: about 3 dozen toasts

BLUEBERRY TEA BUNS

1/3 cup plus 1 tablespoon sugar, divided
1 3/4 cups all-purpose flour
1 teaspoon ground cinnamon
1 teaspoon baking soda
1/2 teaspoon salt
1 can (8 ounces) crushed pineapple in juice, lightly drained
1/4 cup skim milk
3 tablespoons vegetable oil
1/4 cup egg substitute
1 1/2 cups frozen blueberries (do not thaw)
Vegetable cooking spray

Preheat oven to 400 degrees. In a medium bowl, combine 1/3 cup sugar, flour, cinnamon, baking soda, and salt; make a well in center of mixture. Combine pineapple, milk, oil, and egg substitute; add to dry ingredients. Stir just until dry ingredients are moistened. Gently stir in blueberries. Drop batter by heaping tablespoonfuls onto a baking sheet sprayed with cooking spray. Sprinkle remaining 1 tablespoon sugar over batter. Bake 12 to 15 minutes or until golden brown. Serve warm.
Yield: about 24 muffins

LEMON PEPPER-PARMESAN CRACKERS

2 cups all-purpose flour
1 cup grated Parmesan cheese
1 tablespoon dried parsley flakes
2 teaspoons lemon pepper
1 small clove garlic, minced
1 cup chilled butter, cut into pieces

In a medium bowl, combine flour, cheese, parsley, lemon pepper, and garlic until well blended. Using a pastry blender or 2 knives, cut in butter until mixture resembles coarse meal. Shape dough into a ball; wrap in plastic wrap and chill 30 minutes.

Preheat oven to 350 degrees. On a lightly floured surface, use a floured rolling pin to roll out dough to 1/4-inch thickness. Cut out crackers with a 3 x 2 1/2-inch leaf-shaped cookie cutter. Transfer to an ungreased baking sheet and bake 15 to 20 minutes or until golden brown. Serve warm or cool completely on a wire rack.
Yield: about 2 1/2 dozen crackers

ORANGE SURPRISE CUPCAKES

2 packages (3 ounces each) cream cheese, softened
1/4 cup sugar
1 egg white
2/3 cup semisweet chocolate mini chips
1 package (18.25 ounces) orange cake mix
1 1/3 cups water
3 eggs
1/3 cup vegetable oil

Preheat oven to 350 degrees. In a medium bowl, beat cream cheese, sugar, and egg white until fluffy. Stir in chocolate chips. In a large bowl, combine cake mix, water, eggs, and oil. Beat at low speed of an electric mixer 30 seconds. Beat at medium speed 2 minutes. Spoon batter into paper-lined muffin cups, filling each about two-thirds full. Drop a tablespoonful of cream cheese mixture into center of batter in each muffin cup. Bake 18 to 21 minutes or until cake springs back when lightly touched. Transfer cupcakes to a wire rack to cool. Store in an airtight container in refrigerator.
Yield: about 2 dozen cupcakes

COFFEE BREAK CAKE

(shown on page 98)

1 cup crushed chocolate-covered graham crackers
1 cup chopped pecans
2 teaspoons ground cinnamon
1 package (18.25 ounces) yellow cake mix
1 cup water
3 eggs
1/3 cup vegetable oil

1/2 cup sifted confectioners sugar
2 teaspoons milk
1 teaspoon vanilla extract

Preheat oven to 350 degrees. In a small bowl, combine cracker crumbs, pecans, and cinnamon. In a large bowl, combine cake mix, water, eggs, and oil. Beat at low speed of an electric mixer 30 seconds. Beat at medium speed 2 minutes. Pour two-thirds of batter into a greased 10-inch tube pan. Sprinkle one-half of cracker crumb mixture over batter. Pour remaining batter over crumbs. Sprinkle remaining crumb mixture on top. Bake 40 to 45 minutes or until a toothpick inserted in center of cake comes out clean. Cool in pan 15 minutes. Remove from pan and cool completely on a wire rack.

In a small bowl, combine confectioners sugar, milk, and vanilla; stir until smooth. Drizzle glaze over cake.
Yield: about 16 servings

CRANBERRY COFFEE CAKE

CAKE
1/2 cup butter or margarine, softened
1 1/2 cups granulated sugar
2 eggs
1 1/2 teaspoons almond extract
1 teaspoon vanilla extract
2 cups all-purpose flour
1 teaspoon baking powder
1 teaspoon baking soda
1 teaspoon salt
1 cup sour cream
1 cup whole berry cranberry sauce

GLAZE
1 cup confectioners sugar
3 tablespoons milk
1/2 teaspoon almond extract

Preheat oven to 350 degrees. For cake, cream butter and sugar in a large bowl. Beat in eggs and extracts until well blended. In a small bowl, combine flour, baking powder, baking soda, and salt. Stir flour mixture into creamed mixture, alternating with sour cream. Pour half of batter into a greased 9-inch tube pan. Spoon cranberry sauce over batter. Top with remaining batter. Bake 55 to 60 minutes or until a toothpick inserted in center of cake comes out clean. Cool in pan 10 minutes.

For glaze, combine all ingredients in a small bowl, blending well. Remove warm cake from pan and drizzle with glaze.

Yield: 14 to 16 servings

HAZELNUT COFFEE CAKE

CAKE
- 1 cup butter or margarine, softened
- 1^1/$_3$ cups granulated sugar
- 3 eggs
- 1^1/$_2$ teaspoons vanilla extract
- 2^1/$_2$ cups sifted cake flour
- 1 teaspoon baking powder
- 1 teaspoon baking soda
- ^{1}/$_8$ teaspoon salt
- 1^1/$_3$ cups sour cream
- 1^1/$_4$ cups chopped hazelnuts, toasted
- ^{1}/$_2$ cup firmly packed brown sugar
- 1 teaspoon ground cinnamon

ICING
- 2 ounces bittersweet baking chocolate
- 4 teaspoons hazelnut-flavored liqueur
- 1 tablespoon light corn syrup

Preheat oven to 325 degrees. For cake, cream butter and granulated sugar in a large bowl until fluffy. Add eggs and vanilla; beat until smooth. In a medium bowl, combine cake flour, baking powder, baking soda, and salt. Alternately beat dry ingredients and sour cream into creamed mixture, beating just until blended. Spoon one-third of batter into bottom of a greased and floured 9-inch springform pan with a tube insert. In a small bowl, combine hazelnuts, brown sugar, and cinnamon. Sprinkle one-third of hazelnut mixture over batter. Continue layering batter and hazelnut mixture, ending with hazelnut mixture. Bake 55 to 65 minutes or until a toothpick inserted in center of cake comes out clean. Cool cake in pan on a wire rack 10 minutes. Run a knife around edge of pan; remove sides of pan; cool completely. Carefully remove bottom of pan; transfer cake to a serving plate.

For icing, place chocolate, liqueur, and corn syrup in top of a double boiler over hot water. Stirring frequently, cook until chocolate melts and mixture is smooth. Drizzle chocolate mixture over cake. Store in an airtight container.

Yield: about 16 servings

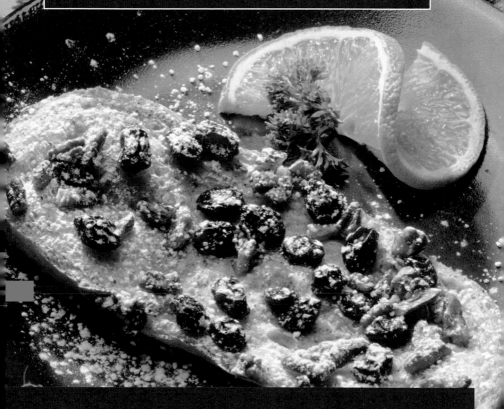

Simply Delicious
BRUNCHES

From hearty pastries to meaty pies and fruity salads you'll find a wide array of tasty foods here to nourish your family. Start the day with delicious entreés, side dishes, fruits, sweets, breads, and beverages.

Oven Baked French Toast, page 108

MUSHROOM PIE

CRUST
- 1 1/2 cups all-purpose flour
- 1/2 teaspoon salt
- 1/2 cup vegetable shortening
- 1/4 cup cold water

FILLING
- 1/4 cup butter or margarine
- 1/2 cup chopped green onions
- 3 cloves garlic, minced
- 10 ounces fresh mushrooms, sliced
- 2 cups shredded Swiss cheese
- 3 eggs
- 1 1/3 cups whipping cream
- 1 teaspoon dried basil leaves, crushed
- 1 teaspoon dried thyme leaves, crushed
- 1 teaspoon salt
- 1/2 teaspoon ground black pepper

Preheat oven to 450 degrees. For crust, combine flour and salt in a medium bowl. Using a pastry blender or 2 knives, cut shortening into dry ingredients until mixture resembles coarse meal. Sprinkle with water; mix until a soft dough forms. On a lightly floured surface, use a floured rolling pin to roll out dough to 1/8-inch thickness. Transfer to an ungreased 9-inch deep-dish pie plate and use a sharp knife to trim edge of dough. Prick bottom of crust with a fork. Bake 5 minutes. Cool completely on a wire rack.

Reduce oven temperature to 375 degrees. For filling, melt butter in a large skillet over medium heat. Add green onions and garlic; cook until onions are tender. Add mushrooms; cook until all liquid has evaporated. Remove from heat. Sprinkle half of cheese over crust. Spoon half of mushroom mixture over cheese. Repeat with remaining cheese and mushroom mixture.

In a medium bowl, whisk eggs, whipping cream, basil, thyme, salt, and pepper. Pour egg mixture into pie crust. Bake 40 to 45 minutes or until a knife inserted in center of pie comes out clean. Let stand 10 minutes before serving. Serve warm or cool slightly, cover, and refrigerate. To reheat, cover and bake in a preheated 350-degree oven 40 to 45 minutes or until heated through.
Yield: 8 to 10 servings

MINTY FRUIT SALAD

- 1 jar (10 ounces) whole maraschino cherries
- 6 oranges, peeled and chopped
- 3 bananas, peeled and sliced
- 1/2 cup pomegranate seeds
- 1/4 cup chopped fresh mint leaves
- 2 tablespoons honey
  Fresh mint leaves to garnish

Drain cherries, reserving juice. In a large bowl, combine cherries, oranges, bananas, pomegranate seeds, and chopped mint. In a small bowl, combine reserved cherry juice and honey. Pour honey mixture over fruit; stir until well coated. Garnish with mint leaves. Serve chilled.
Yield: about six 1-cup servings

easoned with garlic, basil, and thyme and loaded with Swiss cheese, Mushroom Pie makes
flavorful addition to a morning meal. Refreshingly different, Minty Fruit Salad is tossed
ith a sweet mixture of honey and maraschino cherry juice.

Shown on page 5: *A confetti of color, Rice and Barley Pilaf is flavored with bacon and chicken broth. Tender, juicy Peppered Ham is coated with coarse ground pepper and a tangy honey-mustard sauce.*

RICE AND BARLEY PILAF

- 6 slices bacon
- 1 medium onion, chopped
- 1/2 cup chopped celery
- 2 cans (16 ounces each) chicken broth
- 1 cup uncooked brown rice
- 1 cup uncooked barley
- 1 package (10 ounces) frozen green peas
- 2 medium carrots, shredded
- 1/4 cup cooking sherry
- 3/4 teaspoon ground turmeric
- 1/2 teaspoon ground black pepper
- 1 bay leaf

In a large skillet over medium-high heat, cook bacon until crisp. Reserving drippings, remove bacon from pan; set bacon aside. Add onion and celery to bacon drippings; cook until barely tender, stirring frequently. Remove onion mixture from pan and set aside. In same skillet, combine chicken broth, rice, and barley. Cover and cook over medium-low heat 45 minutes or until most of liquid is absorbed. Stir in onion mixture, peas, carrots, sherry, turmeric, pepper, and bay leaf. Reduce heat to low; simmer 10 minutes or until peas are crisp-tender. Remove bay leaf. Crumble bacon on top of pilaf; serve warm.
Yield: 15 to 18 servings

PEPPERED HAM

- 4 pound fully cooked boneless ham
- 1/4 cup honey
- 2 tablespoons prepared mustard
- 1 clove garlic, minced
- 3 tablespoons coarse ground black pepper
- 1/8 teaspoon ground cloves

Preheat oven to 325 degrees. Place ham on a rack in a shallow roasting pan. In a small bowl, combine honey, mustard, garlic, pepper, and cloves. Brush honey mixture over ham. Loosely cover ham with aluminum foil. Bake 1 3/4 to 2 1/4 hour or until heated through. Serve warm.
Yield: about 14 servings

GOLDEN BREAKFAST PUNCH

- 2 tea bags
- 2 cups boiling water
- 3 cups freshly squeezed orange juice
- 2 cups freshly squeezed lemon juice
- 1 1/2 to 2 cups granulated sugar
- 1 quart dry white wine
- 1 cup vodka

Place tea bags in boiling water and steep 5 minutes. Remove tea bags. Add juices and sugar; stir until sugar is dissolved. Cool. Stir in wine and vodka; chill. Serve over ice ring in punch bowl o in glasses filled with ice.
Yield: about 3 quarts punch

Shown on page 5: *Baked Spiced Fruit is a warm compote of spiced apples, peaches, pineapple, and cherries cooked in a cinnamon-brown sugar sauce. Your guests can take a coffee break with hearty Banana-Raisin Bran Muffins.*

BAKED SPICED FRUIT

1 can (29 ounces) peach halves
   in heavy syrup, drained
1 can (20 ounces) pineapple
   slices in fruit juice, drained,
   reserving 3/4 cup of juice
1 jar (about 14 ounces) spiced
   apple rings, drained
1/2 cup drained maraschino cherries
3/4 cup firmly packed brown sugar
1/3 cup butter or margarine
1 teaspoon ground cinnamon
1/4 teaspoon ground cloves
1/4 teaspoon curry powder
4 teaspoons cornstarch
4 teaspoons water

Preheat oven to 350 degrees. Arrange peaches, pineapple slices, apple rings, and maraschino cherries in a 9 x 13-inch baking dish. In a small saucepan over medium heat, combine reserved pineapple juice, brown sugar, butter, cinnamon, cloves, and curry powder. In a small bowl, dissolve cornstarch in water. Stirring pineapple juice mixture frequently, cook 7 to 8 minutes. Stirring constantly, add cornstarch mixture and continue to cook about 2 minutes or until mixture thickens. Pour sauce over fruit. Bake 25 to 30 minutes or until bubbly. Serve warm.

Yield: about 14 servings

BANANA-RAISIN BRAN MUFFINS

1 cup all-purpose flour
3/4 cup whole-wheat flour
1/3 cup sugar
2 teaspoons baking powder
1/2 teaspoon baking soda
1/2 teaspoon salt
2 eggs
1/2 cup buttermilk
1/2 cup vegetable oil
2 medium bananas, mashed
2 cups raisin bran flakes

Preheat oven to 350 degrees. In a medium bowl, combine flours, sugar, baking powder, baking soda, and salt. In a small bowl, whisk eggs, buttermilk, oil, and bananas. Add buttermilk mixture and raisin bran flakes to dry ingredients; stir until ingredients are moistened. Fill paper-lined muffin cups two-thirds full. Bake 25 to 30 minutes or until golden brown. Serve warm.

Yield: about 18 muffins

Shown on page 103: *Flavored with cinnamon, nutmeg, and orange liqueur, Oven-Baked French Toast is sprinkled with raisins and pecans for a delightful treat. Warm Orange Syrup makes a yummy topping.*

OVEN-BAKED FRENCH TOAST

8   1/2-inch-thick slices French bread (about half of a 1-pound loaf)
1/2   cup raisins
1/2   cup chopped pecans
2   cups half and half
6   eggs
1/2   cup orange-flavored liqueur
1   teaspoon ground cinnamon
1/2   teaspoon salt
1/4   teaspoon ground nutmeg
      Sifted confectioners sugar or Orange Syrup (recipe on this page) to serve

Arrange bread slices in a single layer with sides touching in a greased 10 1/2 x 15 1/2-inch jellyroll pan. Sprinkle raisins and pecans over bread. In a medium bowl, whisk half and half, eggs, liqueur, cinnamon, salt, and nutmeg. Pour egg mixture over bread. Cover and refrigerate 8 hours or overnight.

Preheat oven to 400 degrees. Uncover and bake French toast 30 to 35 minutes or until a toothpick inserted in center comes out clean and toast is lightly browned. To serve, dust with confectioners sugar or pour warm Orange Syrup over slices of toast.

Yield: 8 servings

ORANGE SYRUP

1   bottle (12 ounces) pancake syrup
1   teaspoon orange extract

In a small saucepan, heat syrup until hot. Remove from heat; stir in orange extract. Serve warm with Oven-Baked French Toast.

Yield: about 1 1/2 cups syrup

FROZEN PINEAPPLE SALAD

1   can (20 ounces) crushed pineapple, drained
1 1/2   cups softened vanilla ice cream
1 1/2   cups sugar
1   cup sour cream
1   cup chopped walnuts
2   tablespoons freshly squeezed lemon juice
1   can (8 ounces) pineapple chunks, drained to garnish

In a large bowl, combine pineapple, ice cream, sugar, sour cream, walnuts, and lemon juice. Spoon salad evenly into 8 custard cups, cover, and freeze 8 hours or until firm. Before serving, place in refrigerator 1 hour. Garnish with pineapple chunks. Serve chilled.

Yield: 8 servings

Created with fresh vegetables, spicy Italian sausage, and eggs, Italian Sausage Frittata is a filling breakfast casserole.

ITALIAN SAUSAGE FRITTATA

- 1 small onion, thinly sliced
- 1 medium potato, peeled and thinly sliced
- 1 pound Italian sausage, cooked and crumbled
- 3 ounces fresh mushrooms, sliced
- 1 small zucchini, thinly sliced
- 1 small sweet red pepper, sliced into rings
- 12 eggs, beaten
- 1/3 cup freshly shredded Parmesan cheese

Preheat oven to 350 degrees. In a greased 12-inch ovenproof skillet, layer onion, potato, crumbled sausage, mushrooms, zucchini, and red pepper. Pour eggs over vegetables; sprinkle cheese over eggs. Bake 40 to 45 minutes or until eggs are almost set. Place skillet under broiler; broil about 3 minutes or until edges are lightly browned. Cut into wedges and serve immediately.
Yield: 8 to 10 servings

GRANOLA-FRUIT PARFAITS

- 2 cups low-fat granola cereal
- 4 kiwi fruit, peeled and cut into pieces
- 1 can (20 ounces) pineapple chunks, well drained
- 1 package (8 ounces) fat-free cream cheese, softened
- 1 cup fat-free vanilla yogurt

Spoon half of granola into 6 parfait glasses. Arrange half of kiwi fruit and pineapple over granola. Repeat layers with remaining granola and fruit.

In a small bowl, beat cream cheese and yogurt until smooth. Cover cream cheese mixture and parfaits and refrigerate until ready to serve.

To serve, spoon cream cheese mixture over parfaits.

Yield: 6 servings

CHOCOLATE-PEPPERMINT COFFEE MIX

- $1/3$ cup ground coffee
- 1 teaspoon unsweetened chocolate extract
- $1/4$ teaspoon vanilla extract
- $1/8$ teaspoon peppermint extract

Place coffee in a food processor fitted with a steel blade or in a food blender. In a small cup, combine remaining ingredients. With processor running, add flavorings to coffee. Stop processor and scrape sides and bottom of container with a rubber spatula. Process again 10 seconds. Store in airtight container in refrigerator.

Brewing instructions: Place coffee mix in the filter of an automatic drip or percolator coffee maker. Add 6 cups cold water and brew.

Yield: mix for eight 6-ounce servings

CRANBERRY-BLUE CHEESE SALAD

- 2 cans (8 ounces each) pineapple tidbits, undrained
- 1 can (16 ounces) whole berry cranberry sauce
- 1 package (6 ounces) raspberry gelatin
- $1/3$ cup plus 2 tablespoons cream sherry, divided
- 3 ounces blue cheese, crumbled and divided
- $1/2$ very ripe banana, mashed
- 1 teaspoon freshly squeezed lemon juice
- $1/2$ cup whipping cream
- 2 ounces cream cheese, softened Orange peel to garnish

Place a small bowl and beaters from an electric mixer in freezer until well chilled. Place pineapple and cranberry sauce in a medium saucepan; bring to a boil. Remove from heat; add gelatin and stir until gelatin dissolves. Cool 5 minutes. Stir in $1/3$ cup sherry and 2 ounces blue cheese. Pour into an oiled 6-cup mold, cover, and refrigerate until firm.

In a small bowl, combine banana and lemon juice. In chilled bowl, beat whipping cream and cream cheese until stiff peaks form. Beat in remaining 2 tablespoons sherry and 1 ounce blue cheese. Beat in banana mixture. Cover and refrigerate until ready to serve.

To serve, dip bottom of mold into hot water; invert onto a serving plate. Spoon banana mixture over gelatin. Garnish with orange peel.

Yield: about 12 servings

Chock-full of pineapple tidbits, Cranberry-Blue Cheese Salad features an unusual blend of flavors. Crunchy granola, mellow fruit, and a mixture of cream cheese and yogurt are layered to create these wonderful low-fat Granola-Fruit Parfaits.

CREAM CHEESE OMELET

6 eggs
4 ounces cream cheese, softened
1 teaspoon salt
$^1/_2$ teaspoon ground black pepper
$1^1/_2$ tablespoons butter or margarine
6 green onions, finely chopped

In a large bowl, beat eggs, cream cheese, salt, and pepper using an electric mixer. In a large skillet, melt butter over medium heat. Add green onions; sauté until tender. Pour egg mixture into skillet; stir once to mix egg mixture with onions. Cook 3 to 5 minutes or until top is bubbly and edges begin to brown. Using a knife, lift edges of omelet up and tilt skillet to allow egg mixture in center of omelet to run under omelet. Cook 1 minute longer. Use a spatula to fold omelet in half. Reduce heat to low and cook 3 to 5 minutes longer or until omelet is set in center. Transfer to a warm plate, cover, and place in a 200-degree oven until ready to serve. Serve warm.
Yield: about 3 servings

BACON-WALNUT BISCUITS

14 slices bacon, cooked
2 cups all-purpose flour
2 teaspoons baking powder
$^1/_2$ teaspoon baking soda
$^1/_2$ teaspoon salt
$^1/_4$ cup butter or margarine, cut into pieces
$^3/_4$ cup finely ground walnuts
1 cup whipping cream

Preheat oven to 450 degrees. Process bacon in a food processor until finely chopped. In a large bowl, combine flour, baking powder, baking soda, and salt. Using a pastry blender or 2 knives, cut butter into dry ingredients until mixture resembles coarse meal. Stir in walnuts and bacon. Add whipping cream; stir until a soft dough forms. Turn dough onto a lightly floured surface and knead 1 to 2 minutes or until smooth. Using a lightly floured rolling pin, roll out dough to $^1/_2$-inch thickness. Use desired cookie cutters to cut out biscuits. Transfer to a greased baking sheet. Bake 8 to 10 minutes or until light brown. Serve warm.
Yield: about $2^1/_2$ dozen 3-inch biscuits

SPICY TOMATO PUNCH

Spicy Tomato Punch may be made one day in advance.

4 cups tomato juice
1 cup pineapple juice
1 cup orange juice
2 tablespoons prepared horseradish
1 teaspoon ground black pepper
1 teaspoon Worcestershire sauce
1 teaspoon hot pepper sauce
Celery stalks to garnish

In a 2-quart container, combine tomato juice, pineapple juice, orange juice, horseradish, black pepper, Worcestershire sauce, and pepper sauce; stir until well blended. Cover and refrigerate 8 hours or overnight to allow flavors to blend. Serve chilled with celery stalks.
Yield: about 6 cups punch

READY-TO-BAKE ASPARAGUS LOAF

 1 pound fresh asparagus, trimmed
   and cut into 4-inch pieces
 1 package (8 ounces) fresh
   mushrooms, sliced
 2 garlic cloves, minced
 1 tablespoon olive oil
 1½ cups (6 ounces) finely shredded
   Swiss cheese, divided
 ¼ cup chopped fresh dill weed
 1 loaf (16 ounces) unsliced French
   bread
 4 eggs
 1½ cups half and half
 2 teaspoons lemon pepper
 1 teaspoon salt
   Fresh dill sprig to decorate

In a large saucepan, cook asparagus in boiling water 1 minute; drain and rinse in cold water. Pat dry on paper towels; set aside. In a medium skillet over medium heat, sauté mushrooms and garlic in oil until liquid evaporates (about 6 minutes); set aside. In a medium bowl, combine 1 cup cheese and dill weed. Remove crust from bread. Slice bread lengthwise into 3 slices; trim each slice to about 3½ x 8 inches. Place 1 bread slice in bottom of a greased 4½ x 8½-inch baking dish. Place a single layer of asparagus crosswise in baking dish. Layer half of mushroom mixture and half of cheese mixture on asparagus. Repeat layers with 1 bread slice and remaining asparagus, mushroom mixture, and cheese mixture. Place remaining bread slice on top. In a medium bowl, beat eggs, half and half, lemon pepper, and salt. Slowly pour egg mixture over bread. Sprinkle with remaining ½ cup cheese. Decorate with fresh dill. Cover and refrigerate overnight.

To bake and serve: Remove loaf from refrigerator 1 hour before baking. Bake uncovered in a 325-degree oven 60 to 65 minutes or until a knife inserted in center comes out clean and top is golden brown. If top browns too quickly, cover loosely with aluminum foil. Cool uncovered on a wire rack 30 minutes. Cut into 1-inch slices and serve warm.
Yield: 1 loaf, about 8 servings

OVERNIGHT COFFEE CAKE

 1 cup chopped pecans
 ¾ cup firmly packed brown sugar
 1 package (4 ounces) instant
   vanilla pudding mix
 1 teaspoon ground cinnamon
 1 package (25 ounces) frozen
   white yeast roll dough,
   thawed according to package
   directions
 ¾ cup butter or margarine, melted

In a small bowl, combine pecans, brown sugar, pudding mix, and cinnamon. Sprinkle 3 tablespoons sugar mixture in bottom of a greased 10-inch tube pan. Dip each roll in melted butter and then in sugar mixture in bowl, covering each roll completely. Place a single layer of rolls with sides touching in pan. Sprinkle remaining sugar mixture over rolls. Pour remaining butter over rolls. Cover and refrigerate 8 hours or overnight.

Remove pan from refrigerator 30 minutes before baking, leave covered, and place in a warm place (80 to 85 degrees) to allow rolls to rise. Preheat oven to 350 degrees. Uncover and bake 40 to 45 minutes or until golden brown (if top browns too quickly, cover with aluminum foil). Cool in pan 15 minutes. Remove from pan and serve warm.
Yield: about 16 servings

113

CHEESE GRITS CASSEROLE

2 cups milk
1 cup water
3/4 cup quick-cooking grits
3 eggs, beaten
1/2 cup (2 ounces) shredded sharp
    Cheddar cheese
3 tablespoons butter or margarine
1/4 teaspoon salt
1/4 teaspoon ground red pepper
4 ounces cooked ham, finely
    diced
    Sweet red pepper and fresh
    parsley to garnish

Preheat oven to 350 degrees. In a medium saucepan, bring milk and water to a boil over medium heat. Stir in grits. Bring to a boil again and reduce heat to medium-low. Cook, stirring occasionally, 5 to 7 minutes or until thick. Remove from heat and add eggs, cheese, butter, salt, and red pepper; stir until well blended. Stir in ham. Pour into a greased 1½-quart baking dish. Bake 30 to 40 minutes or until top is set and lightly puffed. (We baked our casserole in a tree-shaped ceramic baking dish 50 to 55 minutes or until edges were lightly browned. It was cooled in dish 10 minutes and inverted onto a serving plate. We used a star-shaped aspic cutter to cut stars from sweet red pepper.) Garnish with red pepper and parsley. Serve warm.
Yield: about 8 servings

SPINACH-FETA STRATA

6 croissants, cut in half
    horizontally
6 eggs, beaten
1½ cups milk
1 package (10 ounces) frozen
    chopped spinach, thawed and
    well drained
1/2 teaspoon salt
1/4 teaspoon ground black pepper
1/4 teaspoon ground nutmeg
1½ cups (6 ounces) shredded
    Monterey Jack cheese
7 ounces crumbled feta cheese

Arrange croissant halves with sides overlapping in a greased 9 x 13-inch baking dish. In a medium bowl, combine eggs, milk, spinach, salt, pepper, and nutmeg. Pour over croissants. Sprinkle cheeses over spinach mixture. Cover and refrigerate 8 hours or overnight.
Preheat oven to 350 degrees. Uncover and bake 40 to 45 minutes or until lightly browned. Cut into squares. Serve warm.
Yield: about 15 servings

SAUSAGE-GRITS PIE

CRUST
1½ cups water
1/2 teaspoon garlic powder
1/2 cup quick-cooking grits
1/2 cup (2 ounces) shredded
    Cheddar cheese
1/4 cup all-purpose flour
1 egg, beaten

Featuring a savory cheese grits crust and a hearty filling of eggs, Cheddar cheese, sausage, and green onions, Sausage-Grits Pie makes a delicious main dish.

FILLING

- 6 eggs
- 1/2 teaspoon dry mustard
- 1/2 teaspoon salt
- 1/4 teaspoon ground black pepper
- 1/2 pound ground mild pork sausage, cooked, drained, and crumbled
- 1 cup (4 ounces) shredded Cheddar cheese
- 4 green onions, chopped

For crust, combine water and garlic powder in a medium saucepan. Bring to a boil. Stir in grits and bring to a boil again. Reduce heat to medium-low, cover, and cook 5 to 7 minutes or until thick, stirring occasionally. Remove from heat. In a small bowl, combine cheese, flour, and egg. Stir cheese mixture into grits. Press grits mixture into bottom and 2 inches up sides of a greased 9-inch springform pan.

Preheat oven to 350 degrees. For filling, whisk eggs, mustard, salt, and pepper in a large bowl. Stir in sausage, cheese, and onions. Pour into crust. Bake 45 to 50 minutes or until a knife inserted in center comes out clean. Serve hot or cool completely on a wire rack, cover, and refrigerate.

To reheat, cover and bake in a preheated 350-degree oven 30 to 35 minutes or until heated through. Remove sides of pan. Serve warm.

Yield: 8 to 10 servings

FETA CHEESECAKE

CRUST
- 3/4 cup plain bread crumbs
- 3/4 cup finely ground walnuts
- 1 teaspoon dried oregano leaves
- 5 tablespoons butter or margarine, melted

FILLING
- 2 packages (8 ounces each) cream cheese, softened
- 3/4 cup sour cream
- 2 tablespoons all-purpose flour
- 1/2 teaspoon garlic powder
- 1/4 teaspoon hot pepper sauce
- 4 eggs
- 14 ounces feta cheese, crumbled
  Chopped tomato and walnuts to garnish

Preheat oven to 375 degrees. For crust, combine bread crumbs, walnuts, and oregano in a medium bowl. Stir in melted butter; mix until crumbly. Press mixture into bottom of a greased 9-inch springform pan; set aside.

For filling, beat cream cheese, sour cream, flour, garlic powder, and pepper sauce in a large bowl. Add eggs, 1 at a time, beating well after each addition. Stir in feta cheese. Pour into crust. Bake 35 to 40 minutes or until set in center. Cool in pan 10 minutes; remove sides of pan. Garnish with tomato and walnuts. Serve warm.

Yield: 10 to 12 servings

CHICKEN-CUCUMBER SALAD

- 1 1/2 pounds boneless, skinless chicken breasts
- 1 package (8 ounces) cream cheese, softened
- 1/2 cup sour cream
- 2 tablespoons dry white wine
- 1 1/2 teaspoons garlic powder
- 1 teaspoon salt
- 1/2 teaspoon ground black pepper
- 1/2 teaspoon dried dill weed
- 1/2 teaspoon hot pepper sauce
- 1 cup peeled, diced cucumber
- 1/2 cup chopped green onions
- 4 acorn squash, halved lengthwise and seeded
  Fresh carrot and green pepper slices to garnish

In a medium saucepan, cover chicken with water. Bring to a boil, reduce heat to medium-low, and simmer 30 to 35 minutes or until chicken is cooked; drain. Cool 10 minutes and cut into bite-size pieces.

In a medium bowl, beat cream cheese and sour cream until fluffy. Beat in wine, garlic powder, salt, pepper, dill weed, and pepper sauce. Stir in chicken, cucumber, and green onions. Cut a thin slice off bottom of each squash half so squash will sit level. Spoon chicken salad into each squash half. Garnish with carrot and green pepper slices. Cover and refrigerate until ready to serve.

Yield: 8 servings

CHICKEN SALAD IN PASTRY

PASTRY
- 1 cup (4 ounces) shredded sharp Cheddar cheese
- 1/2 cup butter or margarine, softened
- 1 1/4 cups all-purpose flour
- 1/2 teaspoon salt
- 1/4 teaspoon ground black pepper
- 1/4 teaspoon hot pepper sauce

CHICKEN SALAD
- 2 cans (5 ounces each) chicken, drained
- 1 package (3 ounces) cream cheese, softened
- 1/3 cup sour cream
- 1/4 cup finely chopped celery
- 1 hard-cooked egg, finely chopped
- 1/4 teaspoon salt
- 1/4 teaspoon ground black pepper
  Chopped chives to garnish

Preheat oven to 350 degrees. For pastry, combine cheese and butter in a medium bowl. Add flour, salt, black pepper, and pepper sauce; mix until well blended and crumbly. Knead in bowl until a soft dough forms. Using a tablespoon of dough for each ball, shape dough into 18 balls. Press balls of dough into bottoms and up sides of 18 well-greased 2 1/2-inch tart pans. Prick sides and bottoms with a fork. Bake 20 to 25 minutes or until lightly browned. Cool in pans 10 minutes. Carefully remove pastries from pans and cool completely on a wire rack.

For chicken salad, combine chicken, cream cheese, sour cream, celery, egg, salt, and pepper in a medium bowl. Cover and refrigerate until ready to serve.

To serve, spoon about 1 tablespoon chicken salad into each pastry. Garnish with chives.

Yield: 1 1/2 dozen pastries

CHICKEN PUFFS

- 1/4 cup butter or margarine
- 1/2 cup boiling water
- 1/2 cup all-purpose flour
- 1/4 teaspoon salt
- 2 eggs
- 2/3 cup shredded Swiss cheese
- 1 cup finely chopped cooked chicken
- 1/2 cup chopped almonds
- 1/3 cup mayonnaise
- 1/4 cup finely chopped green pepper
- 1/4 cup finely chopped tomato
- 2 tablespoons white wine
- 1/2 teaspoon seasoned salt
- 1/4 teaspoon ground black pepper

Preheat oven to 400 degrees. In a small saucepan over medium-low heat, melt butter in water. Add flour and salt, stirring until mixture forms a ball. Remove from heat and allow to cool slightly. Add eggs and beat vigorously until smooth. Stir in cheese. Drop dough by heaping teaspoonfuls onto a greased baking sheet. Bake 20 minutes or until golden brown. Remove puffs from oven; cool and split.

Combine remaining ingredients, adding more mayonnaise if needed to moisten. Fill each puff with a heaping teaspoon of chicken mixture.

Yield: about 2 dozen puffs

Apples and brown sugar mingle with smoked sausages to create a special flavor combination in Sausage and Apple Appetizers.

SAUSAGE AND APPLE APPETIZERS

2 tablespoons butter or margarine
1 large onion, chopped
1/2 cup apple jelly
1/2 cup firmly packed brown sugar
2 pounds cocktail-size smoked
   sausages
3 apples, peeled, cored, and sliced
2 tablespoons water
1 tablespoon cornstarch

In a large skillet, melt butter over medium-high heat. Add onion and sauté, stirring constantly, until onion is golden. Stir in apple jelly and brown sugar. Add sausages and reduce heat to medium-low. Cook, stirring occasionally, 20 minutes or until mixture begins to thicken. Add apples, partially cover pan, and cook 10 minutes or until apples are tender. Combine water and cornstarch and stir into mixture in pan. Cook 2 to 3 minutes more or until mixture thickens. Serve warm.
Yield: about 30 appetizers

CREAM CHEESE DEVILED EGGS

9 hard-cooked eggs, shelled
1 package (3 ounces) cream cheese,
   softened
1/2 cup (2 ounces) finely shredded
   Cheddar cheese
1/4 cup sour cream
1/4 cup finely chopped celery
1 tablespoon finely chopped fresh
   parsley
1/2 teaspoon Dijon-style mustard
1/2 teaspoon salt
1/2 teaspoon ground black pepper
   Fresh parsley and paprika to
   garnish

Cut eggs in half lengthwise. Reserving whites, remove yolks and place in a blender or food processor. Add next 8 ingredients; process until well blended. Spoon yolk mixture into a pastry bag fitted with a large star tip; pipe into egg white halves. Garnish with parsley and paprika. Store in an airtight container in refrigerator.
Yield: 1 1/2 dozen deviled eggs

SUNRISE MIMOSAS

2 1/2 cups cranberry juice
1 1/2 cups orange juice
3/4 cup vodka
   Orange slices to garnish

Pour cranberry juice, orange juice, and vodka into a blender and mix. Pour over ice cubes. Garnish with an orange slice o rim of each glass.
Yield: 5 to 6 servings

Cream Cheese Deviled Eggs feature a blend of Cheddar and cream cheeses with crunchy bits of celery. Cheddar cheese and crispy bits of pork make the hearty Cracklin' Biscuits especially tasty.

CRACKLIN' BISCUITS

Bacon or no pork?

8 ounces salt pork, diced
1 package dry yeast
1/4 cup warm water
2 cups buttermilk biscuit mix
2 cups (about 8 ounces) shredded Cheddar cheese
2/3 cup warm milk
1/2 cup dried minced onions

Cook salt pork in a medium skillet over medium-high heat until crisp and golden brown. Transfer salt pork to paper towels to drain.

Preheat oven to 450 degrees. In a small bowl, dissolve yeast in water; let stand 10 minutes. In a medium bowl, combine biscuit mix, cheese, milk, onions, salt pork, and yeast mixture; stir until a soft dough forms. On a lightly floured surface, use a floured rolling pin to roll out dough to 1/2-inch thickness. Use a 2 1/2-inch biscuit cutter to cut out biscuits. Transfer to a greased baking sheet. Bake 10 to 12 minutes or until light brown. Serve warm.
Yield: about 1 dozen biscuits

HEARTY BRUNCH PIE

CRUST
2½ cups all-purpose flour
½ teaspoon salt
¾ cup plus 2 tablespoons butter,
    chilled and cut into pieces
⅓ cup ice water

FILLING
1 pound ground turkey
½ pound mild pork sausage
5 eggs
2 packages (10 ounces each)
    frozen chopped spinach,
    thawed and squeezed dry
4 cups (16 ounces) shredded
    mozzarella cheese
1 cup ricotta cheese
1 teaspoon salt
¼ teaspoon ground black pepper
1 egg yolk
1 tablespoon water
    Red liquid food coloring to
    garnish

Preheat oven to 375 degrees. For crust, sift flour and salt together in a medium bowl. Using a pastry blender or 2 knives, cut butter into flour mixture until mixture resembles coarse meal. Sprinkle ice water over dough, mixing quickly just until dough forms a soft ball. On a lightly floured surface, use a floured rolling pin to roll out ⅔ of dough into a 16-inch-diameter circle. Press dough into a greased 9-inch springform pan. Do not trim edges of dough. Reserve remaining dough for top crust.

For filling, brown turkey and sausage in a large skillet. Drain well and transfer to a large mixing bowl. Stir in 5 eggs, spinach, cheeses, salt, and pepper. Spoon filling into springform pan. Fold edge of crust over filling. For top crust, roll out remaining dough to ¼-inch thickness. Cut out a 9-inch-diameter circle. Mix egg yolk with water in a small bowl; brush on edge of bottom crust. Place top crust over filling and brush yolk mixture over entire top.

To garnish, cut holly leaves from dough scraps and arrange on top of pie. Add 1 teaspoon red food coloring to about 2 tablespoons dough scraps. Form small balls and place in center of holly leaves. Brush garnish with yolk mixture. Bake 1 hour 15 minutes. Cool 10 minutes in pan; remove sides of pan.
Yield: 10 to 12 servings

ORANGE AMBROSIA WITH WINE SAUCE

10 to 12 oranges, peeled and sliced
1 cup shredded coconut, lightly
    toasted
2 packages (4 ounces each) instant
    vanilla pudding mix
1⅓ cups milk
1 cup freshly squeezed orange juice,
    chilled
½ cup sherry
1 cup whipping cream, whipped
    Grated rind of 1 orange

Layer orange slices and coconut in a large serving bowl. Combine pudding mix, milk, orange juice, and sherry. Beat until smooth. Set aside 5 minutes. Fold whipped cream and orange rind into pudding mixture. Sauce may be poured over fruit mixture or served in a separate bowl.
Yield: about 12 servings

CORN BREAD SALAD

6 cups crumbled corn bread
1 pound bacon, cooked, drained, and crumbled
2 cups (8 ounces) shredded Cheddar cheese
2 large tomatoes, chopped
1 can (17 ounces) whole kernel corn, drained
1 cup mayonnaise
1/2 cup chopped green onions
1/2 cup chopped green pepper

In a large bowl, combine all ingredients. Cover and refrigerate until well chilled.
Yield: about 12 servings

HOT BERRY-BRANDY PUNCH

2 packages (12 ounces each) frozen red raspberries, thawed
1 gallon cranberry juice cocktail
2 cups sugar
2 cups blackberry-flavored brandy
1/2 cup raspberry-flavored liqueur

Purée raspberries in a food processor. Strain raspberries; discard seeds and pulp. In a Dutch oven, combine raspberry purée, cranberry juice, sugar, brandy, and liqueur. Bring to a boil; stir until sugar dissolves. Serve warm.
Yield: about 19 1/2 cups punch

SWEET POTATO MUFFINS

2 cups all-purpose flour, sifted
2 teaspoons baking powder
1 teaspoon salt
1/2 teaspoon baking soda
1 1/4 teaspoons ground cinnamon
1/2 teaspoon ground nutmeg
1 cup cooked, mashed sweet potatoes
1 cup granulated sugar
1/2 cup milk
2 eggs
1/4 cup butter, melted
3/4 cup chopped pecans

Sift together flour, baking powder, salt, baking soda, cinnamon, and nutmeg; set aside. In a mixing bowl, combine sweet potatoes, sugar, milk, and eggs. Add dry ingredients and melted butter; mix until well blended. Stir in pecans. Fill greased muffin cups half full. Bake in a preheated 350-degree oven 20 minutes or until a toothpick inserted in center of muffin comes out clean.
Yield: about 24 muffins

SUGARED BACON

1/2 cup firmly packed light brown sugar
4 egg yolks
10 teaspoons Worcestershire sauce
5 teaspoons prepared mustard
20 thin slices bacon
2 cups fine bread crumbs

Beat brown sugar, egg yolks, Worcestershire sauce, and mustard until well blended. Dip bacon in mixture and roll in crumbs. Place bacon on a broiler pan. Bake in a preheated 250-degree oven 20 minutes or until brown and crispy.
Yield: 20 slices bacon

We filled our Pumpkin Yeast Biscuits with slices of smoked turkey. You could also use country ham or thin sausage patties.

PUMPKIN YEAST BISCUITS

2 packages dry yeast
$1/2$ teaspoon granulated sugar
$1/2$ cup warm water
1 cup milk, scalded and cooled
1 cup canned pumpkin
1 cup firmly packed light brown
   sugar
$1/2$ cup butter, melted
6 to 7 cups all-purpose flour
2 teaspoons salt
2 teaspoons pumpkin pie spice
1 teaspoon ground ginger

Dissolve yeast and granulated sugar in warm water. Let stand until bubbly.

In a large mixing bowl, combine yeast mixture, milk, pumpkin, brown sugar, and melted butter. Add flour, salt, pumpkin pie spice, and ginger. Stir until a soft dough forms. Knead on a floured surface until dough is smooth and elastic (about 10 to 12 minutes). Place dough in a greased bowl, turning once to coat. Cover and let rise until doubled in size (about 2 to 3 hours).

On a lightly floured surface, use a floured rolling pin to roll out dough to $1/2$-inch thickness. Cut out biscuits with a floured $11/2$-inch biscuit cutter. Place biscuits close together on a greased baking sheet. Cover and let rise until doubled in size (about 1 hour).

Bake in a preheated 350-degree oven 25 minutes or until golden brown. **Yield:** about 50 biscuits

CRANBERRY BREAKFAST RINGS

2 packages dry yeast
$31/2$ to $41/2$ cups all-purpose flour,
   divided
$11/4$ cups granulated sugar, divided
1 teaspoon salt
1 cup milk
$1/2$ cup butter or margarine
$1/4$ cup water
2 eggs, beaten
1 teaspoon grated lemon rind
1 jar (14 ounces) cranberry-orange
   sauce, divided
1 cup chopped walnuts
2 teaspoons ground cinnamon
$1/2$ cup butter or margarine, melted
   and divided
   Frosting (recipe follows)

In a large bowl, combine yeast, $11/4$ cups flour, $1/2$ cup sugar, and salt. Set aside.

Cranberry Breakfast Rings are as pretty as they are delicious. They also make wonderful hostess gifts!

In a saucepan, combine milk, $1/2$ cup butter, and water; heat until warm. Add to dry ingredients and beat until smooth. Add eggs and $1^1/4$ cups flour, beating again until mixed. Stir in remaining flour and lemon rind. Cover and refrigerate until ready to shape rings.

To make rings, turn dough onto a lightly floured surface and divide in half. Use a floured rolling pin to roll out half of dough into a 14 x 7-inch rectangle. Spread half of cranberry-orange sauce over dough. Combine remaining $3/4$ cup sugar, walnuts, and cinnamon; sprinkle half of mixture over dough. Drizzle with $1/4$ cup melted butter. Beginning with one long side, roll up dough and seal edges. With seam edge down, place dough in a circle on a greased baking sheet. Press ends together to seal. Cut slits two-thirds of the way through ring at 1-inch intervals. Repeat process with remaining half of dough. Cover rings and let rise in a warm place until doubled in size (about 1 hour).

Bake in a preheated 375-degree oven 20 to 25 minutes or until bread sounds hollow when tapped. Frost if desired.
Yield: 2 breakfast rings

FROSTING
  1 cup confectioners sugar
  2 tablespoons warm milk
 $1/2$ teaspoon vanilla extract

Mix all ingredients until smooth; drizzle over rings.

MINI CHEDDAR SOUFFLÉS

1 pound white potatoes, peeled
    and cut into pieces
1/4 cup butter or margarine
1/4 cup all-purpose flour
6 eggs, separated
1/2 teaspoon salt
1/4 teaspoon ground black pepper
1/4 teaspoon cream of tartar
1 3/4 cups (7 ounces) shredded
    sharp Cheddar cheese

In a large saucepan, cover potatoes
with salted water. Bring water to a boil
and cook 25 to 30 minutes or until
potatoes are tender. Drain, reserving
1 1/2 cups potato water. Process potatoes
in a food processor until puréed; leave in
processor.

Preheat oven to 375 degrees. In a large
saucepan, melt butter over medium heat.
Add flour, stirring until smooth. Cook
3 to 4 minutes or until flour begins to
brown. Whisk in reserved potato water.
Bring to a boil. Stirring occasionally,
reduce heat to low and simmer
5 minutes. Add sauce to potato purée
and process until well blended. Transfer
to a large bowl; whisk in egg yolks, salt,
and pepper. In another large bowl, beat
egg whites and cream of tartar until
stiff peaks form. Fold half of egg white
mixture into potato mixture. Fold in
cheese and remaining egg white mixture.
Spoon into a heavily greased miniature
muffin pan, filling each cup three-fourths
full. Bake 25 to 30 minutes or until golden
brown. Serve warm.

Yield: about 7 dozen mini soufflés

HONEY-BAKED HAM

5 to 6 pound fully cooked semi-
    boneless ham
1 1/2 cups apple cider
1 1/2 cups honey, divided
1/4 cup soy sauce
3 tablespoons cornstarch
3 tablespoons water

Preheat oven to 450 degrees. Place
ham in a large roasting pan. Bake
30 minutes or until outside is crisp.
Remove from oven. Reduce oven
temperature to 325 degrees.

In a large bowl, combine cider, 1 cup
honey, and soy sauce; pour over ham.
Cover and bake 2 to 3 hours or until a
meat thermometer registers 140 degrees,
basting ham frequently with cider
mixture. Reserve drippings.

For sauce, combine cornstarch and
water in a small bowl; stir until smooth. In
a medium saucepan, combine reserved
meat drippings and remaining 1/2 cup
honey; bring to a boil. Stirring constantly,
add cornstarch mixture, bring to a boil,
and cook until thickened. Serve warm
sauce with ham.

Yield: 10 to 12 servings

KIELBASA PALMIERS

1 pound kielbasa sausage, finely
    chopped or ground, divided
1 package (17$^{1}/_{4}$ ounces) frozen
    puff pastry dough, thawed and
    divided
1 cup hot and sweet mustard,
    divided

In a skillet, brown sausage over
medium heat. Drain well. Unfold one
sheet of pastry and spread with $^{1}/_{2}$ cup of
mustard. Spread half of the sausage over
the mustard. Roll each long end tightly
and evenly to center of pastry. Repeat
with remaining pastry sheet, mustard,
and sausage. Wrap tightly in aluminum
foil and refrigerate at least 1 hour.
    Preheat oven to 450 degrees. Cut
palmiers crosswise into $^{1}/_{2}$-inch-thick
slices. Place on ungreased baking sheets.
    Bake 15 to 20 minutes or until pastry
is puffed and golden. Serve warm or at
room temperature.
Yield: about 40 palmiers

SMOKED TURKEY SPREAD

1 package (8 ounces) cream cheese,
    softened
1 cup chopped smoked turkey
$^{1}/_{4}$ cup mayonnaise
$^{2}/_{3}$ cup chopped pecans, toasted and
    divided
6 tablespoons chopped fresh parsley,
    divided
$^{1}/_{8}$ teaspoon ground red pepper
    Crackers to seve

Process cream cheese, turkey, and
mayonnaise in a food processor until
well blended. Add $^{1}/_{2}$ cup pecans,
4 tablespoons parsley, and red pepper.
Pulse process until blended. Spoon
into small bowl; garnish with remaining
pecans and 2 tablespoons parsley. Cover
and store in refrigerator. Serve with
crackers.
Yield: about 2$^{1}/_{4}$ cups spread

BRUNCH EGGS

$^1/_2$ cup butter, divided
1 cup minced green onions,
  including tops
$^1/_4$ cup all-purpose flour
$2^1/_2$ cups milk
1 cup (4 ounces) shredded Cheddar
  cheese
$^1/_4$ cup sherry
$^3/_4$ teaspoon seasoned salt
$^1/_2$ teaspoon dry mustard
$^1/_4$ teaspoon curry powder
$^1/_4$ teaspoon ground white pepper
$^1/_4$ teaspoon cayenne pepper
18 eggs
1 cup water
2 tablespoons vegetable oil
  Salt and ground black pepper
$^1/_2$ cup chopped green onions,
  including tops

In a saucepan, melt $^1/_4$ cup butter. Add 1 cup minced green onions and sauté until soft. Remove from heat and blend in flour. Stirring slowly, cook over medium heat 2 minutes. Remove from heat; gradually stir in milk. Return to heat and cook until thickened. Add cheese and stir. Remove from heat; add sherry, seasoned salt, dry mustard, curry powder, white pepper, and cayenne pepper. Cool.

Beat eggs with water. Scramble eggs in remaining $^1/_4$ cup butter and oil in a large skillet until barely set. Salt and pepper to taste. Butter two 2-quart casseroles. Pour a small amount of sauce into bottom of each casserole. Spoon scrambled eggs into casseroles and cover with remainder of sauce. Cover and bake in a preheated 275-degree oven 1 hour. Sprinkle with chopped green onions.
Yield: about 12 servings

TOMATOES STUFFED WITH SPINACH AND ARTICHOKES

6 large tomatoes
$^1/_2$ cup chopped green onions,
  including tops
$^1/_2$ cup plus 3 tablespoons butter or
  margarine, divided
2 packages (10 ounces each)
  frozen chopped spinach
  Salt
1 can (14 ounces) artichoke hearts,
  drained and chopped
1 cup sour cream
1 teaspoon Worcestershire sauce
3 drops hot pepper sauce
$^3/_4$ cup grated Parmesan cheese,
  divided

Wash tomatoes, remove stems, and scoop out seeds (discard); turn upside down to drain.

In a large skillet, sauté onions in $^1/_2$ cup butter. Cook spinach according to package directions; lightly salt and drain. Add spinach, artichoke hearts, sour cream, Worcestershire sauce, and pepper sauce to onions. Stir in $^1/_2$ cup cheese. Stuff tomatoes with spinach mixture and sprinkle with remaining $^1/_4$ cup cheese; dot with remaining 3 tablespoons butter. Bake in a preheated 350-degree oven 20 minutes or until thoroughly heated.
Yield: about 6 servings

BROCCOLI-HAM ROLL

CREAMED HAM
3 tablespoons butter
3 tablespoons all-purpose flour
$^3/_4$ cup chicken broth
2 tablespoons sherry
1 teaspoon Dijon-style mustard
  Salt and ground black pepper

This hearty fare is designed to satisfy big appetites: Brunch Eggs (clockwise from top), Tomatoes Stuffed with Spinach and Artichokes, and Broccoli-Ham Roll.

¹/₂ cup half and half
1¹/₂ cups diced boiled or baked ham
1 can (4 ounces) sliced
mushrooms, drained

BROCCOLI ROLL
4 packages (10 ounces each) frozen
chopped broccoli
¹/₂ cup dry bread crumbs
6 tablespoons butter, melted
Pinch of ground nutmeg
Salt and ground black pepper
4 eggs, separated
8 tablespoons grated Parmesan
cheese, divided

For creamed ham, melt butter in a medium saucepan. Remove from heat and add flour. Stirring slowly, cook over medium heat 2 minutes. Remove from heat; gradually stir in broth, sherry, and mustard. Salt and pepper to taste. Return to heat and cook until mixture thickens. Add half and half, ham, and mushrooms; continue cooking until thoroughly heated. Keep warm while preparing broccoli roll.

For broccoli roll, cook broccoli according to package directions; drain. Cool and finely chop. Butter a 10¹/₂ x 15¹/₂ x 1-inch jellyroll pan and line with waxed paper. Butter waxed paper well and sprinkle with bread crumbs. In a large mixing bowl, combine broccoli, melted butter, and nutmeg; salt and pepper to taste. Beat in egg yolks, one at a time, blending thoroughly after each addition. Beat egg whites until soft peaks form; fold into broccoli mixture. Turn into prepared pan and smooth top. Sprinkle with 4 tablespoons cheese. Bake in a preheated 350-degree oven 12 to 16 minutes or until center feels barely firm when touched.

Place a sheet of buttered waxed paper over the top of the broccoli mixture and invert onto a large baking sheet. Carefully peel away waxed paper. Spread creamed ham over broccoli mixture. Beginning with one long side, gently roll up broccoli mixture. Sprinkle with remaining 4 tablespoons cheese.
Yield: about 12 servings

MINIATURE CORN MUFFINS WITH TURKEY AND RELISH

2 cups buttermilk
2 eggs
1 1/2 cups cornmeal
1/2 cup all-purpose flour
1/4 cup granulated sugar
1 teaspoon baking soda
1 teaspoon salt
1/4 pound sliced, cooked turkey breast
Purchased cranberry relish

Preheat oven to 450 degrees. In a medium mixing bowl, beat buttermilk and eggs. Beat in cornmeal, flour, sugar, baking soda, and salt. Fill lightly greased miniature muffin tins two-thirds full with batter. Bake 10 to 15 minutes or until a muffin springs back when pressed. Remove muffins from pans and cool on wire racks.
Split cooled muffins in half and fill each with a piece of turkey and a small amount of cranberry relish.
Yield: about 45 muffins

FUZZY NAVEL PUNCH

Here's a wonderful punch adaptation of the Fuzzy Navel Cocktail. This is a sparkling, flavorful punch that you will want to make all year long.

9 cups orange juice with pulp
3 cups peach schnapps
1 bottle (750 ml) brut champagne, chilled
Crushed ice or ice ring

Combine orange juice, peach schnapps, and champagne. Pour into a punch bowl and add crushed ice or ice ring.
Yield: about 1 gallon of punch

MEXICAN QUICHES

Green chilies and Monterey Jack cheese add a taste of Mexico to these mouth-watering treats. This recipe freezes well for up to one week. To serve, allow quiches to come to room temperature, then warm in a 325-degree oven.

1/2 cup butter or margarine, softened
1 package (3 ounces) cream cheese, softened
1 cup all-purpose flour
1 cup shredded Monterey Jack cheese
1 can (4 ounces) chopped green chilies
2 eggs, lightly beaten
1/2 cup whipping cream
1/4 teaspoon salt
Ground black pepper to taste

In a medium mixing bowl, combine butter and cream cheese; blend until smooth. Stir in flour. Shape dough into a ball and wrap in waxed paper. Chill 2 to 3 hours.
Preheat oven to 350 degrees. Divide dough into 24 balls and press into lightly greased cups of miniature muffin pans to form shells. Sprinkle cheese and chilies in the bottom of each pastry shell. Combine eggs, cream, salt, and pepper. Pour over cheese and chilies in pastry shells. Bake 30 to 35 minutes.
Yield: 24 quiches

MAKE-AHEAD SAUCY RIBS

5 pounds pork loin back ribs
 Salt
 Ground black pepper
1 cup finely chopped onion
1 cup finely chopped green peper
3 tablespoons vegetable oil
1 bottle (28 ounces) ketchup
1 1/2 cups firmly packed brown sugar
3/4 cup orange marmalade
3/4 cup apple cider vinegar
1 tablespoon hot pepper sauce
1 teaspoon salt
3/4 teaspoon ground black pepper

Preheat oven to 350 degrees. Place rib racks in a single layer in foil-lined baking pans. Sprinkle ribs with salt and pepper. Cover with foil and bake 1 hour or until fully cooked. Let cool.

While ribs are cooking, sauté onion and green pepper in oil in a large saucepan over medium heat until tender. Stir in ketchup, brown sugar, marmalade, vinegar, pepper sauce, 1 teaspoon salt, and 3/4 teaspoon black pepper. Stirring constantly, bring sauce to a simmer. Reduce heat to medium low. Stirring frequently, cook sauce 30 minutes (mixture will be thick). Remove from heat and let cool.

Cut racks into individual ribs. Transfer to a heavy-duty resealable plastic bag. Pour 2 cups sauce over ribs; refrigerate overnight to let ribs marinate. Store remaining sauce in an airtight container in refrigerator.

To serve, preheat oven to 425 degrees. Place ribs in foil-lined baking pans. Spoon sauce from plastic bag over ribs. Bake uncovered 1 hour or until sauce cooks onto ribs, turning every 15 minutes and basting with remaining sauce. Serve warm.
Yield: about 3 dozen ribs

MARMALADE CHEESE TARTS

1 cup butter, softened
2 cups all-purpose flour
1 cup grated sharp Cheddar cheese
3/4 cup orange marmalade
1 egg, lightly beaten

In a medium mixing bowl, combine butter, flour, and cheese. Knead until well blended. Wrap dough in plastic wrap and refrigerate 1 hour.

Preheat oven to 350 degrees. On a lightly floured surface, use a floured rolling pin to roll out dough to 1/8-inch thickness. Cut out dough using a 2-inch round cookie cutter. Place about 1/2 teaspoon marmalade in center of each circle of dough. Fold dough in half and seal edges by pressing with a fork. Transfer tarts to ungreased baking sheets and brush tops with egg. Bake 10 to 15 minutes or until tarts are set and lightly browned. Remove from pans and cool on wire racks.
Yield: about 5 dozen tarts

Crab-Cream Cheese Bake is encased in flaky pastry. It's a savory treat that's sure to become a family favorite.

CRAB-CREAM CHEESE BAKE

1 package (8 ounces) cream cheese, softened
1/4 cup chopped green onions
1/2 teaspoon dried dill weed
1 can (8 ounces) refrigerated crescent dinner rolls
1 can (6 1/2 ounces) crabmeat, drained
1 egg yolk, beaten

Preheat oven to 350 degrees. In a medium bowl, combine cream cheese, onions, and dill weed. Unroll crescent roll dough onto a greased baking sheet, being careful not to separate dough into pieces. Press dough into an 8 x 11-inch rectangle. Spoon crabmeat lengthwise along center of dough. Spoon cream cheese mixture over crabmeat. Fold long edges of dough over cream cheese mixture, slightly overlapping edges; pinch edges together to seal. Place seam side down on baking sheet. Lightly brush top of dough with egg yolk. Cut slits in top of dough. Bake 20 to 22 minutes or until golden brown and flaky. Cut into 1-inch slices and serve warm.
Yield: about 12 servings

COLD SHRIMP, ARTICHOKES, AND MUSHROOMS

7 to 8 pounds shrimp, boiled, peeled, and deveined
3 cans (14 ounces each) artichoke hearts, drained and halved
1 pound fresh mushrooms, sliced
2 cups olive oil
2 cups vegetable oil
1 cup dry sherry
1 cup garlic-flavored vinegar
1 teaspoon salt
3/4 tablespoon Cajun seasoning
3/4 tablespoon hot pepper sauce (optional)
1/4 teaspoon cayenne pepper
6 small red onions, thinly sliced

In a large glass bowl, combine shrimp, artichokes, and mushrooms. In a medium bowl, combine remaining ingredients (except onions). Whisk until blended. Pour over shrimp mixture. Cover tightly and refrigerate for 2 to 3 days, stirring occasionally. Several hours before serving, add onions. Place in a glass serving dish.

Yield: about 60 servings

This flavorful medley of Cold Shrimp, Artichokes, and Mushrooms is seasoned with a peppery marinade.

FETA CHEESE SQUARES

1 1/2 cups cornmeal
1 1/2 cups water
1 1/2 cups milk
 1/4 cup butter or margarine
 1/3 cup finely chopped sun-dried
        tomatoes
 1 cup (4 ounces) shredded sharp
        Cheddar cheese, divided
 1 cup (7 ounces) finely crumbled
        feta cheese, divided
 3 green onions, finely chopped
 1 egg, beaten
 1/2 teaspoon ground red pepper
 1/2 teaspoon dried thyme leaves

Preheat oven to 400 degrees. In a small bowl, combine cornmeal and water. In a large skillet, combine milk, butter, and tomatoes. Bring to a boil; stir in cornmeal mixture. Reduce heat to medium-low. Stirring constantly, cook 5 to 7 minutes or until mixture thickens. Remove from heat. Stir in 1/2 cup Cheddar cheese, 1/2 cup feta cheese, onions, egg, red pepper, and thyme. Spoon into a greased 8 x 11-inch baking pan. Sprinkle remaining cheese evenly over top. Bake 20 to 25 minutes or until cheese begins to brown. Cut into approximately 1-inch squares and serve warm.
Yield: about 4 1/2 dozen squares

FETA CHEESE-VEGETABLE SALAD

DRESSING
 1 cup chopped fresh basil leaves
        or 2 tablespoons dried basil
        leaves, crushed
 3/4 cup balsamic vinegar
 2/3 cup buttermilk
 1/3 cup olive oil
 1 tablespoon Dijon-style mustard
 2 teaspoons salt
 1 teaspoon ground black pepper
 1/2 teaspoon garlic powder

SALAD
 3 cups fresh broccoli flowerets
 3 cups shredded green cabbage
 2 cups thinly sliced zucchini
1 1/2 cups sliced red onions
1 1/2 cups thinly sliced carrots
1 1/2 cups (10 ounces) crumbled
        feta cheese

For dressing, combine basil, vinegar, buttermilk, oil, mustard, salt, pepper, and garlic powder in a 1-pint jar with a tight-fitting lid. Shake until well blended. Refrigerate 8 hours or overnight to allow flavors to blend.

In a large bowl, combine broccoli, cabbage, zucchini, onions, and carrots. Pour dressing over vegetables; stir until well coated. Stir in cheese.
Yield: about 12 cups salad

.IGHT YEAST BISCUITS

1 package dry yeast
2 tablespoons warm water
2 tablespoons sugar, divided
2¹/₂ cups all-purpose flour
¹/₂ teaspoon baking powder
¹/₂ teaspoon baking soda
¹/₂ teaspoon salt
¹/₂ cup butter or margarine,
softened
1 cup buttermilk, warmed
Vegetable cooking spray

In a small bowl, dissolve yeast in
arm water; stir in 1 tablespoon sugar.
a large bowl, combine remaining
tablespoon sugar, flour, baking powder,
aking soda, and salt. Using a pastry
lender or two knives, cut butter into
ry ingredients until mixture resembles
oarse cornmeal. Add buttermilk and
east mixture to dry ingredients; stir until
soft dough forms. Turn onto a lightly
oured surface and knead 4 minutes
until dough becomes smooth and
astic. Place in a large bowl sprayed with
ooking spray, turning once to coat top of
ough. Cover and let rise in a warm place
0 to 85 degrees) 1 to 1¹/₂ hours or until
oubled in size.
Turn dough onto a lightly floured
irface and punch down. Use a floured
lling pin to roll out dough to ¹/₂-inch
ickness. Use a 2-inch-diameter biscuit
utter to cut out biscuits. Place biscuits
inch apart on an ungreased baking
heet. Spray tops with cooking spray,
over, and let rise in a warm place
) to 45 minutes or until doubled in size.
Preheat oven to 400 degrees. Bake
2 to 15 minutes or until golden brown.
erve warm.
eld: about 2 dozen biscuits

ROLLED HERB TOAST

¹/₂ cup butter, melted
1 package (¹/₂ ounce) herb salad
dressing mix
1 teaspoon dried dill weed
¹/₄ teaspoon garlic salt
20 slices thin-sliced bread

Preheat oven to 300 degrees. Combine
melted butter, dressing mix, dill weed,
and garlic salt in a medium bowl. Trim
crusts from bread; flatten each slice with
a rolling pin and roll tightly. Coat each
roll with butter mixture. Place rolls on
an ungreased baking sheet and bake
15 to 20 minutes or until lightly browned,
turning several times. Serve hot.
Toast may be frozen or stored in an
airtight container. Reheat before serving.
Yield: 20 servings

HOT FRUITED TEA

This hot beverage will fill your home with a wonderful spicy aroma. After it is brewed, the tea may be refrigerated and reheated later. For larger crowds, we suggest serving the tea from an electric coffee server.

1^1/$_2$ cups water
^{1}/$_3$ cup unsweetened powdered
    instant tea
1 can (46 ounces) pineapple juice
6 cups orange juice
6 cups lemonade
1^1/$_2$ cups sugar
3 whole nutmegs
3 tablespoons whole cloves
4 2-inch cinnamon sticks
    Sliced oranges or lemons to
    serve

In a large Dutch oven, bring water to a boil; stir in instant tea until dissolved. Stir in pineapple juice, orange juice, lemonade, and sugar, mixing well. Place nutmegs and cloves in center of a small square of cheesecloth and tie corners together to form a bag. Add spice bag and cinnamon sticks to tea. Stirring occasionally, simmer 2 to 3 hours over medium-low heat (do not allow mixture to boil). Remove spice bag and serve hot tea with slices of orange or lemon.
Yield: about 16 cups tea

APPLE-PEAR SKILLET CAKE

1 cup firmly packed brown sugar
6 tablespoons butter or margarine,
    cut into pieces
1 medium unpeeled baking apple,
    cored and sliced
1 medium unpeeled pear, cored
    and sliced
1^1/$_3$ cups all-purpose flour
1 cup granulated sugar
2 teaspoons ground cinnamon
1 ^{1}/$_4$ teaspoons baking soda
^{1}/$_2$ teaspoon salt
2 eggs
^{1}/$_2$ cup sour cream
2 tablespoons vegetable oil
1 teaspoon vanilla extract

Preheat oven to 350 degrees. Place brown sugar and butter in a 10^1/$_2$-inch cast-iron or ovenproof skillet. Place skillet in oven about 5 minutes or until butter melts. Remove skillet from oven and whisk brown sugar mixture until well blended. Arrange fruit slices over brown sugar mixture. In a medium bowl, combine flour, granulated sugar, cinnamon, baking soda, and salt. In a small bowl, whisk eggs, sour cream, oil, and vanilla; beat into flour mixture. Pour batter over fruit; bake 30 to 35 minutes or until a toothpick inserted in center of cake comes out clean. Remove from oven and place on a wire rack to cool 10 minutes. Run knife around edge of cake; invert onto a serving plate. Serve warm.
Yield: about 12 servings

Fresh fruit and a buttery brown sugar topping make Apple-Pear Skillet Cake a sumptuous upside-down delight. It's best when prepared in a cast-iron skillet.

PEACH-APPLE COBBLER WITH WHIPPED CINNAMON SAUCE

CRUST
- 2 cups all-purpose flour
- 1 teaspoon salt
- 2/3 cup vegetable shortening
- 1/2 cup plus 1 tablespoon cold water

FILLING
- 2 1/2 cups peeled, cored, and chopped tart cooking apples (about 3 apples)
- 1 package (16 ounces) frozen unsweetened peach slices, thawed and undrained
- 2 cups granulated sugar
- 1/2 cup chopped walnuts
- 1/4 cup all-purpose flour
- 1/2 teaspoon ground cinnamon
- 1/4 teaspoon ground nutmeg
- 1 egg, beaten
- 1 tablespoon granulated sugar

SAUCE
- 1 cup whipping cream
- 1/4 cup sifted confectioners sugar
- 1/4 teaspoon ground cinnamon

For crust, combine flour and salt in a medium bowl. Using a pastry blender or 2 knives, cut in shortening until mixture resembles coarse meal. Sprinkle with water; mix until a soft dough forms. On a lightly floured surface, use a floured rolling pin to roll out dough to 1/8-inch thickness. Reserving dough scraps, cut a 14-inch circle. Transfer to an ungreased 10-inch deep-dish pie plate. Use a sharp knife to cut out about 10 small leaves from dough scraps. Cover all dough pieces; set aside.

For sauce, place a medium bowl and beaters from an electric mixer in freezer until well chilled.

Preheat oven to 425 degrees. For filling, combine apples, peaches, 2 cups sugar, walnuts, flour, cinnamon, and nutmeg in a large bowl. Pour filling into crust. Fold edges of crust over filling, making overlapping folds every few inches and leaving center of filling uncovered. Brush crust with egg. Place leaves around edges of crust. Brush leaves with egg; sprinkle with 1 tablespoon sugar. Bake 45 to 50 minutes or until crust is golden brown and fruit is tender. If crust becomes too brown, cover with aluminum foil for last 15 to 20 minutes of baking time.

In chilled bowl, whip cream until soft peaks form. Add sugar and cinnamon; beat until stiff peaks form. Place a dollop of sauce in center of cobbler and serve additional sauce with each serving.
Yield: about 12 servings

JAM CAKE SQUARES

CRUST
1 cup all-purpose flour
3 tablespoons sifted confectioners
   sugar
1/4 teaspoon salt
1/2 cup chilled butter or margarine,
   cut into small pieces

TOPPING
2/3 cup strawberry jam or preserves
1 1/4 cups granulated sugar
4 tablespoons all-purpose flour
1/2 teaspoon baking powder
3 eggs
1/4 cup applesauce
   Confectioners sugar

Preheat oven to 350 degrees. For crust, combine flour, confectioners sugar, and salt in a medium bowl. Using a pastry blender or 2 knives, cut in butter until mixture resembles coarse meal. Press into bottom of a greased and floured 8 x 11-inch baking pan. Bake 10 minutes.
For topping, spread jam evenly over hot crust. Bake 10 minutes or until jam is bubbly; set aside. In a medium bowl, combine granulated sugar, flour, and baking powder. Add eggs and applesauce; beat until well blended. Spread topping evenly over jam. Bake 30 to 35 minutes or until golden brown and firm in center. Cool completely on a wire rack. Dust with confectioners sugar. Refrigerate until ready to serve. To serve, cut into 2-inch squares.
Yield: about 1 1/2 dozen squares

WASSAIL PUNCH

1 quart boiling water
4 spiced tea bags
1 gallon apple cider
2 quarts orange juice
1 quart cranberry juice cocktail
1 1/2 cups sugar
12 whole cloves
1 orange
4 cinnamon sticks
1/2 cup small red cinnamon
   candies

In a stockpot, pour boiling water over tea bags; steep 4 minutes. Remove tea bags. Stir in cider, orange juice, cranberry juice, and sugar. Bring to a boil; reduce heat to a simmer. Insert cloves into orange. Add orange, cinnamon sticks, and cinnamon candies to punch. Simmer 30 minutes. Remove orange and cinnamon sticks; serve hot.
Yield: about 32 cups punch

CRANBERRY SANGRIA

1 bottle (750 ml) Burgundy wine
3 cups cranberry juice cocktail
1/4 cup brandy
1/4 cup sugar
1 can (8 ounces) pineapple
    chunks, drained
1 orange, thinly sliced
    Maraschino cherries
    Wooden skewers

Combine wine, cranberry juice, brandy, and sugar in a 2-quart container. Stir until sugar dissolves. Cover and refrigerate until ready to serve. Add ice and pour sangria into glasses. Place pieces of fruit on wooden skewers; place in glasses.
Yield: about 6 cups sangria

FRUIT SALAD WITH YOGURT SAUCE

2 cups plain nonfat yogurt
1 teaspoon sugar-free lemonade-
    flavored soft drink mix
8 cups coarsely chopped fresh fruit

In a small bowl, combine yogurt and soft drink mix; stir until well blended. Store yogurt sauce and fruit in separate airtight containers in refrigerator until ready to serve.

To serve, spoon yogurt sauce over each serving of fruit.
Yield: 8 cups fruit salad

FRUIT WREATH WITH SWEET CHEESE DIP

A pretty tray of fruit and dip is really quick and easy party fare. The wreath may be prepared ahead of time, but keep the cut fruit fresh by sprinkling with lemon juice.

2 packages (8 ounces each)
    cream cheese, softened
1 jar (7 ounces) marshmallow
    creme
1/4 cup milk
1 1/2 teaspoons vanilla extract
1/2 teaspoon ground nutmeg
    Assorted fruits to serve

In a medium mixing bowl, combine cream cheese, marshmallow creme, milk, vanilla, and nutmeg, beating until smooth.

Place dip in a serving bowl. Arrange fruit around bowl.
Yield: about 3 1/2 cups of dip

*This attractive Fruit Wreath with Sweet Cheese Dip was inspired by a Della Robbia wreath.
Served on your prettiest platter, it's sure to gather compliments.*

GREEN BEANS AND NEW POTATOES

2 pounds fresh green beans
2 pounds unpeeled new potatoes, quartered
10 slices bacon
1 onion, chopped
2 cloves garlic, minced
1/2 cup chopped fresh parsley
1/4 cup apple cider vinegar
2 teaspoons dried oregano leaves
1 teaspoon salt
1/2 teaspoon ground black pepper

Wash beans, trim ends, and remove strings. Cut into 1¹/₂-inch pieces. In a Dutch oven, combine green beans and potatoes. Cover with salted water and bring to a boil. Cover and cook until potatoes are tender; drain in a colander.

In a large skillet, cook bacon until crisp. Drain on paper towels; crumble. Add onion and garlic to bacon drippings; cook until onion is tender. Stir in green beans and potatoes, parsley, vinegar, oregano, salt, and pepper. Stirring occasionally, cook until edges of potatoes begin to brown. Stir in crumbled bacon.
Yield: about 12 servings

BAKED PINEAPPLE ORANGES

This tart orange cup may be prepared ahead. We garnished the scalloped edges of the oranges with finely minced parsley.

6 large navel oranges
4 cups crushed pineapple with juice
  Juice of 1 lemon
1/2 cup granulated sugar
1/4 cup firmly packed light brown sugar
1/4 cup sherry
1/2 teaspoon ground nutmeg
1/2 cup finely chopped walnuts

Cut oranges in half and scoop out pulp; reserve orange shells and pulp. Scallop edges of orange shells.

Preheat oven to 350 degrees. In a large saucepan, combine orange pulp, undrained pineapple, lemon juice, and sugars. Stirring frequently, cook over low heat until thickened. Stir in sherry and nutmeg. Spoon orange mixture into shells and sprinkle with chopped walnuts. Bake 20 minutes. Serve at room temperature.
Yield: 12 servings

SWEET POTATO CRESCENT ROLLS

3 1/2 cups all-purpose flour
1/4 cup sugar
1 package dry yeast
1 teaspoon salt
1 cup butter-flavored shortening
1 can (16 ounces) sweet
    potatoes, drained and puréed
1/2 cup milk, at room temperature
1 egg
1 tablespoon vanilla extract

In a large bowl, combine flour, sugar, yeast, and salt; stir until well blended. Using a pastry blender or 2 knives, cut in shortening until mixture resembles coarse meal. Add puréed sweet potatoes, milk, egg, and vanilla; stir until a soft dough forms. Turn dough onto a lightly floured surface and knead 2 to 3 minutes or until smooth. Shape into a ball and place in a greased bowl; grease top of dough. Cover and let rise in a warm place (80 to 85 degrees) 1 hour or until doubled in size.

Preheat oven to 350 degrees. Divide dough in half and shape into 2 balls. On a lightly floured surface, use a floured rolling pin to roll out 1 ball of dough into an 8 x 10-inch rectangle. Fold in half from top to bottom and again from left to right. Roll into an 8 x 10-inch rectangle again. Referring to **Fig. 1**, cut dough into sixteen triangles. Beginning at wide end, roll up each triangle and place on an ungreased baking sheet with point side down. Repeat with remaining dough. Bake 8 to 10 minutes or until golden brown. Serve warm.
Yield: 32 rolls

Fig. 1

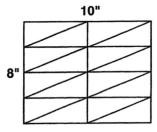

RAISIN-EGGNOG FRENCH TOAST

12 slices raisin bread, dry and firm
2 cups prepared eggnog
1/2 cup butter or margarine
    Confectioners sugar to serve

Cut bread into 1-inch-wide strips, trimming crusts from any long edges of strips. Pour eggnog into a shallow bowl and dip each strip of bread into eggnog, turning each strip over to coat well. Melt butter in a skillet over medium heat. Cook strips of bread on both sides until golden brown. Sprinkle with confectioners sugar to serve.
Yield: about 12 servings

STRAWBERRY-FILLED FRENCH TOAST

FILLING
- 2 packages (8 ounces each) cream cheese, softened
- 1/2 cup sugar
- 1 package (16 ounces) frozen unsweetened strawberries, thawed and drained
- 1 tablespoon vanilla extract
- 1/2 teaspoon ground cinnamon

FRENCH TOAST
- 11 eggs
- 1/2 cup milk
- 1/2 teaspoon salt
- Butter or margarine
- 24 slices white bread
- Confectioners sugar

For filling, beat cream cheese and sugar until fluffy. Add strawberries, vanilla, and cinnamon; stir until well blended.

For French toast, whisk eggs, milk, and salt together until foamy. Melt 1 tablespoon butter in a large skillet over medium heat. For each serving, dip 1 slice bread in egg mixture, turn once to coat, and place in skillet. Spoon about 1/4 cup filling in center of bread. Dip another slice of bread in egg mixture, turn once to coat, and place over filling. Cook 3 to 4 minutes or until underside is lightly browned. Turn and cook 3 to 4 minutes longer or until other side is lightly browned. Transfer to a warm plate, cover with aluminum foil, and place in a 200-degree oven until ready to serve. Add butter to skillet as necessary between batches. To serve, dust each piece of French toast with confectioners sugar.

Yield: 12 servings

POPPY SEED CAKE

CAKE
- 1/2 cup poppy seed
- 1/3 cup milk
- 1 cup butter or margarine, softened
- 1 1/2 cups granulated sugar
- 2 teaspoons grated lemon peel
- 1 1/2 teaspoons lemon extract
- 1 teaspoon vanilla extract
- 4 eggs
- 2 1/4 cups all-purpose flour
- 1 1/2 teaspoons baking powder
- 1/2 teaspoon salt
- 1/2 cup sour cream

GLAZE
- 1/2 cup confectioners sugar
- 1/4 cup lemon juice

Soak poppy seed in milk 1 hour.

Preheat oven to 350 degrees. For cake, cream butter, sugar, lemon peel, and extracts in a large mixing bowl. Beat in eggs, one at a time, beating well after each addition. Drain poppy seed; stir poppy seed into mixture. In a medium bowl, combine flour, baking powder, and salt. Stir flour mixture into creamed mixture, alternating with sour cream. Pour into a greased and floured 9 1/4 x 5 1/4 x 2 1/2-inch loaf pan. Bake 45 to 50 minutes or until a toothpick inserted in center of cake comes out clean.

For glaze, combine confectioners sugar and lemon juice, blending until smooth. Pour over warm cake in pan. Allow cake to cool completely before removing from pan.

Yield: 10 to 12 servings

ORANGE MUFFINS

$^1/_2$ cup shortening
$1^1/_4$ cups Orange Sugar, divided (recipe
    on this page)
 2 eggs
 2 cups all-purpose flour
 1 teaspoon baking soda
 1 cup buttermilk
$^1/_2$ cup golden raisins
$^1/_3$ orange juice

Preheat oven to 350 degrees. In a large bowl, cream shortening and 1 cup Orange Sugar until smooth. Add eggs, beating until fluffy. In a separate bowl, sift together flour and baking soda. Add to creamed mixture along with buttermilk, beating until blended. Stir in raisins. Fill greased and floured muffin pans two-thirds full with batter. Bake 15 to 18 minutes, testing for doneness with a toothpick. While muffins are still warm, brush with orange juice and sprinkle with $^1/_4$ cup Orange Sugar. Store in airtight container.
Yield: about $1^1/_2$ dozen muffins

ORANGE SUGAR

$^2/_3$ cup grated orange peel (about
    7 large oranges)
 4 cups granulated sugar
$1^1/_2$ teaspoons ground cinnamon

Place all ingredients in a blender or food processor fitted with a steel blade. Process until ingredients are completely mixed. Sprinkle over hot cereals or fresh fruit, or substitute for granulated sugar in baking. Store in airtight container in refrigerator.
Yield: about 4 cups of sugar

HOT CRANBERRY-BANANA PUNCH

 1 bottle (48 ounces) cranberry
    juice cocktail
 1 can (6 ounces) frozen
    lemonade concentrate
$^1/_2$ cup firmly packed brown sugar
$2^1/_2$ cups mashed bananas (about
    6 medium bananas)
 1 tablespoon ground allspice
 1 teaspoon ground nutmeg
$^1/_2$ teaspoon ground cinnamon

In a large saucepan or Dutch oven, combine cranberry juice, lemonade, brown sugar, and bananas. Cook over medium-high heat, stirring until well blended. Layer four 4-inch squares of cheesecloth. Place allspice, nutmeg, and cinnamon in center of cheesecloth square and tie with string; add to punch. Stirring occasionally, bring to a boil. Reduce heat to low. Cover and simmer 30 minutes. Remove spice bag. Serve hot.
Yield: about 9 cups punch

ORANGE GLAZED PECANS

1/2 cup granulated sugar
1/2 cup firmly packed brown sugar
1/2 cup sour cream
2 tablespoons frozen orange juice
concentrate, thawed
1 teaspoon orange extract
3 cups unsalted pecan halves,
toasted

Preheat oven to 350 degrees. In a medium saucepan, combine sugars, sour cream, and orange juice. Stirring constantly, cook over medium-low heat until sugars dissolve. Using a pastry brush dipped in hot water, wash down any sugar crystals on sides of pan. Attach candy thermometer to pan, making sure thermometer does not touch bottom of pan. Increase heat to medium and bring to a boil. Cook, without stirring, until syrup reaches soft ball stage (approximately 234 to 240 degrees). Test about 1/2 teaspoon syrup in ice water. Syrup should easily form a ball in ice water but flatten when held in your hand. Remove from heat; stir in orange extract. Add pecans and stir until well coated. Spread pecan mixture on buttered aluminum foil. Allow to dry uncovered at room temperature 24 hours. Break apart and store in an airtight container.
Yield: about 41/4 cups pecans

CHOCOLATE-SOUR CREAM COFFEE CAKE

CAKE
1 cup butter or margarine, softened
2 cups granulated sugar
2 eggs
2 cups all-purpose flour
11/2 teaspoons baking powder
1/2 teaspoon salt
1 cup sour cream
1/2 teaspoon vanilla extract
TOPPING
1 cup chopped pecans
2 tablespoons granulated sugar
1 teaspoon ground cinnamon
CHOCOLATE GLAZE
1/2 cup semisweet chocolate chips
1/4 cup butter or margarine

Preheat oven to 350 degrees. For cake, cream butter and sugar in a large bowl until fluffy. Add eggs, beating until smooth. In a medium bowl, combine flour, baking powder, and salt. Gradually add dry ingredients to creamed mixture, blending well. Gently fold in sour cream and vanilla.

For topping, combine pecans, sugar, and cinnamon in a small bowl.

For chocolate glaze, melt chocolate chips and butter in a small saucepan over low heat, stirring until smooth. Sprinkle 2 tablespoons topping in bottom of greased and floured 9-inch tube pan. Spoon half of cake batter into pan. Sprinkle 4 tablespoons topping over batter and drizzle half of glaze over topping. Spoon remaining batter into pan and sprinkle with remaining topping. Reserve remaining glaze. Bake 1 to 11/4 hours or until a toothpick inserted in center of cake comes out clean. Cool in pan. Transfer to a serving plate. Reheat remaining glaze and drizzle over cake.
Yield: about 16 servings

Layered with a yummy streusel and chocolate filling, this Chocolate-Sour Cream Coffee Cake is indescribably delicious.

CARAMEL-APPLE LOAVES

1 package (18.25 ounces) spice
   cake mix, divided
1 cup quick-cooking oats
3/4 cup firmly packed brown sugar
1/2 cup chopped pecans
1/4 cup butter or margarine, softened
1 1/4 cups applesauce
3 eggs
1 cup chopped dried apples
3 tablespoons caramel ice cream
   topping

Preheat oven to 350 degrees. Grease
three 4 x 8-inch loaf pans and line with
waxed paper; grease waxed paper. In
a medium bowl, combine 2/3 cup dry
cake mix, oats, brown sugar, and pecans.
Using a pastry blender or 2 knives, cut in
butter until mixture is crumbly. In another
medium bowl, beat applesauce and eggs
until well blended. Add dried apples
and remaining cake mix to applesauce
mixture; stir just until blended. Spread
1 cup batter in each prepared pan.
Sprinkle 1/2 cup oat mixture over batter
in each pan. Repeat layers with
remaining batter and oat mixture.
Drizzle 1 tablespoon caramel topping
over oat mixture in each pan. Bake
35 to 40 minutes or until a toothpick
inserted in center of loaf comes out clean.
Cool in pans 20 minutes. Remove from
pans and cool completely on a wire rack.
Store in an airtight container.
Yield: 3 loaves bread

SPICY GINGERBREAD

1/2 cup vegetable shortening
1/2 cup granulated sugar
1 egg
2 1/2 cups all-purpose flour
1 teaspoon baking powder
1 teaspoon ground ginger
1 teaspoon ground allspice
1 teaspoon ground cloves
1 teaspoon ground cinnamon
1/2 teaspoon salt
1 cup molasses
1 cup boiling water
2 tablespoons grated orange rind
   Lemon custard ice cream to serve

In a large mixing bowl, cream
shortening and sugar until well
blended. Add egg and beat. Sift flour,
baking powder, ginger, allspice, cloves,
cinnamon, and salt; add to creamed
mixture, blending well. Add molasses,
water, and orange rind; stir just enough
to blend ingredients. Pour into a greased
and floured 10-inch ring mold or a
9 x 13-inch baking pan. Bake in a
preheated 375-degree oven 30 minutes.
Cool before unmolding. Serve with
lemon custard ice cream.
Yield: about 12 servings

QUICHE MUFFINS

1 container (16 ounces) cottage
    cheese
3 egg whites
5 eggs
$1/4$ cup buttermilk
$1/4$ cup all-purpose flour
1 teaspoon baking powder
$1/4$ teaspoon salt
2 cups (8 ounces) shredded sharp
    Cheddar cheese
10 slices bacon, cooked and
    crumbled
2 green onions, chopped

Preheat oven to 400 degrees. Place cottage cheese in a food processor fitted with a steel blade and process until smooth. Transfer to a large bowl. Process egg whites in food processor until foamy. Add next 5 ingredients and process until smooth. Add egg mixture to cottage cheese. Stir in Cheddar cheese, bacon, and onions. Fill greased large muffin tins $2/3$ full and bake 12 to 15 minutes or until edges are lightly browned.
Yield: about 10 muffins

CHEESY GARDEN CASSEROLE

1 cup diced potato (about 1 medium
    potato)
1 cup diced zucchini squash (about
    1 medium squash)
1 cup diced carrots (about 3 medium
    carrots)
$1/2$ cup diced onion (about 1 medium
    onion)
1 cup water
$1/4$ cup all-purpose flour

2 cups milk
$1/2$ cup butter or margarine, divided
1 teaspoon salt
$1/4$ teaspoon celery seed
$1/4$ teaspoon ground black pepper
4 hard-cooked eggs, thinly sliced
$1/2$ cup shredded sharp Cheddar
    cheese
$1/4$ cup plain bread crumbs

Preheat oven to 400 degrees. In a large skillet, cook potato, squash, carrots, and onion in water over medium-high heat until soft; drain. Reduce heat to medium and return vegetables to skillet. Sprinkle flour over vegetables; stir to blend. Add milk, $1/4$ cup butter, salt, celery seed, and pepper. Cook 10 to 15 minutes, stirring occasionally, until thickened. Pour half of vegetable mixture into a greased 9-inch glass pie plate. Top with sliced eggs and pour remaining vegetable mixture over eggs. Sprinkle cheese over vegetable mixture. Melt remaining $1/4$ cup butter in a small saucepan and stir in bread crumbs. Sprinkle bread crumbs evenly over cheese. Bake 15 to 20 minutes or until cheese is bubbly.
Yield: 8 to 10 servings

Note: Casserole may be assembled 1 day in advance. Cover unbaked casserole and refrigerate. If refrigerated, bake uncovered 25 to 30 minutes or until cheese is bubbly.

Sherried Fruit Cobbler is a mouth-watering mixture of apples, pineapple, peaches, pears, and apricots with brown sugar and sherry.

SHERRIED FRUIT COBBLER

COBBLER
- 1 can (16 ounces) peach halves, drained
- 1 can (16 ounces) pear halves, drained
- 1 can (16 ounces) apricot halves, drained
- 1 can (15¹/₂ ounces) sliced pineapple, drained
- 1 jar (6 ounces) maraschino cherries, drained
- 1 can (21 ounces) apple pie filling
- ¹/₂ cup butter
- ¹/₂ cup firmly packed brown sugar
- 2 tablespoons all-purpose flour
- 1 teaspoon ground cinnamon
- ¹/₂ teaspoon ground nutmeg
- ¹/₄ teaspoon ground allspice
- 1 cup cooking sherry

TOPPING
- ¹/₄ cup butter
- 1 cup graham cracker crumbs

For cobbler, arrange drained fruit and pie filling in a 3-quart casserole dish. Melt butter in a medium saucepan over low heat. Stir in the next 5 ingredients. Stirring constantly, slowly add sherry and cook over medium heat until thickened. Pour over fruit. Cover and chill 8 hours or overnight.

Allow cobbler to come to room temperature. Preheat oven to 350 degrees and bake 20 to 25 minutes or until bubbly.

For topping, melt butter in a small saucepan and stir in graham cracker crumbs. Spread crumbs evenly over cobbler and bake 5 minutes longer or until crumbs are dark brown.

Yield: about 10 servings

Simply Delicious
SUPPERS

What's for supper? Feed your family with hearty meals that are simple to fix and full of tasty goodness. These casual choices for everyday meals include main dishes, grilled foods, casseroles, salads, soups, breads, and more.

Mixed Grill With Cherry Sauce, page 150

MIXED GRILL WITH CHERRY SAUCE

Shown on page 149: Savory Mixed Grill includes morsels of marinated beef, chicken, and shrimp. Served with tangy Cherry Sauce, it satisfies the heartiest of appetites.

GRILLED MEAT

- 1 1/2 pounds filet mignon or rib eye steak
- 1 1/4 pounds boneless, skinless chicken breasts
- 1 pound fresh large shrimp
- 1 cup vegetable oil
- 1 cup sherry
- 1/2 cup soy sauce
- 3 tablespoons honey
- 3 cloves garlic, minced
- 1 teaspoon ground ginger
- 1/4 teaspoon ground black pepper
- Wooden skewers

CHERRY SAUCE

- 2/3 cup plum jam
- 1 teaspoon soy sauce
- 1/4 teaspoon dry mustard
- 1/4 teaspoon ground ginger
- 1 can (16 ounces) pitted dark sweet cherries, drained
- 2 tablespoons water
- 1 tablespoon cornstarch

For grilled meat, cut beef and chicken into 1/2-inch cubes. Peel and devein shrimp. Place chicken, beef, and shrimp in separate resealable plastic bags. Combine next 7 ingredients in a jar. Secure lid on jar and shake well to mix. Pour 1/3 of marinade into each bag and seal. Refrigerate overnight, turning occasionally. (To prevent skewers from burning during cooking, place skewers in a flat dish, cover with water, and soak overnight.)

For cherry sauce, place first 4 ingredients in a blender or food processor fitted with steel blade; process until smooth. Add cherries and process briefly to chop. Refrigerate at least 2 hours to allow flavors to blend.

Preheat oven to 375 degrees. Place chicken, beef, and shrimp on soaked skewers. Place on a rack in a roasting pan, loosely cover with aluminum foil, and bake 25 to 30 minutes.

To serve, heat cherry sauce in a small saucepan over medium heat. Combine water and cornstarch in a small bowl and slowly stir into sauce. Cook 3 to 4 minutes or until sauce thickens, stirring frequently. Serve warm with meat.
Yield: about 25 skewers

EASY RANCH-STYLE POTATOES

- 1 package (5 pounds) frozen potato nuggets
- 1/2 cup vegetable oil
- 3 packages (0.4 ounces each) ranch-style salad dressing mix

Preheat oven to 450 degrees. Place a single layer of potatoes in 2 ungreased jellyroll pans. In a small bowl, combine oil and dressing mix; stir until well blended. Drizzle over potatoes. Bake 30 to 35 minutes or until potatoes are golden brown and crisp, stirring every 10 minutes. Serve warm.
Yield: about 20 servings

Take your meal south of the border with quick-and-easy Chicken Fajitas. Marinate the chicken ahead of time in our special mixture of tequila and spices, then prepare these zesty morsels in minutes.

CHICKEN FAJITAS

1 cup tequila
1/2 cup plus 3 tablespoons vegetable oil, divided
1/2 cup lime juice
1/4 cup tomato paste
2 cloves garlic, minced
1 whole jalapeño pepper
1/2 teaspoon salt
1/2 teaspoon chili powder
1/2 teaspoon ground cumin
11/2 pounds boneless, skinless chicken breasts, cut into strips
10 flour tortillas for fajitas
1 large green pepper, cut into strips
1 large onion, cut into strips
Guacamole, sour cream, salsa, and shredded Cheddar cheese to serve

In a glass bowl or baking dish, combine tequila, 1/2 cup oil, lime juice, tomato paste, garlic, jalapeño pepper, salt, chili powder, and cumin. Blend well. Add chicken, cover, and marinate in refrigerator at least 6 hours or overnight.

Preheat oven to 350 degrees. Wrap tortillas in aluminum foil. Bake 15 minutes while preparing fajitas.

Remove chicken from marinade. In a large heavy skillet over medium-high heat, heat remaining 3 tablespoons oil. Add chicken and cook, stirring constantly, 5 to 7 minutes or until chicken is done. Add green pepper and onion and cook 2 to 3 minutes more, just until vegetables are crisp-tender. Serve with tortillas, guacamole, sour cream, salsa, and cheese.

Yield: 10 fajitas

151

BUFFET BURGERS

2 pounds lean ground beef
1 cup soft bread crumbs
1/2 cup chopped onion
1 egg, lightly beaten
1 tablespoon mayonnaise
1 teaspoon garlic salt
1 teaspoon Italian seasoning
1/4 teaspoon ground black pepper
1 1/2 cups shredded mozzarella cheese
20 small square rolls, heated and split
  Mustard and mayonnaise to serve

Preheat oven to 350 degrees. Combine ground beef, bread crumbs, onion, egg, mayonnaise, garlic salt, Italian seasoning, and pepper; mix well. Press meat mixture into bottom of a 15 1/2 x 10 1/2-inch jellyroll pan to within 1 inch of edges of pan. Bake 20 to 25 minutes; drain. Top meat mixture with cheese and bake 5 to 8 minutes longer or until cheese is melted. Remove from oven and allow to sit (about 5 minutes). Cut meat into 20 squares and place inside split rolls. Serve with mustard and mayonnaise.
Yield: 20 burgers

LONDON BROIL

1/2 cup vegetable oil
1/4 cup lemon juice
2 tablespoons minced onion
1 1/2 teaspoons salt
1 teaspoon granulated sugar
1/2 teaspoon dry mustard
1/2 teaspoon Italian seasoning
1/2 teaspoon ground black pepper
1/4 teaspoon ground ginger
1 clove garlic, minced
1 flank steak (about 2 pounds)
  Purchased hors d'oeuvre-size
    buns, mustard, and mayonnaise
    to serve

Combine all ingredients except steak, blending well. Place steak in a glass or enamel baking dish. Cover with marinade mixture and refrigerate at least 6 hours or overnight, turning steak occasionally.
Preheat broiler. Remove steak from marinade and broil about 5 inches from heat for 5 to 6 minutes on each side. Meat should be rare. Cut steak diagonally across the grain in thin slices. Serve with buns, mustard, and mayonnaise.
Yield: about 36 servings

ZUCCHINI-GREEN PEPPER SLAW

1 1/2 cups mayonnaise
2/3 cup sugar
1/4 cup apple cider vinegar
1 tablespoon salt
1 tablespoon celery seed
1 1/2 teaspoons dry mustard
1 teaspoon ground black pepper
1 small green cabbage,
    quartered and cored
3/4 pound carrots (about 7 small carrots)
4 medium zucchini
4 green onions, sliced
1 green pepper, cut into
    1-inch-long slivers

In a small bowl, combine mayonnaise, sugar, vinegar, salt, celery seed, dry mustard, and black pepper until well blended. Cover and chill until ready to use.
In a food processor fitted with a shredding disc, shred cabbage and carrots. Transfer to a very large bowl. Cut zucchini in half lengthwise and scrape out seeds; shred zucchini. Add zucchini, green onions, green pepper, and mayonnaise mixture to cabbage mixture; stir until well blended. Cover and chill until ready to serve.
Yield: about 8 cups slaw

SQUASH AND WILD RICE SOUP

1/4 cup butter or margarine
1 cup finely chopped onion
1/2 cup finely chopped celery
3 cloves garlic, minced
5 cans (14.5 ounces each) chicken broth
1/2 cup uncooked wild rice
4 cups sliced zucchini
4 cups sliced yellow squash
1/2 cup shredded carrot
1/2 cup uncooked white rice
3/4 teaspoon salt
1/2 teaspoon ground black pepper
3/4 teaspoon dried basil leaves
1/2 teaspoon dried oregano leaves

In a large Dutch oven, melt butter over medium heat. Add onion, celery, and garlic. Stirring frequently, cook about 3 minutes or until vegetables are tender. Add chicken broth and wild rice. Bring mixture to a boil. Reduce heat to medium-low. Cover and cook 30 minutes.

Stir in zucchini, yellow squash, carrot, white rice, salt, and pepper. Increase heat to high and bring mixture to a boil. Reduce heat to low. Cover and simmer 20 minutes or until rice is tender.

Stir in basil and oregano. Serve hot. Store in an airtight container in refrigerator.

Yield: about 12 1/2 cups soup

CHEESY VEGETABLE PIE

This pie is made with previously cooked vegetables, or you may substitute canned or frozen.

1 cup green beans, drained
1 cup green peas, drained
1 cup sliced carrots, drained
1 cup broccoli flowerets
1/2 cup whole kernel corn, drained
1 cup chopped uncooked onion
1/4 cup chopped uncooked green pepper
1 clove garlic, minced
3/4 teaspoon salt
1/4 teaspoon ground black pepper
1 cup sour cream
1 cup (4 ounces) shredded mozzarella cheese
1 tablespoon chopped fresh parsley
1 package (15 ounces) refrigerated pie crusts, at room temperature

Preheat oven to 350 degrees. In a large bowl, combine green beans, green peas, carrots, broccoli, corn, onion, green pepper, garlic, salt, and black pepper; toss until well blended. Stir in sour cream, cheese, and parsley. Press 1 crust into bottom of a 9-inch deep-dish pie plate. Spoon vegetable mixture into crust. Place top crust over vegetables. Crimp edges of crust with a fork. Bake 60 to 65 minutes or until cheese is bubbly and crust is golden brown. If edges of crust brown too quickly, cover with strips of aluminum foil. Allow pie to stand 10 minutes before serving.

Yield: 8 to 10 servings

MEXICAN BEAN SOUP MIX

Keep this mix on hand to simplify preparation. It will yield enough for three different meals.

BEAN SOUP MIX
- 1 pound black beans
- 1 pound red beans
- 1 pound Great Northern beans

SEASONING MIX
- 3 tablespoons dried parsley flakes, divided
- 4$\frac{1}{2}$ teaspoons chili powder, divided
- 3 teaspoons salt, divided
- 1$\frac{1}{2}$ teaspoons crushed dried red pepper flakes, divided
- $\frac{3}{4}$ teaspoon garlic powder, divided
- $\frac{3}{4}$ teaspoon ground black pepper, divided

For bean soup mix, combine all ingredients in a large bowl. Place about 2 heaping cups beans in each of 3 resealable plastic bags.

For seasoning mix, combine 1 tablespoon parsley, 1$\frac{1}{2}$ teaspoons chili powder, 1 teaspoon salt, $\frac{1}{2}$ teaspoon red pepper flakes, $\frac{1}{4}$ teaspoon garlic powder, and $\frac{1}{4}$ teaspoon black pepper in each of 3 small resealable plastic bags.

To prepare, follow Mexican Bean Soup recipe (given on this page).
Yield: about 6 cups bean soup mix and about 6$\frac{1}{2}$ tablespoons seasoning mix

MEXICAN BEAN SOUP

- 1 bag (about 2 cups) Mexican Bean Soup Mix (recipe on this page)
- 1 pound bulk pork sausage
- 2 onions, quartered
- 2 cloves garlic, minced
- 1 can (16 ounces) whole peeled tomatoes
- 1 can (4$\frac{1}{2}$ ounces) chopped green chiles
- 1 bag (about 2 tablespoons) Seasoning Mix (recipe on this page)
  Salt and ground black pepper to taste

Rinse bean soup mix. Place beans in a Dutch oven and cover with water; soak overnight.

In a large skillet, brown sausage, onions, and garlic. Drain beans and return to Dutch oven. Add sausage mixture, tomatoes, green chiles, and seasoning mix to beans. Add enough water to cover. Stirring occasionally, simmer 3 to 4 hours or until beans are tender. Add more water as needed. Salt and pepper to taste.
Yield: 8 to 10 servings

This spicy, Southwestern dinner will be easy to plan when you make the Mexican Bean Soup Mix and Mexican Corn Bread Mix ahead of time. For a sweet finish, serve melt-in-your-mouth Pralines (not shown, recipe on page 156).

MEXICAN CORN BREAD MIX

- 2 cups yellow cornmeal
- 1/2 cup all-purpose flour
- 1 tablespoon sugar
- 2 teaspoons baking powder
- 1 teaspoon salt
- 1 teaspoon ground red pepper
- 1/2 teaspoon baking soda

In a large bowl, combine cornmeal, flour, sugar, baking powder, salt, red pepper, and baking soda. Place in a resealable plastic bag. To prepare, follow Mexican Corn Bread recipe (given on this page).
Yield: about 2 1/2 cups mix

MEXICAN CORN BREAD

- 2 tablespoons butter or margarine
- 1 bag (about 2 1/2 cups) Mexican Corn Bread Mix
- 1 can (12 ounces) beer
- 2 eggs, lightly beaten

Preheat oven to 425 degrees. Place butter in an 8-inch round baking pan or skillet. Place pan in oven to melt butter and to heat pan. In a medium bowl, combine corn bread mix, beer, and eggs. Stir just until blended. Pour into hot pan. Bake 25 to 30 minutes or until lightly browned. Serve warm.
Yield: 6 to 8 servings

PEPPERED CHEESE BUNS

1 package dry yeast
1 cup warm water
3 cups all-purpose flour
1/2 cup grated Romano cheese
2 tablespoons sugar
1 teaspoon garlic powder
1 teaspoon onion powder
1 teaspoon ground black pepper
1/2 teaspoon salt
1 tablespoon olive oil
  Vegetable cooking spray
  Grated Parmesan cheese

In a small bowl, combine yeast and warm water; stir until yeast dissolves. In a medium bowl, combine flour, Romano cheese, sugar, garlic powder, onion powder, pepper, and salt. Add yeast mixture and oil to dry ingredients. Stir until a soft dough forms. Turn onto a lightly floured surface and knead about 5 minutes or until dough becomes smooth and elastic. Place in a medium bowl sprayed with cooking spray, turning once to coat top of dough. Cover and let rise in a warm place (80 to 85 degrees) 1 hour or until doubled in size.

Turn dough onto a lightly floured surface and punch down. For each bun, shape about 3 tablespoons dough into a 4-inch-long roll. Tie each roll into a knot and place on a greased baking sheet. Spray tops of buns with cooking spray, cover, and let rise in a warm place 30 minutes or until doubled in size.

Preheat oven to 375 degrees. Bake 12 to 15 minutes or until golden brown. Transfer to a wire rack. Lightly spray buns with cooking spray; sprinkle with Parmesan cheese. Allow to cool completely. Store in an airtight container.
Yield: about 3 1/2 dozen buns

MACADAMIA NUT PRALINES

2 1/3 cups firmly packed brown sugar
1 can (5 ounces) evaporated milk
2 tablespoons butter or margarine, cut into pieces
1 cup chopped macadamia nuts
1/2 teaspoon maple extract

In a medium microwave-safe bowl, combine sugar and milk; stir until well blended. Drop butter into sugar mixture. Microwave on High 1 to 2 minutes or until butter melts. Stir until smooth. Stir in nuts. Microwave on High 6 minutes, stir, and microwave 3 minutes longer or until candy reaches soft ball stage. (A small amount of syrup should easily form a ball in ice water but flatten when held in your hand. If necessary, continue to microwave, retesting at 30 second intervals.) Stir in maple extract. Drop by heaping tablespoons onto waxed paper. Cool completely. Store in an airtight container.
Yield: about 2 dozen pralines

For this delightful Chicken-Black Bean Casserole, marinate the meat ahead of time. Serve with spicy Peppered Cheese Buns (recipe on page 156).

CHICKEN-BLACK BEAN CASSEROLE

$^2/_3$ cup freshly squeezed lime juice
$^1/_3$ cup olive oil
$^1/_2$ teaspoon ground black pepper
2 teaspoons garlic powder, divided
2 teaspoons salt, divided
1$^1/_2$ pounds boneless, skinless chicken breasts, cut into bite-size pieces
4 cups cooked white rice
2 cans (15 ounces each) black beans
1 cup finely chopped fresh cilantro
1 teaspoon onion powder
1 teaspoon chili powder
1 teaspoon ground cumin

In a medium bowl, whisk lime juice, oil, pepper, 1 teaspoon garlic powder, and 1 teaspoon salt. Add chicken; stir until evenly coated. Cover and refrigerate 2 hours.

In a 2-quart casserole, combine rice, undrained beans, cilantro, onion powder, chili powder, cumin, remaining 1 teaspoon garlic powder, and remaining 1 teaspoon salt; set aside.

Preheat oven to 350 degrees. Using a slotted spoon, place chicken in a large skillet. Cook over medium heat until juices run clear when chicken is pierced with a fork. Stir chicken into rice mixture. Cover and bake 40 to 45 minutes or until heated through.

Yield: about nine 1-cup servings

ROAST TURKEY WITH CRANBERRY-SAUSAGE STUFFING

Cranberries added to the stuffing give this traditional entree a new twist.

1   12- to 14-pound turkey
8   ounces bulk pork sausage
1   cup chopped onion
6   cups crumbled corn bread
4   slices white bread, torn into
      pieces
2¹/₂ cups turkey or chicken broth
1¹/₄ cups coarsely chopped fresh
      cranberries
¹/₂ cup butter, melted
¹/₂ cup chopped celery
2   eggs, lightly beaten
1¹/₂ teaspoons salt
1¹/₂ teaspoons rubbed sage
¹/₂ teaspoon dried rosemary leaves
¹/₂ teaspoon dried thyme leaves
¹/₄ teaspoon ground black pepper

Preheat oven to 325 degrees. Remove giblets and neck from turkey; reserve for another use. Rinse turkey and pat dry with paper towels.

In medium skillet, cook sausage and onion over medium heat until sausage browns; drain. Transfer to a large bowl. Stir in corn bread, white bread, broth, cranberries, melted butter, celery, eggs, salt, sage, rosemary, thyme, and pepper; stir until well blended.

Stuff dressing loosely into neck and body cavities of turkey. (**Note:** Extra dressing may be baked separately in covered baking dish, 30 to 40 minutes or until heated through.) Close cavities with skewers. Tie ends of legs to tail with kitchen twine; lift wing tips up and over back so they are tucked under bird. Place turkey on a rack in a roasting pan with breast side up. Insert a meat thermometer in thickest part of thigh without touching bone. Basting frequently, bake 5¹/₂ to 6¹/₂ hours or until meat thermometer registers 185 degrees and juices run clear when thickest part of thigh is pierced with a fork. Remove skewers and place turkey on a serving platter. Allow to stand 20 minutes before carving.

Yield: 12 to 14 servings

GOLDEN LEMON BISCUITS

2   cups all-purpose flour
2   tablespoons sugar
2   teaspoons baking powder
¹/₂ teaspoon salt
¹/₂ cup chilled butter or margarine
2   eggs, beaten
3   tablespoons milk
2   tablespoons freshly squeezed
      lemon juice
2   teaspoons grated lemon zest

Preheat oven to 400 degrees. In a medium bowl, combine flour, sugar, baking powder, and salt. Using a pastry blender or 2 knives, cut in butter until mixture resembles coarse meal. Stir in eggs, milk, lemon juice, and lemon zest just until blended. On a lightly floured surface, knead dough about 1 minute or until smooth. Roll out dough to ¹/₂-inch thickness; use a 2-inch biscuit cutter to cut out biscuits. Place biscuits 2 inches apart on an ungreased baking sheet. Bake 12 to 15 minutes or until tops are golden brown.

Yield: about 1¹/₂ dozen biscuits

PINEAPPLE RICE

- 3 tablespoons butter or margarine
- 3 tablespoons sesame oil
- 1 cup chopped onion
- 4 cans (14^1/$_2$ ounces each) chicken broth
- 3 cups uncooked brown rice
- 1 teaspoon salt
- ^{1}/$_2$ teaspoon ground black pepper
- 1 can (15^1/$_4$ ounces) pineapple tidbits, drained
- ^{1}/$_4$ cup finely chopped green pepper
- ^{1}/$_4$ cup finely chopped sweet red pepper

In a Dutch oven over medium heat, combine butter and oil. Add onion and cook until onion is tender. Add broth, rice, salt, and pepper. Bring to a boil, reduce heat, cover, and simmer 50 to 60 minutes or until all liquid is absorbed. Stir in remaining ingredients; cook 2 minutes longer.
Yield: about 10 servings

GREEN AUTUMN SALAD WITH ORANGE VINAIGRETTE

ORANGE VINAIGRETTE
- ^{1}/$_4$ cup sugar
- 1 teaspoon dry mustard
- 1 teaspoon paprika
- ^{1}/$_2$ teaspoon salt
- ^{1}/$_4$ cup freshly squeezed orange juice
- 3 tablespoons white vinegar
- 1 teaspoon minced onion
- 1 teaspoon grated orange zest
- ^{3}/$_4$ cup vegetable oil

SALAD
- 12 to 14 cups mixed salad greens (we used arugula, radicchio, and red leaf lettuce)
- 2 medium avocados, peeled, pitted, and sliced
- 1^1/$_2$ cups red seedless grapes
- 1 jar (6 ounces) marinated artichoke hearts, drained and chopped
- 1 small red onion, sliced and separated into rings
- 1 rib celery, chopped
- 4 teaspoons sesame seed, toasted

For orange vinaigrette, combine sugar, dry mustard, paprika, and salt in a blender or food processor. Add orange juice, vinegar, onion, and orange zest to dry ingredients; blend until well mixed. With blender running, slowly pour oil into orange juice mixture. Transfer vinaigrette to an airtight container. Chill until ready to serve.

For salad, combine salad greens, avocado slices, grapes, artichoke pieces, onion rings, and celery in a large bowl. To serve, pour orange vinaigrette over salad and gently toss. Sprinkle with toasted sesame seed. Serve immediately.
Yield: about 12 servings

FESTIVE CORN SALAD

DRESSING
- 1 cup vegetable oil
- 1/3 cup white vinegar
- 1/4 cup finely chopped fresh cilantro
- 2 tablespoons finely minced red onion
- 1 teaspoon salt
- 3/4 teaspoon ground black pepper

SALAD
- 2 packages (16 ounces each) frozen whole kernel yellow corn)
- 1/4 cup water
- 3/4 cup shredded carrots (about 3 small carrots)
- 1/2 cup chopped red onion
- 1/4 cup coarsely chopped fresh cilantro
- 1 to 2 red jalapeño peppers, seeded and finely chopped
  Lettuce leaves to serve
  Avocado slices and fresh cilantro to garnish

For dressing, whisk all ingredients in a small bowl until well blended; cover and set aside.

For salad, combine corn and water in a medium microwave-safe container. Cover and microwave on high power (100%) 10 to 12 minutes or until corn is tender, stirring every 3 minutes. Rinse with cool water and drain. Stir in carrots, onion, chopped cilantro, and jalapeño pepper. Pour dressing over corn mixture; toss to coat. Spoon over lettuce on individual serving plates. Garnish with avocado slices and cilantro.

Yield: about 10 servings

LAYERED MEXICAN CASSEROLE

- 1 pound ground beef
- 1 jar (8 ounces) chunky salsa
- 1 package (1.5 ounces) taco seasoning
- 1 container (12 ounces) cottage cheese
- 1 package (8 ounces) shredded Cheddar cheese, divided
- 2 eggs, beaten
- 10 flour tortillas (about 7-inch diameter), divided
- 1 can (4.5 ounces) chopped green chiles, drained
- 1 can (4 1/4 ounces) chopped ripe olives, drained

Stirring occasionally, brown ground beef in a medium skillet over medium-high heat. Remove from heat; drain. Stir in salsa and taco seasoning.

In a medium bowl, combine cottage cheese, 1 cup Cheddar cheese, and eggs. Grease two 8-inch square baking pans. Place 4 tortillas over bottom and up sides of each pan. Spoon one-fourth of meat mixture and one-fourth of cottage cheese mixture over tortillas in each pan. Place 1 tortilla in center of each pan. Spoon remaining one-fourth of meat mixture and remaining one-fourth of cottage cheese mixture over tortilla in each pan. Sprinkle with green chiles, olives, and remaining 1 cup Cheddar cheese. Cover and store in refrigerator.

To serve, bake covered casserole in a 350-degree oven 45 to 50 minutes or until heated through. Uncover and bake 5 minutes longer or until cheese is bubbly. Serve warm.

Yield: two 8-inch casseroles, about 6 servings each

Plan ahead for a busy night with this spicy Layered Mexican Casserole. The recipe makes enough for two pans—great for a second night or for sharing!

RED PEPPER CREAM SAUCE

¼ cup butter or margarine
1 large sweet red pepper, chopped
¼ cup thinly sliced green onions
3 tablespoons all-purpose flour
½ teaspoon salt
¼ teaspoon ground white pepper
1½ cups half and half
1 tablespoon freshly squeezed
    lemon juice
    Sweet red pepper strips to
    garnish

In a medium saucepan, melt butter over medium heat. Add red pepper and onions; cook until almost tender. Reserve 2 tablespoons pepper mixture. Place remaining pepper mixture in a food processor and purée. Return mixture to saucepan and reduce heat to medium-low. Stirring constantly, add flour, salt, and white pepper to mixture. Cook 2 minutes or until flour is well blended and sauce thickens. While whisking mixture, gradually add half and half and lemon juice. Stir in reserved pepper mixture. Increase heat to medium; continue cooking 5 minutes or until mixture thickens. Garnish with sweet red pepper strips. Serve warm over Pork Tamales (recipe on page 163).
Yield: about 2½ cups sauce

GREEN CHILE CREAM SAUCE

¼ cup butter or margarine
¼ cup thinly sliced green onions
3 cans (4½ ounces each)
    chopped green chiles
2 tablespoons seeded and finely
    chopped fresh jalapeño
    peppers
2 tablespoons all-purpose flour
¼ teaspoon salt
¼ teaspoon ground white pepper
1½ cups half and half
2 teaspoons freshly squeezed lime
    juice

In a medium saucepan, melt butter over medium heat. Add onions; cook until almost tender. Add undrained green chiles and jalapeño peppers; stirring frequently, cook 2 minutes. Reduce heat to medium-low; stirring constantly, add flour, salt, and white pepper to mixture. Cook 1 minute or until flour is well blended and sauce thickens. While whisking mixture, gradually add half and half and lime juice; continue cooking 5 minutes or until mixture thickens. Serve warm over Pork Tamales (recipe on page 163).
Yield: about 3¼ cups sauce

PORK TAMALES

Steamed in corn shucks to seal in the flavor, savory Pork Tamales offer a shredded-meat filling in a traditional masa harina dough. Prepare meat mixture a day ahead for easy assembly of tamales. To accompany the entrée, there are two wonderful toppings, Red Pepper and Green Chile Cream Sauces (recipes on page 162).

7	pound pork shoulder roast, boned, saving bone
2	heads garlic, separated into cloves
9	cups water
1/3	cup plus 1/4 cup chili powder, divided
4	teaspoons cumin seed
3	teaspoons salt, divided
1	package (8 ounces) dried corn shucks
1	package (4.4 pounds) masa harina (about 16 cups)
2	pounds (4 cups) shortening or lard
1	can (14.5 ounces) beef broth

Cut pork into 3-inch pieces. Place meat, bone, and garlic in a stockpot. Add 9 cups water, and more if necessary, to cover meat; bring to a boil over medium-high heat. Reduce heat to medium-low; cover and simmer about 2 hours or until meat is tender. Place meat and liquid in separate containers; discard bone. Shred meat by hand or in a food processor. Place meat in a heavy Dutch oven and stir in 1/3 cup chili powder, cumin seed, and 1 teaspoon salt. Add about 3 cups of reserved liquid to Dutch oven. Stirring frequently, cover and simmer over low heat 1 hour to allow flavors to blend. If necessary, add additional liquid to prevent meat from sticking to pan. Cover and chill meat and reserved liquid overnight in separate containers.

Place corn shucks in warm water about 30 minutes to soften. Clean and separate corn shucks.

For tamale dough, combine masa harina, remaining 1/4 cup chili powder, and remaining 2 teaspoons salt in a large bowl. Cut shortening into masa mixture until it resembles coarse meal. Skim fat from chilled liquid. If necessary, add beef broth to reserved liquid to make 8 cups. Gradually add liquid to mixture, stirring until a soft dough forms that will stick together.

To assemble each tamale, place a softened corn shuck on a flat surface with a long side facing you. Spread about 1/4 cup dough from wide end about 4 1/2 inches along one side.

(Continued on page 164)

(Continued from page 163)

Continue to spread dough, forming a rectangle that covers about two-thirds of the wide end of corn shuck (Fig. 1).

Fig. 1

Spread a heaping tablespoon of meat down center of dough (Fig. 2).

Fig. 2

Roll edge closest to you over meat, rolling back corn shuck enough to expose a small amount of dough (Fig. 3).

Fig. 3

Bring far side toward you until dough edges overlap; wrap corn shuck around tamale. Fold narrow end of corn shuck over tamale. Stand individual tamales in a container or tie in bundles with kitchen string and stand with open ends up (Fig. 4).

Fig. 4

(Note: Tamales may be chilled or frozen at this point and steamed at a later time.)

To steam tamales, stand tamales with open ends up in a steamer basket placed over hot water in a stockpot. Cover and steam 1 to $1^1/2$ hours. Serve warm with Red Pepper Cream Sauce and Green Chile Cream Sauce (recipes on page 162).
Yield: about $5^1/2$ dozen tamales

Jícama and Orange Salad with Lime Dressing is a crisp and colorful combination that includes sweet tart, pomegranate seeds and nutty slivers of Mexican jícama. It's great with Pork Tamales topped with Red Pepper and Green Chile Cream Sauces. (Recipes for the tamale and sauces are on pages 162-164. Tangy Raspberry Lemonade (not shown, recipe on page 166) will have guests asking for more

JÍCAMA AND ORANGE SALAD WITH LIME DRESSING

LIME DRESSING

- 1/2 cup sugar
- 1 tablespoon dry mustard
- 3/4 cup peanut oil
- 6 tablespoons freshly squeezed lime juice
- 1/4 cup honey
- 3 tablespoons water
- 1/4 cup white wine vinegar
- 2 tablespoons chopped fresh cilantro

SALAD

- Leaf lettuce
- 4 to 5 cups peeled, matchsticked jícama
- 5 navel oranges, peeled and sectioned
- Seeds of 2 pomegranates
- Finely chopped, unsalted, dry-roasted peanuts

For lime dressing, combine sugar and dry mustard in a medium bowl. Add oil, lime juice, honey, water, and vinegar; stir until well blended. Stir in cilantro.

For salad, layer ingredients in order given. Serve with lime dressing.

Yield: about 14 servings

RASPBERRY LEMONADE

3 cups sugar
1 cup water
1 package (12 ounces) frozen
   whole red raspberries, thawed
   or 1 cup raspberry juice
1 1/2 cups freshly squeezed lemon
   juice (about 10 to 12 small
   lemons)
1 tablespoon grated lemon zest
5 to 6 cups club soda, chilled
   Lemon slices to garnish

In a medium saucepan, combine sugar and water over medium heat; stir until sugar dissolves. Increase heat to medium-high and bring to a boil. Stirring constantly, boil 1 minute. Pour sugar syrup into a heat-resistant medium bowl and allow to cool.

Press raspberries through a sieve over another medium bowl. Discard seeds and pulp. Add lemon juice, raspberry juice, and lemon zest to sugar syrup; cover and chill.

To serve, combine juice mixture and club soda to taste. Garnish with lemon slices.

Yield: about thirteen 6-ounce servings

FLOUR TORTILLAS

2 cups all-purpose flour
3/4 teaspoon baking powder
1/2 teaspoon salt
1/4 cup vegetable shortening or
   lard
8 tablespoons water

In a medium bowl, combine flour, baking powder, and salt. Using a pastry blender or 2 knives, cut in shortening until mixture resembles coarse meal. Add water, stirring until well blended.

Turn dough onto a lightly floured surface. Gradually sprinkle dough with additional water as necessary to shape into a ball. Knead dough 3 to 5 minutes or until smooth and elastic. Divide dough into 12 balls. Cover with plastic wrap and let rest at room temperature 30 minutes.

Heat an ungreased griddle or large skillet over medium-high heat. Working with 1 ball of dough at a time on a very lightly floured surface, roll into a 7-inch circle. To form a circle, rotate dough and turn over every few strokes of the rolling pin. On hot griddle, cook tortilla about 1 minute on each side or until lightly browned. Transfer tortilla onto a platter and cover with a lid or wrap in a kitchen towel and aluminum foil to retain moisture. Repeat with remaining dough. Wrapped tortillas may be placed in a 200-degree oven for a short period of time to remain warm. To reheat, place foil-wrapped tortillas in a 325-degree oven 15 to 20 minutes.

Yield: twelve 7-inch tortillas

FOUR-CHEESE QUICHES

(Shown on page 5)

1   container (15 ounces) ricotta
      cheese
11 ounces cream cheese, softened
9   eggs
3   tablespoons chopped fresh
      parsley
1   tablespoon stone-ground
      mustard
1/3 cup freshly grated Parmesan
      cheese
2   tablespoons all-purpose flour
1   teaspoon baking powder
1/2 teaspoon salt
3   cups (12 ounces) shredded
      Jarlsberg cheese

Preheat oven to 350 degrees. In a large bowl, beat ricotta cheese and cream cheese until blended. Beat in eggs, parsley, and mustard. In a small bowl, combine Parmesan cheese, flour, baking powder, and salt. Stir dry ingredients into egg mixture; beat until well blended. Stir in Jarlsberg cheese. Pour into 2 greased 9-inch deep-dish pie plates. Bake 33 to 38 minutes or until a knife inserted near center of quiche comes out clean. Allow to stand 10 minutes before serving.
Yield: 2 quiches, about 8 servings each

CORN SALAD WITH ROASTED GARLIC DRESSING

(Shown on page 5)

1   head garlic (about 10 to
      14 cloves)
      Olive oil
2/3 cup mayonnaise
1/2 cup chopped fresh parsley
1   tablespoon Greek seasoning
4   cans (15 1/4 ounces each) whole
      kernel yellow corn, drained
2   cups chopped sweet red pepper
1 1/2 cups chopped green onions

Preheat oven to 400 degrees. To roast garlic, slightly trim tops of garlic cloves. Place garlic head on aluminum foil. Drizzle a small amount of oil on cut edges; wrap in foil. Bake 1 hour. Cool completely.

Press garlic pulp out of each clove and mash in a small bowl. Add mayonnaise, parsley, and Greek seasoning; stir until well blended. In a large bowl, combine corn, red pepper, and green onions; toss with garlic dressing. Cover and chill 2 hours before serving.
Yield: about 9 cups salad

Shown on page 5: Corn Salad with Roasted Garlic Dressing delights the senses with a confetti of veggies tossed in a zippy dressing. Four-Cheese Quiche is incredibly light and flavorful.

HAM HASH

Vegetable cooking spray
1 cup chopped onion
4 cups diced unpeeled red
potatoes
2 cups thinly sliced and chopped
low-fat ham
1 can (4^1/2 ounces) chopped
green chiles
^{1}/4 cup low-fat sour cream
^{3}/4 teaspoon garlic salt
^{1}/2 teaspoon ground cumin

Spray a large nonstick skillet with cooking spray. Sauté onion in skillet over medium-high heat until onion is tender and begins to brown. Reduce heat to medium. Stir in potatoes. Stirring occasionally, cook about 25 minutes or until potatoes are golden brown and almost tender. Stir in ham, undrained chiles, sour cream, garlic salt, and cumin. Stirring occasionally, cook about 5 minutes or until mixture is heated through. Serve warm.
Yield: about 11 servings

CAESAR BREAD SALAD

1 package (8 ounces) herb-
seasoned stuffing
5 cups chopped fresh tomatoes
1^1/2 cups shredded unpeeled
cucumber
1 cup chopped fresh parsley
1 cup fat-free Caesar salad
dressing
1 tablespoon balsamic vinegar
1 tablespoon olive oil

Combine stuffing, tomatoes, cucumber and parsley; stir gently. In a small bowl, combine salad dressing, vinegar, and oil. Stir dressing mixture into salad. Cover and chill 2 hours; serve within 4 hours.
Yield: about 18 servings

CRANBERRY-PEAR AMBROSIA

1^1/4 cups 2% milk, divided
2 tablespoons cornstarch
^{1}/4 cup sugar
^{1}/2 cup frozen unsweetened
shredded coconut, thawed
3 cups unpeeled, cored, and
coarsely chopped red pears
^{2}/3 cup sweetened dried cranberries
1 tablespoon frozen unsweetened
flaked coconut, thawed and
toasted to garnish

In a small bowl, combine ^{1}/4 cup milk and cornstarch; stir until smooth. In a medium saucepan, combine sugar and remaining 1 cup milk; bring to a simmer over medium heat. Whisking constantly, add cornstarch mixture; cook until sauce thickens. Remove from heat; cool.

Stir in ^{1}/2 cup coconut. Gently combine coconut sauce, pears, and cranberries. Cover and refrigerate until well chilled. Garnish with toasted coconut.
Yield: about 8 servings

Cranberry-Pear Ambrosia (clockwise from bottom) is served in a dreamy coconut sauce. Spicy Ham Hash is complemented by zesty Brussels Sprouts in Light Orange Sauce. Replace traditional stuffing with zesty Caesar Bread Salad (not shown), a colorful concoction of fresh tomatoes, cucumber, and herbed stuffing.

BRUSSELS SPROUTS WITH LIGHT ORANGE SAUCE

3   pounds fresh Brussels sprouts
3/4 cup freshly squeezed orange
    juice
6   tablespoons fat-free Italian salad
    dressing
1 1/2 teaspoons grated orange zest
    Grated orange zest to garnish

Trim Brussels sprouts and cut an "X" in stem end of each sprout. Place in a steamer basket over simmering water. Cover and steam about 15 minutes or until sprouts are tender. In a small bowl, combine orange juice, salad dressing, and 1 1/2 teaspoons orange zest. Toss sprouts with orange sauce. Transfer to a serving dish. Garnish with orange zest. Serve warm.
Yield: about 16 servings

OVEN-FRIED CHICKEN

Delicious cold, Oven-Fried Chicken features a zesty herbed breading. It's yummy with Barley-Vegetable Salad.

- 2 pounds boneless skinless chicken breast fillets
  Salt and ground black pepper
- 1¹/₂ cups plain nonfat yogurt
- ¹/₂ cup grated Parmesan cheese
- 1 teaspoon paprika
- 1 teaspoon dried thyme leaves
- ¹/₂ teaspoon garlic powder
- 1¹/₂ cups plain bread crumbs
- 3 tablespoons butter or margarine, melted

Preheat oven to 400 degrees. Sprinkle chicken with salt and pepper. In a small bowl, whisk yogurt, cheese, paprika, thyme, and garlic powder. In another small bowl, combine bread crumbs and butter. Dip chicken, one piece at a time, into yogurt mixture, then place in bread crumb mixture. Spoon bread crumb mixture over chicken, coating well. Place coated pieces of chicken in a greased baking pan. Bake 25 to 30 minutes or until juices run clear when thickest part of chicken is pierced with a fork. Cover and refrigerate until ready to serve. Serve cold.

Yield: about 6 servings

BARLEY-VEGETABLE SALAD

- 4 cups water
- 1 cup uncooked barley
- ³/₄ cup finely diced radishes
- ³/₄ cup finely diced carrots
- ¹/₂ cup peeled and finely diced cucumber
- ¹/₄ cup finely chopped fresh parsley
- 2 tablespoons finely chopped red onion
- 2 tablespoons finely chopped fresh chives
- ¹/₂ cup oil-free Italian salad dressing
- 2 tablespoons lemon juice
- 2 teaspoons dried oregano leaves, crushed
- ¹/₂ teaspoon garlic powder
- ¹/₄ teaspoon salt
- ¹/₄ teaspoon ground black pepper
- 7 ounces feta cheese, crumbled

In a 3-quart saucepan, bring water to a boil; stir in barley. Reduce heat to low; cover and simmer 50 to 55 minutes or until tender. Remove from heat; cool to room temperature.

In a large bowl, combine cooked barley, radishes, carrots, cucumber, parsley, onion, and chives. In a small bowl, whisk salad dressing, lemon juice, oregano, garlic powder, salt, and pepper. Pour over barley mixture; stir until well blended. Stir in cheese. Cover and refrigerate until ready to serve.

Yield: about 7¹/₂ cups salad

CHINESE CHICKEN WINGS

1 1/2 pounds chicken wings, disjointed
       and wing tips discarded
1/2   cup red plum jam
3   tablespoons soy sauce
2   tablespoons prepared horseradish
1   tablespoon prepared mustard
3   to 4 drops hot pepper sauce
       Chinese hot mustard to serve

Preheat oven to 425 degrees. Place wings in a single layer on a baking sheet. Combine jam, soy sauce, horseradish, prepared mustard, and pepper sauce; brush generously over wings. Bake 15 to 20 minutes, basting frequently. Serve with Chinese hot mustard, if desired.
Yield: about 20 chicken wings

CHEESE POCKETS

1   package (10 ounces) refrigerated
       pizza dough
1/4   cup strawberry jam
3/4   cup shredded sharp Cheddar
       cheese
1/4   cup chopped green onion
5   slices bacon, cooked and
       crumbled
1/4   cup chopped pecans

Preheat oven to 400 degrees. Unroll pizza dough and cut into 12 equal pieces. Place 1 teaspoon jam on each piece of dough. Top with cheese, green onion, bacon, and pecans. Brush edges of dough with water. Fold dough over filling and seal edges with fork. Place pockets on a lightly greased baking sheet. Bake 12 to 15 minutes or until golden brown. Serve warm.
Yield: 12 pockets

CRISPY CHICKEN WINGS WITH RANCH-STYLE DIP

1   package (8 ounces) cream
       cheese, softened
1/2   cup sour cream
1   envelope (0.4 ounce) ranch-
       style salad dressing mix
2   pounds chicken wings
1   teaspoon salt
1 1/2 cups corn flake crumbs
3   egg whites

In a small bowl, combine cream cheese, sour cream, and salad dressing mix. Cover and chill until ready to serve.
Preheat oven to 375 degrees. Cut off and discard chicken wing tips. Cut chicken wings in half at joint. Sprinkle with salt; set aside. Place cereal crumbs and egg whites in separate small bowls. Beat egg whites until foamy. Dip chicken pieces, 1 at a time, in egg whites and roll in crumbs. Place on a greased baking sheet. Bake 30 to 40 minutes or until juices run clear when chicken is pierced with a fork. Serve warm with dip.
Yield: 18 to 22 pieces chicken

HAM AND CHEESE BISCUIT TURNOVERS

⅓ cup diced ham (about
    3½ ounces)
⅓ cup shredded Cheddar cheese
2 tablespoons mayonnaise
1 can (7½ ounces) refrigerated
    buttermilk biscuits (10 count)

Preheat oven to 375 degrees. In a small bowl, combine ham, cheese, and mayonnaise. Press each biscuit into a 3-inch-diameter circle. Spoon about 1 tablespoon ham mixture in center of each biscuit and fold over; press edges together. Place on a greased baking sheet. Use scissors to cut slits in tops of turnovers. Bake 12 to 15 minutes or until golden brown. Serve warm.
Yield: 10 turnovers

HUSH PUPPY MUFFINS

1 cup yellow cornmeal
½ cup all-purpose flour
2 teaspoons baking powder
2 teaspoons sugar
1 teaspoon dried dill weed
½ teaspoon salt
1 container (8 ounces) sour cream
2 eggs
¼ cup milk
¼ cup vegetable oil
¼ teaspoon hot pepper sauce
½ cup minced onion

Preheat oven to 425 degrees. Grease and preheat a cast-iron muffin pan. In a large bowl, combine cornmeal, flour, baking powder, sugar, dill weed, and salt. In a small bowl, beat sour cream, eggs, milk, oil, and pepper sauce until well blended.

Add to dry ingredients; stir just until blended. Stir in onion. Fill molds about ⅔ full. Bake 11 to 13 minutes or until edges are golden brown. Serve warm.
Yield: about 1 dozen muffins

ADOBADO SAUCE

2 cans (4 ounces each) chopped
    green chilies
1 cup chicken broth
3 tablespoons butter or margarine
2 medium onions, diced
2 tablespoons ground cumin
2 teaspoons chili powder
2 cloves garlic, minced
¼ cup firmly packed light brown
    sugar
¼ cup orange juice
¼ cup ketchup
2 tablespoons lemon juice

In a blender or food processor, purée chilies. Combine purée with chicken broth and set aside.

In a large skillet, melt butter over medium heat. Add onions and cook 15 minutes, stirring frequently. Blend in cumin, chili powder, and garlic. Stir in chil purée mixture. Reduce heat to medium-low and cook 20 minutes, stirring frequently.

Combine brown sugar, orange juice, ketchup, and lemon juice. Stir into chili mixture. Continue cooking, stirring occasionally, about 15 minutes or until mixture is the consistency of thick purée. Cool slightly. Serve warm or at room temperature.
Yield: about 2¾ cups of sauce

Spicy Cornmeal Chicken Nuggets served with Adobado Sauce can be the foundation of a meal, or they make tasty appetizers for a casual gathering.

CORNMEAL CHICKEN NUGGETS

$^1/_2$ cup cornmeal
1 tablespoon chili powder
2 teaspoons ground cumin
4 boneless, skinless chicken
    breasts, cut into 1-inch cubes
3 tablespoons vegetable oil
    Adobado Sauce to serve (recipe
    on page 172)

Combine cornmeal, chili powder, and cumin; mix well. Add chicken and toss to coat well with mixture. In a large skillet, heat oil over medium heat. Add chicken and cook, stirring frequently, 5 to 6 minutes or until chicken is browned on all sides and done in middle. Serve with Adobado Sauce.

Yield: about 36 nuggets

PORK TENDERLOIN WITH PEACH CHUTNEY GLAZE

PEACH CHUTNEY
- 1 cup peach preserves
- 1/2 cup golden raisins
- 1/4 cup chopped pecans
- 2 tablespoons apple cider vinegar
- 2 teaspoons freshly grated ginger
- 1 teaspoon minced onion

PORK TENDERLOIN
- 1 tablespoon crushed fresh thyme leaves
- 2 cloves garlic, minced
- 2 teaspoons freshly grated ginger
- 1 teaspoon salt
- 1 teaspoon ground black pepper
- 1 pork tenderloin (about 2 pounds) Fresh thyme sprigs and canned peach slices to garnish

For peach chutney, process preserves, raisins, pecans, vinegar, ginger, and onion in a food processor until finely chopped. Transfer ingredients to a medium saucepan over low heat. Stirring frequently, cook 7 to 9 minutes or until mixture is heated through. Remove from heat. Cover and allow flavors to blend.

Preheat oven to 400 degrees. For pork tenderloin, combine thyme, garlic, ginger, salt, and pepper in a small bowl. Rub mixture over pork; place in a roasting pan. Insert meat thermometer into thickest portion of tenderloin. Spooning about 1/3 cup chutney over pork after 30 minutes, bake 40 to 50 minutes or until meat thermometer registers 160 degrees. Transfer tenderloin to a serving platter and allow to stand 10 minutes before slicing. Garnish with thyme sprigs and peach slices. Serve with remaining peach chutney.
Yield: about 10 servings

EASY BAKED BEANS

- 6 slices bacon
- 1 cup chopped onions
- 2 cans (28 ounces each) baked beans
- 2 cans (15.3 ounces each) lima beans, drained
- 1 cup barbecue sauce
- 3/4 cup firmly packed brown sugar
- 2 tablespoons prepared mustard
- 1 tablespoon Worcestershire sauce
- 3/4 teaspoon salt

Preheat oven to 300 degrees. In a large skillet, cook bacon; reserve drippings in skillet. Crumble bacon and set aside. Cook onions in bacon drippings until tender. In a 9 x 13-inch baking dish, combine onions and drippings with beans, barbecue sauce, brown sugar, mustard, Worcestershire sauce, and salt. Stirring occasionally, bake about 2 hours. To serve, stir in bacon. Serve warm.
Yield: about 10 servings

MUSTARD ROLLS

2 packages dry yeast
1/4 cup warm water
1 tablespoon sugar
1 cup milk
2/3 cup prepared mustard
2 tablespoons butter or margarine
4 cups all-purpose flour
  Vegetable cooking spray
1 egg yolk
1 tablespoon water

In a small bowl, combine yeast, 1/4 cup warm water, and sugar; stir until well blended. In a small saucepan, heat milk, mustard, and butter over medium-high heat until butter melts. In a large bowl, combine yeast mixture, milk mixture, and flour. Stir until a soft dough forms. Turn onto a lightly floured surface and knead about 8 minutes or until dough becomes smooth and elastic. Place in a large bowl sprayed with cooking spray, turning once to coat top of dough. Cover and let rise in a warm place (80 to 85 degrees) 1 hour or until doubled in size.

Turn dough onto a lightly floured surface and punch down. Shape dough into 1 1/2-inch balls and place 2 inches apart on a greased baking sheet. Lightly spray tops of rolls with cooking spray. Cover and let rise in a warm place 1 hour or until doubled in size.

Preheat oven to 400 degrees. In a small bowl, whisk egg yolk with 1 tablespoon water; brush over tops of rolls. Bake 12 to 15 minutes or until golden brown. Serve warm with Herbed Beef Brisket.
Yield: about 3 1/2 dozen rolls

HERBED BEEF BRISKET

4 pound beef brisket
12 to 15 cloves garlic, thinly
  sliced
3 tablespoons fennel seed
1 tablespoon all-purpose flour
1 cup hot water
1 teaspoon beef bouillon granules
2 tablespoons Worcestershire
  sauce
1 teaspoon dried marjoram leaves
1 teaspoon dried thyme leaves
1 teaspoon ground oregano
1 teaspoon ground black pepper
  Mustard Rolls (recipe on this page)
  and desired condiments
  to serve

Preheat oven to 325 degrees. Trim excess fat from brisket. Make 1/2-inch-deep cuts in meat across the grain. Insert garlic slices into cuts. Sprinkle fennel seed over top of brisket. Place flour in a large (14 x 20-inch) oven cooking bag; shake to coat bag. Place brisket in bag. Pour water into a small bowl; dissolve bouillon in water. Add Worcestershire sauce, marjoram, thyme, oregano, and pepper to bouillon mixture; pour into cooking bag. Seal and puncture cooking bag according to package directions. Bake 2 1/4 to 2 1/2 hours or until tender. Allow meat to stand in bag 10 to 15 minutes. Remove meat from bag; thinly slice across the grain. Serve warm on Mustard Rolls with desired condiments.
Yield: 30 to 40 appetizers

OVEN-BAKED MINESTRONE SOUP

1½ pounds stew beef, cut into small
      pieces
1   cup chopped onion
2   cloves garlic, minced
2   tablespoons olive oil
1   teaspoon salt
1   teaspoon ground black pepper
3   cans (14½ ounces each) beef
      broth
2¾ cups water
1   can (16 ounces) kidney beans
1   can (14½ ounces) diced
      stewed tomatoes
1½ cups thinly sliced carrots
1   can (6 ounces) whole pitted ripe
      olives
2   cups sliced zucchini
1   cup uncooked small elbow
      macaroni
½   teaspoon dried basil leaves
¼   teaspoon dried thyme leaves
¼   teaspoon dried oregano leaves
¼   teaspoon dried rosemary leaves
¼   teaspoon ground savory
      Freshly shredded Parmesan
      cheese to serve

Preheat oven to 400 degrees. In a large ovenproof Dutch oven, combine beef, onion, garlic, oil, salt, and pepper. Stirring occasionally, bake uncovered 45 minutes. Leaving soup in oven, reduce heat to 350 degrees. Combine beef broth and water in a 2-quart microwave-safe container. Microwave on high power (100%) 10 minutes or until broth mixture begins to boil; add to beef mixture. Stir in undrained beans, undrained tomatoes, carrots, and undrained olives. Cover and bake about 2 hours or until meat is tender. Stir in zucchini, macaroni, and herbs; cover and bake 30 minutes longer or until vegetables are tender. To serve, sprinkle each serving with cheese.

Yield: about 15 cups soup

CRUNCHY BREADSTICK STREAMERS

2   cans (2.8 ounces each) French-
      fried onions, crushed
1   egg, lightly beaten
2   tablespoons milk
1   can (11 ounces) refrigerated
      breadstick dough

Preheat oven to 350 degrees. Place crushed onions on a piece of aluminum foil. In a small bowl, combine egg and milk. Without separating strips, unroll dough onto a flat surface. Cut dough in half crosswise. Brush both sides of dough pieces with egg mixture. Separate dough at perforations to form 16 strips. Roll each strip in onions, lightly pressing onions into dough. Place on a greased baking sheet; twist ends in opposite directions. Bake 13 to 15 minutes or until golden brown. Serve warm.

Yield: 16 breadsticks

Serve Oven-Baked Minestrone Soup for a perfect winter warmer. Old-fashioned Yeast Rolls (top left; recipe on page 178) are just like the ones Grandma would have made. For a flavorful change from dinner rolls, try easy-to-make Crunchy Breadstick Streamers (top right).

OLD-FASHIONED YEAST ROLLS

- 1 cup warm milk
- 1 cup warm water
- 2 packages dry yeast
- 1 tablespoon sugar
- 4 to 5 cups all-purpose flour, divided
- 3 tablespoons butter or margarine, melted
- 2 teaspoons salt
  Vegetable cooking spray
- 1 egg, beaten
- 1 tablespoon milk

In a large bowl, combine warm milk, water, yeast, sugar, and 1 cup flour. Beat mixture until well blended and smooth. Cover and let rise in a warm place (80 to 85 degrees) 1 hour or until doubled in size.

Stir melted butter and salt into yeast mixture. Add 3 cups flour; stir until a soft dough forms. Turn dough onto a lightly floured surface. Knead about 5 minutes or until dough becomes smooth and elastic, using additional flour as necessary. Place in a large bowl sprayed with cooking spray, turning once to coat top of dough. Cover and let rise in a warm place about 2 hours or until tripled in size.

Turn dough onto a lightly floured surface and punch down. Shape dough into 2-inch rolls. Place 2 inches apart on a greased baking sheet. Spray tops of rolls with cooking spray. Cover and let rise in a warm place 1 hour or until almost doubled in size.

Preheat oven to 375 degrees. In a small bowl, combine egg and milk. Brush rolls with egg mixture. Bake 20 to 25 minutes or until rolls are lightly browned. Serve warm or transfer to a wire rack to cool completely.
Yield: about 2 dozen rolls

PASTA ROLLS WITH MARINARA SAUCE

Pasta Rolls and Marinara Sauce may be made one day in advance.

MARINARA SAUCE
- 2 tablespoons olive oil
- 1/2 cup finely chopped onion
- 1 clove garlic, minced
- 1 can (29 ounces) tomato sauce
- 1 can (14 1/2 ounces) Italian-style stewed tomatoes
- 1/2 cup grated Parmesan cheese
- 1 teaspoon dried parsley flakes
- 1 teaspoon sugar
- 1/2 teaspoon dried oregano leaves
- 1/2 teaspoon dried basil leaves
- 1/2 teaspoon dried thyme leaves
- 1/2 teaspoon salt
- 1/4 teaspoon ground black pepper

PASTA ROLLS
- 2 tablespoons olive oil
- 1/2 cup butter or margarine, divided
- 1 cup finely chopped onion
- 2 cloves garlic, minced
- 2 packages (10 ounces each) frozen chopped spinach, thawed and drained
- 1 cup ricotta cheese
- 1 cup grated Parmesan cheese
- 1 teaspoon salt
- 1/2 teaspoon ground black pepper
- 1/2 teaspoon ground nutmeg
- 1 package (16 ounces) lasagna noodles

For marinara sauce, combine oil, onion, and garlic in a large saucepan. Sauté over medium heat until onion is tender. Add tomato sauce, tomatoes, cheese, parsley flakes, sugar, oregano, basil, thyme, salt, and pepper; stir until well blended. Bring to a boil. Reduce heat to low, cover, and simmer 25 to 30 minutes. Pour sauce into a 9 x 13-inch baking dish; set aside.

For pasta rolls, heat oil and 1/4 cup butter in a large skillet over medium heat until butter melts. Add onion and garlic; sauté until onion is tender. Add spinach and continue to cook 10 to 15 minutes or until all liquid has evaporated. Remove from heat and cool to room temperature.

In a large bowl, combine ricotta cheese, Parmesan cheese, salt, pepper, and nutmeg; stir until well blended. Stir in spinach mixture; set aside.

Fill a large saucepan or Dutch oven with water; bring to a boil. Add noodles and cook 8 to 10 minutes or until tender. Drain and rinse with cold water. Spread about 2 tablespoons spinach mixture evenly on each noodle. Use a sharp knife to cut each noodle in half from top to bottom and again from left to right. Beginning with 1 short edge, roll up each piece jellyroll style. Standing rolls on 1 end, place in sauce. Cover and refrigerate 8 hours or overnight to allow flavors to blend.

To serve, preheat oven to 350 degrees. Cover with aluminum foil and bake 25 to 30 minutes or until heated through. Melt remaining 1/4 cup butter in a small saucepan over medium heat. Brush butter lightly over pasta rolls. Serve warm.

Yield: about 6 dozen pasta rolls

CAJUN COLESLAW

1 small head green cabbage, shredded
1 cup chopped walnuts
3/4 cup mayonnaise
1/4 cup red wine vinegar
3 tablespoons Dijon-style mustard
2 teaspoons garlic powder
1 teaspoon ground cayenne pepper

In a large bowl, combine cabbage and walnuts. In a small bowl, whisk together remaining ingredients. Pour mayonnaise mixture over cabbage mixture; stir until well blended. Cover and refrigerate 2 to 3 hours to allow flavors to blend. Store in an airtight container in refrigerator.

Yield: about 6 servings

Pasta Rolls filled with spinach and cheese make impressive hors d'oeuvres. They're served with homemade Marinara Sauce, a zesty blend of tomatoes, onion, garlic, and Italian spices.

ITALIAN LOAF

1 can (10 ounces) refrigerated
   pizza crust dough
4 cups (16 ounces) shredded
   mozzarella cheese
1 pound spicy pork sausage,
   browned and drained
1/2 cup tomato sauce
1 teaspoon dried oregano leaves
1/2 teaspoon dried basil leaves
1 package (10 ounces) frozen
   spinach, thawed and drained
1 egg, lightly beaten
1 jar (7 ounces) diced pimientos,
   drained
1 package (3 ounces) sliced
   pepperoni
12 large pimiento-stuffed green
   olives, cut in half lengthwise

Preheat oven to 400 degrees. Unroll dough and cut off one-fourth of dough crosswise; set aside. Line a greased 5¹/4 x 9¹/4 x 2¹/2-inch loaf pan with the large piece of dough. Moisten the dough with water at corners and press to seal. Place half of cheese on dough in bottom of pan and top with sausage. Spoon tomato sauce over sausage and sprinkle with oregano and basil. In a small bowl, combine spinach with egg and spread over tomato sauce. Layer pimientos on top of spinach and top with remaining cheese. Arrange the pepperoni on top of the cheese layer. Top with olive halves. Cover filling with reserved dough and crimp edges of dough to seal. Cut slits in top of dough to allow steam to escape.

Bake 45 to 50 minutes or until crust is well browned (if crust browns too quickly, cover loosely with aluminum foil). Allow to cool 10 minutes before removing from pan and cutting into slices.
Yield: about 8 servings

BROCCOLI DIP

1 package (10 ounces) frozen
   chopped broccoli, thawed and
   drained
1/2 cup minced fresh parsley
1/2 cup chopped green onions
1 cup chopped celery
1 tablespoon Worcestershire
   sauce
1 teaspoon Greek seasoning
1 cup sour cream
1 cup mayonnaise
1 tablespoon lemon juice
1 loaf (1 pound) round Hawaiian
   bread (found in freezer or deli
   section)
   Chopped fresh parsley to
   garnish
   Crackers to serve

In a large bowl, combine broccoli, minced parsley, green onions, celery, Worcestershire sauce, Greek seasoning, sour cream, mayonnaise, and lemon juice. Cover and refrigerate overnight.

Before serving, cut the top from the loaf of bread. Hollow out the inside of the bread, leaving about a 1-inch shell. Fill hollowed-out bread round with dip. Tear bread from inside of loaf into bite-size pieces. Spread pieces on ungreased baking sheet and toast lightly. Serve with toasted bread or crackers.
Yield: about 3¹/2 cups dip

Light, refreshing Broccoli Dip is especially appealing when served in a hollowed-out loaf of bread.

Spicy Italian Loaf is a colorful treat enlivened with spinach and pimientos.

GREEK PIZZA SQUARES

CRUST
- 2 cups bread flour
- 1 cup whole-wheat flour
- 1 package dry yeast
- 1 teaspoon sugar
- 1 teaspoon salt
- 1¹/₃ cups very warm water
- 1 teaspoon olive oil
- Vegetable cooking spray

TOPPING
- Vegetable cooking spray
- 1 can (14¹/₂ ounces) Italian-style stewed tomatoes
- ¹/₂ cup chopped onion
- ¹/₂ cup chopped green pepper
- 1 teaspoon fennel seed, crushed
- 1 teaspoon garlic powder
- 1 teaspoon salt
- ¹/₂ teaspoon ground black pepper
- 1 can (2¹/₄ ounces) sliced black olives, drained
- 1 cup fat-free shredded mozzarella cheese
- 4 ounces feta cheese, crumbled

For crust, combine flours, yeast, sugar, and salt in a large bowl. Add water and oil; stir until a soft dough forms. Turn onto a lightly floured surface and knead until dough becomes smooth and elastic. Place in a large bowl sprayed with cooking spray, turning once to coat top of dough. Cover and let rise in a warm place (80 to 85 degrees) 1 hour or until doubled in size.

For topping, heat a medium skillet sprayed with cooking spray over medium heat. Add undrained tomatoes to skillet and coarsely chop. Add onion, green pepper, fennel seed, garlic powder, salt, and black pepper to skillet. Stirring occasionally, cook 5 minutes or until liquid evaporates. Remove from heat; stir in olives.

Preheat oven to 375 degrees. Turn dough onto a lightly floured surface and punch down. Press dough into a greased 10¹/₂ x 15¹/₂-inch jellyroll pan. Bake 10 minutes. Remove from oven. Spoon tomato mixture over crust. Sprinkle cheeses over vegetable mixture. Bake 15 to 20 minutes or until cheese is bubbly. Cut into squares and serve warm.

Yield: about 2 dozen appetizers

PARTY PIZZA

- 2 pita breads, split into round halves
- ¹/₄ cup grated Parmesan cheese
- 1 can (14¹/₂ ounces) undrained whole, peeled tomatoes, chopped
- 1 can (6 ounces) tomato paste
- ¹/₂ cup chopped mushrooms
- 1¹/₂ teaspoons Italian seasoning
- 1 teaspoon garlic salt
- ¹/₄ teaspoon minced dried garlic
- 1 pound spicy pork sausage, cooked and drained
- 4 cups shredded mozzarella cheese

Preheat oven to 400 degrees. Place pita bread halves on a large baking sheet. Sprinkle each half with 1 tablespoon Parmesan cheese. Bake 8 to 10 minutes or until lightly toasted.

In a medium saucepan, combine tomatoes, tomato paste, mushrooms, Italian seasoning, garlic salt, and garlic. Stir over medium heat until heated through. Generously spread sauce over bread halves. Top with sausage and mozzarella. Return to oven and bake 10 to 12 minutes or until cheese is bubbly and melted. Cut each pizza into 4 wedges to serve.

Yield: 16 servings

FRIED WON TONS

1 pound ground pork
8 canned water chestnuts, minced
2 cloves garlic, minced
2 green onions, finely chopped
1 teaspoon ground ginger
1/4 teaspoon ground black pepper
1/2 teaspoon garlic salt
1 package (16 ounces) won ton skins
1 egg, lightly beaten
   Vegetable oil
   Plum Dipping Sauce to serve
      (recipe follows)

Combine the pork, water chestnuts, garlic, onions, ginger, pepper, and garlic salt, mixing well. Unwrap won ton skins and cover with damp paper towels to keep skins from drying out. For each won ton, place one won ton skin on work surface with one point facing up. Place 1 heaping teaspoon of filling in center of skin. Bring bottom point up over filling; bring side points over center of filling. Seal seams with egg. Place won tons on a baking sheet; cover with damp paper towels

In a Dutch oven, heat 3 inches of oil to 360 degrees over medium-high heat. Fry won tons, three or four at a time, until golden brown (about 2 to 2 1/2 minutes; do not fry too quickly or the pork centers will not be thoroughly cooked). Drain on paper towels. Serve warm or at room temperature with Plum Dipping Sauce.
Yield: about 50 won tons

PLUM DIPPING SAUCE

1 cup red plum jam
1 clove garlic, minced
3 tablespoons white wine
1 tablespoon Dijon-style mustard
1 1/2 teaspoons dry mustard

Combine all ingredients in a small saucepan over low heat. Stir just until

jam is melted. Serve with Fried Won Tons.
Yield: about 1 cup of sauce

POLYNESIAN MEATBALLS

MEATBALLS
1 1/2 pounds ground pork
1 1/4 pounds ground round
2 cups crushed corn flake cereal
1 cup milk
2 eggs, beaten
3 tablespoons prepared horseradish
3 tablespoons Worcestershire
   sauce
2 teaspoons dry mustard
1 teaspoon salt
1/2 teaspoon ground black pepper

SAUCE
1 cup ketchup
1/2 cup firmly packed brown sugar
1/2 cup water
1/3 cup soy sauce
2 tablespoons honey
2 tablespoons apple cider vinegar
1 teaspoon dry mustard
1 can (8 ounces) crushed
   pineapple, drained

Preheat oven to 450 degrees. For meatballs, combine all ingredients in a large bowl, mixing well. Shape mixture into 1-inch balls. Place on a rack in a shallow baking pan. Bake 12 to 15 minutes or until brown.

For sauce, mix together all ingredients except pineapple in a large saucepan over medium-high heat. Bring to a boil; reduce heat to medium and simmer 10 minutes. Stir in pineapple. Spoon meatballs into sauce, stirring until well coated. Continue to cook 10 to 15 minutes or until heated through. Serve hot.
Yield: about 75 meatballs

TURKEY AND SAUSAGE GUMBO

1/2 cup vegetable oil
3/4 cup all-purpose flour
1 package (1 pound, 2 ounces) frozen sliced okra, thawed
1 cup chopped onion
3/4 cup chopped celery
3/4 cup chopped green onions
1/2 cup chopped green pepper
2 cloves garlic, minced
6 cups turkey stock or canned chicken broth
4 cups chopped cooked turkey
1 pound smoked sausage, sliced
1 can (14 1/2 ounces) diced tomatoes
2 teaspoons hot pepper sauce
1 teaspoon dried thyme leaves
1 teaspoon dried marjoram leaves
1 teaspoon salt
1/2 teaspoon ground black pepper
1/4 teaspoon ground red pepper
2 bay leaves
1 package (16 ounces) frozen cooked and peeled cocktail shrimp, thawed
1 teaspoon filé powder
Cooked rice to serve

Combine oil and flour in a heavy large Dutch oven over medium heat. Stirring constantly, cook 13 to 15 minutes or until mixture forms a brown roux. Reduce heat to medium-low and stir in okra, onion, celery, green onions, green pepper, and garlic. Cook 15 minutes or until vegetables are tender. Stir in turkey stock, turkey, sausage, tomatoes, pepper sauce, thyme, marjoram, salt, black pepper, red pepper, and bay leaves. Increase heat to medium-high and bring to a boil. Reduce heat to low; cover and simmer 1 hour, stirring occasionally. Remove lid and simmer 30 minutes or until desired thickness. Remove from heat; stir in shrimp and filé powder. Remove bay leaves. Serve gumbo over rice.
Yield: about 4 quarts gumbo

CRANBERRY-ORANGE BARBECUE SAUCE
This is a great basting sauce or condiment for poultry and meat.

1 cup whole berry cranberry sauce
1/2 cup firmly packed brown sugar
1/4 cup frozen orange juice concentrate, thawed
2 tablespoons red wine vinegar
1 tablespoon prepared mustard
1 tablespoon Worcestershire sauce
1/2 teaspoon ground black pepper

In a medium saucepan, combine cranberry sauce, brown sugar, juice concentrate, vinegar, mustard, Worcestershire sauce, and pepper over medium heat. Stirring frequently, cook 7 minutes or until heated through.
Yield: about 1 1/2 cups sauce

Loaded with Cajun-style flavor, Turkey and Sausage Gumbo is a delicious way to use leftover turkey. To perk up leftover ham, stir up Tasty Ham Spread to top your favorite crackers.

TASTY HAM SPREAD

- 1 package (3 ounces) cream cheese, softened
- 1/4 cup mayonnaise
- 2 cups ground baked ham
- 2 tablespoons finely chopped sweet pickle
- 1 tablespoon Dijon-style mustard
- 1 teaspoon Worcestershire sauce
  Crackers to serve

In a small bowl, beat cream cheese and mayonnaise until well blended. Stir in ham, pickle, mustard, and Worcestershire sauce. Cover and chill 1 hour. Serve ham spread with crackers.

Yield: about 2 cups spread

MARINATED SHRIMP SALAD

- 1/2 cup white wine vinegar
- 1/3 cup olive oil
- 6 green onions, chopped
- 3 tablespoons chopped fresh parsley
- 1 tablespoon garlic salt
- 2 teaspoons dried basil leaves, crushed
- 1/2 teaspoon ground black pepper
- 1 1/2 pounds large shrimp, cooked, peeled, and deveined
- 1/2 red onion, thinly sliced

In a blender or food processor, process vinegar, oil, green onions, parsley, garlic salt, basil, and pepper until well blended. In a medium bowl, combine shrimp and red onion. Pour vinegar mixture over shrimp mixture; stir until well coated. Cover and refrigerate 8 hours or overnight to allow flavors to blend. Serve chilled.
Yield: about 4 cups salad

SHRIMP SALSA

- 2 1/2 pounds shrimp, cooked, peeled, deveined, and chopped (about 5 cups)
- 1 jar (24 ounces) mild chunky-style salsa
- 2 cups chopped fresh cilantro
- 2 cups finely chopped fresh tomatoes
- 1/4 cup finely chopped red onion
- 2 tablespoons lime juice
  Purchased fat-free tortilla chips to serve

In a large bowl, combine shrimp, salsa, cilantro, tomatoes, onion, and lime juice. Cover and refrigerate 8 hours or overnight to allow flavors to blend. Serve with tortilla chips.
Yield: about 8 cups salsa or 32 servings

HEARTS OF PALM AND SHRIMP SALAD

- 1/2 cup olive oil
- 1/4 cup red wine vinegar
- 1/4 cup water
- 1 tablespoon granulated sugar
- 2 teaspoons lemon juice
- 1 teaspoon Dijon-style mustard
- 1 teaspoon Worcestershire sauce
- 3/4 teaspoon garlic salt
- 1/4 teaspoon ground black pepper
- 3 cans (14 ounces each) hearts of palm, drained
- 1 1/2 pounds large shrimp, cooked, peeled, and deveined
- 6 slices bacon, cooked, drained, and crumbled
  Red cabbage leaves to serve
  Fresh parsley to garnish

In a small bowl, whisk first 9 ingredients until well blended. If desired, cut hearts of palm in half lengthwise. Place hearts of palm, shrimp, and bacon in a 1-gallon resealable plastic bag; pour dressing over. Seal bag and refrigerate 8 hours or overnight to allow flavors to blend.

Reserve dressing. To serve, arrange hearts of palm and shrimp on cabbage leaves on individual serving plates. Pour reserved dressing over each salad. Garnish with parsley.
Yield: about 10 servings

SALMON-CREAM CHEESE CRÊPES

Crêpes can be assembled ahead of time and refrigerated.

CRÊPES

- ²/₃ cup all-purpose flour
- ¼ teaspoon salt
- ¼ teaspoon ground white pepper
- 1 cup evaporated skimmed milk
- 1 egg
- 1 tablespoon reduced-calorie margarine, melted
- Vegetable cooking spray

FILLING

- 1 package (8 ounces) fat-free cream cheese, softened
- 2 tablespoons finely chopped green onions
- 1¹/₂ tablespoons drained capers, rinsed
- 1 teaspoon dried basil leaves
- ¼ teaspoon garlic powder
- ¼ teaspoon ground white pepper
- 3 packages (3 ounces each) smoked salmon, broken into pieces
- Chopped green onion to garnish

For crêpes, combine flour, salt, and white pepper in a medium bowl. Add evaporated milk, egg, and melted margarine; whisk until smooth. Cover and chill 30 minutes.

Lightly spray an 8-inch nonstick skillet with cooking spray. Place pan over medium heat until hot. For each crêpe, spoon about 2 tablespoons batter into pan. Tilt pan to spread batter evenly over bottom of pan to form a 5-inch circle. Cook until lightly browned; turn over and cook 30 seconds longer. Place crêpes between layers of waxed paper.

For filling, combine cream cheese, 2 tablespoons chopped green onions, capers, basil, garlic powder, and white pepper in a medium bowl. Gently stir in salmon. Fill each crêpe with about 2 tablespoons salmon mixture. Roll up crêpes and place, seam side down, in a 9 x 13-inch baking dish. Cover and store crêpes in refrigerator until ready to serve.

To serve, bake covered 20 minutes in a 350-degree oven. Garnish with green onion and serve warm.

Yield: about 12 crêpes

SEAFOOD CHOWDER

- 2 pounds orange roughy, halibut, or haddock fillets, cut into bite-size pieces
- 1 pound bay scallops
- 3 cups water
- 1/4 pound salt pork, diced
- 6 onions, chopped
- 2 tablespoons all-purpose flour
- 2 cups peeled, diced red potatoes
- 2 1/2 cups milk
- 1/2 cup dry white wine
- 1/2 cup finely chopped fresh parsley
- 2 tablespoons butter or margarine
- 1 teaspoon salt
- 1 teaspoon ground black pepper

In a large saucepan, combine fish, scallops, and water; bring to a boil over medium heat. Reduce heat and simmer 30 minutes. Reserving liquid, strain seafood.

In a stockpot, cook salt pork over medium high heat until golden brown. Reserving drippings, transfer salt pork to a medium bowl. Add onions to drippings in stockpot; cook until tender. Add onions to salt pork in bowl. Stir flour into drippings in stockpot and cook 1 minute. Stirring constantly, gradually add reserved seafood liquid. Add potatoes, onion mixture, and seafood. Cover and simmer over medium-low heat 40 to 45 minutes. Stir in remaining ingredients. Cook until heated through (do not boil). Serve warm.

Yield: about 15 servings

CREAM OF SPINACH SOUP

- 1 1/2 cups finely chopped onions
- 1/4 cup butter or margarine
- 2 cloves garlic, minced
- 3 tablespoons all-purpose flour
- 3/4 teaspoon salt
- 1/4 teaspoon ground black pepper
- 3 cups chicken broth
- 2 pounds fresh spinach, washed, stemmed, and drained
- 1 medium potato, chopped
- 1 medium carrot, sliced
- 1 cup half and half
  Bacon pieces and carrot strips to garnish

In a Dutch oven, sauté onions in butter over medium heat until soft. Add garlic; sauté 2 to 3 minutes. Stirring constantly, add flour, salt, and pepper; cook about 3 minutes or until mixture is well blended. Gradually stir in chicken broth. Increase heat to medium high and add spinach, potato, and carrot; bring mixture to a boil. Reduce heat to medium low, cover, and cook until vegetables are tender. Process soup in a food processor until vegetables are finely chopped; return to Dutch oven over medium-low heat. Stirring constantly, gradually add half and half; simmer until heated through. Garnish each serving with bacon and carrot strips.

Yield: about 8 cups soup

CHILLED AVOCADO SOUP

1 medium cucumber, peeled
4 ripe avocados
3 tablespoons freshly squeezed
   lemon juice
2 medium green onions, finely
   chopped
2 tablespoons coarsely chopped
   fresh parsley
2 tablespoons salsa
1 to 2 cloves garlic, minced
1 teaspoon salt
$1/4$ teaspoon ground white pepper
$3^1/2$ cups chicken broth
$1/2$ cup plain yogurt
   Fresh parsley to garnish

Cut cucumber in half lengthwise and remove seeds. Slice half of cucumber and reserve for garnish; coarsely chop remaining half. Cut avocados into pieces and place in a food processor. Sprinkle lemon juice over avocados. Add chopped cucumber, onions, chopped parsley, salsa, garlic, salt, and white pepper; process about 30 seconds or until well blended. Add chicken broth and yogurt; process just until smooth. Place soup in nonmetal container; cover and chill overnight.

To serve, garnish soup with reserved cucumber slices and parsley.
Yield: about 7 cups soup

BACON-CHEESE TOASTS

Spread may be made ahead of time and chilled.

1 package (16 ounces) bacon,
   cooked and finely chopped
3 cups (12 ounces) shredded
   provolone cheese
$1/2$ cup mayonnaise
$2^1/2$ tablespoons finely minced onion
1 loaf (8 ounces) sliced white
   cocktail bread
1 loaf (8 ounces) sliced wheat
   cocktail bread

Preheat oven to 325 degrees. In a medium bowl, combine bacon, cheese, mayonnaise, and onion. Spread about 2 teaspoons mixture on each slice of bread; place on an ungreased baking sheet. Bake 13 to 15 minutes or until cheese mixture is melted and edges of bread are lightly browned.
Yield: about 3 dozen toasts

EGGS BENEDICT

2 English muffins, split in half
   horizontally
8 slices Canadian bacon
4 poached eggs
   Hollandaise Sauce (recipe follows)

Place English muffins on a baking sheet; top each muffin half with 2 slices of Canadian bacon. Bake at 350 degrees for 10 to 15 minutes or until bacon is hot and muffins are toasted. Place each muffin on a serving plate and top with a poached egg and Hollandaise Sauce. Serve immediately.
Yield: 4 servings

HOLLANDAISE SAUCE

3 egg yolks
1/8 teaspoon cayenne pepper
1/4 teaspoon salt
1/2 cup butter, room temperature, cut
     into 1 tablespoon pieces, and
     divided
1 1/2 tablespoons lemon juice

Place egg yolks, cayenne pepper, salt, and 3 tablespoons butter in the top of a double boiler over simmering water. Gradually add lemon juice, stirring until mixture begins to thicken. Add remaining butter, a tablespoon at a time, stirring constantly until sauce is thickened. Serve immediately.
Yield: 3/4 cup sauce

CANDIED APPLES

8 cooking apples (we used Rome
   apples)
1 3/4 cups sugar
3/4 cup water
1 package (9 ounces) small red
   cinnamon candies

Peel, core, and cut apples into eighths. In a Dutch oven, combine sugar, water, and candies. Stirring constantly, cook over medium heat about 10 minutes or until candies dissolve. Add apples and bring to a boil. Cook about 7 minutes or until apples are tender; cool. Cover and store in refrigerator. Serve chilled.
Yield: about 6 1/2 cups apples

TURKEY QUICHE LORRAINE

- 1 unbaked 9-inch pie crust
- 8 slices bacon
- 1/4 cup finely chopped onion
- 1 1/2 cups (about 6 ounces) shredded Gruyère cheese
- 1 cup diced cooked turkey
- 1 1/2 cups half and half
- 4 eggs
- 1/2 teaspoon dry mustard
- 1/4 teaspoon salt

Preheat oven to 350 degrees. Bake crust 8 minutes or until lightly browned. Cook bacon in a medium skillet until crisp; remove bacon, reserving 1 tablespoon drippings in skillet. Drain and crumble bacon; set aside. Sauté onion in reserved drippings over medium-low heat until tender. Sprinkle cheese, turkey, bacon, and onion into bottom of pie crust. In a medium bowl, beat half and half, eggs, dry mustard, and salt until well blended. Pour egg mixture into pie crust. Bake 40 to 50 minutes or until a knife inserted in center of quiche comes out clean. Let stand 5 minutes before serving. Serve warm.

Yield: about 8 servings

SPICY ORANGE PUNCH

- 1 can (12 ounces) frozen orange juice concentrate, thawed
- 1 can (12 ounces) frozen orange-pineapple juice concentrate, thawed
- 2 cups water
- 1 package (0.15 ounces) unsweetened orange-flavored soft drink mix
- 2 teaspoons pumpkin pie spice
- 4 cans (12 ounces each) lemon-lime soft drink, chilled

In a 1 1/2-quart container, combine juice concentrates and water. Add soft drink mix and pumpkin pie spice; whisk until well blended. Cover and chill.

To serve: Place punch mix in a 1-gallon container. Add four 12-ounce cans of chilled lemon-lime soft drink. Stir and serve immediately.

Yield: about 5 cups mix and 11 cups punch

CRANBERRY SALAD

1 envelope unflavored gelatin
1/4 cup cold water
1 package (3 ounces) raspberry
   gelatin
3/4 cup boiling water
1 can (16 ounces) jellied cranberry
   sauce
1 container (16 ounces) sour cream

In a small bowl, sprinkle gelatin over water; let stand 1 minute. In a medium bowl, combine raspberry gelatin and boiling water; stir until gelatin dissolves. Stir in softened gelatin mixture; set aside. Process cranberry sauce in a food processor until smooth. Add sour cream; process just until blended. Whisk cranberry mixture into gelatin. Pour into a lightly oiled 5-cup mold. Cover and chill 4 hours or until firm.
Yield: about 10 servings

FRUITED RICE CREAM

1 jar (6 ounces) red maraschino
   cherries, drained
1 jar (6 ounces) green
   maraschino cherries, drained
2 1/3 cups milk
1 cup uncooked extra long-grain
   rice
1/8 teaspoon salt
2 cups miniature marshmallows
1 package (8 ounces) cream
   cheese, cut into small pieces
   and softened
1/2 cup sweetened condensed milk
1/2 teaspoon almond extract
1/2 teaspoon vanilla extract
2 cups whipping cream, whipped
1/2 cup sliced almonds

Chop cherries and drain on paper towels. Pat cherries dry and set aside. In a heavy medium saucepan, combine milk, rice, and salt over medium-low heat. Stirring frequently to prevent mixture from scorching, cover and cook about 25 to 30 minutes or until rice is tender and most of milk is absorbed. Remove from heat. Without stirring, add marshmallows and cream cheese to rice mixture; cover and let stand 5 minutes. Add sweetened condensed milk and extracts; stir until marshmallows melt and mixture is well blended. Transfer to a large bowl and cool 20 minutes.

Stir cherries into rice mixture. Fold in whipped cream and almonds. Spoon into individual serving dishes. Cover and chill until ready to serve.
Yield: about 8 cups fruited rice

ORANGE-PEACH GELATIN SALAD

2 cups boiling water
1 package (6 ounces) orange
   gelatin
3/4 cup cold water
2 containers (8 ounces each)
   peach yogurt
1 can (16 ounces) peach slices,
   drained
1 can (11 ounces) mandarin
   oranges, drained

In a medium bowl, stir boiling water into gelatin until gelatin dissolves. For top gelatin layer, place 1/2 cup gelatin mixture in a small bowl and stir in cold water. Cover and set aside; do not refrigerate. Stir yogurt into remaining 1 1/2 cups gelatin mixture. Pour yogurt mixture into a 2 1/2-quart serving dish; chill until firm.
Arrange peach and orange slices in a swirled pattern on top of chilled yogurt mixture. Carefully pour reserved gelatin mixture over fruit slices. Chill until firm.
Yield: about 10 servings

SPICY SAUSAGES

1 jar (18 ounces) red plum jam
1/4 cup prepared mustard
1 package (16 ounces) smoked
   cocktail sausages

In a large saucepan over medium-low heat, combine jam and mustard; stir until smooth. Add sausages; stirring occasionally, cook 10 to 15 minutes or until heated through. Serve warm.
Yield: about 4 dozen sausages

CHEESY SPINACH CASSEROLE

3 packages (10 ounces each) frozen
   chopped spinach, cooked and
   squeezed dry
1 tube (6 ounces) jalapeño pepper
   pasteurized process cheese,
   softened
1 container (16 ounces) sour cream
1 can (14 ounces) artichoke hearts
   packed in water, drained and
   finely chopped
1 can (8 ounces) sliced water
   chestnuts, drained and finely
   chopped
1 envelope onion soup mix
2 cups purchased herb-seasoned
   stuffing

Preheat oven to 350 degrees. In a large bowl, combine spinach and cheese until well blended. Stir in sour cream, artichoke hearts, water chestnuts, and soup mix. Spread mixture in a greased 9 x 13-inch baking dish. Sprinkle with stuffing. Bake 30 minutes or until heated through. Serve warm.
Yield: about 14 servings

Gougére is a hearty bread flavored with Cheddar and Swiss cheeses and hot jalapeño peppers.

GOUGÈRE

$^1/_2$ cup butter or margarine
1$^1/_4$ cups all-purpose flour
4 eggs
3 cups shredded sharp Cheddar cheese
1 cup shredded Swiss cheese
$^1/_4$ cup chopped onion
2 jalapeño peppers, chopped
1 clove garlic, minced
$^1/_2$ teaspoon salt
$^1/_4$ teaspoon ground black pepper
$^1/_8$ teaspoon cayenne pepper

Preheat oven to 375 degrees. In a medium saucepan, melt butter over medium heat. Add flour and stir until mixture forms a ball. Remove from heat and continue stirring until mixture cools. Beat in eggs, one at a time, stirring until mixture is slightly glossy and smooth. Stir in remaining ingredients. Pour batter into a greased 10-inch iron skillet. Bake 40 to 45 minutes or until golden brown. Cut bread into slices to serve.
Yield: about 32 slices of bread

Simply Delicious SIDE DISHES

*Side dishes set the mood for every meal! The choice
is yours—casual comfort foods, fresh salads,
impressive dinner dishes, and more.*

Wild Rice Salad, page 205

CREAM OF PUMPKIN SOUP

1 onion, thinly sliced
2 tablespoons butter
2 cups orange juice
2 cups cooked, mashed pumpkin
2 cups chicken broth
$^1/2$ teaspoon ground mace
$^1/2$ teaspoon salt
$^1/4$ teaspoon ground white pepper
$^1/4$ teaspoon ground nutmeg
1 cup half and half
Half and half, toasted walnut halves, and sage leaves to garnish

In a large saucepan, sauté onion in butter until soft. Add orange juice, pumpkin, broth, and seasonings. Simmer 20 minutes. Purée mixture in a food processor or blender until smooth. Return to saucepan and stir in 1 cup half and half. Heat, being careful not to boil. Garnish each serving with a swirl of half and half, walnut halves, and sage leaves. Serve immediately.
Yield: about 8 servings

CREAM OF ARTICHOKE SOUP

$^1/2$ cup chopped green onion
2 carrots, peeled and sliced
2 ribs celery, chopped
$^1/2$ cup butter or margarine, divided
4 cups chicken broth
1 can (14 ounces) artichoke hearts, drained and sliced
1 can (4 ounces) sliced mushrooms, drained
1 bay leaf
$^1/2$ teaspoon ground thyme
$^1/2$ teaspoon ground oregano
$^1/8$ teaspoon cayenne pepper
3 tablespoons all-purpose flour
1 cup whipping cream
Salt and ground black pepper

In large saucepan over medium heat, sauté onion, carrots, and celery in $^1/4$ cup butter. Add chicken broth, artichokes, mushrooms, bay leaf, thyme, oregano, and cayenne. Simmer 15 to 20 minutes. In small skillet, melt remaining $^1/4$ cup butter over low heat. Stir in flour and cook, stirring constantly, until mixture thickens. Stir into artichoke mixture. Slowly add cream. Salt and pepper to taste. Cook 3 to 5 minutes or until slightly thickened and heated through.
Yield: 4 to 6 servings

CURRY-MUSHROOM SOUP

$^3/4$ cup butter or margarine, divided
4 cups (about 12 ounces) sliced fresh mushrooms
1 cup finely chopped onion
$^1/3$ cup all-purpose flour
3 tablespoons curry powder
2 teaspoons garlic powder
2 teaspoons salt
$^1/2$ teaspoon ground black pepper
4 cups milk
2 cups whipping cream
1 package (10 ounces) frozen chopped spinach, thawed and drained
6 slices bacon, cooked and crumbled

In a large skillet, melt $^1/4$ cup butter over medium heat. Add mushrooms and onion; cook until tender. Remove from heat. In a Dutch oven, melt remaining $^1/2$ cup butter over medium heat. Stir in flour, curry powder, garlic powder, salt, and pepper. Cook 2 minutes. Whisking constantly, gradually add milk and whipping cream and cook until thickened. Stir in mushroom mixture and spinach. Cook until heated through. Sprinkle bacon over each serving of soup.
Yield: about nine 1-cup servings

arnished with sage leaves and apple slices, Acorn Squash Soup makes an attractive first
ourse for an elegant dinner. A subtle blend of apples and curry complements the squash
nd adds delicate flavor to this rich soup.

CORN SQUASH SOUP

4   cups water
2   medium acorn squash, scrubbed,
      halved, and seeds removed
1   large onion, sliced
1   sweet yellow pepper, sliced
3   tablespoons butter or margarine
3   apples, peeled, cored, and diced
3   cups chicken broth
1   tablespoon Worcestershire sauce
1   teaspoon curry powder
      Salt and ground black pepper
2   cups half and half

In large saucepan, bring water to a
oil. Add squash, cover, and boil 15 to 20
inutes or until tender. Remove squash
nd allow to cool; reserve liquid.

When cool enough to handle, scoop out
squash with a spoon and discard skin.

In a large saucepan, sauté onion and
yellow pepper in butter until onion is
transparent. Add squash, reserved liquid,
apples, chicken broth, Worcestershire
sauce, and curry. Salt and pepper to taste.
Bring to a boil. Reduce heat to simmer.
Partially cover and cook 15 minutes,
stirring occasionally.

Place squash mixture in a blender or
food processor and purée. Return to
saucepan. Stir in half and half, adjust
seasonings, and cook over medium heat
just until heated through; do not allow
to boil.

Yield: 8 to 10 servings

197

LOBSTER BISQUE

1 gallon water
4 lobster tails (about 4 pounds)
6 tablespoons butter or margarine, divided
$^{1}/_{3}$ cup cognac
$^{1}/_{2}$ cup plus 3 tablespoons chopped green onions, divided
$2^{1}/_{2}$ cups dry white wine
4 cloves garlic, minced
3 tablespoons tomato paste
1 teaspoon dried tarragon leaves
$^{1}/_{2}$ teaspoon dried thyme leaves
$^{1}/_{4}$ teaspoon ground cayenne pepper
2 bay leaves
3 tablespoons all-purpose flour
$2^{1}/_{2}$ cups milk
$^{3}/_{4}$ cup whipping cream
2 egg yolks
1 teaspoon salt
$^{1}/_{4}$ teaspoon ground black pepper
Whipping cream to garnish

In a Dutch oven, heat water to boiling. Add lobster tails, cover, and cook about 12 minutes or until lobster is pink. Remove lobster from water. Reserve 4 cups of water used in cooking lobster tails. When cool enough to handle, remove lobster meat from shells and finely dice; chill.

For stock, melt 3 tablespoons butter in Dutch oven over medium heat. Stir in cognac. Bring mixture to a boil and simmer 3 minutes. Stir in reserved 4 cups water, $^{1}/_{2}$ cup green onions, and next 7 ingredients. Simmer 30 minutes longer. Strain into a large bowl.

In Dutch oven, melt remaining 3 tablespoons butter over medium-high heat. Add remaining 3 tablespoons green onions and sauté 2 minutes. Whisk flour into butter mixture and cook 1 minute longer, stirring constantly. Whisk in stock and next 5 ingredients until blended.

Bring to a boil, reduce heat to medium-low, and simmer 5 minutes. Stir in lobster meat. Simmer 10 to 15 minutes longer or until heated through. Garnish each serving with about 1 tablespoon whipping cream and swirl with a knife. Serve immediately.
Yield: about 8 servings

CREAMY CELERY-POTATO SOUP

6 cups coarsely chopped celery
5 cups peeled and coarsely chopped potatoes
1 cup chopped green onions
3 cans ($14^{1}/_{2}$ ounces each) fat-free chicken broth
2 tablespoons freshly squeezed lemon juice
1 teaspoon dried tarragon leaves
$^{3}/_{4}$ teaspoon salt
$^{1}/_{2}$ teaspoon ground white pepper
1 cup plain low-fat yogurt
2 teaspoons cornstarch
Celery leaves to garnish

In a large Dutch oven, combine celery, potatoes, onions, and chicken broth. Cover and cook over medium-low heat 1 hour or until vegetables are tender. Reserving broth, use a slotted spoon to transfer vegetables to a food processor; purée vegetables. Return puréed vegetables to broth in Dutch oven. Stir in lemon juice, tarragon leaves, salt, and white pepper. Cover and cook over medium-low heat 10 minutes or until mixture begins to simmer (do not boil). Remove soup from heat. In a small bowl, whisk yogurt and cornstarch until well blended. Gradually stir yogurt mixture into soup. Garnish with celery leaves. Serve immediately.
Yield: about 12 cups soup

TORTILLA SOUP
(Shown on page 6)

- 6 cans (14$^{1}/_{2}$ ounces each) chicken broth
- 2 cans (4$^{1}/_{2}$ ounces each) chopped mild green chiles, undrained
- $^{1}/_{3}$ cup fresh mint leaves
- 2 cloves garlic, minced
- 1 teaspoon chili powder
- 1 teaspoon ground cumin
- 1 cup chopped fresh tomatoes
- 2 avocados, peeled, pitted, and chopped
- $^{1}/_{2}$ cup chopped fresh cilantro
- 4 slices bacon, cooked and crumbled
- 3 cups coarsely crushed tortilla chips
  Sour cream and fresh cilantro to garnish

For soup, combine chicken broth, chiles, mint leaves, garlic, chili powder, and cumin in a Dutch oven. Bring to a boil. Reduce heat to medium, cover, and simmer 1 hour.

While broth is simmering, combine tomatoes, avocados, chopped cilantro, and bacon in a medium bowl; set aside. Strain broth and return to pan; bring to a boil again.

To serve, spoon about $^{1}/_{4}$ cup each of avocado mixture and tortilla chips into each bowl. Ladle broth into each bowl. Garnish with sour cream and cilantro. Serve immediately.

Yield: about 12 servings

TOMATO MOUSSE SALAD

- 2 envelopes unflavored gelatin
- $^{1}/_{2}$ cup cold water
- 1 can (10$^{3}/_{4}$ ounces) condensed tomato soup, undiluted
- $^{1}/_{2}$ cup mayonnaise
- 2 tablespoons chopped fresh parsley
- 1 tablespoon lemon juice
- 1 tablespoon dried dill weed
- 2 to 3 drops hot pepper sauce
- 1 cup sour cream
- 1 medium tomato, finely chopped
- $^{1}/_{2}$ cup finely chopped green pepper
- $^{1}/_{2}$ cup peeled chopped cucumber
- $^{1}/_{4}$ cup finely chopped onion
  Avocado slices and sour cream for garnish

Soften gelatin in water. Heat soup in a medium saucepan and add softened gelatin. Whisk in mayonnaise, parsley, lemon juice, dill weed, and pepper sauce. Fold in 1 cup sour cream. Chill mixture until partially set.

Fold in tomato, green pepper, cucumber, and onion. Pour into a well-oiled 9-inch square pan. Chill 4 to 6 hours or until set. Garnish with avocado slices and sour cream.

Yield: 8 to 10 servings

Savory Corn Chowder makes a satisfying light meal or first course. We used a pumpkin and acorn squash halves for our soup tureen and bowls.

CORN CHOWDER

¹/₄ pound salt pork, skin removed
     and thinly sliced
 1 medium onion, chopped
 2 large baking potatoes, peeled and
     chopped
 3 cups water, divided
 1 cup finely crushed cracker crumbs
 3 cups milk
 1 can (17 ounces) creamed corn
1¹/₂ teaspoons salt
 1 teaspoon ground nutmeg

In a large saucepan, fry salt pork with onion until pork is crisp and browned. Stir in potatoes and 2 cups water. Cook over medium heat until potatoes are tender. Combine cracker crumbs and milk; stir into potato mixture. Stir in corn, salt, nutmeg, and remaining 1 cup water. Reduce heat to medium-low and cook, stirring occasionally, 10 minutes or until heated through.

Yield: about 8¹/₂ cups of chowder

A flavorful medley of fresh spinach, beets, lemons, and nuts, Compound Sallet is tossed with a vinaigrette dressing.

COMPOUND SALLET

DRESSING

- 1 cup olive oil
- 1/3 cup red wine vinegar
- 2 tablespoons granulated sugar

SALAD

- 2 bunches fresh spinach, rinsed and torn into pieces
- 1 cup currants
- 1 cup chopped canned red beets
- 1 lemon, peeled, thinly sliced, and seeds removed
- 1 cup toasted slivered almonds
- 1/4 cup drained capers

For dressing, combine oil, vinegar, and sugar in a jar with a tight-fitting lid. Close jar and shake vigorously to blend.

For salad, combine spinach, currants, beets, lemon slices, almonds, and capers in a serving bowl.

To serve, pour dressing over salad and toss.

Yield: about 8 servings

VIRGINIA SALAD

1 package (3 ounces) lime-flavored gelatin
1/2 cup boiling water
1/4 cup minced onion
1/2 cup finely chopped celery
1 container (16 ounces) cottage cheese
2 cups frozen whipped topping, thawed
1/2 cup mayonnaise
1/2 cup chopped walnuts

In a large bowl, dissolve gelatin in water. Stir in remaining ingredients; mix well. Pour into a 2-quart bowl. Cover and refrigerate 8 hours or overnight.
Yield: 8 to 10 servings

MARINATED ONIONS AND OLIVES

1/4 cup olive oil
2 tablespoons freshly squeezed lime juice (about 1 lime)
2 tablespoons white wine vinegar
2 cloves garlic, minced
1 teaspoon dried red pepper flakes
1 teaspoon cumin seed
1 can (6 ounces) small pitted ripe olives, drained
2 jars (3 ounces each) pimiento-stuffed green olives, drained
1 jar (3 ounces) almond-stuffed green olives, drained
2 jars (3 ounces each) cocktail onions, drained
3 tablespoons chopped fresh cilantro

Combine olive oil, lime juice, vinegar, garlic, red pepper flakes, and cumin seed in a medium saucepan. Bring to a boil over medium-high heat. Remove from heat and allow to cool. Stir in olives, onions, and cilantro. Transfer mixture to an airtight container. Chill overnight to allow flavors to blend. Serve at room temperature.
Yield: about 4 cups olives

STRAWBERRY SALAD SUPREME

- 2 packages (3 ounces each) strawberry gelatin
- 2 cups boiling water
- 1 can (20 ounces) crushed pineapple, drained and juice reserved
- 1 package (16 ounces) frozen sweetened strawberries
- 3 bananas, sliced
- 1 envelope (1.4 ounces) whipped topping mix and ingredients to prepare
- 1 package (8 ounces) cream cheese, softened
- 3/4 cup sugar
- 2 eggs, beaten
- 2 tablespoons all-purpose flour
- 1 tablespoon lemon juice
- 1 cup chopped pecans

Place gelatin in a large bowl; add boiling water and stir until gelatin dissolves. Stir in pineapple, strawberries (including juice), and bananas. Pour into a 9 x 13-inch pan; chill until firm.

Prepare whipped topping according to package directions. Blend in cream cheese. Spread on congealed gelatin; cover and chill.

Add enough water to reserved pineapple juice to make 1 cup. Combine pineapple juice mixture, sugar, eggs, flour, and lemon juice in a saucepan over low heat. Cook, stirring constantly, until mixture thickens; chill. Spread over cream cheese layer and sprinkle with pecans.
Yield: 12 to 14 servings

ZESTY GREEN BEAN SALAD

- 2/3 cup bottled chili sauce
- 2 cloves garlic, minced
- 2 tablespoons vegetable oil
- 1 tablespoon chopped fresh parsley
- 1 tablespoon freshly squeezed lemon juice
- 4 cups previously cooked or canned green beans, drained
- 3/4 cup finely chopped green pepper
- 1/2 small red onion, very thinly sliced and separated into rings
  Lettuce leaves
- 8 slices bacon, cooked and crumbled
  Hard-cooked egg, sliced

In a small bowl, combine chili sauce, garlic, oil, parsley, and lemon juice; stir until well blended. In a medium bowl, combine green beans and green pepper. Pour chili sauce mixture over green bean mixture; toss until well coated. Cover and chill 2 hours.

To serve, add onion rings to salad; toss. Line a serving bowl with lettuce leaves. Spoon salad over lettuce. Sprinkle with bacon and top with egg slices.
Yield: about 10 servings

FESTIVE CABBAGE SLAW

11 cups finely shredded green
   cabbage
8 cups finely shredded Savoy
   cabbage
4 cups finely shredded Napa
   cabbage
2¼ cups finely chopped onions
1 cup finely chopped green pepper
1 cup finely chopped sweet red
   pepper
¾ cup finely shredded carrots
2 cups sugar
1¼ cups apple cider vinegar
⅓ cup vegetable oil
1 tablespoon salt
1 tablespoon celery seed
1 teaspoon dry mustard
½ teaspoon ground black pepper

In a very large bowl, combine
cabbages, onions, peppers, and carrots.
In a medium saucepan, combine sugar,
vinegar, oil, salt, celery seed, dry mustard,
and black pepper. Stirring frequently,
cook over medium-high heat about
6 minutes or until mixture comes to
a boil. Pour hot vinegar mixture over
cabbage mixture. Toss until vegetables
are well coated. Cover and chill 8 hours.
Yield: about 13 cups slaw

CRUNCHY COLESLAW

6 cups shredded green cabbage
¾ cup shredded carrots
6 green onions, chopped
½ cup sliced almonds
½ cup lightly salted roasted
   sunflower kernels
1 package (3 ounces) chicken-
   flavored ramen noodle soup
   mix
¼ cup vegetable oil
2 tablespoons sugar
2 tablespoons red wine vinegar
½ teaspoon salt
½ teaspoon ground black pepper

In a large bowl, combine cabbage,
carrots, onions, almonds, and sunflower
kernels. In a small bowl, whisk seasoning
packet from ramen noodles, oil, sugar,
vinegar, salt, and pepper. Pour oil mixture
over cabbage mixture; stir until well
coated. Cover and chill until ready
to serve.
   To serve, crush ramen noodles and stir
into cabbage mixture. Serve immediately.
Yield: about 7 cups coleslaw

WILD RICE SALAD

(Shown on page 195)

VINAIGRETTE
- 1 can (15¼ ounces) pineapple tidbits in juice
- ¼ cup rice wine vinegar
- 1 tablespoon dark sesame oil
- 1 tablespoon vegetable oil
- 1 tablespoon soy sauce
- 2 teaspoons sugar
- ¼ teaspoon ground red pepper

SALAD
- 2 cans (14½ ounces each) chicken broth
- 1 cup uncooked wild rice, rinsed
- 1 cup uncooked basmati rice
- 1½ cups shredded carrots (about 2 carrots)
- ½ cup golden raisins
- ½ cup sliced celery
- 2 tablespoons finely chopped green onion
  Carrot curls to garnish

For vinaigrette, drain pineapple, reserving juice. Set aside pineapple for salad. Combine reserved juice, vinegar, sesame oil, vegetable oil, soy sauce, sugar, and red pepper in a small bowl. Stir until well blended. Cover and let stand at room temperature to let flavors blend.

For salad, combine chicken broth and wild rice in a heavy large saucepan. Bring to a boil over medium-high heat. Stir rice and cover; reduce heat to low and simmer about 30 minutes. Stir in basmati rice and continue to simmer about 20 minutes or until rice is tender. Transfer rice to a 2½-quart serving bowl and allow to cool. Stir after 15 minutes.

Add reserved pineapple, carrots, raisins, celery, and green onion to rice; lightly toss. Pour vinaigrette over salad and lightly toss until salad is coated. Garnish with carrot curls. Serve at room temperature.

Yield: about 11 cups salad

STUFFED BABY BEETS

- 2 jars (16 ounces each) small whole pickled beets, drained
- 1 package (3 ounces) cream cheese, softened
- 2 tablespoons minced sweet pickle
- 1 tablespoon minced onion
- 1 teaspoon freshly squeezed lemon juice
- ⅛ teaspoon salt
- 2 hard-cooked eggs, finely chopped
  Fresh dill weed to garnish

Scoop out a small portion of each beet with a melon baller; set beets aside. In a small bowl, beat cream cheese until fluffy. Stir in pickle, onion, lemon juice, and salt. Stir in eggs. Spoon mixture into a pastry bag fitted with a large open star tip. Pipe filling into beets. Garnish with dill weed.

Yield: about 32 beets

BLACK-EYED PEA SALAD

3 cans (15 ounces each) black-
    eyed peas, drained
1 can (14½ ounces) cut green
    beans, drained
1 cup small cauliflower flowerets
1 small red onion, sliced and
    separated into rings
¼ cup chopped sweet red pepper
½ cup vegetable oil
½ cup white wine vinegar
1 clove garlic, minced
1 teaspoon chili powder
½ teaspoon salt
¼ teaspoon ground black pepper
    Salad greens

In a large bowl, combine black-eyed
peas, green beans, cauliflower, onion
rings, and red pepper. In a small bowl,
combine oil, vinegar, garlic, chili powder,
salt, and black pepper. Pour dressing
over black-eyed pea mixture; toss until
well coated. Cover and chill until ready
to serve.

To serve, place a bed of salad greens
in a serving bowl. Spoon black-eyed pea
mixture over greens.

Yield: 14 to 16 servings

FRESH BROCCOLI-MANDARIN SALAD

1 egg plus 1 egg yolk, lightly
    beaten
½ cup granulated sugar
1½ teaspoons cornstarch
1 teaspoon dry mustard
¼ cup tarragon wine vinegar
¼ cup water
½ cup mayonnaise
3 tablespoons butter or margarine,
    softened
4 cups fresh broccoli flowerets
2 cups sliced fresh mushrooms
1 can (11 ounces) mandarin oranges,
    drained
½ cup raisins
½ cup slivered almonds, toasted
½ large red onion, sliced
6 slices bacon, cooked and
    crumbled

In the top of a double boiler, whisk
together egg, egg yolk, sugar, cornstarch,
and dry mustard. Combine vinegar and
water. Slowly pour into egg mixture,
whisking constantly. Place over
simmering water and cook, stirring
constantly, until mixture thickens.
Remove from heat; stir in mayonnaise
and butter. Chill.

To serve, toss dressing with broccoli,
mushrooms, oranges, raisins, almonds,
onion, and bacon in a serving bowl.

Yield: 10 to 12 servings

Spinach Salad with Warm Dressing features fresh mushrooms, toasted almonds, and crisp bacon. Warming the dressing intensifies its spicy vinegar flavor.

SPINACH SALAD WITH WARM DRESSING

DRESSING

- 1/2 cup red wine vinegar
- 1/2 cup olive oil
- 1/4 cup water
- 2 teaspoons lemon juice
- 1 teaspoon Dijon-style mustard
- 1 teaspoon Worcestershire sauce
- 1 tablespoon granulated sugar
- 3/4 teaspoon garlic salt
- 1/4 teaspoon ground black pepper

SALAD

- 1 bunch fresh spinach, rinsed and torn into pieces
- 1 bunch red leaf lettuce, rinsed and torn into pieces
- 1/2 pound fresh mushrooms, sliced
- 1/2 cup slivered almonds, toasted
- 3 green onions, chopped
- 4 slices bacon, cooked and crumbled

For dressing combine all ingredients in a jar with a tight-fitting lid. Close jar and shake vigorously.

For salad, toss all ingredients together in serving bowl.

To serve, pour dressing into a non-aluminum saucepan and stir over medium heat until heated through. Serve warm dressing with salad.

Yield: 8 to 10 servings

CRANBERRY-FILLED STUFFING RING

CRANBERRY FILLING
- 1 can (16 ounces) whole berry cranberry sauce
- 1/4 cup prepared horseradish
- 2 tablespoons sour cream

STUFFING
- 3/4 cup butter or margarine
- 3 cups coarsely chopped onions (about 2 large onions)
- 1 cup coarsely chopped celery (about 3 ribs celery)
- 4 cups corn bread crumbs
- 5 slices white bread, torn into small pieces (about 4 cups)
- 2 tablespoons rubbed sage
- 2 teaspoons poultry seasoning
- 1 teaspoon salt
- 1/2 teaspoon ground black pepper
- 4 eggs, beaten
- 1 can (14 1/2 ounces) chicken broth

For cranberry filling, combine cranberry sauce, horseradish, and sour cream in a medium saucepan. Bring to a boil over medium heat. Continue to cook, stirring occasionally, 10 to 12 minutes or until filling begins to thicken. Remove from heat; set aside.

For stuffing, melt butter in a large skillet over medium heat. Add onions and celery; sauté until tender. Remove from heat. In a large bowl, combine corn bread crumbs, white bread, sage, poultry seasoning, salt, and pepper. Stir in onion mixture, eggs, and chicken broth.

Preheat oven to 350 degrees. Spread half of stuffing into a heavily greased 10-inch springform tube pan. Bake 30 minutes. Pour filling evenly over baked stuffing. Spread remaining stuffing evenly over filling. Bake 45 to 55 minutes longer or until top is brown. Loosen sides of pan. Invert onto a serving plate. Slice and serve immediately.

Yield: 12 to 16 servings

SAUSAGE-PECAN STUFFING

1 pound mild pork sausage
1 onion, chopped
1 cup coarsely chopped celery
4 cups coarsely crumbled cornbread
3 cups plain croutons
3 apples, peeled, cored, and diced
1 cup chopped pecans
1/2 cup chopped dried apricots
2 tablespoons ground sage
2 teaspoons poultry seasoning
1 teaspoon salt
1/2 teaspoon ground black pepper
4 eggs, beaten
1 can (14 1/2 ounces) chicken broth

In a medium skillet, cook sausage until brown. Reserving drippings, transfer sausage to paper towels to drain; crumble sausage. Add onion and celery to drippings in skillet; cook until tender. Remove from heat. Preheat oven to 375 degrees. In a large bowl, combine next 9 ingredients. Stir in onion mixture, sausage, eggs, and chicken broth. Spoon into a greased 9 x 13-inch baking dish; cover and bake 50 minutes. Uncover and bake 10 minutes longer or until top is brown. Serve warm.
Yield: about 10 servings

CORN BREAD DRESSING WITH DRIED FRUIT

1 1/2 cups dried mixed fruit bits
1/2 cup butter
1 medium onion, chopped
1 cup chopped celery
5 cups corn bread crumbs
2 cups white bread crumbs
1 1/2 cups chicken broth
1 1/2 teaspoons rubbed sage
1 teaspoon poultry seasoning
1 teaspoon salt
1/2 teaspoon ground black pepper
1 egg, lightly beaten

Place fruit in a bowl and add enough water to cover fruit. Cover and allow fruit to sit at room temperature overnight.
Preheat oven to 350 degrees. Melt butter in skillet. Add onion and celery and sauté until onion is transparent. Remove from heat and set aside.
Drain fruit. In a large mixing bowl, combine fruit, sautéed mixture, bread crumbs, chicken broth, sage, poultry seasoning, salt, and pepper, adjusting seasoning as desired. Stir in egg. Spoon dressing into a lightly greased 2-quart baking dish. Cover with aluminum foil and bake 25 to 30 minutes or until dressing is heated through.
Yield: about 10 servings

OYSTER DRESSING

4 cups water
Giblets and neck from turkey
1 cup chopped onion
1 cup chopped celery
1/2 cup butter or margarine
3/4 cup sliced fresh mushrooms
7 cups corn bread crumbs
1/4 cup chopped fresh parsley
2 teaspoons poultry seasoning
2 teaspoons rubbed sage
1 teaspoon salt
2 containers (10 ounces each)
fresh oysters, drained and
chopped
2 eggs, beaten

Place water, giblets, and neck in a medium saucepan; bring to a boil over medium heat. Cover, reduce heat, and simmer 1 hour or until meat is tender. Reserve broth and chop meat.

Preheat oven to 350 degrees. In a medium skillet, sauté onion and celery in butter over medium heat. When vegetables are almost tender, add mushrooms; cook 2 minutes and remove from heat. In a large bowl, combine crumbs, parsley, poultry seasoning, sage, salt, meat, and vegetables. Stir in oysters, eggs, and 2 cups giblet broth, adding additional broth as necessary to moisten. Spoon into a greased 9 x 13-inch baking dish. Cover and bake 45 minutes. Uncover and bake 15 to 20 minutes or until lightly browned. Serve warm.

Yield: 12 to 14 servings

GREEN BEAN AND MUSHROOM BAKE
(Shown on page 222)

1 can (10^3/4 ounces) golden
mushroom soup
2 cups (8 ounces) shredded
Swiss cheese, divided
1 cup sour cream
2 tablespoons white wine
1/2 teaspoon salt
1/2 teaspoon lemon pepper
1/4 teaspoon ground black pepper
8 ounces fresh mushrooms, sliced
3/4 cup finely chopped onion
1 clove garlic, minced
3 tablespoons butter or margarine
3 cans (14^1/2 ounces each)
French-style green beans,
drained
1/3 cup coarsely chopped slivered
almonds

Preheat oven to 325 degrees. In a medium bowl, combine soup, 1 cup cheese, sour cream, wine, salt, lemon pepper, and black pepper. In a large skillet, sauté mushrooms, onion, and garlic in butter over medium heat just until vegetables are tender. Remove from heat and stir in green beans. Stir in soup mixture. Spoon mixture into a greased 9 x 13-inch baking dish. Sprinkle remaining 1 cup cheese over casserole. Sprinkle almonds over casserole. Bake 35 to 45 minutes or until casserole is heated through; serve warm.

Yield: 12 to 14 servings

Corn bread dressing, a Southern great, is given an Eastern Seaboard flavor with fresh shellfish. Moist Oyster Dressing is packed with the flavorful taste of sage and other seasonings.

GREEN BEANS WITH DILL SAUCE

1 cup sour cream, at room temperature
6 slices bacon, cooked and crumbled
1 tablespoon chopped dried chives
1¹/₂ teaspoons lemon pepper
1 teaspoon dried dill weed
Salt
2 packages (10 ounces each) frozen French-style green beans

Combine first 5 ingredients in small saucepan. Salt to taste and set aside (do not refrigerate). Cook green beans according to package directions. Warm sour cream mixture over low heat, stirring constantly. Drain green beans and place about ¹/₂ cup on each serving plate. Indent center of beans with the back of spoon. Place a heaping tablespoon of dill sauce in center of beans.
Yield: about 8 servings

GREEN BEAN SAUTÉ
(Shown on page 6)

¹/₄ cup butter or margarine
1 pound fresh mushrooms, sliced
¹/₂ cup finely chopped onion
2 cloves garlic, minced
1 teaspoon salt
¹/₂ teaspoon ground black pepper
2 cans (16 ounces each) cut green beans, drained
1 cup (7 ounces) crumbled feta cheese

In a large skillet, melt butter over medium heat. Add mushrooms, onion, garlic, salt, and pepper; cook until mushrooms are tender. Add green beans cook 5 to 7 minutes or until heated through. Stir in cheese. Serve hot.
Yield: about 10 servings

WINTER VEGETABLE TRIO

2 pounds rutabagas, peeled and quartered
2 pounds turnips, peeled and quartered
2 pounds russet potatoes, peeled and quartered
1 cup butter or margarine, softened
1 cup whipping cream
2 teaspoons salt
1 teaspoon ground black pepper
Shredded Cheddar cheese and chopped fresh parsley to garnish

In an 8-quart stockpot, cover rutabaga with salted water. Bring to a boil and cook 15 minutes. Add turnips, potatoes, and enough water to cover vegetables. Bring to a boil again and cook until vegetables are tender; drain.
Transfer vegetables to a very large bowl. Add butter, whipping cream, salt, and pepper. Using an electric mixer, beat vegetables until light and fluffy. Garnish with cheese and parsley.
Yield: about 16 servings

CARAMELIZED ONIONS

- 2 pounds pearl onions, peeled
- 1/4 cup butter or margarine
- 2 tablespoons firmly packed brown sugar
- 1 tablespoon grated orange zest
- 1/8 teaspoon salt
- 1/8 teaspoon paprika

In a large saucepan, cover onions with water. Cover and cook over medium-high heat 10 to 12 minutes or until onions are almost tender; drain. In a heavy large skillet, combine onions and butter. Stirring frequently, cook over medium-high heat about 30 minutes or until golden brown. In a small bowl, combine remaining ingredients. Add brown sugar mixture to onions. Stirring constantly, cook until onions are evenly coated and browned. Serve warm.
Yield: about 6 servings

GLAZED BAKED ONIONS

This is a good make-ahead recipe.

- 4 medium onions
  Chicken broth
- 2 packages (10 ounces each) frozen green peas, cooked
- 1/2 cup soft bread crumbs
- 5 tablespoons butter or margarine
- 1/4 cup grated Parmesan cheese
- 2 tablespoons chopped fresh parsley
- 1/2 teaspoon dry mustard
  Melted butter or margarine
  Pimiento strips to garnish

Peel and halve onions. Place in a large saucepan in 2 inches of chicken broth. Bring to a boil, cover, and reduce heat. Simmer 20 minutes or until onions are tender but still firm; drain well. Gently lift out centers of onions, leaving a shell 2 to 3 layers thick. Fill centers with peas.

Combine bread crumbs, 5 tablespoons butter, Parmesan cheese, parsley, and dry mustard. Sprinkle mixture over onions. Drizzle with melted butter. (To serve later, cover onions and chill.) Broil 5 to 7 minutes or until lightly browned. Garnish with pimiento strips.
Yield: 8 servings

LEMON-PARSLEY ASPARAGUS

- 1/2 cup butter, divided
- 1 tablespoon sesame seed
- 1 tablespoon finely minced onion
- 2 tablespoons chopped fresh parsley
- 2 tablespoons freshly squeezed lemon juice
- 1/2 teaspoon grated lemon zest
- 1/2 teaspoon salt
- 1/4 teaspoon ground black pepper
- 4 cans (15 ounces each) asparagus spears, drained
  Lemon zest strips and fresh parsley to garnish

In a medium skillet, combine 2 tablespoons butter, sesame seed, and onion over medium heat. Stirring frequently, cook until sesame seed is lightly browned and onion is tender. Add remaining 6 tablespoons butter, stirring constantly until butter melts. Remove from heat and stir in chopped parsley, lemon juice, lemon zest, salt, and pepper.

Place asparagus in a microwave-safe serving dish. Cover and microwave on high power (100%) 3 to 5 minutes or until heated through, rotating dish halfway through cooking time. Pour butter mixture over asparagus. Garnish with lemon zest strips and parsley. Serve warm.
Yield: 8 to 10 servings

Christmas Cauliflower (top, recipe on page 216) and old-fashioned Corn Pudding (recipe on page 234) will delight the vegetable lovers in your family.

Peas, Mushrooms, and Onions in Cream Sauce (left, recipe below) and Baby Carrots with Horseradish (recipe on page 216) bring color and great taste to the table.

PEAS, MUSHROOMS, AND ONIONS IN CREAM SAUCE

2 tablespoons butter or margarine
2 tablespoons all-purpose flour
1 can (12 ounces) evaporated milk
1 package (10 ounces) frozen green peas, thawed
1 jar (16 ounces) pearl onions, drained
1 jar (4 ounces) pimientos, drained
1 can (4 ounces) button mushrooms, drained
Salt and ground black pepper

Preheat oven to 350 degrees. Melt butter in a large saucepan over medium heat. Stir in flour. Add evaporated milk, stirring constantly. Increase heat and cook until mixture thickens. Remove from heat. Stir in peas, onions, pimientos, and mushrooms. Salt and pepper to taste. Pour into a lightly greased 1$^{1}/_{2}$-quart baking dish. Bake 20 to 25 minutes or until bubbly.
Yield: 6 to 8 servings

BABY CARROTS WITH HORSERADISH

(Shown on page 215)

- 1 package (10 ounces) frozen baby carrots
- 2 cups water
- 1 cup mayonnaise
- 2 tablespoons grated onion
- 2 tablespoons prepared horseradish
- 1/2 teaspoon salt
- 1/4 teaspoon ground black pepper
- 1/4 cup cracker crumbs
- 2 tablespoons butter, cut into small pieces
  Paprika

Cook carrots in water until tender. Drain carrots, reserving 1/4 cup liquid. Combine reserved liquid with next 5 ingredients.

Preheat oven to 375 degrees. Place carrots in lightly greased 8-inch square baking dish. Pour sauce over carrots. Sprinkle with cracker crumbs; dot with butter. Sprinkle with paprika. Bake 15 to 20 minutes or until heated through.
Yield: about 6 servings

CHRISTMAS CAULIFLOWER

(Shown on page 214)

- 2 packages (10 ounces each) frozen chopped broccoli
- 1/2 cup whipping cream
- 1/3 cup chicken broth
- 7 tablespoons butter, melted
- 1/4 cup sour cream
- 1/4 teaspoon ground nutmeg
  Salt and ground black pepper
- 1 large head cauliflower

Cook broccoli according to package directions. Drain well. Place broccoli in blender or food processor. Add whipping

216

cream, chicken broth, butter, sour cream, and nutmeg; purée until smooth. Salt and pepper to taste. Transfer to a saucepan over low heat.

Steam whole cauliflower until tender. Place on a heated serving platter and spoon warm broccoli purée over top of cauliflower.
Yield: 6 to 8 servings

APPLE AND VEGETABLE SAUTÉ

- 1/2 cup butter or margarine
- 5 medium unpeeled turnips, quartered
- 4 medium carrots, cut into 2-inch-long pieces
- 3 medium onions, quartered with root ends intact
- 1 cup firmly packed brown sugar
- 2 unpeeled Granny Smith apples, cored and cut into eighths
- 2 unpeeled Rome apples, cored and cut into eighths
- 1 tablespoon balsamic vinegar
- 1/2 teaspoon salt
- 1/2 teaspoon ground black pepper

Melt butter in a 12-inch-diameter by 2 1/2-inch-deep heavy skillet over medium-high heat. Add turnips to butter; sauté about 5 minutes. Add carrots and onions; cook on 1 side about 10 minutes or until golden brown. Carefully turn vegetables over and brown other side. Sprinkle brown sugar over mixture. Reduce heat to medium; continue to cook about 20 minutes or until vegetables are almost tender. Add apples to vegetables. Cook mixture about 7 to 10 minutes or until apples are completely browned and tender, carefully turning as necessary. Add vinegar, salt, and pepper; toss lightly. Serve immediately.
Yield: 8 to 10 servings

ZUCCHINI-CARROT AU GRATIN

(Shown on page 219)

    3   cups thinly sliced carrots
            (about 4 large carrots)
    7   cups sliced zucchini (about
            2 pounds)
  1/4   cup butter or margarine, cut into
            small pieces
    1   teaspoon salt
  1/2   teaspoon ground black pepper
    6   ounces Gruyère cheese, shredded
  1/2   cup chicken broth

In a large saucepan, cover carrots with water. Bring water to a boil and cook carrots 3 to 5 minutes or until just tender; drain.

Preheat oven to 375 degrees. Place zucchini in a greased 9 x 13-inch glass baking dish. Place carrots over zucchini. Place pieces of butter evenly over carrots. Sprinkle salt, pepper, and cheese evenly over vegetables. Pour chicken broth evenly over top. Cover and bake 20 minutes. Bake, uncovered, 25 to 30 minutes longer or until cheese browns and vegetables are tender. Serve warm.
Yield: 8 to 10 servings

CREAMY MINT CARROTS

(Shown on page 218)

    5   cups thinly sliced carrots (about
            1 1/2 pounds)
    3   cups plus 2 teaspoons water,
            divided
    1   teaspoon cornstarch
    1   cup whipping cream
  1/4   cup firmly packed brown sugar
  1/4   cup chopped fresh mint leaves
    2   tablespoons butter or margarine
    1   teaspoon salt
  1/2   teaspoon ground black pepper

Cover carrots with 3 cups water in a large saucepan; bring to a boil. Cook carrots 3 to 5 minutes or until just tender; drain carrots and return to pan.

In a small bowl, combine cornstarch and 2 teaspoons water; stir until smooth. In a small saucepan, bring cream to a boil. Whisking constantly, add cornstarch mixture to cream, bring to a boil, and cook until thickened. Stir in remaining ingredients. Stir cream mixture into carrots. Serve warm.
Yield: about 10 servings

Creamy Pesto Spinach (recipe on page 220) is presented in tomato cups to create a festive color combination.

Served with a lightly sweetened sauce, Creamy Mint Carrots (recipe on page 217) offer a delightful flavor combination. Colorful Red Cabbage and Apples (recipe on page 220) is simmered in a tangy broth.

Make holiday dinners special with fancy side dishes. Honey-Glazed New Potatoes (top, recipe on page 221) get a hint of sweetness from honey. Fluffy Broccoli Timbales (middle, recipe on page 229) are well seasoned with garlic. Gruyère cheese gives Zucchini-Carrot au Gratin (recipe on page 217) its distinctive flavor.

RED CABBAGE AND APPLES

(Shown on page 218)

$^1/_4$ cup butter or margarine
2 onions, chopped
2 teaspoons salt
$^3/_4$ teaspoon ground black pepper
$^1/_2$ teaspoon ground nutmeg
2 pounds red cabbage, chopped
4 apples, peeled, cored, and
    sliced
1 can (14$^1/_2$ ounces) chicken
    broth
3 tablespoons lemon juice
2 tablespoons apple cider vinegar

In a Dutch oven, melt butter over medium heat. Stir in onions, salt, pepper, and nutmeg; cook until onions are tender. Stir in cabbage, apples, chicken broth, lemon juice, and vinegar; bring to a boil. Reduce heat to medium-low, cover, and simmer 25 to 30 minutes or until cabbage and apples are tender. Serve warm.
Yield: about 12 servings

ENGLISH CHRISTMAS CABBAGE

$^1/_2$ pound bacon
2 cans (14$^1/_2$ ounces each) beef
    broth
$^1/_2$ cup firmly packed brown sugar
$^1/_4$ cup apple cider vinegar
2 teaspoons salt
1 teaspoon ground black pepper
3 pounds red cabbage, shredded

In a Dutch oven, cook bacon over medium-high heat until crisp. Reserving drippings, remove bacon from pan; crumble and set aside. Add beef broth, brown sugar, vinegar, salt, and pepper to bacon drippings in Dutch oven. Cook over medium-high heat, stirring until sugar dissolves and mixture comes to a boil. Add cabbage and bring to a boil. Reduce heat to medium-low, cover, and simmer 30 minutes. Transfer to a serving bowl; sprinkle crumbled bacon over cabbage. Serve hot.
Yield: about 16 servings

CREAMY PESTO SPINACH

(Shown on page 218)

3 medium tomatoes
1 tablespoon salt
2 packages (10 ounces each) frozen
    chopped spinach, thawed and
    squeezed dry
$^1/_4$ cup purchased pesto sauce
$^1/_2$ cup whipping cream
$^2/_3$ cup grated Romano cheese
1 teaspoon ground black pepper
1 tablespoon grated Parmesan
    cheese

Cut tomatoes in half; remove seeds and pulp. Sprinkle salt inside tomato shells and turn upside down on a wire rack to drain 30 minutes. Use a paper towel to pat inside of each tomato dry.

Preheat oven to 400 degrees. In a medium skillet, cook spinach over medium heat 5 to 10 minutes or until heated through. Stir in pesto sauce; cook 2 to 3 minutes longer. Stir in cream; cook until mixture is thick (about 2 minutes). Stir in Romano cheese and pepper. Spoon about $^1/_2$ cup spinach into each tomato shell. Sprinkle Parmesan cheese over top. Bake in a greased 8-inch square baking pan 10 minutes or until heated through. Serve immediately.
Yield: 6 servings

HONEY-GLAZED NEW POTATOES

(shown on page 219)

2½ pounds new potatoes, cut into
     quarters
½   cup butter or margarine
¼   cup water
2   tablespoons honey
1   teaspoon salt
¼   teaspoon ground black pepper

In a large saucepan or Dutch oven, cover potatoes with salted water. Bring water to a boil and cook until potatoes are tender; drain.

In a large skillet, melt butter over medium heat. Stir in water, honey, salt, and pepper. Stirring occasionally, cook 1 layer of potatoes at a time 10 to 12 minutes or until brown. Transfer to serving dish and cover with aluminum foil to keep warm. Serve warm.

Yield: 6 to 8 servings

CARAMELIZED NEW POTATOES

(shown on page 230)

20 small new potatoes
½   cup butter or margarine
½   cup firmly packed brown sugar

Cook unpeeled potatoes in well-salted boiling water 15 to 20 minutes or until tender. Remove from heat, drain, and allow to cool slightly; peel.

Melt butter in a heavy large skillet over medium heat. Stir in brown sugar and cook, stirring constantly, until mixture bubbles and thickens slightly (about minutes). Add potatoes and cook to 3 minutes, stirring constantly until potatoes are thoroughly coated with caramel. Place in a heated serving dish and serve immediately.

Yield: 8 to 10 servings

STUFFED POTATOES

10 small russet potatoes, baked
2   cups fat-free cottage cheese
1   teaspoon salt
¼   teaspoon ground black pepper
2   tablespoons reduced-calorie
     margarine
1   cup finely chopped onions
1   cup chopped fresh mushrooms
1   clove garlic, minced
     Vegetable cooking spray
2   cups (8 ounces) finely shredded
     fat-free Cheddar cheese
¼   cup chopped fresh chives

Preheat oven to 375 degrees. Cut potatoes in half lengthwise. Leaving about ½ inch of pulp on skins, scoop out remaining pulp and place in a large bowl. Add cottage cheese, salt, and pepper to potato pulp; stir until well blended and set aside.

In a medium skillet, melt margarine over medium heat. Add onions, mushrooms, and garlic; cook until onions are tender. Add onion mixture to potato mixture; stir until well blended. Spoon mixture into potato skins and place on a baking sheet sprayed with cooking spray. Sprinkle cheese and chives evenly over stuffed potatoes. Bake 8 to 10 minutes or until cheese is bubbly. Serve warm.

Yield: 20 stuffed potato halves

(Clockwise from top left on plate) Spicy Twice-Baked Sweet Potatoes (recipe on page 224)
feature pineapple and a cinnamony topping. Christmas Succotash (recipe on page 234) add
a sprinkling of crumbled bacon to colorful vegetables. Green Beans with Mushroom Bak
(recipe on page 210) blends almonds, vegetables, and fresh mushrooms.

The sweet-and-sour flavor of Cabbage with Raisins will be a welcome addition to the meal. It's especially colorful served in a hollowed-out pumpkin.

CABBAGE WITH RAISINS

- 1 head (about 2 pounds) red cabbage, quartered
- 1/2 cup raisins
- 1/4 cup butter
- 1/4 cup apple cider vinegar
- 2 tablespoons firmly packed brown sugar

Fill a large saucepan with salted water and bring to a boil. Add cabbage; cover and cook until tender. Remove from heat and drain. Using a large spoon, separate leaves of cabbage. Stir in remaining ingredients. Return saucepan to medium heat and cook 5 minutes.
Yield: 4 to 6 servings

AMBROSIA SWEET POTATOES

- 6 cups cooked sliced sweet potatoes
- 1 orange, sliced
- 1 cup crushed pineapple with juice
- 1/2 cup firmly packed light brown sugar
- 1/2 cup butter, melted
- 1/2 teaspoon salt
- 1/2 cup sweetened shredded coconut

In a buttered 2-quart casserole, alternate layers of potato and orange slices. Mix pineapple, brown sugar, butter, and salt. Pour mixture over potato and orange slices. Sprinkle coconut on top. Bake in a preheated 350-degree oven 30 minutes.
Yield: 8 to 10 servings

SCALLOPED MUSHROOM POTATOES

6 medium unpeeled potatoes
1 1/2 teaspoons salt, divided
1 cup finely chopped onion
1 clove garlic, minced
1/4 cup butter or margarine
1 can (10 3/4 ounces) golden mushroom soup
1 container (8 ounces) sour cream
1/4 teaspoon ground black pepper
8 ounces fresh mushrooms, sliced
1 sweet red pepper, cut into thin rings
3/4 cup coarsely crushed poppy seed crackers
2 tablespoons butter or margarine, melted
1/2 cup shredded Monterey Jack cheese

In a heavy large saucepan, cover potatoes with water and add 1 teaspoon salt. Bring to a boil over medium-high heat. Reduce heat to medium. Cover and cook about 30 minutes or until potatoes are tender. Remove from heat, drain, and cool.

In a heavy medium skillet, sauté onion and garlic in 1/4 cup butter over medium heat until tender. Stir in soup, sour cream, remaining 1/2 teaspoon salt, and black pepper until mixture is well blended. Remove from heat.

Preheat oven to 350 degrees. Peel potatoes and cut into thin slices. Place half of potato slices in a greased 9 x 13-inch baking dish. Place half of mushroom slices over potatoes. Spoon half of soup mixture over vegetables. Layer remaining potatoes, mushrooms, and soup mixture. Place pepper rings over casserole.

In a small bowl, combine cracker crumbs and melted butter. Stir in cheese. Sprinkle mixture over casserole. Bake 30 to 35 minutes or until casserole is hot and bubbly. Serve warm.
Yield: about 12 servings

TWICE-BAKED SWEET POTATOES
(Shown on page 222)

4 sweet potatoes
1/2 cup firmly packed brown sugar
1/4 cup butter or margarine, softened
1 can (8 ounces) crushed pineapple, drained
1/4 teaspoon ground cardamom
1/8 teaspoon ground ginger
1/8 teaspoon salt
1 cup bread crumbs
1/2 teaspoon ground cinnamon
2 tablespoons butter, melted

Preheat oven to 425 degrees. Trim ends and lightly grease potatoes. Bake 45 to 50 minutes or just until tender. Cool potatoes 30 minutes.

Preheat oven to 375 degrees. Cut potatoes in half lengthwise. Scoop out potato pulp, leaving about a 1/4-inch shell. In a medium bowl, combine potato pulp, brown sugar, butter, pineapple, cardamom, ginger, and salt; beat until well blended and fluffy. Spoon potato mixture into potato shells and place on an ungreased baking sheet. In a small bowl, combine bread crumbs and cinnamon. Add melted butter; stir until well blended. Spoon over potatoes. Bake stuffed potatoes 20 minutes or until heated through and topping is golden brown. Serve warm.
Yield: 8 servings

PEACHY SWEET POTATOES
(Shown on page 236)

    2   large sweet potatoes, peeled
        and cut into pieces
    6   cups water
    2   tablespoons firmly packed brown
        sugar
    2   tablespoons butter or margarine,
        softened
    1   teaspoon lemon juice
   1/4 teaspoon salt
   1/4 teaspoon ground cloves
    2   cans (29 ounces each) peach
        halves, drained

In a large saucepan, cook potatoes in
boiling water 25 to 30 minutes or until
tender; drain. Cool to room temperature.
In a large bowl, mash potatoes. Mix in
next 5 ingredients, beating until smooth.
    Preheat oven to 400 degrees. Place
peach halves in an ungreased 9 x 13-inch
baking pan. Using a pastry bag fitted
with a large star tip, pipe potato mixture
into center of each peach half. Bake
15 minutes or until potato mixture is light
brown. Serve immediately.
Yield: 12 to 14 servings

SWEET POTATOES AND CHESTNUTS

    6   large sweet potatoes
    3   apples, peeled, cored, and sliced
    1   can (15.5 ounces) whole chestnuts
        packed in water, drained
   3/4 cup firmly packed brown sugar
    2   teaspoons ground nutmeg
   1/4 cup butter
    1   cup apple cider

In a large saucepan, boil whole,
unpeeled sweet potatoes until tender
(about 20 minutes). Remove from water
and allow to cool.
    Preheat oven to 350 degrees. Peel and
slice sweet potatoes. In a lightly greased
13 x 9 x 2-inch baking pan, layer sweet
potato slices, apples, and chestnuts.
Sprinkle top with brown sugar and
nutmeg; dot with butter. Pour apple cider
over top. Bake 45 minutes or until mixture
is bubbly.
Yield: 8 to 10 servings

CHINESE RICE RING WITH BROCCOLI

RICE

       Vegetable cooking spray
  1 egg, beaten
  2 tablespoons vegetable oil
 1/2 cup diced uncooked pork
 1/2 cup finely chopped fresh
       mushrooms
 1/2 cup finely chopped green onions
  4 cups cooked white rice
 1/2 cup drained canned green peas
 1/4 cup soy sauce

BROCCOLI FILLING

 1/8 cup sesame oil
  3 dried whole red peppers
  2 tablespoons soy sauce
  2 tablespoons rice wine vinegar
  1 tablespoon sugar
  1 teaspoon garlic powder
 1/2 teaspoon ground ginger
  8 cups fresh broccoli flowerets
  1 onion, thinly sliced

For rice, spray a small skillet with cooking spray. Add egg and cook, without stirring, until firm. Place cooked egg on a cutting board and finely chop. In a large skillet, heat oil over medium-high heat. Add pork, mushrooms, and green onions. Stirring constantly, cook 4 to 5 minutes or until pork is cooked. Stir in rice, peas, chopped egg, and soy sauce. Pack hot rice mixture into a 6-cup ring mold sprayed with cooking spray. Cover and place in a 200-degree oven until ready to serve.

For broccoli filling, combine sesame oil and red peppers in a large skillet. Cook over medium heat 3 to 4 minutes. Stir in soy sauce, vinegar, sugar, garlic powder, and ginger. Add broccoli and onion, stirring to coat well. Stirring occasionally, cook until broccoli is tender. Remove from heat; remove peppers. Invert rice ring onto a serving plate and spoon broccoli into center of ring. Serve hot.

Yield: about 12 servings

ALMOND BROCCOLI RING

Broccoli mixture may also be baked in individual custard cups.

  1 package (10 ounces) frozen
       chopped broccoli
  1 package (10 ounces) frozen
       broccoli spears
       Salt
  5 tablespoons margarine, divided
 1/2 cup minced green onions,
       including tops
  3 tablespoons all-purpose flour
 1/4 cup chicken broth
  1 cup sour cream
  3 eggs, lightly beaten
 3/4 cup shredded Swiss cheese
 1/2 cup slivered almonds, toasted
  1 teaspoon salt
 3/4 teaspoon freshly grated nutmeg
 1/2 teaspoon ground black pepper
  1 pint cherry tomatoes

Steam broccoli until tender; drain and lightly salt. Using a sharp knife, finely chop broccoli and set aside.

In a saucepan, melt 3 tablespoons margarine; add onions and sauté lightly. Remove from heat; blend in flour and return to heat. Stirring slowly, cook over medium heat 2 minutes. Remove from heat; add broth and stir. Return to heat and continue to stir as sauce thickens. Lower heat and cook 2 minutes more. Blend in sour cream and heat thoroughly. Stir a few tablespoons of

...autéed cherry tomatoes add a festive touch to this Almond Broccoli Ring, which features a ...elicate blend of flavors.

...auce into beaten eggs; add egg mixture ...o remainder of sauce in pan and cook ... minute, stirring constantly. Blend in ...heese. Add broccoli, almonds, and ...easonings. Spoon mixture into an oiled ...-quart ring mold or eight 5-ounce ...ustard cups. Place in a large baking ...an and add hot water to come halfway ...p sides of mold. Bake in a preheated ...50-degree oven about 50 minutes for mold (30 minutes for custard cups) or until a knife inserted in center comes out clean. When ready to serve, invert onto a serving plate.

Sauté cherry tomatoes in remaining margarine about 5 to 6 minutes. Garnish with tomatoes and fresh herbs or parsley. **Yield:** 8 to 10 servings

BROCCOLI ROULADE WITH HAM

CREAMED HAM
- 3 tablespoons butter
- 3 tablespoons all-purpose flour
- $^3/_4$ cup chicken broth
- 2 tablespoons sherry
- 1 teaspoon Dijon-style mustard
  Salt and ground black pepper
- $^1/_2$ cup half and half
- 1$^1/_2$ cups diced boiled or baked ham
- 1 can (4 ounces) sliced mushrooms, drained

BROCCOLI ROULADE
- 4 packages (10 ounces each) frozen chopped broccoli
- $^1/_2$ cup dry bread crumbs
- 6 tablespoons butter, melted
  Pinch of ground nutmeg
  Salt and ground black pepper
- 4 eggs, separated
- 8 tablespoons grated Parmesan cheese, divided

For creamed ham, melt butter in a medium saucepan. Remove from heat and add flour. Stirring slowly, cook over medium heat 2 minutes. Remove from heat; gradually stir in broth, sherry, and mustard. Salt and pepper to taste. Return to heat and cook until mixture thickens. Add half and half, ham, and mushrooms; continue cooking until thoroughly heated. Keep warm while preparing broccoli roulade.

For broccoli roulade, cook broccoli according to package directions; drain. Cool and finely chop. Butter a 10$^1/_2$ x 15$^1/_2$ x 1-inch jellyroll pan and line with waxed paper. Butter waxed paper well and sprinkle with bread crumbs. In a large mixing bowl, combine broccoli, melted butter, and nutmeg; salt and pepper to taste. Beat in egg yolks, one at a time, blending thoroughly after each addition. Beat egg whites until soft peaks form; fold into broccoli mixture. Turn into prepared pan and smooth top. Sprinkle with 4 tablespoons cheese. Bake in a preheated 350-degree oven 12 to 16 minutes or until center feel barely firm when touched.

Place a sheet of buttered waxed paper over the top of the broccoli mixture and invert onto a large baking sheet. Carefully peel away waxed paper. Spread creamed ham over broccoli mixture. Beginning with one long side, gently roll up broccoli mixture. Sprinkle with remaining 4 tablespoons cheese.
Yield: about 12 servings

RED AND GREEN VEGETABLE MEDLEY
(Shown on page 236)

- 1 large bunch fresh broccoli, cleaned and chopped
- $^3/_4$ cup water
- $^1/_4$ cup butter or margarine
- 3 tablespoons lemon juice
- $^1/_2$ teaspoon dried basil leaves
- $^1/_2$ teaspoon salt
- $^1/_4$ teaspoon ground black pepper
- 1 pint cherry tomatoes, halved

In a large saucepan, cook broccoli in water until tender. Rinse with cold water and drain well. In a large skillet, melt butter over medium-high heat. Stir in broccoli, lemon juice, basil, salt, and pepper. Cook over high heat 1 to 2 minutes, stirring constantly. Add tomatoes and toss. Serve immediately.
Yield: about 6 servings

BROCCOLI TIMBALES

Shown on page 219)

- 1 package (16 ounces) frozen chopped broccoli, thawed
- 1 clove garlic
- 1 1/4 cups whipping cream
- 2 eggs
- 1/2 teaspoon dried basil leaves
- 1/2 teaspoon dried thyme leaves
- 1/2 teaspoon salt
- 1/4 teaspoon ground black pepper

Preheat oven to 325 degrees. Process broccoli and garlic in a food processor until finely chopped. Add whipping cream, eggs, basil, thyme, salt, and pepper; process until puréed. Spoon mixture evenly into 6 custard cups or small ramekins. Place cups in a 9 x 13-inch baking pan and fill pan with hot water to come halfway up sides of cups. Bake 50 to 55 minutes or until a toothpick inserted in center of cups comes out clean. Serve warm.

Yield: 6 servings

ACORN SQUASH RINGS

- 3 unpeeled acorn squash
- 1/4 cup butter or margarine, melted
- 1/2 cup maple syrup
- 1/4 cup firmly packed brown sugar
- 1 1/2 teaspoons ground cardamom

Preheat oven to 375 degrees. Cut each squash in half crosswise and remove seeds. Place squash, cut side down, in a 10 1/2 x 15 1/2 x 1-inch jellyroll pan; pour water into pan to a depth of 1/2 inch. Bake 20 minutes. Remove from oven and allow to cool enough to handle.

Cut squash crosswise into 1/2-inch rings; discard ends. Place rings in 2 greased jellyroll pans. Brush butter onto both sides of squash rings; drizzle with maple syrup. Combine brown sugar and cardamom in a small bowl; sprinkle mixture over squash. Cover pans with aluminum foil and bake 25 minutes. Remove foil and turn each slice. Bake uncovered 20 minutes or until squash is tender, alternating position of pans in oven once during baking. Serve warm.

Yield: about 8 servings

Corn-Stuffed Tomatoes (left) bring exciting new flavor to the table. Caramelized New Potatoes (recipe on page 221) offer a taste of sweetness.

CORN-STUFFED TOMATOES

5 medium tomatoes
2 tablespoons butter or margarine
2 tablespoons all-purpose flour
1 teaspoon salt
1/4 teaspoon ground black pepper
1 cup milk
3 cups frozen corn, cooked in
    salted water and drained
1/2 cup finely chopped green onion
5 slices bacon, cooked and
    crumbled
    Salt and ground black pepper

Cut tomatoes in half. Scoop out as much flesh as possible, invert on paper towels, and drain.

Preheat oven to 350 degrees. Melt butter in saucepan over medium-low heat. Stir in flour, 1 teaspoon salt, and 1/4 teaspoon pepper. Cook until mixture is smooth and bubbly. Slowly pour in milk, stirring constantly. Increase heat to medium and continue cooking and stirring until mixture thickens (about 1 minute). Remove from heat and stir in corn, green onion, and bacon. Salt and pepper to taste. Fill each tomato half with corn mixture and place on baking sheet. Cover with aluminum foil and bake 25 to 30 minutes or just until heated through.
Yield: 10 servings

Sweet onions and mellow cheese are combined to create this delicious Onion-Cheese Casserole (recipe on page 232) with a cracker crumb topping.

ONION-CHEESE CASSEROLE

(Shown on page 231)

2 cups finely crushed butter-flavored crackers (about 45 crackers), divided
1/2 cup butter or margarine, divided
3 pounds onions, thinly sliced
2 tablespoons all-purpose flour
1/2 teaspoon salt
1/2 teaspoon ground black pepper
2 cups milk
1/2 pound pasteurized process cheese, cut into small pieces
Sweet red pepper, cut into rings and fresh jalapeño pepper to garnish

Preheat oven to 350 degrees. Spread 1 cup cracker crumbs in a greased 8 x 11-inch baking dish. In a large skillet, melt 1/4 cup butter over medium heat. Add onions; cook until tender. Spoon onions over cracker crumbs.

In same skillet, melt remaining 1/4 cup butter over medium-high heat. Stir in flour, salt, and pepper; cook 1 minute. Gradually stir in milk. Stirring constantly, cook until thickened. Add cheese and stir until smooth. Pour cheese mixture over onions. Sprinkle remaining 1 cup cracker crumbs over cheese mixture. Bake 25 to 30 minutes or until lightly browned. Garnish with red pepper rings and jalapeño pepper.
Yield: about 12 servings

PEPPERED BLACK-EYED PEA SALAD

1/4 cup olive oil
1/4 cup apple cider vinegar
2 tablespoons granulated sugar
1 tablespoon garlic powder
2 teaspoons hot pepper sauce
2 teaspoons salt
2 teaspoons ground black pepper
1/2 teaspoon ground ginger
4 cans (15 ounces each) black-eyed peas, drained
2 jars (7 ounces each) pickled baby corn, drained and coarsely chopped
1 onion, chopped
1/2 cup finely chopped carrots
1/4 cup chopped green pepper
1 jar (2 ounces) chopped pimiento, drained

Combine first 8 ingredients in a 1-pint jar with a tight fitting lid. Shake until well blended. Refrigerate 8 hours or overnight to allow flavors to blend.

In a large bowl, combine peas, corn, onion, carrots, green pepper, and pimiento. Pour dressing over vegetables and stir until well coated. Refrigerate until ready to serve. Serve chilled.
Yield: about 8 servings

GARLIC CHEESE GRITS

1 cup quick-cooking grits
1 tube (6 ounces) pasteurized process
   cheese food with garlic
1/2 cup butter or margarine
1 container (8 ounces) sour cream
3/4 cup milk
2 eggs
1/8 teaspoon ground red pepper
1 cup (4 ounces) shredded sharp
   Cheddar cheese

Preheat oven to 375 degrees. Cook grits in a large saucepan according to package directions; remove from heat. Add garlic cheese and butter; stir until smooth. In a medium bowl, combine sour cream, milk, eggs, and red pepper; beat until well blended. Gradually stir sour cream mixture into grits mixture. Pour into a greased 2-quart baking dish. Covering with aluminum foil after 30 minutes, bake 50 to 60 minutes or until center is almost set. Uncover grits; sprinkle top with Cheddar cheese and bake 4 minutes longer or until cheese melts. Let stand 15 minutes before serving. Serve warm.
Yield: 10 to 12 servings

CHEESY EGG CASSEROLE
Assemble casserole the night before you plan to serve it.

2 tablespoons butter or margarine,
   softened
6 slices white bread, crusts removed
1/3 cup finely chopped green onions
1 tablespoon vegetable oil
9 eggs
2 1/2 cups half and half
2 cans (7 ounces each) mushroom
   pieces, drained
1 can (4.5 ounces) chopped green
   chiles, drained
1 1/4 teaspoons salt
1/8 teaspoon ground black pepper
2 cups (8 ounces) shredded
   Monterey Jack cheese, divided
1 1/2 cups butter-flavored cracker
   crumbs
   Sweet red pepper ring and chopped
   green onion to garnish

Spread butter over bread slices. Place in bottom of a greased 9 x 13-inch baking dish. In a small skillet, sauté 1/3 cup green onions in oil over medium heat until onions are tender. Beat eggs in a medium bowl. Stir onions, half and half, mushrooms, green chiles, salt, and black pepper into eggs. Stir in 1 1/2 cups cheese. Pour egg mixture over bread slices. Cover and chill overnight.
Preheat oven to 350 degrees. Sprinkle cracker crumbs over top of casserole. Sprinkle remaining 1/2 cup cheese over casserole. Bake 45 minutes or until egg mixture is set and cracker crumbs are golden brown. Garnish with pepper ring and green onions. Serve warm.
Yield: about 12 servings

CHRISTMAS SUCCOTASH
(Shown on page 222)

- 15 slices bacon
- 3/4 cup finely chopped onion
- 2 packages (10 ounces each) frozen whole kernel yellow corn, thawed
- 2 packages (10 ounces each) frozen baby lima beans, thawed
- 1 can (10 ounces) diced tomatoes and green chiles
- 1 1/4 cups bread crumbs
- 2 cups half and half
- 3 eggs
- 1 tablespoon sugar
- 3/4 teaspoon salt
- 1/4 teaspoon ground black pepper

Preheat oven to 375 degrees. In a heavy large skillet, cook bacon over medium heat until crisp. Transfer bacon to paper towels, reserving drippings in skillet. Set aside 6 slices bacon for garnish; crumble remaining bacon. Cook onion in bacon drippings until tender; drain onion. In a large bowl, combine crumbled bacon, onion, corn, lima beans, undrained tomatoes and green chiles, and bread crumbs. In a small bowl, beat half and half and eggs until blended; stir in sugar, salt, and pepper. Stir half and half mixture into vegetable mixture. Pour into a greased 9 x 13-inch baking dish. Cover and bake 1 1/2 hours. Uncover and bake 15 minutes longer. Crumble remaining bacon over casserole to garnish. Serve warm.
Yield: 12 to 14 servings

CORN PUDDING
(Shown on page 214)

- 1/4 cup butter or margarine
- 1/4 cup all-purpose flour
- 1/4 cup finely chopped onion
- 1 tablespoon granulated sugar
- 1 teaspoon salt
- 1 1/2 cups half and half
- 4 cups drained canned corn
- 3 eggs, lightly beaten
- 6 slices bacon, cooked and crumbled
- 1 tablespoon chopped fresh parsley
- 1/4 teaspoon cayenne pepper

Preheat oven to 350 degrees. Melt butter in large saucepan over medium heat. Stir in flour, onion, sugar, and salt. Increase heat to medium-high and cook, stirring constantly, until mixture bubbles. Continuing to stir constantly, add half and half and cook until mixture thickens. Remove from heat. Stir in corn, eggs, bacon, parsley, and cayenne. Pour into a lightly greased 2-quart baking dish. Bake 45 to 50 minutes or until knife inserted in center comes out clean.
Yield: 8 to 10 servings

CORN SOUFFLÉ

1/4 cup butter or margarine
2 tablespoons finely chopped onion
2 tablespoons finely chopped sweet red pepper
2 tablespoons finely chopped sweet yellow pepper
1/4 cup all-purpose flour
1 teaspoon curry powder
1 cup milk
4 eggs, separated
1 package (10 ounces) frozen whole kernel yellow corn, thawed
1 teaspoon salt
1/8 teaspoon ground black pepper
2 tablespoons grated Parmesan cheese

Preheat oven to 350 degrees. In a heavy medium saucepan, melt butter over medium heat; add onion and red and yellow peppers and sauté about 5 minutes or until vegetables are tender. Gradually stir in flour and curry powder until well blended. Add milk, whisking about 2 minutes or until mixture is thick and smooth; remove from heat. In a small bowl, slightly beat egg yolks. Stirring constantly, add a small amount of hot mixture to egg yolks; stir egg mixture back into hot mixture in saucepan. Stir in corn, salt, and black pepper. In a medium bowl, beat egg whites until stiff peaks form. Fold in egg whites. Sprinkle cheese over bottom and sides of a buttered 1 1/2-quart soufflé dish. Spoon corn mixture into dish. Bake 45 to 50 minutes or until soufflé is set. Serve immediately.
Yield: 6 to 8 servings

GRILLED RED ONIONS

4 large red onions, cut crosswise into 1/2-inch slices
1 cup red wine vinegar
1 cup soy sauce
1 cup honey
2 teaspoons garlic powder
1 teaspoon ground black pepper
1/4 cup vegetable oil

Place onions in a 1-gallon resealable plastic bag. In a medium bowl, whisk next 5 ingredients. Pour vinegar mixture into bag and seal. Refrigerate 8 hours or overnight.
Heat oil in a large skillet over medium-high heat. Using a slotted spoon, place onions in skillet and cook until brown on both sides; drain on paper towels. Serve warm.
Yield: about 8 servings

Broccoli and cherry tomatoes seasoned with lemon and basil make up the Red and Green Vegetable Medley (top left, recipe on page 228). Festive Rice Cups (center, recipe below) are mildly flavored with onion and sweet peppers. Our recipe for Peachy Sweet Potatoes (right, recipe on page 225) is an innovative version of a holiday favorite.

FESTIVE RICE CUPS

3   tablespoons butter or margarine
3   tablespoons olive oil
1   cup chopped onion
5   cups chicken broth
2   cups uncooked brown rice
1/2   teaspoon salt
1/4   teaspoon ground turmeric
1/4   teaspoon ground black pepper
1/4   cup chopped sweet red pepper
1/4   cup chopped green pepper

In a large saucepan, melt butter with oil over medium-high heat. Add onion and sauté until golden brown. Add chicken broth, rice, salt, turmeric, and black pepper. Bring to a boil and reduce heat to low. Cover and simmer 50 to 60 minutes or until all liquid is absorbed. Stir in red and green peppers. For each serving, firmly press about 1/2 cup rice mixture into a 3-inch tart mold; invert onto plate. Serve immediately.
Yield: 8 to 10 servings

Chopped apples and sliced carrots lend a crunchy, sweet flavor to Holiday Rice.

HOLIDAY RICE

1¼ cups uncooked long-grain rice
2 tablespoons butter
2 cups chicken broth
½ cup water
1½ teaspoons sugar
¾ teaspoon rubbed sage
½ teaspoon salt
½ teaspoon ground black pepper
1 unpeeled small red apple, cored and chopped
1 unpeeled small green apple, cored and chopped
2 ribs celery, thinly sliced
¾ cup thinly sliced carrots
⅓ cup half and half
⅓ cup sliced almonds
¼ cup golden raisins

In a heavy large skillet, lightly brown rice in butter. Add chicken broth, water, sugar, sage, salt, and pepper. Bring to a boil; cover, reduce heat, and simmer 15 minutes. Stir in apples, celery, carrots, half and half, almonds, and raisins; cook 3 minutes longer. Serve warm.
Yield: 6 to 8 servings

BACON-CHEESE RISOTTO

2 cans (14^1/$_2$ ounces each) fat-
 free chicken broth
3 cups water
 Vegetable cooking spray
1 package (8 ounces) fresh
 mushrooms, sliced
1^1/$_4$ cups chopped sweet red pepper
2 teaspoons minced garlic
2 cups uncooked Arborio rice
^{1}/$_2$ teaspoon salt
1 cup (4 ounces) shredded
 reduced-fat sharp Cheddar
 cheese
6 slices turkey bacon, cooked and
 crumbled

Combine broth and water in a medium
saucepan; bring to a simmer (do not boil).
Keep warm. In a large saucepan sprayed
with cooking spray, sauté mushrooms,
red pepper, and garlic over medium-high
heat about 5 minutes or until tender.
Stirring constantly, add rice and cook
2 minutes. Reduce heat to medium-low.
Add salt and 1 cup broth mixture; stir
constantly until most of liquid is
absorbed. Add remaining broth mixture,
^{1}/$_2$ cup at a time, stirring after each
addition until liquid is absorbed and rice
has a creamy consistency (about
35 minutes). Stir in cheese and bacon;
serve immediately.
Yield: about 15 servings

ONION CASSEROLE

2 large yellow onions, thinly sliced
 and separated into rings, divided
2 large red onions, thinly sliced and
 separated into rings, divided
12 green onions, chopped and
 divided
1 teaspoon ground black pepper,
 divided
10 ounces blue cheese, crumbled
10 ounces (about 2^1/$_2$ cups)
 shredded Havarti cheese
3 tablespoons butter or margarine,
 cut into small pieces
^{3}/$_4$ cup dry white wine

Preheat oven to 350 degrees. In a
greased 9 x 13-inch baking dish, layer
half of yellow, red, and green onions.
Sprinkle ^{1}/$_2$ teaspoon pepper over onions.
Top with blue cheese. Layer remaining
onions and sprinkle remaining pepper
over top. Top with Havarti cheese. Place
butter evenly over cheese. Pour wine over
casserole. Bake 1 hour or until onions
are tender. If cheese browns too quickly,
cover with aluminum foil. Serve hot.
Yield: about 12 servings

*Note: Casserole may be assembled 1 day
in advance and refrigerated. If refrigerated,
increase baking time to 1 hour 15 minutes.*

CHEESY OVEN-ROASTED POTATOES

3 pounds unpeeled red potatoes,
  cut into chunks
6 tablespoons vegetable oil
2 packages (1¼ ounces each)
  cheese sauce mix
1 can (4.5 ounces) chopped
  green chiles
3 tablespoons dried minced onion
1 tablespoon ground cumin
1 tablespoon garlic powder
1½ teaspoons salt
½ teaspoon dried cilantro

Preheat oven to 450 degrees. Place potatoes in a large bowl. In a small bowl, whisk oil and cheese sauce mix until well blended. Stir green chiles, onion, cumin, garlic powder, salt, and cilantro into cheese mixture. Pour mixture over potatoes, stirring until potatoes are well coated. Spread potato mixture in a single layer in a greased 10½ x 15½-inch jellyroll pan. Bake 35 to 45 minutes or until potatoes are tender and golden brown. Serve warm.
Yield: about 12 servings

BAKED BEANS

2 cups dried navy beans
4 cups water
1 medium onion, chopped
2 tablespoons butter
½ cup molasses
½ cup maple syrup
2 teaspoons salt
1 teaspoon dry mustard
1 teaspoon ground ginger
½ teaspoon ground cinnamon

Cover beans with water and allow to soak overnight.

Drain beans and combine with 4 cups water in a 2-quart saucepan. Bring to a boil over high heat. Cover beans, reduce heat, and simmer 2 hours. Drain beans, reserving 2 cups liquid (add additional water to equal 2 cups if necessary).

In a small skillet, sauté onion in butter until onion is limp. Preheat oven to 350 degrees. In a lightly greased 2-quart baking dish, combine beans, sautéed onion, reserved liquid, molasses, syrup, salt, mustard, ginger, and cinnamon. Mix well. Cover and bake 2 hours, stirring occasionally. Add more water to dish if necessary. Uncover and bake 35 to 45 minutes or until top is browned.
Yield: about 8 servings

MEXICAN MACARONI AND CHEESE

1 package (12 ounces) large elbow
    macaroni, cooked
1 can (16 ounces) dark red kidney
    beans, drained
1 can (14.5 ounces) stewed
    tomatoes, drained
1 can (4.5 ounces) chopped green
    chiles
1 can (4^1/4 ounces) chopped ripe
    olives
^{1}/3 cup chopped fresh cilantro
^{1}/4 cup butter or margarine
^{1}/3 cup finely chopped green onions
    (about 4 green onions)
3 tablespoons all-purpose flour
2^1/4 cups warm milk
4 cups (16 ounces) shredded
    Cheddar cheese, divided
1 teaspoon ground cumin
^{1}/4 teaspoon garlic salt
^{1}/8 teaspoon ground red pepper

Preheat oven to 350 degrees. In a large bowl, combine cooked macaroni, kidney beans, tomatoes, green chiles, ripe olives, and cilantro. Melt butter in a large saucepan over medium heat. Sauté green onions in butter just until tender. Remove from heat. Use a slotted spoon to transfer onions to macaroni mixture. Return butter to medium heat; whisk flour into butter until well blended and mixture begins to bubble. Stirring constantly, add warm milk; cook about 6 minutes or until smooth and slightly thickened. Remove from heat and add 3 cups cheese; stir until melted. Stir in cumin, garlic salt, and red pepper. Pour over macaroni mixture. Spoon into a greased 9 x 13-inch baking dish. Sprinkle remaining 1 cup cheese over top. Cover and bake 30 minutes. Uncover and bake 10 minutes or until mixture is bubbly.
Yield: about 14 servings

POSOLE CASSEROLE

2 medium onions, coarsely
    chopped
3 tablespoons vegetable oil
1 medium zucchini, diced
4 cloves garlic, minced
1 tablespoon chili powder
2 teaspoons ground cumin
2 cans (15^1/2 ounces each)
    yellow hominy, drained
1 tablespoon freshly squeezed
    lime juice
^{1}/2 teaspoon salt
^{1}/2 teaspoon ground black pepper
1 cup (4 ounces) combined
    shredded Monterey Jack and
    Cheddar cheese
^{1}/4 cup fresh cilantro leaves, chopped
    Fresh cilantro leaves to garnish

Cook onions in oil in a heavy large skillet over medium-high heat 5 minutes or until onions begin to soften. Stirring frequently, add zucchini, garlic, chili powder, and cumin; cook about 5 minutes or until onions begin to brown. Reduce heat to medium-low. Add hominy, lime juice, salt, and pepper; stir until well blended. Continue cooking until hominy is heated through. Remove from heat. Stir in cheeses and chopped cilantro. Garnish with cilantro leaves. Serve warm.
Yield: about 12 servings

Simply Delicious
EASY DESSERTS

Blueberry-Lemon Tarts, page 244

Apricot Crisp, page 244

Rich flavor in a flash – easy techniques and convenience items like cake mixes and ready-made crusts help you serve these sweets in a hurry!

CREAMY STRAWBERRY PIE

1 package (10 ounces)
  marshmallows
1 package (16 ounces) frozen
  whole strawberries, thawed and
  drained
3 tablespoons strawberry liqueur or
  strawberry juice
1 cup whipping cream, whipped
1 purchased large graham cracker
  pie crust (9 ounces)
  Fresh strawberries to garnish

Place marshmallows in a medium microwave-safe bowl. Microwave on high power (100%) 1$^{1}/_{2}$ to 2 minutes or until marshmallows melt, stirring every 30 seconds. Beat in strawberries and liqueur. Fold in whipped cream. Spoon into crust. Cover and chill. Garnish with strawberries.
Yield: about 10 servings

COCONUT-PINEAPPLE PIE

1$^{1}/_{4}$ cups sugar
  4 eggs
$^{1}/_{4}$ cup butter or margarine, melted
  1 tablespoon lemon juice
$^{1}/_{8}$ teaspoon salt
  1 can (15$^{1}/_{2}$ ounces) crushed
    pineapple, drained
$^{1}/_{2}$ cup finely shredded coconut
  1 9-inch unbaked deep-dish
    pie crust

Preheat oven to 350 degrees. In a large bowl, combine sugar, eggs, melted butter, lemon juice, and salt; beat until well blended. Stir in pineapple and coconut; pour into crust. Bake 45 to 50 minutes or until center is set. Serve warm or transfer to a wire rack to cool. Store in an airtight container in refrigerator.
Yield: about 8 servings

PEANUT BUTTER PIE

$^{3}/_{4}$ cup smooth peanut butter
$^{2}/_{3}$ cup dark corn syrup
$^{2}/_{3}$ cup firmly packed brown sugar
  3 eggs
  3 tablespoons butter or margarine,
    melted
  2 teaspoons vanilla extract
$^{1}/_{8}$ teaspoon salt
  1 9-inch unbaked pie crust
  1 cup coarsely chopped peanuts

Preheat oven to 400 degrees. Combine peanut butter, corn syrup, brown sugar, eggs, melted butter, vanilla, and salt in a large bowl; beat until well blended. Pour into crust. Sprinkle peanuts over filling. Bake 10 minutes. Reduce oven to 350 degrees and bake 35 to 40 minutes or until center is set. Transfer to a wire rack to cool. Store in an airtight container in refrigerator.
Yield: about 8 servings

Coconut-Pineapple Pie (top) is quick to stir up with a few simple ingredients you probably have in your cupboard. Peanut lovers will go nuts over Peanut Butter Pie! Flavored with dark corn syrup and brown sugar, it's packed with smooth peanut flavor.

Shown on page 241: *Frozen lemonade concentrate adds tangy sweetness to Blueberry-Lemon Tarts. The creamy pastries are quick to make using little graham cracker pie crusts. Served warm, Apricot Crisp is a dessert they'll ask for again and again—and it's a snap to create using canned fruit.*

BLUEBERRY-LEMON TARTS

1 can (14 ounces) sweetened condensed milk
1 can (6 ounces) frozen lemonade concentrate, thawed
1 container (8 ounces) frozen non-dairy whipped topping, thawed
4 packages (4 ounces each) of 6 individual-serving graham cracker pie crusts
1 can (21 ounces) blueberry pie filling, chilled
Lemon zest strips to garnish

In a medium bowl, combine sweetened condensed milk and lemonade concentrate. Fold in whipped topping. Spoon about 3 tablespoons lemon mixture into each crust. Cover and chill. To serve, top each tart with 1 heaping tablespoon chilled pie filling. Garnish with lemon zest.
Yield: 2 dozen tarts

APRICOT CRISP

2 cans (17 ounces each) apricot halves in heavy syrup, drained and sliced
2 tablespoons butter or margarine, melted
$1/2$ teaspoon ground cinnamon
$1/2$ teaspoon almond extract
1 cup all-purpose flour
$3/4$ cup firmly packed brown sugar
$1/4$ cup finely chopped pecans
$1/2$ cup butter or margarine
Vanilla ice cream to serve

Preheat oven to 350 degrees. Place apricot slices in a lightly greased 9-inch square baking dish. In a small bowl, combine melted butter, cinnamon, and almond extract. Pour butter mixture over apricots. In a medium bowl, combine flour, brown sugar, and pecans. Using a pastry blender or 2 knives, cut in $1/2$ cup butter until mixture resembles coarse meal. Sprinkle over apricots. Bake 35 to 40 minutes or until topping is golden brown. Serve warm with ice cream.
Yield: about 9 servings

Shown on page 6: Hazelnuts baked in the crust offer an unusually delicious flavor to the tropical taste of Banana Cream Tart. Fresh banana slices are layered under the luscious custard filling, which is quick to prepare in the microwave.

BANANA CREAM TART

CRUST
- 3/4 cup toasted hazelnuts
- 1/2 cup all-purpose flour
- 1/4 cup butter or margarine, softened
- 2 tablespoons firmly packed brown sugar
- 1/4 teaspoon salt

FILLING
- 1/3 cup sugar
- 1/4 cup all-purpose flour
- 1/8 teaspoon salt
- 2 eggs
- 1 3/4 cups half and half
- 1/4 cup butter or margarine, cut into pieces
- 3 tablespoons banana-flavored liqueur
- 1 teaspoon vanilla extract
- 2 bananas
  Banana slices and melted white chocolate to garnish

Preheat oven to 350 degrees. For crust, process all ingredients in a food processor until hazelnuts are coarsely ground and ingredients are well blended. Press mixture into bottom and up sides of an ungreased 9-inch-diameter tart pan with a removable bottom. Bake 11 to 13 minutes or until crust is firm. Cool in pan on a wire rack.

For filling, combine sugar, flour, and salt in a small bowl. In a medium microwave-safe bowl, whisk eggs until frothy. Whisk half and half and dry ingredients into eggs. Add butter. Microwave on medium-high power (80%) 3 minutes; whisk mixture. Continue to microwave until mixture is thick enough to coat the back of a spoon, whisking every 3 minutes. Add liqueur and vanilla; whisk until smooth. Place plastic wrap directly on surface of filling; chill 1 hour.

Slice 2 bananas over bottom of crust. Spoon filling over bananas. To serve, remove sides of pan. Garnish tart with banana slices and drizzle with melted white chocolate. Store in an airtight container in refrigerator.

Yield: about 10 servings

The whole family will love Easy Peach Cobbler, an old-fashioned favorite that you can whip up in a jiffy using canned pie filling. The fruit is spread over the crust, which rises to the top and browns during baking.

EASY PEACH COBBLER

1/2 cup butter or margarine, cut into
     pieces
1 cup sugar
1 cup all-purpose flour
2 teaspoons baking powder
1/2 teaspoon salt
1/2 teaspoon apple pie spice
3/4 cup milk
1 teaspoon almond extract
1 can (21 ounces) peach
     pie filling

Preheat oven to 350 degrees. Place butter pieces in a 7 x 11-inch baking dish. Heat in oven 3 minutes or until butter melts. In a medium bowl, combine sugar, flour, baking powder, salt, and apple pie spice. Add milk and almond extract; stir until well blended. Pour batter over melted butter; do not stir. Spoon pie filling over batter; do not stir. Bake 40 to 45 minutes or until a toothpick inserted in center of cobbler crust comes out clean. Serve warm or transfer to a wire rack to cool.
Yield: about 8 servings

APPLE-CHEDDAR PIE

1 package (11 ounces) pie crust
     mix
1 package (4 ounces) shredded
     sharp Cheddar cheese, at room
     temperature
4 to 5 tablespoons cold water
2 cans (21 ounces each) apple pie
     filling
1/3 cup finely chopped pecans
1/3 cup golden raisins
1/4 cup firmly packed brown sugar
1/2 teaspoon apple pie spice
1/8 teaspoon salt

Using pie crust mix and canned pie filling lets you prepare classic Apple-Cheddar Pie with ease. The crust of this fruit-packed delight is made with sharp Cheddar cheese, and the spiced filling is enriched with pecans and raisins.

Preheat oven to 425 degrees. For crust, process pie crust mix, cheese, and water in a food processor until well blended and dough forms a ball. Divide dough in half and shape into 2 balls. Roll out 1 ball of dough between sheets of plastic wrap. Transfer to a 9-inch deep-dish pie plate. Roll out second ball of dough between plastic wrap for top crust. Cut leaf-shaped pieces of dough from center of top crust and reserve.

In a large bowl, combine pie filling, pecans, raisins, brown sugar, apple pie spice, and salt; pour into crust. Place top crust on filling and flute edges. Arrange reserved dough leaves on crust. Bake 40 to 45 minutes or until filling is bubbly and crust is golden brown. If edges of crust brown too quickly, cover with a strip of aluminum foil. Serve warm or transfer to a wire rack to cool.
Yield: 8 to 10 servings

Chocolate-Cherry Tart (left) is a sweet, nutty delight that has a chocolate cookie crumb crust. Strawberry-Rhubarb Pie can be enjoyed all year-round with frozen sliced rhubarb and canned strawberry pie filling.

STRAWBERRY-RHUBARB PIE

$3/4$ cup sugar
2 tablespoons cornstarch
$1/2$ teaspoon ground cinnamon
1 package (16 ounces) frozen
   sliced rhubarb, thawed
2 cans (21 ounces each) strawberry
   pie filling
2 tablespoons frozen orange juice
   concentrate
1 crust from a 15-ounce package of
   refrigerated pie crusts, at room
   temperature
   Egg white, beaten
   Sugar

Preheat oven to 375 degrees. Combine $3/4$ cup sugar, cornstarch, and cinnamon in a large bowl. Stir in rhubarb until well coated with sugar mixture; allow to stand 15 minutes. Stir pie filling and juice concentrate into rhubarb mixture. Spoon filling into a 9 x 9 x 2-inch baking dish. On a lightly floured surface, unfold pie crust and use a floured rolling pin to roll out crust to about a 12-inch circle. Using a fluted pastry wheel, cut $3/4$-inch-wide strips. Use strips to make lattice top and braided strips around edges of baking dish. Brush crust with egg white and sprinkle with sugar. Bake 50 to 55 minutes or until filling is bubbly and crust is golden brown. Serve warm or transfer to a wire rack to cool.
Yield: 8 to 10 servings

CHOCOLATE-CHERRY TART

FILLING
- 2 cans (14.5 ounces each) tart pitted cherries packed in water
- 1/4 cup cornstarch
- 1 cup sugar
- 1/3 cup chopped toasted slivered almonds
- 1 teaspoon almond extract
- 1/8 teaspoon red liquid food coloring

CRUST
- 1 1/2 cups chocolate wafer cookie crumbs (about 28 cookies)
- 6 tablespoons butter or margarine, melted
  Whipped cream and maraschino cherries to garnish

For filling, drain cherries, reserving 1/2 cup liquid. Combine reserved cherry liquid and cornstarch in a small bowl. Combine drained cherries and sugar in a medium saucepan over medium-high heat. Stirring frequently, cook until sugar dissolves and liquid begins to boil. Stir in cornstarch mixture; reduce heat to medium-low. Continue to cook about 3 minutes or until mixture thickens. Remove from heat; stir in almonds, almond extract, and food coloring. Cover and chill.

For crust, combine cookie crumbs and melted butter in a medium bowl. Press mixture into bottom and up sides of a lightly greased 9-inch-diameter tart pan with a removable bottom. Cover and chill 1 hour or until firm.

Spoon filling into crust. To serve, remove sides of pan. Garnish tart with whipped cream and maraschino cherries.
Yield: about 10 servings

WALNUT-FUDGE PIE

- 1 cup sugar
- 1/2 cup butter or margarine, melted
- 1/2 cup all-purpose flour
- 1/2 cup chopped walnuts
- 2 eggs
- 1/4 cup cocoa
- 8 walnut halves
- 1/4 cup milk chocolate chips
- 1 teaspoon shortening

Combine sugar, butter, flour, chopped walnuts, eggs, and cocoa in a medium bowl; beat until well blended. Spread batter into a greased 9-inch microwave-safe pie plate. Microwave on medium power (60%) 10 to 12 minutes or until almost set in center (do not overbake). Transfer to a wire rack. Arrange walnut halves on pie. Combine chocolate chips and shortening in a small microwave-safe bowl. Microwave on high power (100%) 1 minute or until chocolate softens; stir until smooth. Spoon melted chocolate mixture into a pastry bag fitted with a very small tip. Pipe chocolate onto warm pie in a random pattern of squiggly lines; cool completely.
Yield: about 8 servings

CHOCOLATE-BUTTERSCOTCH PIE

1 can (5 ounces) evaporated milk
1 egg yolk
1 package (6 ounces) semisweet chocolate chips
1 cup butterscotch chips
1 container (8 ounces) frozen non-dairy whipped topping, thawed
1 purchased vanilla wafer crumb pie crust (6 ounces)
Chopped pecans and chocolate sprinkles to garnish

Whisk evaporated milk and egg yolk in a heavy medium saucepan over medium-low heat. Whisking constantly, cook 5 to 6 minutes or until mixture becomes hot and slightly thickened. Reduce heat to low. Add chocolate and butterscotch chips; stir until melted and smooth. Cool to room temperature; fold in whipped topping. Spoon into crust. Garnish with pecans and chocolate sprinkles. Cover and freeze until firm enough to slice.
Yield: about 8 servings

PEANUT BUTTER-BANANA CREAM PIE

$^1/_3$ cup sifted confectioners sugar
$^1/_3$ cup crunchy peanut butter
$^1/_4$ cup plus 2 tablespoons semisweet chocolate mini chips, divided
1 purchased graham cracker pie crust (6 ounces)
1$^1/_4$ cups milk
1 package (3 ounces) vanilla pudding mix
1 package (8 ounces) cream cheese, softened
2 bananas, sliced

Combine confectioners sugar, peanut butter, and $^1/_4$ cup chocolate chips in a small bowl. Lightly press peanut butter mixture over bottom of crust. In a medium saucepan, combine milk and pudding mix. Stirring constantly, cook over medium heat about 8 minutes or until mixture thickens. Remove from heat beat in cream cheese. Arrange banana slices evenly over peanut butter mixture. Pour pudding mixture over bananas. Cover and chill about 1 hour or until set. To serve, sprinkle with remaining 2 tablespoons chocolate chips. Store in an airtight container in refrigerator.
Yield: about 8 servings

VERY BERRY PIE

1 can (21 ounces) cherry pie filling
1 can (21 ounces) blueberry pie
    filling
1 package (12 ounces) frozen
    whole red raspberries, thawed
3/4 cup plus 1 tablespoon sugar,
    divided
1/4 teaspoon plus 1/8 teaspoon
    ground cinnamon, divided
1/4 teaspoon orange extract
1 package (15 ounces)
    refrigerated pie crusts, at room
    temperature

Preheat oven to 400 degrees. For
filling, combine pie fillings, raspberries,
3/4 cup sugar, 1/4 teaspoon cinnamon, and
orange extract in a large bowl. Place
crust in a 9-inch deep-dish pie plate.
Pour filling into crust. Cut triangles in
center of second crust; pull cut edges
back toward center. Place crust over
filling; crimp edges. Combine remaining
tablespoon sugar and 1/8 teaspoon
cinnamon in a small bowl; sprinkle over
crust. Bake 45 to 50 minutes or until filling
is bubbly and crust is golden brown. If
edges of crust brown too quickly, cover
with a strip of foil. Serve warm or transfer
to a wire rack to cool.
Yield: about 10 servings

RICH AND CREAMY PEACH PIE

3/4 cup sugar
1/2 cup all-purpose flour
1/8 teaspoon ground nutmeg
1/8 teaspoon salt
2 cans (16 ounces each) sliced
    peaches, drained
1 teaspoon almond extract

1 9-inch unbaked pie crust
1 cup whipping cream
2 tablespoons sliced almonds

Preheat oven to 350 degrees. Combine
sugar, flour, nutmeg, and salt in a small
bowl; stir in peaches and almond extract.
Spoon peach mixture into crust. Pour
whipping cream over peach mixture.
Bake 50 to 55 minutes or until top is
lightly browned. Sprinkle almonds in
center of pie; bake 5 minutes longer.
Serve warm or transfer to a wire rack
to cool. Store in an airtight container in
refrigerator.
Yield: about 8 servings

EASY SWEET POTATO PIE

1/4 cup butter or margarine, softened
2/3 cup sugar
1 can (16 ounces) cut sweet
    potatoes in syrup, drained
1 can (5 ounces) evaporated milk
2 eggs
1 teaspoon pumpkin pie spice
1 9-inch unbaked deep-dish
    pie crust
    Whipped cream and pumpkin pie
    spice to garnish

Preheat oven to 375 degrees. Cream
butter and sugar in a medium bowl until
fluffy. Add sweet potatoes, evaporated
milk, eggs, and pumpkin pie spice.
Pour into crust. Bake 40 to 45 minutes
or until center is set and crust is lightly
browned. Cool on a wire rack. Garnish
with whipped cream and pumpkin pie
spice. Store in an airtight container in
refrigerator.
Yield: about 8 servings

PRALINE PUMPKIN PIE

1 purchased frozen pumpkin pie
   (1 pound, 10 ounces)
1/4 cup butter or margarine
1/3 cup firmly packed brown sugar
2 tablespoons whipping cream
1/3 cup finely chopped pecans
1/2 teaspoon maple flavoring

Bake pumpkin pie according to package directions. Remove from oven while preparing topping.

Reduce heat to 350 degrees. In a small saucepan, melt butter over medium-high heat. Stir in brown sugar and cream. Bring to a boil, stirring constantly. Remove from heat; stir in pecans and maple flavoring. Pour mixture over hot pie. Bake 5 to 7 minutes or until topping bubbles. Cool to room temperature before serving. Store in an airtight container in refrigerator.
Yield: about 8 servings

CRUNCHY CHOCOLATE-COCONUT PIE

CRUST
1/2 cup semisweet chocolate chips
2 tablespoons butter or margarine
1 1/2 cups crispy rice cereal
1/2 cup flaked coconut

FILLING
1 can (8.5 ounces) cream of
   coconut, chilled
1/2 cup milk
1 package (3.9 ounces) chocolate
   fudge instant pudding mix
   Coconut to garnish

For crust, place chocolate chips in a medium microwave-safe bowl. Microwave on high power (100%) 1 minute or until chocolate softens. Add butter; stir until smooth. Stir in cereal and coconut until well blended. Lightly press mixture into an ungreased 9-inch pie plate. Cover and chill crust.

For filling, combine cream of coconut and milk in a medium bowl. Add pudding mix; beat until thickened. Pour into chilled crust. Cover and chill about 30 minutes or until set. Garnish with coconut.
Yield: about 8 servings

PIÑA COLADA PIE

1 package (3.4 ounces) vanilla
   instant pudding mix
1 1/2 cups liquid piña colada drink
   mixer, chilled
1 package (8 ounces) cream cheese,
   softened
1 can (15 1/4 ounces) pineapple
   tidbits, drained
1/4 cup finely shredded coconut
1 purchased graham cracker pie
   crust (6 ounces)
   Kiwi fruit slices to garnish

In a medium bowl, add pudding mix to drink mixer; beat until thickened. Add cream cheese; beat until smooth. Stir in pineapple and coconut. Spoon into crust. Cover and chill until set. Garnish with kiwi fruit slices.
Yield: about 8 servings

A crispy rice cereal crust adds texture to Crunchy Chocolate-Coconut Pie (top), a dreamy confection created using instant pudding and cream of coconut. Garnished with kiwi fruit slices, Piña Colada Pie combines a tropical drink mixer with cream cheese, coconut, and pineapple.

PUMPKIN STREUSEL CAKE

STREUSEL
- 1/2 cup firmly packed brown sugar
- 1/2 cup finely chopped walnuts
- 1 tablespoon all-purpose flour
- 1 tablespoon butter or margarine, melted
- 1 teaspoon ground cinnamon

CAKE
- 1 package (18.25 ounces) spice cake mix
- 1 package (3.4 ounces) vanilla instant pudding mix
- 1 cup canned pumpkin
- 3 eggs
- 1/2 cup vegetable oil
- 1/2 cup water
- 1 teaspoon vanilla extract
- Confectioners sugar to garnish

For streusel, combine brown sugar, walnuts, flour, melted butter, and cinnamon in a small bowl.

Preheat oven to 350 degrees. For cake, combine cake mix, pudding mix, pumpkin, eggs, oil, water, and vanilla in a large bowl. Beat at low speed of an electric mixer 30 seconds. Beat at medium speed 2 minutes. Pour half of batter into a greased a 10-inch springform pan with fluted tube insert or a 10-inch fluted tube pan; sprinkle streusel mixture over batter. Pour remaining batter into pan. Bake 35 to 42 minutes or until a toothpick inserted in cake comes out clean. Cool in pan 10 minutes. Remove sides of pan and invert onto a serving plate; cool completely. Sift confectioners sugar over cake to garnish.

Yield: about 16 servings

AMARETTO PICNIC CAKE

- 1 cup finely chopped toasted almonds
- 1 package (27.25 ounces) cake mix with streusel topping and glaze mix
- 1 cup brewed amaretto-flavored coffee
- 3 eggs
- 1/4 cup plus 2 tablespoons amaretto, divided
- 1/3 cup vegetable oil
- 1 tablespoon amaretto-flavored non-dairy powdered creamer

Preheat oven to 350 degrees. In a small bowl, combine almonds and package of streusel topping. In a large bowl, combine cake mix, coffee, eggs, 1/4 cup amaretto, oil, and creamer. Beat at low speed of an electric mixer 30 seconds. Beat at medium speed 2 minutes. Sprinkle half of streusel topping mixture into bottom of a greased 10-inch fluted tube pan. Spoon two-thirds of batter over streusel topping. Repeat layers using remaining topping and batter. Bake 40 to 45 minutes or until a toothpick inserted in center of cake comes out clean. Cool in pan 10 minutes. Invert onto a serving plate; cool completely.

Combine package of glaze mix and remaining 2 tablespoons amaretto; drizzle over cake.

Yield: about 16 servings

CREAMY ORANGE-CHOCOLATE CAKE

1 package (18.25 ounces) chocolate fudge cake mix with pudding in the mix
1 cup water
3 eggs
$1/3$ cup vegetable oil
$1/3$ cup plus 1 tablespoon orange-flavored liqueur, divided
1 container (16 ounces) chocolate fudge ready-to-spread frosting
$1/4$ cup orange marmalade
Orange slice and fresh mint leaves to garnish

Preheat oven to 350 degrees. In a large bowl, combine cake mix, water, eggs, oil, and $1/3$ cup liqueur. Beat at low speed of an electric mixer 30 seconds. Beat at medium speed 2 minutes. Pour batter into 3 greased 9-inch round cake pans. Bake 20 to 25 minutes or until a toothpick inserted in center of cake comes out clean. Cool in pans 15 minutes. Remove from pans and cool completely on a wire rack.

Combine frosting, orange marmalade, and remaining 1 tablespoon liqueur in a medium bowl; stir until well blended. Spread glaze between layers and on top of cake. Garnish with orange slice and mint leaves.

Yield: 12 to 14 servings

COOKIES 'N' CREAM CAKE

1 package (18.25 ounces) white cake mix
$1^1/4$ cups water
$1/3$ cup vegetable oil
3 egg whites
$1^1/2$ cups coarsely crushed chocolate sandwich cookies (about 14 cookies), divided
1 package (3 ounces) cream cheese, softened
2 tablespoons butter or margarine, softened
3 cups sifted confectioners sugar
$1/2$ teaspoon vanilla extract
2 to 3 tablespoons milk
Chocolate sandwich cookie halves to decorate

Preheat oven to 350 degrees. In a large bowl, combine cake mix, water, oil, and egg whites. Beat at low speed of an electric mixer 30 seconds. Beat at medium speed 2 minutes. Stir in 1 cup crushed cookies by hand. Pour batter into 2 greased and floured 9-inch round cake pans. Bake 20 to 25 minutes or until a toothpick inserted in center of cake comes out clean. Cool in pans 15 minutes. Remove from pans and cool completely on a wire rack.

In a medium bowl, beat cream cheese and butter until fluffy. Stir in confectioners sugar, vanilla, and enough milk for desired spreading consistency; beat until smooth. Place 1 cake layer, top side down, on a serving plate; spread about one-fourth of icing over layer. Top with remaining cake layer. Spread remaining icing on top and sides of cake. Sprinkle remaining $1/2$ cup crushed cookies on top of cake. Place cookie halves around bottom of cake. Refrigerate in an airtight container.

Yield: 12 to 14 servings

PEACH-ALMOND PASTRIES

1 can (21 ounces) peach pie filling
1/2 cup sliced almonds, toasted
2 tablespoons amaretto
1/2 teaspoon almond extract
1 package (15 ounces) refrigerated
     pie crusts, at room temperature
     Vegetable cooking spray
2 tablespoons sugar
1/2 teaspoon ground cinnamon

Preheat oven to 425 degrees. Using a slotted spoon, remove peaches from pie filling (discard liquid) and place in a food processor. Add almonds, amaretto, and almond extract. Process until peaches are coarsely chopped; set aside.

Cut each pie crust into 8 triangles for a total of 16 triangles. Place 8 triangles on a baking sheet lightly sprayed with cooking spray. Spoon about 3 tablespoonfuls of peach mixture into center of each triangle. Use a heart-shaped aspic cutter to cut hearts in centers of remaining triangles. Place cutout triangles over pie filling. Use a fork to crimp edges of dough together. Combine sugar and cinnamon in a small bowl. Lightly spray tops of pastries with cooking spray; sprinkle with sugar mixture. Bake 20 to 25 minutes or until tops are golden brown. If edges of crust brown too quickly, cover with strips of aluminum foil. Serve warm.
Yield: 8 servings

STRAWBERRY-BANANA CAKE

1 package (18.25 ounces) white
     cake mix
1 package (3 ounces) strawberry
     gelatin
4 eggs
1 cup buttermilk
1/2 cup vegetable oil
1 1/3 cups sliced fresh strawberries,
     divided
1 cup mashed bananas (about
     3 bananas)
1 package (8 ounces) cream cheese,
     softened
1 teaspoon vanilla extract
1 package (16 ounces)
     confectioners sugar
     Banana and strawberry slices and
     whole strawberry to garnish

Preheat oven to 350 degrees. Grease three 9-inch round cake pans and line bottoms with waxed paper. In a large bowl, combine cake mix and gelatin. Add eggs, buttermilk, and oil; beat at low speed of an electric mixer 30 seconds. Beat at medium speed 2 minutes. Add 1 cup strawberries and mashed bananas to cake mixture; beat 1 minute or until well blended. Pour batter into prepared pans. Bake 25 to 30 minutes or until a toothpick inserted in center of cake comes out clean. Cool in pans 15 minutes. Remove from pans and cool completely on a wire rack.

In a medium bowl, beat cream cheese, vanilla, and remaining 1/3 cup strawberries until fluffy. Gradually add confectioners sugar, beating until well blended. Spread icing between layers and on top and sides of cake. Store in an airtight container in refrigerator. Garnish before serving.
Yield: 12 to 14 servings

Make every day a special occasion with a dreamy Strawberry-Banana Cake (bottom) flavored with fresh fruit and strawberry gelatin. The heavenly strawberry-cream cheese icing is inspirational! Prepared with refrigerated pie crusts, the sugar-sprinkled Peach-Almond Pastries are filled with amaretto-laced peaches and toasted almonds.

COCONUT CANDY BAR CAKE

1 cup sugar
1 cup evaporated milk
1/2 cup butter or margarine
24 marshmallows
1 package (14 ounces) flaked coconut
2 9-inch-round devil's food cake layers (prepared from a cake mix)
1 container (16 ounces) chocolate fudge ready-to-spread frosting

In a medium saucepan, combine sugar, evaporated milk, and butter over medium-high heat. Stirring frequently, bring mixture to a boil. Reduce heat to medium; continue to stir and cook 2 minutes. Remove from heat. Stir in marshmallows until melted. Stir in coconut. Chill filling 1 hour.

Cut each cake layer in half to make 4 thin layers. Spread filling evenly between layers. Spread frosting on top and sides of cake. Store in an airtight container in refrigerator.

Yield: 12 to 14 servings

CRANBERRY-ORANGE SQUARES

1 package (18.25 ounces) yellow cake mix
1 cup old-fashioned oats
1/2 teaspoon ground cinnamon
3/4 cup butter or margarine, softened
1 can (16 ounces) whole berry cranberry sauce
1 cup orange marmalade
1 cup chopped walnuts

Preheat oven to 350 degrees. In a large bowl, combine cake mix, oats, and cinnamon. Using a pastry blender or 2 knives, cut in butter until mixture is crumbly. Reserving 1/2 cup oat mixture, firmly press remaining mixture into bottom of a greased 101/2 x 151/2-inch jellyroll pan. In a small bowl, combine cranberry sauce and marmalade. Spread evenly over crust. Combine reserved oat mixture and walnuts. Sprinkle evenly over cranberry mixture; press lightly. Bake 35 to 40 minutes or until golden brown. Cool in pan on a wire rack. Cut into 2-inch squares.

Yield: about 35 squares

COCONUT-BANANA PUDDING

(Shown on page 265)

1 package (3.4 ounces) coconut cream instant pudding mix
2 cups milk
1 banana, mashed
2 tablespoons flaked coconut
2 bananas
24 vanilla wafers, broken into large pieces
Banana slices, chopped pecans, and coconut to serve

In a medium bowl, add pudding mix to milk; beat until thickened. Stir in mashed banana and 2 tablespoons coconut. Slice 2 bananas. Layer vanilla wafer pieces, banana slices, and pudding in 6 individual serving dishes. Cover and chill until ready to serve. To serve, place banana slices, pecans, and coconut over pudding.

Yield: 6 servings

TOPSY-TURVY CAKE

1 cup chopped pecans
1 cup flaked coconut
2 packages (3 ounces each) cream
  cheese, softened
$^1/_3$ cup butter or margarine, softened
1 ounce semisweet baking
  chocolate, melted
1 teaspoon vanilla extract
1 package (16 ounces)
  confectioners sugar
1 package (18.25 ounces) devil's
  food cake mix with pudding in
  the mix
$1^1/_4$ cups water
3 eggs
$^1/_3$ cup vegetable oil

Preheat oven to 350 degrees. Combine
pecans and coconut in a greased
9 x 13-inch baking pan. In a medium
bowl, beat cream cheese and butter
until fluffy; beat in melted chocolate and
vanilla. Add confectioners sugar; continue
to beat until well blended. In a large bowl,
combine cake mix, water, eggs, and oil.
Beat at low speed of an electric mixer 30
seconds. Beat at medium speed
2 minutes. Pour batter over pecan
mixture. Drop tablespoonfuls of cream
cheese mixture over cake batter to within
1 inch of edges. Bake 50 minutes or until
cake pulls away from sides of pan. Cool in
pan 15 minutes. Serve warm. Store in an
airtight container in refrigerator.
Yield: about 16 servings

TAPIOCA-PEACH PARFAITS
(Shown on page 265)

$2^3/_4$ cups milk
$^1/_3$ cup sugar
3 tablespoons quick-cooking
  tapioca
1 egg, beaten
$^1/_2$ teaspoon almond extract
1 can (21 ounces) peach pie filling,
  chilled
2 tablespoons amaretto
  Toasted sliced almonds to garnish

In a medium saucepan, combine milk,
sugar, tapioca, and egg; let stand
5 minutes. Stirring constantly, cook over
medium heat until mixture begins to
boil. Remove from heat; stir in almond
extract. Pour into a medium bowl and
place plastic wrap directly on surface;
chill about 30 minutes or until mixture
thickens.
Combine pie filling and amaretto in a
small bowl. In 4 parfait glasses, alternately
layer tapioca pudding with pie filling
mixture, ending with pie filling mixture.
Garnish with almonds.
Yield: 4 servings

CHOCOLATE SHORTBREAD BARS

1 cup butter, softened
1/3 cup sifted confectioners sugar
1/4 cup firmly packed brown sugar
1 3/4 cups all-purpose flour
1/4 cup cocoa

Preheat oven to 325 degrees. In a large bowl, cream butter and sugars until fluffy. In a small bowl, combine flour and cocoa. Gradually add dry ingredients to creamed mixture; stir just until blended (do not overmix). Press into bottom of a lightly greased 9 x 13-inch baking pan. Prick dough with a fork. Bake 23 to 25 minutes or until edges are lightly browned. Cool in pan on a wire rack 10 minutes. Cut warm shortbread into 1 x 2-inch bars. Cool completely in pan.
Yield: about 4 dozen bars

RUM-RAISIN BARS

1 1/2 cups raisins
1 1/2 cups golden raisins
1/3 cup rum
1/4 cup water
1/2 cup butter or margarine, softened
1/3 cup firmly packed brown sugar
1 cup all-purpose flour
1 cup flaked coconut
1 cup chopped walnuts
1 can (14 ounces) sweetened
   condensed milk

Combine raisins, rum, and water in a heavy small saucepan. Place over medium-high heat and bring to a boil. Remove from heat; cover and allow to stand while preparing crust.
Preheat oven to 350 degrees. Cream butter and brown sugar in a medium bowl until fluffy. Stir in flour until well blended. Press mixture into bottom of a greased 9 x 13-inch baking pan. Bake 10 minutes. Stir coconut and walnuts into raisin mixture; spread over crust. Pour sweetened condensed milk over mixture. Bake 30 minutes or until topping is golden brown. Cool in pan 15 minutes. Cut into 1 1/2-inch squares while warm. Cool completely in pan.
Yield: about 4 dozen bars

Moist and chewy, Rum-Raisin Bars (top right) *are bursting with plump, juicy raisins and* baked coconut. Created with simple ingredients, Chocolate Shortbread Bars are a natural when you have a craving for chocolate. They're great for dunking in milk!

ORANGE-PECAN PUMPKIN BARS

1 package (18.25 ounces) yellow
    cake mix
1/4 cup butter or margarine, melted
1/2 cup finely chopped pecans
3/4 cup orange marmalade, melted
2 packages (3 ounces each) cream
    cheese, softened
1 cup canned pumpkin
1/4 cup firmly packed brown sugar
1 egg
1 teaspoon vanilla extract
1/8 teaspoon salt

Preheat oven to 350 degrees. In a medium bowl, combine cake mix and melted butter (mixture will be crumbly). Stir in pecans. Reserve 1 cup cake mix mixture for topping. Press remaining mixture into bottom of a greased 9 x 13-inch baking pan. Spread marmalade over crust. In a medium bowl, beat cream cheese until fluffy. Add remaining ingredients; beat until smooth. Spread filling over marmalade layer. Sprinkle reserved cake mix mixture over filling. Bake 40 to 45 minutes or until top is lightly browned and filling is set. Cool in pan on a wire rack. Cut into 1 x 2-inch bars. Store in an airtight container in refrigerator.
Yield: about 4 dozen bars

GERMAN CHOCOLATE SQUARES

1 package (18.25 ounces) German
    chocolate cake mix with
    pudding in the mix
1/3 cup vegetable oil
1 egg
1 cup sugar
4 eggs
1/2 teaspoon salt
1 cup light corn syrup
1/4 cup butter or margarine, melted
1 teaspoon vanilla extract
2 cups chopped pecans
1 1/2 cups flaked coconut

Preheat oven to 350 degrees. Combine cake mix, oil, and 1 egg in a medium bowl; stir until well blended. Press mixture into bottom of a greased 9 x 13-inch baking dish. Bake 20 minutes. In a large bowl, beat sugar, 4 eggs, and salt until well blended. Beat in corn syrup, melted butter, and vanilla. Stir in pecans and coconut. Pour filling over hot crust. Bake 30 to 35 minutes or until top is lightly browned and center is set. Cool in pan on a wire rack. Cut into 1 1/2-inch squares.
Yield: about 3 dozen squares

DEATH BY CHOCOLATE

 1 package (21.2 ounces) brownie mix
$1/2$ cup vegetable oil
 2 eggs
$1/4$ cup water
$1/4$ cup coffee-flavored liqueur **or**
     4 tablespoons strongly brewed
     coffee and 1 teaspoon sugar
 3 packages (3.9 ounces each)
     chocolate instant pudding mix
 6 cups milk
$1/2$ teaspoon almond extract
 1 container (12 ounces) frozen
     non-dairy whipped topping,
     thawed
 1 package (9 ounces) snack-size
     chocolate-covered toffee candy
     bars, crushed and divided
     Chocolate curls to garnish

Preheat oven to 350 degrees. Prepare brownie mix with oil, eggs, and water in a large bowl according to package directions. Spread batter into a greased 9 x 13-inch baking pan and bake 24 to 26 minutes. Use a wooden skewer to poke holes about 1 inch apart in top of warm brownies; drizzle with liqueur. Cool completely.

Prepare pudding mixes with milk in a large bowl according to package directions; set aside. In a medium bowl, fold almond extract into whipped topping; set aside. In a 4-quart serving bowl, break half of brownies into bite-size pieces. Sprinkle half of crushed candy bars over brownies. Spread half of pudding over candy pieces. Spread half of whipped topping mixture over pudding layer. Repeat layers, ending with whipped topping mixture. Cover and chill. Garnish with chocolate curls.
Yield: about 20 servings

CREAMY PINEAPPLE-ORANGE DESSERT

 2 cans (11 ounces each) mandarin
     oranges, drained and divided
 1 package (3 ounces) vanilla
     pudding mix
 2 cups milk
 1 can (8 ounces) crushed
     pineapple, drained
 1 package (3 ounces) ladyfingers
     (about 12 ladyfingers)

Reserve several mandarin orange slices for garnish. Combine pudding mix and milk in a medium saucepan. Stirring constantly, cook over medium heat until mixture comes to a full boil. Remove from heat; stir in pineapple and remaining oranges. Cool to room temperature.

Cut ladyfingers in half crosswise. Line sides of a 9 x 2-inch-deep round baking dish with pieces. Cut remaining ladyfingers in half lengthwise and place on bottom of dish. Spread pudding mixture over ladyfingers in bottom of dish. Garnish with reserved orange slices. Cover and chill 1 hour or until firm.
Yield: about 8 servings

Fruity Apple Bread Pudding begins with unseasoned croutons that are soaked in a mixture of milk, applesauce, and spices. Packed with walnuts and raisins, the baked pudding is served with a caramel-whiskey sauce made with purchased ice cream topping. The recipe is on page 266.

Amaretto liqueur adds excitement to Tapioca-Peach Parfaits (top), layered desserts made with peach pie filling and quick-cooking tapioca. A tasty twist on a Southern favorite, Coconut-Banana Pudding combines flaked coconut and mellow bananas with instant coconut cream pudding. Recipes are on pages 258 and 259.

APPLE BREAD PUDDING

(Shown on page 264)

 2 cups milk
 1 cup applesauce
 3/4 cup sugar
 2 eggs
 1 teaspoon vanilla extract
 1 teaspoon apple pie spice
 1 teaspoon ground cinnamon
 1 package (5 ounces) unseasoned
   croutons (about 2 1/2 cups)
 1 cup chopped walnuts
 1/4 cup raisins
 1 container (12.5 ounces) caramel
   ice cream topping
 3 tablespoons whiskey

Preheat oven to 350 degrees. Whisk first 7 ingredients in a large bowl. Stir in croutons, walnuts, and raisins; allow to stand 10 minutes. Pour into a greased 9-inch square baking pan. Bake 50 to 55 minutes or until a knife inserted in center of bread pudding comes out clean. Allow to stand 10 minutes before serving.

Pour caramel topping into a small saucepan. Bring to a boil over medium-high heat. Remove from heat; stir in whiskey. Serve warm sauce over bread pudding.

Yield: about 9 servings

CUSTARD WITH CARAMEL-PECAN TOPPING

 2 cups evaporated milk
 4 eggs
 4 tablespoons firmly packed brown
   sugar
 1 tablespoon vanilla extract
 1 container (12.5 ounces)
   caramel ice cream topping
 1/2 cup chopped pecans

Preheat oven to 325 degrees. In a medium bowl, whisk evaporated milk, eggs, brown sugar, and vanilla. Pour into 6 ungreased 6-ounce custard cups. Place cups in a 9 x 13-inch baking pan. Place pan in oven and fill with hot water about halfway up sides of cups. Bake 30 to 35 minutes or until a knife inserted in center of custard comes out clean. Remove cups from water. Allow custard to cool 10 minutes before removing from cups.

Combine caramel topping and pecans in a small saucepan. Stirring constantly, bring to a boil over medium heat. Remove from heat.

To serve, loosen edges of custard with a knife. Invert onto dessert plates. Spoon warm caramel topping over warm custard.

Yield: 6 servings

HOMESTYLE RICE PUDDING

 3 cups milk
 1 egg yolk, beaten
 1 package (4.4 ounces) custard mix
 1/2 cup raisins, divided
 1 cup cooked rice

In a medium saucepan, combine milk and egg yolk; stir in custard mix. Stirring constantly, bring to a boil over medium heat. Remove from heat. Reserving 2 tablespoons raisins for garnish, stir in rice and remaining raisins. Spoon into serving dishes. Cover and chill. Garnish with reserved raisins.

Yield: about 4 servings

LAYERED CHOCOLATE-ALMOND DELIGHT

1 cup all-purpose flour
2 tablespoons granulated sugar
1/2 cup butter or margarine
1 cup sliced almonds, chopped
1 package (8 ounces) cream cheese, softened
1 cup sifted confectioners sugar
1 container (8 ounces) frozen non-dairy whipped topping, thawed and divided
1 package (3.9 ounces) chocolate instant pudding mix
2²/3 cups milk, divided
1 package (3.4 ounces) vanilla instant pudding mix
3 milk chocolate candy bars with almonds (1.45 ounces each), chopped, to garnish

Preheat oven to 350 degrees. In a medium bowl, combine flour and granulated sugar. Using a pastry blender or 2 knives, cut in butter until mixture resembles coarse meal. Stir in almonds. Press into bottom of a 9 x 13-inch baking dish. Bake 15 to 17 minutes or until edges are lightly browned. Cool in dish on a wire rack.

In a medium bowl, beat cream cheese and confectioners sugar until fluffy. Fold in 1 cup whipped topping. Spread over cooled crust. In a small bowl, add chocolate pudding mix to 1¹/3 cups milk; beat until thickened. Spread pudding over cream cheese mixture layer. In another small bowl, add vanilla pudding mix to remaining 1¹/3 cups milk; beat until thickened. Spread vanilla pudding over chocolate pudding. Cover and chill 15 minutes or until firm.

To serve, spread remaining whipped topping over vanilla pudding. Garnish with chopped candy bars. Cut into 2¹/2-inch squares.
Yield: about 12 servings

CITRUS TRIFLE

1 can (15¹/4 ounces) pineapple tidbits
2 packages (3.4 ounces each) vanilla instant pudding mix
3 cups milk
1 container (8 ounces) sour cream
1 can (11 ounces) mandarin oranges, drained
1 purchased pound cake (16 ounces), cut into bite-size pieces
1 container (8 ounces) frozen non-dairy whipped topping, thawed
2 tablespoons orange-flavored liqueur
Toasted flaked coconut to garnish

Drain pineapple, reserving juice. Combine pudding mixes, milk, and 1/2 cup reserved pineapple juice in a medium bowl. Beat until well blended. Fold in sour cream, oranges, and drained pineapple. Layer one-third of cake pieces in a 3-quart serving bowl; drizzle with one-third of remaining reserved pineapple juice. Spoon one-third of pudding mixture over cake. Repeat layers twice, ending with pudding mixture. Cover and chill at least 3 hours.

To serve, combine whipped topping and liqueur; spread over top of trifle. Garnish with toasted coconut.
Yield: 12 to 14 servings

Creamy Blueberry Squares feature a buttery brown sugar crust covered with sweetened cream cheese and canned pie filling.

CREAMY BLUEBERRY SQUARES

1¹/₄ cups all-purpose flour
 ¹/₂ cup firmly packed brown sugar
 ¹/₂ cup butter or margarine, softened
 ¹/₂ cup chopped pecans
   1 package (8 ounces) cream cheese, softened
 ³/₄ cup granulated sugar
   2 eggs
   1 can (21 ounces) blueberry pie filling
   2 teaspoons lemon juice
     Frozen non-dairy whipped topping, thawed, to garnish

Preheat oven to 350 degrees. For crust, combine flour, brown sugar, butter, and pecans in a medium bowl. Press mixture into bottom of a 9 x 13-inch baking pan. In a medium bowl, beat cream cheese, granulated sugar, and eggs until smooth. Pour cream cheese mixture over crust. Bake 20 to 25 minutes or until filling is set and begins to brown around the edges. Cool in pan 15 minutes on a wire rack.

Combine pie filling and lemon juice in a small bowl. Spread blueberry mixture over cream cheese filling. Cover and chill.

To serve, cut into 2-inch squares. Garnish with whipped topping.
Yield: about 24 servings

Individual Cherry Bread Cups are quick to prepare with maraschino cherries and cubed white bread. A warm pudding and dollops of whipped topping add the finishing touches.

CHERRY BREAD CUPS

2 jars (6 ounces each) maraschino
    cherries, divided
4 slices white bread, cubed
$1/2$ cup sugar
2 eggs, beaten
2 tablespoons butter or margarine,
    melted
1 tablespoon all-purpose flour
1 package (3 ounces) vanilla
    pudding mix
2 cups milk
    Frozen non-dairy whipped
    topping, thawed, to garnish

Preheat oven to 375 degrees. Drain cherries, reserving juice; add enough water to cherry juice to make $2/3$ cup. Coarsely chop cherries. Combine $1/2$ cup cherries, reserved juice mixture, bread cubes, sugar, eggs, melted butter, and flour in a small bowl. Spoon mixture evenly into 6 greased 6-ounce custard cups. Place cups in a 9 x 13-inch baking pan. Place pan in oven and fill with hot water about halfway up sides of cups. Bake 25 to 30 minutes or until edges of mixture begin to pull away from sides of cups. While bread cups are baking, add pudding mix to milk in a medium saucepan. Stirring constantly, cook over medium heat until mixture comes to a full boil. Remove from heat. Stir in remaining cherries.

To serve, spoon warm pudding mixture over each bread cup. Garnish with whipped topping. Serve warm.
Yield: 6 servings

BROWNIE CRÈME BRÛLÉE

1 package (21.5 ounces) brownie
   mix
4 eggs, lightly beaten
1/2 cup brewed coffee
1/4 cup vegetable oil
1/2 cup firmly packed brown sugar
2 tablespoons butter, softened

Preheat oven to 350 degrees. In a medium bowl, combine brownie mix, eggs, coffee, and oil; stir just until blended. Pour batter into 6 lightly greased 6-ounce ramekins. Place ramekins in a 9 x 13-inch baking pan. Place pan in oven and fill with hot water halfway up sides of ramekins. Bake 34 to 36 minutes. Place ramekins on a wire rack to cool while preparing topping. In a small bowl, combine brown sugar and butter until crumbly. Sprinkle about 1 tablespoon mixture over each warm dessert. Place ramekins on a baking sheet 4 inches from broiler and broil about 2 to 3 minutes or until sugar caramelizes. Serve warm.
Yield: 6 servings

CHERRY CREAM CHEESE DESSERT

1 package (8 ounces) cream cheese,
   softened
1 can (14 ounces) sweetened
   condensed milk
1/3 cup lemon juice
1 teaspoon vanilla extract
1 can (21 ounces) cherry pie filling
   Toasted slivered almonds to
   garnish

In a large bowl, beat cream cheese until fluffy. Beat in sweetened condensed milk, lemon juice, and vanilla. Lightly swirl pie filling into cream cheese mixture. Spoon into serving dishes. Cover and chill. Garnish with almonds.
Yield: about 6 servings

DESSERT WAFFLES

1 cup pancake and waffle mix
2 tablespoons sugar
3/4 cup water
1 egg
2 tablespoons butter or margarine,
   melted
1/2 teaspoon vanilla extract
   Vanilla ice cream and strawberry
   ice cream topping to serve

Preheat a Belgian waffle iron. In a medium bowl, combine waffle mix and sugar. Add water, egg, melted butter, and vanilla; stir just until blended. For each waffle, pour about 1/2 cup batter into waffle iron. Bake 3 to 5 minutes or according to manufacturer's instructions until done. Serve warm waffles with ice cream and strawberry topping.
Yield: about 4 waffles

BLUEBERRY-LIME FROZEN DESSERT

3 cups lime sherbet, softened
3/4 cup crushed vanilla wafer crumbs
 (about 20 cookies)
1 pint fresh blueberries

Place a layer of sherbet, cookie crumbs, and blueberries in 4 parfait glasses. Repeat layers, ending with blueberries. Serve immediately.
Yield: 4 servings

FRESH ORANGE-PLUM ICE

3 seedless oranges, peeled and cut
 into bite-size pieces
1 pound fresh plums, quartered
1 cup white grape juice
1/2 cup port wine
1/2 cup sugar
 Cinnamon stick
1/2 teaspoon vanilla extract

In a medium saucepan, combine oranges, plums, grape juice, wine, sugar, and cinnamon stick. Bring to a boil over medium-high heat. Cover saucepan and reduce heat to low, simmering about 15 minutes. Remove from heat. Remove cinnamon stick and place mixture in a food processor. Add vanilla and pulse process until fruit is coarsely chopped and well blended. Pour into a nonmetal container. Cover and freeze until firm. To serve, remove from freezer and allow to soften about 30 minutes.
Yield: about 5 cups fruit ice

FRUIT FIESTA

10 ounces refrigerated sugar cookie
 dough (1/2 of a 20-ounce
 package)
1 package (8 ounces) cream cheese,
 softened
1/3 cup sugar
2 tablespoons plus 2 teaspoons
 orange-flavored liqueur, divided
1/2 teaspoon vanilla extract
4 cups sliced fresh apricots,
 strawberries, bananas, and
 whole blueberries
1/4 cup apricot preserves

Preheat oven to 350 degrees. Press cookie dough into a greased 12-inch pizza pan. Bake 12 to 15 minutes or until dough is lightly browned. Cool pan on a wire rack.

In a medium bowl, beat cream cheese, sugar, 2 tablespoons liqueur, and vanilla until fluffy. Spread over cooled crust. Beginning at outer edge, arrange fruit slices over cream cheese mixture. Melt apricot preserves in a small saucepan over low heat. Remove from heat. Stir in remaining 2 teaspoons liqueur. Brush over fruit. Cover and chill 30 minutes. Cut into wedges to serve.
Yield: about 12 servings

STRAWBERRIES AND BANANAS WITH SABAYON SAUCE

2 egg yolks
2 tablespoons sugar
2 tablespoons sweet Marsala wine
3 tablespoons orange juice
3 bananas, sliced
1 pint fresh strawberries, sliced

Combine egg yolks and sugar in the top of a double boiler over simmering water. Whisking constantly, add wine and cook about 5 minutes or until mixture thickens. Transfer to a small bowl; cover and chill 30 minutes.

In a medium bowl, sprinkle orange juice over banana slices. Add strawberries and toss lightly. To serve, spoon fruit mixture into serving dishes and top with chilled sauce.

Yield: about 5 servings

SPICED POACHED PEARS

6 medium fresh pears
$3/4$ cup water
1 tablespoon lemon juice
Cinnamon stick, broken into 3 pieces
6 cardamom pods, crushed
$1/4$ cup honey
$1/4$ cup butter or margarine
$1/4$ cup firmly packed brown sugar
Fresh mint leaves to garnish

Leaving stems on fruit, peel pears. Core each pear from bottom almost to top, leaving stem end intact. Bring water, lemon juice, cinnamon stick pieces, and cardamom pods to a boil in a large saucepan over high heat. Place pears upright in water. Cover, reduce heat to medium, and simmer 15 to 25 minutes or until pears are tender. Remove pears from saucepan. Discard cinnamon, cardamom pods, and all but $1/4$ cup liquid from saucepan. Add honey, butter, and brown sugar to liquid over medium heat; stir until butter melts. Return pears to saucepan and cook 10 to 15 minutes or until sauce begins to thicken, spooning sauce over pears. Remove pears from sauce. Increase heat to medium-high. Stirring frequently, cook sauce about 4 minutes or until liquid is reduced and sauce is thickened. Spoon 1 tablespoon sauce into each of 6 serving dishes. Place pears on sauce. Spoon 1 teaspoon sauce over each pear. Garnish with mint leaves. Serve immediately.

Yield: 6 servings

SUMMER FRUIT DESSERT

CAKE
1 package (18.25 ounces) lemon cake mix with pudding in the mix
1 cup water
3 eggs
1 package (3 ounces) cream cheese, softened

FILLING
1 package (3 ounces) cream cheese, softened
$1^1/2$ cups milk, divided
1 package (3.4 ounces) lemon instant pudding mix
1 teaspoon grated lemon zest
$1^1/2$ cups frozen non-dairy whipped topping, thawed and divided
$1^1/2$ cups sliced fresh fruit, divided (we used peaches, strawberries, and kiwi fruit)

A lemon-cream cheese filling with a confetti of sliced fruit offers a delicious complement to extra-moist cake in Summer Fruit Dessert. Cake and pudding mixes help you create this luscious treat without a lot of fuss.

Preheat oven to 350 degrees. For cake, combine cake mix, water, eggs, and cream cheese in a large bowl. Beat at low speed of an electric mixer 30 seconds. Beat at medium speed 2 minutes. Pour into a greased 10-inch fluted tube pan. Bake 45 to 50 minutes or until a toothpick inserted in center of cake comes out clean. Cool in pan 15 minutes. Invert onto a wire rack and cool completely.

Place cake on a serving plate. Make a horizontal cut through cake about 2 inches from bottom; set top of cake aside. Use a fork to pull out interior of cake, leaving about a $3/4$-inch shell on sides and bottom of cake.

For filling, beat cream cheese in a large bowl until smooth. Gradually add 1 cup milk, beating until well blended. Add pudding mix, lemon zest, and remaining $1/2$ cup milk; beat until thickened. Fold in $1/2$ cup whipped topping. Spread about half of filling into bottom of cake. Place about 1 cup fruit slices over filling. Spread remaining filling over fruit slices. Replace cake top. Spread remaining whipped topping on cake. Place remaining fruit slices on whipped topping. Serve immediately.

Yield: about 16 servings

LEMON FRUIT DIP

1 package (3 ounces) cream cheese, softened
1 container (8 ounces) lemon yogurt
2 tablespoons sifted confectioners sugar
2 tablespoons lemon juice
1 container (8 ounces) frozen non-dairy whipped topping, thawed
Lemon slice and fresh berry leaves to garnish
Fresh fruit slices to serve

In a medium bowl, beat cream cheese until fluffy. Add yogurt, confectioners sugar, and lemon juice; beat until well blended. Fold in whipped topping. Garnish with lemon slice and berry leaves. Serve with fruit slices. Store in an airtight container in refrigerator.
Yield: about 4 cups dip

BAKED CARAMEL APPLES

6 large red baking apples (we used Rome Beauty apples)
2$^1/_4$ cups oatmeal cookie crumbs, divided
$^3/_4$ cup caramel ice cream topping
$^1/_4$ cup apple juice

Preheat oven to 350 degrees. Core each apple almost to bottom of apple, leaving bottom intact. Using a vegetable peeler, remove a small strip of peel from top of each apple to prevent splitting. Place apples in an ungreased 7 x 11-inch baking dish. Combine 1$^1/_2$ cups cookie crumbs and caramel topping in a small bowl. Spoon cookie crumb mixture into center of each apple. Sprinkle remaining $^3/_4$ cup cookie crumbs over tops of apples. Pour apple juice into baking dish. Bake 35 to 40 minutes or until apples are tender. Serve warm.
Yield: 6 servings

BERRY COMBO

1 cup fresh whole strawberries
1 cup fresh blueberries
1 cup fresh red raspberries
1 cup fresh blackberries
2 teaspoons cornstarch
2 tablespoons cold water
1 cup orange juice
1 tablespoon lemon juice
1 cup sugar
$^1/_2$ teaspoon ground cinnamon
$^1/_8$ teaspoon ground ginger
2 packages (10 ounces each) frozen puff pastry shells, baked according to package directions
Fresh berry leaves to garnish

In a large bowl, combine berries. In a small bowl, combine cornstarch and water. In a medium saucepan, combine juices, sugar, cinnamon, and ginger; whisk until smooth. Stirring constantly, add cornstarch mixture and bring to a boil over medium-high heat. Reduce heat to medium and cook 6 minutes or until mixture begins to thicken. Remove from heat. Pour over berries and toss lightly. Cover and chill 1 hour.

To serve, spoon berry mixture into pastry shells. Garnish with berry leaves.
Yield: 12 servings

PINEAPPLE PASSION

³/₄ cup boiling water
1 package (3 ounces) orange-
   pineapple gelatin
1 cup cold pineapple juice
1 fresh pineapple
1 cup whipping cream

Chill a small bowl and beaters from an electric mixer in freezer. In a large bowl, stir boiling water into gelatin until gelatin dissolves. Stir in pineapple juice. Cover and chill about 1 hour or until gelatin begins to thicken.

Quarter pineapple, remove core, and remove most of fruit, reserving shells. Cut fruit into small pieces. Place fruit in a medium saucepan over medium heat and cook 8 minutes. Remove from heat; drain and allow to cool.

In chilled bowl, beat whipping cream until stiff peaks form. Reserving several pieces of pineapple for garnish, fold whipped cream and remaining pineapple into thickened gelatin. Chill 2 hours or until almost firm.

To serve, spoon mixture into pineapple shells. Garnish with reserved pineapple. Serve immediately.

Yield: 4 servings

FROZEN FRUIT FLUFF

3 cups peeled, sliced ripe peaches
   and nectarines
1¹/₂ tablespoons lemon juice
4 egg whites
¹/₂ cup sugar
   Peach and lemon slices and lemon
   zest strips to garnish

Process fruit slices and lemon juice in a food processor until fruit is finely chopped. In a large bowl, beat egg whites until soft peaks form. Gradually add sugar to egg whites, beating until stiff peaks form. Fold in fruit mixture. Spoon into serving dishes. Freeze until firm. Garnish with peach and lemon slices and lemon zest.

Yield: about 7 servings

BUTTERSCOTCH ICE CREAM SQUARES

1 cup all-purpose flour
1/2 cup butter or margarine, softened
1/4 cup firmly packed brown sugar
1/4 cup quick-cooking oats
1/2 cup chopped pecans
1/2 cup butterscotch ice cream
    topping, divided
1 quart vanilla ice cream, softened

Preheat oven to 400 degrees. In a medium bowl, combine flour, butter, brown sugar, and oats until well blended. Stir in pecans. Spread mixture on an ungreased baking sheet. Stirring every 3 minutes, bake 12 to 15 minutes or until lightly browned. Cool on pan on a wire rack.

Crumble half of oat mixture into a lightly greased 8-inch square baking pan. Drizzle 1/4 cup butterscotch topping over mixture. Spread ice cream over topping. Sprinkle remaining oat mixture over ice cream. Drizzle with remaining 1/4 cup butterscotch topping. Cover and freeze 1 1/2 to 2 hours or until firm. Remove from freezer 10 minutes before serving. Cut into 2-inch squares.

Yield: about 9 servings

TUTTI-FRUTTI SHERBET

2 2/3 cups milk
1 can (5 ounces) evaporated milk
2/3 cup sugar
1 package (0.16 ounces)
    unsweetened punch-flavored
    soft drink mix
1/8 teaspoon salt
1 jar (10 ounces) maraschino
    cherry halves, drained
1 can (8 ounces) crushed
    pineapple, drained
1 banana, sliced

In a large bowl, combine milks, sugar, soft drink mix, and salt; stir until sugar dissolves. Stir in cherry halves, pineapple, and banana slices. Freeze in a 2-quart ice cream freezer according to manufacturer's instructions or cover and freeze until mixture is frozen 1 inch from sides of bowl; stir. Return to freezer until mixture is almost firm. Break up mixture with a spoon; beat with an electric mixer until well blended. Freeze until firm.

Yield: about 1 3/4 quarts sherbet

Garnished with maraschino cherries and miniature chocolate chips, Black Forest Angel Dessert (left) is a quick-to-make confection with chocolate ice cream, angel food cake, and cherry pie filling. Tutti-Frutti Sherbet, a blend of pineapples, cherries, and bananas, gets its tropical taste from fruit punch-flavored soft drink mix.

BLACK FOREST ANGEL DESSERT

4   cups 1-inch cubes of angel food
      cake
1   can (21 ounces) cherry pie filling
1   quart chocolate ice cream,
      softened
1   container (4 ounces) frozen non-
      dairy whipped topping, thawed
      Semisweet chocolate mini chips
      and maraschino cherry halves
      to garnish

Line a 5 x 9-inch loaf pan with plastic wrap. Combine cake pieces and pie filling in a large bowl. Spread half of ice cream in bottom of prepared pan. Spoon cake mixture over ice cream; top with remaining ice cream. Cover and freeze until firm.

To serve, remove dessert from pan and place on a serving dish. Spread whipped topping over top and sides of dessert. Garnish with chocolate chips and cherry halves.

Yield: 8 to 10 servings

ICE CREAM SUNDAE CAKE

(Shown on page 6)

As simple as it is luscious, Ice Cream Sundae Cake is created with alternating layers of pound cake and fruity ice cream. This scrumptious masterpiece will impress even your most discriminating guests.

  1   package (16 ounces) pound
        cake mix
 2/3 cup water
  2   eggs
  1   quart vanilla ice cream, softened
  1   container (11.75 ounces)
        strawberry ice cream topping
  1   can (8 ounces) crushed
        pineapple, drained
 1/4 cup chopped pecans
  2   jars (6 ounces each) maraschino
        cherries
  1   container (12 ounces) non-dairy
        whipped topping, thawed
        Chocolate sprinkles and whole
        maraschino cherries to garnish

Preheat oven to 325 degrees. Combine cake mix, water, and eggs in a large bowl; beat at low speed of an electric mixer 30 seconds. Beat at medium speed 2 minutes. Pour into 3 greased 8-inch round cake pans. Bake 18 to 23 minutes or until a toothpick inserted in center of cake comes out clean. Cool in pans 5 minutes. Remove from pans and cool completely on a wire rack.

In a large bowl, combine ice cream, strawberry topping, pineapple, and pecans. Line two 8-inch round cake pans with plastic wrap. Spread ice cream mixture into prepared pans. Cover and freeze until firm.

Place 1 cake layer on a serving plate. Top with 1 ice cream layer. Repeat with remaining cake and ice cream layers. Freeze until ready to serve.

To serve, process maraschino cherries in a food processor until coarsely chopped; drain. In a medium bowl, fold cherry pieces into whipped topping. Spread mixture over top and sides of cake. Garnish with chocolate sprinkles and whole cherries.

Yield: about 12 servings

TORTILLA ICE CREAM DELIGHTS

 1/4 cup sugar
  1   teaspoon ground cinnamon
        Vegetable oil
  8   flour tortillas (about 6-inch
        diameter)
  1   quart vanilla ice cream
  1   container (12.5 ounces) caramel
        ice cream topping

Combine sugar and cinnamon in a small bowl. In a large skillet, heat 1/4 inch of oil over medium-high heat. Using a sharp knife, cut small slits in centers of tortillas to help keep them flat while frying. Lightly brown both sides of tortillas in oil; drain on paper towels. While still hot, sprinkle 1 side of each tortilla with 1 heaping teaspoon of sugar mixture. With sugar-coated side up, transfer to individual serving plates. Place 1 scoop ice cream on each tortilla. Drizzle about 2 tablespoons caramel topping over each ice cream scoop.

Yield: 8 servings

APRICOT-ALMOND ICE CREAM PIE

    1   cup graham cracker crumbs
    1/4 cup butter or margarine, melted
    3   tablespoons sugar
    3/4 teaspoon almond extract
    1/2 cup sliced almonds, toasted and
        divided
    1   quart vanilla ice cream, softened
    2/3 cup apricot preserves

Preheat oven to 350 degrees. Combine cracker crumbs, melted butter, sugar, and almond extract in a small bowl. Stir in 1/4 cup almonds. Spread 1/4 cup cracker crumb mixture on an ungreased baking sheet. Bake 4 to 5 minutes or until slightly crunchy. Cool on pan; reserve for topping. Press remaining cracker crumb mixture into bottom of a greased 9-inch round cake pan. Spread about half of ice cream over crumb mixture. Spoon apricot preserves over ice cream layer. Sprinkle with 1/8 cup almonds. Cover and freeze about 30 minutes. Spread a second layer of ice cream over almonds. Sprinkle pie with crumb topping and remaining 1/8 cup almonds. Cover and freeze 1 to 1 1/2 hours or until firm. Remove from freezer 10 minutes before serving.
Yield: about 8 servings

CANTALOUPE-RASPBERRY SUNDAES

    2   cantaloupes
    1   pint fresh red raspberries
    1   pint vanilla ice cream
    3/4 cup purchased melba sauce
        Fresh mint leaves to garnish

Cut each cantaloupe in half crosswise. Cut a thin slice from bottom of each cantaloupe half so it will sit flat. Leaving about a 3/4-inch shell, use a melon baller to scoop flesh from cantaloupes. Use a spoon to scoop out additional flesh to smooth insides of cantaloupes. In a medium bowl, combine melon balls and raspberries. Place 2 small scoops of ice cream in each melon half. Top with fruit mixture. Drizzle with melba sauce. Garnish with mint leaves. Serve immediately.
Yield: 4 servings

GO FISH PUDDING

1 cup boiling water
1 package (3 ounces) blue gelatin
1 cup cold water
1 container (8 ounces) frozen non-
    dairy whipped topping, thawed
    Gummi fish to decorate

In a medium bowl, stir boiling water into gelatin until gelatin dissolves. Stir in cold water. Refrigerate about $1^1/2$ hours or until partially set. Fold in whipped topping. Spoon into serving bowls and refrigerate 30 minutes. To serve, decorate with gummi fish.
Yield: about 6 servings

CHOCOLATE-PEANUT BUTTER GORP SNACKS

8 cups round toasted oat cereal
2 cups raisins
1 cup dry-roasted peanuts
1 package (12 ounces) semisweet
    chocolate chips
$1/2$ cup smooth peanut butter

In a large bowl, combine cereal, raisins, and peanuts. Place chocolate chips and peanut butter in a medium saucepan. Stirring constantly, cook over low heat until chocolate melts and mixture is smooth. Pour chocolate mixture over cereal mixture; stir until well coated. Drop about $1^1/2$ tablespoonfuls of mixture into paper muffin cups or onto waxed paper. Use fingers to press mixture together if necessary. Allow chocolate to harden.
Yield: about $4^1/2$ dozen snacks

CREAMY ORANGE CONES
Use your party cups to freeze and serve cones.

$1^1/4$ cups boiling water
1 package (3 ounces) orange
    gelatin
2 cups vanilla ice cream, softened
11 sugar ice-cream cones
    Whipped cream and sprinkles to
    decorate

If using paper cups to hold cones, cut $1^1/4$-inch circles in bottoms of eleven 8-ounce cups. Invert cups onto a jellyroll pan; set aside.
In a medium bowl, stir boiling water into gelatin until gelatin dissolves. Allow mixture to cool 5 minutes. Whisk in ice cream. Chill mixture 20 minutes or until almost set. Spoon into cones; place cones in inverted cups. Freeze until firm. Decorate with whipped cream and sprinkles. Serve immediately.
Yield: 11 servings

CHINATOWN CEREAL SQUARES

 5 cups bite-size square rice cereal
 1 can (3 ounces) chow mein noodles
 1 cup dry-roasted peanuts
 1 package (10.5 ounces) miniature marshmallows
 6 tablespoons butter or margarine
12 ounces vanilla candy coating, chopped

In a large bowl, combine cereal, chow mein noodles, and peanuts. In a large saucepan, combine marshmallows and butter. Cook over low heat until smooth, stirring frequently. Remove from heat and add candy coating; stir until smooth. Pour marshmallow mixture over cereal mixture; stir until well coated. Use greased hands to press mixture into a greased 9 x 13-inch baking dish. Cool completely. Cut into 2-inch squares.
Yield: about 2 dozen squares

PINEAPPLE CREAMSICLES

2 cups vanilla ice cream, softened
1 can (8 ounces) crushed pineapple in juice
7 paper cups (3-ounce size)
7 wooden craft sticks
  Sprinkles to decorate

Combine ice cream and undrained pineapple. Spoon evenly into cups; insert a craft stick into each cup. Freeze until firm. To serve, let stand at room temperature 10 minutes. Remove from cups; roll in sprinkles. Serve immediately.
Yield: 7 servings

RAINBOW COOKIES

1 package (20 ounces) refrigerated sugar cookie dough
  Red, yellow, green, and blue paste food coloring

Divide cookie dough into 4 equal portions. Tint each portion of dough a different color (blend color into dough by kneading or by cutting in with a fork). Between sheets of plastic wrap, shape each piece of dough into a 4 x 8 x 1/4-inch rectangle. Remove plastic wrap. Stack red, yellow, green, and blue rectangles of dough on top of each other. Cover with plastic wrap and freeze 1 hour or until firm.
Preheat oven to 375 degrees. Returning dough to freezer between batches, cut dough into 1/4-inch-thick slices and place on a lightly greased baking sheet. Curve cookies to resemble rainbows. Bake 5 to 7 minutes or until edges begin to brown (do not overbake). Transfer to a wire rack to cool completely.
Yield: about 2 1/2 dozen cookies

of bananas on sides of pan. Bake 6 to 8 minutes or until fillings melt. For each banana, remove peel covering filling and 1 skin segment on each side. Serve warm **Yield:** 6 servings

Banana Boats are packed with a cargo of chocolate and peanut butter chips, marshmallows, and jam.

BANANA BOATS

6 bananas
  Milk chocolate chips
  Miniature marshmallows
  Peanut butter chips
  Strawberry jam

Preheat oven to 400 degrees. For each banana, peel back 1 skin segment in curve of banana without removing peel. Using a small spoon, scoop out a small portion of banana along entire length. Place favorite mixture of fillings in banana; replace peel. Place bananas in an 8-inch square baking pan, propping ends

UPSIDE-DOWN CLOWN CONES

1 container (16 ounces) vanilla ready-to-spread frosting
6 sugar ice-cream cones
  Sprinkles
  Small gumdrops
6 large scalloped-edged cookies (about 3-inch diameter)
6 large scoops vanilla ice cream, firmly frozen
  Orange jelly beans
  Chocolate chips
  Red jelly beans
  Red string licorice

Spread frosting on wide end of cones; roll in sprinkles. Press 1 gumdrop on point of each cone. Place 1 cookie on each of 6 serving plates. Place 1 scoop ice cream on each cookie and invert cones on top of ice cream. Working quickly, press orange jelly beans on sides of ice cream for hair. Press chocolate chips on ice cream for eyes. Cut 3 red jelly beans in half and press on ice cream for noses. Cut small pieces of licorice and press on ice cream for mouths. Place in freezer until ready to serve.
Yield: 6 servings

Any celebration is especially memorable with Upside-Down Clown Cones! These smiley-face delights are simple and fun to make using cookies, candies, and purchased frosting to dress up ice cream and sugar cones.

FROZEN AMARETTO FRUITCAKE

1 package (3.4 ounces) French vanilla instant pudding mix
2 cups milk
2 cups finely crushed amaretto cookies (about 1/2 of a 14.1-ounce tin)
1 cup chopped pecans
1 cup chopped dates
1 cup chopped green and red candied cherries
1 container (8 ounces) non-dairy whipped topping, thawed and divided
2 teaspoons amaretto
  Chopped green and red candied cherries to garnish

In a large bowl, add pudding mix to milk; beat until thickened. Fold in cookie crumbs, pecans, dates, 1 cup candied cherries, and half of whipped topping. Pour mixture into a lightly greased 7-inch springform pan. Cover and freeze overnight.

To serve, run a knife around sides of pan and remove sides. Fold amaretto into remaining whipped topping in a small bowl. Garnish each serving of fruitcake with flavored topping and candied cherries.

Yield: about 12 servings

CHRISTMAS MINCEMEAT BARS

1 package (18.25 ounces) yellow cake mix
2 1/2 cups quick-cooking oats
3/4 cup butter or margarine, melted
1 jar (27 ounces) mincemeat

Preheat oven to 375 degrees. In a medium bowl, combine cake mix, oats, and melted butter (mixture will be crumbly). Reserving 2 cups oat mixture, firmly press remaining mixture into bottom of a lightly greased 9 x 13-inch baking pan. Spread mincemeat over crust. Sprinkle reserved oat mixture over mincemeat. Bake 30 to 35 minutes or until topping is lightly browned. Cool in pan on a wire rack. Cut into 1 x 2-inch bars.

Yield: about 4 dozen bars

PEACHES AND CREAM SAUCE

1/2 cup peach preserves
1 teaspoon lemon juice
1 1/2 cups sour cream
2 tablespoons firmly packed brown sugar
1/2 teaspoon apple pie spice
  Fresh fruit, cake, or custard to serve

Combine peach preserves and lemon juice in a medium bowl. Stir in sour cream, brown sugar, and apple pie spice until well blended. Chill 1 hour to allow flavors to blend. Serve over fruit, cake, or custard. Store in an airtight container.

Yield: about 2 cups sauce

PEANUT BUTTER SAUCE

1 cup firmly packed brown sugar
1 cup whipping cream
1/2 cup crunchy peanut butter
1 teaspoon vanilla extract
  Ice cream or cake to serve

Combine brown sugar and whipping cream in a medium microwave-safe bowl; whisk until smooth. Add peanut butter and microwave on high power (100%) 2 minutes; whisk until melted. Stir in vanilla. Serve warm over ice cream or cake. Store in an airtight container in refrigerator.

Yield: about 2 cups sauce

CHOCOLATE FUDGE SAUCE

2 cans (5 ounces each) evaporated milk
1 package (6 ounces) semisweet chocolate chips
1/2 cup butter or margarine
2 cups sifted confectioners sugar
1 teaspoon vanilla extract
  Ice cream or cake to serve

In a large microwave-safe bowl, combine evaporated milk, chocolate chips, and butter; cover with plastic wrap. Microwave on high power (100%) 5 minutes; carefully remove plastic wrap and stir until smooth. Add confectioners sugar; stir until well blended. Microwave uncovered on high power (100%) 5 minutes, stirring every 2 minutes. Stir in vanilla. Serve warm over ice cream or cake. Store in an airtight container in refrigerator.

Yield: about 2²/3 cups sauce

CRANBERRY-LEMON TRIFLE

(Shown on page 286)

2 packages (4.4 ounces each) custard mix
5 cups milk
1 purchased pound cake loaf (16 ounces)
1/4 cup crème de cassis
1 jar (11 1/4 ounces) lemon curd
2 cans (16 ounces each) whole berry cranberry sauce
  Lemon slice and fresh cranberries to garnish

In a large saucepan, prepare custard mix with milk according to package directions. Cover and chill about 30 minutes.

Cut pound cake into 1/4-inch slices. Place slices on a baking sheet. Sprinkle crème de cassis over slices. Fold lemon curd into custard. Place a layer of custard mixture in a 3 1/2-quart trifle bowl. Place a layer of cake over custard. Spoon a layer of cranberry sauce over cake. Repeat layers, ending with custard on top. Garnish with lemon slice and fresh cranberries. Cover and store in refrigerator.

Yield: about 18 servings

Adult palates will savor elegant Cranberry-Lemon Trifle (top, recipe on page 285), which layers crème de cassis-sprinkled pound cake with custard and cranberry sauce. Zesty Cranberry-Nut Balls will tickle your taste buds! The chewy no-bake candies are prepared with cranberry-orange relish, coconut, and pecans.

CRANBERRY-NUT BALLS

1 cup cranberry-orange relish
1 package (7 ounces) flaked
   coconut
1 cup finely chopped pecans
  Confectioners sugar

Combine cranberry-orange relish, coconut, and pecans in a medium bowl. Chill 2 hours. Shape into 1-inch balls (mixture will be sticky). Roll in confectioners sugar. Store in an airtight container in refrigerator.

Yield: about 3^1/$_2$ dozen candies

Simply Delicious
COOKIES

Springerle, page 323

White Chocolate Cookies, page 324

Chocolate-Orange Logs, page 323

Whether you love them crisp or chewy,
moist or flaky, there's a recipe here to
satisfy everyone's sweet tooth.

SPICY CHRISTMAS TREES

COOKIES
- 1/3 cup butter or margarine, softened
- 1/3 cup vegetable shortening
- 1 1/4 cups sugar
- 1 cup sour cream
- 1/2 cup molasses
- 2 eggs
- 1 teaspoon vanilla extract
- 5 1/4 cups all-purpose flour
- 1/4 cup cocoa
- 1 tablespoon ground cinnamon
- 2 teaspoons baking powder
- 2 teaspoons ground ginger
- 1 teaspoon ground allspice
- 1 teaspoon baking soda
- 1 teaspoon salt

ICING
- 1 cup sifted confectioners sugar
- 1 tablespoon plus 1 teaspoon milk

For cookies, cream butter, shortening, and sugar in a large bowl until fluffy. Add sour cream, molasses, eggs, and vanilla; beat until smooth. In another large bowl, combine flour, cocoa, cinnamon, baking powder, ginger, allspice, baking soda, and salt. Add half of dry ingredients to creamed mixture; stir until a soft dough forms. Stir remaining dry ingredients, 1 cup at a time, into dough; use hands if necessary to mix well. Divide dough into fourths. Wrap in plastic wrap and chill 2 hours or until dough is firm.

Preheat oven to 350 degrees. On a lightly floured surface, use a floured rolling pin to roll out one fourth of dough to slightly less than 1/4-inch thickness. Use 3 1/4 x 4-inch and 2 1/4 x 3 1/4-inch Christmas tree-shaped cookie cutters to cut out cookies. Transfer to a greased baking sheet. Bake 7 to 9 minutes or until firm to the touch. Transfer cookies to a wire rack to cool. Repeat with remaining dough.

For icing, combine confectioners sugar and milk in a small bowl; stir until smooth. Spoon icing into a pastry bag fitted with a small round tip. Pipe outline onto each cookie. Allow icing to harden. Store in an airtight container.

Yield: about 7 dozen cookies

SNOWBALL COOKIES

- 3 cups finely shredded coconut
- 1 package (18 ounces) vanilla candy coating, cut into pieces
- 1 package (16 ounces) chocolate sandwich cookies

Spread coconut on waxed paper. Melt candy coating in a heavy medium saucepan over low heat. Remove from heat. Place each cookie on a fork and dip into candy coating until covered; roll in coconut. Place cookies on waxed paper and allow candy coating to harden.

Yield: about 3 1/2 dozen cookies

Our Spicy Christmas Trees are a yummy after-dinner snack. Their old-fashioned gingerbread taste is sure to please

HAZELNUT COOKIES
(Shown on page 7)

COOKIES
- $3/4$ cup butter or margarine, softened
- $2/3$ cup sugar
- 1 egg
- 1 teaspoon vanilla extract
- $2/3$ cup finely ground hazelnuts
- $2^1/4$ cups all-purpose flour
- $1/4$ teaspoon salt

ICING
- 4 cups confectioners sugar, sifted
- $1/2$ cup plus 1 tablespoon milk
  Brown, pink, black, and yellow
  paste food coloring

Preheat oven to 350 degrees. For cookies, cream butter and sugar in a medium bowl until fluffy. Add egg and vanilla; beat until smooth. Stir in hazelnuts. Add flour and salt; stir until a soft dough forms. On a lightly floured surface, use a floured rolling pin to roll out dough to a 12-inch square. Cut out 1 x 6-inch cookies, cutting one end of each cookie into a point. Transfer to a greased baking sheet. Bake 12 to 15 minutes or until edges are lightly browned. Transfer cookies to a wire rack to cool.

For icing, combine confectioners sugar and milk in a medium bowl; stir until smooth. Transfer $1/4$ cup icing to each of 3 small bowls; tint brown, pink, and black. Tint remaining icing yellow. Refer to photo on page 7 and ice cookies, allowing icing to harden between each color. Store in an airtight container.
Yield: about 2 dozen cookies

GINGERBREAD REINDEER COOKIES

- 1 package (14 ounces) gingerbread mix
- 2 eggs
- $1/4$ cup vegetable oil
  Small pretzel twists
  Brown and red jelly beans

Preheat oven to 350 degrees. In a large bowl, combine gingerbread mix, eggs, and oil; stir until a soft dough forms. For each cookie, place a $1^1/2$-inch ball of dough on a greased baking sheet. Flatten balls into a 3-inch-high oval shape. Use fingers to press in sides of each cookie about one-third from 1 end of cookie to resemble reindeer face. Press pretzels into cookies for "antlers." Press jelly beans into cookies for "eyes" and "noses." Bake 9 to 11 minutes or until bottoms of cookies are firm. Transfer cookies to a wire rack to cool.
Yield: about 1 dozen cookies

COCONUT FRUITCAKE BARS

Shown on page 7)

CRUST
- 12 ounces fruitcake, cut into pieces
- 1/3 cup old-fashioned oats
- 1/3 cup flaked coconut

FILLING
- 1 cup firmly packed brown sugar
- 2 teaspoons all-purpose flour
- 1/2 teaspoon baking powder
- 1/4 teaspoon salt
- 2 eggs
- 1 teaspoon vanilla extract
- 1 1/2 cups flaked coconut
- 1 cup chopped pecans, divided

Preheat oven to 350 degrees. Line a greased 9-inch square baking pan with aluminum foil, extending foil over 2 sides of pan; grease foil. For crust, process fruitcake, oats, and coconut in a food processor until well blended. Press mixture into prepared pan.

For filling, combine brown sugar, flour, baking powder, and salt in a medium bowl. Beat in eggs and vanilla until well blended. Stir in coconut and 1/2 cup pecans. Pour filling over crust. Sprinkle remaining 1/2 cup pecans over filling. Bake 20 to 25 minutes or until almost set in center and golden brown. Cool in pan on a wire rack. Lift from pan using ends of foil. Cut into 1 x 2-inch bars.
Yield: about 2 1/2 dozen bars

BENNE SEED COOKIES

- 1 cup (about 5 ounces) sesame seeds
- 1/4 cup butter or margarine, softened
- 1 cup sugar
- 1 egg
- 1 teaspoon freshly squeezed lemon juice
- 1 teaspoon vanilla extract
- 1/2 cup all-purpose flour
- 1/4 teaspoon salt
- 1/4 teaspoon baking powder

Preheat oven to 350 degrees. Spread sesame seeds on an ungreased baking sheet. Stirring occasionally, bake 5 to 8 minutes or until golden brown. Cool completely on pan.

In a medium bowl, cream butter and sugar until fluffy. Add egg, lemon juice, and vanilla; stir until well blended. In a small bowl, combine flour, salt, and baking powder. Add dry ingredients to creamed mixture and stir until a soft dough forms. Stir in sesame seeds. Drop teaspoonfuls of dough 1 inch apart onto a heavily greased baking sheet. Bake 6 to 8 minutes or until edges are lightly browned. Transfer to a wire rack to cool completely. Store in an airtight container.
Yield: about 5 dozen cookies

Cut in tree shapes and coated with colorful icing, these buttery Christmas Lemon Cookies have lots of holiday appeal. Silvery dragées make pretty "ornaments" for the trees.

CHRISTMAS LEMON COOKIES

COOKIES
   1   cup butter or margarine, softened
   1/2 cup granulated sugar
   1   teaspoon grated dried lemon peel
   2 1/2 cups all-purpose flour

ICING
   2 1/4 cups confectioners sugar
   5   tablespoons milk
       Red and green paste food coloring
       Dragées (for decoration only)

For cookies, cream butter, sugar, and lemon peel in a large bowl until fluffy. Stir in flour; knead dough until a soft ball forms. Cover and chill 30 minutes.

Preheat oven to 300 degrees. On a lightly floured surface, use a floured rolling pin to roll out dough to 1/4-inch thickness. Use a tree-shaped cookie cutter to cut out dough. Transfer cookies to a greased baking sheet. Bake 20 to 25 minutes or until cookies are light brown. Cool on wire rack.

For icing, mix confectioners sugar and milk together in a medium bowl (icing will be thin). Divide icing evenly into 3 small bowls. Tint 1 bowl red, 1 bowl green, and leave 1 bowl white. Pour icing over tops of cookies, smoothing with a spatula. Decorate with dragées. Allow icing to harden. Store in an airtight container. Remove dragées before eating cookies.

Yield: about 3 dozen 5-inch cookies

ightly embossed, Victorian Stamped Cookies are pretty and palate-pleasing.

VICTORIAN STAMPED COOKIES

$^3/_4$ cup butter or margarine, softened
$^3/_1$ cup firmly packed brown sugar
1 egg
1 teaspoon vanilla extract
$^1/_2$ teaspoon butter extract
$2^1/_4$ cups all-purpose flour
$^1/_8$ teaspoon salt

In a large bowl, cream butter and brown sugar until fluffy. Add egg and extracts; beat until smooth. In a medium bowl, combine flour and salt. Add dry ingredients to creamed mixture; stir until soft dough forms. Cover dough and chill 1 hour.

Preheat oven to 350 degrees. Shape dough into 1-inch balls and place 2 inches apart on a greased baking sheet. Flatten balls with 2-inch-diameter cookie stamps (prepared according to manufacturer's directions). Bake 9 to 11 minutes or until bottoms are lightly browned. Transfer cookies to a wire rack to cool. Store in an airtight container.
Yield: about 5 dozen cookies

LEMON SNOWFLAKE COOKIES

COOKIES
- 1/2 cup butter or margarine, softened
- 1 cup sugar
- 1 egg
- 2 tablespoons milk
- 1 teaspoon grated lemon zest
- 1/2 teaspoon lemon extract
- 2 cups all-purpose flour
- 1/2 teaspoon baking soda
- 1/2 teaspoon cream of tartar
- 1/4 teaspoon salt

ROYAL ICING
- 1 3/4 cups sifted confectioners sugar
- 2 tablespoons warm water
- 1 tablespoon meringue powder
- 1/8 teaspoon lemon extract

For cookies, cream butter and sugar in a large bowl until fluffy. Add egg, milk, lemon zest, and lemon extract; beat until smooth. In a small bowl, combine remaining ingredients; add to creamed mixture and stir until a soft dough forms. Wrap in plastic wrap and chill 2 hours or until dough is firm.

Preheat oven to 375 degrees. On a lightly floured surface, use a floured rolling pin to roll out dough to 1/8-inch thickness. Use a 3-inch-diameter fluted-edge cookie cutter to cut out cookies. Transfer to a lightly greased baking sheet. Bake 8 to 10 minutes or until bottoms of cookies are lightly browned. Transfer to a wire rack to cool completely.

For royal icing, beat confectioners sugar, water, meringue powder, and lemon extract in a medium bowl with an electric mixer 7 to 10 minutes or until stiff. Spoon icing into a pastry bag fitted with a small round tip. Pipe snowflake design on each cookie. Allow icing to harden. Store in an airtight container.

Yield: about 2 1/2 dozen cookies

CHOCOLATE CARAMEL BROWNIES

- 1 package (11 ounces) caramel bits or a 14-ounce package of caramels
- 1/2 cup evaporated milk, divided
- 1 package (18.25 ounces) chocolate cake mix
- 3/4 cup butter, melted
- 1 teaspoon vanilla extract
- 1 cup walnuts, chopped

In a medium saucepan, combine caramel bits and 1/4 cup evaporated milk. Stirring constantly, cook over low heat until caramels are melted. Remove from heat and set aside.

Combine remaining 1/4 cup milk, cake mix, butter, and vanilla; stir until blended. Spread half of batter into a foil-lined, lightly greased 9-inch square baking pan. Bake at 350 degrees for 10 minutes; cool pan on a wire rack 5 minutes. Pour caramel mixture over baked brownie layer; sprinkle with walnuts. Spoon remaining batter over walnuts. Bake at 350 degrees for 25 minutes; cool completely in pan on a wire rack. Cover and chill brownies before cutting into 1 x 2-inch bars.

Yield: 32 brownies

A fluted-edge cookie cutter gives tangy Lemon Snowflake Cookies their scalloped border, and a pastry bag is used to pipe the icing.

LEMON CURD TARTS

CRUST

1¼ cups all-purpose flour
2 tablespoons granulated sugar
¼ teaspoon salt
½ cup butter, chilled and cut into pieces
3 tablespoons ice water

LEMON CURD

6 egg yolks
1 cup granulated sugar
½ cup fresh lemon juice
6 tablespoons butter, cut into pieces
1½ tablespoons grated lemon peel
⅛ teaspoon salt
Whipped cream to serve

For crust, sift flour, sugar, and salt into a mixing bowl. Using a pastry blender or two knives, cut butter into flour until mixture resembles coarse meal. Sprinkle ice water over dough, mixing quickly just until dough forms a soft ball. Wrap dough in plastic wrap and refrigerate 1 hour.

On a lightly floured surface, use a floured rolling pin to roll out dough to ⅛-inch thickness. Cut dough into circles about ¼-inch larger than tartlet pans. Press dough into pans; trim excess around edges. Refrigerate 30 minutes.

Preheat oven to 400 degrees. Place small pieces of aluminum foil on dough and weight foil with dried beans or pie weights. Bake 10 minutes. Remove weights and foil and bake 3 to 5 minutes or until very lightly browned. Cool completely before removing tart shells from pans.

For lemon curd, combine all ingredients in a heavy non-aluminum saucepan over medium-low heat. Cook, stirring constantly, until butter melts and mixture thickens slightly. Do not allow mixture to boil. Remove from heat. Transfer mixture to a bowl to cool. Cover and refrigerate at least 2 hours before serving.

To serve, fill tart shells with lemon curd and top with a small amount of whipped cream.

Yield: about 16 tarts

MEXICAN SUGAR COOKIES

¾ cup vegetable oil
2 eggs
1½ teaspoons vanilla extract
1¼ cups sugar, divided
2 cups all-purpose flour
1 teaspoon baking powder
¼ teaspoon salt
1½ teaspoons ground cinnamon

Preheat oven to 400 degrees. In a large bowl, beat oil, eggs, and vanilla until well blended. Add 1 cup sugar; beat until smooth. In a small bowl, combine flour, baking powder, and salt. Add flour mixture to oil mixture; stir until a soft dough forms. In a small bowl, combine remaining ¼ cup sugar and cinnamon. Drop teaspoonfuls of dough into cinnamon-sugar mixture; roll into balls. Place balls 2 inches apart on a greased baking sheet. Flatten cookies with bottom of a glass dipped in cinnamon-sugar mixture. Bake 4 to 6 minutes or until bottoms are lightly browned. Transfer cookies to a wire rack to cool. Store in a cookie tin.

Yield: about 4½ dozen cookies

CHOCOLATE RUM BALLS

1 package (12 ounces) semisweet
   chocolate chips, divided
1/4 cup sour cream
1 tablespoon honey
1/4 teaspoon salt
13/4 cups graham cracker crumbs
1 cup sifted confectioners sugar
3/4 cup ground walnuts
1/2 cup butter or margarine, melted
1/3 cup rum

Combine 1 cup chocolate chips,
sour cream, honey, and salt in a small
saucepan. Stirring constantly, cook over
low heat until smooth. Pour into an
8-inch square pan, cover, and freeze
20 minutes. Shape teaspoonfuls of
chocolate mixture into about 36 balls;
place on aluminum foil and freeze
10 minutes.
   Process remaining 1 cup chocolate
chips in a food processor until finely
ground; transfer to a small bowl and set
aside. In a large bowl, combine cracker
crumbs, confectioners sugar, walnuts,
butter, and rum. Press crumb mixture
around each chocolate ball, forming
1 1/2-inch balls. Immediately roll in ground
chocolate. Store in an airtight container
in refrigerator. Serve chilled.
Yield: about 3 dozen rum balls

CHRISTMAS TREE COOKIES

1 cup butter or margarine, softened
1 cup sugar
2 eggs
1 teaspoon vanilla extract
3 1/3 cups all-purpose flour
1 teaspoon baking powder
1/2 teaspoon salt
1 cup finely crushed hard red
   candies (about 20 candies)

In a large bowl, cream butter and sugar
until fluffy. Add eggs and vanilla; beat
until smooth. In a medium bowl, combine
flour, baking powder, and salt. Add dry
ingredients to creamed mixture; stir until
a soft dough forms. Wrap in plastic wrap
and chill 1 hour.
   Preheat oven to 350 degrees. On a
lightly floured surface, use a floured
rolling pin to roll out dough to 1/8-inch
thickness. Use a 4 1/2-inch tree-shaped
cookie cutter to cut out cookies. Transfer
to a lightly greased aluminum foil-lined
baking sheet. Use a heart-shaped aspic
cutter to cut heart from center of each
cookie. Bake 8 to 10 minutes or until
cookies are firm. Cool completely on pan;
leave cookies on foil to decorate.
   In a small saucepan, melt candies
over medium heat; reduce heat to low.
Spoon melted candies into each heart
cutout. Allow candies to harden. Carefully
remove cookies from foil. Store in an
airtight container.
Yield: about 5 1/2 dozen cookies

RUSSIAN ROCK COOKIES

1 cup butter or margarine, softened
1 cup granulated sugar
1/2 cup firmly packed brown sugar
1/2 cup light corn syrup
1/2 cup buttermilk
3 eggs, beaten
1 teaspoon vanilla extract
3 1/4 cups all-purpose flour, divided
1 package (8 ounces) chopped dates
1 tablespoon ground cinnamon
1 teaspoon ground cloves
1 teaspoon ground nutmeg
1/2 teaspoon baking soda
1/4 teaspoon salt
1 jar (10 ounces) maraschino
    cherries, drained and chopped
2 cups chopped pecans

Preheat oven to 350 degrees. In a large bowl, cream butter and sugars until fluffy. Add corn syrup, buttermilk, eggs, and vanilla; beat until smooth. In a small bowl, combine 1/4 cup flour and dates; stir until dates are coated with flour. In a medium bowl, combine remaining 3 cups flour, cinnamon, cloves, nutmeg, baking soda, and salt. Add dry ingredients to creamed mixture; stir until a soft dough forms. Stir in dates, cherries, and pecans. Drop teaspoonfuls of dough 1-inch apart onto a greased baking sheet. Bake 12 to 15 minutes or until edges are lightly browned. Transfer to a wire rack to cool completely. Store in an airtight container.
Yield: about 8 dozen cookies

ORANGE-MOLASSES CRISPIES

1/3 cup butter or margarine, softened
1/2 cup vegetable shortening
3/4 cup sugar
1/4 cup molasses
2 tablespoons orange-flavored
    liqueur
2 teaspoons grated orange zest
1/2 teaspoon vanilla extract
1 1/2 cups all-purpose flour
1 teaspoon baking soda
1 cup finely chopped walnuts

Preheat oven to 350 degrees. In a large bowl, cream butter, shortening, and sugar until fluffy. Stir in molasses, orange liqueur, orange zest, and vanilla until well blended. In a small bowl, combine flour and baking soda. Add dry ingredients to creamed mixture; stir until a soft dough forms. Stir in walnuts. Drop teaspoonfuls of dough 1-inch apart onto a greased baking sheet. Bake 8 to 10 minutes or until cookies are golden brown. Allow cookies to cool on pan 3 minutes; transfer to a wire rack to cool completely. Store in an airtight container.
Yield: about 5 dozen cookies

RUSSIAN TEACAKES

1 cup butter, softened
$1/2$ cup powdered sugar
1 teaspoon vanilla extract
$2^1/4$ cups all-purpose flour
$1/4$ teaspoon salt
$1/2$ cup finely chopped pecans
Powdered sugar

Preheat oven to 400 degrees. Beat butter, $1/2$ cup powdered sugar, and vanilla until fluffy. Combine flour and salt. Stir flour mixture and pecans into butter mixture. Shape into 1-inch balls. Place on ungreased baking sheets and bake for 8 to 10 minutes or until firm but not brown. Roll in additional powdered sugar while warm. Cool and roll in sugar again.
Yield: $5^1/2$ dozen cookies

APPLE SPICE COOKIES

1 cup vegetable shortening
$2^1/2$ cups granulated sugar
1 cup dark molasses
$4^1/2$ cups all-purpose flour
2 tablespoons baking soda
2 teaspoons salt
$1^1/2$ teaspoons ground cinnamon
1 teaspoon ground cloves
1 teaspoon ground ginger
$1/2$ teaspoon ground nutmeg
$1/2$ cup milk
Granulated sugar
Apple jelly

Preheat oven to 350 degrees. Cream shortening and sugar until fluffy. Add molasses and blend well. In a medium bowl, combine flour, baking soda, salt, cinnamon, cloves, ginger, and nutmeg. Alternately stir dry ingredients and milk into creamed mixture, blending well after each addition. Shape dough into 1-inch balls. Roll balls in sugar and place on ungreased baking sheets. Make a small indentation with thumb in the top of each ball. Use a teaspoon to place a small amount of apple jelly in each indentation. Bake 8 to 10 minutes. Cookies will be very soft, but will harden as they cool. Remove from sheets and cool on wire racks.
Yield: about 7 dozen cookies

COCONUT BELLS

1 cup butter or margarine, softened
1/2 cup firmly packed brown sugar
1/2 cup granulated sugar
1 teaspoon vanilla extract
1 egg
2 1/2 cups all-purpose flour
1/2 teaspoon baking soda
1/2 teaspoon salt
1 teaspoon ground nutmeg
Coconut Filling (recipe follows)
Red and green candied cherry
halves

Beat butter, sugars, vanilla, and egg in a large bowl until well blended. Stir in flour, baking soda, salt, and nutmeg. Wrap in plastic wrap and chill until firm, about 1 hour.

Preheat oven to 375 degrees. On a lightly floured surface, use a floured rolling pin to roll out dough to 1/8-inch thickness. Cut out dough using 2 1/2-inch round cookie cutter. Place on ungreased baking sheets. Place 1/2 teaspoon Coconut Filling in center of each round. Shape into a bell by folding opposite edges together over filling. Pinch top of bell slightly to make it narrower than bottom of bell. Cut each green cherry half into four strips. Place one green cherry strip at bottom of cookie for stem of clapper. Place a red cherry half at bottom of stem for clapper. Bake 10 to 12 minutes or until lightly browned. Remove from sheets and cool on wire racks.
Yield: about 3 dozen cookies

COCONUT FILLING
1/4 cup firmly packed brown sugar
3 tablespoons butter or margarine
1 1/2 tablespoons water
3/4 cup confectioners sugar, sifted
1 can (3 1/2 ounces) shredded
coconut

1 1/2 teaspoons vanilla extract
1/3 cup chopped pecans

In a small saucepan, bring brown sugar, butter, and water to a boil. Remove from heat. Stir in confectioners sugar, coconut, vanilla, and pecans.

ORANGE NUT SQUARES

2 cups old-fashioned oats
1 cup all-purpose flour
3/4 cup firmly packed brown sugar
1 1/4 teaspoons ground cinnamon
divided
1/2 teaspoon baking soda
3/4 cup butter or margarine, melted
1 cup raisins
1/2 cup finely chopped walnuts
1/4 cup orange marmalade
1/2 cup sifted confectioners sugar
1 tablespoon milk

Preheat oven to 350 degrees. In a large bowl, combine oats, flour, brown sugar, 1 teaspoon cinnamon, and baking soda. Stir in melted butter until well blended. Reserving 1 cup oat mixture, press remaining oat mixture into bottom of a greased 8 x 11-inch baking pan. In a medium bowl, combine reserved oat mixture, raisins, walnuts, and marmalade. Spread raisin mixture evenly over oat mixture in pan. Bake 25 to 30 minutes or until lightly browned. While still warm, cut into 1-inch squares. In a small bowl, combine confectioners sugar, remaining 1/4 teaspoon cinnamon, and milk; stir until smooth. Drizzle over warm squares; cool completely in pan. Store in an airtight container.
Yield: about 4 dozen squares

COCONUT-ORANGE SQUARES

CAKE

- 3/4 cup butter or margarine, softened
- 3/4 cup sugar
- 1 can (16 ounces) sliced carrots, drained and mashed
- 1 egg
- 1 1/2 teaspoons grated orange zest
- 1/2 teaspoon vanilla extract
- 1/4 teaspoon orange extract
- 2 cups all-purpose flour
- 2 teaspoons baking powder
- 3/4 teaspoon salt
- 3/4 cup flaked coconut

ICING

- 1 package (8 ounces) cream cheese, softened
- 1/4 cup butter or margarine, softened
- 2 teaspoons milk
- 1/2 teaspoon grated orange zest
- 1/2 teaspoon orange extract
- 1/4 teaspoon vanilla extract
- 3 1/2 cups sifted confectioners sugar
- 1/2 cup toasted flaked coconut to garnish

Preheat oven to 350 degrees. For cake, cream butter and sugar in a large bowl until fluffy. Add carrots, egg, orange zest, and extracts; beat until smooth. In a medium bowl, combine flour, baking powder, and salt. Add dry ingredients to creamed mixture; stir until well blended. Stir in coconut. Pour batter into a lightly greased 9 x 13-inch pan. Bake 20 to 25 minutes or until a toothpick inserted in center of cake comes out clean. Place pan on a wire rack to cool.

For icing, beat cream cheese, butter, milk, orange zest, and extracts in a medium bowl until smooth. Stir in confectioners sugar until smooth. Spread icing over cooled cake. Garnish with toasted coconut. Cut into 2-inch squares.
Yield: about 2 dozen squares

FRESH MINT COOKIES
Prepare dough one day in advance to allow flavors to blend.

- 1 1/2 cups butter or margarine, softened
- 2/3 cup superfine granulated sugar
- 1 egg
- 2 tablespoons minced fresh mint leaves
- 1 tablespoon grated orange zest
- 1/2 teaspoon vanilla extract
- 2 cups all-purpose flour
  Granulated sugar

In a large bowl, cream butter and superfine sugar until fluffy. Add egg, mint leaves, orange zest, and vanilla; beat until smooth. Add flour to creamed mixture; stir until a soft dough forms. Cover dough and chill overnight.

Preheat oven to 350 degrees. Shape dough into 1-inch balls. Place balls 1 inch apart on an ungreased baking sheet; flatten balls with bottom of a glass dipped in granulated sugar. Bake 7 to 9 minutes or until edges are lightly browned. Transfer cookies to a wire rack to cool. Store in an airtight container.
Yield: about 6 dozen cookies

Cut in a wreath shape, Lemon-Iced Apple Cookies are decorated with icing leaves and gold dragées.

LEMON-ICED APPLE COOKIES

COOKIES
- 1 cup butter or margarine, softened
- 3/4 cup sugar
- 1/2 cup apple jelly
- 1 teaspoon vanilla extract
- 3 cups all-purpose flour

ICING
- 4 1/2 cups sifted confectioners sugar
- 3/4 cup milk
- 1 teaspoon lemon extract
  Gold dragées (for decoration only) and purchased green decorating icing with a set of decorating tips to decorate

For cookies, cream butter and sugar in a large bowl until fluffy. Add jelly and vanilla; beat until well blended. Add flour; stir until a soft dough forms. Cover and chill 30 minutes.

Preheat oven to 300 degrees. On a lightly floured surface, use a floured rolling pin to roll out dough to 1/4-inch thickness. Use a 3-inch-wide wreath-shaped cookie cutter to cut out cookies. Transfer to a greased baking sheet. Bake 20 to 25 minutes or until cookies are lightly browned. Transfer cookies to a wire rack to cool completely.

For icing, combine confectioners sugar, milk, and lemon extract in a large bowl; stir until smooth. Ice cookies. Decorate with dragées. Allow icing to harden. Use green decorating icing fitted with a leaf tip to pipe leaves onto cookies. Decorate leaves with dragées. Allow icing to harden. Store in an airtight container. Remove dragées before eating cookies.
Yield: about 4 dozen cookies

PEPPERMINT STOCKINGS

COOKIES
- 3¹/4 cups all-purpose flour
- 1 tablespoon baking powder
- ¹/2 cup butter or margarine, softened
- 1¹/4 cups granulated sugar
- 1 egg
- 2¹/2 teaspoons peppermint extract
- 1 teaspoon vanilla extract
- ¹/4 cup milk

ICING
- 1 cup confectioners sugar
- 2 tablespoons milk
- 1 tablespoon butter, softened
- Red paste food coloring

Preheat oven to 350 degrees. For cookies, combine flour and baking powder in a medium bowl. In a large bowl, cream butter, sugar, egg, and extracts. Add dry ingredients alternately with milk. On a lightly floured surface, use a floured rolling pin to roll out dough to ¹/8-inch thickness. Using desired cookie cutter, cut out dough. Transfer cookies to a lightly greased baking sheet. Bake 8 to 10 minutes or until very lightly browned around edges. Remove from pans and cool on wire racks.

For icing, beat confectioners sugar, milk, and butter until smooth; tint red. Ice cookies as desired.

Yield: about 3 dozen 3-inch-long cookies

Peppermint Stockings make a great snack to set out for Santa, but they're cute for other occasions, too!

CARAMEL GRAHAM CRACKERS

- 24 2¹/2-inch cinnamon graham cracker squares
- ¹/2 cup margarine
- ¹/2 cup butter
- 1 cup firmly packed light brown sugar
- 1 cup chopped pecans

Line a 15¹/2 x 10¹/2 x 1-inch jellyroll pan with foil; cover with single layer of graham crackers. Mix margarine, butter, and brown sugar in a saucepan; bring to a boil and cook 2 minutes. Pour mixture over crackers; sprinkle pecans on top. Bake in a preheated 350-degree oven 12 minutes. Cut into triangles while warm.

Yield: about 4 dozen cookies

APPLE-CINNAMON COOKIES

1 can (21 ounces) apple pie filling
1/2 cup butter or margarine, softened
1/2 cup granulated sugar, divided
1/4 cup firmly packed brown sugar
1 egg
1/2 teaspoon vanilla extract
1 1/2 cups all-purpose flour
1 teaspoon ground cinnamon,
   divided
1/2 teaspoon baking soda
1/2 teaspoon salt
3/4 cup finely chopped walnuts

Preheat oven to 375 degrees. Using a slotted spoon, remove 1 cup apples from pie filling. Set aside remaining pie filling for another use. Process apples in a food processor until finely chopped. In a large bowl, cream butter, 1/4 cup granulated sugar, and brown sugar until fluffy. Add egg and vanilla; beat until smooth. Add chopped apples to creamed mixture; stir until well blended. Sift flour, 1/2 teaspoon cinnamon, baking soda, and salt into a medium bowl. Add dry ingredients to creamed mixture; stir until a soft dough forms. Fold in walnuts. In a small bowl, combine remaining 1/4 cup granulated sugar and 1/2 teaspoon cinnamon; stir until well blended. Drop heaping teaspoonfuls of dough 2-inches apart onto a greased baking sheet. Sprinkle with sugar mixture. Bake 10 to 12 minutes or until edges are lightly browned. Transfer cookies to a wire rack to cool completely. Store in an airtight container.
Yield: about 3 1/2 dozen cookies

PUMPKIN-WALNUT COOKIES

COOKIES
1 cup butter or margarine, softened
1 cup granulated sugar
1 cup canned pumpkin
1 egg
1 teaspoon vanilla extract
2 cups all-purpose flour
1 teaspoon baking powder
1 teaspoon ground cinnamon
1/2 teaspoon ground nutmeg
1/2 teaspoon baking soda
1/2 teaspoon salt
1/4 teaspoon ground allspice
1 cup raisins
1 cup chopped walnuts

ICING
1 cup confectioners sugar
1 package (3 ounces) cream cheese, softened
2 tablespoons water

Preheat oven to 350 degrees. For cookies, cream butter and sugar in a large bowl until fluffy. Add next 3 ingredients, mixing well. In a medium bowl, sift together next 7 ingredients. Add to creamed mixture, mixing well. Stir in raisins and walnuts. Drop by rounded teaspoonfuls onto a greased baking sheet. Bake 12 to 15 minutes or until lightly browned. Cool on a wire rack. For icing, combine all ingredients in a small bowl until smooth. Drizzle icing over cooled cookies. Allow icing to harden. Store in an airtight container.
Yield: about 7 dozen cookies

EGGNOG COOKIES

1 cup butter or margarine, softened
2 cups granulated sugar
1 teaspoon vanilla extract
4 eggs
3 cups all-purpose flour
2 teaspoons baking powder
1/2 teaspoon ground nutmeg
1/2 teaspoon salt

Cream butter, sugar, and vanilla. Beat in eggs, one at a time. Sift dry ingredients together; gradually add to creamed mixture. Cover and refrigerate several hours.

Drop by heaping teaspoonfuls onto ungreased baking sheets. Bake in a preheated 375-degree oven 6 to 8 minutes or until lightly browned around the edges. Cool slightly before removing from baking sheets.
Yield: about 8 dozen cookies

CLOVE COOKIES

1/2 cup butter or margarine, melted
1 cup granulated sugar
1 teaspoon vanilla extract
1 egg
1 cup all-purpose flour
1 teaspoon ground cloves

Stir butter and sugar together; add vanilla. Beat in egg until mixture is smooth. Stir flour and cloves together; blend with butter mixture. Drop teaspoonfuls of dough 2 inches apart onto lightly greased baking sheets. Bake in a preheated 350-degree oven 8 to 10 minutes or until lightly browned. Cool slightly before removing from baking sheets.
Yield: about 4 dozen cookies

CARDAMOM SHORTBREAD

1/2 cup butter or margarine, softened
1/4 cup sugar
1 cup quick-cooking oats
1 teaspoon vanilla extract
2/3 cup all-purpose flour
1 teaspoon ground cardamom

Preheat oven to 350 degrees. In a medium bowl, cream butter and sugar until fluffy. Stir in oats and vanilla. Sift flour and cardamom into a small bowl. Add dry ingredients to creamed mixture; stir until a soft dough forms. Press into a greased 8-inch round shortbread mold or a 9-inch round cake pan. Bake 25 to 30 minutes or until lightly browned. Cool in pan 10 minutes; loosen edges with a knife. Invert onto a cutting board. If necessary, tap edge of pan on cutting board. Cut warm shortbread into wedges. Cool completely. Store in an airtight container.
Yield: 6 to 8 servings

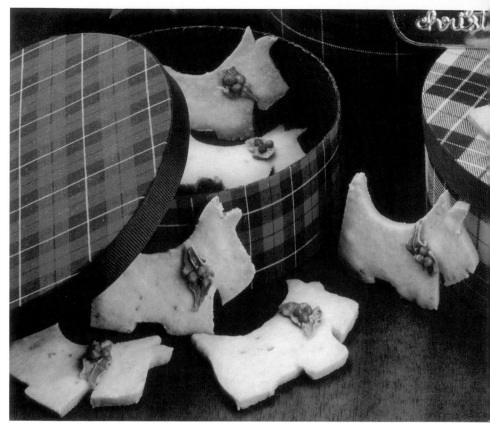

Lads and lassies will love these! Cut in the shape of this beloved dog and adorned with an iced holly "collar," Anise Shortbread Scotties have a delightful licorice flavor.

ANISE SHORTBREAD SCOTTIES

- 1 cup butter, softened
- 1/2 cup confectioners sugar
- 1 1/2 teaspoons crushed anise seed
- 1 teaspoon vanilla extract
- 1/4 teaspoon ground cinnamon
- 2 cups all-purpose flour
  Granulated sugar
  Purchased tubes of green and
    red decorating icing

Cream butter and confectioners sugar until light and fluffy. Beat in anise seed, vanilla, and cinnamon. Stir in flour.

Trace pattern onto tracing paper and cut out. On a lightly floured surface, use a floured rolling pin to roll out dough to 1/4-inch thickness. Place pattern on dough and use a sharp knife to cut around pattern. Transfer cookies to ungreased baking sheets. Sprinkle with granulated sugar. Chill cookies 30 minutes before baking.

Preheat oven to 375 degrees. Bake cookies 5 minutes; reduce heat to 300 degrees and bake 10 minutes more. Remove from pans and cool on wire racks.

Use green and red icing to pipe holly leaves and berries onto cookies.

Yield: about 4 dozen cookies

These international treats (recipes on page 308) are delightful: Mexican Bizcochitos (from left), Belgian Nut Cookies, and French Madeleines.

BIZCOCHITOS
(Shown on page 307)

1 cup butter or margarine, softened
1 cup granulated sugar, divided
1 egg yolk
1 tablespoon milk
2¹/₂ cups all-purpose flour
4¹/₂ teaspoons ground cinnamon, divided
2 teaspoons anise seed
¹/₂ cup white wine

In a large mixing bowl, cream butter, ¹/₂ cup sugar, egg yolk, and milk. In a medium bowl, combine flour, 1¹/₂ teaspoons cinnamon, and anise seed. Add flour mixture to creamed mixture, stirring until combined. Stir in wine. Wrap dough in plastic wrap and chill 2 hours.

Preheat oven to 350 degrees. On a lightly floured surface, use a floured rolling pin to roll out dough to ¹/₈-inch thickness. Cut into desired shapes using a 2-inch cookie cutter. Transfer cookies to lightly greased baking sheets and bake 10 to 12 minutes or until edges are very lightly browned.

In a small bowl, combine remaining ¹/₂ cup sugar and remaining 3 teaspoons of cinnamon. Coat warm cookies with sugar mixture. Store in airtight container.
Yield: about 8 dozen cookies

BELGIAN NUT COOKIES
(Shown on page 307)

³/₄ cup butter, softened
¹/₃ cup granulated sugar
1¹/₂ cups all-purpose flour
1¹/₂ cups ground toasted almonds
1 teaspoon vanilla extract
¹/₈ teaspoon salt
1 cup semisweet chocolate chips
¹/₂ cup raspberry jam

In a large mixing bowl, cream butter and sugar. Add flour, almonds, vanilla, and salt, stirring just until mixture is combined and forms a dough. Divide dough in half and wrap each half in plastic wrap. Refrigerate 1 hour.

Preheat oven to 350 degrees. Roll out dough to ¹/₈-inch thickness between two sheets of waxed paper. Remove top sheet of waxed paper. Using a 2¹/₂-inch-long fluted tart mold or cookie cutter, cut out dough. Place cookies on lightly greased baking sheet. Bake 10 to 12 minutes or until lightly browned around edges. Cool cookies on baking sheet.

Melt chocolate chips in the top of a double boiler over simmering water. Reserving ¹/₄ cup of melted chocolate, spread a thin layer of chocolate on half of the cookies. Spread remaining half of cookies with a thin layer of raspberry jam. With one chocolate side and one raspberry side together, place two cookies together. Place cookies on waxed paper-lined baking sheet. Drizzle tops of cookies with reserved chocolate. Place cookies in refrigerator to set. Store cookies in airtight container in a cool, dry place.
Yield: about 2 dozen cookies

MADELEINES
(Shown on page 307)

2 eggs
¹/₈ teaspoon salt
¹/₂ cup granulated sugar
¹/₂ cup all-purpose flour
¹/₂ cup butter, melted and cooled
Grand Marnier liqueur

Preheat oven to 400 degrees. In a large mixing bowl, combine eggs and salt. Gradually beat in sugar until mixture is thick and lightens in color (about

5 minutes). Fold flour into egg mixture a few tablespoons at a time. Fold in butter a few tablespoons at a time. Spoon 1 tablespoon of batter into each shell of a greased and floured Madeleine pan. Bake 8 to 10 minutes or until a cake springs back when lightly touched. Immediately remove from molds and cool on wire racks. Sprinkle Madeleines with liqueur.
Yield: about 18 Madeleines

Variation: To make chocolate Madeleines, reduce flour to $1/3$ cup and combine flour with 3 tablespoons cocoa. Proceed with recipe as directed.

BUTTER-NUT COOKIES

1	cup butter or margarine, softened
$1^{1}/2$	cups sifted confectioners sugar, divided
1	teaspoon vanilla-butter-nut flavoring
2	cups all-purpose flour
$1/4$	teaspoon salt
$3/4$	cup coarsely ground pecans, toasted

Preheat oven to 375 degrees. In a large bowl, cream butter, $3/4$ cup confectioners sugar, and vanilla-butter-nut flavoring until fluffy. In a small bowl, combine flour and salt. Add dry ingredients and pecans to creamed mixture; stir until well blended. Shape dough into 1-inch balls; place on an ungreased baking sheet. Bake 12 to 14 minutes or until firm to touch and bottoms are lightly browned. When cool enough to handle, roll in remaining $3/4$ cup confectioners sugar. Transfer cookies to waxed paper; allow to cool completely. Roll in confectioners sugar again. Store in an airtight container.
Yield: about $5^{1}/2$ dozen cookies

PECAN PRALINES

2	cups sugar
1	teaspoon baking soda
1	cup buttermilk
1	tablespoon light corn syrup
$3/4$	cup butter, cut into small pieces
2	cups chopped pecans
1	teaspoon vanilla extract

Butter sides of a heavy Dutch oven. Combine sugar and baking soda in buttered pan. Add buttermilk and corn syrup. Stirring constantly, cook over medium-low heat until sugar dissolves. Using a pastry brush dipped in hot water, wash down any sugar crystals on sides of pan. Attach a candy thermometer to pan, making sure thermometer does not touch bottom of pan. Increase heat to medium and bring to a boil. Cook, stirring constantly, until syrup reaches 210 degrees on thermometer; add butter. Continue stirring and cooking mixture until syrup reaches soft-ball stage (approximately 234 to 240 degrees). Test about $1/2$ teaspoon syrup in ice water. Syrup will easily form a ball in ice water but will flatten when held in your hand. Place pan in 2 inches of cold water in sink. Cool to approximately 140 degrees. Using medium speed of an electric mixer, beat candy until thickened and no longer glossy. Quickly stir in pecans and vanilla. Drop by tablespoonfuls onto lightly greased waxed paper. Allow pralines to cool completely. Wrap pralines individually in cellophane or plastic wrap and store in an airtight container.
Yield: about $2^{1}/2$ dozen pralines

Teatime Snowcaps are sweet bar cookies with a pastry crust and a topping of apricot jam, meringue, coconut, and sliced almonds.

TEATIME SNOWCAPS

CRUST
- 3/4 cup vegetable shortening
- 3/4 cup sifted confectioners sugar
- 1 1/2 cups all-purpose flour

TOPPING
- 1 1/2 cups apricot jam
- 3 egg whites
- 3/4 cup sugar
- 3/4 cup coconut, divided
- 1 cup sliced almonds, divided

Preheat oven to 350 degrees. For crust, cream shortening and confectioners sugar in a medium bowl. Stir in flour. Press mixture evenly into bottom of an ungreased 9 x 13-inch baking pan. Bake 12 to 15 minutes or until crust is lightly browned.

For topping, spread jam over hot crust. Beat egg whites until soft peaks form. Gradually beat in sugar, a few tablespoons at a time, until mixture is stiff and glossy. Fold in 1/2 cup coconut and 1/2 cup almonds. Spread mixture over jam. Sprinkle remaining coconut and almonds over top. Bake 20 minutes. Allow to cool. Cut into squares. Store in an airtight container.

Yield: about 35 cookies

The heartwarming taste of home-baked gingerbread is always a favorite. This year, share the goodness with these Gingerbread House Cookies (recipe on page 312).

GINGERBREAD HOUSE COOKIES

(Shown on page 311)

COOKIES
- 1/2 cup butter or margarine, softened
- 1/2 cup firmly packed brown sugar
- 1/2 cup molasses
- 1 egg
- 2 1/2 cups all-purpose flour
- 2 teaspoons ground ginger
- 1 teaspoon ground cinnamon
- 1 teaspoon baking soda
- 1/2 teaspoon ground nutmeg
- 1/4 teaspoon ground cloves
- 1/4 teaspoon salt

ROYAL ICING
- 2 2/3 cups sifted confectioners sugar
- 4 tablespoons warm water
- 2 tablespoons meringue powder
- 1/2 teaspoon lemon extract
- Candies, mints, and gumdrops to decorate

Preheat oven to 350 degrees. For cookies, cream butter and brown sugar in a large bowl until fluffy. Add molasses and egg; beat until smooth. In a medium bowl, combine flour, ginger, cinnamon, baking soda, nutmeg, cloves, and salt. Add dry ingredients to creamed mixture; stir until a soft dough forms. On a lightly floured surface, use a floured rolling pin to roll out dough to 1/4-inch thickness. Use a floured 5 x 7 1/2-inch gingerbread house-shaped cookie cutter to cut out cookies. Transfer to a greased baking sheet. Bake 10 to 12 minutes or until edges are firm. Transfer cookies to a wire rack with waxed paper underneath to cool completely.

For royal icing, beat confectioners sugar, water, meringue powder, and lemon extract in a medium bowl with an electric mixer 7 to 10 minutes or until stiff. Spoon icing into a pastry bag fitted with a medium round tip. Pipe icing onto cookies. Use candies, mints, and gumdrops to decorate cookies as desired. Allow icing to harden. Store in an airtight container.

Yield: 6 cookies

MINT PATTIES

- 1/2 cup butter, melted
- 1 cup granulated sugar
- 1 egg
- 1 3/4 cups all-purpose flour
- 1 teaspoon baking soda
- 1 teaspoon peppermint extract
- 8 ounces chocolate-flavored candy coating
- 1 package (6 ounces) semisweet chocolate chips

Beat butter, sugar, and egg together. Combine flour and baking soda; add to butter mixture. Stir in peppermint extract. Drop by teaspoonfuls onto greased baking sheets. Bake in a preheated 350-degree oven 8 to 10 minutes. Remove from baking sheets and cool on wire racks.

Melt candy coating and chocolate chips in the top of a double boiler over simmering water. Drop each cookie into chocolate to coat. Lift out with a fork, wiping excess chocolate from bottom of cookie. Place on waxed paper and allow chocolate to harden.

Yield: about 3 dozen cookies

CHRISTMAS CANDY CANES

CANDY
4 ounces chocolate candy coating
4 ounces vanilla candy coating
24 small peppermint candy canes

ICING
1 cup confectioners sugar
1 tablespoon milk
Red and green paste food coloring

For candy, melt chocolate and vanilla candy coating in separate small saucepans following package directions. Using tongs, dip half of candy canes in chocolate candy coating. Dip remaining candy canes in vanilla candy coating. Place on a wire rack with waxed paper underneath to cool completely.

For icing, combine confectioners sugar and milk in a small bowl, stirring until smooth. Divide icing in half. Tint 1 bowl red and 1 bowl green. Drizzle icing over candy canes. Allow icing to harden. Store in an airtight container.
Yield: 2 dozen candy canes

CHRISTMAS DIPPED COOKIES

6 ounces chocolate candy coating, cut into pieces
6 ounces vanilla candy coating, cut into pieces
1 package (16 ounces) chocolate sandwich cookies
Tubes of red, green, and white decorating icing

Melt chocolate and vanilla candy coating in separate small saucepans following package directions. Using tongs, dip half of cookies in chocolate candy coating. Dip remaining cookies in vanilla candy coating. Place on a wire rack to cool completely. Use decorating icing to decorate cookies. Allow icing to harden. Store in an airtight container.
Yield: $3^{1}/_{2}$ dozen cookies

MEXICAN CHOCOLATE COOKIES

1 1/2 cups butter, softened
1 3/4 cups granulated sugar
2 eggs, slightly beaten
3 cups all-purpose flour
1 1/2 cups cocoa
1 teaspoon ground cinnamon
1/2 teaspoon ground black pepper
1/4 teaspoon salt
4 to 6 ounces semisweet baking
  chocolate, melted

Cream butter and sugar; add eggs and beat until fluffy. Sift dry ingredients together; gradually add to creamed mixture. Beat until well blended, adding more flour if dough seems too soft. Divide dough into thirds and wrap in plastic wrap; chill at least 1 hour.

On a lightly floured surface, use a floured rolling pin to roll out dough to 1/8-inch thickness; cut out with desired cookie cutters. Place on greased baking sheets. Bake in a preheated 375-degree oven 8 to 10 minutes or until crisp but not darkened. Cool on wire racks; drizzle melted chocolate over cookies.
Yield: about 3 dozen cookies

CHEESECAKE BITES

1 cup all-purpose flour
1/2 cup chopped pecans
1/3 cup firmly packed light brown
  sugar
1/3 cup butter or margarine, melted
1 package (8 ounces) cream cheese,
  softened
1/4 cup granulated sugar
1 egg
2 tablespoons milk
1 tablespoon lemon juice
1 teaspoon vanilla extract

Combine flour, pecans, and brown sugar in a medium bowl. Stir in melted butter until blended. Reserve 1/3 cup of mixture; press remainder into bottom of a greased 8-inch square baking pan. Bake in a preheated 350-degree oven 12 to 15 minutes. Beat cream cheese and granulated sugar until smooth. Beat in remaining ingredients. Pour over baked crust; sprinkle with reserved pecan mixture. Return to oven and bake 25 minutes. Cool slightly; cut into 2-inch squares. Cool completely. Store in an airtight container in refrigerator.
Yield: about 16 squares

DATE BARS

1 cup butter or margarine, softened
2 1/3 cups firmly packed dark brown
  sugar
3 eggs
1 1/2 teaspoons vanilla extract
3 cups all-purpose flour
1 teaspoon baking powder
1/2 teaspoon baking soda
3 cups pitted dates, coarsely
  chopped
1 cup chopped pecans

Cream butter and brown sugar until light and fluffy. Beat in eggs, one at a time. Stir in vanilla. Combine flour, baking powder, and baking soda; gradually add to creamed mixture. Stir in dates and pecans. Spread batter in a greased 13 x 9 x 2-inch baking pan. Bake in a preheated 375-degree oven 25 minutes. Cool in pan and cut into bars.
Yield: about 2 dozen bars

Zippy with a touch of orange zest, Cinnamon-Walnut Biscotti are extra crunchy because they're baked twice—once as a loaf and again as slices.

CINNAMON-WALNUT BISCOTTI

2 cups all-purpose flour
1 cup plus 2 tablespoons sugar, divided
$^1/_2$ teaspoon baking soda
$^1/_2$ teaspoon baking powder
$^1/_4$ teaspoon salt
2 eggs
1 egg yolk
1 teaspoon vanilla extract
1 tablespoon grated orange zest
1$^1/_2$ cups coarsely chopped walnuts, toasted
$^1/_4$ teaspoon ground cinnamon
1 egg
1 teaspoon water

Preheat oven to 300 degrees. Using an electric mixer with a dough hook attachment, combine flour, 1 cup sugar, baking soda, baking powder, and salt in a large bowl until well blended.

(Continued on page 316)

(Continued from page 315)

In a small bowl, whisk 2 eggs, 1 egg yolk, vanilla, and orange zest. Add egg mixture to flour mixture; continue beating until a soft dough forms. Turn onto a lightly floured surface. Add walnuts and knead 3 minutes or until walnuts are evenly distributed. Divide dough in half. On a greased and floured baking sheet, shape each piece of dough into a $2^{1}/_{2}$ x 10-inch loaf, flouring hands as necessary. Allow 3 inches between loaves on baking sheet. In a small bowl, combine remaining 2 tablespoons sugar and cinnamon. In another small bowl, beat 1 egg and water. Brush loaves with egg mixture; sprinkle with sugar and cinnamon mixture. Bake 45 to 50 minutes or until loaves are lightly browned; cool 10 minutes on baking sheet. Cut loaves diagonally into $^{1}/_{2}$-inch slices. Lay cut cookies flat on a baking sheet. Bake 15 minutes, turn cookies over, and bake 15 minutes longer. Transfer cookies to a wire rack to cool completely. Store in an airtight container.

Yield: about $2^{1}/_{2}$ dozen cookies

CHINESE NEW YEAR COOKIES

$^{1}/_{2}$ cup butter or margarine, softened
1 cup sugar
2 eggs
$^{1}/_{2}$ teaspoon vanilla extract
$2^{1}/_{4}$ cups all-purpose flour
2 teaspoons baking powder
1 teaspoon Chinese five-spice powder
1 teaspoon finely chopped crystallized ginger
$^{1}/_{4}$ teaspoon salt

Preheat oven to 375 degrees. In a large bowl, cream butter and sugar until fluffy. Add eggs and vanilla; beat until smooth. In a medium bowl, combine flour, baking powder, Chinese five-spice powder, crystallized ginger, and salt. Add dry ingredients to creamed mixture; stir until a soft dough forms. On a lightly floured surface, use a floured rolling pin to roll out dough to $^{1}/_{8}$-inch thickness. Use a 3-inch-wide animal-shaped cookie cutter (for current Chinese New Year) to cut out cookies. Transfer to an ungreased baking sheet. Bake 8 to 10 minutes or until edges are lightly browned. Transfer to a wire rack to cool completely. Store in an airtight container.

Yield: about 4 dozen cookies

LEMON LACE COOKIES

2 cups butter or margarine, softened
1¼ cups sugar
1 tablespoon grated lemon zest
1 teaspoon lemon extract
1 teaspoon vanilla extract
3 cups quick-cooking oats
2 cups all-purpose flour
½ teaspoon salt
Confectioners sugar

In a large bowl, cream butter and sugar until fluffy. Beat in lemon zest and extracts. In a medium bowl, combine oats, flour, and salt. Add dry ingredients to creamed mixture; stir until a soft dough forms. Cover and chill 30 minutes. Preheat oven to 350 degrees. Shape dough into 1-inch balls; place about 2 inches apart on an ungreased baking sheet. Flatten balls with bottom of glass dipped in confectioners sugar. Bake 9 to 11 minutes or until edges are lightly browned. Cool cookies on baking sheet 1 minute; transfer to a wire rack to cool completely. Store in an airtight container.
Yield: about 8 dozen cookies

PEPPERMINT SNOWBALLS

1¼ cups crushed peppermint candies
     (about 45 round candies)
1⅓ cups sugar, divided
½ cup butter or margarine, softened
¼ cup vegetable shortening
2 eggs
1 teaspoon peppermint extract
¾ teaspoon vanilla extract
2½ cups all-purpose flour
¼ teaspoon salt

Preheat oven to 350 degrees. In a food processor, finely grind peppermint candies and ⅓ cup sugar to a powdery consistency; transfer to a small bowl. In a large bowl, cream butter, shortening, and remaining 1 cup sugar until fluffy. Add eggs and extracts; beat until smooth. In a medium bowl, combine flour and salt. Add dry ingredients to creamed mixture; stir until a soft dough forms. Shape dough into 1-inch balls. Roll balls in candy mixture. For best results, place 6 cookies at a time on an ungreased baking sheet. Bake 8 minutes; immediately roll hot cookies in candy mixture. Transfer to a wire rack to cool completely. Repeat with remaining dough. Store in an airtight container.
Yield: about 5½ dozen cookies

SUGAR COOKIE ORNAMENTS

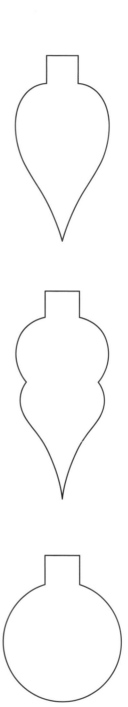

3/4   cup confectioners sugar
1/2   cup butter or margarine, softened
1   egg yolk
1   teaspoon vanilla extract
1/2   teaspoon almond extract
1 1/4   cups all-purpose flour
1/2   teaspoon baking soda
1/4   teaspoon cream of tartar
1/8   teaspoon salt
      Purchased tubes of decorating
        icing, candy sprinkles, and
        dragées (for decoration only)
      Nylon line (to hang cookies)

In a large mixing bowl, combine
confectioners sugar, butter, egg yolk, and
extracts, beating until fluffy. In a medium
bowl, combine flour, baking soda, cream
of tartar, and salt. Stir flour mixture into
butter mixture. Wrap dough in plastic
wrap. Chill at least 2 hours.
   Preheat oven to 350 degrees. On a
lightly floured surface, use a floured
rolling pin to roll out dough to 1/8-inch
thickness. Use miniature cookie cutters
or patterns to cut out dough. (To use
patterns, trace patterns onto tracing
paper and cut out. Place patterns on
dough and use a sharp knife to cut
around patterns.) Transfer cookies to
a lightly greased baking sheet. Bake
5 to 7 minutes or until very lightly
browned. Use a toothpick to make
a hole for hanger in top of each warm
cookie. Transfer cookies to a wire rack
to cool. Referring to photo, decorate
cookies with icing, candy sprinkles, and
dragées. Use nylon line to hang cookies
from tree. Remove dragées before
eating cookies.
Yield: about 5 dozen cookies

eminiscent of the days when tree decorations were often cookies or candies, this
*iniature feather tree adorned with delicious Sugar Cookie Ornaments makes a charming
ift or home accent.

WALNUT BUTTER COOKIES

1 cup chopped walnuts
2 cups all-purpose flour
1/4 teaspoon baking soda
1/8 teaspoon salt
1 cup chilled butter or margarine
1/2 cup granulated sugar
1 egg yolk
2 1/2 teaspoons vanilla extract
   Sifted confectioners sugar

Preheat oven to 350 degrees. To toast walnuts, spread evenly on an ungreased baking sheet. Stirring occasionally, bake 5 to 8 minutes or until darker in color. Cool completely on baking sheet. Process walnuts in a food processor until finely ground.

In a large bowl, combine flour, baking soda, and salt. Using a pastry blender or 2 knives, cut butter into flour mixture until mixture resembles coarse meal. Add ground walnuts, granulated sugar, egg yolk, and vanilla; stir until a soft dough forms. Shape dough into 1-inch balls and place 2 inches apart on a greased baking sheet. Press balls with back of a fork in a crisscross pattern to form 1/4-inch-thick cookies. Bake 15 to 20 minutes or until edges are lightly browned. Transfer cookies to a wire rack with waxed paper underneath. Dust warm cookies with confectioners sugar; cool completely. Dust with confectioners sugar again. Store in an airtight container.
Yield: about 5 dozen cookies

LEMON BARS

2 1/4 cups all-purpose flour, divided
2 1/4 cups confectioners sugar, divided
1 cup butter or margarine, melted
2 cups granulated sugar
4 eggs, slightly beaten
1 teaspoon baking powder
2 cups coconut
1/4 cup plus 3 to 4 tablespoons lemon juice, divided

Combine 2 cups flour and 1/2 cup confectioners sugar. Add melted butter; mix well. Spread mixture in a greased 13 x 9 x 2-inch baking pan. Bake in a preheated 350-degree oven 20 to 25 minutes.

Stir granulated sugar and eggs together. Combine baking powder and remaining 1/4 cup flour; add to sugar mixture. Stir in coconut and 1/4 cup lemon juice. Pour over baked crust. Return to oven and bake 30 minutes; cool.

Combine remaining 1 3/4 cups confectioners sugar and remaining 3 to 4 tablespoons lemon juice; pour over baked mixture. Cut into bars.
Yield: about 2 dozen bars

MERINGUE DELIGHTS

1 egg white
3/4 cup firmly packed dark brown sugar
1 tablespoon all-purpose flour
   Pinch of salt
1 cup pecans, chopped

Beat egg white until stiff. Add brown sugar and beat until blended. Stir in flour, salt, and pecans. Drop teaspoonfuls of mixture 2 inches apart onto greased baking sheets. Bake in a preheated 325-degree oven 10 minutes. Cool slightly before removing from baking sheets.
Yield: about 3 dozen cookies

HONEY BARS

1/2 cup butter or margarine, softened
11/2 cups firmly packed brown sugar
1/3 cup honey
1 egg
1 teaspoon vanilla extract
13/4 cups all-purpose flour
11/2 teaspoons baking powder
1/2 teaspoon baking soda
1/4 teaspoon salt
1 cup chopped pecans, toasted

Preheat oven to 350 degrees. In a large bowl, cream butter and brown sugar until fluffy. Add honey, egg, and vanilla; beat until smooth. In a small bowl, combine dry ingredients. Add to creamed mixture; stir until well blended. Stir in pecans. Spread batter into a lightly greased 9 x 13-inch baking pan. Bake 28 to 30 minutes or until mixture starts to pull away from sides of pan. Cool in pan 15 minutes. Cut into 2-inch squares while warm; cool completely in pan. Store in an airtight container.
Yield: about 2 dozen bars

BUTTER PECAN COOKIES
(Shown on page 322)

1/2 cup plus 2 tablespoons butter, softened and divided
11/2 cups coarsely chopped pecans
1/2 cup granulated sugar, divided
6 tablespoons firmly packed brown sugar
1 egg
1/2 teaspoon vanilla extract
11/2 cups all-purpose flour
1/2 teaspoon baking soda
1/2 teaspoon salt

Preheat oven to 375 degrees. In a large skillet, melt 2 tablespoons butter over medium heat. Stir in pecans and cook 10 to 15 minutes or until nuts are dark brown. Remove from heat and stir in 2 tablespoons granulated sugar. Cool to room temperature.
Cream remaining 1/2 cup butter, remaining 6 tablespoons granulated sugar, and brown sugar in a large bowl until fluffy. Beat in egg and vanilla. Sift next 3 ingredients into a small bowl. Add dry ingredients to creamed mixture, stirring until a soft dough forms. Fold in pecans. Drop by tablespoonfuls onto a greased baking sheet. Bake 8 to 10 minutes or until edges are brown. Cool on wire rack. Store in an airtight container.
Yield: about 2 dozen cookies

Brown-sugary Butter Pecan Cookies (recipe on page 321) are packed with nuts.

CHOCOLATE-ORANGE LOGS

(Shown on page 287)

COOKIES
- 1 cup butter or margarine, softened
- 1 cup sugar
- 1 egg
- 1 teaspoon grated orange zest
- 2$1/4$ cups all-purpose flour
- 1 teaspoon baking powder

ICING
- $1/2$ cup semisweet chocolate chips
- 1 teaspoon vegetable shortening
- $1/4$ teaspoon orange extract
- $3/4$ cup finely chopped pecans

For cookies, cream butter and sugar in a large bowl until fluffy. Add egg and orange zest; beat until smooth. In a medium bowl, combine flour and baking powder. Add dry ingredients to creamed mixture; stir until a soft dough forms.

Spoon mixture into a pastry bag fitted with a large star tip (we used tip #6B). Pipe 2$1/2$-inch strips of dough 2 inches apart onto an ungreased baking sheet. Chill cookies 30 minutes.

Preheat oven to 375 degrees. Bake about 8 minutes or until golden and firm. Allow cookies to cool on pan 2 minutes; transfer to a wire rack to cool completely.

For icing, place chocolate chips and shortening in a small microwave-safe bowl; microwave on medium power (50%) 3 minutes or until chips are soft. Stir chips until smooth; stir in orange extract. Dip one end of each cookie in chocolate mixture and then in pecans. Place on waxed paper; allow chocolate to harden. Store in an airtight container.

Yield: about 5 dozen cookies

SPRINGERLE

(Shown on page 287)
Make cookies at least 2 weeks in advance to allow flavor to develop.

- 4 eggs
- 2 cups sugar
- 1 teaspoon grated lemon zest
- 1 teaspoon anise extract **or**
  2 teaspoons anise seed, crushed
- 3$3/4$ cups all-purpose flour
- 1 teaspoon baking powder

In a large bowl, beat eggs at high speed of an electric mixer 1 minute. Gradually add sugar, beating at high speed 10 minutes. Add lemon zest and anise extract. In a medium bowl, combine flour and baking powder. Stir dry ingredients into egg mixture (dough will be stiff). Shape dough into 2 balls. Wrap in plastic wrap and chill 1 hour.

Work with 1 ball of dough at a time. On a lightly floured surface, use a floured rolling pin to roll out dough into a $1/4$-inch-thick rectangle the width of a springerle rolling pin. Pressing firmly, roll designs into dough using springerle rolling pin (or press dough into individual cookie molds). If using rolling pin, cut out cookies along design lines (a pizza cutter works well). Place cookies on a lightly greased baking sheet; allow to stand uncovered at room temperature overnight.

Preheat oven to 350 degrees. Place baking sheet in oven; immediately reduce temperature to 300 degrees. Bake 15 to 20 minutes or until bottoms are lightly browned. Transfer cookies to a wire rack to cool completely. Store in an airtight container.

Yield: about 7$1/2$ dozen cookies

WHITE CHOCOLATE COOKIES

(Shown on page 287)

- ³/₄ cup butter or margarine, softened and divided
- ¹/₄ cup vegetable shortening
- ¹/₂ cup granulated sugar
- ¹/₂ cup firmly packed brown sugar
- 1 egg yolk
- ¹/₂ teaspoon vanilla extract
- 1¹/₃ cups plus 6 tablespoons all- purpose flour, divided
- ¹/₂ teaspoon baking powder
- ¹/₈ teaspoon salt
- ¹/₂ cup coarsely chopped walnuts
- 2 ounces white chocolate, coarsely chopped
- 1 tablespoon chocolate-flavored syrup

In a large bowl, beat ¹/₂ cup butter and shortening until well blended; add sugars and beat until fluffy. Add egg yolk and vanilla; beat until smooth. In a small bowl, combine 1¹/₃ cups flour, baking powder, and salt. In a food processor, process walnuts and chocolate until finely ground. Add dry ingredients and walnut mixture to creamed mixture; stir until a soft dough forms. Wrap in plastic wrap and chill 1 to 2 hours.

Preheat oven to 350 degrees. Shape chilled dough into ³/₄-inch balls; place 2 inches apart on an ungreased baking sheet. Flatten cookies with bottom of a glass dipped in 2 tablespoons flour. In a small bowl, mix remaining ¹/₄ cup butter, remaining 4 tablespoons flour, and syrup; stir until well blended.

Spoon chocolate mixture into a pastry bag fitted with a small round tip. Pipe tree design onto each cookie. Bake 8 to 10 minutes or until edges are lightly browned. Transfer to a wire rack to cool completely. Store in airtight container.
Yield: about 6 dozen cookies

CANDIED PINEAPPLE COOKIES

- ¹/₂ cup butter or margarine
- ¹/₃ cup firmly packed brown sugar
- ¹/₄ cup apple juice
- 2 tablespoons molasses
- 2 cups all-purpose flour
- 2 teaspoons ground cinnamon
- ¹/₂ teaspoon baking soda
- 1 package (4 ounces) candied pineapple, finely chopped
- ¹/₂ cup chopped walnuts

Preheat oven to 350 degrees. In a large bowl, cream butter and brown sugar until fluffy. Add apple juice and molasses, beating until smooth. In a medium bowl, sift together flour, cinnamon, and baking soda. Stir dry ingredients into creamed mixture. Stir in candied pineapple and walnuts. Shape dough into a ball, cover, and refrigerate 1 hour.

On a lightly floured surface, use a floured rolling pin to roll out dough to ³/₄-inch thickness. Use a floured 1-inch biscuit cutter to cut out dough. Transfer cookies to a greased baking sheet. Bake 12 to 15 minutes or until light brown.
Yield: about 4 dozen cookies

CASHEW-FUDGE TARTS

PASTRY
- 3 cups all-purpose flour
- 6 tablespoons sugar
- 1½ cups butter or margarine, softened

FILLING
- 1 can (14 ounces) sweetened condensed milk
- 1 egg
- 1 tablespoon hot water
- 1 teaspoon instant coffee granules
- 1 package (6 ounces) semisweet chocolate chips, melted
- 2 tablespoons all-purpose flour
- 1 teaspoon vanilla extract
- ¼ teaspoon baking powder
- 1½ cups lightly salted dry-roasted cashews, coarsely chopped and divided

For pastry, combine flour and sugar in a medium bowl. Using a pastry blender or 2 knives, cut butter into dry ingredients until mixture resembles coarse meal. Knead until a soft dough forms. Shape ½ tablespoonfuls of dough into balls. Press balls of dough into bottoms and up sides of greased miniature muffin pans.

Preheat oven to 350 degrees. For filling, whisk sweetened condensed milk and egg in a medium bowl. In a small bowl, combine water and coffee; stir until coffee dissolves. Add coffee mixture, chocolate chips, flour, vanilla, and baking powder to milk mixture; beat with an electric mixer until smooth. Stir in 1 cup cashews. Spoon about 1 tablespoon filling into each pastry.

Sprinkle remaining ½ cup cashews evenly over filling. Bake 25 to 30 minutes or until set in center. Cool in pans 10 minutes. Transfer to a wire rack to cool completely. Store in an airtight container.
Yield: about 5½ dozen tarts

FILBERT COOKIES

- 1 cup butter, softened
- 1 cup granulated sugar
- 2 cups all-purpose flour
- 2 teaspoons vanilla extract
- ¼ teaspoon salt
- 1 cup finely ground filberts
  Confectioners sugar
  Pastel Glaze (recipe follows)

Cream butter and granulated sugar; stir in flour, vanilla, and salt. Add filberts and mix well. Shape teaspoonfuls of dough into balls. Place balls 1 inch apart on ungreased baking sheets; flatten slightly. Bake in a preheated 300-degree oven 18 to 20 minutes. Cool slightly, then roll in confectioners sugar. Cookies may also be iced with Pastel Glaze.
Yield: about 6 dozen cookies

PASTEL GLAZE
The flavor of our glaze can be changed by substituting orange or lemon juice for the water.

- 3 to 4 tablespoons hot water
  Red food coloring
- 2½ cups confectioners sugar, sifted

Add water and food coloring gradually to sugar. (**Note:** Be careful to add only a few drops of color at a time.) Beat mixture until smooth; drizzle or pour over cookies.

FRUITCAKE CHRISTMAS COOKIES

1/2 cup butter or margarine, softened
1 cup granulated sugar
1 egg, beaten
1/2 teaspoon baking soda
1/4 cup sour milk
13/4 to 2 cups all-purpose flour
1/2 teaspoon salt
3/4 cup chopped candied cherries
3/4 cup chopped dates
3/4 cup chopped pecans
    Buttercream Frosting (recipe
        follows)
    Red and green candied cherries
        to decorate

Cream butter and sugar; stir in egg. Stir together baking soda and sour milk; gradually add to creamed mixture. (Note: Milk may be soured by stirring 1 tablespoon lemon juice or vinegar into scant 1/4 cup whole milk.) Combine flour and salt; gradually add to creamed mixture. Stir in fruit and pecans until well blended. Drop teaspoonfuls of dough onto greased baking sheets. Bake in a preheated 350-degree oven 10 to 12 minutes. Cool cookies on wire racks.
    Spread Buttercream Frosting on cookies and decorate with red and green cherries.
Yield: about 3 dozen cookies

BUTTERCREAM FROSTING
2 cups confectioners sugar
2 tablespoons butter or margarine
1 tablespoon milk
1 teaspoon vanilla extract

Blend all ingredients until smooth. Add more milk or sugar as necessary to achieve spreading consistency.

ALMOND CRISPS

2/3 cup plus 2 tablespoons finely
    ground blanched almonds
1/2 cup granulated sugar
1/2 cup butter or margarine
2 tablespoons whipping cream
1 tablespoon all-purpose flour

Combine all ingredients in a 10-inch skillet. Cook over low heat, stirring constantly, until butter is melted and mixture is blended. Keep skillet warm over very low heat. Drop heaping teaspoonfuls of mixture 2 inches apart onto a greased baking sheet. (Note: Bake only 4 cookies at a time.) Bake in a preheated 350-degree oven 5 minutes or until golden. Use a spatula to loosen and turn cookies over; quickly roll each one around the handle of a wooden spoon. If cookies become too firm to roll, reheat in oven a minute to soften. Cool rolled cookies on wire racks. Repeat until all batter is used, greasing baking sheet each time. Store cookies in an airtight container.
Yield: about 2 1/2 dozen cookies

CREAM CHEESE SPRITZ

1 cup vegetable shortening
1 package (3 ounces) cream cheese,
    softened
1 cup granulated sugar
1 egg yolk
1 teaspoon vanilla extract
2 1/2 cups all-purpose flour, sifted
1/2 teaspoon salt
1/4 teaspoon ground cinnamon
    Food coloring, if desired
    Dragées (for decoration only)

Cream shortening and cream cheese. Gradually add sugar and mix well. Beat in egg yolk and vanilla. Sift flour with salt

nd cinnamon; gradually add to
creamed mixture. Tint with food coloring,
if desired. Fill cookie press and form
cookies on ungreased baking sheets.
Bake in a preheated 350-degree oven
12 to 15 minutes. Cool before removing
from baking sheets. Decorate with
dragées. Remove dragées before
eating cookies.
Yield: about 6 dozen cookies

PEANUT BUTTER SURPRISES

- 1 cup butter or margarine, softened
- 1 cup crunchy peanut butter
- $3/4$ cup firmly packed brown sugar
- $3/4$ cup granulated sugar
- 2 eggs
- $1^1/2$ teaspoons vanilla extract
- $2^1/2$ cups all-purpose flour
- 1 teaspoon baking powder
- 1 teaspoon baking soda
- $1/2$ teaspoon salt
- 2 cups coarsely chopped miniature
  peanut butter cups

Preheat oven to 350 degrees.
Cream butter, peanut butter, sugars,
eggs, and vanilla until fluffy. Sift flour,
baking powder, baking soda, and salt
together. Gradually stir dry ingredients
into creamed mixture. Stir in chopped
peanut butter cups. Drop by heaping
teaspoonfuls onto ungreased baking
sheets. Bake 12 to 15 minutes or until
lightly browned. Remove from sheets
and cool on wire racks.
Yield: about 5 dozen cookies

ALMOND FINGERS

- 1 cup butter or margarine, softened
- $1/2$ cup firmly packed brown sugar
- $1/2$ cup granulated sugar
- 1 egg yolk, lightly beaten

- $1/2$ teaspoon vanilla extract
- $1/2$ teaspoon almond extract
- $2^1/4$ cups all-purpose flour
- 1 package (6 ounces) semisweet
  chocolate chips
- 1 cup finely chopped almonds

Preheat oven to 350 degrees. Cream
butter and sugars together until fluffy.
Beat in egg yolk and extracts. Stir in flour.
Shape teaspoonfuls of dough into 2-inch-
long rolls. Place on lightly greased baking
sheets. Bake 10 to 12 minutes or until
very lightly browned around the edges.
Remove from sheets and cool on wire
racks.
Melt chocolate chips. Dip ends of each
cookie $1/2$ inch into melted chocolate.
Roll ends in chopped almonds. Allow
chocolate to harden.
Yield: about 5 dozen cookies

SHORTBREAD

- 1 cup butter, softened
- $1/2$ cup granulated sugar
- $2^1/2$ cups all-purpose flour, sifted

Cream butter; gradually add sugar and
blend until light and fluffy. Stir in flour
until well blended. Cover with waxed
paper and chill for several hours.
Work with half of dough at a time and
store remainder in refrigerator. Press
dough into a cookie mold or use a floured
rolling pin to roll out dough on a lightly
floured surface to $1/2$-inch thickness; cut
out with desired cookie cutters. Place
on ungreased baking sheets. Bake in a
preheated 300-degree oven 30 minutes.
Cool slightly before removing from
sheets.
Yield: about $3^1/2$ dozen cookies

Purchased icing and candies make it a snap to transform store-bought cookies into fun holly-trimmed Wreath Cookies and poinsettia-adorned Gift Box Cookies. Rolled cookies dipped in candy coating and topped with almond "flames" stand upright on chocolate sandwich cookies to make our unique Candle Cookies.

CANDLE COOKIES

Vanilla candy coating
1 package (5¹/₂ ounces) Pepperidge Farms Pirouette cookies
Purchased green decorating icing
Chocolate sandwich cookies
Whole almonds

Melt candy coating in a small saucepan according to package directions. Using tongs, dip each Pirouette cookie into candy coating. Place on a wire rack with waxed paper underneath; let coating harden.

Using a large star tip, pipe icing in a small circle onto 1 side of each sandwich cookie. Press 1 end of a dipped cookie into icing. Using a small amount of icing, secure 1 almond in remaining end of dipped cookie. Allow icing to harden. Store in an airtight container.
Yield: about 1¹/₂ dozen cookies

GIFT BOX COOKIES

Purchased red and green
decorating icing
1 package (10 ounces) square
shortbread cookies
Gold dragées (for decoration only)

Using a small leaf tip, pipe green
icing onto each cookie to resemble
ribbon. Using a small round tip, pipe
red icing onto each cookie to resemble
a poinsettia. Place a dragée in center of
each flower. Allow icing to harden. Store
in an airtight container. Remove dragées
before eating cookies.
Yield: about 3¹/₂ dozen cookies

WREATH COOKIES

1 package (11 ounces) wreath-
shaped cookies
Purchased green decorating icing
Small red cinnamon candies

Using a small leaf tip, pipe icing onto
each cookie to resemble leaves. Place
candies in center of leaves. Allow icing to
harden. Store in an airtight container.
Yield: about 2¹/₂ dozen cookies

ORANGE COOKIES WITH CHOCOLATE FILLING

COOKIES
1 cup vegetable shortening
1 cup granulated sugar
2 eggs
3 tablespoons orange juice
concentrate
2 tablespoons grated orange peel

1 teaspoon vanilla extract
4¹/₂ cups all-purpose flour
1 teaspoon baking soda
¹/₂ teaspoon baking powder
¹/₂ teaspoon salt
¹/₂ cup buttermilk

FILLING
1 cup semisweet chocolate chips,
melted
2 tablespoons whipping cream
2¹/₂ teaspoons orange extract

For cookies, cream shortening, sugar,
eggs, orange juice concentrate, orange
peel, and vanilla in a large mixing bowl.
Combine dry ingredients and stir into
creamed mixture, alternating with
buttermilk. Divide dough in half and
wrap in plastic wrap. Refrigerate at least
2 hours or until well chilled.
Preheat oven to 375 degrees. On a
lightly floured surface, use a floured
rolling pin to roll out dough to 1/8-inch
thickness. Using 2-inch round cookie
cutter, cut out dough. Transfer cookies
to a lightly greased baking sheet. Bake
6 to 8 minutes or until very lightly
browned around edges. Remove from
pans and cool on wire racks.
For filling, combine all ingredients,
blending until smooth. Spread a thin
layer of filling on bottoms of half of
cookies and place remaining cookies
on top of filling. Chill 5 minutes or until
chocolate hardens.
Yield: about 4 dozen cookies

ALMOND CHRISTMAS TREES

1¼ cups butter or margarine, softened
⅔ cup granulated sugar
2 cups all-purpose flour
1½ cups finely ground almonds
1 teaspoon ground cinnamon
¼ teaspoon ground nutmeg
½ teaspoon vanilla extract
½ teaspoon almond extract
   Raspberry jam
   Confectioners sugar

Cream butter and granulated sugar until light and fluffy. Stir in flour, almonds, cinnamon, nutmeg, and extracts. Wrap dough in plastic wrap and chill 1 hour.

Preheat oven to 375 degrees. Divide dough in half. On a lightly floured surface, use a floured rolling pin to roll out half of dough to ⅛-inch thickness. Using a 4½-inch tree-shaped cookie cutter, cut out 24 trees. Place cookies on a lightly greased baking sheet. Roll out remaining half of dough and cut out 24 additional trees. Using a drinking straw, randomly cut a few holes for "ornaments" in second batch of cookies. Place cookies on lightly greased baking sheets. If there is any extra dough, roll out and cut an even number of trees, making holes in half of them. Bake 8 to 10 minutes or until lightly browned. Remove from sheets and cool on wire racks.

Spread each solid tree with a layer of raspberry jam. Place a tree with holes on top of jam layer and dust with confectioners sugar.

Yield: about 2 dozen cookies

SUGAR COOKIES

½ cup butter or margarine, softened
1 cup granulated sugar
1 egg
1½ teaspoons vanilla extract
½ teaspoon almond extract
2 cups all-purpose flour
½ teaspoon baking powder
¼ teaspoon salt
   Icing (recipe follows)

Cream butter and sugar until light and fluffy. Beat in egg and extracts. Sift together dry ingredients. Gradually add dry ingredients to creamed mixture, blending well. Wrap dough in plastic wrap and chill at least 1 hour.

Preheat oven to 400 degrees. On a lightly floured surface, use a floured rolling pin to roll out dough to ⅛-inch thickness. Cut out dough using desired cookie cutters. Place cookies on lightly greased baking sheets. Bake 8 to 10 minutes or until edges are lightly browned. Remove from sheets and cool on wire racks. Ice and decorate cookies, if desired.

Yield: about 3 dozen cookies

ICING
2¼ cups confectioners sugar, sifted
⅓ cup milk
½ teaspoon vanilla extract
   Red and green food coloring (optional)

Combine all ingredients, blending until smooth. Dip tops of cookies in icing; place on wire racks to dry. If desired, divide remaining icing and add food coloring to icing, stirring to blend well. Spoon into pastry bags fitted with small, round tips. Decorate tops of cookies.

CHOCOLATE BRANDY DROPS

1 cup butter or margarine, softened
1 cup confectioners sugar
1/2 cup granulated sugar
1 cup semisweet chocolate chips, chilled
3 cups all-purpose flour
1 1/2 cups brandy
1 cup finely chopped pecans

Preheat oven to 350 degrees. In a large bowl, cream butter and sugars until fluffy. In a food processor fitted with a steel blade, process chocolate chips until finely chopped. Add chocolate and remaining ingredients to creamed mixture, stirring until a soft dough forms. Drop by teaspoonfuls onto a greased baking sheet. Bake 12 to 15 minutes or until light brown. Cool completely on a wire rack. Store in an airtight container.
Yield: about 3 dozen cookies

SCOTCHIES

1 cup butter or margarine, softened
1 cup confectioners sugar
2 1/2 cups all-purpose flour
6 tablespoons Scotch whiskey
1/2 cup butterscotch chips, chilled
1 cup finely chopped pecans
Confectioners sugar

Preheat oven to 350 degrees. In a large bowl, cream butter and sugar until fluffy. Add flour and whiskey, stirring until a soft dough forms. In a food processor fitted with a steel blade, process butterscotch chips until finely chopped. Stir chopped chips and pecans into dough. Shape tablespoonfuls of dough into crescent shapes and place on a greased baking sheet. Bake 12 to 15 minutes or until lightly browned. Roll cookies in confectioners sugar immediately after removing from oven. Cool completely on a wire rack. Roll in confectioners sugar again.
Yield: about 4 1/2 dozen cookies

PECAN THIMBLE COOKIES

2 cups all-purpose flour
1 1/4 cups chopped pecans
1 cup butter, softened
1/4 cup granulated sugar
1/4 cup firmly packed brown sugar

Process flour and pecans in a food processor until pecans are very finely chopped. In a medium bowl, beat butter and sugars until light and fluffy. Stir in flour mixture. Wrap dough in plastic wrap and refrigerate overnight.
Preheat oven to 300 degrees. On a lightly floured surface, use a floured rolling pin to roll out dough to 1/4-inch thickness. Use a thimble to cut out cookies. Transfer to a foil-lined baking sheet. Bake 10 to 12 minutes or until very lightly browned.
Yield: about 50 dozen cookies

Variation: Cookies may be rolled out as directed above and cut out using desired cookie cutters. Bake 20 to 25 minutes.
Yield: about 5 dozen 2 1/2-inch cookies

Moist, chewy Peanut Butter Brownies are made with extra-crunchy peanut butter so they're packed with nutty flavor.

PEANUT BUTTER BROWNIES

¹/₄ cup butter or margarine, melted
¹/₂ cup granulated sugar
¹/₂ cup firmly packed brown sugar
2 eggs
1 teaspoon vanilla extract
¹/₂ cup all-purpose flour
¹/₂ teaspoon baking powder
¹/₂ teaspoon salt
¹/₂ cup extra-crunchy peanut butter

Preheat oven to 350 degrees. In a medium bowl, combine butter and sugars. Add eggs and vanilla; beat until smooth. In a small bowl, combine flour, baking powder, and salt. Add dry ingredients to creamed mixture; stir just until dry ingredients are moistened. Stir in peanut butter. Spread batter in a greased 8 x 11-inch baking pan. Bake 20 to 25 minutes or until set in center. Cool completely in pan. Cut into 2-inch squares.

Yield: about 1¹/₂ dozen brownies

Simply Delicious
SNACKS

Butterscotch Bran Muffins, page 350

*Got the munchies? Grab a bite at any hour
and keep your energy up! Choose from fast-to-fix
treats and always-on-hand favorites.*

Orange-Date-Nut Loaves, page 347

SMOKED PARMESAN ALMONDS

1 egg white
1 cup whole unsalted almonds
2 tablespoons butter or margarine
$^1/_4$ cup grated Parmesan cheese
2 teaspoons liquid smoke flavoring
1 teaspoon salt

Preheat oven to 350 degrees. In a small bowl, beat egg white until foamy. Stir in almonds, coating well.

In a small saucepan, melt butter over medium heat. Stir in remaining ingredients. Add almonds to butter mixture, stirring until well coated. Pour onto an ungreased baking sheet. Bake 25 to 30 minutes or until cheese is brown. Cool completely on pan. Store in an airtight container.
Yield: about 1 cup almonds

RASPBERRY NUT BARS

$1^1/_2$ cups butter or margarine, softened
2 cups granulated sugar
2 egg yolks
1 teaspoon vanilla extract
4 cups all-purpose flour
$1^1/_3$ cups finely chopped pecans
1 jar (12 ounces) raspberry preserves

Preheat oven to 350 degrees. In a large bowl, cream butter and sugar until fluffy. Beat in egg yolks and vanilla. Mix in flour and pecans, stirring until a soft dough forms. Divide dough in half. Press half of dough into a greased 9 x 13-inch glass baking dish. Spread preserves evenly over dough. Place remaining dough on a sheet of waxed paper. Dust with flour and use a floured rolling pin to roll out dough to a 9 x 13-inch rectangle. Place dough over preserves, patching if necessary to completely cover preserves. Bake 40 to 45 minutes or until golden brown. Cool completely in dish. Cut into 1 x 3-inch bars. Store in an airtight container.
Yield: about 3 dozen bars

Checkerboard Walnuts are luscious bites of coconut covered with vanilla or chocolate candy coating. Raspberry Nut Bars (right) have a jam filling.

CHECKERBOARD WALNUTS

2 cups flaked coconut
1/2 cup granulated sugar
2 tablespoons light corn syrup
1/8 teaspoon salt
1 egg white
1/4 teaspoon coconut extract
24 walnut halves
4 ounces chocolate-flavored almond bark
4 ounces vanilla-flavored almond bark

In a large saucepan, combine coconut, sugar, corn syrup, and salt. Cook over medium heat, stirring constantly, 5 to 6 minutes or until candy thickens and coconut is light brown. Whisk egg white in a small bowl until foamy.

Add egg white to coconut mixture. Stirring constantly, cook 5 to 6 minutes longer or until mixture becomes stiff and very sticky. Remove from heat and stir in coconut extract. Cool to room temperature.

Dip fingers in cold water and shape coconut mixture into 1-inch balls. Place on waxed paper; press 1 walnut half on top of each coconut ball. Refrigerate 1 hour or until firm.

Melt chocolate and vanilla almond bark in separate small saucepans following package directions. Dip bottom half of each candy in chocolate or vanilla bark, completely covering coconut. Return to waxed paper and cool completely. Store at room temperature in an airtight container.

Yield: about 2 dozen candies

CHOCOLATE GRANOLA CANDIES

2$^1/_2$ cups granola cereal with fruit
and nuts
$^3/_4$ cup diced mixed dried fruits and
raisins
12 ounces chocolate-flavored
candy coating, cut into pieces

In a medium bowl, combine cereal and dried fruits and raisins. In a heavy medium saucepan, melt candy coating over low heat; remove from heat. Stir cereal mixture into melted chocolate. Drop teaspoonfuls of mixture into foil candy cups. Place candies in refrigerator to harden. Store in an airtight container in a cool, dry place.
Yield: about 5 dozen pieces candy

PEANUT BUTTER CRUNCH BALLS

4 cups miniature marshmallows
$^1/_2$ cup butter or margarine
$^1/_2$ cup smooth peanut butter
3 cups round toasted oat cereal
1 cup unsalted peanuts
1 cup red and green candy-coated
chocolate pieces

In a medium saucepan, melt together marshmallows, butter, and peanut butter over low heat, stirring constantly until smooth. Remove mixture from heat. Cool 15 minutes.

In a large bowl, mix cereal, peanuts, and candy-coated chocolate pieces. Pour syrup over cereal mixture, stirring until evenly coated. Roll mixture into 2-inch balls and cool completely on waxed paper. Store in an airtight container.
Yield: about 3 dozen crunch balls

NUT-CRACKER SWEETS

1 package (12 ounces) semisweet
chocolate chips
3 tablespoons ground cinnamon
1 cup unsalted cashews
1 cup oyster crackers

Melt chocolate chips in a medium saucepan over low heat. Stir in cinnamon. Fold in cashews and crackers. Drop by heaping teaspoonfuls onto waxed paper. Cool completely. Store in an airtight container.
Yield: about 2$^1/_2$ dozen candies

HARD CANDY SANTAS AND LOLLIPOPS

(Shown on page 338)

- 2 cups granulated sugar
- 1 cup water
- 2/3 cup light corn syrup
- 1 teaspoon oil-based flavoring for candy making
- 1/2 to 1 teaspoon candy coloring
  Purchased lollipop sticks

In a large saucepan, combine sugar, water, and corn syrup over medium-high heat. Without stirring, cook to hard crack stage (300 degrees on a candy thermometer). Remove from heat and stir in flavoring and coloring.

For Santas, use balls of aluminum foil to prop oiled two-piece metal candy molds upright on a baking sheet. Pour mixture into molds. When mixture is hard, but not thoroughly cooled, remove candies from molds.

For molded lollipops, pour mixture into oiled metal lollipop molds. Quickly insert lollipop sticks into indentations before mixture hardens. When mixture is hard, but not thoroughly cooled, remove lollipops from molds.

For round lollipops, pour mixture into 3- to 4-inch circles on an oiled baking sheet. Quickly insert lollipop sticks into circles before mixture hardens. When lollipops are thoroughly cooled, remove from baking sheet.

Yield: about four 3-inch-high Santas, fifteen 1 1/2-inch molded lollipops, or ten round lollipops

PEPPERMINT-ORANGE PATTIES

(Shown on page 338)

- 7 cups sifted confectioners sugar
- 1 can (14 ounces) sweetened condensed milk
- 1/2 cup butter, softened
- 1 1/2 teaspoons orange extract
- 1/2 teaspoon peppermint extract
- 14 ounces chocolate-flavored candy coating
- 8 ounces semisweet chocolate chips (about 1 1/3 cups)

In a large mixing bowl, combine first five ingredients. Blend until smooth. Cover and refrigerate mixture overnight.

Use lightly greased hands to shape mixture into 1-inch balls and flatten to make patty shapes. Place patties on a jellyroll pan lined with waxed paper. Freeze patties at least 30 minutes.

In a heavy medium saucepan, melt candy coating and chocolate chips over low heat. Remove chocolate mixture from heat. Working with 1 dozen patties at a time, place each patty on a fork and spoon chocolate mixture over top until covered. Transfer patties to a jellyroll pan lined with waxed paper. Chill until chocolate hardens. Store in an airtight container in a cool place.

Yield: about 8 dozen candies

Variation: To make peppermint drops, eliminate orange extract and increase peppermint extract to 1 teaspoon. Proceed as directed. Shape mixture into 1-inch balls, but do not flatten into patty shapes. Continue with recipe as directed.

This sweet selection contains old-fashioned confections made with modern ease. Clockwise from top left: Our collection includes delicious Peppermint-Orange Patties (recipe on page 337) and soft, chewy Gumdrops with a crystallized sugar coating. Our Never-Fail Divinity always turns out right because we substitute marshmallow creme for egg whites. Hard Candy Santas and Lollipops (recipe on page 337) are favorite candies, and Rum-Raisin Fudge is spiked with marinated raisins.

NEVER-FAIL DIVINITY
(Shown on page 338)

1½ cups granulated sugar
½ cup water
2 tablespoons light corn syrup
⅛ teaspoon salt
1 jar (7 ounces) marshmallow creme
1½ teaspoons vanilla extract
1 cup chopped pecans

In a large saucepan, combine sugar, water, corn syrup, and salt. Cook over medium-high heat to hard ball stage (250 degrees on a candy thermometer). Place marshmallow creme in a large mixing bowl. Beating constantly, gradually add syrup to marshmallow creme. Beat until stiff peaks form. Beat in vanilla and pecans. Quickly drop by heaping teaspoonfuls onto waxed paper. Store in an airtight container.
Yield: about 2 dozen candies

RUM-RAISIN FUDGE
(Shown on page 338)

1 cup raisins
½ cup dark rum
2½ cups granulated sugar
1 cup evaporated milk
½ cup butter or margarine
2 cups semisweet chocolate chips
1 jar (7 ounces) marshmallow creme
½ cup chopped pecans
1 teaspoon rum extract

In a small bowl, combine raisins and rum. Cover and marinate overnight at room temperature.

In a heavy large saucepan, combine sugar, evaporated milk, and butter. Cook over medium heat, stirring constantly, until mixture reaches soft ball stage (238 degrees on a candy thermometer). Remove from heat. Stir in chocolate chips, marshmallow creme, pecans, rum extract, and raisin mixture. Spread mixture into a lightly greased 10 x 8 x 2-inch baking pan. Cool and cut into squares.
Yield: about 4 dozen pieces of fudge

GUMDROPS
(Shown on page 338)

4 tablespoons unflavored gelatin
1 cup cold water
1½ cups boiling water
4 cups granulated sugar
½ teaspoon desired flavoring: lemon extract, orange extract, peppermint extract, etc.
3 to 4 drops desired food coloring
Granulated sugar

In a large saucepan, soften gelatin in cold water 5 minutes. Stir in boiling water until gelatin is dissolved. Stir in sugar and bring mixture to a boil over medium-high heat. Boil 25 minutes, stirring frequently. Pour mixture into two 8 x 8-inch pans. To each pan add ½ teaspoon desired flavoring and desired food coloring (do not add color for clear gumdrops). Stir until combined. Cover and refrigerate pans overnight.

Using a knife dipped in hot water, cut gelatin mixture into 1-inch cubes. Roll in granulated sugar until well coated. Place gumdrops on a sheet of waxed paper and allow to sit at room temperature two days to crystallize. Store in airtight containers.
Yield: about 10 dozen candies

BUTTERMILK FUDGE

2 cups sugar
1 cup buttermilk
1/2 cup butter or margarine
1 tablespoon light corn syrup
1 teaspoon baking soda
1 teaspoon vanilla extract
1/2 cup chopped walnuts

Butter sides of a heavy large saucepan or Dutch oven. Combine sugar, buttermilk, butter, corn syrup, and baking soda in pan. Stirring constantly, cook over medium-low heat until butter melts and sugar dissolves. Using a pastry brush dipped in hot water, wash down any sugar crystals on sides of pan. Attach a candy thermometer to pan, making sure thermometer does not touch bottom of pan. Increase heat to medium and bring to a boil. Cook, without stirring, until mixture reaches soft-ball stage (approximately 234 to 240 degrees). Test about 1/2 teaspoon mixture in ice water. Mixture should easily form a ball in ice water but flatten when held in your hand. Remove from heat. Add vanilla; do not stir. Cool to approximately 200 degrees. Using medium speed of an electric mixer, beat until fudge thickens and begins to lose its gloss. Stir in walnuts. Pour into a buttered 8-inch square baking pan. Cool completely. Cut into 1-inch squares. Store in an airtight container in refrigerator.
Yield: about 4 dozen pieces fudge

IRISH CREAM FUDGE

1 cup finely chopped walnuts
4 cups granulated sugar
1 cup evaporated milk
1/3 cup light corn syrup
6 tablespoons butter or margarine
2 tablespoons honey
1/2 teaspoon salt
1/2 cup Irish Cream liqueur
1 1/2 cups (9 ounces) semisweet
   chocolate chips, melted

Spread nuts evenly in bottom of a greased 8 x 11-inch baking dish. Grease sides of a large stockpot. Combine next 6 ingredients in stockpot and cook over medium-low heat, stirring constantly until sugar dissolves. Using a pastry brush dipped in hot water, wash down any sugar crystals on sides of pan.
Attach candy thermometer to pan, making sure thermometer does not touch bottom of pan. Increase heat to medium and bring to a boil. Do not stir while syrup is boiling. Cook until syrup reaches soft ball stage (approximately 234 to 240 degrees). Test about 1/2 teaspoon syrup in ice water. Syrup should easily form a ball in ice water, but flatten when held in your hand.
Place stockpot in 2 inches of cold water in sink. Add liqueur to syrup; do not stir until syrup cools to approximately 110 degrees. Add chocolate and beat fudge using medium speed of an electric mixer until it is no longer glossy and thickens. Pour over nuts. Allow to cool completely. Cut into 1-inch squares. Store in an airtight container in refrigerator.
Yield: about 7 dozen squares fudge

FUDGY PEANUT BUTTER BITES

 4 cups sugar
 1 cup evaporated milk
 1/3 cup corn syrup
 6 tablespoons butter or margarine
 2 tablespoons honey
 1/2 teaspoon vanilla extract
 1 package (6 ounces) semisweet
   chocolate chips
 1 1/2 cups crunchy peanut butter

Butter sides of a large saucepan or Dutch oven. Combine sugar, evaporated milk, corn syrup, butter, and honey in saucepan. Stirring constantly, cook over medium-low heat until sugar dissolves. Using a pastry brush dipped in hot water, wash down any sugar crystals on sides of pan. Attach a candy thermometer to pan, making sure thermometer does not touch bottom of pan. Increase heat to medium and bring to a boil. Cook, without stirring, until mixture reaches soft-ball stage (approximately 234 to 240 degrees). Test about 1/2 teaspoon mixture in ice water. Mixture will easily form a ball in ice water but flatten when held in your hand. Place pan in 2 inches of cold water in sink. Add vanilla; do not stir until mixture cools to approximately 120 degrees Stir in chocolate chips. Using medium speed of an electric mixer, beat fudge until thickened and no longer glossy. Divide fudge in half. Place each half on a separate piece (22 inches long) of plastic wrap. Use a greased rolling pin to roll each half of fudge into a 5 x 18-inch rectangle. Spread 3/4 cup peanut butter lengthwise along center of each rectangle. Fold long edges of each rectangle over peanut butter to form an 18-inch-long roll; pinch edges to seal. Wrap in plastic wrap and refrigerate until firm. Cut into 1/2-inch slices. Store in an airtight container in refrigerator.

Yield: about 6 dozen pieces fudge

TOASTED ALMOND TOFFEE

1 cup butter
1 cup sugar
1/3 cup water
1 tablespoon light corn syrup
2 1/4 cups slivered almonds, toasted,
    coarsely chopped, and divided
1/2 teaspoon vanilla extract
1 cup semisweet chocolate mini
    chips, divided

Line 2 baking sheets with aluminum foil; grease foil. Butter sides of a very heavy large saucepan. Combine butter, sugar, water, and corn syrup in saucepan. Stirring constantly, cook over medium-low heat until sugar dissolves. Using a pastry brush dipped in hot water, wash down any sugar crystals on sides of pan. Attach a candy thermometer to pan, making sure thermometer does not touch bottom of pan. Increase heat to medium and bring to a boil. Cook, without stirring, until mixture reaches hard-crack stage (approximately 300 to 310 degrees). Test about 1/2 teaspoon mixture in ice water. Mixture will form brittle threads in ice water and will remain brittle when removed from the water. Remove from heat and stir in 1 cup almonds and vanilla. Spread mixture onto 1 prepared baking sheet. Sprinkle 1/2 cup chocolate chips over hot toffee; spread melted chocolate. Sprinkle 1/2 cup almonds over chocolate. Invert toffee onto second baking sheet.

Sprinkle second side with remaining 1/2 cup chocolate chips; spread melted chocolate. Sprinkle remaining almonds over chocolate; press into chocolate. Chill 1 hour or until chocolate hardens. Break into small pieces. Store in an airtight container in a cool place.
Yield: about 1 1/2 pounds toffee

CASHEW TOFFEE

40 unsalted saltine crackers
1 cup butter or margarine
1 cup firmly packed brown sugar
2 cups chopped unsalted cashews
1 package (12 ounces) semisweet
    chocolate chips

Preheat oven to 400 degrees. Arrange a single layer of crackers with sides touching in the bottom of a foil-lined 11 x 17-inch shallow baking pan. In a small saucepan, combine butter and brown sugar over medium heat. Cook, stirring constantly, until syrup reaches hard ball stage (250 to 268 degrees). Remove from heat and stir in cashews. Pour syrup over crackers and bake 5 minutes. Remove from oven and sprinkle chocolate chips evenly over crackers. As chocolate melts, spread evenly over candy. Refrigerate 30 minutes or until candy hardens. Break candy into pieces. Store at room temperature in an airtight container.
Yield: about 1 pound candy

MIXED NUT BRITTLE

1 1/2 cups sugar
1/2 cup light corn syrup
1/4 cup water
1 1/2 tablespoons butter or margarine
1/2 teaspoon salt
3/4 cup lightly salted mixed nuts
1 teaspoon baking soda

Butter sides of a 3-quart heavy saucepan. Combine sugar, corn syrup, and water in saucepan. Stirring constantly, cook over medium-low heat until sugar dissolves. Using a pastry brush dipped in hot water, wash down any sugar crystals on sides of pan. Attach a candy thermometer to pan, making sure thermometer does not touch bottom of pan. Increase heat to medium and bring to a boil. Cook, without stirring, until mixture reaches hard-crack stage (approximately 300 to 310 degrees) and turns light golden in color. Test about 1/2 teaspoon mixture in ice water. Mixture should form brittle threads in ice water and remain brittle when removed from the water. Remove mixture from heat and add butter and salt; stir until butter melts. Add nuts and baking soda (syrup will foam); stir until baking soda dissolves. Pour candy into a buttered 10 1/2 x 15 1/2-inch jellyroll pan. Using a buttered spatula, spread candy to edges of pan. Allow to cool completely. Break into pieces. Store in an airtight container.
Yield: about 1 1/2 pounds brittle

MICROWAVE PEANUT BRITTLE

1 cup granulated sugar
1/2 cup light corn syrup
1 cup dry-roasted peanuts
1 teaspoon butter or margarine
1 teaspoon vanilla extract
1/2 teaspoon salt
1 1/2 teaspoons baking soda

In a 2-quart microwave-safe dish, combine sugar and corn syrup. Microwave on high power 4 minutes. Stir in peanuts. Microwave on high power 3 to 5 minutes or until light golden brown. Stir in butter, vanilla, and salt. Microwave on high power 1 to 2 minutes. Stir in baking soda until mixture foams. Quickly pour onto a greased baking sheet. Cool and break into pieces. Store in an airtight container.
Yield: about 3 cups candy

PEANUT BUTTER SPREAD

1 jar (16 ounces) peanut butter
1 cup miniature semisweet chocolate chips
1/2 cup chopped miniature marshmallows
1/2 cup chopped salted peanuts
2 tablespoons honey
Graham cracker bears or vanilla wafers to serve

Combine all ingredients in a microwave-safe container, blending well. Microwave on high power 1 minute and gently stir to swirl mixture. (Do not overcook; chocolate will soften when stirred.) Store in airtight container. Serve with graham cracker bears or vanilla wafers.
Yield: about 3 cups spread

343

PEANUT BUTTER DIVINITY

2 cups sugar
1/2 cup light corn syrup
1/2 cup water
1/8 teaspoon salt
2 egg whites
1 teaspoon vanilla extract
1 cup crunchy peanut butter

Butter sides of a large saucepan or Dutch oven. Combine sugar, corn syrup, water, and salt in saucepan. Stirring constantly, cook over medium-low heat until sugar dissolves. Using a pastry brush dipped in hot water, wash down any sugar crystals on sides of pan. Attach a candy thermometer to pan, making sure thermometer does not touch bottom of pan. Increase heat to medium and bring to a boil.

While syrup mixture is boiling, use highest speed of an electric mixer to beat egg whites in a large bowl until stiff peaks form; set aside.

Cook syrup mixture, without stirring, until mixture reaches firm-ball stage (approximately 242 to 248 degrees). Test about 1/2 teaspoon mixture in ice water. Mixture will roll into a firm ball in ice water but will flatten if pressed when removed from the water. While beating egg whites at low speed, slowly pour hot mixture into egg whites. Add vanilla and increase speed of mixer to high. Continue to beat until candy is no longer glossy. Fold in peanut butter. Pour into a buttered 8-inch square baking dish. Allow to harden. Cut into 1-inch squares. Store in an airtight container in refrigerator.
Yield: about 5 dozen squares divinity

PECAN LACE COOKIES

1 cup finely chopped pecans
1/2 cup butter or margarine, softened
1/2 cup firmly packed brown sugar
2 tablespoons rum, divided
2 tablespoons whipping cream
1/3 cup semisweet chocolate chips
1/4 cup all-purpose flour
1/4 teaspoon salt
1/8 teaspoon baking soda
1 cup quick-cooking oats

Preheat oven to 350 degrees. To toast pecans, spread evenly on an ungreased baking sheet. Stirring occasionally, bake 5 to 8 minutes or until darker in color. Cool completely on baking sheet.

In a large bowl, cream butter and brown sugar until fluffy. Beat in 1 tablespoon rum. In a small saucepan, bring whipping cream to a boil over medium heat. Reduce heat to medium-low. Stir in remaining 1 tablespoon rum and simmer 2 to 3 minutes. Remove from heat; add chocolate chips and stir until smooth. Add chocolate mixture to creamed mixture and stir until well blended. Sift flour, salt, and baking soda into a medium bowl. Stir dry ingredients into chocolate mixture. Fold in oats and toasted pecans. Drop heaping teaspoonfuls of dough 4 inches apart onto a greased baking sheet. Use fingers to press each cookie into a 2-inch-diameter circle. Bake 8 minutes (cookies will be soft); cool on baking sheet 3 minutes. Transfer cookies to a wire rack to cool completely. Store in an airtight container.
Yield: about 4 dozen cookies

Peanut Butter Divinity is a delicious variation of a favorite holiday candy. Light and delicate, Pecan Lace Cookies have a chocolaty flavor.

ROCKY ROAD MOUSSE

This mousse is a wonderful adult version of the classic treat. It makes plenty for a hungry crowd!

4 eggs, separated
1/2 cup brewed coffee
1 teaspoon vanilla extract
3 cups semisweet chocolate chips
3/4 cup sugar, divided
1 tablespoon water
1/4 teaspoon cream of tartar
1/8 teaspoon salt
1 cup whipping cream
1 1/2 cups miniature marshmallows
1 cup sliced almonds, toasted

In top of a double boiler, combine egg yolks, coffee, and vanilla. Whisking constantly, cook over simmering water until mixture reaches 160 degrees on a thermometer (about 8 to 10 minutes). Gradually stir in chocolate chips, whisking until smooth. Transfer to a large bowl. In top of a double boiler, combine egg whites, 1/2 cup sugar, water, cream of tartar, and salt. Whisking constantly, cook over simmering water until mixture reaches 160 degrees (about 10 to 12 minutes). Transfer to a large bowl and beat until stiff. Gradually adding remaining 1/4 cup sugar, beat whipping cream in a large bowl until stiff. Fold egg white mixture into whipped cream mixture. Fold into chocolate mixture. Stir in marshmallows and almonds. Pour mousse into a serving bowl. Cover and chill until set.
Yield: 10 to 12 servings

DATE PINWHEELS

(Photo on page 348)

1/2 cup butter or margarine, softened
1 cup firmly packed brown sugar
1 egg
1 1/2 teaspoons vanilla extract
2 cups all-purpose flour
1/2 teaspoon baking soda
1/2 teaspoon salt
1/2 teaspoon ground cinnamon
1/4 teaspoon ground nutmeg
1 package (8 ounces) chopped dates
1/2 cup water
1/4 cup granulated sugar
1/4 teaspoon ground cinnamon

In a large bowl, cream butter, brown sugar, egg, and vanilla. In a separate bowl, combine flour, baking soda, salt, 1/2 teaspoon cinnamon, and nutmeg. Stir flour mixture into creamed mixture. Cover and refrigerate dough at least 2 hours or until well chilled.

In a saucepan, combine dates, water, granulated sugar, and 1/4 teaspoon cinnamon over low heat. Cook, stirring constantly, until thickened; cool.

Preheat oven to 350 degrees. Divide dough into three equal parts. Roll each third of dough into a rectangle 8 x 10 inches and 1/4 inch thick. Spread one third of date mixture over each rectangle. Starting with one long end, roll up dough. Cut into 1/2 inch thick slices. Place on lightly greased baking sheets. Bake 14 to 16 minutes or until lightly browned. Cool on wire racks.
Yield: about 5 dozen cookies

GOLDEN GINGERBREAD

1/2 cup butter or margarine, softened
1/2 cup firmly packed brown sugar
2 eggs
1/2 cup molasses
2 cups all-purpose flour
1 teaspoon ground cinnamon
3/4 teaspoon baking powder
1/2 teaspoon baking soda
1/4 teaspoon ground cloves
1/2 cup hot strongly brewed coffee
1/3 cup golden raisins
1/4 cup finely chopped crystallized
   ginger
1 tablespoon grated orange zest

Preheat oven to 350 degrees. Grease a 5 x 9-inch baking pan and line with waxed paper. In a large bowl, cream butter and brown sugar until fluffy. Add eggs and molasses; beat until smooth.

In a small bowl, combine flour, cinnamon, baking powder, baking soda, and cloves. Alternately add dry ingredients and coffee to creamed mixture; stir until well blended. Stir in raisins, ginger, and orange zest. Pour batter into prepared pan.

Bake 45 to 55 minutes or until a toothpick inserted in center of bread has a few crumbs clinging and top is golden brown. Cool in pan 10 minutes. Serve warm or cool completely.

Yield: 1 loaf bread

ORANGE-DATE-NUT LOAVES

(Shown on page 333)

1 package (16 ounces) pound
   cake mix
2/3 cup vegetable oil
1/2 cup sweetened condensed milk
2 eggs
1 teaspoon orange extract
2 cups chopped pecans
1 package (8 ounces) chopped
   dates

Preheat oven to 325 degrees. In a large bowl, beat cake mix, oil, sweetened condensed milk, eggs, and orange extract at low speed of an electric mixer 30 seconds. Beat at medium speed 2 minutes. Stir in pecans and dates. Spoon batter into 2 greased and floured 5 x 9-inch loaf pans. Bake 1 hour to 1 hour 10 minutes or until a toothpick inserted in center of bread comes out with only a few crumbs attached. Cool in pans 10 minutes. Remove from pans and cool completely on a wire rack.

Yield: 2 loaves bread

Date Pinwheels (recipe on page 346) are easy-to-make refrigerator cookies that have all the good, spicy flavor of Grandma's traditional version.

Nestled in a cocoa-mocha crust, Macadamia Nut Fudge Tart is a chocolate lover's delight!

MACADAMIA NUT FUDGE TART

CRUST
- 1³/4 cups all-purpose flour
- ¹/3 cup cocoa
- ¹/4 cup granulated sugar
- ¹/8 teaspoon salt
- ³/4 cup butter or margarine, chilled and cut into pieces
- ¹/2 cup strongly brewed coffee, chilled

FILLING
- 1 package (6 ounces) semisweet chocolate chips, melted
- ²/3 cup granulated sugar
- 2 tablespoons butter or margarine, melted
- 2 tablespoons milk
- 2 teaspoons coffee-flavored liqueur
- 2 eggs, beaten
- ¹/2 cup chopped macadamia nuts

For crust, combine first 4 ingredients in a large bowl. Using a pastry blender or two knives, cut butter into dry ingredients until mixture resembles coarse meal. Add coffee and knead until a soft dough forms. Cover and chill 8 hours or overnight.

On a lightly floured surface, use a floured rolling pin to roll out dough to an 11-inch circle. Press into a greased 9-inch tart pan. Chill at least 1 hour.

Preheat oven to 350 degrees. For filling, combine first 5 ingredients in a large bowl. Add eggs, beating until smooth. Fold in nuts. Pour batter into tart shell. Bake 30 to 40 minutes or until top is dry and firm (inside will be soft). Cool completely in pan.

Yield: about 16 servings

These Shapes Foretell...

Foretell a sweet Noel with a basket of candy cane-shaped rolls! Baked in this festive form, our delicious Cardamom Bread Twists (recipe on page 371) are brushed with a light coffee glaze.

BUTTERSCOTCH BRAN MUFFINS

(Shown on page 333)

1/2 cup butterscotch chips
4 ounces cream cheese
   Vegetable cooking spray
1 package (7 ounces) bran muffin
   mix
1/3 cup milk
1 egg, beaten

In a small saucepan, melt butterscotch chips over low heat. Stir in cream cheese until well blended; remove from heat.
Preheat oven to 400 degrees. Line 9 muffin pan cups with paper muffin cups; spray paper cups with cooking spray. In a medium bowl, combine muffin mix, milk, egg, and half of butterscotch mixture; stir just until moistened. Spoon batter into prepared muffin cups, filling each about two-thirds full. Bake 15 to 18 minutes or until a toothpick inserted in center of muffin comes out clean. Cool in pan 10 minutes; transfer muffins to a wire rack. Spread remaining butterscotch mixture over tops of warm muffins. Serve warm.
Yield: 9 muffins

BLUEBERRY-LEMON MUFFINS

2 cups all-purpose flour
1 tablespoon baking powder
1/2 teaspoon salt
3/4 cup granulated sugar
1 egg, lightly beaten
4 tablespoons butter or margarine,
   melted
1 cup milk
1 teaspoon vanilla extract
1 1/2 teaspoons grated lemon peel
1 1/2 cups blueberries, fresh or frozen,
   rinsed

Preheat oven to 450 degrees. Sift together flour, baking powder, salt, and sugar. Combine egg, butter, milk, and vanilla. Stir liquid ingredients into dry ingredients just until moistened. Stir in lemon peel and blueberries. Fill lightly greased muffin tins three-quarters full. Bake 20 minutes or until golden brown.
Yield: 1 dozen muffins

ALMOND MUFFINS

1⅓ cups all-purpose flour
½ cup firmly packed brown sugar
1 teaspoon baking powder
½ teaspoon baking soda
¼ teaspoon salt
1 cup plus 2 tablespoons chopped
   sliced almonds, toasted and
   divided
½ cup buttermilk
¼ cup butter or margarine, melted
2 eggs, beaten
½ teaspoon vanilla extract
½ teaspoon almond extract

Preheat oven to 350 degrees. In a medium bowl, combine flour, brown sugar, baking powder, baking soda, and salt. Stir in 1 cup almonds. Make a well in center of mixture. In a small bowl, combine buttermilk, melted butter, eggs, and extracts. Add to dry ingredients; stir just until moistened. Spoon batter into paper-lined muffin cups, filling each about one-half full. Sprinkle remaining 2 tablespoons almonds over muffins. Bake 20 to 25 minutes or until lightly browned and a toothpick inserted in center of muffin comes out clean. Remove from pan. Serve warm or cool on wire rack. Store in an airtight container.
Yield: about 1 dozen muffins

GRANNY'S APPLE MUFFINS

1 cup granulated sugar
⅓ cup vegetable shortening
1 egg
1 teaspoon vanilla extract
¼ cup milk
1 teaspoon salt
1½ cups all-purpose flour
1 teaspoon baking soda
2 cups peeled and chopped apples
   Granulated sugar

Preheat oven to 375 degrees. In a medium mixing bowl, cream 1 cup sugar and shortening. Beat in egg. Stir in vanilla and milk. In another bowl, combine salt, flour, and baking soda. Stir into creamed mixture. Blend in apples. Fill each cup of a lightly greased 12-cup muffin tin ⅔-full with batter. Sprinkle sugar over batter. Bake 20 to 25 minutes or until lightly browned and a muffin springs back when lightly pressed.
Yield: 1 dozen muffins

Chocolate Bread Pudding is an old-fashioned favorite with a chocolate twist! A drizzling c̸ warm Caramel Sauce makes the moist dessert irresistible.

CHOCOLATE BREAD PUDDING WITH CARAMEL SAUCE

BREAD PUDDING
- 1 can (10 biscuits) refrigerated buttermilk biscuits, baked according to package directions
- 2 cups milk
- 2 eggs
- 2 tablespoons butter or margarine, melted
- 2 teaspoons vanilla extract
- ³/₄ cup sugar
- ¹/₄ cup cocoa
- ¹/₂ cup semisweet chocolate chips

CARAMEL SAUCE
- ¹/₂ cup butter or margarine
- ¹/₂ cup firmly packed brown sugar
- ¹/₂ cup granulated sugar
- ¹/₂ cup evaporated milk
- 1 tablespoon vanilla extract

Preheat oven to 350 degrees. For bread pudding, tear baked biscuits into bite-size pieces. In a large bowl, combine biscuits and milk; set aside. In a medium bowl, beat eggs, melted butter, and vanilla until well blended. Add sugar and cocoa; beat until well blended. Stir in chocolate chips. Add chocolate mixture to biscuit mixture; stir until well blended Pour into a greased 8-inch square glass baking dish. Bake 55 to 60 minutes or until set in center and edges pull away from sides of pan.

For caramel sauce, combine butter, sugars, and milk in a medium saucepan. Stirring constantly, cook over low heat until butter melts and sugars dissolve. Increase heat to medium and bring to a boil. Stirring constantly, boil about 9 minutes or until thickened. Remove from heat; stir in vanilla. Cut warm bread pudding into squares and serve with warm sauce.

Yield: about 9 servings

PEANUT BUTTER-CHEESE SHORTIES

8 ounces mild Cheddar cheese, grated
1 1/4 cups all-purpose flour
3/4 cup smooth peanut butter
1/4 cup butter or margarine, softened
1/4 cup water
1/2 teaspoon salt

Preheat oven to 400 degrees. In a large mixing bowl, combine cheese, flour, peanut butter, butter, water, and salt until well blended. On a lightly floured surface, use a floured rolling pin to roll out dough to 1/8-inch thickness. Using a pastry wheel or knife dipped in flour, cut dough into 1/2 x 2-inch strips. Transfer strips to lightly greased baking sheets. Bake 10 to 15 minutes or until golden brown. Cool before removing from pans. Store in an airtight container.

Yield: about 9 dozen shorties

CHOCOLATE SPLURGE

1/2 cup butter or margarine, softened
3/4 cup sifted confectioners sugar
1 egg
1/2 cup cocoa
3 ounces semisweet baking chocolate, melted
2 tablespoons crème de menthe liqueur
4 cups (about 14 ounces) chocolate mint-flavored cookies, broken into small pieces
Sweetened Whipped Cream to serve (recipe below)

In a medium mixing bowl, beat butter, confectioners sugar, and egg until creamy. Blend in cocoa, chocolate, and liqueur. Stir in cookie pieces. Turn mixture into a plastic wrap-lined 8-inch round pan. Cover and chill until firm (1 to 2 hours). Serve with Sweetened Whipped Cream.

Yield: 8 to 10 servings

SWEETENED WHIPPED CREAM

1 cup whipping cream
1/2 cup granulated sugar
1 1/2 teaspoons vanilla extract

Place all ingredients in a large mixing bowl. Beat at high speed until soft peaks form.

OLIVE-CREAM CHEESE BAGELS

1 cup milk, scalded
1 package (3 ounces) cream
   cheese, softened
$^1/_4$ cup butter or margarine
1 tablespoon sugar
1 teaspoon salt
1 package dry yeast
2 eggs
$^1/_2$ cup sliced green olives
4 cups all-purpose flour
   Cream cheese to serve

In a medium saucepan, combine milk, cream cheese, butter, sugar, and salt. Cook over medium-low heat, stirring occasionally, until mixture reaches 115 degrees. Remove from heat; transfer to a large bowl. Add yeast and stir until dissolved. Let stand 3 minutes. Whisk eggs into milk mixture. Stir in olives. Gradually stir in flour. Turn onto a lightly floured surface and knead 5 to 10 minutes or until dough becomes smooth and elastic. Shape into a ball and place in a greased bowl. Grease top of dough, cover, and let rise in a warm place (80 to 85 degrees) 30 minutes.

Turn dough onto a lightly floured surface and punch down. For each bagel, pinch off about 2 tablespoons dough and shape into a 5-inch-long roll. Form dough into a ring, overlap ends, and pinch ends to seal. (Or, using a floured rolling pin, roll out dough to $^1/_2$-inch thickness. Use a 2-inch biscuit cutter to cut out dough. Use the end of a wooden spoon to punch a hole through center of each bagel.) Place on a greased baking sheet. Cover and let rise in a warm place 10 minutes or until puffy.

Preheat oven to 400 degrees. Fill a large saucepan with water; bring to a boil. Drop 4 to 5 bagels at a time into boiling water and cook 3 minutes, turning once. Transfer to a greased baking sheet. Bake 25 to 30 minutes or until golden brown. Serve warm or at room temperature with cream cheese.
Yield: about $2^1/_2$ dozen bagels

GINGERBREAD CUTOUTS

$^1/_2$ cup vegetable shortening
2 tablespoons granulated sugar
1 egg
1 cup dark molasses
1 cup boiling water
$2^1/_4$ cups all-purpose flour
1 teaspoon baking soda
$^1/_2$ teaspoon salt
$1^1/_2$ teaspoons ground ginger
1 teaspoon ground cinnamon
$^1/_2$ teaspoon ground cloves
   Ice cream to serve

Preheat oven to 325 degrees. In a large mixing bowl, cream shortening, sugar, and egg. Blend in molasses and water. Combine flour, baking soda, salt, ginger, cinnamon, and cloves; add to molasses mixture. Beat until smooth. Pour into a 15 x 10 x 1-inch waxed paper-lined jellyroll pan. Bake 30 to 35 minutes or until cake springs back when touched in center. Cool cake in pan. Cut out shapes using desired cookie cutters (smaller shapes were cut from scraps using 1-inch-long cookie cutters). Serve with ice cream.
Yield: about 3 dozen 3-inch cutouts

CHOCOLATE SWIRL BANANA BREAD

1/2 cup vegetable shortening
1/2 cup granulated sugar
1/2 cup firmly packed brown sugar
2 eggs
1 1/2 cups mashed bananas (about 3 bananas)
1 teaspoon vanilla extract
2 cups all-purpose flour
1 teaspoon baking soda
1 teaspoon salt
2 ounces semisweet baking chocolate, melted
1 cup chopped walnuts, toasted

Preheat oven to 325 degrees. Grease two 3 3/4 x 7 1/2-inch loaf pans. Line bottoms of pans with waxed paper; grease waxed paper. In a large bowl, cream shortening and sugars until fluffy. Add eggs, 1 at a time, beating well after each addition. Add bananas and vanilla; beat just until blended. In a small bowl, combine flour, baking soda, and salt. Add dry ingredients to creamed mixture; stir until well blended. Remove 3/4 cup batter and place in a small bowl; stir in melted chocolate. Stir walnuts into remaining plain batter. Spoon nut batter into prepared pans. Drop chocolate batter by tablespoonfuls over nut batter. Swirl batters with a knife. Bake 58 to 62 minutes or until a toothpick inserted in center of bread comes out clean. Cool in pans on a wire rack 10 minutes. Remove from pans and cool completely on a wire rack. Store in an airtight container.
Yield: 2 loaves bread

MINIATURE HONEY-ROASTED PEANUT CHEESECAKES

2 cups crushed chocolate-covered graham crackers
3 packages (8 ounces each) cream cheese, softened
1 1/2 cups honey
1 cup peanut butter
1 cup whipping cream
2 teaspoons vanilla extract
4 eggs
1 cup chopped roasted peanuts
1 cup miniature semisweet chocolate chips

Preheat oven to 325 degrees. Line bottoms of four 5-inch springform pans with aluminum foil. Lightly grease pans and foil. Press 1/2 cup graham cracker crumbs into bottom of each pan; set aside.

In a large mixing bowl, beat cream cheese until smooth. Beat in honey, peanut butter, whipping cream, and vanilla. Beat in eggs until well blended. Stir in peanuts and chocolate chips. Divide mixture evenly between the four pans. Bake 40 to 45 minutes or until centers are set. Cool to room temperature. Cover and refrigerate overnight.

To remove each springform, use a knife to loosen sides of cheesecake from pan; remove sides. Store in refrigerator.
Yield: 4 cheesecakes

Brown Sugar Shortbread is delicious served with Spiced Coffee (mix recipe on page 366). These nutty cookies also make a nice gift when you bake them in the shape of your gift box.

BROWN SUGAR SHORTBREAD

2 cups all-purpose flour
1 cup pecans
¹/₈ teaspoon salt
1 cup butter or margarine, softened
¹/₂ cup firmly packed brown sugar

Place flour, pecans, and salt in a blender or food processor fitted with a steel blade. Process until mixture is a fine powder. In a large bowl, cream butter and brown sugar until fluffy. Add dry ingredients to creamed mixture; stir until a soft dough forms. Cover and chill 8 hours or overnight.

Preheat oven to 300 degrees. For cookie pattern, place desired gift box on tracing paper. Use a pencil to draw around box. Cut out pattern ³/₈ inch inside drawn line. On a lightly floured surface, use a floured rolling pin to roll out dough to ¹/₄-inch thickness. Place pattern on dough and use a sharp knife to cut around pattern. Transfer cookies to a greased baking sheet. Bake 20 to 25 minutes or until light brown. Cool completely on a wire rack. Store in an airtight container.
Yield: about 1 dozen 5-inch cookies

etty and pink, Marshmallow-Mint Sandwiches are quick-and-easy treats that children ill love.

MARSHMALLOW-MINT SANDWICHES

2   packages (12¹/₂ ounces each)
       fudge-covered graham crackers
2   envelopes unflavored gelatin
1   cup cold water, divided
¹/₄ cups granulated sugar
¹/₂ teaspoons peppermint extract
1   teaspoon vanilla extract
       Red paste food coloring
1   ounce vanilla-flavored candy
       coating and red paste food
       coloring to decorate

Line the bottom of an ungreased
3 x 9 x 2-inch baking pan with
5 graham crackers, top sides down. In
large mixing bowl, soften gelatin in
2 cup water; set aside. In a saucepan,
ombine remaining ¹/₂ cup water and
sugar. Bring to a boil and boil 2 minutes.
Stir sugar mixture into gelatin, blending
well. Refrigerate 10 minutes.

Beat gelatin mixture at highest speed
of an electric mixer until mixture turns
white and becomes thick like meringue.
Beat in extracts; tint pink. Pour mixture
over crackers. Top mixture with
36 crackers, top sides up. Refrigerate
about 1 hour or until set.

Using a sharp knife dipped in hot
water, cut into sandwiches using cookie
tops as guidelines.

If desired, melt candy coating; tint pale
pink. Drizzle candy coating over tops
of cookies to decorate. Store at room
temperature.
Yield: 36 cookies

FRUITCAKE COOKIES

1 package (15 ounces) sugar
  cookie mix and ingredients
  required to prepare cookies
1³/₄ cups chopped fruitcake

Preheat oven to 375 degrees. In a medium bowl, mix cookie dough according to package directions. Stir in fruitcake pieces. Drop rounded teaspoonfuls of dough 2 inches apart onto an ungreased baking sheet. Bake 6 to 8 minutes or until edges are lightly browned. Transfer cookies to a wire rack to cool completely. Store in an airtight container.
Yield: about 4 dozen cookies

PECAN SANDIES

1¹/₄ cups all-purpose flour
¹/₂ cup butter, softened
¹/₂ cup ground toasted pecans
¹/₃ cup firmly packed brown sugar
1 teaspoon vanilla extract

Combine all ingredients in a medium mixing bowl, blending well. Wrap dough in plastic wrap and refrigerate 1 hour.
Preheat oven to 350 degrees. On a lightly floured surface, use a floured rolling pin to roll out dough to ¹/₄-inch thickness. Using a 1-inch-wide heart-shaped cookie cutter, cut out dough. Transfer cookies to ungreased baking sheets. Bake 10 to 15 minutes or until golden brown. Remove from pans and cool on wire racks.
Yield: about 6 dozen cookies

OLIVER TWISTS

2 jars (2 ounces each) crystallized
  ginger
¹/₂ cup butter or margarine, softened
¹/₄ cup honey
1 cup granulated sugar
2 eggs
3¹/₄ cups all-purpose flour
1¹/₂ teaspoons baking powder
¹/₂ teaspoon salt
  Granulated sugar

In a blender or food processor, process ginger until very finely chopped; set aside.
In a large mixing bowl, cream butter, honey, and sugar until light and fluffy. Beat in eggs until smooth. Stir in ginger. In a medium bowl, combine flour, baking powder, and salt. Stir flour mixture into creamed mixture. Wrap dough in plastic wrap and refrigerate overnight.
Preheat oven to 325 degrees. Roll small amounts of dough into ¹/₄ x 10-inch ropes; form into pretzel shapes. Transfer cookies to lightly greased baking sheets and sprinkle cookies with sugar. Bake 20 to 25 minutes or until lightly browned (Cookies will be slightly firm to touch and will become crisper as they cool.) Remove cookies from pans and cool on wire racks. Store in an airtight container.
Yield: about 3 dozen cookies

CHOCOLATE MERINGUE CUPCAKES

CRUST
16 2-inch-diameter chocolate wafer
    cookies, finely ground
 3 tablespoons butter or margarine,
    melted
 1 teaspoon ground cinnamon

FILLING
 3 egg whites
2/3 cup sugar
1/2 teaspoon ground cinnamon
1/2 cup semisweet chocolate chips
1/2 cup chopped pecans

For crust, combine cookie crumbs, butter, and cinnamon in a medium bowl; stir until well blended. Line a muffin pan with foil muffin cups. Press about teaspoons mixture into bottom of each muffin cup.

Preheat oven to 325 degrees. For filling, beat egg whites in a large bowl until foamy. Gradually adding sugar and cinnamon, beat until stiff. Fold in chocolate chips and pecans. Spoon about tablespoons filling into each muffin cup. Bake 30 to 35 minutes or until lightly browned and set in center. Cool completely in pan. Store in an airtight container.

Yield: about 1 1/2 dozen cupcakes

FUDGE POUND CAKE

1/2 cup butter or margarine, softened
1 3/4 cups granulated sugar
 2 teaspoons vanilla extract
 3 eggs
1 3/4 cups all-purpose flour
2/3 cup cocoa
 2 teaspoons baking powder
1/2 teaspoon baking soda
 1 cup sour cream

Preheat oven to 325 degrees. In a large mixing bowl, cream butter, sugar, and vanilla. Beat in eggs.

In a small bowl, combine flour, cocoa, baking powder, and baking soda. Stir flour mixture into butter mixture, alternating with sour cream. Pour into a greased 9 x 5 x 3-inch loaf pan. Bake 1 hour 20 minutes or until a toothpick inserted in center comes out clean. Cool 10 minutes in pan; remove from pan and cool completely.

Yield: 12 to 14 servings

A parade of animal cutouts on the edge of the top crust gives sweet appeal to tart cranberry-apple Calico Pie (recipe on page 363).

Baked with a swirl of nutty cinnamon filling, Walnut Coffee Cake (recipe on page 362) s generously topped with nuts and a sweet glaze.

WALNUT COFFEE CAKE
(Shown on page 361)

FILLING
- 1 cup chopped walnuts
- 2 tablespoons sugar
- $1/2$ teaspoon ground cinnamon

CAKE
- 1 cup butter or margarine, softened
- 2 cups sugar
- 2 eggs
- $1/2$ cup milk
- $1^1/2$ cups all-purpose flour
- $1^1/2$ teaspoons baking powder
- $1/2$ teaspoon salt
- 1 cup sour cream
- $1/2$ teaspoon vanilla extract

GLAZE
- $3/4$ cup sifted confectioners sugar
- 1 tablespoon butter or margarine, melted
- 1 tablespoon milk
- 1 teaspoon vanilla extract
- $1/2$ cup chopped walnuts

Preheat oven to 350 degrees. For filling, combine walnuts, sugar, and cinnamon in a small bowl.

For cake, cream butter and sugar in a large bowl until fluffy. Add eggs and milk; beat until smooth. Sift flour, baking powder, and salt into a medium bowl. Gradually add dry ingredients to creamed mixture, beating until well blended. Beat in sour cream and vanilla. Spoon half of batter into a greased and floured 10-inch tube pan. Spoon filling evenly over batter in pan. Spoon remaining batter over filling; swirl with a knife. Bake 1 hour to 1 hour 15 minutes, testing for doneness with a toothpick.

Cool 10 minutes in pan. Remove from pan and cool completely on a wire rack.

For glaze, combine confectioners sugar and butter in a small bowl. Add milk and vanilla; stir until smooth. Drizzle glaze over cake. Sprinkle walnuts over glaze.

Yield: about 16 servings

SUGARED NUTS

- 1 egg white
- $1/2$ cup granulated sugar
- $1/2$ teaspoon ground cinnamon
- 2 cans (11 ounces each) lightly salted mixed nuts

Preheat oven to 225 degrees. In a medium bowl, beat egg white until foamy. Stir in sugar, cinnamon, and nuts, coating well. Spread on a greased baking sheet. Bake 1 hour, stirring every 15 minutes. Cool completely. Store in an airtight container.

Yield: About 6 cups

CALICO PIE

(shown on page 360)

We used the scraps of dough and miniature cookie cutters to cut out little dogs and cats to decorate the edge and center of the pie. Just bake the cutouts separately for 10 minutes. When the pie is cool, use a little corn syrup to "glue" the cutouts around the edge.

CRUST
2 1/4   cups all-purpose flour
1/2   teaspoon salt
3/4   cup plus 2 tablespoons chilled
          butter, cut into pieces
1/3   cup ice water

FILLING
1 1/2   cups sugar
    1   cup golden raisins
1 1/2   cups peeled, cored, and
          chopped apple
    1   cup whole berry cranberry sauce
    3   tablespoons lemon juice
1/2   teaspoon salt
1/2   teaspoon ground cinnamon
1/4   teaspoon ground cloves
1/4   teaspoon ground ginger

Preheat oven to 400 degrees. For crust, sift flour and salt into a medium bowl. Using a pastry blender or 2 knives, cut in butter into flour until mixture resembles coarse meal. Sprinkle water over dough, mixing quickly just until dough forms a ball (dough will be soft). Divide dough in half. On a lightly floured surface, use a floured rolling pin to roll out one half of dough. Place the dough in an ungreased 9-inch pie pan. Roll out remaining half of dough. If using miniature cookie cutters, center and cut holes in center of top crust; set aside.

For filling, combine sugar, raisins, apple, cranberry sauce, lemon juice, salt, cinnamon, cloves, and ginger in a medium bowl. Pour into pie shell. Top pie with remaining dough. Trim and crimp edges of pie. If not using miniature cookie cutters, cut slits in top of pie for steam to escape. Bake 35 to 40 minutes or until crust is golden brown. Serve warm or at room temperature.
Yield: 8 servings

IRISH CREAM CAKES

CAKES
    1   package (18.25 ounces) white cake
          mix
1 1/2   cups Irish cream liqueur
    1   cup miniature semisweet
          chocolate chips
    4   eggs
    1   package (6 ounces) instant vanilla
          pudding mix
1/2   cup vegetable oil

GLAZE
    3   cups confectioners sugar
    1   cup Irish cream liqueur

Preheat oven to 350 degrees. For cakes, combine cake mix, liqueur, chocolate chips, eggs, pudding mix, and oil in a large mixing bowl; blend well. Pour into 10 greased and floured 1-cup metal gelatin or cake molds. Bake 25 to 30 minutes or until cake springs back when lightly touched.

For glaze, combine confectioners sugar and liqueur in a small bowl; blend well. While cakes are still warm in molds, poke holes in cakes; pour glaze over. Allow cakes to cool in molds at least 2 hours before removing.
Yield: 10 miniature cakes

CHOCOLATE WAFFLES WITH CINNAMON-MARSHMALLOW TOPPING

WAFFLES
- 1/2 cup butter or margarine, softened
- 1 cup sugar
- 1/2 cup milk
- 2 eggs
- 1 teaspoon vanilla extract
- 1 1/2 cups sifted cake flour
- 2 teaspoons baking powder
- 1/4 teaspoon salt
- 2 ounces semisweet baking chocolate, melted

TOPPING
- 1 jar (7 ounces) marshmallow creme
- 2 tablespoons light corn syrup
- 1/2 teaspoon clear vanilla extract (used in cake decorating)
- 1/4 teaspoon ground cinnamon
  Shaved semisweet baking chocolate to garnish

For waffles, preheat waffle iron. In a large bowl, cream butter and sugar until fluffy. Add milk, eggs, and vanilla; beat until smooth. In a medium bowl, combine cake flour, baking powder, and salt. Add dry ingredients and melted chocolate to creamed mixture and blend (do not overmix). For each waffle, pour about 1/2 cup batter into waffle iron. Bake 5 to 7 minutes or according to manufacturer's instructions.

For topping, heat marshmallow creme and corn syrup over medium-low heat in a medium saucepan until marshmallow creme is smooth. Stir in vanilla and cinnamon. Serve waffles hot with warm topping. Garnish with shaved chocolate.
Yield: about six 7-inch waffles

MOCHA CHOCOLATE MOUSSE

- 1 package (6 ounces) instant chocolate pudding mix
- 1 package (1 1/4 ounces) whipped dessert topping mix
- 2 teaspoons instant coffee granules
- 2 1/3 cups milk (do not use skim or low fat)

Combine ingredients in a large mixing bowl. Beat with electric mixer at high speed until fluffy. Serve immediately, or chill until serving.
Yield: 6 to 8 servings

Chocolate Waffles are a delightful alternative to typical morning fare. Drizzled with creamy Cinnamon-Marshmallow Topping, they can be a unique and elegant dessert, too!

CHERRY-ALMOND WREATH

BREAD
- 1 package dry yeast
- 1/4 cup warm water
- 1/2 cup butter or margarine, softened
- 1/4 cup warm milk
- 2 tablespoons sugar
- 1 teaspoon ground cardamom
- 1/2 teaspoon salt
- 3 to 3 1/2 cups all-purpose flour, divided
- 2 eggs
  Vegetable cooking spray

FILLING
- 1/2 cup sugar
- 1/2 cup almond paste
- 1/3 cup butter or margarine, softened
- 1 teaspoon almond extract
- 3/4 cup red and green candied cherries, divided
- 1/2 cup sliced almonds, toasted

ICING
- 1 cup sifted confectioners sugar
- 2 tablespoons milk
- 1/4 teaspoon almond extract

For bread, dissolve yeast in warm water in a large bowl. Stir in butter, milk, sugar, cardamom, salt, and 1 cup flour. Stir in eggs and enough remaining flour to form a soft dough. Turn onto a lightly floured surface and knead 5 minutes or until dough becomes smooth and elastic. Place in a large bowl sprayed with cooking spray, turning once to coat top of dough. Cover and let rise in a warm place (80 to 85 degrees) 1 hour or until doubled in size.

For filling, combine sugar, almond paste, butter, and almond extract in a small bowl until well blended. Set aside.

Turn dough onto a lightly floured surface and punch down. Use a floured rolling pin to roll out dough to a 9 x 30-inch rectangle. Spread filling over dough to within 1/2 inch of edges; sprinkle with 1/2 cup cherries and almonds. Beginning at 1 long edge, roll up dough jellyroll style; pinch seam to seal. Cut dough in half lengthwise; turn cut sides up. Wrap dough halves around each other with cut sides up. Place dough on a greased baking sheet; shape into a wreath and pinch ends together to seal. Place remaining 1/4 cup cherries on top of wreath. Spray with cooking spray. Cover loosely with plastic wrap and let rise in a warm place about 30 minutes or until doubled in size.

Preheat oven to 350 degrees. Bake 30 to 40 minutes or until lightly browned. Transfer to a wire rack to cool completely.

For icing, combine confectioners sugar, milk, and almond extract in a small bowl; stir until smooth. Drizzle icing over bread. Allow icing to harden.

Yield: about 20 servings

SPICED COFFEE MIX
(Shown on page 356)
- 4 cups firmly packed brown sugar
- 2 cups coffee-flavored liqueur
- 1 1/2 cups non-dairy powdered creamer
- 1 1/2 teaspoons ground cinnamon
- 1 teaspoon ground allspice

In a large bowl, combine brown sugar, liqueur, creamer, cinnamon, and allspice using lowest speed of an electric mixer. Cover and chill overnight.

To serve, spoon 1 tablespoon coffee mix into a mug. Stir in 6 ounces desired hot beverage such as coffee, cocoa, or milk. Store coffee mix in an airtight container in refrigerator.

Yield: about 4 cups of coffee mix

CHEDDAR CHEESE SPREAD

2 cups shredded Cheddar cheese
1 package (8 ounces) cream cheese, softened
1 tablespoon prepared horseradish
2 to 3 drops hot pepper sauce
6 slices bacon, cooked and crumbled

Combine Cheddar cheese, cream cheese, horseradish, and pepper sauce in the top of a double boiler over simmering water. Stir constantly until cheeses are melted and mixture is smooth. Remove from heat and stir in bacon. Cool and store in an airtight container in refrigerator.
Yield: about 3 cups of spread

CRUNCHY CANDIED PICKLES

1 quart hamburger dill pickle slices
2 cups granulated sugar
1/2 cup tarragon wine vinegar
1 teaspoon celery seed
1 teaspoon dry mustard
1/2 teaspoon crushed dried red pepper flakes
1/8 teaspoon garlic salt

Drain pickles in colander; rinse. Combine remaining ingredients in saucepan and bring to a boil. Remove from heat and cool. Pack pickles into two pint jars with lids and pour syrup over pickles. Cover jars and refrigerate at least 6 to 8 hours to allow flavors to blend. Store in refrigerator.
Yield: 2 pints of pickles

HOT AND SWEET MUSTARD

1 cup apple cider vinegar
4 eggs, lightly beaten
1/2 cup granulated sugar
1/2 cup butter or margarine, melted
1 can (2 ounces) dry mustard
1 1/2 teaspoons cayenne pepper
1 teaspoon salt

Combine vinegar, eggs, sugar, butter, dry mustard, cayenne, and salt in the top of a double boiler over simmering water. Whisking constantly, cook until thickened (about 10 minutes). Cool and store in an airtight container in refrigerator.
Yield: about 2 cups of mustard

CANDIED BABY DILLS

1 quart miniature dill pickles
2 cups granulated sugar
1/2 cup apple cider vinegar
1 tablespoon fancy pickling spice
1/2 teaspoon garlic salt

Drain pickles in colander; rinse. Combine remaining ingredients in a large saucepan and bring to a boil. Remove from heat and cool. Pack pickles into heat-resistant jars with lids and pour syrup over pickles. Refrigerate overnight to allow flavors to blend. Store in refrigerator.
Yield: 2 pints of pickles

BRAIDED ORANGE BREAD

BREAD
4¹/₂ cups all-purpose flour
2 packages quick-rising dry yeast
1¹/₂ teaspoons salt
6 tablespoons butter or margarine
¹/₂ cup milk
¹/₂ cup water
1 egg
1 teaspoon vanilla extract

FILLING
1 cup butter or margarine
2 cups firmly packed brown sugar
2 cups finely chopped walnuts
2 tablespoons ground cinnamon
1 tablespoon grated dried orange
   peel

GLAZE
2 tablespoons frozen orange juice
   concentrate, thawed
2 tablespoons granulated sugar

For bread, combine first 3 ingredients in a large bowl, mixing well. In a medium saucepan, melt butter over medium heat; stir in milk and water. Heat mixture to approximately 130 degrees. Remove from heat. Whisk egg and vanilla into milk mixture. Stir milk mixture into dry ingredients; knead until a soft dough forms. Turn dough onto a lightly floured surface and knead about 5 minutes or until dough becomes elastic. Divide dough in half, cover, and let rest at room temperature.

For filling, combine all ingredients in a medium saucepan. Bring to a boil over medium heat, stirring constantly until sugar dissolves (about 3 minutes). Remove from heat; set aside.

For glaze, combine orange juice and sugar in a small bowl. Stir until sugar dissolves; set aside.

On a lightly floured surface, use a floured rolling pin to roll out each half of dough to a 6 x 20-inch rectangle. Spread half of filling evenly over each rectangle. Cut each rectangle into three 2-inch wide strips. With filling sides together, fold strips in half lengthwise. Braid 3 strips of dough together; join ends to form a circle. Repeat for remaining strips of dough. Transfer to a greased baking sheet. Cover and set in a warm place (80 to 85 degrees). Let rise 30 minutes or until doubled in size.

Preheat oven to 375 degrees. Bake 8 to 9 minutes; brush generously with glaze. Bake 4 to 5 minutes longer or until golden brown. Remove from oven; brush with remaining glaze. Cool completely on a wire rack. Store in an airtight container.

Bread may be served at room temperature or warm. To reheat, preheat oven to 350 degrees. Bake uncovered on an ungreased baking sheet 3 to 5 minutes or until heated through.
Yield: 2 bread rings

CANDIED CHRISTMAS POPCORN

Make two batches; tint one green and one red.

Vegetable cooking spray
16 cups popped popcorn
2 cups sugar
1/2 cup light corn syrup
2 teaspoons almond extract
1 teaspoon salt
1 teaspoon baking soda
Red and green paste food coloring

Spray inside of a 14 x 20-inch oven cooking bag with cooking spray. Place popcorn in bag. In a 2-quart microwave-safe bowl, combine sugar and corn syrup. Microwave on high power (100%) 2 minutes or until mixture boils. Stir and microwave 2 minutes longer. Stir in almond extract, salt, and baking soda; tint red or green. Pour syrup over popcorn; stir and shake until well coated. Microwave on high power 3 minutes, stirring and shaking after each minute. Spread on aluminum foil sprayed with cooking spray; cool. Store in an airtight container.

Yield: about 17 cups candied popcorn

It only takes a few minutes to make a batch of microwave Candied Christmas Popcorn, and it's sure to be a favorite with holiday snackers.

CARAMEL CRACKERS
(Shown on page 7)

  2 packages (9 ounces each) small
       butter-flavored crackers
  1 cup dry-roasted peanuts
  1 cup granulated sugar
  1/2 cup butter or margarine
  1/2 cup light corn syrup
  1 teaspoon vanilla extract
  1 teaspoon baking soda

Preheat oven to 250 degrees. Combine crackers and peanuts in a greased large shallow baking pan. In a saucepan, bring sugar, butter, and corn syrup to a boil and cook 5 minutes. Remove from heat; add vanilla and baking soda. Pour caramel mixture over crackers and peanuts; stir well. Bake 1 hour, stirring every 15 minutes. Pour onto waxed paper and break apart; allow to cool. Store in an airtight container.
Yield: about 9 cups of snack mix

CINNAMON-APPLE POPCORN
(Shown on page 7)

  2 cups chopped dried apples
  10 cups popped popcorn
  2 cups pecan halves
  4 tablespoons butter, melted
  2 tablespoons firmly packed brown
       sugar
  1 teaspoon ground cinnamon
  1/4 teaspoon ground nutmeg
  1/4 teaspoon vanilla extract

Preheat oven to 250 degrees. Place apples in a large shallow baking pan. Bake 20 minutes. Remove pan from oven and stir in popcorn and pecans. In a small bowl, combine remaining ingredients. Drizzle butter mixture over popcorn mixture, stirring well. Bake 30 minutes, stirring every 10 minutes. Pour onto waxed paper to cool. Store in an airtight container.
Yield: about 14 cups of snack mix

SEASONED PRETZELS

  6 cups pretzels (mix shapes if
       desired)
  1/2 cup butter or margarine, melted
  1 package (1 ounce) ranch-style
       party dip mix
  1 tablespoon Worcestershire sauce
  1/2 teaspoon seasoned salt

Preheat oven to 250 degrees. Place pretzels in a large shallow baking pan. In a small bowl, combine butter, dip mix, Worcestershire sauce, and salt. Pour butter mixture over pretzels; stir well. Bake 1 hour, stirring every 15 minutes. Pour onto waxed paper to cool. Store in an airtight container.
Yield: about 6 cups of snack mix

CARAMEL CORN PUFFS
(Shown on page 7)

  1 package (10.9 ounces) puffed corn
       cereal
  1 cup pecan halves
  1 cup granulated sugar
  1/2 cup butter or margarine
  1/2 cup light corn syrup
  1 teaspoon vanilla extract
  1 teaspoon baking soda

Preheat oven to 250 degrees. Combine cereal and pecans in a greased large shallow baking pan. In a saucepan, bring sugar, butter, and corn syrup to a boil and cook 5 minutes. Remove from heat; add vanilla and baking soda. Pour caramel mixture over cereal and pecans; stir well. Bake 1 hour, stirring every 15 minutes. Pour onto waxed paper and break apart; allow to cool. Store in an airtight container.

Yield: about 10 cups of snack mix

CARDAMOM BREAD TWISTS

(Shown on page 349)

3^1/$_4$ cups milk
^{1}/$_2$ cup butter or margarine, softened
2 cups granulated sugar, divided
3 eggs
2 teaspoons ground cardamom
1^1/$_2$ teaspoons salt
3 packages quick-rising dry yeast
^{1}/$_2$ cup warm water
12 cups all-purpose flour
1 cup hot brewed coffee

In a medium saucepan, bring milk to a boil; remove from heat and cool to room temperature. In a very large mixing bowl, cream butter and 1^1/$_2$ cups sugar until fluffy. Add next 3 ingredients, mixing until smooth. Dissolve yeast in water. Add milk and yeast mixture to creamed mixture; mix until well blended. Add flour 2 cups at a time, mixing thoroughly after each addition.

Preheat oven to 350 degrees. On a lightly floured surface, knead dough until soft and pliable. Use a floured rolling pin to roll out dough to ^{1}/$_2$-inch thickness. Cut dough into 1 x 9-inch strips. Twist 2 strips together into a candy cane shape and transfer to an ungreased baking sheet. Repeat with remaining strips of dough.

For glaze, dissolve remaining sugar in coffee; set aside. Bake bread 30 minutes; brush with glaze. Bake 5 to 10 minutes longer or until golden brown. Store in an airtight container.

Yield: about 2^1/$_2$ dozen rolls

CARAMEL CRISPY TREATS

3 bags (14 ounces each) caramels
1^1/$_2$ sticks butter
1 can sweetened condensed milk
1 box (10 ounces) crisp rice cereal
1 package (10 ounces) large marshmallows

Melt caramel, butter, and milk in double boiler or microwave. Dip marshmallows into caramel mixture using a fork; roll in cereal and put on wax paper. Refrigerate until firm.

Yield: 40 treats

CRUNCHY SNACK MIX

Here is our version of the traditional cereal snack mix. This mixture freezes well, so it may be made in advance.

- $1/2$ cup butter or margarine, melted
- 1 package Caesar garlic cheese salad dressing mix
- 1 tablespoon Worcestershire sauce
- 1 teaspoon seasoned salt
- 4 cups bite-size shredded wheat cereal
- 3 cups chow mein noodles
- 2 cups unblanched whole almonds
- 2 cups walnut halves

Preheat oven to 250 degrees. In a small bowl, combine butter, salad dressing mix, Worcestershire sauce, and seasoned salt; stir to blend. In a large bowl, combine the remaining ingredients. Pour butter mixture over cereal mixture, stirring until thoroughly coated. Pour onto a baking sheet and bake 1 hour, stirring every 15 minutes; cool in pan. Store in a tightly sealed container.
Yield: about 11 cups snack mix

ORIENTAL SNACK MIX

- 2 cups small pretzels
- $1^1/2$ cups golden raisins
- 1 cup chow mein noodles
- 1 cup salted peanuts
- 11 ounces vanilla baking chips
- 1 teaspoon vegetable shortening

In a large mixing bowl, combine pretzels, raisins, chow mein noodles, and peanuts. In a heavy medium saucepan, melt baking chips and shortening over low heat. Remove from heat and quickly stir into pretzel mixture. Spread mixture on a lightly greased baking sheet. Refrigerate 10 minutes or until set.

Break candy into bite-size pieces. Store in airtight container.
Yield: about 2 $3/4$ pounds candy

SUGARED CRANBERRY TRAIL MIX

- 1 cup whole almonds
- 2 cups small pretzels
- 1 cup dried cranberries
- 1 egg white
- $1/2$ cup sugar
- $1/2$ teaspoon ground cinnamon
- $1/2$ teaspoon salt

Preheat oven to 350 degrees. To toast almonds, spread almonds evenly on an ungreased baking sheet. Bake 7 to 8 minutes or until almonds are slightly darker in color. Cool completely on baking sheet.

Reduce oven temperature to 225 degrees. In a large bowl, combine almonds, pretzels, and cranberries. In a small bowl, beat egg white until foamy. Pour over pretzel mixture; toss until well coated. In another small bowl, combine sugar, cinnamon, and salt. Sprinkle over pretzel mixture; toss until well coated. Spread evenly on a greased baking sheet. Bake 1 hour, stirring every 15 minutes. Cool completely on baking sheet. Store in an airtight container.
Yield: about 5 cups trail mix

HEARTS OF LETTUCE WITH CAESAR DRESSING

DRESSING
1²/3 cups olive oil
1 cup (4 ounces) shredded
  Parmesan cheese
²/3 cup white wine vinegar
1 tube (1³/4 ounces) anchovy paste
2 tablespoons lemon juice
3 cloves garlic, minced
2 teaspoons Worcestershire sauce
1 teaspoon salt
1 teaspoon ground black pepper
¹/2 teaspoon dry mustard

CROUTONS
1 cup butter or margarine
1 teaspoon garlic powder
¹/2 teaspoon salt
¹/2 loaf French bread, cut into
  cubes (about 4³/4 cups)

SALAD
2 heads iceberg lettuce
8 green onions
8 cherry tomatoes, halved
  Fresh parsley

For dressing, combine all ingredients in a 2-pint jar with a tight fitting lid. Shake until well blended. Refrigerate 8 hours or overnight to allow flavors to blend.

For croutons, preheat oven to 350 degrees. In a large skillet, combine butter, garlic powder, and salt. Cook over medium heat until butter melts. Stir in bread cubes. Spread evenly in a jellyroll pan. Stirring occasionally, bake 20 to 25 minutes or until bread is golden brown. Transfer to paper towels to cool completely.

For salad, cut heads of lettuce lengthwise into eight 1-inch slices. Place slices of lettuce on individual plates. Arrange green onions, tomatoes, and parsley on lettuce. Pour dressing over salads. Sprinkle croutons over salads.
Yield: 8 servings

ITALIAN OIL AND PASTA

FLAVORED OIL
3 cups olive oil
3 tablespoons dried Italian herb
  seasoning

Place oil and seasoning in a small glass bowl. Cover and allow to sit in a cool place 3 days. Store in an airtight container. Use in Pasta Salad recipe.

PASTA SALAD
6 tablespoons Flavored Oil
3 tablespoons lemon juice
3 tablespoons white wine vinegar
1 clove garlic, minced
1 teaspoon Dijon-style mustard
1 teaspoon salt
¹/2 teaspoon dry mustard
¹/2 teaspoon ground black pepper
1 package (6 ounces) pasta
¹/2 cup sliced stuffed green olives
¹/3 cup chopped celery
¹/3 cup chopped sweet red pepper
2 tablespoons thinly sliced green
  onion

Combine Flavored Oil, lemon juice, vinegar, garlic, Dijon-style mustard, salt, dry mustard, and black pepper in a small bowl; set aside. Prepare pasta according to package directions. Drain and rinse with cold water. Place in a medium bowl. Add olives, celery, red pepper, onion, and oil mixture to pasta; stir until well coated. Store in an airtight container in refrigerator.
Yield: about 3 cups flavored oil and about 5 cups pasta salad

Tossed with a luscious blend of honey, ginger, and orange juice, Gingered Fruit Salad is pleasingly different.

GINGERED FRUIT SALAD

Gingered Fruit Salad may be made one day in advance.

- 1 can (20 ounces) pineapple chunks, drained
- 1 package (16 ounces) frozen unsweetened peach slices, thawed
- 1 cup coarsely chopped fresh pear (about 1 medium pear)
- 1 cup coarsely chopped apple (about 1 medium apple)
- ¹/₄ cup honey
- 2 tablespoons orange juice concentrate, thawed
- 2 teaspoons ground ginger

In a large bowl, combine pineapple chunks, peach slices, pear, and apple. In a small bowl, combine honey, orange juice, and ginger. Pour over fruit; toss until well coated. Cover and refrigerate 8 hours or overnight. Serve chilled.

Yield: about 8 servings

SOFT BREADSTICKS
(Shown on page 7)

1 1/2 cups warm water
2 tablespoons granulated sugar
1 package dry yeast
1 1/4 teaspoons salt
4 1/2 cups all-purpose flour
1 egg
1 tablespoon water
Coarse salt or margarita salt

In a large mixing bowl, combine 1 1/2 cups warm water, sugar, yeast, and 1 1/4 teaspoons salt. Stir to dissolve sugar and yeast; allow to sit 5 minutes. Gradually stir in flour, blending well to make a smooth dough. Turn out dough on a lightly floured surface and knead until smooth and elastic, 8 to 10 minutes. Divide dough into 28 equal pieces. Roll each piece into an approximately 8 x 1/4-inch breadstick. Place on a greased baking sheet.

In a small bowl, combine egg with 1 tablespoon water. Brush mixture over breadsticks and sprinkle with coarse salt. Cover and let rise 25 minutes.

Preheat oven to 425 degrees. Bake 15 to 20 minutes or until brown. Remove from pan and cool on wire rack.

Yield: 28 breadsticks

MADEIRA CHEESE SPREAD
(Shown on page 7)

1/2 cup Madeira wine
1/3 cup butter, melted
14 ounces Gouda cheese
1 cup sour cream
1 teaspoon salt
1/8 teaspoon cayenne pepper

In a small bowl, combine wine and butter. In a food processor or blender, combine cheese, sour cream, salt, and cayenne. Process until smooth. With motor running, gradually add wine mixture, blending until smooth. Refrigerate 24 hours before serving to allow flavors to blend.

Yield: about 2 1/2 cups spread

BOURSIN CHEESE SPREAD

2 packages (8 ounces each) cream cheese, softened
1 cup butter, softened
2 cloves garlic, minced
1 teaspoon dried oregano leaves
1 teaspoon dried basil leaves
1/4 teaspoon dried dill weed
1/4 teaspoon dried marjoram leaves
1/4 teaspoon dried thyme leaves
1/4 teaspoon ground black pepper
Crackers to serve

Combine all ingredients, blending until smooth. Cover and refrigerate overnight to allow flavors to blend. Serve at room temperature with crackers.
Yield: about 3 cups spread

SWEET CHEESE DIP FOR FRUIT
Keep the cut fruit fresh by sprinkling with lemon juice.

2 packages (8 ounces each) cream cheese, softened
1 jar (7 ounces) marshmallow creme
1/4 cup milk
1 1/2 teaspoons vanilla extract
1/2 teaspoon ground nutmeg
Assorted fruits to serve

In a medium mixing bowl, combine cream cheese, marshmallow creme, milk, vanilla, and nutmeg, beating until smooth. Serve dip with freshly cut fruits.
Yield: about 3 1/2 cups dip

HUMMUS DIP

2 cans (15 ounces each) chick-peas, drained
1/2 cup olive oil
3 tablespoons freshly squeezed lemon juice
2 cloves garlic, coarsely chopped
1 tablespoon tahini (ground sesame seed)
1 tablespoon coarsely chopped onion
1 tablespoon minced fresh parsley
1/4 teaspoon salt
1/4 teaspoon ground black pepper
1/8 teaspoon curry powder
Sliced black olives, fresh parsley, and red onion wedges to garnish
Pita bread triangles to serve

Process chick-peas, oil, lemon juice, garlic, tahini, onion, parsley, salt, pepper, and curry powder in a food processor until smooth. Spoon hummus into a serving dish. Garnish with black olives, parsley, and red onion wedges. Serve at room temperature with pita bread triangles.
Yield: about 3 cups dip

SPICY BLACK BEAN DIP

Dip may be made one day in advance.

3 cans (15 ounces each) black
   beans, drained
1/2 cup peeled and coarsely
   chopped cucumber
1/4 cup finely chopped fresh cilantro
2 tablespoons minced sweet red
   pepper
2 tablespoons minced sweet
   yellow pepper
2 tablespoons minced green
   pepper
2 tablespoons minced red onion
2 tablespoons freshly squeezed
   lime juice
1 jalapeño pepper, seeded
2 teaspoons dried basil leaves
1 teaspoon ground black pepper
1/2 teaspoon garlic powder
1/2 teaspoon ground cumin
1/4 teaspoon salt
1/4 teaspoon hot pepper sauce
1/4 cup shredded sharp Cheddar
   cheese to garnish
   Tortilla chips or crackers to serve

Process beans, cucumber, cilantro, red pepper, yellow pepper, green pepper, onion, lime juice, jalapeño pepper, basil, black pepper, garlic powder, cumin, salt, and pepper sauce in a food processor until puréed. Transfer to a 1 1/2-quart casserole dish. Cover and refrigerate 8 hours or overnight to allow flavors to blend.

To serve, preheat oven to 350 degrees. Cover and bake 15 to 20 minutes or until heated through. Sprinkle cheese over bean dip. Serve with chips or crackers.

Yield: about 4 1/2 cups bean dip

BACON-CHEESE RING

The potent flavors of sharp Cheddar cheese, green onion, and bacon will make this cheese spread a favorite. Top each bite with a small amount of strawberry preserves for a really different treat.

1 package (12 ounces) bacon
1 pound extra sharp Cheddar
   cheese, shredded
1 bunch green onions, finely
   chopped
2 cups mayonnaise
1 teaspoon cayenne pepper
1/2 cup toasted slivered almonds
   Strawberry preserves and crackers
   or French bread slices to serve

Fry bacon until crisp. Drain well and crumble into small pieces. In a medium mixing bowl, combine bacon, cheese, green onions, mayonnaise, and cayenne pepper; mix thoroughly. Place almonds in the bottom of an oiled 7-cup ring mold; press cheese mixture into mold. Refrigerate overnight.

Unmold cheese ring onto platter. Place a small custard cup filled with strawberry preserves in the center of the ring. Serve with crackers or French bread slices.

Yield: 20 to 25 servings

A batch of Green Chile-Corn Dip offers Southwestern flavor.

GREEN CHILE-CORN DIP

1/2   cup plus 2 tablespoons drained
      canned whole kernel corn,
      divided
1   cup nonfat cottage cheese
2   tablespoons picante sauce
1/4   teaspoon garlic powder
1/8   teaspoon ground cumin
1   can (4 1/2 ounces) chopped
      green chiles
4   tablespoons diced sweet red
      pepper, divided
      Tortilla chips to serve

Process 1/2 cup corn, cottage cheese, picante sauce, garlic powder, and cumin in a food processor until puréed. Transfer to a medium bowl. Stir in chiles, 2 tablespoons red pepper, and remaining 2 tablespoons corn. Garnish with remaining 2 tablespoons red pepper. Cover and chill. Serve chilled with chips.
Yield: about 2 1/3 cups dip

Simply Delicious
PARTY SNACKS

Mushrooms in Cream Cheese Pastry, page 382
Cheesy Pepper Rice Squares, page 383

Creamy dips, spicy sausage rolls, crunchy snack mixes, decadent cookies…your guests will reach for these goodies again and again! This collection of foods and beverages for casual entertaining includes appetizers, snacks, sweets, drinks, and choices for kids, too.

PIZZA BITES

DOUGH
- 1 package dry yeast
- 1 cup warm water
- 1 teaspoon sugar
- 2 tablespoons vegetable oil
- 1 teaspoon salt
- 2½ cups all-purpose flour, divided
  Vegetable cooking spray

TOPPINGS
- 5 plum tomatoes, thinly sliced and divided
- 1 sweet yellow pepper, thinly sliced
- 1 to 2 ounces feta cheese, crumbled
- 1 to 2 cloves garlic, minced
- 1 teaspoon dried basil leaves
- 4 tablespoons olive oil, divided
- 2 ounces Canadian bacon, cut into bite-size pieces
- 1 sweet red pepper, thinly sliced
- 1 green pepper, thinly sliced
- 1 small onion, thinly sliced and separated into rings
- 1 can (2¼ ounces) sliced black olives, drained
- 2 tablespoons finely chopped fresh cilantro **or** 2 teaspoons dried cilantro
- ½ teaspoon ground cumin
- 1 cup (4 ounces) shredded mozzarella cheese

For dough, dissolve yeast in warm water in a medium bowl. Add sugar, oil, salt, and 2 cups flour; stir until a soft dough forms. Turn onto a lightly floured surface; adding remaining ½ cup flour, knead 5 minutes or until dough becomes smooth and elastic. Place in a medium bowl sprayed with cooking spray, turning once to coat top of dough. Cover and let rise in a warm place (80 to 85 degrees) 1 hour or until doubled in size.

Preheat oven to 400 degrees. Using half of dough, shape into eight 1½-inch balls. On a lightly floured surface, use a floured rolling pin to roll out each ball into a 5-inch circle. Transfer dough circles to an ungreased baking sheet.

For toppings, place half of tomato slices on dough circles. Layer yellow pepper, feta cheese, garlic, and basil over tomato slices; drizzle 2 tablespoons olive oil evenly over toppings. Repeat procedure with remaining dough, layering with remaining tomato slices, Canadian bacon, red and green peppers, onion rings, black olives, cilantro, cumin, and mozzarella cheese. Drizzle with remaining 2 tablespoons olive oil. Bake 20 to 25 minutes. Cut each pizza into 4 wedges. Serve warm.

Yield: 64 pizza bites

Awaken the table with Festive Shrimp Appetizer! The shrimp and vegetables are tossed in a zesty oil and vinegar mixture.

FESTIVE SHRIMP APPETIZER

2 pounds medium shrimp, cooked, peeled, and deveined
1 medium white onion, cut into bite-size pieces
1 large sweet red pepper, cut into bite-size pieces
1 large green pepper, cut into bite-size pieces
1 jar (5 ounces) stuffed green olives, drained
1/2 cup olive oil
1/4 cup white rice vinegar
3/4 teaspoon red peppercorns
1/2 teaspoon green peppercorns

In a large bowl, combine shrimp, onion, red and green peppers, olives, olive oil, vinegar, and peppercorns; lightly toss until well coated. Cover and refrigerate overnight to allow flavors to blend. Serve chilled.
Yield: about 7 cups shrimp

Shown on page 379: *Mushrooms in Cream Cheese Pastry (top) have a filling of fresh mushrooms and Parmesan cheese. Made with red peppers and green chiles, Cheesy Pepper Rice Squares are smothered with two kinds of cheese.*

MUSHROOMS IN CREAM CHEESE PASTRY

2¹/₂ cups all-purpose flour
  ³/₄ teaspoon salt, divided
  2 packages (8 ounces each) cream cheese, softened
  ³/₄ cup butter or margarine, softened
  12 ounces fresh mushrooms, quartered
  ¹/₂ cup freshly grated Parmesan cheese
  2 tablespoons dry white wine
  2 tablespoons chopped fresh parsley
  2 tablespoons chopped pimiento
  1 clove garlic, minced
  1 teaspoon dried marjoram leaves
  ¹/₈ teaspoon ground white pepper
  ¹/₈ teaspoon dry mustard
  1 egg, beaten

In a medium bowl, combine flour and ¹/₂ teaspoon salt. Using a pastry blender or 2 knives, cut in cream cheese and butter until mixture resembles coarse meal. Lightly knead dough. Divide dough in half and wrap in plastic wrap; chill 1 hour.

In a food processor, process mushrooms, Parmesan cheese, wine, parsley, pimiento, garlic, marjoram leaves, remaining ¹/₄ teaspoon salt, white pepper, and dry mustard until coarsely chopped. Allow mushroom mixture to stand 15 minutes; drain in a colander.

Preheat oven to 400 degrees. On a lightly floured surface, use a floured rolling pin to roll out half of dough to ¹/₈-inch thickness. Use a 3-inch-diameter fluted-edge cookie cutter to cut out dough. For each dough circle, place a scant teaspoon of mushroom filling on half of circle; brush edge of remaining half of circle with beaten egg. Fold dough over filling. Use a floured fork to crimp edges of dough together and to prick top of pastry. Place on an ungreased baking sheet. Bake 15 to 20 minutes or until lightly browned. Serve warm.

Unbaked pastries may be placed on a baking sheet and frozen. Store frozen pastries in an airtight container. Bake frozen pastries 20 to 25 minutes in a preheated 400-degree oven.
Yield: about 5 dozen pastries

CHEESY PEPPER RICE SQUARES

4 cups cooked white rice
1 1/2 cups (6 ounces) shredded
  Monterey Jack cheese,
  divided
1 1/2 cups (6 ounces) shredded
  Cheddar cheese, divided
1 cup sour cream
2 cans (4 ounces each) whole
  green chiles, drained
1 jar (7 ounces) roasted red
  peppers, drained

Preheat oven to 325 degrees. In a medium bowl, combine rice, 1 cup Monterey Jack cheese, 1 cup Cheddar cheese, and sour cream until well blended. Firmly press half of rice mixture into bottom of a greased 7 x 11-inch baking pan. Cut green chiles open; place over rice mixture. Press remaining rice mixture over green chiles. Place roasted red peppers over rice mixture. Bake uncovered 25 to 30 minutes; sprinkle remaining cheese over red peppers. Bake 5 minutes longer or until cheese melts. Place pan on a wire rack and allow to cool 15 minutes. Cut into 2-inch squares. Serve warm.
Yield: about 15 servings

SAUSAGE-CREAM CHEESE SQUARES

2 cans (8 ounces each)
  refrigerated crescent rolls
2 packages (8 ounces each)
  cream cheese, softened
1/2 teaspoon dried basil leaves,
  crushed
1/4 teaspoon garlic powder
1 1/2 pounds mild pork sausage,
  cooked, drained, and
  crumbled
12 ounces provolone cheese,
  shredded (about 3 cups)
3/4 cup finely chopped sweet red
  pepper

Preheat oven to 350 degrees. Unroll 1 can of crescent roll dough into 2 long rectangles. Place on a greased baking sheet. With long sides touching, form an 8 x 13-inch rectangle, pressing edges to seal. Repeat for remaining can of rolls, using a second greased baking sheet. Bake 12 to 15 minutes or until golden brown. Remove from oven.
In a medium bowl, beat cream cheese, basil, and garlic powder using an electric mixer. Spread cream cheese mixture evenly over baked dough. Sprinkle sausage, provolone cheese, and sweet red pepper evenly over cream cheese mixture. Bake 5 to 7 minutes or until cheese melts. Cut into 2-inch squares. Serve warm.
Yield: about 4 dozen appetizers

CINNAMON-GRAHAM POPCORN

10 cups popped popcorn
$^1/_2$ cup golden raisins
2 cups graham cracker cereal
1 cup miniature marshmallows
1 cup chopped dried dates
$^1/_4$ cup butter or margarine, melted
$^1/_4$ cup firmly packed brown sugar
2 teaspoons ground cinnamon
$^1/_2$ teaspoon ground ginger
$^1/_2$ teaspoon ground nutmeg

Preheat oven to 250 degrees. Combine popcorn, raisins, cereal, marshmallows, and dates in large roasting pan; stir well. Combine remaining ingredients in a small bowl. Stir into popcorn mixture. Bake 20 minutes, strirring once. Allow to cool. Store in an airtight container.
Yield: about 14 cups popcorn mix

LAYERED PIZZA DIP

1 package (8 ounces) cream cheese, softened
$^1/_2$ cup sour cream
$^1/_4$ cup freshly grated Parmesan cheese
$^1/_2$ teaspoon garlic salt
$^1/_2$ cup prepared pizza sauce
$^3/_4$ cup shredded mozzarella cheese
1 package ($3^1/_2$ ounces) sliced pepperoni, finely chopped
Toasted pita bread wedges to serve

Preheat oven to 350 degrees. In a small bowl, beat cream cheese until fluffy. Stir in sour cream, Parmesan cheese, and garlic salt. Spread into a lightly greased 9-inch pie plate. Spread pizza sauce over cream cheese mixture. Sprinkle mozzarella cheese over pizza sauce and top with pepperoni. Bake about 20 minutes or until heated through. Serve warm with pita bread.
Yield: about 3 cups dip

Store-bought taco seasoning mix gives Fiesta Snack Mix zesty appeal.

SPICY JALAPEÑO SPREAD

4 cups (16 ounces) shredded sharp Cheddar cheese
1 cup mayonnaise
1 medium white onion, finely chopped
1/2 cup chopped green onion
6 jalapeño peppers, chopped
2 cloves garlic, minced
1 teaspoon garlic salt
Crackers to serve

In a large bowl, combine cheese, mayonnaise, white onion, green onion, peppers, garlic, and garlic salt; stir until well blended. Refrigerate overnight to allow flavors to blend before serving. Serve with crackers.
Yield: about 4 1/2 cups spread

FIESTA SNACK MIX

1 can (7 1/2 ounces) corn chips
1 can (12 ounces) salted mixed nuts
1/4 cup butter or margarine, melted
1/4 cup grated Parmesan cheese
2 teaspoons taco seasoning mix

Preheat oven to 325 degrees. In a large bowl, combine corn chips and nuts. In a small bowl, combine melted butter, cheese, and taco seasoning mix. Pour over corn chip mixture. Stir until well coated. Spread mixture evenly on a baking sheet. Bake 12 minutes. Cool completely. Store in an airtight container.
Yield: about 6 cups snack mix

Shown on page 8: *Sweet, crisp apple and pear slices are the perfect complement to the piquant character of Blue Cheese and Port Wine Spread. Prepared with crabmeat and sweet red pepper, Deviled Crab Eggs are delectable enticements.*

BLUE CHEESE AND PORT WINE SPREAD

1 package (3 ounces) cream cheese, softened
¼ cup butter, softened
8 ounces soft, mild blue cheese, at room temperature
3 tablespoons tawny Port wine
¼ teaspoon ground white pepper
¾ cup finely chopped toasted walnuts
  Crackers and apple and pear slices to serve

Process cream cheese and butter in a food processor until blended. Add blue cheese, wine, and pepper; process until well blended. Transfer to a small bowl; stir in walnuts. Serve at room temperature with crackers and apple and pear slices.
Yield: about 2¼ cups spread

DEVILED CRAB EGGS

1 dozen hard-cooked eggs, chilled
1 can (6 ounces) lump crabmeat, drained
½ cup mayonnaise
2 tablespoons finely minced sweet red pepper
1½ tablespoons finely minced onion
2 teaspoons prepared mustard
1½ teaspoons freshly squeezed lemon juice
½ teaspoon chopped fresh dill weed
¼ teaspoon salt
¼ teaspoon hot pepper sauce
⅛ teaspoon ground black pepper
  Fresh dill weed and chopped sweet red pepper to garnish

Cut eggs in half lengthwise. In a medium bowl, mash egg yolks. Add crabmeat, mayonnaise, red pepper, onion, mustard, lemon juice, dill weed, salt, pepper sauce, and black pepper to egg yolks. Stir until crabmeat is broken into small pieces and mixture is well blended. Spoon yolk mixture into a pastry bag fitted with a large star tip. Pipe yolk mixture into egg white halves. Chill until ready to serve. Garnish with dill weed and red pepper.
Yield: 24 deviled eggs

Light, cool Cucumber Dip makes a colorful appetizer when paired with fresh vegetables.

CUCUMBER DIP

- 1 large cucumber, peeled and seeded
- 1 container (8 ounces) fat-free cottage cheese
- ¼ cup chopped pecans
- 1 teaspoon lemon juice
- 1 package (1 ounce) fat-free ranch salad dressing mix
- 2 tablespoons fat-free mayonnaise
- 1 teaspoon garlic powder
- 1 teaspoon onion powder

  Small carrot and fresh parsley to garnish

  Fresh vegetables to serve

Process cucumber, cottage cheese, pecans, lemon juice, dressing mix, mayonnaise, garlic powder, and onion powder in a food processor until cucumber and pecans are finely chopped. Transfer to an airtight container and refrigerate until well chilled. Garnish with carrot and parsley. Serve with fresh vegetables.

Yield: about 2 cups dip or 16 servings

SHRIMP SPREAD

Shrimp spread should be made 1 day in advance.

1¹/₂   pounds cooked, peeled, and deveined shrimp
1   package (8 ounces) cream cheese, softened
¹/₄   cup finely chopped onion
2   tablespoons sour cream
2   teaspoons sweet pickle relish
1¹/₂   teaspoons Dijon-style mustard
1¹/₂   teaspoons hot pepper sauce
  Crackers or bread to serve

Reserve several shrimp for garnish. Finely chop remaining shrimp. In a large bowl, combine chopped shrimp, cream cheese, onion, sour cream, pickle relish, mustard, and hot pepper sauce; stir until well blended. Cover and refrigerate 8 hours or overnight to allow flavors to blend.

To serve, garnish with reserved shrimp. Serve with crackers or bread.

Yield: about 4 cups spread

SHRIMP BUNDLES

1   package (8 ounces) fat-free cream cheese, softened
¹/₄   cup cooking sherry
¹/₄   cup finely chopped green onions
1   teaspoon dried tarragon leaves, crushed
¹/₂   teaspoon garlic powder
¹/₂   teaspoon salt
¹/₂   teaspoon ground black pepper
9   sheets frozen phyllo pastry, thawed according to package directions
  Olive oil cooking spray
3   dozen medium shrimp, cooked, peeled, and deveined

Preheat oven to 375 degrees. In a medium bowl, combine cream cheese, sherry, onions, tarragon, garlic powder, salt, and pepper; stir until well blended. Lightly spray each sheet of phyllo pastry with cooking spray. Stack 3 sheets of pastry on top of each other; cut into twelve 4-inch squares. Spoon a heaping teaspoonful of cheese mixture in center of each pastry square. Place 1 shrimp over cheese mixture on each pastry square. Bring corners of pastry squares together and twist. Place on a baking sheet sprayed with cooking spray. Lightly spray each bundle with cooking spray. Repeat with remaining pastry sheets, cheese mixture, and shrimp. Bake 6 to 8 minutes or until lightly browned. Serve warm.

Yield: 3 dozen shrimp bundles

SAVORY PARTY BITES

1 pound hot pork sausage
1 package (8 ounces) cream
   cheese, softened
1/2 cup finely chopped onion
1/3 cup chopped fresh parsley
3 tablespoons prepared mustard
1/4 teaspoon garlic powder
1 can (10 ounces) chopped
   sauerkraut, drained
1/2 cups all-purpose baking mix
1/4 cups bread crumbs
1/2 teaspoons paprika

Process uncooked sausage, cream cheese, onion, parsley, mustard, and garlic powder in a food processor just until blended. Add sauerkraut; pulse process until blended. Transfer mixture to a large bowl. Stir in baking mix. Cover and chill 1 hour.

Preheat oven to 350 degrees. In a small bowl, combine bread crumbs and paprika. Shape sausage mixture into 1-inch balls. Roll each ball in bread crumb mixture. Place on a lightly greased baking sheet. Bake 23 to 26 minutes or until golden brown. Serve warm.

Yield: about 8 dozen appetizers

SESAME-PARMESAN ROUNDS

2 cups all-purpose flour
1/2 teaspoon ground red pepper
1/8 teaspoon salt
1 cup butter, softened
1 cup freshly grated Parmesan
   cheese
1 egg white
1 teaspoon water
1/4 cup sesame seeds, toasted

Preheat oven to 350 degrees. In a medium bowl, combine flour, red pepper, and salt; set aside. In a large bowl, combine butter and cheese; beat until well blended. Add dry ingredients to creamed mixture; stir until well blended. On a lightly floured surface, use a floured rolling pin to roll out dough to 1/8-inch thickness. Use a 1 1/2-inch biscuit cutter to cut out dough. Transfer to a greased baking sheet. In a small bowl, beat egg white and water until blended. Brush dough with egg white mixture and sprinkle with sesame seeds. Bake 12 to 14 minutes or until bottoms are lightly browned. Serve warm. To reheat crackers, place in a 325-degree oven about 2 minutes.

Yield: about 8 dozen crackers

CIRCUS MIX

2 cups honey-flavored toasted
oat cereal
1 cup raisins
1 cup unsalted peanuts or
Peanut M&M's® candies
2 cups miniature marshmallows
1/2 cup milk chocolate chips
1/2 cup peanut butter flavored chips

Combine all ingredients in a large bowl.
Store in an airtight container.
Yield: about 7 cups mix

CRANBERRY-CHAMPAGNE COCKTAILS

1 quart cranberry juice cocktail,
chilled
1 bottle (750 ml) champagne,
chilled

Combine cranberry juice and
champagne in a 2-quart pitcher; stir until
well blended. Serve chilled.
Yield: about nine 6-ounce servings

MARINATED MOZZARELL

1 pound mozzarella cheese, cut
into thin 2-inch squares
1/4 cup olive oil
2 tablespoons finely chopped
fresh parsley
1 teaspoon garlic powder
1 teaspoon onion powder
1 teaspoon dried oregano leaves,
crushed
1/4 teaspoon ground black pepper
Fresh basil leaves to garnish
Bagel chips or crackers to serve

Place cheese in a single layer in a
10 1/2 x 15 1/2-inch jellyroll pan. In a smal
bowl, whisk oil, parsley, garlic powder,
onion powder, oregano, and pepper.
Pour over cheese. Cover and refrigerate
8 hours or overnight to allow flavors to
blend, turning slices occasionally.
Arrange slices on a serving plate;
garnish with fresh basil. Serve with bag
chips or crackers.
Yield: about 3 dozen cheese squares

Delicious with bagel chips or crackers, slices of Marinated Mozzarella get a mellow flavor from herbs and olive oil.

ROASTED RED PEPPER DIP

2 large sweet red peppers
1/2 cup fat-free mayonnaise
1/2 cup fat-free sour cream
1 tablespoon minced onion
2 teaspoons chopped fresh
    parsley
1 small clove garlic, minced
1/2 teaspoon white wine vinegar
1/4 teaspoon ground white pepper
1/4 teaspoon celery salt
1/4 teaspoon salt
    Low-fat crackers to serve

To roast red peppers, cut in half lengthwise and remove seeds and membranes. Place skin side up on an ungreased baking sheet; use hand to flatten peppers. Broil about 3 inches from heat about 10 minutes or until peppers are blackened. Immediately seal peppers in a plastic bag and allow to steam 10 to 15 minutes. Remove charred skin and finely chop peppers.

In a medium bowl, combine chopped roasted red peppers, mayonnaise, sour cream, onion, parsley, garlic, vinegar, white pepper, celery salt, and salt. Stir until well blended. Cover and chill 1 hour to allow flavors to blend. Serve at room temperature with crackers.
Yield: about 2 cups dip

CINNAMON POPCORN SNACK MIX

10 cups popped popcorn, cooked
    without salt or fat
2 egg whites
1 cup granulated sugar
1 teaspoon ground cinnamon
1 teaspoon salt

Preheat oven to 225 degrees. Place popcorn in a large bowl. In a small bowl, beat egg whites until stiff. Beat in sugar, cinnamon, and salt. Spoon egg white mixture over popcorn; stir until well coated. Spread evenly on a greased baking sheet. Bake 1 hour, stirring every 15 minutes. Cool completely on pan. Store in an airtight container.
Yield: about 8 cups snack mix

TORTILLA CHIPS

1 package (12 count) fresh corn
    tortillas
    Vegetable oil
1 tablespoon salt
1 clove garlic, minced

Cut each tortilla into 6 wedges. Pour oil into a skillet to a depth of 1 inch. Heat oil to 360 degrees over medium-high heat. Fry tortillas, a few at a time, about 1 minute or until crisp. Drain on paper towels. Place salt and garlic in a plastic bag. Add chips and shake well. Serve warm or at room temperature.
Yield: 6 dozen chips

AKED TACO DIP

1   can (16 ounces) refried beans
1/2   teaspoon ground cumin
1/2   teaspoon garlic salt
1/2   teaspoon onion powder
1/2   pound lean ground beef
1/2   cup chopped onion
1/2   cup taco sauce
1/2   cups (6 ounces) shredded
        Cheddar cheese
      Tortilla chips to serve

Preheat oven to 350 degrees. In a small
owl, combine beans, cumin, garlic salt,
d onion powder. Spread mixture in
ttom of a lightly greased 9-inch pie
ate. In a small skillet, cook ground
ef and onion over medium heat until
eat is browned; drain well. Layer meat
ixture, taco sauce, and cheese over
an mixture. Bake 25 to 30 minutes
  until heated through and cheese is
elted. Serve warm with chips.
eld: about 3 1/2 cups dip

ESTY TOMATO JUICE

1   can (48 ounces) tomato juice
1/2   cup lemon juice
1/4   cup Worcestershire sauce
2   tablespoons juice from canned
        or bottled jalapeño peppers
1/2   teaspoons hot pepper sauce
1/2   teaspoon onion juice

Combine tomato juice, lemon juice,
orcestershire sauce, pepper juice,
epper sauce, and onion juice; stir well.
ore in refrigerator.
eld: about 6 servings

NACHO CHEESE SNACK MIX

6   cups rice cereal squares
4   cups cheese snack sticks
2   cups small pretzels
2   cups mixed nuts
1/2   cup butter, melted
1   tablespoon Worcestershire
        sauce
1   package (1 1/4 ounces) cheese
        sauce mix
2   teaspoons chili powder
1/4   teaspoon ground red pepper

Preheat oven to 250 degrees. Combine
cereal, cheese sticks, pretzels, and nuts
in a large roasting pan. In a small bowl,
combine melted butter, Worcestershire
sauce, cheese sauce mix, chili powder,
and red pepper. Pour over cereal mixture;
stir until well coated. Bake 30 minutes,
stirring every 10 minutes. Spread on
waxed paper to cool. Store in an airtight
container.
Yield: 14 cups snack mix

TEA PARTY SNACKS

HAM AND CHEESE SANDWICHES

- 4 ounces (¹/₂ of an 8-ounce container) soft cream cheese
- 1¹/₂ teaspoons ranch-style dressing mix
- 6 slices very thin-sliced white bread, crusts removed
- 4 ounces thin-sliced ham
  Carrot strips to garnish

In a small bowl, combine cream cheese and dressing mix until well blended. Cover and chill overnight to allow flavors to blend.

Spread cream cheese mixture on 1 side of each bread slice. Place ham slices over cream cheese mixture on half of bread slices. Top with remaining bread slices. Cut each sandwich into quarters. To garnish, use a party pick to secure a carrot strip on each sandwich.
Yield: 12 small sandwiches

PEPPERONI AND CHEESE SANDWICHES

- 2 tablespoons mayonnaise
- 2 tablespoons prepared mustard
- 12 slices very thin-sliced white bread
- 3¹/₂ ounces white American cheese slices
- 24 slices pepperoni (about 1 ounce)
  Miniature sweet pickles to garnish

In a small bowl, combine mayonnaise and mustard until well blended. Use a 2-inch biscuit cutter to cut 2 circles from each bread slice.

Spread mayonnaise mixture on 1 side of each bread round. Use a 1¹/₂-inch biscuit cutter to cut circles from cheese slices. Alternately layer 2 pepperoni slices and 2 cheese slices between bread rounds. To garnish, use a party pick to secure a pickle on each sandwich.
Yield: 12 small sandwiches

PEANUT BUTTER AND BANANA SANDWICHES

- 6 slices cinnamon-raisin bread
- 2 tablespoons smooth peanut butter
- 1 banana

Use a 1¹/₂-inch biscuit cutter to cut 4 circles from each bread slice. Spread about ¹/₄ teaspoon peanut butter on 1 side of each bread round. Cut banana into ¹/₄-inch slices and place on half of bread slices. Top with remaining bread slices.
Yield: 12 small sandwiches

CHICKEN NUGGET SNACKS

- ¹/₂ cup ketchup
- ¹/₄ cup firmly packed brown sugar
- ¹/₄ cup honey
- 1 tablespoon apple cider vinegar
- 1 tablespoon prepared mustard
- 1 package (13.5 ounces) frozen chicken nuggets
  Seedless grapes and pineapple tidbits to garnish

In a small bowl, combine ketchup, brown sugar, honey, vinegar, and mustard; stir until smooth. Set sauce aside.

rve Cherry-Apple Punch with a tasty assortment of tiny Tea Party Snacks. The array of ?ats is made with delicious fillers of ham, cheeses, pepperoni, peanut butter, and banana. ?pped with fruit, chicken nuggets are accompanied by a tangy sweet-and-sour sauce.

Preheat oven to 425 degrees. Bake ⸱icken nuggets on an ungreased baking ⸱eet according to package directions. ⸱ garnish, use a party pick to secure a ⸱ape and a pineapple tidbit on each ⸱arm nugget. Serve with sauce for ⸱pping.
eld: about 2 dozen snacks and 1 cup ⸱uce

HERRY-APPLE PUNCH
ake punch the day of party.

1 cup boiling water
1 package (3 ounces) cherry
      gelatin

1 can (6 ounces) frozen pink
      lemonade concentrate,
      thawed
3 cups apple juice
2 cans (12 ounces each) cherry-
      lemon-lime soda, chilled

In a medium bowl, stir boiling water into gelatin until gelatin dissolves. In a large container, combine gelatin, lemonade concentrate, and apple juice. Cover and chill 2 hours. To serve, stir in cherry-lemon-lime soda. Serve immediately.
Yield: about 7$^1/_2$ cups punch

CHEESY SNACK MIX

14 cups (about 20 ounces) small
pretzels
1 cup butter or margarine
1 cup grated Parmesan cheese
3 packages (1.25 ounces each)
cheese sauce mix
2 packages (1 ounce each)
ranch-style salad dressing mix
1 teaspoon garlic powder

Preheat oven to 350 degrees. Place
pretzels in a large bowl. In a medium
saucepan, melt butter over medium heat.
Remove from heat. Stir in remaining
ingredients. Pour over pretzels; stir until
well coated. Transfer to two ungreased
baking sheets. Bake 10 to 12 minutes
or until golden brown. Cool completely
on baking sheets. Store in an airtight
container.
Yield: about 15$^1/_2$ cups snack mix

PARTY CHEESE ROLLS
Make several recipes and freeze.

5 dozen small finger rolls (about
2$^1/_2$ inches long)
2 cups (8 ounces) shredded
sharp Cheddar cheese
2 cups (8 ounces) shredded mild
Cheddar cheese
1 can (4$^1/_2$ ounces) ripe olives,
chopped
6 hard-cooked eggs, chopped
1 can (4 ounces) green chiles,
chopped
1 cup tomato sauce
1 teaspoon celery salt
1 medium onion, finely chopped
1 cup butter, softened

Preheat oven to 400 degrees. Split
rolls in half. Using a small spoon, scoop
out centers of rolls; reserve half of
the crumbs. In a large bowl, combine
remaining ingredients; add reserved
crumbs. Stuff rolls with mixture. Bake
10 to 15 minutes. Serve immediately.
To make ahead, unbaked rolls can
be placed in an airtight container and
frozen. To bake after freezing, thaw
completely, wrap in foil, and heat.
Yield: 60 rolls

THREE-CHEESE SANDWICH ROLLS

1 package dry yeast
1 tablespoon sugar
1/4 cup warm water
2 1/2 to 3 cups all-purpose flour,
    divided
1 teaspoon salt
3 tablespoons butter or
    margarine, melted
2 eggs
1 cup ricotta cheese
3/4 cup (6 ounces) shredded
    cheddar cheese
3/4 cup (6 ounces) shredded
    Monterey Jack cheese with
    jalapeño peppers
  Vegetable cooking spray
1 egg yolk
1 teaspoon water

In a small bowl, dissolve yeast and sugar in warm water. In a large bowl, combine 2 1/2 cups flour and salt. Add melted butter, eggs, cheeses, and yeast mixture to dry ingredients; stir until a soft dough forms. Turn onto a lightly floured surface. Knead 3 to 5 minutes or until dough becomes smooth and elastic, using additional flour as necessary. Place in a large bowl sprayed with cooking spray, turning once to coat top of dough. Cover and let rise in a warm place (80 to 85 degrees) 1 hour or until doubled in size.

Turn dough onto a lightly floured surface and punch down. Divide dough into 10 equal pieces; shape into 2 x 4-inch rolls. Place rolls 2 inches apart on a greased baking sheet. Spray tops of rolls with cooking spray, cover, and let rise in a warm place 1 hour or until doubled in size.

Preheat over to 350 degrees. Beat egg yolk and water in a small bowl; brush over rolls. Bake 20 to 25 minutes or until golden brown. Serve warm or transfer to a wire rack to cool completely.
Yield: 10 rolls

HORSERADISH BEEF ROLLS

1/2 cup fat-free cottage cheese
2 tablespoons prepared
    horseradish
2 teaspoons Dijon-style mustard
1 pound thinly sliced lean
    cooked roast beef
2 cans (10 biscuits each)
    refrigerated buttermilk
    biscuits
  Vegetable cooking spray

Preheat oven to 450 degrees. For sauce, process cottage cheese, horseradish, and mustard in a small food processor until smooth. Cut or fold each slice of roast beef into a 3-inch square. On a lightly floured surface, use a floured rolling pin to roll each biscuit into a 4-inch square. Spread a heaping teaspoonful of sauce over biscuit. Place two 3-inch squares of roast beef over sauce. Roll up biscuit and place, seam side down, on a baking sheet sprayed with cooking spray. Bake 8 to 10 minutes or until golden brown. Serve warm with remaining sauce.
Yield: 20 beef rolls

Savory Stuffed Potatoes feature a flavorful mushroom and onion filling topped with cheese and chives.

STUFFED POTATOES

10 small russet potatoes, baked
 2 cups fat-free cottage cheese
 1 teaspoon salt
 $1/4$ teaspoon ground black pepper
 2 tablespoons reduced-calorie
     margarine
 1 cup finely chopped onions
 1 cup chopped fresh mushrooms
 1 clove garlic, minced
     Vegetable cooking spray
 2 cups (8 ounces) finely
     shredded fat-free Cheddar
     cheese
 $1/4$ cup chopped fresh chives

Preheat oven to 375 degrees. Cut potatoes in half lengthwise. Leaving about $1/2$ inch of pulp on skins, scoop out remaining pulp and place in a large bowl. Add cottage cheese, salt, and pepper to potato pulp; stir until well blended and set aside.

In a medium skillet, melt margarine over medium heat. Add onions, mushrooms, and garlic; cook until onions are tender. Add onion mixture to potato mixture; stir until well blended. Spoon mixture into potato skins and place on a baking sheet sprayed with cooking spray. Sprinkle cheese and chives evenly over stuffed potatoes. Bake 8 to 10 minutes or until cheese is bubbly. Serve warm.
Yield: 20 stuffed potato halves

Ham and Swiss or Roast Beef and Cheddar Party Loaves satisfy hearty appetites. The recipes are on page 400.

Horseradish Beef Rolls (recipe on page 397) are easy to make with canned biscuits.

ROAST BEEF AND CHEDDAR PARTY LOAVES

(Shown on page 399)

$1/3$ cup mayonnaise
3 tablespoons Dijon-style mustard
$2^1/2$ tablespoons Worcestershire sauce
1 tablespoon dried minced onion
1 package (16 ounces) 2 small French bread loaves
8 ounces thinly sliced roast beef
6 ounces thinly sliced Cheddar cheese

In a small bowl, combine mayonnaise, mustard, Worcestershire sauce, and onion until well blended. Split loaves in half lengthwise. Spread inside of each loaf with mayonnaise mixture. Layer bottom halves with roast beef and cheese. Place top halves on loaves. Wrap in aluminum foil and store in refrigerator until ready to serve.

To serve, bake loaves in foil in a 350-degree oven 15 to 20 minutes or until bread is warm and cheese is melted. Cut into 1-inch slices. Serve warm.
Yield: 2 party loaves, about 12 servings each

HAM AND SWISS PARTY LOAVES

(Shown on page 399)

$1/2$ cup butter or margarine, softened
3 tablespoons Dijon-style mustard
2 tablespoons Worcestershire sauce
$1^1/2$ tablespoons dried minced onion
1 package (16 ounces) 2 small French bread loaves
8 ounces thinly sliced ham
6 ounces thinly sliced Swiss cheese

In a small bowl, combine butter, mustard, Worcestershire sauce, and onion until well blended. Split loaves in half lengthwise. Spread inside of each loaf with butter mixture. Layer bottom halves with ham and cheese. Place top halves on loaves. Wrap in aluminum foil and store in refrigerator until ready to serve.

To serve, bake loaves in foil in a 350-degree oven 15 to 20 minutes or until bread is warm and cheese is melted. Cut into 1-inch slices. Serve warm.
Yield: 2 party loaves, about 12 servings each

CHEESY MINIATURE QUICHES

2 cups all-purpose flour
1/2 cup butter or margarine, melted
1 1/2 teaspoons salt
3/4 teaspoon ground red pepper
4 cups (16 ounces) shredded sharp Cheddar cheese
4 eggs
3/4 cup milk
8 ounces bacon, cooked and crumbled
1/2 cup frozen chopped spinach, thawed and squeezed dry
Optional garnishes: cucumber slices, carrot curls, green onion brushes, red onion shreds, tomato peel, sweet red pepper, dill weed, celery leaves, celery slices, and green onion curls

Process flour, melted butter, salt, and red pepper in a food processor until combined. Add cheese; process until well blended. Shape dough into 1 1/2-inch balls. Press dough into bottom and up sides of greased 2 1/2-inch tart pans.
Preheat oven to 350 degrees. In a medium bowl, whisk eggs and milk. Stir in bacon and spinach. Spoon tablespoon filling into each pastry shell. Bake 20 to 25 minutes or until center is set. Cool in pans 5 minutes. Remove from pans; garnish. Serve warm.
Yield: about 3 dozen quiches

BEEF SATÉ WITH HOT PEANUT DIPPING SAUCE

HOT PEANUT DIPPING SAUCE
1/4 cup smooth peanut butter
1/4 cup beef broth
2 tablespoons peanut oil
1 tablespoon soy sauce
1 tablespoon seasoned rice wine vinegar
1 teaspoon dark sesame oil
1 teaspoon freshly grated ginger
1/2 teaspoon crushed red pepper flakes

BEEF SATÉ
3/4 cup seasoned rice wine vinegar
1/3 cup peanut oil
1/3 cup soy sauce
3 cloves garlic, minced
1 tablespoon firmly packed brown sugar
1 tablespoon grated fresh ginger
1 teaspoon crushed red pepper flakes
2 pounds flank steak, trimmed of fat and partially frozen
Six-inch-long bamboo skewers

For hot peanut dipping sauce, combine all ingredients in a food processor; process until well blended. Transfer to a small bowl; cover and let stand at room temperature 2 hours to allow flavors to blend. Store in refrigerator.
(Continued on page 402)

(Continued from page 401)
For beef saté, combine vinegar, oil, soy sauce, garlic, brown sugar, ginger, and red pepper flakes in a large bowl; stir until well blended. Slice chilled meat diagonally across the grain into thin slices. Place beef strips in marinade and refrigerate overnight. Soak bamboo skewers in water overnight.

Bring sauce to room temperature. Thread marinated beef strips onto skewers. Broil or grill about 4 inches from heat 5 to 6 minutes; turning once after 3 minutes. Serve warm with sauce.

Yield: about 1/2 cup sauce and about 4 dozen appetizers

ROASTED GARLIC

6 large heads garlic
1 loaf (8 ounces) 2 1/2-inch-diameter French bread, cut into 1/4-inch slices

Preheat oven to 375 degrees. Remove the outermost papery skin from each head of garlic, leaving cloves of garlic intact. Slice across stem end of each garlic head. Place garlic heads in a baking dish; cover with heavy aluminum foil. Bake about 1 hour. Allow garlic to cool 10 to 15 minutes before serving. Place French bread slices on a baking sheet. Toast in a 375-degree oven 5 minutes, turning slices over after 3 minutes. To serve, press garlic pulp out of each clove and spread on toast.

Yield: about 50 servings

CURRIED BLUE CHEESECAKE

1 1/4 cups butter-flavored cracker crumbs
1/4 cup freshly grated Parmesan cheese
1/4 cup butter or margarine, melted
3 packages (8 ounces each) cream cheese, softened
4 eggs
1/2 cup mayonnaise
1/2 cup finely minced onion
1 tablespoon lemon juice
3/4 teaspoon curry powder
1/2 teaspoon Worcestershire sauce
8 ounces blue cheese, crumbled
Purchased chutney to garnish
Crackers to serve

Preheat oven to 300 degrees. In a medium bowl, combine cracker crumbs, Parmesan cheese, and melted butter. Press into bottom of a greased 9-inch springform pan. In a large bowl, beat cream cheese until fluffy. Add eggs, 1 at a time, beating 2 minutes after each addition. Continue beating while adding mayonnaise, onion, lemon juice, curry powder, and Worcestershire sauce; beat until well blended. Stir in blue cheese. Pour filling over crust. Bake 1 1/2 hours. Turn oven off. With oven door partially open, leave cheesecake in oven 1 hour. Transfer to a wire rack to cool. Remove sides of pan. Spoon chutney over top of cheesecake. Serve chilled or at room temperature with crackers.

Yield: about 50 servings

Garnished with chutney and served with crackers, Curried Blue Cheesecake (clockwise from top left) *is a robust appetizer. Simple Roasted Garlic is a buttery-soft spread for toasted slices of French bread. Terrific grilled or broiled, skewers of Marinated Beef Saté get extra flavor from Hot Peanut Dipping Sauce* (recipes on page 401).

CHICKEN PIES

FILLING
1 cup frozen hash brown
    potatoes
1 cup (about $1/2$ pound) finely
    chopped uncooked chicken
1 large onion finely chopped
$1/4$ cup shredded carrot
$1/4$ cup finely chopped turnip
2 teaspoons garlic powder
$1/2$ teaspoon salt
$1/2$ teaspoon ground black pepper

PASTRY
4 cups all-purpose flour
2 teaspoons salt
1 cup butter-flavored shortening
1 cup ice water
$1/2$ cup butter or margarine, melted

For filling, combine potatoes, chicken, onion, carrot, turnip, garlic powder, salt, and pepper in a large bowl; stir until well blended. Cover and refrigerate until ready to use.

Preheat oven to 375 degrees. For pastry, sift flour and salt into a large bowl. Using a pastry blender or 2 knives, cut shortening into flour mixture until mixture resembles coarse meal. Slowly add water, mixing until a soft dough forms. Turn dough onto a lightly floured surface and use a floured rolling pin to roll out dough to $1/4$-inch thickness. Use a 3-inch heart-shaped cookie cutter to cut out an even number of heart shapes. Transfer half of heart shapes to a greased baking sheet; spoon about 2 tablespoons filling in center of each heart shape. Place remaining heart shapes over filling.

To seal, crimp edges with a fork. Brush tops with melted butter. Bake 45 to 50 minutes or until golden brown. Transfer to a wire rack to cool completely. Store i an airtight container in refrigerator.

To serve, preheat oven to 350 degrees Bake uncovered 10 to 15 minutes or unt heated through.

Yield: about $1 1/2$ dozen pies

STUFFED SNOW PEAS

Stuffed snow peas may be prepared sever hours ahead of time. Just wrap airtight an refrigerate until needed.

$1/2$ pound fresh snow peas
1 package (8 ounces) cream
    cheese, softened
2 tablespoons mayonnaise
1 teaspoon dried dill weed
1 teaspoon dried chives
$1/2$ teaspoon seasoned salt
$1/2$ teaspoon lemon pepper

Blanch snow peas in lightly salted boiling water 2 to 3 minutes. Drain and rinse in cold water to stop cooking.

In a medium bowl, combine cream cheese, mayonnaise, dill weed, chives, salt, and lemon pepper; beat until smooth. Using a sharp knife, split each snow pea open along straight edge. Place cheese mixture in a pastry bag fitted with a small star tip. Pipe cheese mixture inside each snow pea.

Yield: about 40 snow peas

CRAB AU GRATIN

2 tablespoons cornstarch
2 tablespoons water
1 1/2 cups milk
1/4 pound pasteurized process
  cheese
2 egg yolks
1/2 teaspoon salt
1/4 teaspoon ground black pepper
1/8 teaspoon ground red pepper
1 1/2 pounds lump crabmeat
  Paprika and fresh parsley to
  garnish

In a small bowl, combine cornstarch and water. In a medium saucepan, combine next 6 ingredients. Stirring constantly, cook over medium heat until mixture boils; add cornstarch mixture and cook until thickened. Stir in crabmeat. Spoon into 5-inch seashells. Garnish with paprika and parsley.
Yield: about 6 servings

PINEAPPLE WINE COOLERS

1 quart pineapple juice
1 bottle (750 ml) dry white wine
1 cup vodka
1 cup granulated sugar
  Pineapple chunks and
  maraschino cherries with
  stems on wooden skewers
  to garnish

In a 2 1/2-quart container, combine first 4 ingredients; stir until sugar dissolves. Chill; serve over ice. Garnish with pineapple and cherries.
Yield: about ten 6-ounce servings

SHRIMP TOAST

1/2 pound shrimp, peeled,
  deveined, and minced
6 canned water chestnuts,
  minced
1 tablespoon minced red onion
1 egg
1 tablespoon white wine
1 teaspoon ground ginger
1/2 teaspoon salt
1/8 teaspoon freshly ground black
  pepper
1 1/2 teaspoons cornstarch
  dissolved in 1 tablespoon
  water
6 slices day-old bread
  Vegetable oil for frying

In a small bowl, combine shrimp, water chestnuts, onion, egg, wine, ginger, salt, pepper, and cornstarch mixture, blending well. Trim crusts from bread. Spread shrimp mixture evenly onto bread. Cut each slice of bread in half diagonally. Cut in half again to form triangles.

In a skillet, heat 2 inches of oil to 360 degrees. Gently place bread, shrimp side up, in hot oil. Fry 1 minute, turn, and fry 15 seconds or until golden brown. Drain on paper towels. Serve immediately.
Yield: 24 toasts

Salad greens make a leafy bed for "Nine-Patch" Cobb Salad, which is served with a tangy vinaigrette. The salad toppings — including bacon, cheeses, eggs, and vegetables — are outlined with pepper strips to create the look of a patchwork quilt.

"NINE-PATCH" COBB SALAD

VINAIGRETTE

- $1/2$ cup vegetable oil
- $1/4$ cup white wine vinegar
- 1 tablespoon orange juice
- 1 teaspoon sugar
- $1/2$ teaspoon salt
- $1/2$ teaspoon dried tarragon leaves, crushed
- $1/8$ teaspoon ground black pepper

SALAD

- 10 cups torn assorted salad greens
- $1/2$ cup chopped radishes (about 5 radishes)
- $1/2$ cup (2 ounces) finely shredded Cheddar cheese
- $1/2$ small red onion, chopped
- $1/2$ cup chopped avocado (about 1 avocado), sprinkled with 2 teaspoons freshly squeezed lemon juice
- $1/2$ cup chopped fresh tomato (about 1 medium tomato)
- $1/2$ cup chopped hard-cooked eggs (about 2 eggs)

½ cup finely shredded carrot
   (about 1 medium carrot)
½ cup (2 ounces) crumbled blue
   cheese
8 slices bacon, cooked and
   crumbled
1 green pepper, cut into 3-inch
   strips

For vinaigrette, combine oil, vinegar, orange juice, sugar, salt, tarragon, and black pepper in a small bowl. Stir until well blended. Cover and allow to sit at room temperature 1 hour for flavors to blend.

For salad, place salad greens in a 9 x 9 x 2-inch serving dish. Place the following ingredients on salad greens to form 9 equal squares: radishes, Cheddar cheese, onion, avocado, tomato, eggs, carrot, blue cheese, and bacon. Outline squares with green pepper strips. Serve with vinaigrette.

Yield: 12 to 14 servings

CHERRY TOMATOES WITH PESTO MAYONNAISE

1 cup mayonnaise
1 cup purchased pesto sauce
1 pint cherry tomatoes, halved

In a medium bowl, combine mayonnaise and pesto sauce; stir until well blended. Cover and chill. Serve with cherry tomato halves.

Yield: about 2 cups pesto mayonnaise

DOUBLE DILL DIP

1 cup coarsely chopped
   refrigerated kosher dill
   pickles
1 package (8 ounces) cream
   cheese, softened
¼ cup sour cream
1 tablespoon fresh dill weed
⅛ teaspoon ground red pepper
   Fresh dill weed to garnish
   Corn chips to serve

Process pickles in a food processor until finely chopped. Add remaining ingredients and process until well blended. Cover and chill 2 hours. Garnish with dill weed. Serve with chips.

Yield: about 2 cups dip

Cherry Tomatoes with Pesto Mayonnaise are extra-easy appetizers!

SPIRITED CIDER

For a non-alcoholic version of this "spirited" drink, serve without the peach schnapps.

3   cinnamon sticks (3 inches long), cut into pieces
1   tablespoon whole cloves
1   tablespoon whole allspice berries
1   apple, cored and cut into rings
1   orange, sliced
1   bottle (48 ounces) unsweetened apple cider
    Peach schnapps
    Cinnamon sticks to garnish

Place cinnamon stick pieces, cloves, and allspice in the center of a square of cheesecloth and tie corners together to make a bag. Combine all ingredients except schnapps in a 2-quart saucepan or slow cooker. Simmer over low heat at least 2 hours to allow flavors to blend. Remove spice bag and fruit. Add 1 jigger (3 tablespoons) peach schnapps to each 8-ounce serving of hot cider. Garnish with cinnamon sticks.
Yield: about six 8-ounce servings

STRAWBERRY WINE PUNCH

$^1/_2$ cup sugar
$^1/_4$ cup water
2   packages (10 ounces each) frozen sweetened sliced strawberries, partially thawed
2   bottles (750 ml each) red wine, chilled
1   bottle (2 liters) lemon-lime soda, chilled

In a small saucepan, combine sugar and water over medium-high heat. Stirring frequently, bring to a boil. Remove from heat and cool. Cover and chill syrup until ready to serve.
To serve, place strawberries in a $1^1/_2$-gallon container. Pour wine and lemon-lime soda over strawberries; carefully stir to break up strawberries. Sweeten punch to taste by adding 1 tablespoon syrup at a time; stir well after each addition. Serve immediately.
Yield: about 16 cups punch

PEAR WINE

4   ripe Bartlett pears
1   bottle (750 ml) dry white wine
$^1/_4$ cup sugar

Wash and core pears; cut into small cubes. Combine pears, wine, and sugar in a large glass bowl; stir until sugar dissolves. Pour into wine bottle and chill 3 days to allow flavors to blend. Serve chilled.
Yield: about 3 cups wine

SPARKLING LIME SPRITZER

2 cups boiling water
1/4 cup lime-flavored gelatin
1 liter dry white wine
1 cup vodka
2 tablespoons lime juice
1 liter ginger ale, chilled
   Fresh lime slices and maraschino
      cherries on wooden skewers
      to garnish

In a small bowl, combine water and gelatin; stir until gelatin dissolves. In a 3-quart container, combine gelatin mixture, wine, vodka, and lime juice. Cover and refrigerate until well chilled. Stir in ginger ale. Serve over ice. Garnish with lime slices and cherries.
Yield: about fifteen 6-ounce servings

MEXICAN-STYLE HOT CHOCOLATE

1/4 cup cocoa
1/4 cup warm water
1 quart milk
1 cup granulated sugar
3 eggs, separated
   Pinch of salt
1 teaspoon vanilla extract

In a medium bowl, stir together cocoa and water until smooth. Stir in milk, sugar, egg yolks, and salt. In a large bowl, beat egg whites until stiff peaks form. With electric mixer running, slowly add chocolate mixture and beat until well blended. Pour into a large saucepan. Stirring constantly, cook over medium heat until mixture coats the back of a metal spoon (do not boil). Remove from heat. Stir in vanilla. Serve immediately.
Yield: about eight 6-ounce servings

SPICED IRISH COFFEE

1/3 cup plus 2 tablespoons sugar,
   divided
1/4 teaspoon ground cinnamon
2 cups skim milk
2 cinnamon sticks
1 whole nutmeg, crushed
2 1/2 quarts hot, strongly brewed
   coffee
3 tablespoons fat-free non-dairy
   powdered creamer
2/3 cup Irish whiskey
   Fat-free frozen whipped
      topping, thawed to garnish

In a small bowl, combine 2 tablespoons sugar and ground cinnamon; set aside. Combine remaining 1/3 cup sugar, milk, cinnamon sticks, and nutmeg in a Dutch oven. Cook over medium-low heat, stirring until sugar dissolves. Stir in coffee and creamer. Cover and heat 5 minutes to allow flavors to blend. Remove from heat; strain and discard cinnamon sticks and nutmeg. Stir in Irish whiskey. Pour into 8-ounce Irish coffee glasses. Garnish each serving with 1 tablespoon whipped topping and sprinkle with sugar-cinnamon mixture. Serve immediately.
Yield: about 12 cups coffee

CHERRY COCOA MIX

6¹/₄ cups nonfat dry milk powder
1 jar (16 ounces) non-dairy
   powdered creamer
1 package (16 ounces) chocolate
   mix for milk
1 package (16 ounces)
   confectioners sugar
¹/₂ cup cocoa
2 packages (0.13 ounces each)
   unsweetened cherry-
   flavored soft drink mix
   Whipped cream and
   maraschino cherries with
   stems to garnish

In a very large bowl, combine dry milk, creamer, chocolate mix, confectioners sugar, cocoa, and soft drink mix. To serve, combine 2¹/₂ heaping tablespoons cocoa mix with 6 ounces hot water. Garnish each serving with whipped cream and a cherry.
Yield: about 15 cups cocoa mix

STRAWBERRY FIZZ

3 packages (10 ounces each)
   frozen sweetened sliced
   strawberries
3 cartons (8 ounces each)
   strawberry yogurt
2 tablespoons sugar
4 cans (12 ounces each)
   strawberry-flavored soft drink,
   chilled

Process frozen strawberries, yogurt, and sugar in a food processor until smooth. Spoon strawberry mixture into a punch bowl; stir in soft drink. Serve immediately.
Yield: about 16 cups punch

CONFETTI CANDY

2 cups sugar
1 cup light corn syrup
¹/₂ cup water
¹/₄ teaspoon cotton candy-
   flavored oil
7 teaspoons assorted colors of
   coarse decorating sugars
   (we used red, green, yellow,
   orange, pink, blue, and purple)

Lightly grease a 10¹/₂ x 15¹/₂-inch jellyroll pan. Butter sides of a heavy 3-quart saucepan. Combine sugar, corn syrup, and water in pan. Stirring constantly, cook over medium-low heat until sugar dissolves. Using a pastry brush dipped in hot water, wash down any sugar crystals on sides of pan. Attach a candy thermometer to pan, making sure thermometer does not touch bottom of pan. Increase heat to medium-high and bring to a boil. Cook, without stirring, until syrup reaches hard-crack stage (approximately 300 to 310 degrees). Test about ¹/₂ teaspoon syrup in ice water. Syrup will form brittle threads in ice water and will remain brittle when removed from the water. Remove from heat and stir in cotton candy oil. Immediately pour into prepared pan. Quickly sprinkle decorating sugars over candy. Allow candy to cool completely; break into pieces. Store in an airtight container.
Yield: about 1¹/₄ pounds candy

Welcome guests with mugs of warming Cherry Cocoa. A sprinkling of colorful sugar gives Confetti Candy added sparkle!

HOT BERRY TEA

1 whole orange
10 cups water
4 regular-size tea bags
2 cinnamon sticks
1 teaspoon whole cloves
2 cans (12 ounces each) frozen cranberry-raspberry-strawberry juice beverage concentrate
1 cup firmly packed brown sugar
Orange slices to serve

Peel whole orange in one continuous strip; set peel aside and reserve orange meat for another use. Place water, tea bags, cinnamon sticks, cloves, and orange peel in a heavy large saucepan. Bring to a simmer over medium-high heat. Cover and continue to simmer 15 minutes. Strain tea into a Dutch oven; discard tea bags, orange peel, and spices. Add concentrate and brown sugar; stir over medium-low heat until sugar dissolves and tea is hot. Serve hot with orange slices.
Yield: about seventeen 6-ounce servings

ROSEMARY TEA

$^1/_2$ cup tea leaves
1 tablespoon dried rosemary leaves

Process tea leaves and rosemary in a food processor until finely ground. Store in an airtight container.
To brew tea, place 1 teaspoon tea for each 8 ounces of water in a warm teapot. Bring water to a rolling boil and pour over tea. Steep tea 5 minutes; strain. Serve hot or over ice.
Yield: about $^1/_3$ cup tea leaves

IMPERIAL CHAMPAGNE COCKTAILS

2 cups tropical fruit punch drink
2 cups orange juice
1 cup peach schnapps
1 bottle (750 ml) champagne, chilled

In a $2^1/_2$-quart container, combine fruit punch, orange juice, and schnapps. Cover and refrigerate until well chilled.
To serve, stir in champagne. Serve chilled.
Yield: about ten 6-ounce servings

PICED TEA

4 tablespoons black or Earl Grey
    tea leaves
1/2 teaspoon nutmeg
1/2 teaspoon cinnamon
1/2 teaspoon allspice
4 cups boiling water
4 cups cranberry juice
6 cups fresh orange juice or 1 can
    (12 ounces) frozen orange juice,
    reconstituted

Pour boiling water over tea and spices.
>ver and let stand 15 to 20 minutes;
ain. Add cranberry juice and orange
ice to tea. Sweeten to taste with sugar
artificial sweetener. Serve hot or iced.
eld: 14 cups

CHOCOLATE YOGURT SHAKES

2 cups chocolate milk
2 cups chocolate frozen yogurt,
    softened
2 cups crushed ice
1/2 cup chocolate syrup

In a blender, combine all ingredients;
process until well blended. Serve
immediately.
Yield: about eight 6-ounce servings

ORANGE-PINEAPPLE PUNCH

Punch must be made 1 day in advance.

2 quarts water
2 cans (20 ounces each)
   crushed pineapple in juice,
   undrained
3 cups sugar
3 ripe bananas, mashed
1 can (12 ounces) frozen orange
   juice concentrate, thawed
1 can (6 ounces) frozen
   lemonade concentrate,
   thawed
1 package (0.14 ounce)
   unsweetened orange-
   flavored soft drink mix
1 bottle (1 liter) ginger ale,
   chilled
1 jar (10 ounces) maraschino
   cherries, drained

In a 6-quart container, combine water, pineapple, sugar, bananas, juice concentrates, and soft drink mix. Place punch in a covered container and freeze.

Remove punch from freezer 4 hours before serving to partially thaw.

To serve, break into chunks. Add ginger ale and cherries; stir until slushy.

Yield: about 20 cups punch

"BEARY" CUTE POPCORN SNACKS

16 cups popped popcorn
4 cups miniature marshmallows
1/4 cup butter or margarine
2 tablespoons milk
1/2 cup smooth peanut butter
1 tablespoon vanilla extract
1 teaspoon salt
   Semisweet chocolate mini
   chips
   Small red cinnamon candies
   Ribbon to decorate

Place popcorn in a very large bowl. In a medium saucepan, combine marshmallows, butter, and milk. Stirring constantly, cook over low heat until marshmallows are melted. Remove from heat and stir in peanut butter, vanilla, and salt. Pour marshmallow mixture over popcorn and stir until evenly coated. With lightly greased hands, press about 1/2 cup popcorn mixture into a 4 1/2-inch-high bear-shaped mold. Transfer to waxed paper. Press 2 chocolate chips and 1 candy onto popcorn bear for eyes and nose. Repeat with remaining popcorn mixture, chocolate chips, and candies. Cool completely. Tie ribbon around neck of each bear. Store in an airtight container.

Yield: about 17 popcorn snacks

"Beary" Cute Popcorn Snacks are shaped in a mold and decorated with candies. Kids will love slushy Orange-Pineapple Punch.

Shown on page 8: *Instead of the usual chips and dips, tempt partygoers with our crunchy Tropical Granola Snack Mix and flavorful Cinnamon Candy Corn.*

CINNAMON CANDY CORN

6 quarts popped white popcorn
1³/₄ cups sugar
1 cup butter or margarine
¹/₂ cup light corn syrup
¹/₂ teaspoon salt
3 cups miniature marshmallows
¹/₄ teaspoon cinnamon-flavored oil
¹/₄ teaspoon red liquid food coloring

Preheat oven to 250 degrees. Place popcorn in a greased large roasting pan. In a large saucepan, combine sugar, butter, corn syrup, and salt. Stirring constantly, cook over medium heat 8 to 10 minutes or until mixture boils. Boil 2 minutes without stirring. Remove from heat; add marshmallows. Stir until marshmallows melt. Stir in cinnamon oil and food coloring. Pour syrup over popcorn, stirring until well coated. Bake 1 hour, stirring every 15 minutes. Spread on lightly greased aluminum foil to cool. Store in an airtight container.
Yield: about 25 cups candy corn

TROPICAL GRANOLA SNACK MIX

4 cups graham cereal squares
4 cups round toasted oat cereal
1 package (6 ounces) dried pineapple chunks (about 1¹/₄ cups)
1 package (5 ounces) dried banana chips (about 1¹/₂ cups)
1 cup dried coconut chips
1 cup sunflower kernels
1 cup golden raisins
³/₄ cup slivered almonds
³/₄ cup firmly packed brown sugar
¹/₃ cup vegetable oil
6 tablespoons frozen orange juice
3 tablespoons honey

Preheat oven to 300 degrees. In a large roasting pan, combine cereals, pineapple chunks, banana chips, coconut chips, sunflower kernels, raisins, and almonds. In a small bowl, combine brown sugar, oil, juice concentrate, and honey; stir until well blended. Pour over cereal mixture; stir until well coated. Stirring every 10 minutes, bake 40 to 45 minutes or until lightly browned (mixture will be slightly moist). Spread on waxed paper and allow to cool. Store in an airtight container in a cool place.
Yield: about 14 cups snack mix

PECAN BUTTER SPREAD

1¹/₄ cups chopped pecans
2 tablespoons peanut oil
8 ounces Brie cheese, rind removed
1 package (3 ounces) cream cheese, softened
2 tablespoons sherry
¹/₄ teaspoon salt
Crackers or apples and Roasted Pecans (recipe on this page) to serve

Process pecans and peanut oil in a food processor until smooth. Add Brie cheese, cream cheese, sherry, and salt; process until mixture is completely blended. Store in an airtight container in refrigerator. Serve at room temperature with crackers or apple slices topped with Roasted Pecans.
Yield: about 1¹/₂ cups spread

CINNAMON DIP

1 package (8 ounces) cream cheese, softened
2 tablespoons milk
1 teaspoon vanilla extract
2 tablespoons firmly packed brown sugar
1 teaspoon ground cinnamon
¹/₄ teaspoon ground nutmeg
Apples or cookies to serve

In a medium bowl, beat cream cheese, milk, vanilla extract, brown sugar, cinnamon, and nutmeg until smooth. Store in an airtight container in refrigerator. Serve with apple slices or cookies.
Yield: about 1 cup dip

ROASTED PECANS

1 cup pecan halves
1 tablespoon butter, melted
Salt

Preheat oven to 200 degrees. In a small bowl, combine pecans and butter. Pour nuts onto a baking sheet and bake 1 hour, stirring every 15 minutes. Drain on paper towel; sprinkle with salt. Cool completely. Store in an airtight container.
Yield: 1 cup pecans

CINNAMON SNACK MIX

3 cups apple-cinnamon-flavored cereal
2 cups pecan halves
1 cup whole almonds
1 cup chow mein noodles
2 egg whites
1 cup sugar
2 tablespoons ground cinnamon
¹/₂ teaspoon salt

Preheat oven to 225 degrees. In a large bowl, combine cereal, pecans, almonds, and noodles; spread on a greased baking sheet. In a small bowl, combine egg whites, sugar, cinnamon, and salt. Pour over dry ingredients, stirring to coat well. Bake 35 to 40 minutes, stirring frequently to break apart. Pour onto waxed paper to cool. Store in an airtight container.
Yield: about 9 cups snack mix

CRISPY APPLE SQUARES

1 can (21 ounces) apple pie
   filling
$^1/_2$ cup sugar
$1^1/_2$ teaspoons ground cinnamon
1 package (12 ounces) wonton
   wrappers
   Vegetable oil

Process pie filling in a food processor until coarsely chopped. In a medium bowl or a large plastic bag, combine sugar and cinnamon; set aside. For each apple square, place 1 wonton wrapper on a flat surface. Spoon 1 rounded teaspoonful apple pie filling into center of wrapper. Moisten points of wrapper with water. Fold 2 opposite points over filling; press to seal. Fold 2 remaining points over filling; press to seal. Place squares, sealed side down, on a baking sheet. (Filled squares can be covered with plastic wrap and chilled until ready to fry.) Heat oil in a deep-fat fryer or deep skillet. With sealed side down, place a single layer of squares in hot oil. Fry, turning once, until filling is heated through and wrapper is golden brown. Drain on paper towels. Toss hot squares in sugar mixture until well coated. Serve warm.
Yield: about 4 dozen apple squares

FRUIT TRIFLE WITH HONEY-YOGURT DRESSING

2 cans ($15^1/_4$ ounces each)
   pineapple rings in juice
3 containers (8 ounces each)
   lemon yogurt
$^1/_2$ cup honey
3 navel oranges, peeled, sliced
   into rings, and divided
3 small grapefruit, peeled, sliced
   into rings, and divided
5 kiwi fruit, peeled, sliced, and
   divided
1 pound seedless red grapes,
   divided
1 pound seedless green grapes,
   divided
2 cups miniature marshmallows,
   divided
   Lemon slices to garnish

Drain pineapple rings, reserving juice; set rings aside. In a medium bowl, combine yogurt, honey, and $^1/_3$ cup reserved pineapple juice; cover and chill.

In a 4-quart trifle bowl, layer half of each of the following: orange slices, grapefruit slices, kiwi fruit slices, pineapple rings, red grapes, green grapes, and marshmallows. Repeat layers with remaining fruit and marshmallows. Cover and chill until ready to serve. Garnish honey-yogurt dressing with lemon slices and serve with fruit salad.
Yield: about 16 cups fruit salad and about $3^1/_4$ cups dressing

FRUITCAKE BITES

1/2 cup dark rum
1/4 cup golden raisins
1/4 cup raisins
1/4 cup butter or margarine,
     softened
1/2 cup firmly packed brown sugar
2 eggs, beaten
1 1/2 cups all-purpose flour
1 1/2 teaspoons baking soda
1 teaspoon ground cinnamon
1 teaspoon ground nutmeg
1/2 teaspoon ground allspice
3 tablespoons milk
1/2 cup chopped green candied
     cherries
1/2 cup chopped red candied
     cherries
1/2 cup chopped dates
2 cups chopped pecans

In a small bowl, combine rum and raisins. Let stand at room temperature 1 hour.

Preheat oven to 275 degrees. In a large bowl, cream butter and brown sugar until fluffy. Add eggs; beat until smooth. In a small bowl, combine flour, baking soda, and spices. Stir dry ingredients into creamed mixture. Stir in milk and raisin mixture. Stir in cherries, dates, and pecans. Fill paper-lined miniature muffin cups about two-thirds full. Bake 10 to 15 minutes or until top of muffin springs back when lightly touched. Transfer to a wire rack to cool. Store in an airtight container.
Yield: about 5 dozen muffins

CARAMELIZED CAKE SQUARES

2 cups butter or margarine
2 cups firmly packed brown sugar
1 purchased (7-inch diameter)
     angel food cake, cut into
     1-inch cubes
4 cups finely chopped pecans

In a large saucepan, combine butter and brown sugar over medium heat. Stirring constantly, cook until sugar dissolves. Increase heat to medium high and bring to a boil. Cook until mixture reaches soft-ball stage (234 to 240 degrees); remove from heat. Using tongs, dip cake cubes in mixture; roll in pecans. Place on waxed paper to cool completely. Store in an airtight container.
Yield: about 5 dozen cake squares

PLUM ICE CREAM SAUCE

1/4 cup cocoa
1/4 cup hot water
1 jar (18 ounces) plum jam or
     preserves
1 teaspoon vanilla extract
1/2 cup finely chopped walnuts

In a small bowl, stir together cocoa and water until cocoa dissolves. In a small saucepan, melt jam over medium-low heat, stirring occasionally. Add cocoa mixture and vanilla; stir until well blended. Stir in walnuts. Remove from heat. Serve warm or cold over ice cream. Store in an airtight container in refrigerator.
Yield: about 2 1/4 cups sauce

RASPBERRY FUDGE BROWNIES

1/2 cup butter or margarine,
    softened
1 cup sugar
3 eggs
1 jar (12 ounces) raspberry jam,
    divided
18 chocolate wafer cookies (2-inch
    diameter), finely ground
1/2 cup all-purpose flour
1 cup (6 ounces) semisweet
    chocolate chips
1 cup chopped walnuts

Preheat oven to 350 degrees. In a large bowl, cream butter and sugar until fluffy. Add eggs and 1/2 cup jam, beating until smooth. Add ground cookies and flour; mix well. Pour batter into a greased 8 x 11-inch baking dish. Sprinkle chocolate chips evenly over batter. Bake 35 to 40 minutes or until a toothpick inserted in center comes out clean. In a small saucepan, melt remaining jam over low heat, stirring constantly. Stir in walnuts. Pour jam mixture over brownies. Cool completely in pan. Cut into 2-inch squares. Store in an airtight container.

Yield: about 1 1/2 dozen brownies

CHOCOLATE SNOWBALL COOKIES

1 1/2 cups (9 ounces) semisweet
    chocolate chips
1 package (8 ounces) cream
    cheese, cut into small pieces
1 1/2 teaspoons vanilla extract
3 cups finely ground chocolate
    wafer cookies (about
    64 cookies)
1 cup finely ground pecans
    Confectioners sugar, sifted

In a large saucepan, melt chocolate chips over low heat, stirring constantly. Add cream cheese and vanilla, stirring until smooth. Remove from heat. Stir in cookie crumbs and pecans. Shape into 1-inch balls; roll in confectioners sugar. Cover and refrigerate 8 hours or until firm. Roll balls in confectioners sugar again. Store in an airtight container in refrigerator.

Yield: about 6 dozen cookies

Raspberry Fudge Brownies make mouth-watering treats! Walnuts and raspberry jam enhance the rich bars.

A chocolate lover's version of the traditional holiday beverage, Chocolate Eggnog is served with a garnish of ground nutmeg. Coated with confectioner's sugar, Chocolate Snowball Cookies are no-bake delights.

CHOCOLATE EGGNOG

1   quart prepared eggnog
$^1/_2$ cup chocolate syrup
$^1/_4$ teaspoon ground nutmeg
1   tablespoon vanilla extract
    Ground nutmeg to garnish

In a large saucepan, combine eggnog, chocolate syrup, and $^1/_4$ teaspoon nutmeg. Stirring occasionally, cook over medium-low heat 20 to 25 minutes or until heated through (do not boil). Remove from heat; stir in vanilla. To serve, pour into cups; sprinkle lightly with nutmeg. Serve warm.
Yield: about six 6-ounce servings

WHITE CHOCOLATE MACADAMIA COOKIES

1/2 cup butter or margarine, softened
1/2 cup vegetable shortening
3/4 cup firmly packed brown sugar
1/2 cup granulated sugar
1 egg
1 1/2 teaspoons vanilla extract
2 cups all-purpose flour
1 teaspoon baking soda
1/2 teaspoon salt
1 package (6 ounces) white baking chocolate, cut into chunks
1 jar (7 ounces) macadamia nuts, coarsely chopped

Preheat oven to 350 degrees. In a large bowl, cream butter, shortening, and sugars until fluffy. Add egg and vanilla; beat until smooth. In a medium bowl, combine flour, baking soda, and salt. Add dry ingredients to creamed mixture; stir until a soft dough forms. Stir in white chocolate and macadamia nuts. Drop teaspoonfuls of dough 2 inches apart onto an ungreased baking sheet. Bake 8 to 10 minutes or until lightly browned. Transfer cookies to a wire rack to cool. Store in an airtight container.
Yield: about 4 1/2 dozen cookies

GINGERBREAD COOKIES

1 cup butter or margarine, softened
1 1/4 cups firmly packed brown sugar
3 eggs
1 cup honey
8 1/2 cups all-purpose flour
2 tablespoons plus 2 teaspoons ground cinnamon
4 teaspoons ground ginger
2 teaspoons baking soda
1 teaspoon salt
Purchased white decorating icing, raisins, and candy-coated chocolate pieces to decorate

Preheat oven to 350 degrees. In a large bowl, cream butter and sugar until fluffy. Add eggs and honey; mix until smooth. In a large bowl, sift together flour, cinnamon, ginger, baking soda, and salt. Add dry ingredients to creamed mixture; knead in bowl until a soft dough forms. Divide dough in half. On a lightly floured surface, use a floured rolling pin to roll out each half of dough to 1/4-inch thickness. Use gingerbread boy cookie cutter to cut out cookies. Place cookies 1 inch apart on a greased baking sheet. Bake 8 to 10 minutes or until edges begin to brown. Transfer to a wire rack to cool completely. Store in an airtight container until ready to decorate. To decorate cookies, use icing to secure raisins and candy-coated chocolate pieces on cookies for eyes, noses, and buttons. Use a round tip to pipe icing on cookies for mouths.
Yield: about 2 dozen 7-inch cookies

CARAMEL-PECAN BROWNIES

1 package (18.25 ounces)
    German chocolate cake mix
    with pudding in the mix
2/3 cup butter or margarine,
    melted
2/3 cup evaporated milk, divided
1/2 cup pecans, chopped
1 package (14 ounces) caramels
1 package (6 ounces) semisweet
    chocolate chips

Preheat oven to 350 degrees. In a medium bowl, combine cake mix, butter, /3 cup evaporated milk, and pecans. Spread half of mixture into a greased 9 x 13-inch baking pan; reserve remaining mixture. Bake 10 minutes or until slightly firm; set aside.

Microwave caramels and remaining /3 cup evaporated milk in a 2-quart microwave-safe dish on medium power (50%) 5 to 7 minutes or until caramels melt, stirring after 3 minutes. Sprinkle chocolate chips over cake; spread melted caramel mixture over chocolate chips. Break up reserved cake mix mixture and drop over top of cake; bake 20 to 24 minutes or until almost set. Cool brownies; cut into 2-inch squares. Store in an airtight container.
Yield: about 2 dozen brownies

MEXICAN CHOCOLATE BROWNIES

1 cup cocoa
3/4 cup butter or margarine, melted
1 1/4 cups all-purpose flour
1/2 teaspoon salt
3 cups sugar
7 eggs, lightly beaten
1 tablespoon vanilla extract
2 1/2 teaspoons ground cinnamon
1 teaspoon freshly ground black
    pepper

Preheat oven to 350 degrees. In a small bowl, combine cocoa with butter, stirring until smooth. In a large bowl, combine flour, salt, and sugar. Stir in cocoa mixture, eggs, vanilla, cinnamon, and pepper. Pour into a lightly greased 9 x 13 x 2-inch baking pan and bake 35 to 40 minutes or until center is set.
Yield: about 2 dozen brownies

CHOCOLATE-PECAN COOKIES
(Shown on page 424)

3/4 cup butter or margarine,
    softened
1 cup firmly packed brown sugar
1 egg yolk
1 teaspoon vanilla extract
1 1/2 cups all-purpose flour
1/3 cup cocoa
1 cup finely chopped pecans
    Pecan halves

Preheat oven to 350 degrees. In a medium bowl, cream butter and sugar. Beat in egg yolk and vanilla. In a small bowl, combine flour and cocoa. Add dry ingredients to creamed mixture; stir until a soft dough forms. Stir in chopped pecans. Drop heaping teaspoonfuls of dough 1 inch apart onto a greased baking sheet. Press 1 pecan half into each cookie. Bake 8 to 10 minutes or until firm. Transfer to a wire rack to cool completely. Store in an airtight container.
Yield: about 5 dozen cookies

Everyone will love these chocolaty treats! The Chocolate Chip-Mocha Bars have a rich coffee flavor, and Chocolate-Pecan Cookies (recipe on page 423) are chock-full of nuts.

CHOCOLATE CHIP-MOCHA BARS

2 tablespoons instant coffee granules
2 tablespoons hot water
1 box (18.25 ounces) yellow cake mix
1 cup firmly packed brown sugar
¹/₂ cup butter or margarine, softened
2 eggs
2 teaspoons vanilla extract
3 cups (one 12-ounce and one 6-ounce package) semisweet chocolate chips, divided

Preheat oven to 350 degrees. In a medium bowl, combine coffee and water. Add cake mix, sugar, butter, eggs, and vanilla to coffee mixture; beat until smooth. Stir in 2 cups chocolate chips. Spoon batter into a greased 9 x 13-inch baking pan. Bake 40 to 45 minutes or until edges begin to pull away from sides of pan. Cool completely in pan. Cut into 1 x 2-inch bars.

Place remaining 1 cup chocolate chips in a disposable pastry bag. Microwave on medium power (50%) for 30-second intervals until melted. Cut the end of the bag to make a small hole. Drizzle chocolate over bars. Allow chocolate to harden. Store in an airtight container.
Yield: about 3 dozen bars

Simply Delicious
PARTY FOODS

When it's time to party, it's time to munch and sip!
Satisfy your guests' cravings with this big assortment of
appetizers and drinks. There are tasty bites, creamy dips,
spicy teas, rich coffees, and more!

Christmas Cheese Star, page 454

APPLE-CINNAMON CHEESE BALL

1 package (8 ounces) cream cheese, softened
1/2 cup apples from Apple-Cinnamon Wine (recipe on this page)
1/4 cup chopped pecans
1/4 teaspoon ground cinnamon
    Chopped pecans
    Sugar cookies to serve

In a medium bowl, combine cream cheese, apples, 1/4 cup pecans, and cinnamon. Shape into a ball and roll in pecans. Wrap cheese ball in plastic wrap and refrigerate 8 hours or overnight to allow flavors to blend.

To serve, let stand at room temperature 20 to 30 minutes or until softened. Serve with sugar cookies.
Yield: 1 cheese ball

HONEY-RUM COFFEE

1 can (12 ounces) evaporated milk
6 tablespoons honey
1 1/2 quarts strongly brewed hot coffee
1/2 cup dark rum

In a Dutch oven, combine evaporated milk and honey. Stirring occasionally, cook over medium-high heat until milk is warm. Add coffee; stir until well blended. Remove from heat. Stir in rum. Serve hot.
Yield: about ten 6-ounce servings

APPLE-CINNAMON WINE

1 bottle (750 ml) dry white wine
3 medium Granny Smith apples, peeled, cored, and finely chopped (about 4 1/2 cups)
1/2 cup sugar
1/2 teaspoon ground cinnamon

In a 2-quart container, combine wine, apples, sugar, and cinnamon; stir until sugar dissolves. Cover and refrigerate 1 month to allow flavors to blend.

Use cheesecloth to strain wine, reserving 1/2 cup apples for Apple-Cinnamon Cheese Ball if desired (recipe on this page). Serve wine chilled.
Yield: about 3 cups wine

RASPBERRY WINE

3 cups frozen unsweetened raspberries, thawed
1/4 cup granulated sugar
1 bottle (750 ml) dry white wine

In a large bowl, combine raspberries and sugar, stirring until well coated. Stir in wine until sugar is dissolved. Cover and chill 5 days. Strain wine through a fine sieve; discard raspberries or save for another use. Store wine in refrigerator. Serve chilled.
Yield: about 3 cups wine

What a combo! Apple-Cinnamon Wine has a mellow, fruity flavor. The Apple-Cinnamon Cheese Ball, made using fruit from the wine, is terrific with cookies or vanilla wafers.

427

PEPPERMINT ICE CREAM PUNCH

1 jar (8 ounces) red maraschino cherries, drained
12 round peppermint candies
2 half-gallons vanilla ice cream, softened and divided
1 cup coarsely crushed peppermint candies (about 30 round candies), divided
48 ounces cherry-lemon-lime soft drink, chilled

Place cherries and whole peppermint candies in bottom of a 6-cup ring mold. In a large bowl, combine 1 half-gallon ice cream and $^1/_2$ cup crushed candies. Spoon ice cream mixture over cherries and candies in mold. Cover and freeze 4 hours or until firm.

In a large bowl, combine remaining half-gallon ice cream and $^1/_2$ cup crushed candies; cover and store in freezer.

To serve, spoon peppermint ice cream mixture into punch bowl. Stirring constantly, pour soft drink over ice cream mixture until blended. Dip mold into warm water to loosen ice cream ring. Place ice cream ring in punch.
Yield: about 16 cups punch

APPLE BRANDY

2 cups chopped red apples (do not peel)
3 3-inch long cinnamon sticks
2 tablespoons water
2$^1/_2$ cups granulated sugar
2 cups brandy
3 cups dry white wine

In a medium saucepan, combine apples, cinnamon, and water. Cover and cook over medium heat 10 minutes. Add sugar and stir until dissolved. Remove from heat and cool. In a large glass container with lid, combine the apple mixture with the brandy and wine. Cover tightly and store 3 weeks in a cool, dark place. Shake the container every 3 days to blend.

After 3 weeks, drain the liquid through a strainer or doubled layer of cheesecloth into a glass bowl. Pour the liquid into a glass bottle. Cover bottle tightly and store in a cool, dark place for 2 weeks.
Yield: about 1$^1/_2$ quarts of brandy

PINEAPPLE FROST

3 cups pineapple sherbet, softened
2 cans (8 ounces each) crushed pineapple, drained
2 cups half and half
$^2/_3$ cup light corn syrup
1 quart ginger ale, chilled

Process sherbet, pineapple, half and half, and corn syrup in a food processor until pineapple is very finely chopped. Pour into a medium metal or plastic bowl. Cover and freeze until firm.

Remove from freezer one hour before serving. To serve, place pineapple mixture in a 3-quart container; add ginger ale and stir to make a slush.
Yield: about 9$^1/_2$ cups punch

CRANBERRY FREEZER DAIQUIRIS

2 to 3 cups crushed ice
1 can (16 ounces) jellied cranberry
   sauce
1 can (10 ounces) frozen
   strawberry daiquiri mix
1¼ cups rum
2 tablespoons grenadine syrup
   Fresh or frozen whole
   strawberries to garnish

In a blender or food processor,
combine crushed ice, cranberry sauce,
daiquiri mix, rum, and grenadine syrup;
blend until slushy. Store in an airtight
container in freezer. To serve, garnish
with strawberries.
Yield: about seven 6-ounce servings

SUNRISE MIMOSAS
(Shown on page 8)

2½ cups cranberry juice
1½ cups orange juice
¾ cup vodka
   Orange slices to garnish

Pour cranberry juice, orange juice, and
vodka into a blender and mix. Pour over
ice cubes. Garnish with an orange slice on
rim of each glass.
Yield: 5 to 6 servings

LAMB'S WOOL

3 apples, peeled, cored,
   and chopped
3 tablespoons butter or margarine
3 bottles (12 ounces each) dark
   beer
½ cup firmly packed brown sugar
1 teaspoon ground cinnamon
1 teaspoon ground ginger
½ teaspoon ground nutmeg

Preheat oven to 350 degrees. Place
apples in baking dish; dot with butter.
Bake 30 minutes.
In a large saucepan, combine apples,
beer, brown sugar, and spices. Cook,
stirring occasionally, over medium-low
heat until heated through. Serve warm.
Yield: 6 to 8 servings

Cinnamon, cloves, and fruit juices make Spicy Christmas Drink a delicious winter warmer.

SPICY CHRISTMAS DRINK

  2 cups water
  $^1/_2$ cup sugar
  3 cinnamon sticks
  1 teaspoon whole cloves
  1 gallon apple cider
  1 can (12 ounces) frozen
      orange juice concentrate
  1 can (12 ounces) frozen
      pineapple juice concentrate
  1 can (6 ounces) frozen
      lemonade concentrate

Combine water and sugar in a stockpot. Stirring constantly, cook over medium-high heat 4 minutes or until sugar dissolves. Reduce heat to low. Add cinnamon sticks and cloves; cover and cook 15 minutes. Remove cinnamon and cloves. Stir in apple cider and orange, pineapple, and lemonade concentrates; heat until hot. Serve hot.
Yield: about 22 cups drink

Variation: Add 1 tablespoon apple brandy to each serving of prepared hot drink.

SOUTHERN EGGNOG

You'll love our eggnog. It begins with a cooked custard made in advance. We've also included a version for those who prefer eggnog without alcohol.

  1 cup sugar, divided
 12 large eggs, separated
 $^1/_2$ teaspoon salt
  1 quart milk
 $^1/_4$ cup water
 $^3/_4$ teaspoon cream of tartar
  2 cups whipping cream
 $^1/_2$ cup brandy
 $^1/_2$ cup dark rum
    Freshly grated nutmeg

In top of a double boiler, combine $^1/_2$ cup sugar, egg yolks, and salt. Gradually stir in milk. Cook over simmering water until mixture thickens and coats the back of a metal spoon. Remove from heat and cool. Pour mixture into an airtight container and chill.

In top of double boiler, combine egg whites, remaining $^1/_2$ cup sugar, water, and cream of tartar. Whisking constantly, cook over simmering water until a thermometer reaches 160 degrees (about 10 minutes). Transfer egg white mixture to a large bowl; beat until stiff peaks form. Cover and chill mixture.

In a large bowl, beat whipping cream until stiff peaks form. Pour egg yolk mixture into punch bowl. Stir in brandy and rum. (For eggnog without alcohol, omit brandy and rum; stir in 2 teaspoons rum extract and 1 cup whipping cream.) Fold in egg white mixture and whipped cream. Sprinkle with nutmeg.
Yield: about $3^1/_2$ quarts eggnog

A holiday party isn't complete without rich, creamy Southern Eggnog.

ALMOND MERINGUES

2 cups slivered almonds, toasted
2 cups confectioners sugar
3 egg whites
1 tablespoon amaretto
1 teaspoon almond extract
1/4 teaspoon salt

Preheat oven to 300 degrees. Line baking sheet with parchment paper. Process almonds and confectioners sugar in a large food processor until almonds are finely ground. In a large bowl, combine egg whites, amaretto, almond extract, and salt. Beat until stiff peaks form. Gradually fold almond mixture into egg white mixture. Drop teaspoonfuls of batter onto prepared baking sheet. Bake 12 to 15 minutes or until cookies are lightly browned. Turn oven off and leave door closed 15 minutes. Transfer cookies to a wire rack to cool. Store in an airtight container.
Yield: about 5 1/2 dozen cookies

RAISIN-WALNUT PINWHEELS

1 sheet (from a 17 1/4-ounce package) frozen puff pastry dough, thawed
1/3 cup granulated sugar
1 tablespoon ground cinnamon
1/4 cup butter or margarine
1/2 cup raisins
1/2 cup finely chopped walnuts
1 egg yolk, beaten

Preheat oven to 350 degrees. On a lightly floured surface, use a floured rolling pin to roll out pastry to an 8 x 12-inch rectangle. In a small bowl, combine sugar and cinnamon and set aside. In a small saucepan, melt butter. Add raisins and walnuts, stirring until well coated. Spread raisin mixture evenly over pastry. Sprinkle sugar mixture evenly over raisin mixture. Beginning at 1 long edge, roll up pastry. Brush egg yolk on long edge to seal. Place on a greased baking sheet. Bake 20 to 25 minutes or until golden brown. Cool completely. Cut into 1-inch slices.
Yield: about 12 pinwheels

HOT CAPPUCCINO PUNCH

3 cups brewed coffee, room temperature
3 cups half and half
1/2 cup cream of coconut
1/2 cup rum
1/2 cup brandy

Combine all ingredients in a large saucepan. Cook over medium heat until mixture begins to boil. Remove from heat. Serve immediately.
Yield: about ten 6-ounce servings

Warm and creamy with a hint of coconut, Hot Cappuccino Punch is laced with rum and brandy. It's a perfect complement to flaky Raisin-Walnut Pinwheels.

MACADAMIA NUT TARTS

CRUST
1 1/2 cups butter or margarine,
    softened
2/3 cup granulated sugar
2 1/2 teaspoons grated dried lemon
    peel
3 cups all-purpose flour
1/2 cup cornstarch
1/2 teaspoon salt

TOPPING
1/2 cup plus 2 tablespoons butter or
    margarine
1/2 cup firmly packed brown sugar
1/3 cup honey
3 cups macadamia nuts
2 1/2 tablespoons whipping cream

Preheat oven to 350 degrees. For crust, cream butter, sugar, and lemon peel in a large bowl until fluffy. In a medium bowl, sift together next 3 ingredients. Stir dry ingredients into creamed mixture, mixing just until dough is crumbly. On a lightly floured surface, use a floured rolling pin to roll out dough to 1/4-inch thickness. Use a 3-inch biscuit cutter to cut out dough. Transfer dough to greased 2 1/2-inch- diameter tart pans. Prick with a fork. Bake 16 to 18 minutes or until light brown. Cool in pan 10 minutes; turn onto a wire rack to cool completely.

For topping, combine first 3 ingredients in a medium saucepan. Stir constantly over medium-high heat until mixture comes to a boil. Boil 1 minute, without stirring, until mixture thickens and large bubbles begin to form. Remove from heat; stir in nuts and cream. Spoon about 2 tablespoons mixture into each tart crust. Cool completely.

Yield: about 20 tarts

PUMPKIN PIE SQUARES

CRUST
1 3/4 cups all-purpose flour
1 1/4 cups granulated sugar
2 teaspoons baking powder
1/2 teaspoon salt
1/2 cup plus 2 tablespoons butter or
    margarine, chilled and cut into
    pieces
2 eggs, beaten

FILLING
2 eggs
1/4 cup firmly packed brown sugar
1 can (30 ounces) pumpkin pie mix
2/3 cup milk
1 tablespoon pumpkin pie spice
1 teaspoon ground cinnamon
1 teaspoon ground nutmeg

FROSTING
1 cup butter or margarine
1 cup firmly packed brown sugar
1/2 teaspoon ground cinnamon
1 1/2 cups chopped walnuts

Preheat oven to 350 degrees. For crust, sift together first 4 ingredients in a large bowl. Using a pastry blender or 2 knives, cut butter into flour until mixture resembles coarse meal. Add eggs, stirring until a soft dough forms. Press into bottom of a greased 9 x 13-inch baking pan. Bake 15 to 20 minutes or until golden brown.

For filling, beat eggs in a large bowl until foamy. Add brown sugar, beating until smooth. Stir in remaining ingredients, mixing well. Pour filling over crust. Bake 30 to 40 minutes or until center is set.

For frosting, combine first 3 ingredients in a medium saucepan over medium heat. Stir constantly 3 to 5 minutes or until syrup thickens. Stir in walnuts. Pour frosting evenly over warm filling. Cool completely. Cut into approximately 2-inch squares.
Yield: about 2 dozen squares

PECAN NUGGETS

1 cup firmly packed brown sugar
2 tablespoons all-purpose flour
1 tablespoon cornstarch
1 tablespoon dark rum
1 egg white
1/8 teaspoon cream of tartar
1/8 teaspoon salt
2 cups pecan halves

Preheat oven to 300 degrees. In a medium mixing bowl, combine brown sugar, flour, cornstarch, and rum. In a separate bowl, beat egg white with cream of tartar and salt until stiff peaks form. Stir one-third of the egg white mixture into the rum mixture; fold in the remaining egg white mixture. Stir in pecans. Drop individual pecan halves coated with mixture 2 inches apart onto a lightly greased baking sheet. Bake 12 to 15 minutes or until puffed and golden brown. Remove from pan and cool on wire rack.
Yield: about 6 dozen nuggets

CHOCOLATE MOCHA BROWNIES

1 cup firmly packed brown sugar
3/4 cup butter or margarine
2 tablespoons instant coffee granules
1 tablespoon hot water
2 eggs
2 tablespoons vanilla extract
2 cups all-purpose flour
2 teaspoons baking powder
1/2 teaspoon salt
4 ounces semisweet baking chocolate, broken into small pieces
4 ounces white chocolate, broken into small pieces

In a medium saucepan, melt sugar and butter over medium-low heat. Dissolve coffee in hot water and stir into butter mixture. Cool to room temperature.
Preheat oven to 350 degrees. Beat eggs and vanilla into butter mixture. In a large bowl, sift together next 3 ingredients. Stir butter mixture into dry ingredients. Fold in chocolate pieces. Pour batter into a greased 8 x 11-inch baking pan. Bake 25 to 30 minutes or until light brown. Cool in pan. Cut into 1 1/2-inch squares.
Yield: about 3 dozen brownies

CHERRY CORDIAL FUDGE

3/4 cup milk
2 cups granulated sugar
2 ounces unsweetened baking
   chocolate
2 tablespoons light corn syrup
2 tablespoons butter or margarine,
   cut into small pieces
1 jar (6 ounces) maraschino
   cherries, drained and halved
2 teaspoons vanilla extract

In a medium saucepan, combine first 4 ingredients. Cook over medium heat, stirring constantly, until mixture is smooth and comes to a boil. Reduce heat to low, cover pan, and boil 2 to 3 minutes. Uncover and stir to blend ingredients. Continue to boil uncovered, without stirring, until syrup reaches soft ball stage (234 to 240 degrees). Remove from heat. Add butter; do not stir until syrup cools to 110 degrees. Add cherries and vanilla, stirring until mixture thickens and is no longer glossy. Pour into greased 8-inch square pan. Chill until firm; cut into 1-inch squares.
Yield: about 5 dozen pieces of fudge

MARMALADE COOKIES

2 cups all-purpose flour
1 teaspoon baking powder
1 cup butter or margarine, chilled
   and cut into pieces
1 cup finely ground almonds
3/4 cup granulated sugar
2 tablespoons lemon juice
1/2 cup orange marmalade
6 ounces chocolate-flavored
   almond bark

In a large bowl, sift flour and baking powder together. With a pastry blender or 2 knives, cut butter into flour mixture until mixture resembles coarse meal. Stir in next 3 ingredients; knead dough until a soft ball forms. Cover and chill 1 hour.

Preheat oven to 375 degrees. On a lightly floured surface, use a floured rolling pin to roll out dough to 1/8-inch thickness. Use a 3-inch round cookie cutter to cut out 48 cookies. Transfer cookies to a greased baking sheet. Bake 10 to 12 minutes or until lightly browned. Cool on baking sheet.

Spread marmalade on half the cookies; top with remaining cookies. In a small saucepan, melt almond bark following package directions. Dip half of each sandwich cookie into almond bark. Cool on waxed paper.
Yield: 2 dozen cookies

APRICOT FOLDOVERS

FILLING
1 cup chopped dried apricots
1 cup firmly packed brown sugar
1/2 cup water
2 tablespoons all-purpose flour

PASTRY
21/2 cups all-purpose flour
1/2 teaspoon salt
3/4 cup plus 2 tablespoons butter or
   margarine, chilled and cut into
   pieces
1 package (3 ounces) cream
   cheese, cut into pieces
1/3 cup ice water

For filling, mix all ingredients together in a medium saucepan over medium heat and bring to a boil. Cook, stirring constantly, 8 to 10 minutes or until filling thickens. Cool completely.

Light up the season with these fruity delights: Spread with orange marmalade and dipped in chocolate, Marmalade Cookies (in tin) taste as good as they look. Tiny Apricot Foldovers have a sweet filling of dried fruit. Cherry Cordial Fudge is a rich blend of chocolate and maraschino cherries.

Preheat oven to 350 degrees. For pastry, sift flour and salt together into a medium bowl. Using a pastry blender or 2 knives, cut butter and cream cheese into flour until mixture resembles coarse meal. Sprinkle ice water over dough, mixing quickly just until dough forms a soft ball. On a lightly floured surface, use a floured rolling pin to roll out dough into a ¼-inch-thick rectangle. Use a pastry wheel to cut dough into 2-inch squares. Transfer dough to a greased baking sheet. Spoon about 1 teaspoon of filling into the center of each square. Fold dough in half diagonally over filling to form a triangle; use a fork to crimp edges together. Bake 15 to 20 minutes or until golden brown. Cool completely on a wire rack. Store in an airtight container.
Yield: about 4 dozen cookies

COCONUT POUND CAKE

CAKE
- 1½ cups butter or margarine, softened
- 3 cups sugar
- 6 eggs
- 3 cups all-purpose flour
- ¼ teaspoon baking soda
- 1 container (8 ounces) sour cream
- 1 teaspoon coconut extract
- 1 teaspoon rum extract
- 1 cup flaked coconut

SYRUP
- 1 cup water
- 1 cup sugar
- 1 teaspoon almond extract

Preheat oven to 325 degrees. For cake, cream butter and sugar in a large bowl. Add eggs, 1 at a time, beating well after each addition. Sift flour and baking soda into a medium bowl. Alternately beat dry ingredients, sour cream, and extracts into creamed mixture. Stir in coconut. Spoon batter into a greased 10-inch fluted tube pan. Bake 1¼ to 1½ hours or until a toothpick inserted in center of cake comes out clean. Cool cake in pan 15 minutes.

For syrup, combine water and sugar in a medium saucepan. Stirring frequently, cook over medium-high heat 5 minutes. Remove from heat and stir in almond extract. Before removing cake from pan, brush about one-third of warm syrup on cake. Invert cake onto a serving plate. Brush remaining syrup on cake. Allow cake to cool completely. Store in an airtight container.

Yield: about 16 servings

ORANGE CHEESECAKES
(Shown on page 440)

- 12 vanilla wafers
- 1½ cups (12 ounces) fat-free cream cheese, softened
- 1 cup fat-free sour cream
- ½ cup sugar
- ½ cup egg substitute
- 2 tablespoons all-purpose flour
- 2 teaspoons orange extract
- 1 can (11 ounces) mandarin oranges, well drained
- 2 tablespoons orange marmalade

Preheat oven to 350 degrees. Place 1 vanilla wafer into bottom of each paper-lined cup of a muffin pan. In a medium bowl, beat cream cheese until fluffy. Add sour cream, sugar, egg substitute, flour, and orange extract; beat until smooth. Spoon cheese mixture over vanilla wafers, filling each cup full. Bake 18 minutes. Turn oven off and leave in oven 2 minutes. Leaving oven door ajar, leave in oven 15 minutes longer. Cool completely in pan.

In a small bowl, combine oranges and marmalade. Spoon orange mixture on top of each cheesecake. Loosely cover and store in refrigerator. Serve chilled.

Yield: 1 dozen cheesecakes

SINLESS BROWNIES
(Shown on page 440)

1^1/$_2$ cups sugar
 1 cup all-purpose flour
 ^{1}/$_3$ cup cocoa
 ^{1}/$_2$ teaspoon baking powder
 ^{1}/$_4$ teaspoon salt
 ^{1}/$_4$ cup egg substitute
 ^{1}/$_4$ cup water
 1 egg white
 2 tablespoons reduced-calorie
     margarine, softened
 1 tablespoon vanilla extract
     Vegetable cooking spray

Preheat oven to 350 degrees. In a medium bowl, combine sugar, flour, cocoa, baking powder, and salt. Add egg substitute, water, egg white, margarine, and vanilla; stir until well blended. Spoon batter into an 8-inch square baking pan sprayed with cooking spray. Bake 25 to 30 minutes or until dry on top and set in center. Cut into 2-inch squares.
Yield: about 16 brownies

DATE MUFFINS WITH HARD SAUCE
(Shown on page 440)

MUFFINS
1^1/$_4$ cups chopped toasted pecans
 1 package (8 ounces) chopped
     dates
 1 cup granulated sugar
 3 eggs, beaten
 ^{1}/$_2$ cup all-purpose flour
 ^{1}/$_2$ teaspoon salt
 ^{1}/$_2$ teaspoon ground cinnamon
 ^{1}/$_4$ teaspoon ground nutmeg

HARD SAUCE
 2 cups sifted confectioners sugar
 ^{1}/$_2$ cup butter, softened
 1 teaspoon vanilla extract

Preheat oven to 350 degrees. For muffins, combine all ingredients in a large mixing bowl. Stir just until all ingredients are moistened. Fill lightly greased miniature muffin tins two-thirds full with batter. Bake 15 minutes or until tops are very lightly browned and a muffin springs back when lightly pressed. Remove from tins and cool on wire racks.

For hard sauce, combine all ingredients in a medium bowl and beat until smooth. Spread hard sauce on tops of muffins.
Yield: about 4 dozen muffins

Chewy Date Muffins (recipe on page 439) are packed with pecans. Top them with a hard sauce and gumdrop holly berries for a delectable difference.

Sinless Brownies (recipe on page 439) are moist, chewy treats. Mandarin oranges and marmalade add color to low-fat Orange Cheesecakes (recipe on page 438).

Little open-faced sandwiches make great finger foods: Mini Bagels with Dilled Shrimp Spread (top, recipe on page 442) are flavored with dill and garlic. Sun-Dried Tomato Spread is delicious on Melba toast with ricotta cheese.

SUN-DRIED TOMATO SPREAD

1 cup sun-dried tomatoes
  Boiling water
5 tablespoons olive oil
2 tablespoons red wine vinegar
1 tablespoon capers
2 cloves garlic, minced
2 teaspoons Italian seasoning
1 teaspoon salt
  Melba toast and ricotta cheese
    to serve

Place tomatoes in a small bowl and add boiling water to cover. Allow to sit 15 minutes; drain.

Place tomatoes in a food processor and purée. Add oil, vinegar, capers, garlic, Italian seasoning, and salt. Process until well blended and mixture is still slightly coarse. Adjust seasonings, if desired. Store in a jar in refrigerator until ready to serve.

To serve, spread Melba toast with ricotta cheese and top with sun-dried tomato spread.

Yield: about 1 cup spread

MINI BAGELS WITH DILLED SHRIMP SPREAD

(Shown on page 441)

1/2 pound cooked shrimp, peeled, deveined, and finely chopped
1 package (8 ounces) cream cheese, softened
2 tablespoons mayonnaise
2 tablespoons sherry
1 tablespoon lemon juice
2 cloves garlic, minced
1/2 teaspoon salt
1/2 teaspoon lemon pepper
1/2 teaspoon dried dill weed
20 mini bagels, split, to serve

Combine all ingredients in a small bowl, blending well. Cover and chill at least 1 hour before serving with mini bagels.
Yield: about 2 cups spread

SUGARED WALNUTS

A brown sugar coating makes these crispy nuts a sweet treat.

8 cups water
4 cups English walnut halves
1/2 cup firmly packed light brown sugar
Vegetable oil

In a large pan, bring water to a boil. Add walnuts and boil for 1 minute. Drain walnuts and rinse in very hot water; drain again. Place warm walnuts in a bowl and add brown sugar. Stir until sugar is melted.
In a heavy skillet, heat 1 inch of oil to 320 degrees on a candy thermometer. Cook 2 cups of walnuts at a time 3 to 4 minutes. (Do not overcook.) Drain on paper towels. Store in airtight containers.
Yield: 4 cups walnuts

MONTEREY CHEESE CRISPS

You won't believe how easy these are to make. A sprinkling of cayenne pepper gives them an added bite.

1 pound Monterey Jack cheese, softened (use only Monterey Jack cheese)
Cayenne pepper or chili powder

Cut cheese into 1/4-inch-thick slices, then cut slices into circles using a 1 1/2-inch round cookie cutter. Place cheese rounds 3 inches apart on an ungreased non-stick baking sheet (cheese will spread while baking). Sprinkle with cayenne or chili powder. Bake in a preheated 400-degree oven 10 minutes or until golden brown. (Do not overbake.) Remove crisps with a spatula and cool on paper towels. Store in airtight containers.
Yield: 36 to 42 crisps

SPICY PECANS

1/2 cup butter
3 tablespoons steak sauce
6 drops hot pepper sauce
4 cups pecan halves
Cajun seasoning

Melt butter in a 15 1/2 x 10 1/2-inch jellyroll pan in a preheated 200-degree oven. Add steak sauce and pepper sauce; stir in pecans. Spread pecans on pan and bake 1 hour. Stir often while baking. Drain on paper towels and sprinkle with Cajun seasoning. Store in airtight containers.
Yield: 4 cups pecans

MARINATED OLIVES

These stuffed olives fortified with vinegar and herbs give party flavor to an everyday treat. The recipe can easily be doubled for larger crowds.

1 jar (8 ounces) pimiento-stuffed
  green olives, drained
1/4 cup tarragon wine vinegar
1/4 cup olive oil
1 tablespoon dried chives
1 clove garlic, minced
1/4 teaspoon whole black
  peppercorns

Place olives in a glass container with a lid. Combine remaining ingredients and pour over olives. Secure lid on jar and shake to coat olives well. Marinate at room temperature 2 days, shaking jar daily. Drain before serving.
Yield: about 1 cup olives

MARINATED VEGETABLES

1 1/2 cups vegetable oil
1/2 cup sherry wine vinegar
1/2 cup olive oil
1 1/2 teaspoons dry mustard
1 teaspoon salt
1 teaspoon dried tarragon leaves
1/2 teaspoon dried lemon peel
1 1/2 cups pickled okra, drained
1 1/2 cups baby corn, drained
8 to 10 cherry peppers

For dressing, combine vegetable oil, vinegar, olive oil, dry mustard, salt, tarragon, and lemon peel until well blended. Place okra, baby corn, and cherry peppers in a jar with a tight-fitting lid. Pour dressing over vegetables; shake to blend. Allow mixture to marinate overnight at room temperature.
Yield: about 4 1/2 cups vegetables

MEXICAN CHEESE CRACKERS

1 package (14 1/2 ounces) cheese
  crackers
1/2 cup butter or margarine, melted
1 package taco seasoning mix
1 tablespoon Worcestershire sauce
1/2 teaspoon seasoned salt

Preheat oven to 250 degrees. Place crackers in a large shallow baking pan. In a small bowl, combine butter, taco seasoning mix, Worcestershire sauce, and salt. Pour butter mixture over crackers; stir well. Bake 1 hour, stirring every 15 minutes. Pour onto waxed paper to cool. Store in an airtight container.
Yield: about 6 cups snack mix

These cheesy appetizers will be the hit of the party! (Clockwise from top) Greek Potato Skins are topped with feta cheese and herbs. Mini Hot Browns (recipe on page 446) feature a creamy mixture of turkey, bacon, and Cheddar. Ham Pinwheels (recipe on page 446) are good-tasting roll-ups accented with crunchy almonds and a touch of hot pepper sauce.

GREEK POTATO SKINS

3　medium baking potatoes,
　　scrubbed
　　Olive oil
4　ounces feta cheese, crumbled
1¹/₂　teaspoons dried oregano leaves
¹/₂　teaspoon dried basil leaves
¹/₄　teaspoon dried rosemary leaves
¹/₂　teaspoon garlic salt

Preheat oven to 400 degrees. Prick potatoes and rub with oil. Bake potatoes 1 hour or until done.

Cool potatoes slightly. Preheat oven to 450 degrees. Cut potatoes in half lengthwise. Leaving about a ¹/₄-inch shell, scoop out pulp (reserve pulp for another use, if desired). Cut skins in half lengthwise again; then cut skins in half crosswise. Place skins on a baking sheet and brush generously with oil. Bake 5 minutes. Combine remaining ingredients. Remove skins from oven and top with cheese mixture. Drizzle with more oil. Broil 2 to 3 minutes or until cheese is bubbly.
Yield: 24 potato skins

Cajun Canapés (left) are stuffed with zesty sausage and cheese. Showy yet simple to make, Cornucopia Appetizers (recipe on page 447) have olives and cocktail onions tucked inside rolls of spicy salami and Havarti cheese.

CAJUN CANAPÉS

2 cans (10 biscuits per can)
   refrigerated buttermilk biscuits
¹/₂ pound mild pork sausage, cooked
   and drained
1¹/₂ cups (6 ounces) shredded sharp
   Cheddar cheese
¹/₄ cup chopped green pepper
¹/₄ cup mayonnaise
2 green onions, chopped
2 teaspoons lemon juice
¹/₂ teaspoon salt
¹/₂ teaspoon paprika
¹/₄ teaspoon cayenne pepper
¹/₄ teaspoon garlic powder
¹/₄ teaspoon ground thyme

Place biscuits 1 inch apart on a greased baking sheet. Following baking time and temperature listed on package directions, bake biscuits, turning over halfway through baking time. Allow to cool. Using a melon ball cutter, scoop out center of each biscuit.

Preheat oven to 400 degrees. In a large bowl, mix together remaining ingredients. Spoon about 1 tablespoon of mixture into each hollowed biscuit. Place on baking sheet and bake 8 to 10 minutes or until heated through. Serve warm.
Yield: 20 canapés

Note: Filled biscuits may be refrigerated overnight before baking. If refrigerated, decrease oven temperature to 325 degrees and bake 12 to 15 minutes or until golden brown and cheese melts.

MINI HOT BROWNS
(Shown on page 444)

    3   tablespoons butter or margarine
    3   tablespoons all-purpose flour
  1/2   cup shredded sharp Cheddar
          cheese
    1   cup milk
  1/2   teaspoon salt
  1/2   teaspoon ground white pepper
 11/2   cups finely diced cooked
          turkey breast
    8   slices bacon, cooked and
          crumbled
   20   slices thinly sliced white bread
  3/4   cup freshly grated Parmesan
          cheese

In a medium saucepan, melt butter over medium-low heat. Whisk in flour, blending well. Add Cheddar cheese, whisking constantly until smooth. Increase heat to medium. Whisking constantly, slowly add milk; cook 4 to 5 minutes or until sauce is thick and smooth. Remove from heat and stir in salt, white pepper, turkey, and bacon; set aside.

Preheat broiler. Trim crusts from bread and cut each slice into four squares. Place bread on baking sheets and toast 1 side under broiler.

Spread a heaping tablespoon of turkey mixture on untoasted side of each piece of bread. Place on baking sheets. Sprinkle with Parmesan cheese. Broil a few seconds or until cheese melts and mixture begins to bubble. Serve warm.
Yield: 80 appetizers

HAM PINWHEELS
(Shown on page 444)

    1   package (8 ounces) cream
          cheese, softened
  1/4   cup chopped black olives
    2   tablespoons chopped toasted
          almonds
    2   tablespoons mayonnaise
    2   tablespoons chopped green
          onion
    1   tablespoon sherry
    1   teaspoon dry mustard
  1/2   teaspoon paprika
  1/4   teaspoon salt
  1/4   teaspoon freshly ground black
          pepper
  1/8   teaspoon ground red pepper
    3   to 4 drops hot pepper sauce
    5   rectangular slices (about
          5 ounces) baked ham

Beat cream cheese until smooth. Stir in olives, almonds, mayonnaise, green onion, sherry, dry mustard, paprika, salt, black pepper, red pepper, and pepper sauce. Spread mixture on ham slices. Beginning at 1 long edge, roll up ham slices jellyroll style. Place, seam side down, on baking sheet. Freeze 30 minutes. Remove from freezer and slice each roll into about 8 pieces. Insert a toothpick through each slice.
Yield: about 40 pinwheels

LIGHT ARTICHOKE SPREAD
(Shown on page 448)

1 can (13³/₄ ounces) artichoke
   hearts, drained and chopped
1 cup fat-free mayonnaise
1 cup grated Parmesan cheese
2 teaspoons garlic powder
   Crackers or bread to serve
2 fresh artichokes (optional)

Preheat oven to 350 degrees. In a medium bowl, combine artichoke hearts, mayonnaise, cheese, and garlic powder; stir until well blended. Transfer to a 1-quart casserole. Cover and bake 15 to 20 minutes or until heated through. Serve with crackers or bread.

If desired, spread may be served in fresh artichokes.

To prepare artichokes, fill a large saucepan with water; bring to a boil. Add fresh artichokes and boil 5 to 8 minutes or until leaves soften. Drain and cool to room temperature. Using a sharp knife, remove stem. Leaving 2 to 3 layers of leaves, hollow out inside of each artichoke. Spoon warm spread into center of each artichoke.

Yield: about 3 cups spread

CORNUCOPIA APPETIZERS
(Shown on page 445)

¹/₂ pound Havarti cheese, sliced
   paper-thin
¹/₄ pound Genoa salami, sliced
   paper-thin
24 cocktail onions
24 pimiento-stuffed green olives

Cut cheese slices slightly smaller than salami slices. For each appetizer, place 1 cheese slice on top of each salami slice. Roll into a cone shape. Place 1 onion and 1 olive inside and secure with a toothpick. Refrigerate 1 hour or until firm. Remove toothpicks before serving.

Yield: 24 appetizers

BRIE PUFFS
(Shown on page 448)

1 package (17¹/₄ ounces) frozen
   puff pastry dough, thawed
1 jar (12 ounces) strawberry
   preserves or jam
8 ounces Brie cheese, trimmed of
   rind and softened
2 tablespoons cooking sherry

Preheat oven to 350 degrees. On a lightly floured surface, use a 1¹/₂-inch biscuit cutter to cut out rounds from each pastry sheet. Place on an ungreased baking sheet and bake 15 to 20 minutes or until golden brown. Transfer to a wire rack to cool completely.

Carefully slice tops off puffs. Spoon about ¹/₂ teaspoon preserves onto bottom half of each puff. In a large bowl, combine cheese and sherry until well blended. Spoon about ¹/₂ teaspoon cheese mixture over preserves. Replace tops.

Yield: about 6 dozen puffs

Calorie-conscious guests will enjoy Light Artichoke Spread (top). Strawberry preserves add sweetness to Brie Puffs (lower right). Cranberry Meatballs have a tangy sauce. (Recipes are on pages 447 and 450.)

Miniature Crab Cakes (recipe on page 451) are breaded with a crunchy corn flake coating and baked. The fresh Tartar Sauce gets its tangy flavor from dill pickles, scallions, capers, and creamed horseradish.

CRANBERRY MEATBALLS

(Shown on page 448)

Cranberry Meatballs may be made one day in advance.

MEATBALLS
- 1 pound lean ground beef
- 3/4 cup plain bread crumbs
- 1/2 cup tomato juice
- 2 tablespoons prepared horseradish
- 1 egg, beaten
- 1 tablespoon Worcestershire sauce
- 1 tablespoon minced fresh parsley
- 1 teaspoon salt
- 1/4 teaspoon ground black pepper

SAUCE
- 1 tablespoon cornstarch
- 1 tablespoon water
- 1 can (16 ounces) whole berry cranberry sauce
- 1/3 cup firmly packed brown sugar
- 1 tablespoon freshly squeezed lime juice

Preheat oven to 350 degrees. For meatballs, combine meat, bread crumbs, tomato juice, horseradish, egg, Worcestershire sauce, parsley, salt, and pepper in a large bowl; stir until well blended. Shape into 1-inch balls and place in an ungreased 9 x 13-inch baking dish. Bake about 30 minutes or until meat browns. Place meatballs on paper towels to drain; set aside.

For sauce, dissolve cornstarch in water in a small bowl; stir until smooth. In a large skillet, combine cranberry sauce, brown sugar, and lime juice. Stirring constantly, cook over medium heat until sugar dissolves. Stirring constantly, add cornstarch mixture and cook until sauce thickens. Stir in meatballs. Transfer to a 2-quart casserole. Cover and refrigerate 8 hours or overnight to allow flavors to blend.

To serve, preheat oven to 350 degrees. Cover and bake 30 to 35 minutes or until heated through. Serve warm.

Yield: about 4 dozen meatballs

SAUSAGE BITES

- 1 pound mild pork sausage
- 1/2 cup finely chopped onion
- 1/3 cup finely chopped green pepper
- 1/3 cup plain bread crumbs
- 1 egg
- 1/4 cup Dijon-style mustard
- 1 package (17 1/4 ounces) frozen puff pastry dough, thawed
- 1 cup (4 ounces) shredded sharp Cheddar cheese
- 1 egg

Preheat oven to 400 degrees. In a large bowl, combine sausage, onion, green pepper, bread crumbs, and 1 egg; stir until well blended. Shape into eight 5-inch-long rolls. Place on a broiler pan and bake 30 to 35 minutes or until sausage is fully cooked and brown. Transfer to paper towels and cool to room temperature.

Preheat oven to 425 degrees. Spread mustard evenly over each pastry sheet. Sprinkle cheese evenly over mustard. Cut each pastry sheet in half from top to bottom and again from left to right. Place 1 sausage roll near 1 long edge of a pastry quarter. Roll up jellyroll style. Beat 1 egg in a small bowl. Brush edge of pastry with egg to seal. Place pastry, sealed edge down, on a greased baking sheet. Repeat for remaining sausage rolls. Bake 20 to 25 minutes or until pastry is brown. Cut into 1-inch slices and serve warm.

Yield: about 3 dozen sausage bites

MINIATURE CRAB CAKES WITH TARTAR SAUCE
(Shown on page 449)

Crab cakes may be prepared one day in advance and refrigerated until ready to bake.

TARTAR SAUCE

- 2 cups mayonnaise
- 2/3 cup finely chopped dill pickles
- 4 tablespoons freshly squeezed lemon juice
- 4 tablespoons finely minced scallions (use white and a small portion of green tops)
- 2 tablespoons drained capers, chopped
- 1/2 teaspoon creamed horseradish
- 1/2 teaspoon hot pepper sauce

CRAB CAKES

- 3 cans (6 ounces each) crabmeat, drained
- 1/2 cup finely chopped green pepper
- 1/2 cup finely chopped sweet red pepper
- 3 tablespoons minced onion
- 2 teaspoons minced fresh parsley
- 1 egg, beaten
- 1/2 cup finely crushed butter-flavored crackers (about 12 crackers)
- 1/4 teaspoon salt
- 1/8 teaspoon ground black pepper
- 3/4 cup corn flake crumbs

For tartar sauce, combine mayonnaise, pickles, lemon juice, scallions, capers, horseradish, and pepper sauce in a small bowl; stir until well blended. Reserve 1/3 cup for crab cakes; refrigerate remaining sauce until ready to serve.

Preheat oven to 350 degrees. For crab cakes, combine crabmeat, green and red peppers, onion, reserved 1/3 cup tartar sauce, parsley, egg, cracker crumbs, salt, and black pepper in a medium bowl. Carefully blend ingredients, just until mixed. Use 1 tablespoon of crab mixture to form each patty. Roll in corn flake crumbs until well coated. Place on an ungreased baking sheet. Bake 20 to 25 minutes or until golden brown. Serve warm with tartar sauce.

Yield: about 40 crab cakes and about 2 1/3 cups tartar sauce

A combination of spinach, parsley, walnuts, and cheeses makes this Layered Christmas Cheese Loaf (recipe on page 455) a luscious spread for French bread.

Broccoli flowerets form a wreath of green atop this delectable Cheese Cracker Vegetable Dip (recipe on page 454).

CHRISTMAS CHEESE STAR
(Shown on page 425)

2¹/₂ cups (10 ounces) shredded sharp Cheddar cheese
1 container (12 ounces) cottage cheese
1 package (8 ounces) cream cheese, softened
1 jar (4 ounces) diced pimientos, drained
2 tablespoons dried minced onion
¹/₂ teaspoon garlic powder
¹/₂ teaspoon ground red pepper
Sweet red pepper, cucumber, and parsley to garnish
Crackers to serve

Line a 1-quart star-shaped mold with plastic wrap. In a large bowl, combine cheeses, pimientos, onion, garlic powder, and ground red pepper using an electric mixer. Spoon into prepared mold. Cover and chill 1 hour. Invert mold onto a serving plate. Remove plastic wrap. Cover and refrigerate until ready to serve.

To serve, let stand at room temperature 20 to 30 minutes or until softened. Use a small star-shaped aspic cutter to cut stars from sweet red pepper. Garnish cheese star with cucumber slices, red pepper stars, and parsley. Serve with crackers or bread.

Yield: about 3³/₄ cups cheese spread

CHEESE CRACKER VEGETABLE DIP
(Shown on page 453)

This dip looks especially pretty garnished with a wreath of broccoli and topped with tiny chili pepper "lights."

1²/₃ cups Cheddar cheese snack cracker crumbs, divided
3 tablespoons butter or margarine, melted
1 carton (16 ounces) sour cream
1 package (3 ounces) cream cheese, softened
¹/₄ cup chopped pimientos
¹/₄ cup finely chopped green pepper
2 teaspoons Italian salad dressing mix
1 teaspoon Worcestershire sauce
¹/₄ teaspoon cayenne pepper
Assorted fresh vegetables to serve

Combine 1¹/₃ cups cracker crumbs and melted butter; mix well. Press half of crumb mixture into bottom of a buttered 8-inch round springform pan.

Combine next seven ingredients, blending well. Spread one half of sour cream mixture over cracker crumb crust. Sprinkle remaining buttered cracker crumbs over sour cream mixture; spread remaining sour cream mixture over crumbs. Sprinkle remaining ¹/₃ cup cracker crumbs over top. Cover and refrigerate 6 hours or overnight.

To serve, remove sides of springform pan and serve with assorted fresh vegetables for dipping.

Yield: 15 to 20 servings

LAYERED CHRISTMAS CHEESE LOAF

(Shown on page 452)

A simple garnish of fresh herbs and pink peppercorns adds a colorful touch to this elegant loaf.

2 packages (8 ounces each) cream
   cheese, softened
1/4 cup butter or margarine, softened
3 tablespoons milk
2 packages (10 ounces each)
   frozen chopped spinach,
   thawed and drained
2 cups lightly packed fresh parsley,
   stems removed
1/2 cup chopped walnuts
1/2 cup vegetable oil
1 tablespoon fresh lemon juice
2 cloves garlic, minced
1 teaspoon dried basil leaves
1 teaspoon dried oregano leaves
1 1/2 cups grated Parmesan cheese
   French bread slices to serve

In a mixing bowl, beat cream cheese, butter, and milk until smooth. Set aside.

In a blender or food processor, combine spinach, parsley, walnuts, vegetable oil, lemon juice, garlic, basil, and oregano. Process until smooth. Add Parmesan cheese and blend thoroughly.

Line a 7 1/2 x 3 1/2 x 2-inch loaf pan with plastic wrap. Spread one-third of cream cheese mixture evenly in bottom of the pan. Top with half of spinach mixture, spreading evenly. Repeat layers, ending with cream cheese mixture. Cover and refrigerate 3 to 4 hours or overnight.

Unmold and carefully remove plastic wrap. Garnish as desired. Serve with slices of French bread.

Yield: 35 to 40 servings

GREEN ONION CHEESE BALLS

2 cups (8 ounces) shredded
   sharp Cheddar cheese
2 cups (8 ounces) shredded
   Monterey Jack cheese
1 package (8 ounces) cream
   cheese, softened
1 cup finely chopped green onions
2 teaspoons hot pepper sauce
   Chili powder
   Crackers to serve

Combine cheeses, green onions, and pepper sauce in a large bowl. Beat with electric mixer until well blended. Shape cheese mixture into 3 balls. Roll in chili powder. Serve with crackers.

Yield: 3 cheese balls, about 1 cup each

BACON AND LETTUCE STUFFED TOMATOES

20 cherry tomatoes
   Salt
1/2 cup finely chopped lettuce
1/3 cup mayonnaise
10 slices bacon, cooked and
   crumbled
1/4 cup chopped green onion
   Salt and ground black pepper
   to taste

Cut the top off of each tomato. Scoop out pulp and seeds. Salt inside of each tomato. Invert tomatoes and drain 15 minutes.

In a small bowl, combine remaining ingredients. Fill each tomato with mixture.

Yield: 20 stuffed tomatoes

BLUE CHEESE MOUSSE
(Shown on page 460)

2 envelopes unflavored gelatin
1/4 cup cold water
2 cups sour cream
1 1/2 cups small curd cream-style cottage cheese
1 package (4 ounces) crumbled blue cheese
Grapes for garnish
Crackers or gingersnaps to serve

Combine gelatin and cold water in the top of a double boiler, stirring to soften. Place over boiling water and stir until gelatin dissolves. In a blender or food processor, combine gelatin mixture, sour cream, cottage cheese, and blue cheese. Process until smooth. Pour into a lightly oiled 3 1/2-cup decorative mold or small loaf pan. Chill until firm. Unmold and garnish with grapes. Serve with crackers or gingersnaps.
Yield: 25 to 30 servings

CARNITAS

1 pound bulk pork sausage
1/2 cup diced onion
1/2 cup diced green pepper
3 tablespoons ketchup
2 teaspoons chili powder
1/2 teaspoon ground cumin
1/8 teaspoon ground cloves
24 miniature taco shells
Shredded Cheddar cheese and shredded lettuce to serve

In a skillet over medium heat, cook sausage with onion and green pepper; drain well. Stir in ketchup, chili powder, cumin, and cloves. Cook 3 minutes, stirring constantly. Drain again. Serve mixture in taco shells with cheese and lettuce.
Yield: 24 miniature tacos

MUSHROOM CROUSTADES

36 thin slices wheat bread, cut into 3-inch rounds
1/4 cup butter or margarine
1/3 cup finely chopped green onion
8 ounces fresh mushrooms, finely chopped
2 tablespoons all-purpose flour
1 tablespoon minced fresh parsley
1/2 teaspoon salt
1/8 teaspoon cayenne pepper
1 pound bulk pork sausage, cooked and drained
1 cup whipping cream
2 teaspoons lemon juice
3 tablespoons freshly grated Parmesan cheese

Preheat oven to 400 degrees. Carefully fit bread into lightly greased miniature muffin tins, pressing gently into sides to form cups. Bake 8 to 10 minutes or until firm to touch.
In a large skillet, melt butter over medium-high heat. Add green onion and sauté 3 to 4 minutes. Stir in mushrooms and cook, stirring constantly, 10 to 15 minutes or until most of liquid is evaporated. Stir in flour, parsley, salt, and cayenne until well blended. Stir in sausage and whipping cream and bring to a low boil. Reduce heat to medium-low and simmer about 10 minutes or until mixture thickens. Stir in lemon juice and remove from heat. Let cool slightly.
Preheat oven to 350 degrees. Spoon filling evenly into bread cups. Sprinkle cheese over tops. Bake 8 to 10 minutes or until cheese melts. Serve warm.
Yield: 36 croustades

These tiny tidbits are packed with flavor: Mushroom and Chicken Pastries (clockwise from left) are easy to make with purchased puff pastry dough. Carnitas are miniature tacos with a sausage filling. Mushroom Croustades offer a creamy combination of sausage and mushrooms in a toasted bread cup.

MUSHROOM AND CHICKEN PASTRIES

2   cans (5 ounces each) chunk white
     chicken, drained and chopped
1   cup finely chopped fresh
     mushrooms
1/3 cup mayonnaise
1/4 cup minced onion
2   tablespoons Worcestershire sauce
2   tablespoons minced fresh parsley
1   teaspoon garlic salt
1   teaspoon lemon pepper
1/2 teaspoon grated lemon peel
1   package (17 1/4 ounces) frozen puff
     pastry dough, thawed

Combine all ingredients except puff pastry dough. Blend well, cover, and refrigerate until ready to use.

Preheat oven to 350 degrees. Unfold puff pastry dough. Using a 2-inch round cookie cutter, cut out dough. Place circles on lightly greased baking sheet and bake 15 to 20 minutes or until puffed and golden. Cool slightly and use a sharp knife to cut off tops of pastries; set aside. Remove soft inner dough from pastries. Fill with chicken mixture; replace tops.
Yield: about 40 pastries

457

VEGETABLE PATÉ

2   packages (8 ounces each)
      Neufchâtel cheese, softened
3/4 cup fat-free sour cream
2   tablespoons all-purpose flour
4   eggs
2   cloves garlic, minced
2   tablespoons freshly squeezed
      lemon juice
1   teaspoon chili powder
1   teaspoon salt
1/2 teaspoon ground black pepper
1/4 teaspoon paprika
1/4 teaspoon hot pepper sauce
1   cup (4 ounces) shredded sharp
      Cheddar cheese
1/2 cup finely chopped broccoli
1/2 cup peeled and finely chopped
      carrots
1/4 cup finely chopped green onions
1   cup chopped tomato
2   teaspoons dried parsley flakes
      Crackers or bread to serve

Preheat oven to 375 degrees. In a large bowl, beat Neufchâtel cheese, sour cream, and flour using an electric mixer. Add eggs, 1 at a time, beating well after each addition. Add garlic, lemon juice, chili powder, salt, pepper, paprika, and pepper sauce; stir until well blended. Fold in Cheddar cheese, broccoli, carrots, and green onions. Pour into a greased 9-inch springform pan. Bake 35 to 45 minutes or until set in center. Cool completely on a wire rack. Remove sides of pan, cover, and refrigerate until well chilled.

To serve, place tomato on top of paté. Lightly sprinkle with parsley flakes. Serve with crackers or bread.
Yield: about 16 servings

HOT MACADAMIA DIP
The rich flavor of macadamia nuts enhances this creamy dip that is served bubbling hot.

11 ounces (one 8-ounce and one
      3-ounce package) cream cheese,
      softened
2   tablespoons milk
1   jar (2 1/2 ounces) dried chipped
      beef, shredded
1/3 cup finely chopped onion
1/3 cup finely chopped green pepper
1   clove garlic, minced
1/2 teaspoon ground black pepper
1/4 teaspoon ground ginger
3/4 cup sour cream
1/2 cup coarsely chopped macadamia
      nuts
1   tablespoon butter or margarine
      Crackers to serve

Preheat oven to 350 degrees. Combine cream cheese and milk, blending until completely smooth. Stir in chipped beef, onion, green pepper, garlic, black pepper, and ginger. Fold in sour cream. Pour beef mixture into a glass pie plate or shallow baking dish. In a small skillet, sauté nuts in butter until thoroughly glazed. Sprinkle nuts over beef mixture. Bake 20 to 25 minutes or until heated through. Serve hot with crackers.
Yield: 12 to 15 servings

ULTIMATE CHILI DIP

A combination of cheese, beef, and chili seasonings makes this a hearty dip.

- 2 pounds ground round
- 1 cup chopped onion
- 2 cloves garlic, minced
- 1 package (2 pounds) processed American cheese, cut into pieces
- 1 can (16 ounces) undrained chili beans
- ¾ cup evaporated milk
- 2 packages (1¾ ounces each) chili seasoning mix
- ¼ cup chopped jalapeño peppers
  Tortilla or corn chips to serve

Cook meat, onion, and garlic in a large Dutch oven over medium heat until meat is brown; drain. Add cheese, beans, evaporated milk, chili seasoning, and jalapeño peppers to meat mixture; stir. Cook over medium heat, stirring often, until thoroughly blended and heated through. Serve warm in a chafing dish with tortilla or corn chips.

Yield: about 10 cups dip

POTATO COINS

(Shown on page 460)

- 2 pounds new potatoes
  Seasoned salt
  Sour cream
  Desired toppings (see list)

Preheat oven to 350 degrees. Wash potatoes. Place potatoes on a baking sheet and cover with aluminum foil. Bake 30 to 45 minutes or until tender.

To serve, slice each potato crosswise into ¼-inch-thick slices. With a small spoon, scoop out a small portion of the center of each potato slice, creating a small cavity. Sprinkle potatoes with seasoned salt. Fill cavity with sour cream and any of the toppings listed below. Serve warm.

Yield: about 30 slices

TOPPING VARIATIONS
Red, gold, or black caviar
Crumbled bacon
Chopped onion sautéed in butter
Shredded cheeses
Chopped green onion
Fresh herbs

HOT SEAFOOD DIP

(Shown on page 8)

- 2 cans (14 ounces each) artichoke hearts, drained and coarsely chopped
- 2¼ cups mayonnaise
- 2 cups grated Parmesan cheese
- 2 cans (6 ounces each) lump crabmeat, drained
- ⅓ cup seasoned bread crumbs
- 1½ teaspoons garlic salt
- 1 teaspoon lemon pepper
  Crackers to serve

Preheat oven to 325 degrees. In a medium mixing bowl, combine all ingredients, blending well. Pour into a greased 3-quart baking dish. Bake 20 to 25 minutes or until heated through. Serve warm or at room temperature with crackers.

Yield: about 6 cups dip

Elegant Blue Cheese Mousse (recipe on page 456) has a delicate taste that's delightful with crackers or gingersnaps.

Potato Coins (recipe on page 459) have bacon, caviar, shredded cheese, and green onion nestled in beds of sour cream.

Creamy garlic-flavored Aioli Dip (recipe on page 462) is wonderful with fresh vegetables, seafood, or French bread.

TOMATILLO SALSA

1 small onion, quartered
1/4 cup water
1/4 teaspoon salt
1¼ pounds fresh tomatillos, husked and washed (about 12 tomatillos)
1/2 cup coarsely chopped green pepper
2 jalapeño peppers, seeded
2 tablespoons chopped fresh cilantro
1 tablespoon freshly squeezed lime juice
1 clove garlic, coarsely chopped
Tortilla chips to serve

In a medium saucepan, combine onion, water, and salt over medium heat; cover and cook about 5 minutes or until onion is soft. Add whole tomatillos, green pepper, and jalapeño peppers to saucepan. Reduce heat, cover, and cook 15 minutes or until tomatillos are tender; drain. Process tomatillo mixture, cilantro, lime juice, and garlic in a food processor until coarsely chopped. Pour into a serving dish; cover and allow to stand 1 hour for flavors to blend. Serve at room temperature with tortilla chips.
Yield: about 3 cups salsa

AIOLI DIP
(Shown on page 461)

3 cloves garlic, minced
1/4 cup lemon juice
2 egg yolks, beaten
1 teaspoon Dijon-style mustard
1/4 teaspoon salt
1/8 teaspoon ground white pepper
1/8 teaspoon cayenne pepper
1½ cups olive oil
See serving suggestions at end of recipe

In a food processor or blender, purée garlic. Add next 6 ingredients; process until smooth. With the motor running, slowly pour oil into mixture in a steady stream. Continue processing until mixture becomes thick and firm. Chill until ready to serve.
Serve with artichoke hearts, hearts of palm, blanched snow peas, carrots, cauliflower, strips of green pepper, cherry tomatoes, zucchini, hard-cooked eggs, chunks of cooked lobster, cooked shrimp, or chunks of French bread.
Yield: about 2 cups dip

PESTO VEGETABLE DIP

1¹/₂ cups chopped fresh parsley
³/₄ cup grated Parmesan cheese
¹/₄ cup pine nuts
¹/₄ cup olive oil
1 cup mayonnaise
1 cup sour cream
1 clove garlic
1 teaspoon seasoned salt
¹/₄ teaspoon ground black pepper
Fresh vegetables to serve

Place first 4 ingredients in a blender or food processor fitted with a steel blade. Process until mixture resembles coarse meal. Add remaining ingredients and process until smooth. Serve with fresh vegetables.
Yield: about 3 cups dip

SESAME SPREAD WITH TOASTED PITA CHIPS

1 can (15 ounces) garbanzo
    beans, drained
¹/₃ cup tahini (sesame seed paste)
¹/₃ cup lemon juice
¹/₄ cup chopped green onion
1 tablespoon minced fresh parsley
1 clove garlic, minced
¹/₄ teaspoon salt
¹/₄ teaspoon ground black pepper
Pita bread
Coconut, chutney, toasted slivered
    almonds, and golden raisins
    to serve

Combine first 8 ingredients in a blender or food processor and process until smooth. Spoon mixture into a small bowl; cover and refrigerate at least 1 hour before serving.
Preheat oven to 450 degrees. Separate pita rounds in half. Cut each circle into 8 wedges. Place on ungreased baking sheet. Bake 5 to 8 minutes or until lightly browned and crisp. Serve sesame spread on pita chips topped with coconut, chutney, almonds, or golden raisins.
Yield: about 1¹/₂ cups spread

CHILLED ASPARAGUS MOUSSE

(Shown on page 8)

- 1/4 cup butter or margarine
- 1/4 cup all-purpose flour
- 1 1/2 cups milk, warmed
- 1/2 cup whipping cream, warmed
- 1/4 cup water
- 1 envelope unflavored gelatin
- 1 tablespoon Dijon-style mustard
- 1 teaspoon dried dill weed
- 1 teaspoon salt
- 1 teaspoon lemon juice
- 1/2 teaspoon ground black pepper
- 2 packages (8 ounces each) frozen asparagus spears, thawed and drained well
- Large tomato to garnish

Melt butter in a medium saucepan over medium heat; stir in flour. Cook about 2 minutes or until light brown. Add milk and cream, stirring constantly until sauce is thick and smooth. Remove from heat. In a small saucepan, combine water and gelatin over low heat, stirring until gelatin is dissolved. Stir gelatin mixture, mustard, dill weed, salt, lemon juice, and pepper into sauce. Using a food processor fitted with a steel blade, process asparagus until finely chopped. Stir asparagus into sauce. Pour mixture into a greased 2-quart mold. Chill overnight.

To remove from mold, dip in hot water up to rim of mold and invert onto a serving plate.

For tomato rose garnish, remove peel from tomato in 1-inch-wide strips. Roll 1 piece of peel into a cone shape, then surround with another piece. Continue with remaining pieces of peel until rose is desired size. Secure with a toothpick and place on top of mousse.

Yield: 12 to 14 servings

PISTACHIO CHEESE BALL

- 2 packages (8 ounces each) cream cheese, softened
- 3 tablespoons finely chopped green onion
- 3 tablespoons finely chopped fresh parsley
- 1 teaspoon paprika
- 1/4 teaspoon grated lemon peel
- 1/2 teaspoon salt
- 1/2 teaspoon freshly ground pepper
- 3/4 cup shelled, salted pistachios, finely chopped

In a medium mixing bowl, combine all ingredients except pistachios; blend well. Form into a ball. Place pistachios on waxed paper; roll ball in pistachios until well covered. Wrap tightly in plastic wrap and refrigerate 2 hours or until firm.

Yield: 1 cheese ball or approx. 2 cups cheese spread

FESTIVE CHEESE BALL

1 package (8 ounces) Neufchâtel
   cheese, softened
1/2 cup finely chopped celery
1/3 cup grated Parmesan cheese
1/4 cup shredded carrot
2 tablespoons mayonnaise
2 tablespoons dried minced onion
   Sweet red and yellow peppers
   and green onions to garnish
   Crackers to serve

In a medium bowl, combine first 6 ingredients. On a serving plate, shape cheese mixture into a 1-inch-high by 5-inch-diameter circle. Cover and refrigerate 8 hours or overnight to allow flavors to blend.

Garnish cheese ball with peppers and tops of green onions. To serve, let stand at room temperature 20 to 30 minutes or until softened. Serve with crackers.

Yield: 1 cheese ball

PESTO DIP

1 jar (0.6 ounces) dried
   crushed basil leaves
1/4 cup olive oil
1 teaspoon garlic powder
1/4 teaspoon salt
2 tablespoons plus 2 teaspoons
   grated Parmesan cheese
1/4 cup pine nuts
1 carton (16 ounces) sour cream

Place first 4 ingredients in a food processor fitted with a steel blade and process until smooth. Add cheese and nuts; process until smooth. Transfer to a large bowl. Add sour cream; stir until well blended. Store in an airtight container in refrigerator. Serve with crackers or fresh vegetables.

Yield: about 2 cups dip

For a zesty snack that takes just minutes to make, serve make-ahead South of the Border Salsa with tortilla chips.

SOUTH OF THE BORDER SALSA

Keep this salsa in the refrigerator to serve drop-in guests.

- 1 can (28 ounces) whole tomatoes with liquid, chopped
- $^1/_2$ cup olive oil
- $^1/_2$ cup minced fresh parsley
- 1 medium onion, minced
- $^1/_4$ cup chopped jalapeño peppers
- 2 cloves garlic, minced
  Tortilla chips to serve

Combine tomatoes, olive oil, parsley, onion, peppers, and garlic in a non-metallic container. Refrigerate overnight to allow flavors to blend. Serve with tortilla chips.

Yield: about 3 cups salsa

Light, crispy Tortilla Wedges are the perfect accompaniment for Florentine Dip, a tasteful blend of spinach, cheese, and artichoke hearts. (Recipes are on page 468.)

467

FLORENTINE DIP
(Shown on page 467)

- 1 package (10 ounces) frozen chopped spinach, thawed and squeezed dry
- 1 package (3 ounces) cream cheese, softened
- 1/2 cup sour cream
- 2 tablespoons minced green onion
- 2 teaspoons prepared horseradish
- 1 jalapeño pepper, seeded and chopped
- 1/2 teaspoon salt
- 1/4 teaspoon ground black pepper
- 1/2 cup shredded sharp Cheddar cheese, divided
- 1/2 cup shredded Monterey Jack cheese, divided
- 1 jar (6 ounces) marinated artichoke hearts, drained and chopped
  Tortilla Wedges to serve (recipe on this page)

Preheat oven to 350 degrees. In a large mixing bowl, combine first 8 ingredients, blending until smooth. Stir in 1/4 cup Cheddar cheese and 1/4 cup Monterey Jack cheese. Spread mixture into a greased 9-inch pie plate. Arrange chopped artichoke hearts around edge of plate. Bake 15 to 20 minutes. Sprinkle remaining cheeses on top and bake 5 minutes longer or until bubbly. Serve warm with Tortilla Wedges.

Yield: about 3 cups dip

TORTILLA WEDGES
(Shown on page 467)

- 12 large flour tortillas
  Vegetable oil

Cut each tortilla into 8 wedges. Pour oil into a 10-inch skillet to a depth of 1/2 inch and heat to 350 degrees. Fry tortilla wedges, 2 at a time, about 10 seconds on each side or until light brown. Drain on paper towels.

Yield: 96 tortilla wedges

Note: Tortilla wedges may be made 1 day in advance and stored in an airtight container.

SPINACH PUFFS
(Shown on page 8)

- 1 sheet (from a 17 1/4-ounce package) frozen puff pastry dough, thawed
- 1 package (12 ounces) frozen spinach soufflé, thawed
- 1 egg, lightly beaten
  Grated Parmesan cheese

Preheat oven to 350 degrees. Unfold puff pastry sheet and cut lengthwise into three equal rectangles. Cut each rectangle into four equal pieces. Place on an ungreased baking sheet and bake 20 to 25 minutes or until golden brown and puffed. Remove tops from puffs and pull out soft dough. Fill each rectangle with about 2 tablespoons of softened soufflé. Replace tops and brush with egg. Sprinkle with Parmesan cheese. Bake 20 minutes. Cut each puff in half diagonally. Serve warm.

Yield: 24 puffs

POPPY SEED CHICKEN

- 1 package (12 ounces) spinach egg noodles
- 2 tablespoons olive oil
- 2 pounds thick-sliced delicatessen chicken breast, cut into bite-size pieces (about 6 cups)
- 2 cans (10³/₄ ounces each) cream of chicken soup
- 1¹/₂ cups sour cream
- 1 can (8 ounces) sliced water chestnuts, drained
- ¹/₂ cup cooking sherry
- 1 teaspoon dried tarragon leaves
- ¹/₂ teaspoon ground white pepper
- ¹/₈ teaspoon ground red pepper
- 1 cup butter-flavored cracker crumbs
- 2 teaspoons poppy seed
- 6 tablespoons butter, melted

In a large saucepan, cook noodles according to package directions. Drain cooked noodles and toss with olive oil. Place noodles in two 7 x 11-inch greased glass baking dishes, spreading noodles up side of dishes. In a medium bowl, combine chicken, soup, sour cream, water chestnuts, sherry, tarragon, and peppers. Pour soup mixture over noodles. Sprinkle cracker crumbs and poppy seed over soup mixture. Pour melted butter over crackers. Cover and store in refrigerator.

To serve: Bake uncovered in a preheated 325-degree oven 55 to 60 minutes or until heated through.

Yield: 2 casseroles, about 6 servings each

GLAZED GINGER PORK

(Shown on page 470)

Cooked ahead and served cold, this ginger-flavored pork is an easy dish for entertaining.

- ¹/₄ cup soy sauce
- ¹/₄ cup dry white wine
- 2 tablespoons honey
- 1 tablespoon freshly grated ginger
- 1 clove garlic, minced
- 1 (3-pound) boneless pork loin roast
- ³/₄ cup currant jelly
- Sweet mustard to serve

For marinade, combine soy sauce, wine, honey, ginger, and garlic. Place roast in marinade. Cover and marinate roast in the refrigerator 6 hours or overnight, turning several times.

When ready to cook, remove roast from container and place on a rack in a shallow baking pan. Insert meat thermometer. Reserve 3 to 4 tablespoons of marinade for glaze; the remainder will be used for basting. Basting several times with marinade during cooking, bake in a preheated 300-degree oven 2 hours or until thermometer reaches 175 degrees.

For glaze, combine 3 to 4 tablespoons reserved marinade with jelly in a small saucepan. Stirring constantly, bring to a boil over medium-high heat; boil 1 minute. Set aside to cool.

After roast is cooked, spoon glaze over meat until it is completely coated. Refrigerate until ready to serve. Slice roast paper thin. Serve with sweet mustard.

Yield: about 50 slices

Tangy Glazed Ginger Pork (left, recipe on page 469) and Marmalade Meatballs will keep your guests coming back for more.

MARMALADE MEATBALLS

Bake these in batches and freeze for an upcoming party.

- 1 egg
- 1/2 cup water
- 1 pound finely ground chuck
- 1 cup water chestnuts, finely chopped
- 1/2 cup bread crumbs
- 2 teaspoons horseradish
- 1/4 teaspoon salt
- 2/3 cup orange marmalade
- 1/3 cup water
- 2 tablespoons soy sauce
- 2 tablespoons lemon juice
- 1 clove garlic, finely minced

In a medium bowl, beat egg and 1/2 cup water. Blend in ground chuck, water chestnuts, bread crumbs, horseradish, and salt. (**Note:** For tender meatballs, do not overmix.) Shape mixture into balls about 3/4 inch in diameter. Place meatballs on a foil-lined baking sheet. Bake in a preheated 350-degree oven 30 minutes or until lightly browned.

While meatballs are cooking, make sauce by combining remaining ingredients in a saucepan. Heat slowly, stirring often.

Place cooked meatballs in a serving dish and cover with sauce. If making in advance, place meatballs and sauce in a covered container and refrigerate. Heat slowly before serving.

Yield: about 24 servings

Simply Delicious
GIFTS FOR FRIENDS

Amaretto-Cinnamon Nut Mix, page 491

What could be more personal than presenting friends with their favorite foods, whether it's to satisfy their sweet tooth or nourish their health! To honor all your loved ones, here are wonderful candies, cookies, cakes, casseroles, soups, breads, jams, and more.

471

CARAMEL FUDGE

To have a friend, it helps to know how to be a friend. With our luscious Caramel Fudge and some pretty bags, you can make lots of sweet friendship gifts.

4 cups granulated sugar
1 cup evaporated milk
1/3 cup light corn syrup
6 tablespoons butter or margarine
2 tablespoons honey
1/2 teaspoon vanilla extract
1 cup chopped pecans

Butter sides of a large stockpot. Combine first 5 ingredients in pot and cook over medium-low heat, stirring constantly until sugar dissolves. Using a pastry brush dipped in hot water, wash down any sugar crystals on sides of pot. Attach candy thermometer to pot, making sure thermometer does not touch bottom of pot. Increase heat to medium and bring to a boil. Do not stir while syrup is boiling. Cook until syrup reaches soft ball stage (approximately 234 to 240 degrees). Test about 1/2 teaspoon syrup in ice water. Syrup should easily form a ball in ice water but flatten when held in your hand. Place pot in 2 inches of cold water in sink. Add vanilla; do not stir until syrup cools to approximately 110 degrees. Using medium speed of an electric mixer, beat fudge until it is no longer glossy and thickens. Pour into a buttered 8 x 11-inch baking dish. Sprinkle pecans evenly on top. Cool completely in pan.

Cut into 1-inch squares. Store in an airtight container in refrigerator.
Yield: about 7 dozen pieces fudge

TRILLIONAIRE CANDY

1 container (12 1/2 ounces) caramel topping
1 cup finely chopped pecans
3 dozen round butter-flavored crackers
1 package (12 ounces) semisweet chocolate chips

In a medium saucepan, combine caramel topping and pecans over medium heat. Stirring constantly, bring to a boil and cook 3 to 5 minutes longer or until mixture thickens. Remove from heat and allow to cool 5 minutes. Spoon about 1 1/2 teaspoons caramel mixture on top of each cracker. Refrigerate 1 hour or until firm. In a small saucepan, melt chocolate chips over low heat, stirring constantly. Remove from heat. Using tongs, dip bottom of each cracker in chocolate. Transfer to waxed paper and refrigerate 1 hour or until chocolate is firm. Store in an airtight container in refrigerator.
Yield: 3 dozen candies

I am wealthy in my friends.

—William Shakespeare

Trillionaire Candy will be a luxurious indulgence for a lucky friend! Unbelievably easy to make, the sweet treats are created by coating butter crackers with golden caramel, dark chocolate, and crunchy pecans.

MAPLE DIVINITY

Light, airy Maple Divinity is a delightful, old-fashioned treat for an old friend. Present it in a keepsake box adorned with photocopies of treasured photographs.

    2   cups granulated sugar
    1/2 cup light corn syrup
    1/2 cup water
    1/8 teaspoon salt
    2   egg whites
    1   teaspoon maple flavoring
    1   cup chopped walnuts

Grease sides of a large stockpot. Combine first 4 ingredients in stockpot over medium-low heat, stirring constantly until sugar dissolves. Syrup will become clear. Using a pastry brush dipped in hot water, wash down any sugar crystals on sides of stockpot. Attach candy thermometer to stockpot, making sure thermometer does not touch bottom of stockpot. Increase heat to medium and bring to a boil. Do not stir while syrup is boiling.

When syrup reaches approximately 240 degrees, use highest speed of an electric mixer to beat egg whites in a large bowl until stiff.

Continue to cook syrup until it reaches firm-ball stage (approximately 246 to 260 degrees). Test about 1/2 teaspoon syrup in ice water. Syrup will form a firm ball in ice water but will flatten if pressed when removed from water. While beating egg whites at low speed, slowly pour syrup into egg whites. Add maple flavoring and increase speed of mixer to high. Continue to beat until candy is no longer glossy and a stationary column forms when beaters are lifted. Fold in nuts. Pour into a greased 8 x 11-inch baking dish. Allow to harden. Cut into 1-inch squares. Store in an airtight container.

Yield: about 7 dozen squares divinity

RUM-RAISIN BALLS

Tuck these nutty cookies into an elegant fabric bag.

    1 1/2 cups granulated sugar, divided
    1   cup chopped walnuts
    1   cup sweetened shredded
        coconut
    1   cup raisins
    2   eggs, beaten
    1   teaspoon rum-flavored extract

Preheat oven to 350 degrees. In a large bowl, combine 1 cup sugar and remaining ingredients; stir until well blended. Spoon into a greased 8-inch square baking dish. Bake 20 to 25 minutes, stirring occasionally. Cool on a wire rack 10 minutes. Using damp hands, shape into 1-inch balls; roll in remaining sugar. Store in an airtight container.

Yield: about 2 1/2 dozen balls

JELLY BEAN BRITTLE

With colorful jelly beans substituted for peanuts, traditional brittle becomes a sweet surprise for children.

1 1/2 cups jelly beans
   3 cups granulated sugar
   1 cup light corn syrup
 1/2 cup water
   3 tablespoons butter or
       margarine
   1 teaspoon salt
   2 teaspoons baking soda

Spread jelly beans evenly on greased aluminum foil. Grease sides of a large stockpot. Combine next 3 ingredients over medium-low heat; stir constantly until sugar dissolves. Using a pastry brush dipped in hot water, wash down any sugar crystals on sides of pot. Attach candy thermometer to pot, making sure thermometer does not touch bottom of pot. Increase heat to medium and bring to a boil. Do not stir while syrup is boiling. Continue to cook until syrup reaches hard crack stage (approximately 300 to 310 degrees) and turns golden brown. Test about 1/2 teaspoon syrup in ice water. Syrup should form brittle threads in ice water and remain brittle when removed from water. Remove from heat and add butter and salt; stir until butter melts. Add soda (syrup will foam); stir until soda dissolves. Pour syrup over jelly beans. Using 2 greased spoons, pull edges of warm candy until stretched thin. Cool completely on foil. Break into pieces. Store in an airtight container.
Yield: about 2 pounds brittle

Friendship begins with one smile.

PEANUT BUTTER-HONEY SPREAD

This cinnamon-spiced spread is great on graham crackers or cookies. It's cute to give in a jar decorated with a heart label and topped with a circle of fabric secured to the lid with a ribbon or string.

1 cup smooth peanut butter
1 cup honey
1 teaspoon ground cinnamon

Combine all ingredients in a large bowl using medium speed of an electric mixer. Store in an airtight container. Serve with crackers or cookies. Include serving suggestions with gift.
Yield: about 2 cups spread

CHOCOLATE-DIPPED FORTUNE COOKIES

1 cup (6 ounces) semisweet
    chocolate chips
1 box (3¹/₂ ounces) purchased
    fortune cookies

In a small saucepan, melt chocolate over low heat, stirring constantly. Remove from heat. Dip ¹/₂ of each cookie in chocolate. Transfer to a wire rack with waxed paper underneath to cool completely. Store in an airtight container
Yield: about 1 dozen cookies

A coating of dark chocolate gives store-bought fortune cookies a gourmet look and taste. To deliver the crispy treats, spell out our special message on a take-out carton using letters cut from magazines.

Strawberry Gem Cookies are a delectable way to show someone that you think they are a jewel!

STRAWBERRY GEM COOKIES

1 cup butter or margarine, softened
¹/₄ cup granulated sugar
2 tablespoons water
1 teaspoon vanilla extract
2 cups all-purpose flour
¹/₄ teaspoon salt
2 cups unsweetened shredded coconut
¹/₂ cup red shelled pistachios, finely chopped
Confectioners sugar
¹/₂ cup strawberry jam

Preheat oven to 350 degrees. In a large bowl, cream butter and sugar until fluffy. Stir in water and vanilla. In a medium bowl, sift together flour and salt. Gradually add flour mixture to creamed mixture; stir until a soft dough forms. Fold in coconut and pistachios. Shape dough into 1-inch balls and place 2 inches apart on a greased baking sheet. Using the end of a wooden spoon, make a depression in the center of each cookie. Bake 15 to 20 minutes or until light brown. Transfer to a wire rack. Dust warm cookies with confectioners sugar. Spoon about ¹/₂ teaspoon jam into center of each cookie. Allow to cool completely. Store in an airtight container.
Yield: about 3 dozen cookies

Choose thy friends like thy books, few but choice.

—James Howell

HAZELNUT CHEWIES

1 cup butter or margarine, softened
2/3 cup firmly packed brown sugar
1/2 cup granulated sugar
2 tablespoons vegetable oil
1 tablespoon corn syrup
2 eggs
2 teaspoons vanilla extract
2 cups all-purpose flour
3/4 teaspoon baking powder
1/4 teaspoon salt
1 cup sweetened shredded coconut
1 cup finely chopped hazelnuts

Preheat oven to 350 degrees. In a large bowl, cream butter and sugars until fluffy. Add next 4 ingredients; beat until smooth. In a medium bowl, sift together next 3 ingredients. Add dry ingredients to creamed mixture; stir until a soft dough forms. Fold in coconut and hazelnuts. Drop teaspoonfuls 2 inches apart onto a greased baking sheet. Bake 10 to 12 minutes or until brown. Transfer to a wire rack to cool completely. Store in an airtight container.
Yield: about 7 1/2 dozen cookies

CARAMEL-MACADAMIA NUT COOKIES

1 1/2 cups macadamia nuts, coarsely chopped
1 cup butter or margarine, softened
3/4 cup firmly packed brown sugar
1 egg
1 tablespoon corn syrup
1 teaspoon vanilla extract
2 cups all-purpose flour

Preheat oven to 350 degrees. Spread macadamia nuts evenly on an ungreased baking sheet. Stirring occasionally, bake 10 to 15 minutes or until nuts begin to brown. Remove from oven; cool to room temperature.
In a large bowl, cream butter and sugar until fluffy. Add next 3 ingredients; stir until smooth. Add flour; stir until well blended. Fold in macadamia nuts. Drop tablespoonfuls 2 inches apart onto a greased baking sheet. Bake 10 to 12 minutes or until golden brown. Transfer to a wire rack to cool completely. Store in an airtight container.
Yield: about 3 dozen cookies

What better way to brighten someone's day than with a batch of homemade cookies nestled in a pretty cloth! The sweet, nutty taste of Caramel-Macadamia Nut Cookies will provide a friend with delicious proof of your devotion. The simple cloth will serve as a lasting reminder of your kindness.

Shown on page 9: *A batch of star-spangled cookies is sure to boost the morale of a loved one in the military who's based far from home. For a special delivery, trim your cookie box in patriotic colors, too.*

HONEY-ALMOND COOKIES

COOKIES
- 1 cup butter or margarine, softened
- 1/3 cup butter-flavored shortening
- 1/3 cup vegetable oil
- 2 cups granulated sugar
- 2 eggs
- 1/3 cup honey
- 1 teaspoon almond extract
- 1 cup quick-cooking rolled oats
- 4 cups all-purpose flour

ICING
- 7 cups confectioners sugar
- 1/2 cup plus 2 tablespoons plus 2 teaspoons milk
- Blue and red paste food coloring
- 1 tablespoon water

For cookies, cream butter, shortening, oil, and sugar in a large bowl until fluffy. Add eggs, honey, and almond extract; beat until smooth. Add oats and flour; knead until a soft dough forms. Cover and refrigerate 1 hour.

Preheat oven to 350 degrees. On a lightly floured surface, use a floured rolling pin to roll out dough to 1/4-inch thickness. Place a piece of tracing paper over heart and star patterns and trace; cut out. Place patterns on dough and use a sharp knife to cut out an equal number of heart-shaped and star-shaped cookies. Transfer to a greased baking sheet. Bake 10 to 12 minutes or until light brown. Transfer to a wire rack to cool completely.

For icing, combine sugar and milk in a large bowl; beat until smooth. Transfer 3/4 cup icing to a small bowl; tint blue and cover. Transfer 1/2 cup white icing to another small bowl; add water and stir until smooth. Tint red and cover. Cover remaining icing. Ice star-shaped cookies blue and heart-shaped cookies white. Allow icing to harden. Use a small round paintbrush and red icing to paint wavy lines on heart-shaped cookies. Allow icing to harden. Store in an airtight container.

Yield: about 7 dozen 3-inch cookies

PRALINE TEA CAKES

These delicious Praline Tea Cakes will enhance an intimate conversation shared over a cup of tea.

CAKES
- 1 cup butter or margarine, softened
- 1 cup granulated sugar
- 6 eggs
- 1 teaspoon maple-flavored extract
- 1 cup finely crushed vanilla wafer cookies
- 1 teaspoon baking powder
- 1/2 teaspoon salt
- 1/2 teaspoon dried grated orange peel

TOPPING
- 2 cups chopped pecans
- 1 cup butter or margarine
- 1 cup firmly packed brown sugar

Preheat oven to 350 degrees. For cakes, cream butter and sugar in a large bowl until fluffy. Add eggs and maple extract; beat until smooth. Add remaining ingredients; stir until well blended. Pour batter evenly into 12 greased and floured shortcake tins. Bake 15 to 20 minutes or until a toothpick inserted in center comes out clean. Cool in pan 10 minutes; invert onto a wire rack to cool completely.

For topping, preheat oven to 350 degrees. Spread pecans evenly on an ungreased baking sheet and bake 10 to 15 minutes, stirring occasionally. Remove from oven. In a medium saucepan, combine butter and sugar over medium heat. Stirring constantly, bring to a boil and cook 2 to 3 minutes or until mixture thickens. Stir in pecans. Spoon about 2 tablespoons topping into center of each cake. Allow to cool completely. Store in an airtight container.

Yield: 1 dozen cakes

ORANGE THINS

These crisp Orange Thins make a light, tasty dessert for an impromptu picnic. Pack them for a friend in a decorative lunch box, along with a sandwich or salad.

- $1/2$ cup butter or margarine, softened
- $1/2$ cup granulated sugar
- 1 tablespoon frozen orange juice concentrate, thawed
- $1/2$ teaspoon vanilla extract
- $1/2$ teaspoon orange-flavored extract
- $1/2$ teaspoon dried grated orange peel
- 1 cup all-purpose flour
- $1/4$ teaspoon salt
- $1/2$ cup chopped walnuts

Preheat oven to 350 degrees. In a large bowl, cream butter and sugar until fluffy. Add next 4 ingredients; mix until smooth. In a blender or food processor fitted with a steel blade, process remaining ingredients until walnuts are finely ground. Add dry ingredients to creamed mixture; stir until a soft dough forms. Shape into $1/2$-inch balls and place 2 inches apart on a greased baking sheet. Flatten each ball with a spatula. Bake 8 to 10 minutes or until brown. Transfer to a wire rack to cool completely. Store in an airtight container.
Yield: about 3 dozen cookies

GINGER-PEANUT BUTTER COOKIES

- 1 cup butter or margarine, softened
- $1/3$ cup butter-flavored shortening
- $1/3$ cup vegetable oil
- 2 cups granulated sugar
- 2 eggs
- 1 teaspoon vanilla extract
- 1 cup smooth peanut butter
- 5 cups all-purpose flour
- 1 teaspoon ground ginger
- $1/2$ teaspoon salt

Preheat oven to 350 degrees. In a large bowl, cream first 4 ingredients until fluffy Add eggs and vanilla; beat until smooth. Stir in peanut butter. In another large bowl, sift together remaining ingredients Add dry ingredients to creamed mixture; knead until a soft dough forms.

On a lightly floured surface, use a floured rolling pin to roll out dough to $1/4$-inch thickness. Use a cookie cutter to cut out cookies. Transfer to a greased baking sheet. Bake 10 to 12 minutes or until golden brown. Transfer to a wire rack to cool completely. Store in an airtight container.
Yield: about 6 dozen cookies

When a dear friend is moving away, remind her to keep in touch with a dainty photo album and a batch of Forgotten Cookies. The meringue treats practically bake themselves while being "forgotten" in a low-temperature oven.

FORGOTTEN COOKIES

1 cup chopped pecans
4 egg whites
1/2 teaspoon cream of tartar
1 cup sifted confectioners sugar
2 teaspoons vanilla extract

Preheat oven to 350 degrees. Spread pecans evenly on an ungreased baking sheet. Stirring occasionally, bake 10 to 15 minutes. Remove from oven; cool to room temperature.

Reduce oven temperature to 200 degrees. In a large bowl, beat egg whites until foamy. Add cream of tartar; beat until soft peaks form. Gradually add sugar, beating until stiff peaks form. Stir in vanilla. Fold in pecans. Drop by tablespoonfuls onto a waxed paper-lined baking sheet. Bake 2 hours 30 minutes to 2 hours 40 minutes or until golden yellow. Cool completely on baking sheet. Carefully peel away waxed paper. Store in an airtight container.
Yield: about 3¹/₂ dozen cookies

KEY LIME PIE

Because friends are the key to a happy life, we keep them close to our hearts. Express this sentiment to a friend by presenting our creamy Key Lime Pie along with a heart-shaped key ring or other trinket.

CRUST
1¹/2 cups all-purpose flour
 ¹/2 teaspoon salt
 ¹/2 cup vegetable shortening
 ¹/4 cup cold water

FILLING
 4 egg yolks
 1 can (14 ounces) sweetened
   condensed milk
 ¹/3 cup freshly squeezed lime
   juice (juice of about 3 limes)
   Green food coloring (optional)

MERINGUE
 4 egg whites
 ¹/2 teaspoon cream of tartar
 ¹/2 cup granulated sugar

Preheat oven to 450 degrees. For crust, sift flour and salt together in a medium bowl. Using a pastry blender or 2 knives, cut in shortening until mixture resembles coarse meal. Sprinkle water over mixture; mix until a soft dough forms. On a lightly floured surface, use a floured rolling pin to roll out dough to ¹/8-inch thickness. Transfer to a 9-inch pie plate and use a sharp knife to trim edges of dough. Prick crust with a fork. Bake 8 minutes. Cool completely on a wire rack.

Reduce oven temperature to 325 degrees. For filling, combine egg yolks, condensed milk, and lime juice in a medium saucepan over low heat. Cook, stirring constantly, until mixture reaches 160 degrees (about 10 minutes). Remove from heat. If desired, tint green.

For meringue, beat egg whites and cream of tartar in a large bowl until foamy using highest speed of an electric mixer. Gradually add sugar; beat until stiff peaks form.

Pour filling into crust. Spread meringue evenly over filling. Bake 25 to 30 minutes or until meringue is brown. Cool completely on a wire rack. Cover and refrigerate until ready to present.
Yield: 8 to 10 servings

RING OF GOLD APRICOT CAKE

CAKE
 1 cup butter or margarine,
   softened
 2 cups granulated sugar
 5 eggs
 ¹/2 cup apricot jam
 ¹/2 cup sour cream
 1 teaspoon vanilla extract
 2 cups all-purpose flour
 1 teaspoon baking soda
 ¹/2 teaspoon salt
 2 cups sweetened shredded
   coconut
 1 cup finely chopped pecans
 1 package (8 ounces) dried
   apricots, finely chopped

GLAZE
 ¹/2 cup apricot jam
 2 tablespoons apricot nectar

Preheat oven to 350 degrees. For cake, cream butter and sugar in a large owl until fluffy. Add eggs 1 at a time, beating well after each addition. Stir in next 3 ingredients. In a medium bowl, sift together next 3 ingredients. Stir dry ingredients into creamed mixture. Fold in remaining ingredients. Pour batter into a greased and floured 10-inch tube pan. Bake 45 to 55 minutes or until a toothpick inserted in center comes out clean. Cool in pan 10 minutes; turn onto a wire rack to cool completely.

For glaze, combine jam and nectar in a small saucepan over medium heat; stir until well blended. Pour evenly over top of cake. Store in an airtight container. **Yield:** about 20 servings

BLUEBERRY STICKY BUNS
(Shown on page 486)

3	cups all-purpose flour
1/2	cup granulated sugar
2	packages active dry yeast
1	teaspoon salt
1 1/4	cups butter or margarine, softened and divided
1/2	cup buttermilk
1/4	cup milk
1	teaspoon vanilla extract
2	eggs
2	cups firmly packed brown sugar, divided
1	cup fresh blueberries
4	teaspoons ground cinnamon
1	cup chopped pecans
1/2	cup honey

In a large bowl, combine first 4 ingredients. In a small saucepan, combine 1 cup butter and next 3 ingredients over medium-low heat. Stir until mixture reaches 130 degrees (butter may not be completely melted). Remove from heat; whisk in eggs. Stir egg mixture into dry ingredients; knead until a soft dough forms. Turn dough onto a lightly floured surface. Knead about 5 minutes or until dough becomes elastic and pliable. Form into a ball; place in a greased bowl. Grease top of dough, cover, and refrigerate 2 hours or until well chilled. In a small bowl, stir together 1 cup brown sugar, blueberries, and cinnamon; set aside. In another small bowl, stir together remaining brown sugar, pecans, and honey. Spoon a heaping tablespoon pecan mixture into the bottoms of 12 greased jumbo muffin tins; set aside.

(Continued on page 486)

A friend is one
to whom we cling,
though many leagues
of space separate us.

—J.E. Dinger

(Continued from page 485)

Turn dough onto a lightly floured surface; knead 2 to 3 minutes or until smooth. Using a floured rolling pin, roll out dough to a 10 x 18-inch rectangle. Sprinkle blueberry mixture evenly over dough. Beginning with 1 long edge, roll dough tightly jelly-roll fashion. Cut evenly into 12 slices. Place 1 slice of dough over pecan mixture in each muffin tin. In a small saucepan, melt remaining butter over medium heat. Brush tops of slices with melted butter. Cover and let rise in a warm place (80 to 85 degrees) 1 hour or until doubled in size.

Preheat oven to 350 degrees. Bake 35 to 40 minutes or until golden brown. Turn onto waxed paper to cool completely. Store in an airtight container. Give with serving instructions.

Sticky buns may be served warm or at room temperature. To reheat, preheat oven to 350 degrees. Bake uncovered on a greased baking sheet 3 to 5 minutes or until heated through.

Yield: 1 dozen buns

Whether near or far, true friends always stick together. To commemorate such a relationship, why not bake a batch of yummy Blueberry Sticky Buns! Topped with a sweet honey-pecan glaze, the rolls are simply bursting with blueberries.
Recipe begins on page 485.

Friendship is a sheltering tree, and these realistic Acorn Cookies are a perfect fall friendship gift. Accented with chocolate, nuts, and a clove "stem," the almond treats are sweetened with brown sugar and spiced with cinnamon.

ACORN COOKIES

1 cup butter or margarine, softened
1¹/₂ cups firmly packed brown sugar
1 teaspoon almond extract
1 envelope unflavored gelatin
2 tablespoons hot water
2 cups all-purpose flour
¹/₂ teaspoon ground cinnamon
¹/₄ teaspoon salt
3¹/₄ cups finely ground almonds
1 cup (6 ounces) semisweet chocolate chips
1 cup finely chopped almonds
Whole cloves

Preheat oven to 375 degrees. In a large bowl, cream butter and sugar until fluffy. Beat in almond extract. In a small bowl, dissolve gelatin in water. Add to creamed mixture; stir until well blended. In a medium bowl, sift together next 3 ingredients. Add dry ingredients to creamed mixture; stir until a soft dough forms. Fold in ground almonds. Shape dough into 1-inch diameter acorn shapes. Transfer to a greased baking sheet. Bake 10 to 12 minutes or until light brown. Transfer to a wire rack to cool completely.

Melt chocolate chips in a small saucepan over low heat; remove from heat. Dip wide end of each cookie in chocolate; roll chocolate-dipped end in chopped almonds. For stem, insert the round end of 1 clove into the chocolate-dipped end of each cookie. Allow chocolate to harden. Store in an airtight container.

Yield: about 6 dozen cookies

CRUNCHY CHEESE BALL

Two surprise ingredients—ramen noodles and sunflower seeds—lend a crisp, nutty flavor to this Crunchy Cheese Ball. Green onions and parsley add a touch of color. To deliver the gift, tuck it in a fabric-lined basket with some crackers.

- 1 package (3 ounces) chicken-flavored ramen noodle soup
- 2 packages (8 ounces each) cream cheese, softened
- 1 cup sour cream
- 1/2 cup dry-roasted shelled sunflower seeds
- 4 green onions, chopped
- 1/3 cup dried parsley flakes

In a food processor fitted with a steel blade, process noodles, contents of seasoning packet, and next 4 ingredients until well blended. Divide mixture in half. Shape each half into a ball. Roll in parsley. Wrap in plastic wrap and refrigerate. Give with serving instructions.

To serve, let stand at room temperature 20 to 30 minutes or until softened. Serve with crackers or bread.
Yield: 2 cheese balls

SUNSHINE PUNCH

- 3 bananas, peeled and cut into pieces
- 1 can (6 ounces) frozen lemonade concentrate, thawed
- 4 cups water
- 2 cups red grape juice
- 1 can (6 ounces) frozen pineapple juice concentrate, thawed

In a blender or food processor fitted with a steel blade, process bananas and lemonade concentrate until well blended. Transfer to a 3-quart container. Add remaining ingredients; stir until well blended. Cover and refrigerate. Serve chilled.
Yield: about 2 1/2 quarts punch

ONION-SESAME SNACK MIX

- 3 cups oyster crackers
- 2 cups dry-roasted peanuts
- 1/2 cup butter or margarine
- 1 package (1 ounce) dry onion soup mix
- 1/4 cup sesame seeds

Preheat oven to 350 degrees. In a large bowl, combine crackers and peanuts. In a small saucepan, melt butter over medium heat. Remove from heat; stir in remaining ingredients. Pour over cracker mixture; toss until well coated. Spread evenly on a baking sheet. Bake 10 to 12 minutes or until light brown. Cool completely in pan. Store in an airtight container.
Yield: about 5 cups snack mix

SPICY VEGETABLE SALSA

With its combination of fresh ingredients, this Spicy Vegetable Salsa will warm up any meeting among friends. A variety of seasonings and vegetables gives the chunky sauce its mild zesty flavor.

- 1/2 cup spicy vegetable juice
- 1 tablespoon lime juice
- 1 tablespoon lemon juice
- 1 tablespoon orange juice
- 1 tablespoon red wine vinegar
- 2 teaspoons ground dried basil leaves
- 1/2 teaspoon ground cumin
- 1/2 teaspoon ground black pepper
- 1/4 teaspoon hot pepper sauce
- 1/4 teaspoon salt
- 1 clove garlic, minced
- 2 tablespoons minced sweet red pepper
- 2 tablespoons minced green pepper
- 2 tablespoons minced sweet yellow pepper
- 2 tablespoons minced unpeeled cucumber
- 2 tablespoons minced red onion
- 2 tablespoons minced fresh cilantro

In a medium bowl, combine first 11 ingredients; stir until well blended. Stir in remaining ingredients. Cover and refrigerate 8 hours or overnight to allow flavors to blend. Serve with meat or chips. Include serving suggestions with gift.
Yield: about 1 cup salsa

SPICY CHEESE SNACK MIX

- 1 box (9 ounces) miniature saltine crackers
- 1/2 cup butter or margarine
- 2 packages (1 1/4 ounces each) cheese sauce mix
- 1/2 cup grated Parmesan cheese
- 1/2 teaspoon cayenne pepper

Preheat oven to 350 degrees. Pour crackers into a large bowl. In a small saucepan, melt butter over medium heat. Remove from heat; stir in remaining ingredients. Pour over crackers; toss until well coated. Transfer to a baking sheet. Bake 10 to 12 minutes or until light brown. Transfer to paper towels to cool. Store in an airtight container.
Yield: about 4 cups snack mix

When friends meet, hearts warm.

Friends who are a work of art will think this gift is a real masterpiece. You simply add a spicy coating to ready-made pretzels and present them in a tin decorated with a photocopy of a famous painting.

CURRIED PRETZELS

  1 bag (10 ounces) Bavarian
      pretzels
  3 tablespoons butter or
      margarine
 $^1/_2$ teaspoon curry powder
 $^1/_4$ teaspoon seasoned salt

Preheat oven to 225 degrees. Place a single layer of pretzels on a baking sheet. In a small saucepan, melt butter over medium heat. Add remaining ingredients; stir until well blended. Using a pastry brush, brush butter mixture on each pretzel. Bake 20 to 25 minutes or until dry to the touch. Cool completely on pan. Store in an airtight container. **Yield:** about $2^1/_2$ dozen pretzels

TRAIL MIX

 $^1/_2$ cup dry-roasted peanuts
 $^1/_2$ cup whole almonds
 $^1/_2$ cup raisins
 $^1/_2$ cup granola cereal
 $^1/_2$ cup stick pretzels
  1 can (14 ounces) sweetened
      condensed milk

Preheat oven to 300 degrees. In a large bowl, combine first 5 ingredients. Pour condensed milk over mixture; toss until well coated. Transfer to a greased 9 x 13-inch baking pan. Bake 25 to 30 minutes, stirring occasionally. Transfer to aluminum foil to cool completely. Break into pieces. Store in an airtight container in refrigerator. **Yield:** about 4 cups trail mix

Delivered in a jar decorated with epoxy-covered nuts and bolts, Amaretto-Cinnamon Nut Mix is a creative way to say "I'm nuts about you!"

AMARETTO-CINNAMON NUT MIX

- ¹/₄ cup butter or margarine
- ¹/₂ cup granulated sugar, divided
- ¹/₂ teaspoon ground cinnamon
- 2 tablespoons amaretto liqueur
- 1 cup unsalted whole almonds

Preheat oven to 425 degrees. In a small saucepan, melt butter over medium heat. Stir in ¹/₄ cup sugar and cinnamon. Bring to a boil, stirring constantly until sugar dissolves. Boil sugar mixture 3 minutes longer. Remove from heat. Add liqueur; stir until well blended. Stir in almonds. Spread evenly on a greased baking sheet. Bake 5 to 8 minutes or until dark brown. Roll in remaining sugar; transfer to aluminum foil to cool completely. Store in an airtight container.

Yield: about 1 cup nut mix

A friend is the hope of the heart.

ORANGE-CHOCOLATE CHIFFON CAKE

Bake this light and airy cake in a heart-shaped pan for a sentimental gift. A rich dark chocolate glaze enhances the delicate flavor of the cake, while orange peel rosettes add a fragrant accent.

CAKE
- 1 cup all-purpose flour
- 2/3 cup granulated sugar
- 1 1/2 teaspoons baking powder
- 1/4 teaspoon salt
- 2 eggs, separated
- 1/2 cup milk
- 1/4 cup vegetable oil
- 2 tablespoons frozen orange juice concentrate, thawed
- 1 teaspoon dried grated orange peel
- 1 teaspoon vanilla extract
- 1/4 teaspoon cream of tartar

GLAZE
- 2 ounces unsweetened chocolate
- 2 tablespoons butter or margarine
- 1 1/2 cups confectioners sugar
- 1 teaspoon vanilla extract
- 3 tablespoons plus 1 teaspoon hot water
- 2 oranges for garnish

Preheat oven to 350 degrees. For cake, sift together first 4 ingredients in a large bowl. Add egg yolks and next 5 ingredients. Beat until well blended using medium speed of an electric mixer set aside.

In another large bowl, beat egg whites until foamy. Add cream of tartar and beat until stiff peaks form. Gently fold egg white mixture into egg yolk mixture. Pour into a greased and floured 8-inch heart-shaped pan. Bake 25 to 30 minutes or until a toothpick inserted in center of cake comes out clean. Leaving cake in pan, turn cake upside down on a wire rack to cool completely. Using cake pan as a pattern, cut a heart-shaped piece of cardboard. Place cooled cake on cardboard.

For glaze, melt chocolate and butter in a small saucepan over low heat; stir until smooth. Remove from heat; add sugar and vanilla. Stir until crumbly. Add water and stir until smooth. Spread glaze on sides and top of cake.

For garnish, cut one 1/8 x 4-inch strip of orange peel. Tie into a bow; set aside. For roses, remove remaining peel from oranges in 1-inch wide strips. Roll 1 strip of peel into a cone shape, then surround with another strip. Continue with remaining strips of peel until rose is desired size. Secure with toothpick. Repeat for remaining 2 roses. Arrange roses and bow on cake. Cover until ready to present.

Yield: about 10 servings

They are rich who have true friends.

—Thomas Fuller

CHOCOLATE-FILLED BUTTER CAKE

CAKE
- 1/2 cup butter or margarine, softened
- 1/3 cup firmly packed brown sugar
- 1/4 cup milk
- 1 1/2 teaspoons vanilla extract
- 1 cup all-purpose flour
- 1/8 teaspoon salt

FILLING
- 1/4 cup semisweet chocolate chips
- 1 tablespoon butter or margarine
  Whole almonds for garnish

Preheat oven to 350 degrees. In a large bowl, cream butter and sugar until fluffy. Add milk and vanilla; mix until well blended. In a medium bowl, sift together flour and salt. Add dry ingredients to creamed mixture; stir until well blended.

For filling, melt chocolate chips and butter in a medium saucepan over low heat; stir until smooth. Remove from heat. Spread 1/2 of batter evenly into a greased and floured 7-inch springform pan. Spread filling evenly over batter. Spread remaining batter over filling. Place almonds on top of batter. Bake 40 to 45 minutes or until edges are brown. Cool in pan 10 minutes; transfer to a wire rack to cool completely. Store in an airtight container.

Yield: about 6 servings

NO-BAKE BROWNIES

When a friend needs a little attention, the heart tells us to respond immediately. With these delicious No-Bake Brownies, it's easy to create a thoughtful treat, even when your time is short.

- 1 can (14 ounces) sweetened condensed milk
- 1 box (12 ounces) vanilla wafer cookies, finely crushed
- 1/2 cup chopped walnuts
- 1 ounce unsweetened chocolate, melted
- 1/2 cup semisweet chocolate chips, melted

In a large bowl, mix first 4 ingredients together until well blended using lowest speed of an electric mixer. Spread mixture evenly into a greased 9-inch diameter cake pan. Spread melted chocolate chips over top. Cover and refrigerate 1 hour or until firm. Cut into wedges to serve. Store in an airtight container in refrigerator.

Yield: about 10 to 12 brownies

If you need to say "I goofed," here's a lighthearted way to make amends: No-Fail Microwave Fudge in a box decorated with comics!

NO-FAIL MICROWAVE FUDGE

- 3$^1/_2$ cups confectioners sugar
- $^1/_2$ cup cocoa
- $^1/_4$ teaspoon salt
- $^1/_2$ cup butter or margarine, cut into pieces
- $^1/_4$ cup milk
- 1 tablespoon vanilla extract
- 1 cup candy-coated chocolate pieces

In a large microwave-safe bowl, combine first 3 ingredients; stir until well blended. Drop butter into sugar mixture. Microwave on High 1 to 2 minutes or until butter melts. Add milk, stirring until smooth. Microwave on High 1 minute longer. Stir in vanilla and chocolate pieces. Pour into a buttered 8-inch square baking pan. Chill 1 hour or until firm. Cut into 1-inch squares. Store in an airtight container.

Yield: about 5 dozen squares fudge

ROCKY ROAD TART

CRUST
- 1 cup granulated sugar
- 1 cup all-purpose flour
- 1 cup finely ground almonds
- 1 teaspoon baking powder
- 1/2 cup butter or margarine
- 2 ounces unsweetened chocolate
- 1 teaspoon vanilla extract

FILLING
- 6 ounces (two 3-ounce packages) cream cheese, softened
- 1/2 cup granulated sugar
- 1/4 cup butter or margarine, softened
- 2 tablespoons all-purpose flour
- 1 egg
- 1/2 teaspoon vanilla extract
- 1/2 cup slivered almonds
- 1 cup (6 ounces) semisweet chocolate chips
- 2 cups miniature marshmallows

Preheat oven to 350 degrees. For crust, combine first 4 ingredients in a medium bowl. In a small saucepan, melt butter and chocolate over low heat, stirring until smooth. Add chocolate mixture and vanilla to dry ingredients; stir until dough is crumbly. Press evenly into bottom of a greased and floured 9-inch springform pan.

For filling, beat cream cheese, sugar, and butter in a medium bowl until fluffy. Beat in next 3 ingredients. Fold in almonds and chocolate chips. Spoon batter evenly over crust. Bake 40 to 45 minutes or until a toothpick inserted in center comes out clean. Spread marshmallows evenly over top.

We all know that friendship makes the rough road smooth, so our Rocky Road Tart is a fitting gift for someone who makes your journey through life a little easier.

Bake 4 to 5 minutes longer or until marshmallows are light brown. Cool in pan 10 minutes. Remove sides of pan; cool completely. Store in an airtight container.

Yield: 8 to 10 servings

PINEAPPLE CAKE

Express your affection for a one-in-a-million friend with this extra-flavorful Pineapple Cake. Crushed pineapple, chopped walnuts, and sour cream, along with a hint of nutmeg and vanilla, give the moist cake its delicious taste.

CAKE
1³/4 cups all-purpose flour
1 teaspoon baking powder
1 teaspoon baking soda
1/2 teaspoon salt
1 teaspoon ground nutmeg
3/4 cup firmly packed brown sugar
1 cup drained, canned crushed pineapple
1/2 cup finely chopped walnuts
1 cup sour cream
1/3 cup vegetable oil
1 egg
2 teaspoons vanilla extract

ICING
6 cups confectioners sugar
6 tablespoons milk

Preheat oven to 350 degrees. For cake, sift together first 5 ingredients in a large bowl. Stir in next 3 ingredients. Add remaining ingredients; blend well using medium speed of an electric mixer. Pour batter into a greased and floured 9 x 13-inch baking pan. Bake 35 to 40 minutes or until a toothpick inserted in center of cake comes out clean. Cool completely on a wire rack.

For icing, combine sugar and milk in a large bowl; beat until smooth. Spread icing over top of cake and allow to harden. Cover with plastic wrap.
Yield: 12 to 14 servings

APPLE NUT TART

Make this special tart for someone who is the apple of your eye.

CRUST
1/3 cup butter or margarine, softened
1/2 cup granulated sugar
1 egg
1/2 teaspoon vanilla extract
1 cup all-purpose flour
1/3 cup finely ground almonds

FILLING
1/4 cup half and half
1 tablespoon cornstarch
1 can (21 ounces) apple pie filling
1/2 teaspoon ground cinnamon

TOPPING
1/2 cup slivered almonds
1 tablespoon granulated sugar
1/2 teaspoon ground cinnamon

Preheat oven to 350 degrees. For crust, cream butter and sugar in a large bowl until fluffy. Beat in egg and vanilla. Add flour and almonds; stir until a soft dough forms. Press into bottom and up sides of a greased 11-inch tart pan. Prick with a fork. Bake 10 minutes. Cool completely on a wire rack.

For filling, stir half and half and cornstarch together in a small bowl until smooth. In a small saucepan, combine pie filling and cinnamon. Cook over medium heat, stirring until heated through. Add half and half mixture to pie filling, stirring constantly until mixture begins to boil and thickens. Pour into crust.

For topping, combine all ingredients in small bowl. Sprinkle evenly over filling. Bake 20 to 25 minutes or until crust is golden brown. Remove from pan and cool completely on a wire rack. Store in an airtight container.

Yield: 8 to 10 servings

Ꭺ good neighbor, like an apron, is comfortable, protecting, and always appreciated a lot.

—Claudia Rohling

BLACKBERRY CUPCAKES

For a neighborly gift, present these wonderfully moist and fruity cupcakes along with a pretty apron.

1	cup butter or margarine, softened
3/4	cup granulated sugar
2	eggs
1	cup blackberry jam
3/4	teaspoon vanilla extract
1 3/4	cups all-purpose flour
1/8	teaspoon salt
1/2	cup whipping cream
1	cup chopped pecans
	Confectioners sugar

Preheat oven to 350 degrees. In a large bowl, cream butter and granulated sugar until fluffy. Add eggs 1 at a time, beating well after each addition. Beat in jam and vanilla. In a medium bowl, sift together flour and salt. Add dry ingredients alternately with whipping cream to creamed mixture; stir until well blended. Fold in pecans. Spoon batter into paper-lined muffin tins, filling each tin 2/3 full. Bake 30 to 35 minutes or until a toothpick inserted in center comes out clean. Transfer to a wire rack to cool completely. Dust with confectioners sugar. Store in an airtight container.

Yield: about 2 dozen cupcakes

I relish your friendship.

BLUEBERRY RELISH

1 bag (16 ounces) frozen
   unsweetened blueberries,
   thawed and drained well
1 apple, peeled, cored, and
   coarsely chopped
1 cup finely chopped pecans
$1/2$ cup granulated sugar
2 teaspoons apple cider vinegar
1 teaspoon ground allspice
$1/2$ teaspoon ground cinnamon
4 teaspoons lemon juice

In a large saucepan, combine first
7 ingredients. Stirring constantly, bring
to a boil over medium heat. Remove
from heat. Add lemon juice; stir until
well blended. Following Sealing Jars
instructions, page 505, fill jar. Store in
refrigerator. Serve with meat or bread.
Include serving suggestions with gift.
Yield: about 1 pint relish

BLACKBERRY CHUTNEY

2 tablespoons hot water
1 teaspoon unflavored gelatin
1 tablespoon vegetable oil
$1/4$ cup finely chopped celery
2 tablespoons finely chopped
   onion
1 package (16 ounces) frozen
   blackberries, thawed
$1/4$ cup red wine vinegar
3 tablespoons honey
2 tablespoons granulated sugar
$1/2$ teaspoon ground cinnamon

In a small bowl, combine water and
gelatin; stir until dissolved. In a medium
saucepan, heat oil over medium heat.
Add celery and onion; sauté until tender.
Add remaining ingredients; stir until
well blended. Bring to a boil; remove
from heat. Stir gelatin mixture into
blackberry mixture. Following Sealing
Jars instructions, page 505, fill jar. Store
in refrigerator. Serve with meat or bread.
Include serving suggestions with gift.
Yield: about 1 pint chutney

STRAWBERRY PIE

CRUST
$1^{1}/2$ cups all-purpose flour
$1/2$ teaspoon salt
$1/2$ cup vegetable shortening
4 tablespoons cold water

FILLING
1 box (3 ounces) strawberry-
   flavored gelatin
1 cup water
$1/2$ cup whipping cream
1 package (8 ounces) cream
   cheese, softened
1 cup confectioners sugar
1 pint strawberries, capped and
   sliced

GLAZE
1 teaspoon cornstarch
1 teaspoon water
3 tablespoons apple jelly
   Red food coloring

Preheat oven to 450 degrees. For crust,
sift together flour and salt in a medium

The perfect gift for your "sweetie pie," our Strawberry Pie features a creamy filling nestled in a flaky pastry shell.

bowl. Using a pastry blender or 2 knives, cut in shortening until mixture resembles a coarse meal. Sprinkle water over mixture; mix until a soft dough forms. On a lightly floured surface, use a floured rolling pin to roll out dough to ⅛-inch thickness. Transfer to a 9-inch pie pan and use a sharp knife to trim edges of dough. Prick crust with a fork. Bake 12 to 15 minutes or until light brown. Cool completely on a wire rack.

For filling, combine gelatin and water in a medium saucepan over medium heat, stirring until gelatin dissolves. Remove from heat. In a chilled large bowl, whip cream until stiff peaks form.

In another large bowl, beat cream cheese and sugar until fluffy. Beat whipped cream and cream cheese mixture together. Stir in gelatin. Spoon filling evenly into cooled crust. Arrange strawberries over filling.

For glaze, melt jelly in a small saucepan over medium heat. Combine cornstarch and water in a small bowl to form a paste. Whisk into jelly; remove from heat. Stir in 1 or 2 drops food coloring. Pour glaze evenly over strawberries. Chill 1 hour or until pie is set in center. Store in an airtight container in refrigerator. Serve chilled.
Yield: 8 to 10 servings

Friendship is the breathing rose, with sweets in every fold.

—Oliver Wendell Holmes

ROSE PETAL JAM

1²/₃ cups granulated sugar
1¹/₃ cups water
2 cups firmly packed fragrant rose petals from pesticide-free blossoms (about 15 large roses), washed
1 teaspoon rose flower water (available at gourmet food stores)
1 box (1³/₄ ounces) pectin
Red food coloring (optional)

In a large stockpot, combine sugar and water over medium-high heat; stir constantly until sugar dissolves. Stir petals and rose flower water into syrup. Bring to a rolling boil. Add pectin; stir until dissolved. Bring to a rolling boil again and boil 1 minute longer. Remove from heat; skim off foam. If desired, tint with food coloring. Following Sealing Jars instructions, page 505, pour into jars. Store in refrigerator.
Yield: about 1 pint jam

GRAPE JAM

1¹/₂ pounds (about 3 cups) red seedless grapes
2¹/₄ cups granulated sugar
1 cup water
1 tablespoon grated dried orange peel
1 box (1³/₄ ounces) pectin

In a large stockpot, combine first 4 ingredients over medium-high heat; stir constantly until sugar dissolves. Bring to a rolling boil. Add pectin; stir until dissolved. Bring to a rolling boil again and boil 1 minute longer. Remove from heat; skim off foam. Following Sealing Jars instructions, page 505, pour into jars Store in refrigerator.
Yield: about 2 pints jam

GRAPE-WINE JAM

1¹/₂ pounds (about 3 cups) red seedless grapes
2¹/₄ cups granulated sugar
1 cup dry red wine
1 tablespoon grated dried orange peel
1 box (1³/₄ ounces) pectin

In a large stockpot, combine first 4 ingredients over medium-high heat; stir constantly until sugar dissolves. Bring to a rolling boil. Add pectin; stir until dissolved. Bring to a rolling boil again and boil 1 minute longer. Remove from heat; skim off foam. Following Sealing Jars instructions, page 505, pour into jars. Store in refrigerator.
Yield: about 2 pints jam

ROSE PETAL TEA

2 cups firmly packed fragrant rose petals from pesticide-free blossoms (about 15 large roses), washed and patted dry
1 cup tea leaves

Preheat oven to 200 degrees. Place rose petals on an ungreased baking sheet. Leaving oven door slightly open, dry petals in oven 3 to 4 hours or until completely dry, stirring occasionally. In a food processor fitted with a steel blade, process rose petals and tea leaves until finely chopped. Store in an airtight container. Give with instructions for brewing tea.

To brew tea, place 1 teaspoon tea for each 8 ounces of water in a warm teapot. Bring water to a rolling boil and pour over tea. Steep tea 5 minutes, stir, and strain. Serve hot or chilled.
Yield: about 3 cups tea

RASPBERRY COCOA MIX

3 cups instant hot cocoa mix
1 package (0.13 ounces) unsweetened raspberry-flavored soft drink mix

Combine ingredients in a medium bowl; stir until well blended. Store in an airtight container. Give with serving instructions.

To serve, stir 2 heaping tablespoonfuls into 8 ounces hot water.
Yield: about 3 cups cocoa mix

You're the cream in my coffee.

CHOCOLATE-MALT COFFEE CREAMER

2 cups instant hot cocoa mix
2/3 cup nondairy powdered coffee creamer
2/3 cup malted milk mix
1/2 teaspoon ground cinnamon

Combine all ingredients in a large bowl; stir until well blended. Store in an airtight container. Give with serving instructions.

To serve, stir 2 heaping teaspoonfuls into 8 ounces hot coffee.
Yield: about 3 cups creamer

NIGHTCAP COFFEE MIX

2/3 cup nondairy powdered coffee creamer
1/3 cup instant coffee granules
1/3 cup granulated sugar
1 teaspoon ground cardamom
1/2 teaspoon ground cinnamon

Combine all ingredients in a medium bowl; stir until well blended. Store in an airtight container. Give with serving instructions.

To serve, spoon 1 heaping tablespoon coffee mix into 8 ounces hot coffee. Stir until well blended.
Yield: about 1 1/3 cups coffee mix

These fruity sugars make sweet little gifts. Flavored with powdered soft drink mixes, the sugars are a refreshing addition to iced tea, or you can serve them with cereal or fruit for an eye-opening breakfast treat. They can also be substituted for ordinary sugar in favorite recipes.

LEMON SUGAR

2 cups granulated sugar
1 package (0.31 ounces) unsweetened lemonade-flavored soft drink mix

In a small bowl, combine sugar and drink mix; stir until well blended. Store in an airtight container. Give with serving instructions.

Sprinkle sugar over cereal or fresh fruit, or stir into tea. Flavored sugar may also be substituted for granulated sugar in baking.

Yield: about 2 cups sugar

STRAWBERRY-BANANA SUGAR

2 cups granulated sugar
1 package (0.20 ounces) unsweetened strawberry-banana soft drink mix

In a small bowl, combine sugar and drink mix; stir until well blended. Store in an airtight container. Give with serving instructions.

Sprinkle sugar over cereal or fresh fruit, or stir into tea. Flavored sugar may also be substituted for granulated sugar in baking.

Yield: about 2 cups sugar

You add sweetness to my life.

FORGET-ME-NOT TEA

1 jar (15 ounces) instant orange breakfast drink mix
1 cup granulated sugar
1 cup unsweetened instant tea mix
$1/2$ cup presweetened lemonade mix
1 package (0.14 ounces) unsweetened cherry-flavored soft drink mix
2 teaspoons ground cinnamon
1 teaspoon ground nutmeg

In a large bowl, combine all ingredients; mix well. Store in an airtight container. Give with serving instructions.

To serve, stir 2 heaping tablespoons tea mix into 8 ounces hot or cold water.

Yield: about 4 cups tea mix

BLUEBERRY WINE

This delicious beverage is easy to make by adding fruit and sugar to white wine.

1 bottle (720 ml) dry white wine
3 cups unsweetened frozen blueberries, thawed
$1/4$ cup granulated sugar

Combine all ingredients in a large bowl; stir until sugar dissolves. Cover and chill 3 days to allow flavors to blend. Store in an airtight container in refrigerator. Serve chilled.

Yield: about 4 cups wine

> *New-made friendships,*
> *like new wine,*
> *Age will mellow*
> *and refine.*
>
> —Joseph Parry

WINE PUNCH

2   bottles (720 ml each) dry white wine
2   cans (12 ounces each) frozen pineapple juice concentrate, thawed
1   can (6 ounces) frozen lemonade concentrate, thawed
1   can (6 ounces) frozen orange juice concentrate, thawed
1   jar (10 ounces) maraschino cherries

In a 1 gallon container, combine first 4 ingredients, stirring until well blended. Stir in cherries. Cover and chill 8 hours or overnight to allow flavors to blend. Serve chilled.
Yield: about 3 quarts punch

A bottle of creamy Mint Cordial can help you tell someone special that you were meant to be friends. Thick and frothy, the drink has a cool, refreshing flavor.

MINT CORDIAL

1   can (14 ounces) sweetened condensed milk
1¹/₂   cups whipping cream
1   cup peppermint schnapps
2   teaspoons vanilla extract

Pour all ingredients into a blender and blend until smooth. Store in an airtight container in refrigerator. Shake well before serving. Serve chilled.
Yield: about 4 cups liqueur

LEMON JELLY

8 medium lemons, peeled,
  seeded, and coarsely chopped
7 cups water
4 1/2 cups granulated sugar
1 box (1 3/4 ounces) pectin
  Yellow food coloring

Combine lemons and water in a large stockpot over medium-high heat. Bring to a boil; reduce heat to medium. Simmer uncovered 45 minutes. Strain fruit mixture, reserving liquid. If necessary, add additional water to reserved liquid to equal 2 1/2 cups. Combine liquid and sugar in stockpot over medium heat; stir until sugar dissolves.

Increase heat to medium-high and bring to a rolling boil. Add pectin; stir until dissolved. Bring to a rolling boil again and boil 1 minute longer. Remove from heat; skim off foam. Tint to desired color.

Following Sealing Jars instructions, page 505, pour into jars. Store in refrigerator.

Yield: about 3 pints jelly

RADISH JELLY

2 cups (about two 6-ounce bags)
  finely chopped radishes
2 1/2 cups granulated sugar
3/4 cup water
1 box (1 3/4 ounces) pectin
2 teaspoons prepared
  horseradish

In a large stockpot, combine first 3 ingredients over medium-high heat; stir constantly until sugar dissolves. Bring to a rolling boil. Add pectin; stir until

dissolved. Bring to a rolling boil again and boil 1 minute longer. Remove from heat; skim off foam. Stir in horseradish. Following Sealing Jars instructions, page 505, pour into jars. Store in refrigerator. Serve with cream cheese and crackers or meat. Include serving suggestions with gift.

Yield: about 2 pints jelly

ORANGE CURD

1 cup milk
1 cup whipping cream
1/2 cup frozen orange juice
  concentrate, thawed
1 vanilla bean, cut in half
  lengthwise
6 egg yolks
2/3 cup granulated sugar
1 tablespoon all-purpose flour

In a large saucepan, combine first 4 ingredients over medium heat. Bring to a boil; remove from heat. Cover and let stand 15 minutes. Remove vanilla bean and use a sharp knife to scrape black seeds from bean into milk mixture. Return bean to milk mixture.

In a medium bowl, whisk remaining ingredients together until smooth. Add 1/2 cup milk mixture to egg mixture; stir until well blended. Add egg mixture to remaining milk mixture in saucepan. Stirring constantly, cook over medium-low heat 7 to 10 minutes or until mixture coats the back of a spoon. Do not boil. Remove from heat; strain mixture. Store in an airtight container in refrigerator. Serve with cookies, muffins, or toast.

Yield: about 2 1/2 cups orange curd

He who plants kindness, gathers love.

—Basil the Great

PUMPKIN BUTTER

1 can (16 ounces) pumpkin
1 tablespoon pumpkin pie spice
4¹/₂ cups granulated sugar
1 box (1³/₄ ounces) pectin

In a large saucepan, combine first 3 ingredients over medium heat; stir constantly until sugar dissolves. Bring to a rolling boil. Add pectin; stir until dissolved. Bring to a rolling boil again and boil 1 minute longer. Remove from heat; skim off foam. Following Sealing Jars instructions, below, pour into jars. Store in refrigerator. Serve with bread or muffins. Include serving suggestions with gift.
Yield: about 2 pints pumpkin butter

SEALING JARS: To seal jars, wash jars, lids, and screw rings in soapy water; rinse well. Place jars on a rack in a large Dutch oven. Place lids and screw rings in a saucepan; cover jars, lids, and screw rings with water. Bring both pans to a boil; boil 10 minutes. Remove from heat, leaving jars, lids, and screw rings in hot water until ready to use.

Immediately before filling, remove jars from hot water and drain well. Fill hot jars to within ¹/₄ inch of tops; wipe jar rims and threads. Quickly cover with lids; screw the rings on tightly. Invert jars 5 minutes; turn upright. If food is to be canned, use water-bath method as directed by the USDA. If food is not canned, store in refrigerator.

PESTO SALAD SPRINKLES

16 slices white bread, lightly toasted
1 package (¹/₂ ounce) pesto sauce mix
¹/₂ cup butter or margarine, melted
¹/₄ cup olive oil

Preheat oven to 375 degrees. Trim and discard crusts; cut bread into ¹/₂-inch cubes. In a large bowl, combine remaining ingredients; stir until well blended. Add bread and toss until well coated. Spread evenly on an ungreased baking sheet. Bake 12 to 15 minutes or until golden brown and crunchy. Store in an airtight container.
Yield: about 4 cups salad sprinkles

PUMPKIN PUDDING

2 cups milk
1 box (3 ounces) vanilla pudding mix (do not use instant)
1 can (16 ounces) pumpkin
1 teaspoon pumpkin pie spice

Combine milk and pudding mix in a medium saucepan. Cook over medium heat, stirring constantly, until mixture coats the back of a spoon (about 15 minutes). Remove from heat. Add remaining ingredients; stir until smooth. Store in an airtight container in refrigerator.
Yield: about 3 cups pudding

Here's a sweet gift for a friend who's a lot like you. Two-Berry Jam combines blackberries and raspberries in a spread that's perfect with biscuits or English muffins.

TWO-BERRY JAM

1   cup frozen blackberries,
       thawed and drained
1   cup frozen raspberries, thawed
       and drained
4   cups granulated sugar
1   package (3 ounces) liquid
       pectin

In a large stockpot, combine first 3 ingredients over medium-high heat. Bring to a rolling boil, stirring constantly until sugar dissolves. Stir in pectin. Bring to a rolling boil again and boil 1 minute longer. Remove from heat; skim foam from top. Following Sealing Jars instructions, page 505, fill jars. Store in refrigerator.

Yield: about 2 pints jam

RAINBOW FRUIT SALAD

- 1 can (14 ounces) sweetened condensed milk
- 1/4 cup frozen lemonade concentrate, thawed
- 1 can (16 ounces) mandarin oranges, drained
- 1 can (20 ounces) pineapple chunks, drained
- 2 kiwifruit, peeled and sliced
- 1 pint strawberries, capped and sliced

In a large bowl, stir together condensed milk and lemonade using medium speed of an electric mixer. Add remaining ingredients; stir by hand until fruit is well coated. Store in an airtight container in refrigerator.
Yield: about 10 servings

BLUE CHEESE DRESSING

- 3/4 cup olive oil
- 1/4 cup red wine vinegar
- 3 tablespoons Dijon-style mustard
- 2 green onions, finely chopped
- 1 teaspoon garlic powder
- 1 teaspoon salt
- 1/2 teaspoon ground black pepper
- 4 ounces blue cheese, crumbled

In a blender or a food processor fitted with a steel blade, process first 7 ingredients until smooth. Transfer to a small bowl; stir in cheese. Cover and chill 8 hours or overnight to allow flavors to blend. Store in an airtight container in refrigerator.
Yield: about 1 1/2 cups salad dressing

SUNSHINE PARFAITS

A friend who always brightens your day will be thrilled by this cheerful gift.

- 4 cups water, divided
- 1 box (3 ounces) orange-flavored gelatin
- 1 box (3 ounces) lemon-flavored gelatin
- 1 cup sour cream, divided
- 1 can (11 ounces) mandarin oranges, drained
- 1 can (8 ounces) pineapple tidbits, drained
  Whipped cream and fresh mint leaves for garnish (optional)

In a small saucepan, bring 2 cups water to a boil over high heat. Remove from heat. Add orange gelatin; stir until dissolved. Repeat with remaining water and lemon gelatin.

Pour 1/2 of orange gelatin into a small bowl. Add 1/2 cup sour cream; stir until well blended. Repeat for lemon gelatin. Add mandarin oranges to remaining orange gelatin. Add pineapple to remaining lemon gelatin. Cover and chill all gelatin mixtures until partially set.

Pour orange-sour cream mixture evenly into 4 tall glasses. Layer mandarin orange mixture, lemon-sour cream mixture, and pineapple mixture evenly into glasses. Cover and refrigerate until set. If desired, garnish with whipped cream and fresh mint leaves before giving gift.
Yield: 4 parfaits

TUNA AMANDINE CASSEROLE

2 tuna steaks (about 1¹/₄ pounds)
1 teaspoon salt, divided
¹/₂ teaspoon ground black pepper, divided
2 tablespoons vegetable oil
¹/₂ cup sliced almonds
¹/₄ cup butter or margarine
1 large onion, chopped
3 tablespoons all-purpose flour
2 cups milk
2 cups cooked rice
1 lemon, cut into thin slices (for garnish)

Rinse tuna steaks with cold water; pat dry with paper towels. Sprinkle both sides of tuna steaks evenly with ¹/₂ teaspoon salt and ¹/₄ teaspoon pepper. In a large skillet, heat oil over medium heat. Add tuna steaks and cook until brown and flaky, turning once. Transfer to paper towels to drain; set aside. Add next 3 ingredients to oil in skillet; sauté until onion is tender. Sprinkle flour and remaining salt and pepper evenly over onion mixture; stir until well blended. Continue to cook until flour begins to brown. Gradually stir in milk. Stirring constantly, bring to a boil and cook 3 to 5 minutes or until sauce thickens. Remove from heat.

Spoon rice into a 3-quart casserole. Break tuna steaks into pieces and place over rice. Pour sauce evenly over tuna. Garnish with sliced lemon. Cover and refrigerate until ready to present. Give with serving instructions.

To serve, preheat oven to 350 degrees. Cover and bake 25 to 30 minutes or until heated through.
Yield: 6 to 8 servings

WHITE CHILI

2 tablespoons vegetable oil
1 medium white onion, finely chopped
1 can (4 ounces) chopped green chilies
2 teaspoons garlic powder
2 teaspoons salt
2 teaspoons ground cumin
2 teaspoons ground oregano
2 teaspoons ground coriander
¹/₂ teaspoon cayenne pepper
2 cans (15.8 ounces each) great northern beans (do not drain)
2 cans (10¹/₂ ounces each) chicken broth
2 cans (5 ounces each) chicken, drained

In a large stockpot, heat oil over medium heat. Add onion; sauté until brown. Add next 7 ingredients; stir until well blended. Stir in remaining ingredients. Bring to a boil; reduce heat to low and simmer 15 to 20 minutes. Store in an airtight container in refrigerator. Give with serving instructions.

To serve, transfer chili to a large stockpot. Cook over medium heat 10 to 15 minutes or until heated through.
Yield: 8 to 10 servings

A meal becomes a feast when shared with friends.

SALMON POT PIE

CRUST
- 2 cups all-purpose flour
- 1 teaspoon salt
- 2/3 cup vegetable shortening
- 6 tablespoons cold water

FILLING
- 2 tablespoons vegetable oil
- 2 salmon steaks (about 10 ounces)
- 1 teaspoon salt, divided
- 1/2 teaspoon ground black pepper, divided
- 3 tablespoons all-purpose flour
- 1 teaspoon garlic powder
- 1 teaspoon dried rosemary, crushed
- 2 cups milk
- 2 cans (16 ounces each) mixed vegetables, drained
- 1 egg, beaten

For crust, sift together flour and salt in a medium bowl. Using a pastry blender or 2 knives, cut shortening into flour mixture until mixture resembles coarse meal. Sprinkle water over mixture. Knead until a soft dough forms. On a lightly floured surface, use a floured rolling pin to roll out 2/3 of dough to 1/4-inch thickness. Transfer rolled dough to a 1/2-quart round casserole (dough will drape over sides of dish). Cover casserole and remaining dough with plastic wrap.

Preheat oven to 400 degrees. For filling, heat oil in a large skillet over medium heat. Sprinkle salmon evenly with 1/2 teaspoon salt and 1/4 teaspoon pepper. Place salmon in skillet and cook until flaky, turning once. Transfer to paper towels. Add remaining salt and pepper and next 3 ingredients to skillet; stir to make a paste. Gradually add milk; stir until smooth. Stir in vegetables. Stirring constantly, bring to a boil; cook 3 to 5 minutes or until sauce thickens. Remove skin and bones from fish. Break into pieces and stir into sauce. Pour filling into crust. Fold edges of crust over filling. Brush edges with egg. On a lightly floured surface, use a floured rolling pin to roll remaining dough to 1/4-inch thickness for top crust. Place crust over filling. Bake 45 to 50 minutes or until brown. Cool completely on a wire rack. Cover and refrigerate until ready to present. Give with serving instructions.

To serve, preheat oven to 350 degrees. Cover and bake 25 to 30 minutes or until heated through.

Yield: about 8 servings

CHICKEN TURNOVERS

1 tablespoon sesame oil
6 green onions, chopped
1/2 pound fresh mushrooms, chopped
3 cloves garlic, minced
1/2 teaspoon salt
1/4 teaspoon ground black pepper
1 can (5 ounces) chicken, drained
1 package (17 1/4 ounces) frozen puff pastry dough, thawed according to package directions
4 ounces Havarti cheese, grated

Preheat oven to 350 degrees. In a large skillet, heat oil over medium heat. Add next 5 ingredients; sauté until onions are brown. Stir in chicken. Remove from heat.

On a lightly floured surface, use a floured rolling pin to roll out each sheet of pastry to an 8 x 12-inch rectangle. Using a sharp knife, cut pastry into 4-inch squares. Spoon about 1 tablespoon chicken mixture into center of each square. Sprinkle about 2 teaspoons cheese over chicken mixture. Fold pastry over chicken and cheese, forming a triangle. Crimp edges together with a fork. Transfer to a greased baking sheet. Bake 20 to 25 minutes or until brown. Transfer to a wire rack to cool completely. Store in an airtight container in refrigerator. Give with serving instructions.

Turnovers may be served at room temperature or reheated. To reheat, preheat oven to 350 degrees. Bake uncovered on an ungreased baking sheet 8 to 10 minutes or until heated through.
Yield: 1 dozen turnovers

CHICKEN PAPRIKA

1/2 cup butter or margarine
1 medium onion, chopped
1/2 cup chopped celery
1 teaspoon dried minced garlic
2 teaspoons paprika
1 teaspoon salt
1/2 teaspoon ground black pepper
2 cans (5 ounces each) chicken, drained
1/2 cup all-purpose flour
1 can (10 1/2 ounces) chicken broth
1 cup half and half
2 cups cooked rice

In a large stockpot, melt butter over medium heat. Add next 3 ingredients and sauté until onion and celery are tender. Stir in next 4 ingredients. Sprinkle flour evenly over chicken mixture; stir until well blended. Cook until heated through. Stirring constantly, gradually add chicken broth and cook until mixture begins to thicken. Stir in half and half and rice. Cook 5 to 10 minutes or until heated through. Remove from heat. Transfer to a 2-quart casserole. Cover and refrigerate until ready to present. Give with serving instructions.

To serve, preheat oven to 350 degrees. Bake covered 25 to 30 minutes or until heated through.
Yield: 6 to 8 servings

CHICKEN-ONION SOUP

Shown on page 9: When someone is ailing, a friend's smiling face can help speed the recovery. You'll be a sure cure when you deliver Chicken-Onion Soup, an old home remedy with zesty new flavor.

4 tablespoons butter or margarine
2 tablespoons olive oil
5 medium onions, coarsely chopped
4 cloves garlic, minced
3 tablespoons all-purpose flour
1 tablespoon Dijon-style mustard
1 teaspoon granulated sugar
1 teaspoon salt
1 teaspoon ground black pepper
1/2 teaspoon ground thyme
6 cans (14 1/2 ounces each) beef broth
1 1/2 cups dry white wine
3 cans (5 ounces each) chicken, drained
1/3 cup cognac

In a large stockpot, heat butter and oil over medium-high heat. Add onions and garlic; sauté until tender. Add next 7 ingredients; stir until well blended. Gradually stir in beef broth and wine. Stir in chicken. Bring to a boil; reduce heat to low and simmer 30 minutes. Remove from heat. Stir in cognac. Store in an airtight container in refrigerator. Give with serving instructions.

To serve, transfer soup to a large stockpot. Cook over medium heat 15 to 20 minutes or until heated through, stirring occasionally.

Yield: about 12 servings

TORTELLINI SALAD

2 packages (9 ounces each) refrigerated cheese-filled tortellini (we used spinach and plain tortellini)
6 ounces pepperoni, cut into pieces
3/4 cup olive oil
1/2 cup white wine vinegar
6 green onions, coarsely chopped
3 tablespoons chopped fresh parsley
1 tablespoon garlic salt
2 teaspoons dried crushed basil
1 teaspoon salt
1/4 teaspoon ground black pepper

Cook tortellini according to package directions. Drain and rinse with cold water. Transfer tortellini to a large bowl; add pepperoni. In a blender or food processor fitted with a steel blade, process remaining ingredients until well blended. Pour oil mixture over tortellini mixture; toss until well coated. Cover and refrigerate 8 hours or overnight to allow flavors to blend.

Yield: 8 to 10 servings

The greatest medicine is a true friend.

—Sir William Temple

This dreamy Seventh Heaven Layered Salad will be a blessing for a busy friend who's hosting a luncheon or dinner party.

SEVENTH HEAVEN LAYERED SALAD

DRESSING
- 1 package (8 ounces) cream cheese, softened
- 1 cup mayonnaise
- 1 cup sour cream
- 1 teaspoon dried ground basil leaves
- 1/2 teaspoon garlic powder
- 1/2 teaspoon onion powder

SALAD
- 1/2 head iceberg lettuce, chopped
- 2 large tomatoes, chopped
- 1 large cucumber, sliced
- 4 large carrots, peeled and sliced
- 10 green onions, finely chopped
- 2 cups (8 ounces) grated sharp Cheddar cheese
- 1 pound bacon, cooked and crumbled

For dressing, combine all ingredients in a medium bowl; blend well using medium speed of an electric mixer. Cover and set aside.

For salad, layer vegetables and cheese in desired order in a trifle bowl or large glass container. Spread dressing evenly over vegetables. Garnish with crumbled bacon. Cover and store in refrigerator.
Yield: about 10 servings

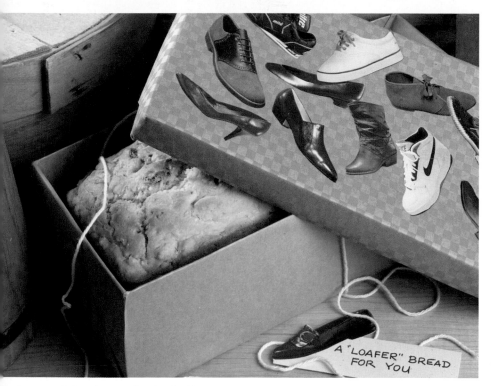

A decorated shoe box with a loaf of hearty Bacon Batter Bread is a lighthearted way to let a special friend know that no one else could take his or her place in your heart.

BACON BATTER BREAD

1   pound bacon
3   cups all-purpose flour
1/4 cup granulated sugar
2   tablespoons baking powder
2   teaspoons salt
3   eggs
1/2 teaspoon liquid smoke
      flavoring
1 1/2 cups milk

In a large skillet, cook bacon over medium heat until crisp. Transfer to paper towels to drain; reserve 1/3 cup bacon drippings. Cool bacon to room temperature, crumble, and set aside.

Preheat oven to 350 degrees. In a large bowl, combine next 4 ingredients. In a medium bowl, whisk together reserved bacon drippings and next 3 ingredients. Add egg mixture to dry ingredients; stir just until moistened. Fold in bacon. Pour batter into a greased 5 x 9-inch loaf pan. Bake 45 to 50 minutes or until a toothpick inserted in center comes out clean. Cool in pan 10 minutes; turn onto a wire rack to cool completely. Store in an airtight container.
Yield: 1 loaf bread

BLACK-EYED PEA SOUP

A friend who's fond of homestyle cooking will love this Southern gift. Our easy Black-Eyed Pea Soup is loaded with chunks of pepper, tomato, onion, and bacon. Teamed with Cheddar Johnny Cakes, the spicy dish makes a hearty meal.

- 6 slices bacon
- 1 large onion, finely chopped
- 1 clove garlic, minced
- 1 teaspoon salt
- 1/2 teaspoon ground black pepper
- 1 can (4 ounces) chopped jalapeño peppers
- 4 cans (15.8 ounces each) black-eyed peas
- 2 cans (14 1/2 ounces each) beef stock
- 1 can (10 ounces) diced tomatoes and green chilies

In a large stockpot, cook bacon over medium heat until crisp. Transfer to paper towels to drain; crumble bacon. Add next 5 ingredients to bacon drippings in pot; sauté until onion is brown. Add bacon and remaining ingredients. Increase heat to medium-high and bring to a boil. Remove from heat. Store in an airtight container in refrigerator. Give with serving instructions.

To serve, transfer soup to a stockpot. Cook over medium-high heat 10 to 15 minutes or until heated through, stirring occasionally. Serve with Cheddar Johnny Cakes (recipe follows).

Yield: 12 to 14 servings

CHEDDAR JOHNNY CAKES

- 1 cup all-purpose flour
- 1 cup cornmeal
- 4 teaspoons baking powder
- 1 teaspoon salt
- 1/2 teaspoon baking soda
- 1 egg
- 1 1/2 cups buttermilk
- 1/4 cup butter or margarine, melted
- 1 1/2 cups (6 ounces) grated sharp Cheddar cheese
- 1/2 cup vegetable oil

In a large bowl, stir together first 5 ingredients. In a medium bowl, whisk together next 3 ingredients. Add egg mixture to dry ingredients; stir just until moistened. Fold in cheese.

In a large skillet, heat oil over medium heat. Drop tablespoonfuls of batter into hot oil. Turning once, cook 3 to 4 minutes or until brown. Transfer to paper towels to drain. Store in an airtight container in refrigerator. Give with serving instructions.

To serve, preheat oven to 350 degrees. Bake uncovered 5 to 8 minutes or until heated through. Serve with Black-Eyed Pea Soup.

Yield: about 1 1/2 dozen Johnny Cakes

"Bee" my honey.

ANGEL BISCUITS

2 1/2 cups biscuit baking mix
 1/2 cup sweetened shredded
     coconut
   1 cup whipping cream
   2 tablespoons butter or
     margarine, melted

Preheat oven to 450 degrees. In a large bowl, combine baking mix and coconut. Add cream and stir until well blended. Turn dough onto a lightly floured surface and knead about 1 minute. Use a floured rolling pin to roll out dough to 1/2-inch thickness. Use a floured 2-inch biscuit cutter to cut out dough. Place biscuits 2 inches apart on a greased baking sheet and brush tops with melted butter. Bake 7 to 10 minutes or until light brown. Transfer to a wire rack to cool completely. Store in an airtight container. Give with serving instructions.
To serve, preheat oven to 350 degrees. Cover and bake 3 to 5 minutes or until heated through.
Yield: about 1 1/2 dozen biscuits

ORANGE HONEY

   1 cup honey
1 1/2 teaspoons orange-flavored
     extract

In a small bowl, combine honey and extract; stir until well blended. Store in an airtight container. Give with serving instructions.
Serve with bread, crackers, cake, or ice cream. Flavored honey may be substituted for plain honey in baking.
Yield: about 1 cup honey

SPAGHETTI BREAD

3 1/2 ounces (1/2 of 7-ounce
     package) thin spaghetti,
     cooked, drained, and rinsed
     with cold water
   2 cups all-purpose flour
   1 cup whole wheat flour
 1/3 cup grated Parmesan cheese
   1 package active dry yeast
   1 tablespoon granulated sugar
   1 teaspoon garlic salt
 1/2 teaspoon dried basil leaves
 1/2 teaspoon dried oregano leaves
1 1/2 cups warm water
   1 tablespoon olive oil

In a large bowl, combine first 9 ingredients. In a medium bowl, whisk together water and oil. Gradually add oil mixture to dry ingredients; knead until a soft dough forms. Turn dough onto a lightly floured surface and knead about 5 minutes or until dough becomes elastic and pliable. Place dough in a greased bowl; grease top of dough. Cover and let rise in a warm place (80 to 85 degrees) 1 hour or until doubled in size. Turn dough onto a lightly floured surface and punch down. Shape into a loaf and place in a greased 5 x 9-inch loaf pan. Grease top of dough. Cover and let rise in a warm place 1 hour or until doubled in size.
Preheat oven to 350 degrees. Bake 30 to 35 minutes or until brown and bread sounds hollow when tapped. Transfer to a wire rack to cool completely. Store in an airtight container.
Yield: 1 loaf bread

Make your best friend feel like a winner with a hearty loaf of homemade Onion-Pecan Bread topped with a blue ribbon.

ONION-PECAN BREAD

    3   cups all-purpose flour
    1   package active dry yeast
 1¹/2   teaspoons granulated sugar
 1¹/2   teaspoons salt
  ³/4   cup finely chopped pecans
  ¹/2   cup finely chopped red onion
    1   cup plus 1 tablespoon milk
  ¹/4   cup butter

Sift first 4 ingredients together in a large bowl. Stir in pecans and onion. In a small saucepan, combine milk and butter over medium-low heat. Stir occasionally until milk mixture reaches 130 degrees (butter may not be completely melted). Stir milk mixture into dry ingredients; knead until a soft dough forms.

Turn dough onto a lightly floured surface. Knead about 5 minutes or until dough becomes elastic and pliable. Form into a ball. Place dough in a greased bowl, grease top of dough, and cover. Let rise in a warm place (80 to 85 degrees) 1 hour or until doubled in size. Punch down dough and form into a loaf shape. Transfer to a greased 5 x 9-inch loaf pan. Grease top of dough and cover. Let rise in a warm place 1 hour or until doubled in size.

Preheat oven to 375 degrees. Bake 35 to 40 minutes or until golden brown. Invert onto a wire rack to cool completely. Store in an airtight container. **Yield:** 1 loaf bread

Simply Delicious
FOOD GIFTS

Irish Soda Bread Mix, page 544

Looking for gifts that say you care?
Treat loved ones to ready-to-fix mixes
that make something delicious!

INSTANT CHOCOLATE MOUSSE MIX

    1   package (6 ounces) instant
        chocolate pudding mix
    1   package (1 1/4 ounces) whipped
        dessert topping mix
 2 1/3 cups milk to serve

Combine pudding mix and topping mix in a small bowl. Place mousse mix in a resealable plastic bag. Give with serving instructions.

To serve: Combine mousse mix and 2 1/3 cups milk in a large mixing bowl. Beat with electric mixer at high speed until fluffy. Serve immediately or chill until ready to serve.
Yield: 6 to 8 servings

Variations: For Mocha Mousse, add 2 teaspoons instant coffee granules to dry mix. For Mint Mousse, add 1/4 teaspoon peppermint extract to dry mix.

CHOCOLATE CUPS
Chocolate cups also make perfect containers for chocolate mousse or fresh fruit.

    4   ounces semisweet baking chocolate
    1   tablespoon butter
    8   foil muffin cups
        Ice cream, Irish Smoothie
        (recipe on this page), and
        fresh sweet cherries to serve

In a heavy small saucepan, melt chocolate and butter over low heat, stirring constantly (do not overheat).

Cool until slightly thickened. Place 1 tablespoon chocolate mixture in a foil cup; spread over bottom and sides. Place another foil cup on top of chocolate and press lightly. Repeat with remaining chocolate mixture. Refrigerate or freeze until firm. Give with serving instructions.
Yield: 4 chocolate cups

To serve: Carefully remove foil liners. Fill each chocolate cup with ice cream; top with Irish Smoothie and a cherry.

IRISH SMOOTHIE
Delicious stirred into coffee or poured over ice cream that is served in Chocolate Cups (recipe on this page).

    2   cups whipping cream
    1   cup sweetened condensed milk
  3/4   cup Irish whiskey
  1/2   cup brandy
    2   tablespoons chocolate syrup
    1   tablespoon instant coffee
        granules
    1   teaspoon vanilla extract
    1   teaspoon almond extract

Combine whipping cream, condensed milk, whiskey, brandy, chocolate syrup, coffee granules, and extracts in a blender until well mixed. Pour into gift containers. Cover and store in refrigerator. Give with serving instructions for Chocolate Cups.
Yield: about 4 1/4 cups liqueur

stant Chocolate Mousse Mix will delight the chocolate lovers on your gift list. All they ave to do to enjoy this creamy treat is add milk and beat until fluffy.

or a tasty surprise, present some Chocolate Cups for serving ice cream. Include a bottle of ch, creamy Irish Smoothie to pour over the treat or to stir into coffee.

SPECIAL CHERRY COBBLER TOPPING

Present with a fresh pound cake or ice cream.

1 can (16 ounces) pitted dark cherries in heavy syrup
3 tablespoons sugar
1 tablespoon cornstarch
1 teaspoon freshly squeezed lemon juice
2 tablespoons Chambord (raspberry-flavored liqueur)
  Pound cake to serve

Drain cherries, reserving $1/2$ cup syrup. Process cherries in a food processor until coarsely chopped. In a small saucepan, combine cherries, sugar, cornstarch, lemon juice, and reserved cherry syrup. Stirring constantly, cook over medium-low heat until mixture comes to a boil. Continuing to stir, cook 1 minute or until mixture thickens. Remove from heat and stir in liqueur. Store in an airtight container in refrigerator. Give with serving instructions.

Yield: about $1^1/_3$ cups topping

To serve: Pour warm topping over pound cake or ice cream.

APPLE CRISP KIT

2 cups all-purpose flour
1 cup firmly packed brown sugar
1 cup old-fashioned oats
$1/2$ teaspoon ground cinnamon
$1/2$ teaspoon salt
$1/4$ teaspoon ground nutmeg
1 cup chilled butter or margarine
1 cup chopped pecans
4 cans (21 ounces each) apple pie filling to give

In a large bowl, combine flour, brown sugar, oats, cinnamon, salt, and nutmeg. Using a pastry blender or 2 knives, cut in butter until mixture resembles coarse meal. Stir in pecans. Divide topping into 2 resealable plastic bags; store in refrigerator. Give each bag of topping with 2 cans apple pie filling and serving instructions.

Yield: about 7 cups topping

To serve: Spread 2 cans apple pie filling in a lightly greased 9 x 13-inch baking dish. Sprinkle topping over apples. Bake in a 400-degree oven 19 to 21 minutes or until filling bubbles and topping is golden brown. Serve warm.

Yield: about 12 servings

NUTTY ICE CREAM CRUMBLE

2 cups all-purpose flour
1 cup butter or margarine, softened
1 cup chopped pecans
$1/2$ cup firmly packed brown sugar
$1/2$ cup quick-cooking oats

Preheat oven to 400 degrees. In a medium bowl, combine all ingredients. Spread in an ungreased 10 x 15-inch jellyroll pan. Bake 15 minutes or until lightly browned, stirring once halfway through baking. Cool in pan. Store in an airtight container. Give with a purchased ice cream sauce and serving instructions.
Yield: about 5 cups topping

To serve: Sprinkle over ice cream topped with a purchased sauce.

PEACH-AMARETTO YOGURT FLAVORING

1 jar (18 ounces) peach jam or
    preserves
$1/4$ cup amaretto liqueur
$1/4$ cup chopped pecans
$1/8$ teaspoon amaretto-flavored oil
    (used for candy making)

In a small saucepan, melt jam over low heat, stirring occasionally. Remove from heat. Add liqueur, pecans, and amaretto-flavored oil; stir until well blended. Store in an airtight container in refrigerator. Give with vanilla-flavored yogurt and serving instructions.
Yield: about $13/4$ cups yogurt flavoring

To serve: Stir $1/4$ cup yogurt flavoring into one 8-ounce carton vanilla-flavored yogurt.

TASTY FRUIT DIP MIX

1 cup firmly packed brown sugar
3 tablespoons chopped crystallized
    ginger
2 teaspoons ground cinnamon
    Apples to give

Process brown sugar, ginger, and cinnamon in a food processor until ginger is finely chopped. Store in an airtight container. Give with apples and serving instructions.
Yield: about $11/4$ cups mix

To serve: In a small bowl, beat 3 tablespoons mix into one 8-ounce package softened cream cheese until well blended. Cover and chill 1 hour to let flavors blend. Serve with pieces of fruit.
Yield: about 1 cup spread

CHRISTMAS COOKIE KITS

1 cup butter or margarine, softened
1/2 cup vegetable shortening
5 cups all-purpose flour
2 1/2 cups granulated sugar
1 cup firmly packed brown sugar
2 teaspoons baking powder
1 teaspoon salt
Cookie cutters and red and green decorating sugars to give with mixes

In a small bowl, beat butter and shortening until fluffy. In a large bowl, combine flour, granulated sugar, brown sugar, baking powder, and salt. Using a pastry blender or 2 knives, cut butter mixture into dry ingredients until mixture resembles coarse meal. Divide cookie mix in half and place in 2 resealable plastic bags. Store in refrigerator. Give each mix with a 3-inch star-shaped cookie cutter, decorating sugars, and recipe for Christmas Cookies.
Yield: about 11 1/2 cups cookie mix

CHRISTMAS COOKIES
1 bag (about 5 3/4 cups) Cookie Mix
1 egg
1/4 cup water
1 teaspoon vanilla extract

Preheat oven to 375 degrees. In a large bowl, combine cookie mix, egg, water, and vanilla; stir until a soft dough forms. On a lightly floured surface, use a floured rolling pin to roll out dough to 1/4-inch thickness. Use cookie cutter to cut out cookies. Transfer to a greased baking sheet. Sprinkle cookies with decorating sugar. Bake 6 to 8 minutes or until bottoms are lightly browned. Transfer cookies to a wire rack to cool. Store in an airtight container.
Yield: about 3 1/2 dozen cookies

PRALINES

1 3/4 cups granulated sugar
1 1/4 cups firmly packed brown sugar
1 cup evaporated milk
1/2 cup butter or margarine
2 tablespoons dark corn syrup
4 cups pecan halves

In a heavy large saucepan, combine granulated sugar, brown sugar, evaporated milk, butter, and corn syrup. Stirring occasionally, bring to a boil over medium heat. Attach a candy thermometer to pan, making sure themometer does not touch bottom of pan. Cook, without stirring, until mixture reaches soft-ball stage (approximately 234 to 240 degrees). Test about 1/2 teaspoon of mixture in ice water. Mixture will easily form a ball in ice water but will flatten when held in your hand. Transfer to a heat-resistant medium bowl and beat with an electric mixer about 5 minutes. Stir in pecans. Drop by teaspoonfuls onto waxed paper; cool completely. Store in an airtight container. Present a dozen or so in a decorated gift jar.
Yield: about 48 small pralines

GINGERBREAD MIX
Shown on page 9)

7¹/₂ cups all-purpose flour
1¹/₄ cups granulated sugar
¹/₂ cup firmly packed brown sugar
3 tablespoons ground cinnamon
2 tablespoons baking powder
2 tablespoons finely chopped
    crystallized ginger
1 tablespoon ground ginger
1 teaspoon salt
2 teaspoons baking soda
2 teaspoons dried orange peel
1 teaspoon ground cloves
2 cups vegetable shortening

In a very large bowl, combine flour, sugars, cinnamon, baking powder, crystallized ginger, ground ginger, salt, baking soda, orange peel, and cloves. Using a pastry blender or 2 knives, cut in shortening until mixture resembles coarse meal. Store in an airtight container in a cool place. To give, place about 3¹/₄ cups mix in each of four 1-quart resealable plastic bags; give with Gingerbread Cookie Instructions.
Yield: about 13 cups mix (4 gifts)

Gingerbread Cookie Instructions:
Make Your Own Gingerbread Boys!
1. Pour mix into large bowl.
2. Add ¹/₄ cup molasses, 2 tablespoons brewed coffee, and 1 lightly beaten egg; beat until well blended.
3. Roll out dough to ¹/₈-inch thickness on a floured surface. Cut out with cookie cutter.
4. Place 1 inch apart on an ungreased baking sheet; bake 6 to 8 minutes at 375 degrees.
Yield: about 12 cookies

SLICE-AND-BAKE COOKIES

³/₄ cup butter or margarine, softened
1¹/₄ cups sugar
1 egg
1 teaspoon vanilla extract
2 cups all-purpose flour
¹/₂ teaspoon salt

In a large bowl, cream butter and sugar until fluffy. Add egg and vanilla; beat until smooth. In a small bowl, combine flour and salt. Add dry ingredients to creamed mixture; stir until a soft dough forms. Divide dough in half. Place each half on plastic wrap. Use plastic wrap to shape dough into two 8-inch-long rolls. Chill 3 hours or until firm (if rolls have flattened, reshape into a round shape). Give with baking instructions.
Yield: 2 rolls of dough

To bake: Preheat oven to 375 degrees. Cut dough into ¹/₄-inch slices. Place 1 inch apart on a lightly greased baking sheet. Bake 6 to 8 minutes or until bottoms are lightly browned. Transfer cookies to a wire rack to cool. Store in an airtight container.
Yield: about 2¹/₂ dozen cookies from each roll

GIANT SNOWMAN COOKIE KIT

5 cups all-purpose flour
3¹/₂ cups sugar
2 teaspoons baking powder
1 teaspoon salt
1¹/₂ cups vegetable shortening
   Candy corn, black jelly beans, and
   cherry string twist licorice to
   decorate

In a large bowl, combine flour, sugar, baking powder, and salt. Using a pastry blender or 2 knives, cut shortening into dry ingredients until mixture resembles coarse meal. Divide cookie mix in half and place in 2 resealable plastic bags. Store in refrigerator. Give each bag of mix with a 7-inch-wide x 9-inch-high gingerbread boy cookie cutter, cookie decorations, and recipe for Snowman Cookies.
Yield: about 11 cups cookie mix (5¹/₂ cups in each bag)

SNOWMAN COOKIES

   Cookie Mix (5¹/₂ cups)
1 egg
¹/₄ cup water
1 teaspoon vanilla extract
   Confectioners sugar

Preheat oven to 375 degrees. In a large bowl, combine cookie mix, egg, water, and vanilla; stir until well blended. Shape into a ball. On greased aluminum foil, use a rolling pin dusted with confectioners sugar to roll out dough to ¹/₄-inch thickness. Transfer foil with dough to baking sheet. Use cookie cutter to cut out cookie; remove dough scraps. Bake 10 to 12 minutes or until bottom is lightly browned. Transfer cookie on foil to a flat surface to decorate. Decorate warm cookie with candies. Use candy corn for nose, jelly bean halves for eyes and buttons, and 3 strings of licorice for scarf. Repeat with remaining dough and candies to make 3 additional snowmen. Allow cookies to cool before removing from foil.

Shape remaining dough into 4 balls; place on a greased baking sheet. Press into ¹/₄-inch-thick "snowballs." Bake 7 to 9 minutes or until bottoms are lightly browned. Store in an airtight container.
Yield: about 4 large snowman cookies and 4 snowball cookies

What a fun gift for a family! This Giant Snowman takes shape from our Cookie Kit, which includes cookie mix and assorted candies to decorate the cookie. Each batch yields enough dough to make four snowmen—and several snowballs, too! For a cool presentation, pack the supplies in decorated bags and place the sacks, a cookie cutter, and baking instructions in a ribbon-tied basket.

BAKING SPICE

- 6 tablespoons ground cinnamon
- 1 tablespoon ground allspice
- 2 teaspoons ground nutmeg
- 1 teaspoon ground cloves
- $1/2$ teaspoon ground ginger

In a medium bowl, combine cinnamon, allspice, nutmeg, cloves, and ginger. Substitute baking spice in cake, muffin, or bread recipes that use any of the above spices. Can also be sprinkled on hot cereal or toast. Give with recipe for Spice Coffee Cake (recipe on this page).
Yield: about $1/2$ cup baking spice

SPICE COFFEE CAKE

- 2 cups all-purpose flour
- 1 cup firmly packed brown sugar
- $1^1/4$ teaspoons Baking Spice, divided (recipe on this page)
- $1/2$ cup chilled butter or margarine, cut into pieces
- 1 cup buttermilk
- 1 teaspoon baking soda
- 1 egg
- 1 teaspoon vanilla extract
- $1/2$ cup chopped walnuts

Preheat oven to 350 degrees. In a large bowl, combine flour, brown sugar, and 1 teaspoon baking spice. Using a pastry blender or 2 knives, cut in butter until mixture resembles coarse meal. Reserve $1/2$ cup of crumb mixture. In a small bowl, combine buttermilk and baking soda. Add buttermilk mixture, egg, and vanilla to remaining crumb mixture; stir just until moistened. Pour batter into a greased 9-inch square baking pan. Combine reserved crumb mixture, walnuts, and remaining $1/4$ teaspoon baking spice. Sprinkle over batter. Bake 27 to 30 minutes or until a toothpick inserted in center of cake comes out clean. Cool cake in pan 15 minutes. Cut into 2-inch squares and serve warm.
Yield: about 16 servings

FUNNEL CAKE MIX

- 1 cup all-purpose flour
- 1 teaspoon baking powder
- $1/4$ teaspoon salt
- $1/2$ teaspoon ground cinnamon

Combine all ingredients, stirring well. Store in an airtight container. Give mix with instructions for making Funnel Cakes.
Yield: 1 cup of mix, enough for 6 Funnel Cakes

To make Funnel Cakes: Pour vegetable oil into a skillet to a depth of 1 inch. Heat oil to 360 degrees over medium-high heat. In a small bowl, combine 1 egg with $3/4$ cup of milk. Add 1 cup Funnel Cake Mix and beat with fork until smooth. Holding finger under funnel opening, pour about $1/4$ cup of batter into funnel. Allow batter to pour from funnel into hot oil, moving funnel in a circle to form a spiral shape. Fry 1 minute, turn cake, and continue frying until golden brown. Remove to paper towels to drain. Sprinkle with confectioners sugar.
Yield: 6 Funnel Cakes

MOCHA-CHOCOLATE CHIP CAKE MIX

CAKE MIX
- 1 package (18$^1/_4$ ounces) devil's food cake mix with pudding in the mix
- 1 cup semisweet chocolate mini chips
- 1$^1/_2$ tablespoons instant coffee granules

ICING MIX
- 2 cups confectioners sugar
- 3 tablespoons cocoa
- 1 teaspoon instant coffee granules

For cake mix, combine cake mix, chocolate chips, and coffee granules. Store in an airtight container.

For icing mix, sift confectioners sugar, cocoa, and coffee granules into a small bowl. Store in an airtight container.

Give mixes with baking instructions.

Yield: 1 cake mix and 1 icing mix

To bake: Preheat oven to 350 degrees. In a large bowl, combine cake mix, 1$^1/_3$ cups water, 3 eggs, and $^1/_4$ cup vegetable oil; beat until well blended. Pour batter into a greased 9 x 13-inch baking pan. Bake 30 to 34 minutes or until a toothpick inserted in center of cake comes out clean. Cool cake in pan.

Combine icing mix and $^1/_4$ cup boiling water in a small bowl; stir until smooth. If necessary, add a few more drops of water at a time until icing is desired consistency. Pour icing over cake. Let cake cool. Store cake in an airtight container.

Yield: 12 to 15 servings

SPICY GRANOLA CUPCAKE MIX

Surprise a terrific family with a bag of this Spicy Granola Cupcake Mix! It's a cinch to toss together, and delivery is easy when you pack it in a handmade fabric bag tied with a torn-fabric bow and a silk flower. Write the baking instructions on an appliquéd recipe card for an extra homey touch.

- 1 package (18$^1/_4$ ounces) yellow cake mix
- 2 cups granola cereal with nuts and dried fruit
- 1 teaspoon ground cinnamon
- $^1/_8$ teaspoon ground cloves

In a large bowl, combine cake mix, cereal, cinnamon, and cloves. Divide mixture into 2 resealable plastic bags (about 2$^1/_2$ cups in each bag). Give with baking instructions.

Yield: about 5 cups mix (2 gifts)

To bake: Preheat oven to 350 degrees. Combine bag of cupcake mix, $^2/_3$ cup water, 2 eggs, and 2 tablespoons oil in a medium bowl; beat until well blended. Fill paper-lined muffin cups about three-fourths full. Bake 18 to 20 minutes or until a toothpick inserted in center of cupcake comes out clean and tops are golden brown. Serve warm.

Yield: about 1 dozen cupcakes

SPICED CRANBERRY TEA MIX

1 cup unsweetened powdered instant tea
1 cup sugar
$^1/_2$ cup orange-flavored powdered instant breakfast drink
2 packages (3 ounces each) cranberry gelatin
1 teaspoon ground cinnamon
1 teaspoon ground allspice

Process all ingredients in a food processor until well blended. Store in a resealable plastic bag. Give with serving instructions.
Yield: about $2^1/_2$ cups mix (1 gift)

To serve: Pour 6 ounces hot water over 2 tablespoons tea mix; stir until well blended.

FRUITY TEA MIX

1 cup sweetened powdered instant tea mix with lemon flavor
$^1/_2$ cup sugar
1 package (0.16 ounce) unsweetened punch-flavored soft drink mix
1 package ($7^1/_2$ ounces) fruit-shaped fruit-flavored candy

In a medium bowl, combine tea, sugar, soft drink mix, and candy. Store in an airtight container. Give with serving instructions.
Yield: about 2 cups mix

To serve: Pour 8 ounces hot or cold water over 2 tablespoons tea mix; stir until well blended.

HEARTWARMING TEA MIX

1 jar (15 ounces) orange-flavored powdered instant breakfast drink
1 cup sugar
1 cup unsweetened powdered instant tea
$^1/_2$ cup presweetened lemonade-flavored soft drink mix
1 teaspoon pineapple extract
1 teaspoon coconut extract

Process orange drink, sugar, tea, lemonade mix, and extracts in a food processor until well blended. Give with serving instructions.
Yield: about $4^1/_4$ cups tea mix

To serve: Pour 6 ounces hot water over 1 rounded tablespoon tea mix; stir until well blended.

LEMONY CRANBERRY JUICE MULLS

$^1/_3$ cup brown sugar, firmly packed
4 (3- to 4-inch) cinnamon sticks, broken into pieces
3 teaspoons whole allspice
2 whole nutmegs, crushed
3 teaspoons grated lemon peel
4 large lemons
4 2-inch squares of fine-mesh cheesecloth
Cotton String

For mull mixture, combine all ingredients except lemons in a small bowl. To make each lemon basket, refer to photo and vertically cut a $^1/_4$-inch wide strip at center of lemon for the handle, cutting through only half of the lemon.

Packed with brown sugar and spices, Lemony Cranberry Juice Mulls make a wonderful hot drink when added to cranberry juice. Give several in a colorful bag, or use them as party favors. Your good taste will be appreciated sip after sip!

Cut horizontally from each tip of the lemon to the handle. Remove wedges from both sides; scoop out pulp.

For mulls, divide mull mixture in fourths and spoon into four 2-inch squares of cheesecloth; wrap cheesecloth around mixture and tie with string. Place spice bundles in lemon baskets. Wrap mulls in plastic wrap; tie with ribbon. Store in refrigerator. Give with

instructions for making mulled cranberry juice.
Yield: 4 mulls

To make mulled cranberry juice: Place 1 mull and 1¹/₂ quarts cranberry juice in a large saucepan. Bring to a boil; simmer 15 minutes.

MULLED TEA BAG

2½ teaspoons loose tea leaves
1 teaspoon coarsely crushed
   cinnamon stick
½ teaspoon dried orange peel
¼ teaspoon dried lemon peel
3 whole allspice berries
2 whole cloves
   5-inch square of fine-mesh
   cheesecloth
   Cotton string

Place tea leaves, cinnamon pieces, orange peel, lemon peel, allspice, and cloves on cheesecloth square. Bring corners together and tie with string to form a bag. Give with serving instructions.
Yield: 1 tea bag

To serve: Place tea bag in a mug and add 6 ounces boiling water; steep 4 to 5 minutes.

MINT TEA MIX

1½ cups loose tea leaves
1 jar (0.25 ounce) dried mint leaves
2 tablespoons dried orange peel
2 tablespoons whole cloves

Combine tea leaves, mint leaves, orange peel, and cloves in a medium bowl; stir until well blended. Store in an airtight container. Give with serving instructions.
Yield: about 1¾ cups tea mix

To serve: For 1 cup of tea, place 1 teaspoon tea mix in an individual tea infuser. Pour 1 cup boiling water over tea mix. Allow tea to steep 3 to 5 minutes. Remove infuser; serve hot.
For 1 quart of tea, place 2 tablespoons tea mix in a teapot. Pour 1 quart boiling water over tea mix. Allow tea to steep 3 to 5 minutes. Strain tea; serve hot.

ORANGE-NUTMEG TEA MIX

1 cup unsweetened powdered
   instant tea
1 cup sugar
1 package (0.15 ounce)
   unsweetened orange-flavored
   soft drink mix
1 teaspoon ground nutmeg

In a small bowl, combine instant tea, soft drink mix, and nutmeg; stir until well blended. Store in an airtight container. Give with serving instructions.
Yield: about 1⅔ cups tea mix

To serve: Pour 6 ounces hot or cold water over 2 tablespoons tea mix; stir until well blended.

LEMON-RASPBERRY SLEEPY TEA MIX

    1 cup decaffeinated lemon-flavored
       artificially sweetened powdered
       instant tea mix
    1 package (0.3 ounce) sugar-free
       raspberry gelatin

Combine tea mix and gelatin in a resealable plastic bag. Glve with serving instructions.

Yield: about 1 cup tea mix

To serve: Pour 6 ounces hot water over 1 to 2 teaspoons tea mix; stir until well blended.

CHOCOLATE-ALMOND COFFEE MIX

    1   cup non-dairy powdered
        creamer
    1   cup sugar
    1/2 cup instant coffee granules
    1/2 cup cocoa
    1   teaspoon almond extract

Process creamer, sugar, coffee granules, cocoa, and almond extract in a food processor until well blended. Store in an airtight container. Give with serving instructions.

Yield: about 2 cups coffee mix

To serve: Pour 6 ounces hot water over 2 heaping teaspoons coffee mix. Stir until well blended.

BRANDIED SPICE COFFEE

    1/3 cup ground coffee
    1/2 teaspoon brandy extract
    1 1/2 three-inch-long cinnamon sticks
    1/4 teaspoon whole cloves
    1/4 teaspoon whole allspice

Place coffee in a food processor. With processor running, add brandy extract. Stop and scrape sides of container with a spatula. Process 10 seconds longer. Place mix in a resealable plastic bag; add cinnamon sticks, cloves, and allspice. Store in refrigerator. Give with serving instructions.

Yield: mix for eight 6-ounce servings

To serve: Place mix in filter of an automatic drip coffee maker. Add 6 cups water and brew.

Welcome winter by sharing steaming cups of Strawberry-Vanilla Drink. The mix is fun to present in a snowman canister crafted from a recycled 32-ounce mayonnaise jar.

STRAWBERRY-VANILLA DRINK MIX

- 1 package (25.6 ounces) nonfat dry milk powder
- 1 package (16 ounces) confectioners sugar
- 2 jars (8 ounces each) French vanilla-flavored non-dairy powdered creamer
- 1 package (15 ounces) strawberry mix for milk
- 1 jar (11 ounces) non-dairy powdered creamer
- 1/2 teaspoon salt

In a very large bowl, combine all ingredients; stir until well blended. Store in an airtight container. Give 2 cups mix with serving instructions.
Yield: about 20 cups drink mix (10 gifts)

To serve: For a hot drink, pour 6 ounces hot water over 3 heaping tablespoons drink mix; stir until well blended.

For a cold strawberry-vanilla shake, place 6 ounces cold water, 3 heaping tablespoons drink mix, and 1 to 2 scoops vanilla ice cream in a blender. Blend until desired consistency.

After a winter jaunt outside, what could be more warming than a cup of steaming Malted Cocoa? Surprise a snowbird friend with this chill-busting mix packaged in a jolly snowman bag that's easy and fun to make.

MALTED COCOA MIX

1 package (25.6 ounces) nonfat
   dry milk powder
6 cups miniature marshmallows
1 container (16 ounces) instant
   cocoa mix for milk
1 jar (13 ounces) malted milk
   powder
1 cup sifted confectioners sugar
1 jar (6 ounces) non-dairy
   powdered creamer
1/2 teaspoon salt

In a very large bowl, combine dry milk, marshmallows, cocoa mix, malted milk powder, confectioners sugar, creamer, and salt; stir until well blended. Store in an airtight container in a cool place. Give 2 cups mix with serving instructions.
Yield: about 20 cups mix (10 gifts)

To serve: Pour 6 ounces hot water over 1/3 cup cocoa mix; stir until well blended.

SPICY COCOA MIX

3¹/2 cups firmly packed brown sugar
  2 cups cocoa
  2 teaspoons ground cinnamon
  ¹/2 teaspoon ground nutmeg
  ¹/2 teaspoon ground cloves
  ¹/4 teaspoon salt

Process brown sugar, cocoa, cinnamon, nutmeg, cloves, and salt in a food processor until well blended. Store in an airtight container. Give with serving instructions.
Yield: about 5 cups cocoa mix

To serve: Pour 6 ounces hot milk over 1¹/2 tablespoons cocoa mix; stir until well blended. Serve warm.

PINEAPPLE CIDER MIX

  1 package (7.4 ounces) apple cider mix (10 envelopes)
  1 package (3 ounces) pineapple gelatin
  2 packages (0.15 ounce each) unsweetened orange-pineapple-flavored soft drink mix
  2 cups sugar

In a medium bowl, combine apple cider mix, gelatin, soft drink mix, and sugar. Store in an airtight container. Give with serving instructions.
Yield: about 3¹/4 cups mix

To serve: Pour 6 ounces hot water over 2 tablespoons cider mix; stir until well blended.

SPICY CHRISTMAS DRINK MIX

  4 cups water
  1 cup sugar
  5 cinnamon sticks
  2 teaspoons whole cloves
  2 cans (12 ounces each) frozen orange juice concentrate
  2 cans (12 ounces each) frozen pineapple juice concentrate
  1 can (12 ounces) frozen lemonade concentrate

Combine water and sugar in a large saucepan. Stirring constantly, cook over medium-high heat 4 minutes or until sugar dissolves. Reduce heat to low. Add cinnamon sticks and cloves; cover and cook 15 minutes. Strain mixture into a large heatproof container; discard cinnamon and cloves. Stir in orange, pineapple, and lemonade concentrates. Store in an airtight container in refrigerator. Give 2 cups mix with serving instructions.
Yield: about 12 cups mix (6 gifts)

To serve: Heat ¹/4 cup drink mix with 6 ounces apple cider; serve hot. For a variation, add 1 tablespoon apple brandy to each serving of prepared hot drink.

FRUIT PUNCH MIX

  1 can (46 ounces) pineapple juice
  1 can (12 ounces) frozen limeade concentrate, thawed
  2 cups water
  1 cup rum
  1 cup peppermint schnapps
    Green liquid food coloring

In a 3-quart container, combine first 5 ingredients; tint green. Pour evenly into two 1 1/2-quart or 1.5-liter containers. Cover and store in refrigerator. Give instructions for making punch with each container.
Yield: 3 quarts drink mix, enough to make 2 recipes of punch

To make punch: In a large punch bowl, stir together 1 1/2 quarts chilled drink mix and 12 ounces chilled lemon-lime soft drink. If desired, add ice cubes and garnish with fresh mint.
Yield: about nine 6-ounce servings

SPICY POPCORN SEASONING

     3 tablespoons dried parsley flakes
2 1/2 tablespoons chili powder
     2 tablespoons garlic salt
     1 tablespoon dried chives
     2 teaspoons onion powder

Combine all ingredients in a small bowl. Store in an airtight container. Give with serving instructions.
Yield: about 1/2 cup seasoning mix

To serve: Combine 1/3 cup butter or margarine and 1 tablespoon seasoning mix in a small microwave-safe bowl. Cover and microwave on medium power (50%) 1 minute or until butter melts. Drizzle over 15 cups popped popcorn; toss to coat popcorn.

MICROWAVE POPCORN SEASONING MIX

1/2 cup freshly grated Parmesan cheese
  1 teaspoon paprika
  1 teaspoon dried Italian herb seasoning
1/2 teaspoon garlic powder
1/4 teaspoon ground red pepper
  8 bags (3 1/2 ounces each) unpopped microwave popcorn

In a small bowl, combine Parmesan cheese, paprika, Italian seasoning, garlic powder, and red pepper until well blended. Place 1 tablespoon seasoning mix in each of 8 small plastic bags. Store in refrigerator. Give 1 bag of popcorn and serving instructions with each bag of seasoning mix.
Yield: about 1/2 cup seasoning mix

To serve: Microwave a 3 1/2-ounce bag of microwave popcorn according to package directions. Open bag carefully to avoid steam. Sprinkle seasoning mix (1 tablespoon) over popcorn; hold top of bag closed and shake until popcorn is coated.

Refreshing Friendship Fruit Sauce makes a scrumptious addition to our tasty muffins. Your gift recipient can use the jar of sauce you include in the basket to make more muffins or as a topping for ice cream or pound cake. They can even use the sauce to start a batch of their own. What a wonderfully versatile recipe!

FRIENDSHIP FRUIT SAUCE

YEAST STARTER
- 1 cup sugar
- 2 packages dry yeast
- 1 can (15 1/4 ounces) pineapple chunks in heavy syrup

FRUIT SAUCE
- 1 recipe yeast starter
- 1 can (15 1/4 ounces) pineapple chunks in heavy syrup
- 4 cups sugar, divided
- 1 can (16 ounces) sliced peaches in syrup
- 1 can (14 ounces) apricot halves in syrup, cut in half
- 1 jar (10 ounces) maraschino cherries

For yeast starter, combine sugar, yeast, and undrained pineapple in a 1-quart nonmetal container with a loose-fitting lid. Stir several times during first day to make sure sugar and yeast dissolve. Let mixture stand 2 weeks at room temperature; stir daily.

For fruit sauce, place yeast starter in a 1-gallon nonmetal container with a loose-fitting lid. Add undrained pineapple and 1 cup sugar. Let fruit mixture stand 1 week at room temperature; stir daily.

For week 2, add undrained peaches and 1 cup sugar; stir daily.

For week 3, add undrained apricot pieces and 1 cup sugar; stir daily.

For week 4, add undrained cherries and remaining 1 cup sugar; stir daily.

At end of fourth week, let mixture stand 3 days longer at room temperature; stir daily. Fruit sauce is now ready to use. Serve over ice cream, pound cake, or use in Friendship Fruit Muffins (recipe on this page). Reserve at least 1 1/2 cups fruit sauce to start a new batch of sauce.

To replenish fruit sauce, add 1 can undrained fruit (alternating types of fruit) and 1 cup sugar every week. Stir mixture daily. Let mixture stand 3 days at room temperature before using.

For each gift, give 1 1/2 cups fruit sauce, replenishing instructions, and muffin recipe.

Yield: about 10 cups fruit sauce

FRIENDSHIP FRUIT MUFFINS

- Vegetable cooking spray
- 1 cup drained fruit from Friendship Fruit Sauce (recipe on this page)
- 1/2 cup syrup from Friendship Fruit Sauce
- 1 cup sugar, divided
- 1/2 teaspoon ground cinnamon
- 1 cup butter, melted
- 1 container (8 ounces) sour cream at room temperature
- 2 cups self-rising flour

Preheat oven to 350 degrees. Line a muffin pan with paper muffin cups. Spray cups with cooking spray. In a small bowl, combine fruit, syrup, 1/2 cup sugar, and cinnamon. In a medium bowl, combine melted butter and sour cream. Add flour and remaining 1/2 cup sugar to sour cream mixture; stir just until moistened. Spoon 2 tablespoons batter into prepared muffin cups. Spoon 1 tablespoon fruit mixture over batter. Bake 30 to 35 minutes or until golden brown. Serve warm.

Yield: about 1 1/2 dozen muffins

SOURDOUGH STARTER FOR SOURDOUGH BREAD

3 cups all-purpose flour, divided
1 teaspoon active dry yeast
2 cups hot water
1 cup lukewarm water

DAY 1
In a medium bowl, combine 2 cups of the flour with yeast; stir. Stir in the hot water until mixture is blended. Cover the bowl with a clean towel and allow the mixture to sit at room temperature 24 hours.

DAY 2
Stir the mixture. After 12 hours, stir the mixture again. Allow mixture to sit at room temperature another 12 hours.

DAY 3
Stir in the lukewarm water and remaining flour until blended. Cover the bowl with the towel and allow to sit at room temperature 24 hours.

DAY 4
The starter is now ready to be used. Store loosely covered in a glass container with a non-metal lid in the refrigerator.

To maintain Sourdough Starter: Stir the starter at least once a week. For each 1 cup of starter that is removed, stir in 1 cup flour and 1 cup lukewarm water (if the starter is not used every few weeks, remove 1 cup of starter and replace as directed above). Cover and allow the starter to sit at room temperature overnight. Then store loosely covered in a glass container with a non-metal lid in the refrigerator.

SOURDOUGH BREAD

Give one loaf of bread and a crock of Sourdough Starter, along with replenishing instructions and bread recipe.

1 package active dry yeast
$3/4$ cup lukewarm water, divided
1 cup Sourdough Starter (recipe on this page)
2 tablespoons honey
3 tablespoons butter, melted
1 tablespoon salt
$3^1/2$ cups all-purpose flour

Dissolve the yeast in $1/4$ cup water. In a large mixing bowl, combine remaining $1/2$ cup water, starter, honey, butter, dissolved yeast, and salt, blending well. Stir in flour by hand. On a lightly floured surface, knead dough 6 to 8 minutes. If necessary, add just enough extra flour to prevent dough from being sticky. Place dough in a lightly greased bowl, turning dough to coat top. Cover with plastic wrap and allow to rise until doubled in bulk, about $1^1/2$ hours.

Punch down dough and divide in half. Shape each half into a round loaf and place on a lightly greased baking sheet 4 inches apart. Cover with plastic wrap and allow to rise until doubled in bulk, about 1 hour.

Preheat the oven to 400 degrees. Bake 15 minutes, reduce the heat to 375 degrees and bake 20 to 25 minutes longer, or until the bread sounds hollow when tapped. Remove loaves from pan and cool on wire racks.
Yield: 2 loaves

SOURDOUGH STARTER FOR MOLASSES BREAD

Give with recipe for Sourdough Molasses Bread and instructions for replenishing.

    2 cups warm milk
    2 cups all-purpose flour
    1 package active dry yeast

Combine all ingredients in a very large non-metal container; stir until well blended. Loosely cover with cheesecloth and let stand in a warm place (80 to 85 degrees) 24 hours. Give with recipe for Sourdough Molasses Bread and instructions for replenishing.

To replenish starter, stir in equal amounts of flour and warm water (80 to 85 degrees) to replace the mixture used. (For example, if 1 cup starter is used, replace with $1/2$ cup flour and $1/2$ cup warm water.) Let stand in a warm place at least 24 hours before using. If starter is not used every 3 to 5 days, remove 1 cup starter and replenish as directed. Store loosely covered in refrigerator. Bring to room temperature before using.
Yield: about 4 cups starter

SOURDOUGH MOLASSES BREAD

    8 cups all-purpose flour, divided
    2 cups warm water
    2 cups warm milk
    1 cup Sourdough Starter (recipe
       on this page)
    1 tablespoon butter or margarine,
       melted
    1 package active dry yeast
    1 cup whole wheat flour
 $1/2$ cup granulated sugar
 $1/4$ cup molasses
    2 teaspoons salt
    2 teaspoons baking soda

In a large bowl, combine $2^1/2$ cups all-purpose flour and next 4 ingredients. Stir in yeast and set aside 30 minutes. Add wheat flour and next 4 ingredients; stir until well blended. Gradually add remaining all-purpose flour; knead until a soft dough forms. Turn dough onto a lightly floured surface; knead until dough becomes pliable and elastic. Shape dough into 4 loaves and place in greased 5 x 9-inch loaf pans. Grease tops of loaves. Let rise in a warm place (80 to 85 degrees) 1 hour or until doubled in size.

Preheat oven to 350 degrees. Bake 25 to 30 minutes or until brown. Transfer to a wire rack to cool completely. Store in an airtight container.
Yield: 4 loaves bread

SOURDOUGH STARTER FOR BAGUETTES

1 package dry yeast
2¹/₂ cups warm water, divided
2 cups all-purpose flour
3 tablespoons sugar
¹/₂ teaspoon salt

In a large nonmetal bowl, dissolve yeast in ¹/₂ cup warm water. With a wooden spoon, combine remaining 2 cups warm water, flour, sugar, and salt. Loosely cover bowl or transfer starter into a 1¹/₂-quart pitcher with lid, keeping spout open. Place container in a warm place (80 to 85 degrees) free of drafts 3 days. Stir mixture several times each day.

To use starter, remove amount needed for recipe. To replenish starter, stir in ²/₃ cup warm water and ²/₃ cup flour for each ²/₃ cup starter that is removed. Let stand at room temperature overnight and then store in refrigerator. Use and replenish starter every 7 to 10 days.
Yield: about 4 cups starter

SOURDOUGH BAGUETTES

Give one loaf of bread and a batch of Sourdough Starter, along with replenishing instructions and bread recipe.

4¹/₂ to 5 cups all-purpose flour, divided
1 cup plus 2 tablespoons warm water
²/₃ cup Sourdough Starter, at room temperature (recipe on this page)
³/₄ teaspoon salt
Vegetable cooking spray
1 tablespoon yellow cornmeal
1 egg white
1 tablespoon water

In a large nonmetal bowl, use a wooden spoon to combine 2¹/₂ cups flour, warm water, and starter. Cover mixture loosely with plastic wrap and let rest in a warm place (80 to 85 degrees) 5 hours or until doubled in size.

Stir in 2 cups flour and salt. Turn dough onto a lightly floured surface. Knead 5 minutes or until dough becomes smooth and elastic, adding additional flour as necessary. Place in a large bowl sprayed with cooking spray, turning once to coat top of dough. Cover loosely with plastic wrap and let rise in a warm place 12 hours or until doubled in size.

Turn dough onto a lightly floured surface and punch down. Knead dough 2 to 3 minutes; divide into thirds. Shape each piece of dough into a 12-inch-long loaf. Place loaves on a baking sheet that has been lightly greased with cooking spray and sprinkled with cornmeal. Spray loaves with cooking spray. Loosely cover loaves with plastic wrap and let rise in a warm place 4 hours or until doubled in size.

Preheat oven to 400 degrees. Use a sharp knife to make diagonal cuts across tops of loaves. In a small bowl, lightly beat egg white and water; brush on loaves. Bake about 20 to 25 minutes or until bread is golden brown and sounds hollow when tapped.

Serve warm or transfer to a wire rack to cool completely. Store in an airtight container.
Yield: 3 loaves bread

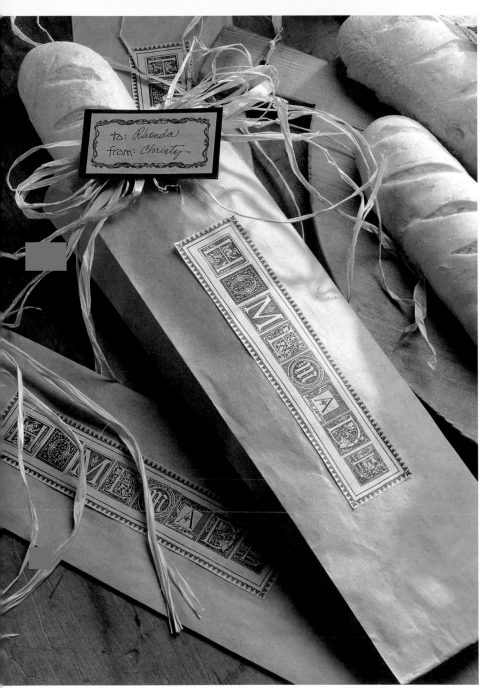

Nothing tastes better than fresh homemade bread! Our Sourdough Baguettes lend French charm to even the simplest meal. Present baked loaves in decorated brown bottle bags. You can also include a batch of the starter so your friends can enjoy the baguettes time after time!

HERB BREAD

3 tablespoons granulated sugar
1 package dry yeast
1/4 cup warm water
6 cups all-purpose flour, divided
2 tablespoons dried basil leaves
1 tablespoon dried parsley flakes
2 teaspoons salt
4 eggs
1 1/4 cups warm milk
2 tablespoons vegetable oil
Basil Butter to serve (recipe follows)

Stir sugar and yeast into warm water; let stand 5 minutes. In large mixing bowl, combine 4 cups flour, basil, parsley, and salt. Separate 1 egg (reserve egg yolk). Add remaining 3 eggs to egg white and beat with fork until frothy. Stir in yeast mixture, milk, and oil. Stir liquid mixture into flour mixture and beat until smooth. Stir in remaining 2 cups flour to make a stiff dough. Turn dough onto a lightly floured surface and knead 8 to 10 minutes or until smooth and elastic. Place in greased bowl, turning once to grease top. Cover and let rise until doubled in size (about 1 hour). Punch down dough and let rise until doubled again (about 1 hour).

Divide dough into three equal parts; roll each part into a rope about 18 inches long. Braid ropes and place on greased baking sheet. Press each end firmly together; tuck ends under loaf to seal. Cover and let rise until doubled in size (about 1 hour).

Beat reserved egg yolk with fork and brush over braid. Bake in a preheated 375-degree oven 40 to 45 minutes or until light golden brown. Remove from baking sheet and cool on wire rack. Serve with Basil Butter.

Yield: 1 braided loaf

BASIL BUTTER
1 cup butter, softened
3 tablespoons dried basil leaves

In mixing bowl, combine butter and basil. Chill before serving.

MINCED PUMPKIN BREAD

This spicy, moist bread is excellent sliced and served with whipped cream cheese.

1 cup vegetable oil
3 cups granulated sugar
4 eggs
2 1/2 cups cooked pumpkin
1 1/2 cups chopped pecans
1 1/4 cups mincemeat
3 1/4 cups all-purpose flour
2 teaspoons baking soda
1 1/2 teaspoons salt
1 1/2 teaspoons ground nutmeg
1 teaspoon ground cinnamon
1 teaspoon baking powder

Blend oil and sugar. Add eggs, pumpkin, pecans, and mincemeat. Combine dry ingredients; stir into sugar mixture until well blended. Spoon mixture into three greased and floured 9 x 5-inch pans. Bake in a preheated 350-degree oven 50 minutes or until a toothpick inserted in center comes out clean. Cool in pans 30 minutes. (Freezes well.)

Yield: 3 loaves of bread

LEMON NUT BREAD

1 cup butter, softened
1/2 cups granulated sugar
4 eggs, separated
3 1/2 tablespoons grated lemon peel
3 cups cake flour, sifted
2 1/2 teaspoons baking powder
1 teaspoon salt
1/2 cups finely chopped walnuts
1 cup milk
1 tablespoon lemon juice
Citrus Glaze (recipe follows)

Cream butter and sugar, beating until fluffy. Add egg yolks, one at a time, beating well after each addition. Stir in lemon peel. Combine flour, baking powder, salt, and walnuts. Stir flour mixture into butter mixture. Stir in milk and lemon juice. Beat egg whites until stiff; fold one-half of whipped egg whites at a time into butter mixture. Spoon mixture into two greased and floured x 5-inch pans. Bake in a preheated 50-degree oven 40 to 45 minutes or until a toothpick inserted in center comes out clean. Cool in pans 10 minutes. Remove bread from pans and cool on wire racks. Glaze if desired.
Yield: 2 loaves of bread

CITRUS GLAZE
1/4 cup **each** lemon juice, orange juice, and pineapple juice
2 tablespoons butter
2 1/2 cups confectioners sugar

Heat juices and butter. Stir in confectioners sugar; blend until smooth. Spoon glaze over bread.

CRUSTY NUTMEG BREAD
Freshly grated nutmeg gives this butter-flavored bread a spicy taste.

3 cups all-purpose flour, sifted and divided
2 1/4 cups firmly packed light brown sugar, divided
3/4 cup butter, softened and divided
3/4 cup chopped pecans, divided
2 eggs
1 teaspoon freshly grated nutmeg
1 teaspoon vanilla extract
1 cup sour cream
1 1/2 teaspoons baking soda

For topping, combine 1/4 cup each of flour, brown sugar, butter, and pecans. Set aside.

Cream remaining butter and brown sugar, beating until light and fluffy. Beat in eggs, nutmeg, and vanilla. Combine sour cream and baking soda in a separate bowl; stir into butter mixture. Stir in remaining flour and pecans. Spoon mixture into two greased and floured 9 x 5-inch pans. Sprinkle with reserved topping. Bake in a preheated 350-degree oven 45 to 50 minutes or until a toothpick inserted in center comes out clean. Cool in pans 10 minutes. Remove bread from pans and cool on wire racks.
Yield: 2 loaves of bread

A gift of Irish Soda Bread Mix will delight a friend who loves to bake.

IRISH SODA BREAD MIX

(Also shown on page 517)

- 3 cups all-purpose flour
- $3/4$ cup quick-cooking oats
- 6 tablespoons dry buttermilk powder
- $1/4$ cup sugar
- 1 teaspoon baking soda
- $1/2$ teaspoon baking powder
- $1/2$ teaspoon salt
- $2/3$ cup chilled butter or margarine, cut into pieces
- 1 cup raisins

In a large bowl, combine flour, oats, buttermilk powder, sugar, baking soda, baking powder, and salt. Using a pastry blender or 2 knives, cut in chilled butter until mixture resembles coarse meal.

Stir in raisins. Place mix in a resealable plastic bag. Store in refrigerator. Give with serving instructions.

Yield: about $6^1/2$ cups bread mix (makes 1 loaf bread)

To serve: Store bread mix in refrigerator until ready to prepare. Preheat oven to 350 degrees. In a medium bowl, combine bread mix and $1^1/2$ cups water; stir just until a soft dough forms. Spoon dough into a greased $1^1/2$-quart ovenproof bread crock or a 5 x 9-inch loaf pan. Smooth top of dough. Bake 1 to $1^1/4$ hours or until top is browned and a wooden skewer inserted in center of bread comes out clean. Cool in crock 10 minutes. Remove from crock and serve warm or transfer to a wire rack to cool completely. Store in an airtight container.

To give others a fast and nutritious start to the day, bundle up a bag of Hearty Pancake Mix.

HEARTY PANCAKE MIX

1 cup old-fashioned oats
2 cups all-purpose flour
1¹/₂ cups whole-wheat flour
1 cup dry buttermilk powder
¹/₃ cup sugar
3 tablespoons baking powder
1 tablespoon baking soda
1 teaspoon dried orange peel
1 cup raisins
1 cup sliced almonds, toasted

Process oats in a food processor until coarsely ground. Add flours, buttermilk powder, sugar, baking powder, baking soda, and orange peel; process until blended. Transfer dry ingredients to a large bowl. Stir in raisins and almonds. Divide into 2 resealable plastic bags. Give with serving instructions.
Yield: about 6¹/₄ cups pancake mix

To serve: Grease and preheat griddle. Combine 1 bag pancake mix, 1²/₃ cups water, 1 egg, and 3 tablespoons vegetable oil in a medium bowl. Stir just until moistened. For each pancake, pour about ¹/₄ cup batter onto griddle. Cook until top of pancake has a few bubbles and bottom is golden brown. Turn with a spatula and cook until remaining side is golden brown. Serve warm pancakes with syrup.
Yield: about 18 pancakes

ALMOND PANCAKE MIX

3 cups nonfat dry milk powder
2 1/2 cups all-purpose flour
1 cup whole-wheat flour
1 cup finely ground almonds
1/3 cup baking powder
1/3 cup sugar
2 teaspoons salt

In a large bowl, combine dry milk, flours, almonds, baking powder, sugar, and salt until well blended. Store in a resealable plastic bag. Give with recipe for pancakes.
Yield: about 7 1/2 cups pancake mix, enough for 3 batches of pancakes

To make pancakes: In a medium bowl, combine 2 1/2 cups pancake mix, 1 1/4 cups water, 1 egg, and 2 tablespoons vegetable oil. Stir just until moistened. Heat a greased griddle over medium heat. For each pancake, pour about 1/4 cup batter onto griddle and cook until top of pancake is full of bubbles and underside is golden brown. Turn with a spatula and cook until remaining side is golden brown. Regrease griddle as necessary. Serve with butter and syrup.
Yield: about 1 dozen 5-inch pancakes

CHEESE SPREADS
(Shown on page 9)

Each of these savory spreads is made by adding ingredients to the Basic Spread. Miniature flowerpots make cute gift containers.

BASIC SPREAD
2 packages (8 ounces each)
cream cheese, softened
1/2 cup sour cream
3 tablespoons mayonnaise

Beat cream cheese, sour cream, and mayonnaise in a medium bowl until smooth. Use Basic Spread to make each of the following recipes.
Yield: about 2 2/3 cups spread

GARLIC
1 cup Basic Spread
1 1/2 teaspoons garlic salt
1 teaspoon Fines Herbes
1/8 teaspoon hot pepper sauce
Fines Herbes to garnish

Combine basic spread, garlic salt, 1 teaspoon Fines Herbes, and pepper sauce in a small bowl; stir until well blended. Transfer to a serving container; sprinkle with Fines Herbes to garnish. Serve with assorted crackers.

CHEESE
1 cup Basic Spread
1/3 cup grated Parmesan cheese
1 teaspoon Worcestershire sauce
3/4 teaspoon onion salt
Grated Parmesan cheese to garnish

Combine basic spread, 1/3 cup Parmesan cheese, Worcestershire sauce, and onion salt; stir until well blended. Transfer to a serving container; sprinkle with Parmesan cheese to garnish. Serve with assorted crackers or wedges of red apple.

ALMOND

2/3 cup Basic Spread
1/4 cup butter, softened
1/4 cup sugar
1/8 cup golden raisins
1/8 cup slivered almonds
    Raisins or almonds to garnish

Combine basic spread, butter, sugar, 1/8 cup raisins, and 1/8 cup almonds; stir until well blended. Transfer to a serving container; sprinkle with raisins or almonds to garnish. Serve with assorted fruits or crackers.

ORIENTAL BROCCOLI SLAW KIT

Broccoli slaw mix can be found with packaged salad greens.

1/4 cup butter
1 cup chopped walnuts
1 package (3 ounces) chicken-
    flavored ramen noodle soup mix
2 tablespoons vegetable oil
2 tablespoons sugar
2 tablespoons balsamic vinegar
2 tablespoons soy sauce
1/2 teaspoon ground black pepper
1 package (16 ounces) shredded
    broccoli slaw mix
1/2 cup sliced green onions

In a medium skillet over medium heat, melt butter. Add walnuts. Crush noodles and add to mixture. Stirring constantly, cook until mixture browns (about 10 minutes). Drain on paper towels; cool and set aside.

In a small saucepan, combine seasoning packet from ramen noodles, oil, sugar, vinegar, soy sauce, and pepper. Stirring constantly, cook over medium heat until sugar dissolves; cool.

In a large bowl, combine slaw mix and green onions. Place dressing mixture in an airtight container and noodle mixture and slaw mixture in separate resealable plastic bags; store in refrigerator. Give with serving instructions.

Yield: about 6 cups slaw mixture, about 2 cups noodle mixture, and about 1/2 cup dressing

To serve: Combine noodle mixture and slaw mixture in a large bowl. Add dressing; stir until well coated. Serve immediately.

Yield: about 7 cups slaw

FISH FRY COATING MIX

1 1/2 cups yellow cornmeal
1/4 cup all-purpose flour
1 tablespoon lemon pepper
2 teaspoons salt
1 teaspoon onion powder
1/2 teaspoon paprika

In a large bowl, combine all ingredients. Store in an airtight container. Give with fish frying instructions.
Yield: about 1 3/4 cups mix

To prepare fried fish: Dip fish in buttermilk and roll in coating mix. To cook, pour oil into a Dutch oven to a depth of 2 to 3 inches. Heat to 375 degrees. Fry coated fish, one piece at a time, about 4 to 6 minutes or until golden brown.

ITALIAN CRACKED PEPPER SEASONING

Give to your favorite "grill master" with a couple of handy new cooking utensils.

1/2 cup cracked black pepper
1 teaspoon dried basil leaves
1 teaspoon dried thyme leaves
1 teaspoon dried oregano leaves
1 teaspoon dried sage leaves
1/2 teaspoon dried rosemary leaves

Combine all ingredients in a resealable plastic bag. Use to season meats before baking or grilling.
Yield: about 1/2 cup seasoning

GARLIC MUSTARD

8 cloves garlic, peeled
1 tablespoon olive oil
1 jar (8 ounces) Dijon-style mustard
1/2 teaspoon dried basil leaves
1/4 teaspoon dried oregano leaves

Preheat oven to 325 degrees. Place garlic in a small baking dish and drizzle with oil. Roast garlic 20 to 30 minutes, stirring frequently, until garlic is soft. Mash garlic, removing any tough pieces. Combine mashed garlic with remaining ingredients; cover and refrigerate overnight to allow flavors to blend.
Yield: about 1 cup mustard

These tempting toppings are great for baked potatoes.

BAKED POTATO KIT

BACON-CHEDDAR TOPPING
  1 cup sour cream
^{2}/3 cup finely shredded Cheddar
       cheese
^{1}/2 cup cooked and crumbled bacon
  2 tablespoons finely chopped green
       onion

Yield: about 1 ^{1}/2 cups topping

GARLIC-PEPPER BUTTER
^{1}/2 cup butter, softened
  2 small cloves garlic, minced
^{1}/2 teaspoons freshly ground black
       pepper

Yield: about ^{1}/2 cup topping

LOW-FAT SALSA TOPPING
^{1}/4 cup fat-free sour cream
^{1}/4 cup thick salsa
  2 tablespoons chopped ripe olives
  1 tablespoon finely chopped green
       onion

Yield: about ^{1}/2 cup topping

  6 uncooked baking potatoes to give
       with toppings

For each topping, combine ingredients in a small bowl; stir until well blended. Cover and store in refrigerator. Give toppings with baking potatoes.

PASTA FAGIOLI SOUP MIX

2 tablespoons dried minced onion
1 tablespoon dried parsley flakes
1 tablespoon sugar
1 tablespoon celery salt
1 tablespoon sweet pepper flakes
2 teaspoons chicken bouillon
   granules
2 teaspoons dried Italian seasoning
1 1/2 teaspoons salt
1/2 teaspoon paprika
1/2 teaspoon garlic powder
1/2 teaspoon ground black pepper
1 package (16 ounces) dried
   cranberry beans and 1 cup
   ditalini pasta to give

In a small bowl, combine minced onion, parsley flakes, sugar, celery salt, pepper flakes, chicken bouillon, Italian seasoning, salt, paprika, garlic powder, and black pepper. Pour seasoning mix into a small jar with lid. Place beans and pasta in separate plastic bags. Give seasoning mix, beans, and pasta with serving instructions.
Yield: about 1/2 cup seasoning mix

To serve: Rinse and sort dried beans. In a large Dutch oven, combine beans and 12 cups water. Cover and bring to a boil over medium-high heat. Reduce heat to medium-low and cook 1 1/4 hours. Stir in seasoning mix, pasta, 2 cans (14 1/2 ounces each) diced tomatoes, and 1 can (8 ounces) tomato sauce. Cover and simmer 30 minutes or until beans are tender. Serve warm.
Yield: about 13 cups soup

LENTIL SOUP MIX

2 cups dried lentils
1 tablespoon chicken bouillon
   granules
1 tablespoon onion powder
1 teaspoon ground cumin
1 teaspoon celery salt
3/4 teaspoon salt
1/2 teaspoon garlic powder
1/2 teaspoon dried thyme leaves
1/2 teaspoon ground black pepper
1/4 teaspoon dried lemon peel
1 bay leaf

Place lentils in a resealable plastic bag. In a small bowl, combine chicken bouillon, onion powder, cumin, celery salt, salt, garlic powder, thyme, pepper, lemon peel, and bay leaf. Transfer seasoning mixture to a small cellophane bag. Give with serving instructions.
Yield: about 3 tablespoons seasoning mix

To serve: Rinse lentils. In a Dutch oven, cover lentils with 2 quarts water. Bring to a boil over medium-high heat. Reduce heat to medium low. Stirring occasionally, cover and simmer 15 minutes or until lentils are barely tender. Stir in seasoning mix. Cover and simmer 30 minutes longer or until lentils are tender. Serve warm.
Yield: about 7 cups soup

SAVORY BREADSTICKS

3/4 cup butter or margarine
1/2 tablespoon instant beef bouillon
  granules
1 tablespoon dried parsley flakes
1/8 teaspoon dried marjoram leaves
2 packages (41/2 ounces each)
  prepared breadsticks
2 tablespoons grated Parmesan
  cheese

Melt butter in a jellyroll pan. Stir
in bouillon, parsley, and marjoram.
Roll breadsticks in butter mixture and
sprinkle with cheese. Bake in a preheated
400-degree oven 10 minutes. Store in an
airtight container.
Yield: 30 breadsticks

DILLY OYSTER CRACKERS

1 package (1.6 ounces) ranch-style
  salad dressing mix
1 tablespoon dried dill weed
1/2 teaspoon garlic powder
1 box (16 ounces) unseasoned
  oyster crackers
1 cup vegetable oil

In a large bowl, combine dressing
mix, dill weed, and garlic powder. Add
crackers and blend thoroughly. Pour oil
over mixture and stir thoroughly; allow
crackers to absorb oil and seasonings.
Store in an airtight container.
Yield: about 8 cups

PARMESAN-HERB NIBBLES
(Shown on page 552)

1 cup all-purpose flour
1/2 teaspoon baking powder
1/4 teaspoon salt
1/8 teaspoon cayenne pepper
1 teaspoon Fines Herbes
  (in grocery spice section)
1/3 cup butter or margarine
2/3 cup grated Parmesan cheese
3 egg yolks
2 teaspoons water

Preheat oven to 400 degrees. In a large
bowl, sift together first 4 ingredients.
Stir in herbs. With a pastry blender or
2 knives, cut in butter and cheese until
mixture resembles a coarse meal. Stir in
egg yolks and water. Place dough on a
lightly floured surface and knead until
smooth, about 2 minutes. Roll out dough
to 1/8-inch thickness. With a paring knife,
cut dough vertically into 1-inch wide
strips; cut 1-inch wide strips horizontally
to make small squares. Carefully lift
squares from surface with flat side of
knife and place on greased baking sheets.
Bake 8 to 10 minutes or until lightly
browned. Cool completely before storing
in airtight container. Give with Potato
Soup Mix (recipe on page 552).
Yield: about 6 dozen squares

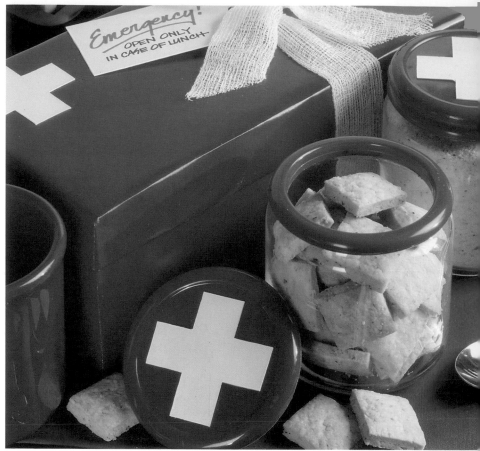

Perfect for office workers, Potato Soup Mix and a jar of Parmesan-Herb Nibbles (recipe on page 551) will come in handy when bad weather or a hectic schedule makes going out inconvenient.

POTATO SOUP MIX

1³/₄ cups instant mashed potatoes
1¹/₂ cups nonfat dry milk
  2 tablespoons instant chicken
       bouillon
  2 teaspoons dried minced onion
1¹/₂ teaspoons seasoned salt
  1 teaspoon dried parsley
¹/₄ teaspoon dried whole thyme
¹/₄ teaspoon ground white pepper
¹/₈ teaspoon turmeric

Combine all ingredients in a large bowl, mixing until completely blended. Store in airtight container. Give with Parmesan-Herb Nibbles (recipe on page 551).
Yield: about 2¹/₂ cups of mix

To serve: Place ¹/₄ cup soup mix in a soup bowl or mug. Add 1 cup boiling water and stir until smooth. Let soup sit 1 to 2 minutes to thicken slightly.

Mexican Corn Bread goes great with Mexican Bean Soup (recipe on page 554).

MEXICAN CORN BREAD MIX

    2 cups yellow cornmeal
$^1/_2$ cup all-purpose flour
    1 tablespoon sugar
    2 teaspoons baking powder
    1 teaspoon salt
    1 teaspoon ground red pepper
$^1/_2$ teaspoon baking soda

In a large bowl, combine cornmeal, flour, sugar, baking powder, salt, red pepper, and baking soda. Place in a resealable plastic bag. Give mix with recipe for Mexican Corn Bread.
Yield: about $2^1/_2$ cups mix

MEXICAN CORN BREAD

    2 tablespoons butter or margarine
    1 bag (about $2^1/_2$ cups) Mexican Corn
        Bread Mix (recipe on this page)
    1 can (12 ounces) beer
    2 eggs, lightly beaten

Preheat oven to 425 degrees. Place butter in an 8-inch round baking pan or skillet. Place pan in oven to melt butter and to heat pan. In a medium bowl, combine corn bread mix, beer, and eggs. Stir just until blended. Pour into hot pan. Bake 25 to 30 minutes or until lightly browned. Serve warm.
Yield: 6 to 8 servings

MEXICAN BEAN SOUP MIX

BEAN SOUP MIX
  1 pound black beans
  1 pound red beans
  1 pound great Northern beans

SEASONING MIX
  3 tablespoons dried parsley flakes, divided
  4$^{1}/_{2}$ teaspoons chili powder, divided
  3 teaspoons salt, divided
  1$^{1}/_{2}$ teaspoons crushed dried red pepper flakes, divided
  $^{3}/_{4}$ teaspoon garlic powder, divided
  $^{3}/_{4}$ teaspoon ground black pepper, divided

For bean soup mix, combine all ingredients in a large bowl. Place about 2 heaping cups beans in each of 3 resealable plastic bags.

For seasoning mix, combine 1 tablespoon parsley, 1$^{1}/_{2}$ teaspoons chili powder, 1 teaspoon salt, $^{1}/_{2}$ teaspoon red pepper flakes, $^{1}/_{4}$ teaspoon garlic powder, and $^{1}/_{4}$ teaspoon black pepper in each of 3 small resealable plastic bags.

Give 1 bag of beans with 1 bag of seasoning mix and recipe for Mexican Bean Soup (recipe on this page).
Yield: about 6 cups bean soup mix and about 6$^{1}/_{2}$ tablespoons seasoning mix

MEXICAN BEAN SOUP
(Shown on page 553)

Great served with Mexican Corn Bread (mix recipe on page 553).

  1 bag (about 2 cups) Mexican Bean Soup Mix (recipe on this page)
  1 pound bulk pork sausage
  2 onions, quartered
  2 cloves garlic, minced
  1 can (16 ounces) whole peeled tomatoes
  1 can (4$^{1}/_{2}$ ounces) chopped green chiles
  1 bag (about 2 tablespoons) Seasoning Mix (recipe on this page)
  Salt and ground black pepper to taste

Rinse bean soup mix. Place beans in a Dutch oven and cover with water; soak overnight.

In a large skillet, brown sausage, onions, and garlic. Drain beans and return to Dutch oven. Add sausage mixture, tomatoes, green chiles, and seasoning mix to beans. Add enough water to cover. Stirring occasionally, simmer 3 to 4 hours or until beans are tender. Add more water as needed. Salt and pepper to taste.
Yield: 8 to 10 servings

PIZZA SAUCE AND CRUST MIX

2 large ripe tomatoes, peeled,
   seeded, and quartered
1 cups tomato sauce
1/3 cup tomato paste
2 teaspoons Italian seasoning
1 teaspoon garlic salt
1 teaspoon granulated sugar
1/4 teaspoon ground black pepper
4 cups biscuit baking mix

For sauce, use a blender or food processor fitted with a steel blade to coarsely chop tomatoes. Transfer tomatoes to a mixing bowl. Place remaining ingredients, except baking mix, in processor; blend until smooth. Add to tomatoes, mixing well. Cover and store in refrigerator.

For crust mix, place biscuit mix in a resealable plastic bag. Give Pizza Sauce and Crust Mix with recipe for Pizza (recipe on this page).

Yield: about 2 cups sauce and 4 cups crust mix, enough for two 12-inch pizzas

PIZZA

2 cups Crust Mix (recipe on this page)
1/2 cup cold water
1/2 grated Parmesan cheese
1 cup Pizza Sauce (recipe on this page)
1 1/2 cups (6 ounces) grated mozzarella
   cheese
1/4 pound pepperoni, sliced
Chopped green pepper, onion,
   olives, and mushrooms

Preheat oven to 425 degrees. In a medium bowl, combine Crust Mix with cold water. Beat with a wooden spoon about 20 strokes. Pat dough into a greased 12-inch pizza pan. Sprinkle with Parmesan cheese. Spread with Pizza Sauce and top with remaining ingredients. Bake 20 to 25 minutes until crisp around the edges.

Yield: one 12-inch pizza

HERBED FOCACCIA KIT

DOUGH MIX
- 3^3/$_4$ cups all-purpose flour
- ^{1}/$_4$ cup freshly grated Parmesan cheese
- 1 package dry yeast
- 1 teaspoon sugar
- 1 tablespoon dried rosemary leaves
- 2 teaspoons dried minced onion
- 1 teaspoon salt
- ^{1}/$_2$ teaspoon garlic powder
- ^{1}/$_2$ teaspoon ground black pepper

TOPPING MIX
- 2 tablespoons freshly grated Parmesan cheese
- 1 teaspoon dried rosemary leaves
- ^{1}/$_4$ teaspoon garlic powder
- Olive oil to give

For dough mix, combine all ingredients in a medium bowl. Store in an airtight container.

For topping mix, combine cheese, rosemary, and garlic powder in a small bowl. Store in an airtight container in refrigerator. Give with a bottle of olive oil and serving instructions.

To serve: In a large bowl, combine dough mix, 1^1/$_2$ cups very warm water, and 1 tablespoon olive oil; stir until a soft dough forms. Turn dough onto a lightly floured surface. Knead about 5 minutes or until dough becomes smooth and elastic. Cover and allow dough to rest 10 minutes.

Divide dough in half and press each half into a 9-inch-diameter circle on a lightly greased baking sheet. Drizzle each dough circle with about 1 teaspoon olive oil and sprinkle with topping mix. Cover with plastic wrap and let rise in a warm place (80 to 85 degrees) 45 minutes or until almost doubled in size.

Preheat oven to 425 degrees. Make indentations in dough with fingertips. Bake 14 to 18 minutes or until crust is golden brown. Serve warm with olive oil.
Yield: 2 focaccia rounds

PIZZA KITS
The Pizza Kits recipe makes 3 gifts; each gift makes two 12-inch pizzas.

PIZZA DOUGH MIX
- 11^1/$_4$ cups all-purpose flour, divided
- 3 packages dry yeast, divided
- 3 teaspoons sugar, divided
- 1^1/$_2$ teaspoons salt, divided

PIZZA SAUCE
- 3 tablespoons olive oil
- 1 cup finely chopped onion
- 5 cloves garlic, minced
- 1 green pepper, chopped
- 1 can (29 ounces) tomato sauce
- 3 large ripe tomatoes, peeled and chopped (about 2 cups)
- 1 jar (6 ounces) sliced mushrooms, drained
- 1 can (6 ounces) tomato paste
- 2 cans (2^1/$_4$ ounces each) sliced ripe olives, drained
- 2 tablespoons chopped fresh basil leaves
- 2 tablespoons chopped fresh oregano leaves
- ^{3}/$_4$ teaspoon salt
- ^{1}/$_2$ teaspoon ground black pepper
- ^{1}/$_2$ teaspoon sugar
- ^{1}/$_4$ teaspoon crushed red pepper flakes
- Three 8-ounce packages shredded mozzarella cheese and three 8.5-ounce packages pepperoni slices to give with gifts

For pizza dough mix, combine the following ingredients in each of 3 resealable plastic bags: 3³/₄ cups flour, 1 package yeast, 1 teaspoon sugar, and ¹/₂ teaspoon salt.

For pizza sauce, heat oil in a large Dutch oven over medium-low heat. Add onion, garlic, and green pepper. Stirring frequently, cook until vegetables are tender. Add tomato sauce, tomatoes, mushrooms, tomato paste, olives, basil, oregano, salt, black pepper, sugar, and red pepper flakes; simmer uncovered 20 minutes or until thickened. Remove from heat and cool. Place 2¹/₂ cups sauce in each of 3 containers. Cover and store sauce in refrigerator.

For each gift, give 1 bag Pizza Dough Mix, 1 container (2¹/₂ cups) Pizza Sauce, 1 package (8 ounces) shredded mozzarella cheese, 1 package (8.5 ounces) pepperoni slices, and recipe for Pepperoni-Veggie Pizza (recipe on this page).

In a large bowl, combine Pizza Dough Mix, very warm water, and oil; stir until a soft dough forms. Turn dough onto a lightly floured surface. Knead about 5 minutes or until dough becomes smooth and elastic, using additional flour as necessary. Cover and allow dough to rest 10 minutes. Divide dough in half and press into 2 lightly greased 12-inch pizza pans. Cover and let rise in a warm place (80 to 85 degrees) 30 minutes.

Preheat oven to 425 degrees. Bake crusts 10 minutes. Spread 1¹/₄ cups Pizza Sauce over each partially baked crust. Place pepperoni slices on each pizza. Sprinkle 1 cup mozzarella cheese over each pizza. Bake 10 to 12 minutes or until crust is lightly browned and cheese is melted.

Yield: two 12-inch pizzas

PEPPERONI-VEGGIE PIZZA

   1   bag Pizza Dough Mix (recipe
         on page 556; bag packaging
         quantities on this page)
1¹/₂   cups very warm water
   2   tablespoons vegetable oil
   1   container (2¹/₂ cups) Pizza Sauce
         (recipe on page 556)
   1   package (8.5 ounces) pepperoni
         slices
   1   package (8 ounces) shredded
         mozzarella cheese

An after-caroling party is the perfect place to deliver this Ready-To-Cook Holiday Pizza.

READY-TO-COOK HOLIDAY PIZZA

1   package dry yeast
1/2 teaspoon sugar
1 1/2 cups warm water
2   tablespoons vegetable oil
2   to 2 1/4 cups all-purpose flour,
      divided
1 1/2 cups whole-wheat flour
1   teaspoon salt
1   pound Italian sausage
1/2 cup prepared pizza sauce, divided
2   cups (8 ounces) shredded
      Mozzarella cheese, divided
1   jar (2.5 ounces) sliced
      mushrooms, drained and
      divided
1   can (2.25 ounces) sliced black
      olives, drained and divided
      Sweet red pepper, green pepper,
      and yellow pepper to decorate

In a small bowl, dissolve yeast and sugar in 1 1/2 cups warm water. Stir oil into yeast mixture. In a medium bowl, combine 1 1/2 cups all-purpose flour, whole-wheat flour, and salt. Add yeast mixture to dry ingredients; stir until a soft dough forms. Turn onto a lightly floured surface and knead 5 minutes or until dough becomes smooth and elastic, using additional flour as necessary. Cover and let dough rest 10 minutes. Divide dough in half and press into 2 lightly greased 12-inch pizza pans. Cover and let rise in a warm place (80 to 85 degrees) 30 minutes.

Preheat oven to 425 degrees. Bake crusts 7 minutes or just until dry. Place on a wire rack to cool.

In a medium skillet, brown sausage; drain, crumble, and set aside. Transfer cooled crusts to 12-inch-diameter cardboard circles. Spread half of pizza sauce over each crust. Layer each pizza with half of sausage, cheese, mushrooms, and olives. Slice red and green peppers into rings. Use a 3/4-inch- and a 1 1/2-inch-wide star-shaped cookie cutter to cut out yellow pepper stars. Place pepper pieces on pizzas. Cover tightly with plastic wrap. Store in refrigerator. Give with serving instructions.

Yield: two 12-inch pizzas, about 8 servings each

To serve: Preheat oven to 425 degrees. Remove plastic wrap and slide pizza off cardboard onto a pizza pan or baking sheet. Bake 22 to 25 minutes or until heated through and cheese melts.

RED BEANS AND RICE MIX

SEASONING MIX
- 1 tablespoon dried sweet pepper flakes
- 1 tablespoon dried minced onion
- 2 teaspoons seasoned salt
- 1 teaspoon granulated sugar
- 1 teaspoon ground cumin
- 1/2 teaspoon dried minced garlic
- 1/2 teaspoon celery seed
- 1/4 teaspoon cayenne pepper
- 1/4 teaspoon crushed red pepper flakes
- 1 bay leaf

BEANS AND RICE MIX
- 2 cups (about 1 pound) dried red beans
- 1 cup uncooked long grain white rice

For seasoning mix, combine all ingredients in a small bowl. Place in a small, resealable plastic bag.

For beans and rice mix, fill a pint canning jar with red beans. Fill a resealable plastic bag with rice.

Give bag of seasoning mix with jar of beans and bag of rice. Include cooking directions for Red Beans and Rice (recipe on this page).

Yield: enough for 1 recipe of Red Beans and Rice

RED BEANS AND RICE

- 2 cups dried red beans
- 1 ham bone
- 1 bag Seasoning Mix (recipe on this page)
- 2 cups water
- 1 cup uncooked long grain white rice
- 1 teaspoon salt
- 1 pound spicy smoked sausage, sliced
- Salt and ground black pepper to taste

Wash beans. Place beans in a Dutch oven; cover with water and soak overnight.

The following day, add ham bone and seasoning mixture to beans. If necessary, add additional water to cover beans. Cook, partially covered, over medium-low heat 3 to 4 hours. About 30 minutes before serving, combine 2 cups water, rice, and 1 teaspoon salt in a saucepan and bring to a boil. Reduce heat to low. Cover pan and cook 30 minutes without lifting lid. About 20 minutes before serving, add sausage to beans; salt and pepper to taste. Serve over rice.

Yield: 4 to 6 servings

DOG BONES

Don't forget your four-legged friends when it comes to gift giving.

2^1/$_4$ cups whole-wheat flour
  ^{1}/$_2$ cup nonfat dry milk powder
  1 egg
  ^{1}/$_2$ cup vegetable oil
  1 beef bouillon cube dissolved in
        ^{1}/$_2$ cup hot water
  1 tablespoon firmly packed brown
        sugar

Preheat oven to 300 degrees. In a large bowl, combine all ingredients, stirring until well blended. Knead dough 2 minutes. On a floured surface, use a floured rolling pin to roll out dough to ^{1}/$_4$-inch thickness. Use a 2^1/$_2$-inch-long bone-shaped cookie cutter to cut out bones. Bake 30 minutes on an ungreased baking sheet. Remove from pan and cool on wire rack. Store in an airtight container.
Yield: about 4 dozen dog bones

FAVORITE PETS' SNACK MIXES

DOG SNACK MIX
  Combine a variety of dry dog food and dog treats to yield 6 cups. Store in an airtight container.

CAT SNACK MIX
  Combine a variety of dry cat food and cat treats to yield 6 cups. Store in an airtight container.

SPECIAL DOG TREAT MIX

  2 cups whole-wheat flour
  1 cup all-purpose flour
  1 cup yellow cornmeal
  ^{1}/$_2$ cup nonfat dry milk powder
  ^{1}/$_2$ teaspoon garlic powder
  1 package (3 ounces) beef jerky
        dog treats, finely chopped
  ^{1}/$_2$ cup shredded Cheddar cheese

In a large bowl, combine flours, cornmeal, dry milk, and garlic powder. Stir in beef jerky pieces and cheese. Store in an airtight container in refrigerator. Give with recipe for Special Dog Treats (recipe on this page).
Yield: about 5 cups mix (2 gifts)

SPECIAL DOG TREATS

2^1/$_2$ cups Special Dog Treat Mix
  ^{1}/$_3$ cup vegetable oil
  ^{1}/$_4$ cup plus 2 tablespoons beef or
        chicken broth
  1 egg

Preheat oven to 300 degrees. In a large bowl, combine mix, oil, broth, and egg; stir until well blended. On a lightly floured surface, pat dough to ^{3}/$_8$-inch thickness. Use a 1^7/$_8$ x 3^5/$_8$-inch bone-shaped cookie cutter to cut out treats. Transfer to an ungreased baking sheet. Bake 20 to 22 minutes or until firm and bottoms are lightly browned. Transfer treats to a wire rack to cool. Store in an airtight container in refrigerator.
Yield: about 1 dozen dog treats

A simple combination of kitchen staples and bird seed, this mix is sure to attract a flock of feathered friends! It's a natural gift choice for friends who are cuckoo about bird-watching.

BIRD-WATCHING MIX

- 1 cup bacon drippings
- 1 cup cornmeal
- 1/4 cup molasses or corn syrup
- 1/4 cup fruit preserves
- 1 cup peanut butter
- 1 cup mixed wild bird seed

In a heavy medium saucepan, melt bacon drippings over medium heat; remove from heat. Stir in cornmeal, molasses, and preserves. Add peanut butter and bird seed; stir until well blended. Spread a heaping cup of mixture into each of three 4¹/₂-inch-diameter plant saucers. Cover and store in a cool place.

Yield: about 3¹/₂ cups bird mix (3 gifts)

METRIC EQUIVALENTS

The recipes that appear in this cookbook use the standard United States method for measuring liquid and dry or solid ingredients (teaspoons, tablespoons, and cups). The information on this chart is provided to help cooks outside the U.S. successfully use these recipes. All equivalents are approximate.

METRIC EQUIVALENTS FOR DIFFERENT TYPES OF INGREDIENTS

A standard cup measure of a dry or solid ingredient will vary in weight depending on the type of ingredient. A standard cup of liquid is the same volume for any type of liquid. Use the following chart when converting standard cup measures to grams (weight) or milliliters (volume).

Standard Cup	Fine Powder	Grain	Granular	Liquid Solids	Liquid
	(ex. flour)	(ex. rice)	(ex. sugar)	(ex. butter)	(ex. milk)
1	140 g	150 g	190 g	200 g	240 ml
¾	105 g	113 g	143 g	150 g	180 ml
⅔	93 g	100 g	125 g	133 g	160 ml
½	70 g	75 g	95 g	100 g	120 ml
⅓	47 g	50 g	63 g	67 g	80 ml
¼	35 g	38 g	48 g	50 g	60 ml
⅛	18 g	19 g	24 g	25 g	30 ml

USEFUL EQUIVALENTS FOR LIQUID INGREDIENTS BY VOLUME

¼ tsp					=	1 ml	
½ tsp					=	2 ml	
1 tsp					=	5 ml	
3 tsp	=	1 tbls		= ½ fl oz	=	15 ml	
		2 tbls	= ⅛ cup	= 1 fl oz	=	30 ml	
		4 tbls	= ¼ cup	= 2 fl oz	=	60 ml	
		5⅓ tbls	= ⅓ cup	= 3 fl oz	=	80 ml	
		8 tbls	= ½ cup	= 4 fl oz	=	120 ml	
		10⅔ tbls	= ⅔ cup	= 5 fl oz	=	160 ml	
		12 tbls	= ¾ cup	= 6 fl oz	=	180 ml	
		16 tbls	= 1 cup	= 8 fl oz	=	240 ml	
	1 pt	= 2 cups	= 16 fl oz	=	480 ml	
	1 qt	= 4 cups	= 32 fl oz	=	960 ml	
				33 fl oz	=	1000 ml	= 1 l

USEFUL EQUIVALENTS FOR DRY INGREDIENTS BY WEIGHT

(To convert ounces to grams, multiply the number of ounces by 30.)

1 oz	=	1⁄16 lb	=	30 g
4 oz	=	¼ lb	=	120 g
8 oz	=	½ lb	=	240 g
12 oz	=	¾ lb	=	360 g
16 oz	=	1 lb	=	480 g

USEFUL EQUIVALENTS FOR LENGTH

(To convert inches to centimeters, multiply the number of inches by 2.5.)

1 in			=	2.5 cm		
6 in	= ½ ft		=	15 cm		
12 in	= 1 ft		=	30 cm		
36 in	= 3 ft	= 1 yd	=	90 cm		
40 in			=	100 cm	=	1 m

USEFUL EQUIVALENTS FOR COOKING/OVEN TEMPERATURES

	Fahrenheit	Celsius	Gas Mark
Freeze Water	32° F	0° C	
Room Temperature	68° F	20° C	
Boil Water	212° F	100° C	
Bake	325° F	160° C	3
	350° F	180° C	4
	375° F	190° C	5
	400° F	200° C	6
	425° F	220° C	7
	450° F	230° C	8
Broil			Grill

SIMPLY DELICIOUS CHOCOLATE • RECIPE INDEX

SIMPLY DELICIOUS BREADS & MUFFINS • RECIPE INDEX

SIMPLY DELICIOUS BRUNCHES • RECIPE INDEX

SIMPLY DELICIOUS SUPPERS • RECIPE INDEX

SIMPLY DELICIOUS SIDE DISHES • RECIPE INDEX

SIMPLY DELICIOUS EASY DESSERTS • RECIPE INDEX

SIMPLY DELICIOUS COOKIES • RECIPE INDEX

SIMPLY DELICIOUS SNACKS • RECIPE INDEX

SIMPLY DELICIOUS PARTY SNACKS • RECIPE INDEX

SIMPLY DELICIOUS PARTY FOODS • RECIPE INDEX

SIMPLY DELICIOUS GIFTS FOR FRIENDS • RECIPE INDEX

SIMPLY DELICIOUS FOOD GIFTS • RECIPE INDEX